ISCO-88

International Standard Classification of Occupations

International Standard Classification of Occupations

ISCO-88

International Labour Office   Geneva

ILO
International Standard Classification of Occupations: ISCO-88
Geneva, International Labour Office, 1990
/ISCO/, /Occupational classification/ /Index/, /Occupational description/s. 13.11.1
ISBN 92-2-106438-7

Published in French under the title: *Classification internationale type des professions,*
édition 1988 *(CITP-88)* (ISBN 92-2-206438-0), Geneva, 1991
Also published in Spanish under the title: *Clasificación internacional uniforme de
ocupaciones,* edición de 1988 *(CIUO-88)* (ISBN 92-2-306438-4), Geneva, 1991

ILO Cataloguing in Publication Data

Printed in Belgium

VAN

PREFACE

This volume, the *International Standard Classification of Occupations 1988* (ISCO-88), replaces that issued in 1968 and reprinted for the fifth time in 1986.

The history of the development of the International Standard Classification of Occupations (ISCO) goes back several decades and has always been closely connected with the work of the International Conference of Labour Statisticians, which meets under the auspices of the International Labour Organisation. It was in 1921 that the need for an international standard classification of occupations was initially discussed, but the first positive step towards its establishment was the adoption of a provisional classification of nine major groups by the Seventh International Conference of Labour Statisticians in 1949. In 1952 the ILO published the *International Classification of Occupations for Migration and Employment Placement*, with detailed descriptions of 1,727 occupations based on the national classifications of eight industrialised countries. The publication of the first edition of ISCO took place in 1958, and a revised edition followed in 1968.

The present edition, ISCO-88, was adopted as Resolution III — Resolution concerning the revision of the International Standard Classification of Occupations — by the Fourteenth International Conference of Labour Statisticians on the sixth day of November 1987.

ISCO-88, like its predecessors, has been developed to facilitate international comparisons of occupational statistics and to serve as a model for countries developing or revising their national occupational classifications.

If ISCO-88 represents an improvement over previous editions of international occupational classifications it is because the ILO Bureau of Statistics, in particular Eivind Hoffmann and Mirjana Matejovic-Scott who worked on the project, was able to benefit from accumulated national and international experience as well as from collaboration with experts from different countries.

In addition to the thanks due to the members of the Thirteenth and Fourteenth Conferences of Labour Statisticians, special thanks should go to all those participating at the four meetings of experts which took place in 1985 and 1986 at different stages of the work, and in particular to Mr. Brian Embury, from the Australian Bureau of Statistics, who shared his vast experience in the field of occupational classifications in a most generous and indefatigable manner.

Thanks are also due to all the colleagues at the ILO Bureau of Statistics who directly or indirectly contributed to the completion of this volume.

CONTENTS

INTRODUCTION

The revised International Standard Classification of Occupations (ISCO-88) provides a system for classifying and aggregating occupational information obtained by means of population censuses and other statistical surveys, as well as from administrative records.

ISCO-88 is a revision of the International Standard Classification of Occupations 1968, which it supersedes. The revision was carried out in line with the recommendations and decisions of the Thirteenth and Fourteenth International Conferences of Labour Statisticians, held at the International Labour Office, Geneva, in 1982 and 1987. The Fourteenth ICLS endorsed ISCO-88 and recommended that: "In collecting and processing statistics classified by occupation, ... each country should ensure the possibility of conversion into the ISCO-88 system, to facilitate international use of occupational information." Thus, ISCO-88 is one of the standards of international labour statistics.

MAIN OBJECTIVES

ISCO-88 has three main aims. The first is to facilitate international communication about occupations by supplying national statisticians with a tool to make national occupational data available internationally.

The second is to make it possible for international occupational data to be produced in a form which can be useful for research as well as for specific decision-making and action-oriented activities, such as those connected with international migration or job placement.

The third aim is to serve as a model for countries developing or revising their national occupational classifications. It should be emphasised that, while serving as a model, ISCO-88 is not intended to replace any existing national classification of occupations, as the occupational classifications of individual countries should fully reflect the structure of the national labour market.[1] However, countries whose occupational classifications are already aligned to ISCO-88 in concept and structure will find it easier to develop necessary procedures for making their occupational statistics internationally comparable.

It should also be noted that, in many cases, countries will wish to develop in their national classifications finer structural and definition details than those contained in ISCO-88. In certain cases they may wish to include coded information on Job Content

---

[1]   The ILO Bureau of Statistics is at present preparing a manual on how to develop and use national occupational classifications.

Factors and detailed occupational descriptions, which are of particular interest for wage settlements, vocational guidance and training, placement services, or analysis of occupation-specific morbidity and mortality.

CONCEPTUAL FRAMEWORK

The framework necessary for designing and constructing ISCO-88 has been based on two main concepts: the concept of the kind of work performed or *job*, and the concept of *skill*.

Job – defined as a set of tasks and duties executed, or meant to be executed, by one person – is the *statistical unit* classified by ISCO-88. A set of jobs whose main tasks and duties are characterised by a high degree of similarity constitutes an *occupation*. Persons are classified by occupation through their relationship to a past, present or future job.

Skill – defined as the ability to carry out the tasks and duties of a given job – has, for the purposes of ISCO-88 the two following dimensions:

(a) *Skill level* – which is a function of the complexity and range of the tasks and duties involved; and

(b) *Skill specialisation* – defined by the field of knowledge required, the tools and machinery used, the materials worked on or with, as well as the kinds of goods and services produced.

On the basis of the skill concept thus defined, ISCO-88 occupational groups were delineated and further aggregated.

Bearing in mind the international character of the classification, only four broad skill levels were defined. They were given operational definitions in terms of the educational categories and levels which appear in the *International Standard Classification of Education* (ISCED), COM/ST/ISCED (Paris, Unesco, 1976).

The use of ISCED categories to define the four skill levels does not imply that the skills necessary to perform the tasks and duties of a given job can be acquired only through formal education. The skills may be, and often are, acquired through informal training and experience. In addition, it should be emphasised that the focus in ISCO-88 is on the skills required to carry out the tasks and duties of an occupation – and not on whether a worker having a particular occupation is more or less skilled than another worker in the same occupation.

Therefore, as a rule, the following operational definitions of the four ISCO-88 skill levels apply where the necessary occupational skills are acquired through formal education or vocational training.

(a) *The first ISCO skill level* was defined with reference to ISCED category 1, comprising primary education which generally begins at the age of 5, 6 or 7 and lasts about five years.

(b) *The second ISCO skill level* was defined with reference to ISCED categories 2 and 3, comprising first and second stages of secondary education. The first stage begins at the age of 11 or 12 and lasts about three years, while the second stage begins at the age of 14 or 15 and also lasts about three years. A period of on-the-job training and experience may be necessary, sometimes formalised in apprenticeships. This period may supplement the formal training or replace it partly or, in some cases, wholly.

(c) *The third ISCO skill level* was defined with reference to ISCED category 5, (category 4 in ISCED has been deliberately left without content) comprising education which begins at the age of 17 or 18, lasts about four years, and leads to an award not equivalent to a first university degree.

(d) *The fourth ISCO skill level* was defined with reference to ISCED categories 6 and 7, comprising education which also begins at the age of 17 or 18, lasts about three, four or more years, and leads to a university or postgraduate university degree, or the equivalent.

Unavoidably, some subjective judgement was involved in determining the skill levels of occupations, or occupational groups, in the structure of ISCO-88. Many national classifications and national circumstances have been examined to gather data for this purpose, and it is hoped that the decisions made reflect prevailing situations and main trends.

DESIGN AND STRUCTURE

The conceptual approach adopted for ISCO-88 resulted in a pyramid whose hierarchical structure consists of ten major groups at the top level of aggregation, subdivided into 28 sub-major groups, 116 minor groups, and 390 unit groups.

Table 1. ISCO-88 major groups with number of sub-groups and skill levels

Major groups	Sub-major groups	Minor groups	Unit groups	ISCO skill level
1. Legislators, senior officials and managers	3	8	33	--
2. Professionals	4	18	55	4th
3. Technicians and associate professionals	4	21	73	3rd
4. Clerks	2	7	23	2nd
5. Service workers and shop and market sales workers	2	9	23	2nd
6. Skilled agricultural and fishery workers	2	6	17	2nd
7. Craft and related trades workers	4	16	70	2nd
8. Plant and machine operators and assemblers	3	20	70	2nd
9. Elementary occupations	3	10	25	1st
0. Armed forces	1	1	1	--
Totals	28	116	390	

As can be seen from the above table, out of the ten major groups, eight have been linked to the four ISCO skill levels – which, as mentioned earlier, were given operational definitions by reference to the educational categories and levels of the International Standard Classification of Education. The concept of skill level was not applied in the case of Major group 1, *Legislators, senior officials and managers*, and Major group 0, *Armed forces*. The reason for this was that, based on information from national sources, skills for executing tasks and duties of occupations belonging to each of these two major groups vary to such an extent that it would be impossible to link them with any of the four broad ISCO-88 skill levels.

Further sub-divisions of ISCO-88 occupational groups, providing successively finer detail, were carried out on the basis of skill specialisation, defined by reference to the field of knowledge required, the tools and machinery used, the materials worked on or with, as well as the kinds of goods and services produced.

The 28 sub-major groups, at the second ISCO-88 level of aggregation, represent an innovation in the sense that all of the preceding international occupational classifications have had a substantial numerical gap in the number of groups at their first and second levels of aggregation. For instance, in the case of ISCO-68 there were eight groups at the first level of aggregation followed by 83 groups at the second level. This presented an imbalance in the number of groups needed, on the one hand, for the presentation of the occupational structure in broad terms and for cross-classifying with variables such as industry or detailed age groups and, on the other hand, for presenting the occupational structure without cross-classifying, or when cross-classifying with variables such as sex or broad age groups.

The 390 unit groups, representing the most detailed level of the ISCO-88 structure, in most cases consist of more than one occupation. In national circumstances, the number and delineation between occupations will, to a large extent, depend on the size of the economy and the level of economic development, the level and type of technology, work organisation and historical circumstances. For this reason detailed descriptions of the occupations belonging to each of the 390 unit groups have not been developed for ISCO-88. However, a selection is being made among the 1,506 detailed occupational descriptions which were included in ISCO-68. Those found to be still relevant will be published in a companion volume to ISCO-88.

For each of the groups at the four levels of aggregation of ISCO-88 a code number, a title and a brief description of the content is provided. In the case of the unit groups, the main tasks of the occupations belonging to each of them are briefly described and some of the relevant occupational titles are listed as examples. In most cases examples are also given of the occupations which, although related in some way to those belonging to the unit group in question, are classified elsewhere. This has been done in order to clarify possible ambiguities and to highlight the ISCO-88 conceptual approach and characteristics of its structure.

Detailed descriptions of the occupational groups at the four levels of aggregation are followed by the ISCO-88 index of occupational titles. Three separate listings of the index are provided. The first is according to ISCO-88 numerical order, the second by ISCO-68 numerical order, and the third is an alphabetical list of occupational titles. The index reflects the results of a recoding and recasting of the ISCO-68 "Expanded alphabetical list of titles". For further details the reader is referred to the "Notes on the ISCO-88 index of occupational titles" which precede the index.

While revising the index, every effort was made to take into consideration the conceptual and structural differences between the two classifications, and, where possible, to make appropriate modifications, including some new index entries. However, some of the shortcomings of the ISCO-68 index — such as unevenness of detail when naming specialisations relating to a given generic occupational title — have been carried over to the present index. The user should bear in mind that the main aim of the present index is to indicate the content of each group within the ISCO-88 structure, and that the index makes no claim to being exhaustive. The Bureau of Statistics of the ILO intends, by using the latest national sources of occupational titles, to compile an extended and updated version of the ISCO-88 index for later publication. It is hoped that any shortcomings in the present index will be dealt with satisfactorily in the later version.

SUMMARY OF MAJOR GROUPS

The following briefly outlines ISCO-88 major groups, and is meant to facilitate the interpretation of the classification. The information given here should not be regarded as a substitute for the more detailed descriptions of occupational groups which the volume contains.

1. Legislators, senior officials and managers

This major group includes occupations whose main tasks consist of determining and formulating government policies, as well as laws and public regulations, overseeing their implementation, representing governments and acting on their behalf, or planning, directing and co-ordinating the policies and activities of enterprises and organisations, or departments. Reference to skill level has not been made in defining the scope of this major group, which has been divided into three sub-major groups, eight minor groups and 33 unit groups, reflecting differences in tasks associated with different areas of authority and different types of enterprises and organisations.

2. Professionals

This major group includes occupations whose main tasks require a high level of professional knowledge and experience in the fields of physical and life sciences, or social sciences and humanities. The main tasks consist of increasing the existing stock of knowledge, applying scientific and artistic concepts and theories to the solution of problems, and teaching about the foregoing in a systematic manner. Most occupations in this major group require skills at the fourth ISCO skill level. This major group has been divided into four sub-major groups, 18 minor groups and 55 unit groups, reflecting differences in tasks associated with different fields of knowledge and specialisation.

3. Technicians and associate professionals

This major group includes occupations whose main tasks require technical knowledge and experience in one or more fields of physical and life sciences, or social sciences and humanities. The main tasks consist of carrying out *technical work* connected with the application of concepts and operational methods in the above-mentioned fields, and in teaching at certain educational levels. Most occupations in this major group require skills at the third ISCO skill level. This major group has been divided into four sub-major groups, 21 minor groups and 73 unit groups, reflecting differences in tasks associated with different fields of knowledge and specialisation.

4. Clerks

This major group includes occupations whose main tasks require the knowledge and experience necessary to organise, store, compute and retrieve information. The main tasks consist of performing secretarial duties, operating word processors and other office machines, recording and computing numerical data, and performing a number of customer-oriented clerical duties, mostly in connection with mail services, money-handling operations and appointments. Most occupations in this major group require skills at the second ISCO skill level. This major group has been divided into two sub-major groups, seven minor groups and 23 unit groups, reflecting differences in tasks associated with different areas of specialisation.

5. Service workers and shop and market sales workers

This major group includes occupations whose main tasks require the knowledge and experience necessary to provide personal and protective services, and to sell goods in shops or at markets. The main tasks consist of providing services related to travel, housekeeping, catering, personal care, protection of individuals and property, and to maintaining law and order, or selling goods in shops or at markets. Most occupations in this major group require skills at the second ISCO skill level. This major group has been divided into two sub-major groups, nine minor groups and 23 unit groups, reflecting differences in tasks associated with different areas of specialisation.

6. Skilled agricultural and fishery workers

This major group includes occupations whose tasks require the knowledge and experience necessary to produce farm, forestry and fishery products. The main tasks consist of growing crops, breeding or hunting animals, catching or cultivating fish, conserving and exploiting forests and, especially in the case of market-oriented agricultural and fishery workers, selling products to purchasers, marketing organisations or at markets. Most occupations in this major group require skills at the second ISCO skill level. This major group has been divided into two sub-major groups, six minor groups and 17 unit groups, reflecting differences in tasks associated with different areas of specialisation, and differences between market-oriented and subsistence agricultural and fishery workers.

7. Craft and related trades workers

This major group includes occupations whose tasks require the knowledge and experience of skilled trades or handicrafts which, among other things, involves an understanding of materials and tools to be used, as well as of all stages of the production process, including the characteristics and the intended use of the final product. The main tasks consist of extracting raw materials, constructing buildings and other structures and making various products as well as handicraft goods. Most occupations in this major group require skills at the second ISCO skill level. This major group has been divided into four sub-major groups, 16 minor groups and 70 unit groups, reflecting differences in tasks associated with different areas of specialisation.

8. Plant and machine operators and assemblers

This major group includes occupations whose main tasks require the knowledge and experience necessary to operate and monitor large scale, and often highly automated, industrial machinery and equipment. The main tasks consist of operating and monitoring mining, processing and production machinery and equipment, as well as driving vehicles and driving and operating mobile plant, or assembling products from component parts. Most occupations in this major group require skills at the second ISCO skill level. This major group has been divided into three sub-major groups, 20 minor groups and 70 unit groups, reflecting differences in tasks associated with different areas of specialisation.

9. Elementary occupations

This major group covers occupations which require the knowledge and experience necessary to perform mostly simple and routine tasks, involving the use of hand-held tools and in some cases considerable physical effort, and, with few exceptions, only limited personal initiative or judgement. The main tasks consist of selling goods in streets, doorkeeping and property watching, as well as cleaning, washing, pressing, and working as labourers in the fields of mining, agriculture and fishing, construction and manufacturing. Most occupations in this major group require skills at the first ISCO skill level. This major group has been divided into three sub-major groups, ten minor groups and 25 unit groups, reflecting differences in tasks associated with different areas of work.

0. Armed forces

Members of the armed forces are those personnel who are currently serving in the armed forces, including auxiliary services, whether on a voluntary or compulsory basis, and who are not free to accept civilian employment. Included are regular members of the army, navy, air force and other military services, as well as conscripts enrolled for military training or other service for a specified period, depending on national requirements. Excluded are persons in civilian employment of government establishments concerned with defence issues; police (other than military police); customs inspectors and members of border or other armed civilian services; persons who have been temporarily withdrawn from civilian life for a short period of military training or retraining, according to national requirements, and members of military reserves not currently on active service. Reference to a skill level has not been used in defining the scope of this major group.

APPROACHES TO SOME SPECIFIC ISSUES

National differences in educational requirements

However broad the skill levels of an international occupational classification may be, the presumed skill level of a particular occupation, or a group of occupations, may not correspond exactly to that determined by the educational requirements of some countries. On the basis of the information received in the course of work on ISCO-88, as well as on the basis of the discussions held by the Fourteenth International Conference of Labour Statisticians, it became apparent that differences in formal educational requirements were most prominent in the cases of some of the *teaching, health and social services occupations*. In some countries it is necessary to have a university degree in order to be able to practise these occupations, while in other countries lower-level educational certificates are considered sufficient. In order to accommodate these differences, parallel occupational groups were created in ISCO-88 Major groups 2 and 3, – *Professionals* and *Technicians and associate professionals*, respectively. The codes and titles of these groups are as follows:

Major group 2, Professionals

2230 Nursing and midwifery professionals
2331 Primary education teaching professionals

2332 Pre-primary education teaching professionals
2340 Special education teaching professionals
2446 Social work professionals

Major group 3, Technicians and associate professionals

3231 Nursing associate professionals
3232 Midwifery associate professionals
3310 Primary education teaching associate professionals
3320 Pre-primary education teaching associate professionals
3330 Special education teaching associate professionals
3460 Social work associate professionals

This means that, in accordance with educational requirements, when grouping national occupational data according to the ISCO-88 structure, countries will be able to classify nursing, midwifery, teaching and social services occupations either into Major group 2, *Professionals*, or into Major group 3, *Technicians and associate professionals*, as appropriate.

Occupations with a broad range of tasks and duties

Differences in the range of tasks and duties belonging to the *same occupation* are, at national level, mostly determined by the size of the establishment. For instance, in a small establishment typing and filing may be combined with the duties of a receptionist into one single job, while in a bigger enterprise they may constitute two or three separate jobs. At international level, although it is acknowledged that factors such as tradition or collective agreements may play an important part, the existence of these differences is mostly linked to the level of economic development, with its simple patterns of labour division.

Occupational classifications – national as well as international – define occupations, and occupational groups, by reference to the most common combinations of tasks and duties, and therefore face a problem when, in the case of some occupations, the range of tasks and duties does not correspond to those specified in the classification.

In such cases ISCO-88 suggests application of the following rules:

(a) In cases where the tasks and duties performed require skills usually obtained through different levels of training and experience, jobs should be classified in

accordance with those tasks and duties which require *the highest level of skills*. For instance a job which consists of driving a van and delivering goods should be classified in Unit group 8322, *Car, taxi and van drivers*.

(b) In cases where the tasks and duties are connected with different stages of the production and distribution of goods process, tasks and duties related to *the production stage* should take priority over associated ones, such as those related to the sales and marketing of the same goods, their transportation or the management of the production process – unless one of these tasks and duties predominates. For example, a baker who bakes bread, makes pastries and sells these products should not be classified as a sales person, but as a baker, which means, in ISCO-88 terms, Unit group 7412, *Bakers, pastry-cooks and confectionery makers*.

Technology and skills

Developments in technology, particularly those which led to mass-production methods, have had a profound effect on the skills that are needed according to whether a product is made by a craft worker or manufactured through the application of one of the latest techniques. For instance, skills required to perform the tasks of a smith or a tailor are different from those required to perform the tasks of a machine-operator in an enterprise engaged in metalworking or in the mass-production of textile garments.

Broadly speaking, a smith or a tailor has to know the materials, tools, sequence of tasks performed, and the characteristics and intended use of the final product. A machine-operator, on the other hand, has to know how to use very sophisticated machinery and equipment, how to recognise and signal, or eliminate, problems before they start to affect output in a serious way, or how to react if something goes wrong with the machine itself. In addition, a machine-operator should have a level of skill and breadth of training which would allow retraining costs to be minimal when product specifications change or when new technology is introduced.

In ISCO-88 the delineation between Major groups 7 and 8 reflects these differences in the type of skills required. Major group 7, *Craft and related trades workers*, classifies craft-oriented and artisanal occupations – such as mason, carpenter, mechanic, baker, potter, decorative painter, wood-carver – while Major group 8, *Plant and machine operators and assemblers*, classifies machine-oriented occupations.

Coexistence of two agricultural sectors

Inequalities in the economic development of different countries, or regions within the same country, have resulted in the coexistence of two agricultural sectors, of which one is characterised by low-skilled subsistence farming while the other often has a highly automated production process and, as a result, achieves high productivity with relatively few workers. These differences are reflected in ISCO-88 through a distinction made in Major group 6, *Skilled agricultural and fishery workers*, between, on the one hand, skilled market-oriented farmers and agricultural workers, and, on the other, those who are engaged in subsistence farming. The aim of this distinction is to reflect important skill differences existing in the two sectors, as well as to improve the quality of the data needed to undertake analyses and make decisions concerning rural development.

Occupations and women

In most countries the number and proportion of women in the labour force has increased over the past two decades, and it is highly probable that this trend will continue. However, this positive numerical increase has not been accompanied by an equal distribution of various jobs between men and women, nor by equal earnings. Women workers tend to cluster in lower-skilled jobs, and their wages in most sectors lag behind those of men performing the same tasks and duties.

Occupation is one of the main variables which denotes the situation of women in the labour force. It is therefore important that occupational categories of a given occupa-tional classification be delineated in a way which will not obscure but promote detail and clarity of information on sex composition of jobs. In ISCO-88 atttention is paid to this issue, especially in the case of groups where occupations characterised by the predomin-ance of women workers are classified, such as Major group 4, *Clerks*, Major group 5, *Service workers and shop and market sales workers*, and Major group 9, *Elementary occupations*.

Occupations in the informal sector

The need to identify occupations in the informal sector was taken into consideration in the structure of ISCO-88, especially in the delineation of the unit groups. The following unit groups may be particularly useful for classifying informal sector occupations: Unit groups 7331 and 7332 entitled *Handicraft workers in wood and related materials*, and *Handicraft workers in textile, leather and related materials*, respectively, as well as Unit groups 9111, *Street food vendors*, 9112, *Street vendors, non-food products*, and 9120, *Shoe cleaning and other street services elementary occupations*.

Occupations and status in employment

ISCO-88, unlike its predecessor, does not take into consideration whether a worker is a working proprietor or not, as this and similar attributes of the labour force, such as being an employer or an employee etc., reflect sta-tus in employment and not the tasks and duties of the worker, and therefore should be dealt with in a separate *Status in employment classification*.

NOTES ON SOME PARTICULAR OCCUPATIONS

Technical occupations are classified separately from professional occupations in Major group 3, *Technicians and associate professionals*. Thus, *Technician, biology* is classified in Unit group 3211, *Life science technicians*, while *Technician, engineering/mining* is classified in Unit group 3117, *Mining and metallurgical technicians*.

Quality inspecting occupations, whose main tasks are to ensure compliance with the quality standards and specifications of manufacturers, are classified in Unit group 3152, *Safety, health and quality inspectors*. On the other hand, testers and checkers, whose main tasks consist of a mechanical inspection of the goods produced which, in most cases, amounts to simple visual checking, are classified with workers producing these goods.

Supervising occupations, as well as those of a foreman/woman, which are mainly concerned with the control of the professional or technical quality of the *work* done, are classified together with the jobs whose tasks they supervise. However, if the main tasks and duties of a job consist of planning, organising, controlling and directing the daily work activities of a group of subordinate workers, the occupation should be considered as a managerial occupation and classified in the appropriate group belonging either to Sub-major group 12 or 13, *Corporate managers* or *General managers*, respectively.

Coaching occupations primarily concerned with *on-the-job training* by continuous observation, assessment and guidance are classified with the occupations whose workers they instruct, in particular trade, craft or machine-operating tasks.

Teaching occupations mainly concerned with giving *private lessons* are classified with other teachers at the corresponding institutional level. It should be noted that driving, flying, sailing and related instructors are classified in Unit group 3340, *Other teaching associate professionals*.

Occupations concerned with *research and development* are classified according to the field of specialisation in Major group 2, *Professionals*. When a researcher is also exercising a teaching profession, he or she should be classified as a teacher, at the appropriate educational level.

Apprentices and trainees are classified according to the tasks and duties actually performed, and not, as is the case with some occupational classifications, according to their future occupation.

MAPPING NATIONAL OCCUPATIONAL CLASSIFICATIONS INTO ISCO-88

Comparisons of occupations among countries or regions demand that national occupational statistics be converted to international standards. This is usually achieved by mapping the national occupational categories into a common international classification system, ISCO-88. International comparability of occupational statistics can also be achieved by using the international classification system to recode the original responses elicited by the occupational questions in censuses or other surveys. However, this latter method normally cannot be used because of the high costs involved.

Mapping one classification into another is equivalent to coding each group in the first classification to the most appropriate group in the other. The validity of the mapping is in inverse proportion to the aggregated level at which the mapping is done. That is why it is recommended that mapping should be carried out at the lowest level of aggregation of each of the two classifications, i.e. national occupational classification (NOC) and ISCO-88.

In the process of mapping, the three following situations are those most frequently encountered:

(a) The NOC group, at the lowest level of aggregation, belongs unambiguously to one of the ISCO-88 unit groups. This is, of course, the simplest situation and, if the NOC, both conceptually and structurally, has a base similar to ISCO-88, it is likely to be the most usual situation.

(b) The NOC group, at the lowest level of aggregation, differs in occupational content from the most relevant ISCO-88 unit group, but the difference in the content does not prevent the NOC group from being validly mapped into an ISCO-88 group at one of the higher levels of aggregation. For example: NOC classifies glass engravers and etchers together with glass and ceramics decorative painters in the *same* lowest level aggregation group, while ISCO-88 classifies these occupations in *two* unit groups, but in both classifications subsequent aggregation of these occupations is carried out in the same manner.

(c) The way of grouping certain occupations is different in NOC from that applied in ISCO-88, and, as a result, an existing NOC group cannot validly be mapped into any of the ISCO-88 groups. For example: at the lowest aggregation level, NOC classifies farmers, farm managers and farm labourers in one single group, while ISCO-88 classifies these occupations in three separate unit groups belonging to three different minor, sub-major and major groups.

If internationally available occupational statistics have to be produced at the minor group aggregation level of ISCO-88, or any of the higher ones, then no problem arises in the situation described under *(b)* above. If the information has to be produced at the level corresponding to ISCO-88 unit groups, in that case, as well as in the situation described under *(c)* above, *the following rules should be applied in order of priority as they are described*:

The *numerical dominance rule,* according to which, on the basis of the additional information available from economic and other statistics, or from sectoral experts, estimates or judgement should be made concerning the relative importance of the occupations classified in the NOC group. If approximately 80 per cent or more of the jobs classified in the NOC group belong to a particular ISCO-88 group, then the whole NOC group should be classified in this ISCO-88 group.

The *skill level rule,* according to which the occupational mix of the NOC group should be analysed on the basis of the ISCO-88 skill-level concept. The mapping into an ISCO-88 group should then be carried out on the basis of the occupations found to be the most skilled.

The *production rule,* according to which, for the purposes of mapping into ISCO-88, in the occupational mix of a NOC group production occupations will have priority over sales or managerial occupations.

MAJOR, SUB-MAJOR, MINOR AND UNIT GROUP TITLES

MAJOR GROUP 1
LEGISLATORS, SENIOR OFFICIALS AND MANAGERS

11 LEGISLATORS AND SENIOR OFFICIALS

111 LEGISLATORS

1110 Legislators

112 SENIOR GOVERNMENT OFFICIALS

1120 Senior government officials

113 TRADITIONAL CHIEFS AND HEADS OF VILLAGES

1130 Traditional chiefs and heads of villages

114 SENIOR OFFICIALS OF SPECIAL-INTEREST ORGANISATIONS

1141 Senior officials of political-party organisations

1142 Senior officials of employers', workers' and other economic-interest organisations

1143 Senior officials of humanitarian and other special-interest organisations

12 CORPORATE MANAGERS[1]

121 DIRECTORS AND CHIEF EXECUTIVES

1210 Directors and chief executives

122 PRODUCTION AND OPERATIONS DEPARTMENT MANAGERS

1221 Production and operations department managers in agriculture, hunting, forestry and fishing

1222 Production and operations department managers in manufacturing

1223 Production and operations department managers in construction

1224 Production and operations department managers in wholesale and retail trade

1225 Production and operations department managers in restaurants and hotels

1226 Production and operations department managers in transport, storage and communications

1227 Production and operations department managers in business services

1228 Production and operations department managers in personal care, cleaning and related services

1229 Production and operations department managers not elsewhere classified

123 OTHER DEPARTMENT MANAGERS

1231 Finance and administration department managers

1232 Personnel and industrial relations department managers

1233 Sales and marketing department managers

1234 Advertising and public relations department managers

1235 Supply and distribution department managers

1236 Computing services department managers

1237 Research and development department managers

1239 Other department managers not elsewhere classified

13 GENERAL MANAGERS[2]

131 GENERAL MANAGERS

1311 General managers in agriculture, hunting, forestry and fishing

1312 General managers in manufacturing

1313 General managers in construction

---

[1] This group is intended to include persons who – as directors, chief executives or department managers – manage enterprises or organisations, or departments, requiring a total of three or more managers.

[2] This group is intended to include persons who manage enterprises, or in some cases organisations, on their own behalf, or on behalf of the proprietor, with some non-managerial help and the assistance of no more than one other manager who should also be classified in this sub-major group as, in most cases, the tasks will be broader than those of a specialised manager in a larger enterprise or organisation. Non-managerial staff should be classified according to their specific tasks.

1314 General managers in wholesale and retail trade

1315 General managers of restaurants and hotels

1316 General managers in transport, storage and communications

1317 General managers of business services

1318 General managers in personal care, cleaning and related services

1319 General managers not elsewhere classified

MAJOR GROUP 2
PROFESSIONALS

21 PHYSICAL, MATHEMATICAL AND ENGINEERING SCIENCE PROFESSIONALS

211 PHYSICISTS, CHEMISTS AND RELATED PROFESSIONALS

2111 Physicists and astronomers

2112 Meteorologists

2113 Chemists

2114 Geologists and geophysicists

212 MATHEMATICIANS, STATISTICIANS AND RELATED PROFESSIONALS

2121 Mathematicians and related professionals

2122 Statisticians

213 COMPUTING PROFESSIONALS

2131 Computer systems designers and analysts

2132 Computer programmers

2139 Computing professionals not elsewhere classified

214 ARCHITECTS, ENGINEERS AND RELATED PROFESSIONALS

2141 Architects, town and traffic planners

2142 Civil engineers

2143 Electrical engineers

2144 Electronics and telecommunications engineers

2145 Mechanical engineers

2146 Chemical engineers

2147 Mining engineers, metallurgists and related professionals

2148 Cartographers and surveyors

2149 Architects, engineers and related professionals not elsewhere classified

22 LIFE SCIENCE AND HEALTH PROFESSIONALS

221 LIFE SCIENCE PROFESSIONALS

2211 Biologists, botanists, zoologists and related professionals

2212 Pharmacologists, pathologists and related professionals

2213 Agronomists and related professionals

222 HEALTH PROFESSIONALS (except nursing)

2221 Medical doctors

2222 Dentists

2223 Veterinarians

2224 Pharmacists

2229 Health professionals (except nursing) not elsewhere classified

223 NURSING AND MIDWIFERY PROFESSIONALS

2230 Nursing and midwifery professionals

23 TEACHING PROFESSIONALS

231 COLLEGE, UNIVERSITY AND HIGHER EDUCATION TEACHING PROFESSIONALS

2310 College, university and higher education teaching professionals

232 SECONDARY EDUCATION TEACHING PROFESSIONALS

2320 Secondary education teaching professionals

233 PRIMARY AND PRE-PRIMARY EDUCATION TEACHING PROFESSIONALS

2331 Primary education teaching professionals

2332 Pre-primary education teaching professionals

234 SPECIAL EDUCATION TEACHING PROFESSIONALS

2340 Special education teaching professionals

235 OTHER TEACHING PROFESSIONALS

2351 Education methods specialists

2352 School inspectors

2359 Other teaching professionals not elsewhere classified

24 OTHER PROFESSIONALS

241 BUSINESS PROFESSIONALS
2411 Accountants
2412 Personnel and careers professionals
2419 Business professionals not elsewhere classified

242 LEGAL PROFESSIONALS
2421 Lawyers
2422 Judges
2429 Legal professionals not elsewhere classified

243 ARCHIVISTS, LIBRARIANS AND RELATED INFORMATION PROFESSIONALS
2431 Archivists and curators
2432 Librarians and related information professionals

244 SOCIAL SCIENCE AND RELATED PROFESSIONALS
2441 Economists
2442 Sociologists, anthropologists and related professionals
2443 Philosophers, historians and political scientists
2444 Philologists, translators and interpreters
2445 Psychologists
2446 Social work professionals

245 WRITERS AND CREATIVE OR PERFORMING ARTISTS
2451 Authors, journalists and other writers
2452 Sculptors, painters and related artists
2453 Composers, musicians and singers
2454 Choreographers and dancers
2455 Film, stage and related actors and directors

246 RELIGIOUS PROFESSIONALS
2460 Religious professionals

MAJOR GROUP 3
TECHNICIANS AND ASSOCIATE PROFESSIONALS

31 PHYSICAL AND ENGINEERING SCIENCE ASSOCIATE PROFESSIONALS

311 PHYSICAL AND ENGINEERING SCIENCE TECHNICIANS
3111 Chemical and physical science technicians
3112 Civil engineering technicians
3113 Electrical engineering technicians
3114 Electronics and telecommunications engineering technicians
3115 Mechanical engineering technicians
3116 Chemical engineering technicians
3117 Mining and metallurgical technicians
3118 Draughtspersons
3119 Physical and engineering science technicians not elsewhere classified

312 COMPUTER ASSOCIATE PROFESSIONALS
3121 Computer assistants
3122 Computer equipment operators
3123 Industrial robot controllers

313 OPTICAL AND ELECTRONIC EQUIPMENT OPERATORS
3131 Photographers and image and sound recording equipment operators
3132 Broadcasting and telecommunications equipment operators
3133 Medical equipment operators
3139 Optical and electronic equipment operators not elsewhere classified

314 SHIP AND AIRCRAFT CONTROLLERS AND TECHNICIANS
3141 Ships' engineers
3142 Ships' deck officers and pilots
3143 Aircraft pilots and related associate professionals
3144 Air traffic controllers
3145 Air traffic safety technicians

315 SAFETY AND QUALITY INSPECTORS
3151 Building and fire inspectors
3152 Safety, health and quality inspectors

32 LIFE SCIENCE AND HEALTH ASSOCIATE PROFESSIONALS

321 LIFE SCIENCE TECHNICIANS AND RELATED ASSOCIATE PROFESSIONALS
3211 Life science technicians
3212 Agronomy and forestry technicians
3213 Farming and forestry advisers

322 MODERN HEALTH ASSOCIATE PROFESSIONALS (except nursing)
3221 Medical assistants
3222 Sanitarians
3223 Dieticians and nutritionists
3224 Optometrists and opticians
3225 Dental assistants
3226 Physiotherapists and related associate professionals
3227 Veterinary assistants
3228 Pharmaceutical assistants
3229 Modern health associate professionals (except nursing) not elsewhere classified

323 NURSING AND MIDWIFERY ASSOCIATE PROFESSIONALS
3231 Nursing associate professionals
3232 Midwifery associate professionals

324 TRADITIONAL MEDICINE PRACTITIONERS AND FAITH HEALERS
3241 Traditional medicine practitioners
3242 Faith healers

33 TEACHING ASSOCIATE PROFESSIONALS

331 PRIMARY EDUCATION TEACHING ASSOCIATE PROFESSIONALS
3310 Primary education teaching associate professionals

332 PRE-PRIMARY EDUCATION TEACHING ASSOCIATE PROFESSIONALS
3320 Pre-primary education teaching associate professionals

333 SPECIAL EDUCATION TEACHING ASSOCIATE PROFESSIONALS
3330 Special education teaching associate professionals

334 OTHER TEACHING ASSOCIATE PROFESSIONALS
3340 Other teaching associate professionals

34 OTHER ASSOCIATE PROFESSIONALS

341 FINANCE AND SALES ASSOCIATE PROFESSIONALS
3411 Securities and finance dealers and brokers
3412 Insurance representatives
3413 Estate agents
3414 Travel consultants and organisers
3415 Technical and commercial sales representatives
3416 Buyers
3417 Appraisers, valuers and auctioneers
3419 Finance and sales associate professionals not elsewhere classified

342 BUSINESS SERVICES AGENTS AND TRADE BROKERS
3421 Trade brokers
3422 Clearing and forwarding agents
3423 Employment agents and labour contractors
3429 Business services agents and trade brokers not elsewhere classified

343 ADMINISTRATIVE ASSOCIATE PROFESSIONALS
3431 Administrative secretaries and related associate professionals
3432 Legal and related business associate professionals
3433 Bookkeepers
3434 Statistical, mathematical and related associate professionals
3439 Administrative associate professionals not elsewhere classified

344 CUSTOMS, TAX AND RELATED GOVERNMENT ASSOCIATE PROFESSIONALS
3441 Customs and border inspectors
3442 Government tax and excise officials
3443 Government social benefits officials
3444 Government licensing officials
3449 Customs, tax and related government associate professionals not elsewhere classified

345 POLICE INSPECTORS AND DETECTIVES
3450 Police inspectors and detectives

346 SOCIAL WORK ASSOCIATE PROFESSIONALS
3460 Social work associate professionals

347 ARTISTIC, ENTERTAINMENT AND SPORTS ASSOCIATE PROFESSIONALS
3471 Decorators and commercial designers
3472 Radio, television and other announcers

3473	Street, night-club and related musicians, singers and dancers		**348**	**RELIGIOUS ASSOCIATE PROFESSIONALS**
3474	Clowns, magicians, acrobats and related associate professionals		3480	Religious associate professionals
3475	Athletes, sportspersons and related associate professionals			

MAJOR GROUP 4
CLERKS

41 OFFICE CLERKS

411 SECRETARIES AND KEYBOARD-OPERATING CLERKS

4111 Stenographers and typists

4112 Word-processor and related operators

4113 Data entry operators

4114 Calculating-machine operators

4115 Secretaries

412 NUMERICAL CLERKS

4121 Accounting and bookkeeping clerks

4122 Statistical and finance clerks

413 MATERIAL-RECORDING AND TRANSPORT CLERKS

4131 Stock clerks

4132 Production clerks

4133 Transport clerks

414 LIBRARY, MAIL AND RELATED CLERKS

4141 Library and filing clerks

4142 Mail carriers and sorting clerks

4143 Coding, proof-reading and related clerks

4144 Scribes and related workers

419 OTHER OFFICE CLERKS

4190 Other office clerks

42 CUSTOMER SERVICES CLERKS

421 CASHIERS, TELLERS AND RELATED CLERKS

4211 Cashiers and ticket clerks

4212 Tellers and other counter clerks

4213 Bookmakers and croupiers

4214 Pawnbrokers and money-lenders

4215 Debt-collectors and related workers

422 CLIENT INFORMATION CLERKS

4221 Travel agency and related clerks

4222 Receptionists and information clerks

4223 Telephone switchboard operators

MAJOR GROUP 5
SERVICE WORKERS AND SHOP AND MARKET SALES WORKERS

51 PERSONAL AND PROTECTIVE SERVICES WORKERS

511 TRAVEL ATTENDANTS AND RELATED WORKERS

5111 Travel attendants and travel stewards

5112 Transport conductors

5113 Travel guides

512 HOUSEKEEPING AND RESTAURANT SERVICES WORKERS

5121 Housekeepers and related workers

5122 Cooks

5123 Waiters, waitresses and bartenders

513 PERSONAL CARE AND RELATED WORKERS

5131 Child-care workers

5132	Institution-based personal care workers	5162	Police officers
5133	Home-based personal care workers	5163	Prison guards
5139	Personal care and related workers not elsewhere classified	5169	Protective services workers not elsewhere classified

514 OTHER PERSONAL SERVICES WORKERS

5141	Hairdressers, barbers, beauticians and related workers
5142	Companions and valets
5143	Undertakers and embalmers
5149	Other personal services workers not elsewhere classified

515 ASTROLOGERS, FORTUNE-TELLERS AND RELATED WORKERS

5151	Astrologers and related workers
5152	Fortune-tellers, palmists and related workers

516 PROTECTIVE SERVICES WORKERS

5161	Fire-fighters

52 MODELS, SALESPERSONS AND DEMONSTRATORS

521 FASHION AND OTHER MODELS

5210	Fashion and other models

522 SHOP SALESPERSONS AND DEMONSTRATORS

5220	Shop salespersons and demonstrators

523 STALL AND MARKET SALESPERSONS

5230	Stall and market salespersons

MAJOR GROUP 6
SKILLED AGRICULTURAL AND FISHERY WORKERS

61 MARKET-ORIENTED SKILLED AGRICULTURAL AND FISHERY WORKERS

611 MARKET GARDENERS AND CROP GROWERS

6111	Field crop and vegetable growers
6112	Tree and shrub crop growers
6113	Gardeners, horticultural and nursery growers
6114	Mixed-crop growers

612 MARKET-ORIENTED ANIMAL PRODUCERS AND RELATED WORKERS

6121	Dairy and livestock producers
6122	Poultry producers
6123	Apiarists and sericulturists
6124	Mixed-animal producers
6129	Market-oriented animal producers and related workers not elsewhere classified

613 MARKET-ORIENTED CROP AND ANIMAL PRODUCERS

6130	Market-oriented crop and animal producers

614 FORESTRY AND RELATED WORKERS

6141	Forestry workers and loggers
6142	Charcoal burners and related workers

615 FISHERY WORKERS, HUNTERS AND TRAPPERS

6151	Aquatic-life cultivation workers
6152	Inland and coastal waters fishery workers
6153	Deep-sea fishery workers
6154	Hunters and trappers

62 SUBSISTENCE AGRICULTURAL AND FISHERY WORKERS

621 SUBSISTENCE AGRICULTURAL AND FISHERY WORKERS

6210	Subsistence agricultural and fishery workers

MAJOR GROUP 7
CRAFT AND RELATED TRADES WORKERS

71 EXTRACTION AND BUILDING TRADES WORKERS

711 MINERS, SHOTFIRERS, STONE CUTTERS AND CARVERS

7111 Miners and quarry workers

7112 Shotfirers and blasters

7113 Stone splitters, cutters and carvers

712 BUILDING FRAME AND RELATED TRADES WORKERS

7121 Builders, traditional materials

7122 Bricklayers and stonemasons

7123 Concrete placers, concrete finishers and related workers

7124 Carpenters and joiners

7129 Building frame and related trades workers not elsewhere classified

713 BUILDING FINISHERS AND RELATED TRADES WORKERS

7131 Roofers

7132 Floor layers and tile setters

7133 Plasterers

7134 Insulation workers

7135 Glaziers

7136 Plumbers and pipe fitters

7137 Building and related electricians

714 PAINTERS, BUILDING STRUCTURE CLEANERS AND RELATED TRADES WORKERS

7141 Painters and related workers

7142 Varnishers and related painters

7143 Building structure cleaners

72 METAL, MACHINERY AND RELATED TRADES WORKERS

721 METAL MOULDERS, WELDERS, SHEET-METAL WORKERS, STRUCTURAL-METAL PREPARERS, AND RELATED TRADES WORKERS

7211 Metal moulders and coremakers

7212 Welders and flamecutters

7213 Sheet-metal workers

7214 Structural-metal preparers and erectors

7215 Riggers and cable splicers

7216 Underwater workers

722 BLACKSMITHS, TOOL-MAKERS AND RELATED TRADES WORKERS

7221 Blacksmiths, hammer-smiths and forging-press workers

7222 Tool-makers and related workers

7223 Machine-tool setters and setter-operators

7224 Metal wheel-grinders, polishers and tool sharpeners

723 MACHINERY MECHANICS AND FITTERS

7231 Motor vehicle mechanics and fitters

7232 Aircraft engine mechanics and fitters

7233 Agricultural- or industrial-machinery mechanics and fitters

724 ELECTRICAL AND ELECTRONIC EQUIPMENT MECHANICS AND FITTERS

7241 Electrical mechanics and fitters

7242 Electronics fitters

7243 Electronics mechanics and servicers

7244 Telegraph and telephone installers and servicers

7245 Electrical line installers, repairers and cable jointers

73 PRECISION, HANDICRAFT, PRINTING AND RELATED TRADES WORKERS

731 PRECISION WORKERS IN METAL AND RELATED MATERIALS

7311 Precision-instrument makers and repairers

7312 Musical-instrument makers and tuners

7313 Jewellery and precious-metal workers

732 POTTERS, GLASS-MAKERS AND RELATED TRADES WORKERS

7321 Abrasive wheel formers, potters and related workers

7322 Glass-makers, cutters, grinders and finishers

7323 Glass engravers and etchers

7324 Glass, ceramics and related decorative painters

733 HANDICRAFT WORKERS IN WOOD, TEXTILE, LEATHER AND RELATED MATERIALS

7331 Handicraft workers in wood and related materials

7332 Handicraft workers in textile, leather and related materials

734 PRINTING AND RELATED TRADES WORKERS

7341 Compositors, typesetters and related workers

7342 Stereotypers and electrotypers

7343 Printing engravers and etchers

7344 Photographic and related workers

7345 Bookbinders and related workers

7346 Silk-screen, block and textile printers

74 OTHER CRAFT AND RELATED TRADES WORKERS

741 FOOD PROCESSING AND RELATED TRADES WORKERS

7411 Butchers, fishmongers and related food pre-parers

7412 Bakers, pastry-cooks and confectionery makers

7413 Dairy-products makers

7414 Fruit, vegetable and related preservers

7415 Food and beverage tasters and graders

7416 Tobacco preparers and tobacco products makers

742 WOOD TREATERS, CABINET-MAKERS AND RELATED TRADES WORKERS

7421 Wood treaters

7422 Cabinet-makers and related workers

7423 Woodworking-machine setters and setter-operators

7424 Basketry weavers, brush makers and related workers

743 TEXTILE, GARMENT AND RELATED TRADES WORKERS

7431 Fibre preparers

7432 Weavers, knitters and related workers

7433 Tailors, dressmakers and hatters

7434 Furriers and related workers

7435 Textile, leather and related pattern-makers and cutters

7436 Sewers, embroiderers and related workers

7437 Upholsterers and related workers

744 PELT, LEATHER AND SHOEMAKING TRADES WORKERS

7441 Pelt dressers, tanners and fellmongers

7442 Shoe-makers and related workers

MAJOR GROUP 8
PLANT AND MACHINE OPERATORS AND ASSEMBLERS

81 STATIONARY-PLANT AND RELATED OPERATORS

811 MINING- AND MINERAL-PROCESSING-PLANT OPERATORS

8111 Mining-plant operators

8112 Mineral-ore- and stone-processing-plant operators

8113 Well drillers and borers and related workers

812 METAL-PROCESSING-PLANT OPERATORS

8121 Ore and metal furnace operators

8122 Metal melters, casters and rolling-mill operators

8123 Metal-heat-treating-plant operators

8124 Metal drawers and extruders

813 GLASS, CERAMICS AND RELATED PLANT OPERATORS

8131 Glass and ceramics kiln and related machine operators

8139 Glass, ceramics and related plant operators not elsewhere classified

814 WOOD-PROCESSING- AND PAPERMA-KING-PLANT OPERATORS

8141 Wood-processing-plant operators

8142 Paper-pulp plant operators

8143 Papermaking-plant operators

815 CHEMICAL-PROCESSING-PLANT OPERATORS

8151 Crushing-, grinding- and chemical-mixing-machinery operators

8152 Chemical-heat-treating-plant operators

8153 Chemical-filtering- and separating-equipment operators

8154 Chemical-still and reactor operators (except petroleum and natural gas)

8155 Petroleum- and natural-gas-refining-plant operators

8159 Chemical-processing-plant operators not elsewhere classified

816 POWER-PRODUCTION AND RELATED PLANT OPERATORS

8161 Power-production plant operators

8162 Steam-engine and boiler operators

8163 Incinerator, water-treatment and related plant operators

817 AUTOMATED-ASSEMBLY-LINE AND INDUSTRIAL-ROBOT OPERATORS

8171 Automated-assembly-line operators

8172 Industrial-robot operators

82 MACHINE OPERATORS AND ASSEMBLERS

821 METAL- AND MINERAL-PRODUCTS MACHINE OPERATORS

8211 Machine-tool operators

8212 Cement and other mineral products machine operators

822 CHEMICAL-PRODUCTS MACHINE OPERATORS

8221 Pharmaceutical- and toiletry-products machine operators

8222 Ammunition- and explosive-products machine operators

8223 Metal finishing-, plating- and coating-machine operators

8224 Photographic-products machine operators

8229 Chemical-products machine operators not elsewhere classified

823 RUBBER- AND PLASTIC-PRODUCTS MACHINE OPERATORS

8231 Rubber-products machine operators

8232 Plastic-products machine operators

824 WOOD-PRODUCTS MACHINE OPERATORS

8240 Wood-products machine operators

825 PRINTING-, BINDING- AND PAPER-PRODUCTS MACHINE OPERATORS

8251 Printing-machine operators

8252 Bookbinding-machine operators

8253 Paper-products machine operators

826 TEXTILE-, FUR- AND LEATHER-PRODUCTS MACHINE OPERATORS

8261 Fibre-preparing-, spinning- and winding-machine operators

8262 Weaving- and knitting-machine operators

8263 Sewing-machine operators

8264 Bleaching-, dyeing- and cleaning-machine operators

8265 Fur- and leather-preparing-machine operators

8266 Shoemaking- and related machine operators

8269 Textile-, fur- and leather-products machine operators not elsewhere classified

827 FOOD AND RELATED PRODUCTS MACHINE OPERATORS

8271 Meat- and fish-processing-machine operators

8272 Dairy-products machine operators

8273 Grain- and spice-milling-machine operators

8274 Baked-goods, cereal and chocolate-products machine operators

8275 Fruit-, vegetable- and nut-processing-machine operators

8276 Sugar production machine operators

8277 Tea-, coffee-, and cocoa-processing-machine operators

8278 Brewers-, wine and other beverage machine operators

8279 Tobacco production machine operators

828 ASSEMBLERS

8281 Mechanical-machinery assemblers

8282 Electrical-equipment assemblers

8283 Electronic-equipment assemblers

8284 Metal-, rubber- and plastic-products assemblers

8285 Wood and related products assemblers

8286 Paperboard, textile and related products assemblers

829 OTHER MACHINE OPERATORS AND ASSEMBLERS

8290 Other machine operators and assemblers

83 DRIVERS AND MOBILE-PLANT OPERATORS

831 LOCOMOTIVE-ENGINE DRIVERS AND RELATED WORKERS

8311 Locomotive-engine drivers

8312 Railway brakers, signallers and shunters

832 MOTOR-VEHICLE DRIVERS

8321 Motor-cycle drivers

8322 Car, taxi and van drivers

8323 Bus and tram drivers

8324 Heavy truck and lorry drivers

833 AGRICULTURAL AND OTHER MOBILE-PLANT OPERATORS

8331 Motorised farm and forestry plant operators

8332 Earth-moving- and related plant operators

8333 Crane, hoist and related plant operators

8334 Lifting-truck operators

| **834** | **SHIPS' DECK CREWS AND RELATED WORKERS** | 8340 | Ships' deck crews and related workers |

MAJOR GROUP 9
ELEMENTARY OCCUPATIONS

91 SALES AND SERVICES ELEMENTARY OCCUPATIONS

911 STREET VENDORS AND RELATED WORKERS

9111 Street food vendors

9112 Street vendors, non-food products

9113 Door-to-door and telephone salespersons

912 SHOE CLEANING AND OTHER STREET SERVICES ELEMENTARY OCCUPATIONS

9120 Shoe cleaning and other street services elementary occupations

913 DOMESTIC AND RELATED HELPERS, CLEANERS AND LAUNDERERS

9131 Domestic helpers and cleaners

9132 Helpers and cleaners in offices, hotels and other establishments

9133 Hand-launderers and pressers

914 BUILDING CARETAKERS, WINDOW AND RELATED CLEANERS

9141 Building caretakers

9142 Vehicle, window and related cleaners

915 MESSENGERS, PORTERS, DOORKEEPERS AND RELATED WORKERS

9151 Messengers, package and luggage porters and deliverers

9152 Doorkeepers, watchpersons and related workers

9153 Vending-machine money collectors, meter readers and related workers

916 GARBAGE COLLECTORS AND RELATED LABOURERS

9161 Garbage collectors

9162 Sweepers and related labourers

92 AGRICULTURAL, FISHERY AND RELATED LABOURERS

921 AGRICULTURAL, FISHERY AND RELATED LABOURERS

9211 Farm-hands and labourers

9212 Forestry labourers

9213 Fishery, hunting and trapping labourers

93 LABOURERS IN MINING, CONSTRUCTION, MANUFACTURING AND TRANSPORT

931 MINING AND CONSTRUCTION LABOURERS

9311 Mining and quarrying labourers

9312 Construction and maintenance labourers: roads, dams and similar constructions

9313 Building construction labourers

932 MANUFACTURING LABOURERS

9321 Assembling labourers

9322 Hand packers and other manufacturing labourers

933 TRANSPORT LABOURERS AND FREIGHT HANDLERS

9331 Hand or pedal vehicle drivers

9332 Drivers of animal-drawn vehicles and machinery

9333 Freight handlers

MAJOR GROUP 0
ARMED FORCES

01 ARMED FORCES

011 ARMED FORCES

0110 Armed forces

MAJOR GROUP **1**
LEGISLATORS, SENIOR OFFICIALS AND MANAGERS

Legislators, senior officials and managers determine, formulate, direct or advise on government policies, as well as those of special-interest organisations, formulate laws, public rules and regulations, represent governments and act on their behalf, oversee the interpretation and implementation of government policies and legislation, or plan, direct, and co-ordinate the policies and activities of enterprises or organisations, or their internal departments or sections.

Tasks performed by legislators, senior officials and managers usually include: determining, formulating or advising on policies of national, state, regional or local governments; formulating laws, public rules and regulations; representing governments and acting on their behalf; overseeing the interpretation and implementation of government policies and legislation; performing similar tasks on behalf of political parties, trade unions, and other special-interest organisations; planning, directing and co-ordinating the policies and activities of enterprises or organisations, or their internal departments or sections. Supervision of other workers may be included.

Occupations in this major group are classified into the following sub-major groups:

11   Legislators and senior officials

12   Corporate managers [1]

13   General managers [2]

Note
In some case where specific professional, technical or operational skills and knowledge may be required of workers at legislative, administrative or managerial level, it may be difficult to decide whether a particular job belongs in this or another major group. In such cases, additional information on the main tasks of the job in question is essential. If the main tasks require the operational application of specific professional knowledge or a particular technical skill, then the job belongs in a different major group. If, however, professional knowledge or technical skill serve only as a basis for legislative, administrative or managerial tasks, then the job belongs in this major group. For example, if the main tasks of a job consist of diagnosing and treating illnesses, the job belongs in Major group 2, *Professionals*. However, if one of the main tasks is to allocate research and development funds on the basis of medical knowledge, then the job belongs in this major group.

[1] This group is intended to include persons who – as directors, chief executives or department managers – manage enterprises or organisations, or their internal departments, requiring a total of three or more managers.
[2] This group is intended to include persons who manage enterprises, or in some cases organisations, on their own behalf, or on behalf of the proprietor, with some non-managerial help and the assistance of no more than one other manager who should also be classified in this sub-major group as, in most cases, the tasks will be broader than those of a specialised manager in a larger enterprise or organisation. Non-managerial staff should be classified according to their specific tasks.

SUB-MAJOR GROUP **11**
LEGISLATORS AND SENIOR OFFICIALS

Legislators and senior officials determine, formulate or advise on and direct government policies, make, ratify, amend and repeal laws, public rules and regulations, represent governments and act on their behalf, oversee the interpretation and implementation of government policies and legislation, or carry out similar tasks on behalf of special-interest organisations.

Tasks performed by workers in this sub-major group usually include: determining and formulating, or advising on and directing policies of national, state, regional or local governments; making, ratifying, amending, or repealing laws, public rules and regulations; representing governments and acting on their behalf; overseeing the interpretation and implementation of government policies and legislation by government or intergovernmental departments and agencies; performing similar functions for political parties, trade unions, and other special-interest organisations, including negotiations on behalf of suchlike organisations, their members and clients. Supervision of other workers may be included.

Occupations in this sub-major group are classified into the following minor groups:

111   **Legislators**

112   **Senior government officials**

113   **Traditional chiefs and heads of villages**

114   **Senior officials of special-interest organisations**

Note

In some cases where specific professional, technical or operational skills and knowledge may be required of workers at legislative and administrative level, it may be difficult to decide whether a particular job belongs in this or another sub-major group. In such cases, additional information on the main tasks of the job in question is essential. If the main tasks require the operational application of specific professional knowledge or a particular technical skill, then the job belongs in a different sub-major group. If, however, professional knowledge or technical skill serve only as a basis for legislative or administrative tasks, then the job belongs in this sub-major group. For example, if the main tasks of a job consist of diagnosing and treating illnesses, the job belongs in Major group 2, *Professionals*. However, if one of the main tasks is to allocate research and development funds from a government budget, on the basis of medical knowledge, then the job belongs in this sub-major group.

MINOR GROUP **111**
LEGISLATORS

Legislators determine, formulate, and direct policies of national, state, regional or local governments, and make, ratify, amend or repeal laws, public rules and regulations.

Tasks performed usually include: presiding over or participating in the proceedings of legislative assemblies and administrative councils of national, state, regional or local governments; determining, formulating, and directing policies of national, state, regional or local governments; making, ratifying, amending or repealing laws, public rules and regulations. Supervision of other workers may be included.

Occupations in this minor group are classified into the following unit group:

1110   Legislators

1110   LEGISLATORS

Legislators determine, formulate, and direct policies of national, state, regional or local governments, and make, ratify, amend or repeal laws, public rules and regulations.

Tasks include –

(a)   presiding over or participating in the proceedings of legislative bodies and administrative councils of national, state, regional or local governments or legislative assemblies;

(b)   determining, formulating, and directing policies of national, state, regional or local governments;

(c)   making, ratifying, amending or repealing laws, public rules and regulations within the framework of a Constitution determining their powers and fields of jurisdiction;

(d)   serving on government administrative boards or official committees;

(e)   promoting the interests of the constituencies which they represent;

(f)   as members of the government, directing senior administrators and officials of government departments and agencies in the interpretation and implementation of government policies;

(g)   performing related tasks;

(h)   supervising other workers.

Examples of the occupations classified here:

- Minister, government
- President, government
- Prime minister
- Secretary, government/legislative
- Senator

Some related occupations classified elsewhere:

- Secretary, government/non-legislative, – 1120

MINOR GROUP **112**
SENIOR GOVERNMENT OFFICIALS

Senior government officials advise governments on policy matters, oversee the interpretation and implementation of government policies and legislation, represent their country abroad, or carry out similar tasks in intergovernmental organisations.

Tasks performed usually include: advising national, state, regional or local governments on policy questions; overseeing the interpretation and implementation of government policies and legislation; representing their country abroad; performing similar tasks in intergovernmental organisations. Supervision of other workers may be included.

Occupations in this minor group are classified into the following unit group:

1120   Senior government officials

Note

Senior government officials who manage a government-owned or government-controlled industrial, public utility, transport or other such business enterprise or organisation, or perform tasks similar to those of 122, *Production and operations department managers,* or, 123, *Other department managers,* are classified into Sub-major group 12, *Corporate managers*[1] or 13, *General managers*[2] as appropriate.

Further possible subdivisions of this minor group into unit groups should reflect the particular policy areas in which government administrators are working and about which they may need thorough knowledge and understanding in order to carry out their tasks. Dif-
ferent areas of government functions are defined and classified in the *Classification of the functions of government (COFOG),* issued by the United Nations Statistical Office in 1980 (Statistical papers, Series M, No. 70). One possible subdivision of policy areas would be the following: 1. General public services (COFOG major group 01) 2. Defence, public order and safety affairs (COFOG major groups 02 + 03) 3. Educational, cultural and religious affairs (COFOG major groups 04 + 08) 4. Health, social security and welfare affairs (COFOG major groups 05 + 06) 5. Housing and community amenities affairs (COFOG major group 07) 6. Energy and economic affairs and services (COFOG major groups 09 + 10 + 11 + 12 + 13)

1120   SENIOR GOVERNMENT OFFICIALS

Senior government officials advise governments on policy matters, oversee the interpretation and implementation of government policies and legislation by government departments and agencies, represent their country abroad and act on its behalf, or carry out similar tasks in intergovernmental organisations.

Tasks include –

(a)   advising national, state, regional or local governments on policy matters;

(b)   advising on the preparation of government budgets, laws and regulations, including amendments;

(c)   overseeing the interpretation and implementation of government policies and legislation by government departments and agencies;

(d)   representing their country abroad;

(e)   performing similar tasks in intergovernmental organisations;

(f)   performing related tasks;

(g)   supervising other workers.

---

[1] See footnote 1 at beginning of Major group 1.   [2] See footnote 2 at beginning of Major group 1.

Examples of the occupations classified here:
- Administrator, government
- Administrator, intergovernmental organisation
- Ambassador
- Consul-general
- Secretary, government/non-legislative

MINOR GROUP **113**
TRADITIONAL CHIEFS AND HEADS OF VILLAGES

Traditional chiefs and heads of villages perform a variety of legislative, administrative and ceremonial tasks and duties, determined by ancient traditions, as well as by the division of rights and responsibilities between village chiefs and the local, regional and national authorities.

Tasks performed usually include: allocating the use of communal land and other resources among households in the community; collecting and distributing surplus production of the community or village; settling disputes between members of the community or village; disciplining members of the community or village for violation of rules and customs; performing ceremonial duties in connection with births, marriages, deaths, harvests and other traditional feasts; representing the community or village on local or regional councils; being responsible for informing the community or village about government rules and regulations. Supervision of other workers may be included.

Occupations in this minor group are classified into the following unit group:

1130   Traditional chiefs and heads of villages

1130   TRADITIONAL CHIEFS AND HEADS OF VILLAGES

Traditional chiefs and heads of villages perform a variety of legislative, administrative and ceremonial tasks and duties, determined by ancient traditions, as well as by the division of rights and responsibilities between village chiefs and the local, regional and national authorities.

Tasks include –

(a) allocating the use of communal land and other resources among households in the community or village;

(b) collecting and distributing surplus production of the community or village;

(c) settling disputes between members of the community or village;

(d) disciplining members of the community or village for violation of rules and customs;

(e) perfoming ceremonial duties in connection with births, marriages, deaths, harvests and other traditional feasts;

(f) representing the community or village on local or regional councils;

(g) being responsible for informing the community or village about government rules and regulations;

(h) performing related tasks;

(i) supervising other workers.

Examples of the occupations classified here:
- Chief, village
- Head, village

MINOR GROUP **114**
SENIOR OFFICIALS OF SPECIAL-INTEREST ORGANISATIONS

Senior officials of special-interest organisations determine, formulate and direct the implementation of policies of special-interest organisations, such as political-party organisations, trade unions, employers' organisations, trade and industry associations, humanitarian or charity organisations, or sports associations, and represent their organisations and act on their behalf.

Tasks performed usually include: determining and formulating the policies, rules and regulations of the organisation; negotiating on behalf of the organisation, its members and relevant special-interest groups; promoting the interests of the organisation, its members and relevant special-interest groups before the legislature, government or general public; planning, organising and directing sections charged with implementing the organisation's policies, rules and regulations. Supervision of other workers may be included.

Occupations in this minor group are classified into the following unit groups:

1141   Senior officials of political-party organisations

1142   Senior officials of employers', workers' and other economic-interest organisations

1143   Senior officials of humanitarian and other special-interest organisations

Note
Senior officials of special-interest organisations who manage a business enterprise owned or controlled by a special-interest organisation, or perform tasks similar to those of 122, *Production and operations department managers*, or 123, *Other department managers*, are classified into Sub-major group 12, *Corporate managers*[1] or 13, *General managers*[2] as appropriate.

1141   SENIOR OFFICIALS OF POLITICAL-PARTY ORGANISATIONS

Senior officials of political-party organisations determine and formulate policies, rules and regulations of political-party organisations, direct their application, represent these organisations and act on their behalf.

Tasks include –

(a)   determining and formulating the political-party's policies, rules and regulations;

(b)   negotiating on behalf of the political party and its members;

(c)   planning and organising campaigns, on behalf of the political party, for the election of its candidates to political offices;

---

[1] See footnote 1 at beginning of Major group 1.   [2] See footnote 2 at beginning of Major group 1.

(d) planning and organising campaigns to recruit and educate political party members;

(e) planning, organising and directing sections charged with implementing the political-party's policies, rules and regulations;

(f) performing related tasks;

(g) supervising other workers.

Examples of the occupations classified here:

- Leader, political party
- President, political party
- Senior official, political party

1142 SENIOR OFFICIALS OF EMPLOYERS', WORKERS' AND OTHER ECONOMIC-INTEREST ORGANISATIONS

Senior officials of employers', workers' and other economic-interest organisations determine and formulate policies, rules and regulations of their respective organisations, direct their application, represent these organisations and act on their behalf.

Tasks include –

(a) deciding and formulating the organisation's policies, rules and regulations;

(b) negotiating on behalf of the organisation and its members;

(c) promoting the interests of the organisation and its members before the legislature, government or general public;

(d) planning and organising campaigns to recruit and educate members;

(e) planning, organising and directing sections charged with implementing the organisation's policies, rules and regulations;

(f) performing related tasks;

(g) supervising other workers.

Examples of the occupations classified here:

- Secretary-general, employers' organisation
- Secretary-general, trade union
- Senior official, employers' organisation
- Senior official, trade union

1143 SENIOR OFFICIALS OF HUMANITARIAN AND OTHER SPECIAL-INTEREST ORGANISATIONS

Senior officials of humanitarian and other special-interest organisations determine and formulate policies, rules and regulations of humanitarian organisations, sports associations or other special-interest organisations, direct their application, represent these organisations and act on their behalf.

Tasks include –

(a) determining and formulating the organisation's policies, rules and regulations;

(b) negotiating on behalf of the organisation, its members and relevant special-interest groups;

(c) promoting the interests of the organisation and its members before the legislature, government or general public;

(d) planning and organising campaigns to recruit and educate members;

(e) planning, organising and directing sections charged with implementing the organisation's policies, rules and regulations;

(f) performing related tasks;

(g) supervising other workers.

Examples of the occupations classified here:

- Secretary-general, environment protection organisation
- Secretary-general, wild life protection organisation
- Senior official, special-interest organisation

SUB-MAJOR GROUP **12**
CORPORATE MANAGERS[1]

Corporate managers determine and formulate policies and plan, direct and co-ordinate the activities of enterprises and organisations, or their internal departments or sections.

Tasks performed by workers in this sub-major group usually include: determining and formulating policies; planning, directing and co-ordinating the activities of the business enterprise or other organisation as a whole, or of their internal departments or sections. Supervision of other workers may be included.

Occupations in this sub-major group are classified into the following minor groups:

121   Directors and chief executives

122   Production and operations department managers

123   Other department managers

Note
In some cases where specific professional, technical or operational skills and knowledge may be required of workers at managerial level, it may be difficult to decide whether a particular job belongs in this or another sub-major group. In such cases, additional information on the main tasks of the job in question is essential. If the main tasks require the operational application of specific professional knowledge or a particular technical skill, then the job belongs in a different sub-major group. If, however, professional knowledge or technical skill serve only as a basis for managerial tasks, then the job belongs in this sub-major group. For example, if the main tasks of a job consist of diagnosing and treating illnesses, the job belongs in Major group 2, *Professionals*. However, if one of the main tasks is to allocate research and development funds for various projects within an enterprise or organisation on the basis of medical knowledge, then the job belongs in this sub-major group.

Professionals and technicians who, as consultants, advise enterprises and organisations on general or specialised management, or on operational functions, should be classified into Major group 2, *Professionals*, or 3, *Technicians and associate professionals*, as appropriate.

MINOR GROUP **121**
DIRECTORS AND CHIEF EXECUTIVES

Directors and chief executives head enterprises or organisations (except special-interest organisations) and, with the help of at least two other managers, determine and formulate policies, plan, direct and co-ordinate the activities of enterprises or organisations, usually within the guidelines set up by a board of directors or a governing body to whom they are answerable for the operations undertaken and results obtained.

Tasks performed usually include: determining and formulating policies, planning, directing and co-ordinating the general functioning of the enterprise or organisation, with the help of at least two other managers and, as a rule, within guidelines set up by a

---

[1] See footnote 1 at beginning of Major group 1.

board of directors or a governing body; reviewing the operations and results of the enterprise or organisation; reporting on results to the board of directors or to the governing body; representing the enterprise or organisation in its dealings with outside bodies, including government and other authorities. Supervision of other workers may be included.

Occupations in this minor group are classified into the following unit group:

1210   Directors and chief executives

1210   DIRECTORS AND CHIEF EXECUTIVES

Directors and chief executives head enterprises or organisations (except special-interest organisations) and, with the help of at least two other managers, determine and formulate policies and plan, direct and co-ordinate the general functioning of the enterprise or organisation usually within the guidelines set up by a board of directors or a governing body, to whom they are answerable for the operations undertaken and results obtained.

Tasks include –

(a) determining and formulating policies of the enterprise or organisation;

(b) planning, directing and co-ordinating the general functioning of the enterprise or organisation;

(c) determining and directing a particular policy, through consultation with subordinate managers;

(d) reviewing the operations and results of the enterprise, or organisation, and reporting to governing bodies;

(e) representing the enterprise or organisation in its dealings with outside bodies, including government or other authorities;

(f) performing related tasks;

(g) supervising other workers.

Examples of the occupations classified here:
- Chief executive, enterprise
- Director-general, enterprise
- Director-general, organisation
- Managing director, enterprise
- Managing director, organisation
- President, organisation

MINOR GROUP **122**
PRODUCTION AND OPERATIONS DEPARTMENT MANAGERS

Production and operations department managers of enterprises or organisations requiring a total of three or more managers, plan, direct and co-ordinate activities concerning the production of goods or the provision of services, under the broad guidance of directors and chief executives and in consultation with managers of other departments or sections.

Tasks performed usually include: planning, directing and co-ordinating activities concerning the production of goods or the provision of services by the enterprise or organisation; directing daily operations; overseeing the selection, training and performance of staff; reviewing the results and reporting them to directors and chief executives; liaising with managers of other departments; representing their department in its dealings with other parts of the organisation or with outside bodies. Supervision of other workers may be included.

Occupations in this minor group are classified into the following unit groups:

1221 Production and operations department managers in agriculture, hunting, forestry and fishing

1222 Production and operations department managers in manufacturing

1223 Production and operations department managers in construction

1224 Production and operations department managers in wholesale and retail trade

1225 Production and operations department managers in restaurants and hotels

1226 Production and operations department managers in transport, storage and communications

1227 Production and operations department managers in business services

1228 Production and operations department managers in personal care, cleaning, and related services

1229 Production and operations department managers not elsewhere classified

Note
The unit groups defined in this minor group classify jobs of production and operations department managers found in nine broad areas of economic activities. To define these areas in more detail, the following references can be made to the *International standard classification of all economic activities (ISIC)*, issued by the United Nations Secretariat, ST/ESA/STAT/SER.M/4/REV.3/ADD.2, New York, 1988.

- Unit Group 1221 refers to the jobs of *Production and operations department managers* which are found in enterprises classified in ISIC tabulation category A *Agriculture, hunting, and forestry*, and B *Fishing*.
- Unit Group 1222 refers to the jobs of *Production and operations department managers* which are found in enterprises classified in ISIC tabulation category C *Mining and quarrying*, D *Manufacturing*, and E *Electricity, gas and water supply*.
- Unit Group 1223 refers to the jobs of *Production and operations department managers* which are found in enterprises classified in ISIC tabulation category F *Construction*.
- Unit Group 1224 refers to the jobs of *Production and operations department managers* which are found in enterprises classified in ISIC tabulation category G *Wholesale and retail trade; Repair of motor vehicles, motor cycles and personal and household goods.*

- Unit Group 1225 refers to the jobs of *Production and operations department managers* which are found in enterprises classified in ISIC tabulation category H *Hotels and Restaurants*.
- Unit Group 1226 refers to the jobs of *Production and operations department managers* which are found in enterprises classified in ISIC tabulation category I *Transport, storage and communication*.
- Unit Group 1227 refers to the jobs of *Production and operations department managers* which are found in enterprises classified in ISIC tabulation categories J *Financing intermediation* and K *Real estate, renting and business activities*.
- Unit Group 1228 refers to the jobs of *Production and operations department managers* which are found in enterprises classified in ISIC divisions 90 *Sewage and refuse disposal, sanitation and similar activities*, and 93 *Other service activities*, and in tabulation category P *Private households with employed persons*.
- Unit Group 1229 refers to the jobs of *Production and department managers* which are found in the enterprises or organisations classified into ISIC tabulation categories L *Public administration and defence; compulsory social security*, excluding class 7522 *Defence activities*, M *Education*, N *Health and social work*, Q *Extra-territorial organisations and bodies*, and in division 92 *Recreational, cultural and sporting activities*.

1221 PRODUCTION AND OPERATIONS DEPARTMENT MANAGERS IN AGRICULTURE, HUNTING, FORESTRY AND FISHING

Production and operations department managers in agriculture, hunting, forestry and fishing plan, direct and co-ordinate those activities of farming and related enterprises which are concerned with the production of goods, under the broad guidance of the directors and chief executives, and in consultation with managers of other departments or sections.

Tasks include –

(a) planning, directing and co-ordinating activities concerning the production of goods;

(b) ensuring the efficient use of resources and the fulfilment of production quotas;

(c) planning and directing daily operations;

(d) controlling expenditure;

(e) establishing and directing operational and administrative procedures;

(f) overseeing the application of work safety and related procedures;

(g) overseeing the selection, training and performance of staff;

(h) representing the department in its dealings with other parts of the enterprise or with outside bodies;

(i) performing related tasks;

(j) supervising other workers.

Examples of the occupations classified here:

- Department manager, production and operations/agriculture
- Department manager, production and operations/fishing
- Department manager, production and operations/forestry
- Department manager, production and operations/hunting

Some related occupations classified elsewhere:

- Farmer, field crop – 6111
- Farmer, livestock – 6121
- General manager, agriculture – 1311
- Managing director, enterprise/agriculture – 1210

1222 PRODUCTION AND OPERATIONS DEPARTMENT MANAGERS IN MANUFACTURING

Production and operations department managers in manufacturing plan, direct and co-ordinate those activities of the enterprise which are concerned with the production of goods, under the broad guidance of the directors and chief executives, and in consultation with managers of other departments or sections.

Tasks include –

(a) planning, directing and co-ordinating activities concerning the manufacture of goods, or extraction of solid minerals from underground and surface mines and quarries, or the production and distribution of electricity, gas and water;

(b) ensuring the efficient use of resources and the fulfilment of production quotas;

(c) planning and directing daily production operations;

(d) controlling expenditure;

(e) establishing and directing operational and administrative procedures;

(f) overseeing the application of work safety and related procedures;

(g) overseeing the selection, training and performance of staff;

(h) representing the department in its dealings with other parts of the enterprise or with outside bodies;

(i) performing related tasks;

(j) supervising other workers.

Examples of the occupations classified here:

- Department manager, production and operations/manufacturing

Some related occupations classified elsewhere:

- General manager, manufacturing – 1312
- Managing director, enterprise/manufacturing – 1210

1223 PRODUCTION AND OPERATIONS DEPARTMENT MANAGERS IN CONSTRUCTION

Production and operations department managers in construction plan, direct and co-ordinate those activities of the enterprise which are concerned with construction work, under the broad guidance of the directors and chief executives, and in consultation with managers of other departments or sections.

Tasks include –
(a) planning, directing and co-ordinating activities concerning construction work;
(b) ensuring the efficient use of resources and the fulfilment of production quotas;
(c) planning and directing daily production operations;
(d) controlling expenditure;
(e) establishing and directing operational and administrative procedures;
(f) overseeing the application of work safety and related procedures;
(g) overseeing the selection, training and performance of staff;
(h) representing the department in its dealings with other parts of the enterprise or with outside bodies;
(i) performing related tasks;
(j) supervising other workers.

Examples of the occupations classified here:
- Department manager, production and operations/construction

Some related occupations classified elsewhere:
- General manager, construction – 1313
- Managing director, enterprise/construction – 1210

1224 PRODUCTION AND OPERATIONS DEPARTMENT MANAGERS IN WHOLESALE AND RETAIL TRADE

Production and operations department managers in wholesale and retail trade plan, direct and co-ordinate those activities of the enterprise which are concerned with trade, under the broad guidance of the directors and chief executives, and in consultation with managers of other departments or sections.

Tasks include –
(a) planning, directing and co-ordinating activities concerning trade carried out by the enterprise;
(b) ensuring the efficient use of resources and the fulfilment of trade quotas;
(c) planning and directing daily trade operations;
(d) controlling expenditure;
(e) establishing and directing operational and administrative procedures;
(f) overseeing the application of work safety and related procedures;
(g) overseeing the selection, training and performance of staff;
(h) representing the department in its dealings with other parts of the enterprise or with outside bodies;
(i) performing related tasks;
(j) supervising other workers.

Examples of the occupations classified here:
- Department manager, production and operations/retail trade
- Department manager, production and operations/wholesale trade

Some related occupations classified elsewhere:
- General manager, retail trade – 1314
- Managing director, enterprise/wholesale trade – 1210

1225 PRODUCTION AND OPERATIONS DEPARTMENT MANAGERS IN RESTAURANTS AND HOTELS

Production and operations department managers in restaurants and hotels plan, direct and co-ordinate those activities of the enterprise which are concerned with the provision of accommodation, catering and related services, under the broad guidance of the directors and chief executives, and in consultation with managers of other departments or sections.

Tasks include –
(a) planning, directing and co-ordinating activities concerning the provision of

accommodation, catering and related services;

(b) ensuring the efficient use of resources and the fulfilment of schedules;

(c) planning and directing daily operations;

(d) controlling expenditure;

(e) establishing and directing operational and administrative procedures;

(f) overseeing the application of work safety and related procedures;

(g) overseeing the selection, training and performance of staff;

(h) representing the department in its dealings with other parts of the enterprise or with outside bodies;

(i) performing related tasks;

(j) supervising other workers.

Examples of the occupations classified here:

- Department manager, production and operations/hotel
- Department manager, production and operations/restaurant

Some related occupations classified elsewhere:

- General manager, restaurant – 1315
- Managing director, enterprise/hotel – 1210

1226 PRODUCTION AND OPERATIONS DEPARTMENT MANAGERS IN TRANSPORT, STORAGE AND COMMUNICATIONS

Production and operations department managers in transport, storage and communications plan, direct and co-ordinate those activities of the enterprise which are concerned with providing relevant services, under the broad guidance of the directors and chief executives, and in consultation with managers of other departments or sections.

Tasks include –

(a) planning, directing and co-ordinating activities concerning the provision of relevant services;

(b) ensuring the efficient use of resources and the fulfilment of service quotas;

(c) planning and directing daily service operations;

(d) controlling expenditure;

(e) establishing and directing operational and administrative procedures;

(f) overseeing the application of work safety and related procedures;

(g) overseeing the selection, training and performance of staff;

(h) representing the department in its dealings with other parts of the enterprise or with outside bodies;

(i) performing related tasks;

(j) supervising other workers.

Examples of the occupations classified here:

- Department manager, production and operations/communications
- Department manager, production and operations/storage
- Department manager, production and operations/transport

Some related occupations classified elsewhere:

- General manager, storage – 1316
- Managing director, enterprise/communications – 1210
- Managing director, enterprise/transport – 1210

1227 PRODUCTION AND OPERATIONS DEPARTMENT MANAGERS IN BUSINESS SERVICES

Production and operations department managers in business services plan, direct and co-ordinate those activities of the enterprise which are concerned with providing external business services, under the broad guidance of the directors and chief executives, and in consultation with managers of other departments or sections.

Tasks include –

(a) planning, directing and co-ordinating activities concerning the provision of external business services such as banking, insurance, real estate, data processing, market research, accounting, architecture, engineering, building cleaning, technical testing and analysis, advertising or packaging;

(b) ensuring the efficient use of resources and the fulfilment of schedules;

(c) planning and directing daily operations;

(d) controlling expenditure;

(e) establishing and directing operational and administrative procedures;

(f) overseeing the application of work safety and related procedures;

(g) overseeing the selection, training and performance of staff;

(h) representing the department in its dealings with other parts of the enterprise or with outside bodies;

(i) performing related tasks;

(j) supervising other workers.

Examples of the occupations classified here:

- Department manager, production and operations/business services

Some related occupations classified elsewhere:

- General manager, business services – 1317
- Managing director, enterprise/business services – 1210

1228 PRODUCTION AND OPERATIONS DEPARTMENT MANAGERS IN PERSONAL CARE, CLEANING, AND RELATED SERVICES

Production and operations department managers in personal care, cleaning, and related services plan, direct and co-ordinate those activities of the enterprise which are concerned with providing relevant services, under the broad guidance of the directors and chief executives, and in consultation with managers of other departments or sections.

Tasks include –

(a) planning, directing and co-ordinating activities concerning the provision of relevant services;

(b) ensuring the efficient use of resources and the fulfilment of schedules;

(c) planning and directing daily trade operations;

(d) controlling expenditure;

(e) establishing and directing operational and administrative procedures;

(f) overseeing the application of work safety and related procedures;

(g) overseeing the selection, training and performance of staff;

(h) representing the department in its dealings with other parts of the enterprise or with outside bodies;

(i) performing related tasks;

(j) supervising other workers.

Examples of the occupations classified here:

- Department manager, production and operations/cleaning
- Department manager, production and operations/personal care

Some related occupations classified elsewhere:

- General manager, personal care – 1318
- Managing director, enterprise/cleaning – 1210

1229 PRODUCTION AND OPERATIONS DEPARTMENT MANAGERS NOT ELSEWHERE CLASSIFIED

This unit group covers department managers not classified elsewhere in Minor group 122, *Production and operations department managers.*

For instance here should be classified those who plan, direct and co-ordinate activities of the enterprise or organisation concerning government administrative and other operations, public or private education services, health and social work services, recreational, cultural, and sporting events and services, and operations of extra-territorial organisations and bodies.

In such cases tasks would include –

(a) planning, directing and co-ordinating government operations concerning public service activities, such as control of the money supply or taxation schemes, various government business regulations, as well as civil service administration and related activities;

(b) planning, directing and co-ordinating activities concerning the administration and operation of foreign affairs and public order and safety activities;

(c) planning, directing and co-ordinating activities concerning the administration and operation of government-funded social security schemes;

(d) planning, directing and co-ordinating activities concerning public or private education;

(e) planning, directing and co-ordinating activities concerning health and social services;

(f) planning, directing and co-ordinating activities concerning recreational, cultural and sporting operations and events;

(g) planning, directing and co-ordinating activities concerning the operations of extra-territorial organisations and bodies;

(h) performing related tasks;

(i) supervising other workers.

Examples of the occupations classified here:
- Dean
- Department manager, production and operations/extra-territorial organisations
- Department manager, production and operations/health
- Department manager, production and operations/recreation
- Head teacher

Some related occupations classified elsewhere:
- General manager, education – 1319
- General manager, recreation – 1319
- Managing director, enterprise/health – 1210
- Managing director, organisation/extra-territorial organisations – 1210

MINOR GROUP **123**
OTHER DEPARTMENT MANAGERS

Other department managers of enterprises or organisations requiring a total of three or more managers, plan, direct and co-ordinate particular activities, under the broad guidance of the directors and chief executives, and in consultation with managers of other departments or sections.

Tasks performed usually include: planning, directing and co-ordinating activities of their department; directing daily operations; overseeing the selection, training, and performance of staff; reviewing the results and reporting them to directors and chief executives; liaising with managers of other departments; representing the department in its dealings with other parts of the organisation or with outside bodies.

Occupations in this minor group are classified into the following unit groups:

1231 Finance and administration department managers

1232 Personnel and industrial relations department managers

1233 Sales and marketing department managers

1234 Advertising and public relations department managers

1235 Supply and distribution department managers

1236 Computing services department managers

1237 Research and development department managers

1239 Other department managers not elsewhere classified

1231 FINANCE AND ADMINISTRATION DEPARTMENT MANAGERS

Finance and administration department managers plan, direct and co-ordinate the internal administration or financial operations of the enterprise or organisation, under the broad guidance of the directors and chief executives, and in consultation with managers of other departments or sections.

Tasks include –
(a) planning, directing and co-ordinating the internal administration or financial operations of the enterprise or organisation;
(b) assessing the financial situation of the enterprise or organisation, preparing budgets and overseeing various financial operations;
(c) controlling expenditure and ensuring the efficient use of resources;
(d) establishing and directing operational and administrative procedures;
(e) planning and directing daily operations;
(f) overseeing the selection, training and performance of staff;
(g) representing the department in its dealings with other parts of the organisation or with outside bodies;
(h) performing related tasks;
(i) supervising other workers.

Examples of the occupations classified here:
- Department manager, administration
- Department manager, finance

1232 PERSONNEL AND INDUSTRIAL RELATIONS DEPARTMENT MANAGERS

Personnel and industrial relations department managers plan, direct and co-ordinate policies concerning personnel and the industrial relations activities of the enterprise or organisation, under the broad guidance of the directors and chief executives, and in consultation with managers of other departments or sections.

Tasks include –
(a) planning, directing and co-ordinating policies concerning personnel and the industrial relations activities of the enterprise or organisation;
(b) planning and organising procedures for recruitment, training, promotion, determination of wage structures and negotiations about wages, liaison and consultation with workers, and related personnel matters;
(c) overseeing safety, health and related programmes and activities, with the participation of all concerned;
(d) controlling expenditure and ensuring the efficient use of resources;
(e) establishing and directing operational and administrative procedures;
(f) planning and directing daily operations;
(g) overseeing the selection, training and performance of staff;
(h) representing the department in its dealings with other parts of the organisation or with outside bodies;
(i) performing related tasks;
(j) supervising other workers.

Examples of the occupations classified here:
- Department manager, industrial relations
- Department manager, personnel

1233 SALES AND MARKETING DEPARTMENT MANAGERS

Sales and marketing department managers plan, direct and co-ordinate the sales and marketing activities of the enterprise or organisation, under the broad guidance of the directors and chief executives, and in consultation with managers of other departments or sections.

Tasks include –
(a) planning, directing and co-ordinating the sales and marketing activities of the enterprise or organisation;
(b) planning and organising special sales and marketing programmes based on sales records and market assessments;
(c) determining price lists, discount and delivery terms, sales promotion budgets, sales methods, special incentives and special campaigns;
(d) controlling expenditure and ensuring the efficient use of resources;

(e) establishing and directing operational and administrative procedures;

(f) planning and directing daily operations;

(g) overseeing the selection, training and performance of staff;

(h) representing the department in its dealings with other parts of the organisation or with outside bodies;

(i) performing related tasks;

(j) supervising other workers.

Examples of the occupations classified here:
- Department manager, marketing
- Department manager, sales

1234 ADVERTISING AND PUBLIC RELATIONS DEPARTMENT MANAGERS

Advertising and public relations department managers plan, direct and co-ordinate the advertising, public relations and public information activities of the enterprise or organisation, under the broad guidance of the directors and chief executives, and in consultation with managers of other departments or sections.

Tasks include –

(a) planning, directing and co-ordinating the advertising and public relations activities of the enterprise or organisation;

(b) negotiating advertising contracts with officials of newspapers, radio and television stations, sports and cultural organisations and advertising agencies;

(c) planning and managing information programmes to inform legislators, the mass media and the general public about the plans, accomplishments and points of view of the enterprise or organisation;

(d) planning and managing fund-raising activities for educational, humanitarian and other non-profit-making organisations;

(e) controlling expenditure and ensuring the efficient use of resources;

(f) establishing and directing operational and administrative procedures;

(g) planning and directing daily operations;

(h) overseeing the selection, training and performance of staff;

(i) representing the department in its dealings with other parts of the organisation or with outside bodies;

(j) performing related tasks;

(k) supervising other workers.

Examples of the occupations classified here:
- Department manager, advertising
- Department manager, public relations

1235 SUPPLY AND DISTRIBUTION DEPARTMENT MANAGERS

Supply and distribution department managers plan, direct and co-ordinate the supply and distribution activities of the enterprise or organisation, under the broad guidance of the directors and chief executives, and in consultation with managers of other departments or sections.

Tasks include –

(a) planning, directing and co-ordinating the supply, storage and distribution activities of the enterprise or organisation;

(b) negotiating purchase contracts, agreeing a suitable price with suppliers and ensuring the quality of the goods purchased;

(c) planning and installing systems for inventory control;

(d) controlling expenditure and ensuring the efficient use of resources;

(e) establishing and directing operational and administrative procedures;

(f) planning and directing daily operations;

(g) overseeing the selection, training and performance of staff;

(h) representing the department in its dealings with other parts of the organisation or with outside bodies;

(i) performing related tasks;

(j) supervising other workers.

Examples of the occupations classified here:
- Department manager, distribution
- Department manager, supplies

1

1236 COMPUTING SERVICES DEPARTMENT MANAGERS

Computing services department managers plan, direct and co-ordinate the computing services of the enterprise or organisation, under the broad guidance of the directors and chief executives, and in consultation with managers of other departments or sections.

Tasks include –

(a) planning, directing and co-ordinating the computing services of the enterprise or organisation;

(b) directing the selection, installation, use and maintenance of computing equipment and software and the purchase of externally provided computing services;

(c) planning the overall data processing policies of the enterprise or organisation and co-ordinating the search for alternatives;

(d) controlling expenditure and ensuring the efficient use of resources;

(e) establishing and directing operational and administrative procedures;

(f) planning and directing daily operations;

(g) overseeing the selection, training and performance of staff;

(h) representing the department in its dealings with other parts of the organisation or with outside bodies;

(i) performing related tasks;

(j) supervising other workers.

Examples of the occupations classified here:

- Department manager, computing services

1237 RESEARCH AND DEVELOPMENT DEPARTMENT MANAGERS

Research and development department managers plan, direct and co-ordinate the research and development activities of the enterprise or organisation, under the broad guidance of the directors and chief executives, and in consultation with managers of other departments or sections.

Tasks include –

(a) planning, directing and co-ordinating research and development activities, in-house or commissioned from external research organisations, to develop new or improved technical processes, products or utilisation of materials for the enterprise or organisation;

(b) planning the overall research and development programme of the enterprise or organisation, specifying goals and budgetary requirements;

(c) controlling expenditure and ensuring the efficient use of resources;

(d) establishing and directing operational and administrative procedures;

(e) planning and directing daily operations;

(f) overseeing the selection, training and performance of staff;

(g) representing the department in its dealings with other parts of the organisation or with outside bodies;

(h) performing related tasks;

(i) supervising other workers.

Examples of the occupations classified here:

- Department manager, research and development

1239 OTHER DEPARTMENT MANAGERS NOT ELSEWHERE CLASSIFIED

This unit group covers department managers not classified elsewhere in Minor group 123, *Other department managers*.

SUB-MAJOR GROUP 13
GENERAL MANAGERS[1]

General managers head various small business undertakings which they manage on their own behalf, or on behalf of the proprietors, with the assistance of no more than one other manager and some non-managerial help.

Tasks performed by workers in this sub-major group usually include: planning, formulating and implementing policies; managing daily operations and reviewing their results; negotiating with suppliers, customers and other enterprises; planning and controlling the use of resources and the selection of staff; reporting to owners, if any; supervising other workers.

Occupations in this sub-major group are classified into the following minor group:

131   General managers

MINOR GROUP 131
GENERAL MANAGERS

General managers head various small business undertakings which they manage on their own behalf, or on behalf of the proprietors, with the assistance of no more than one other manager and some non-managerial help.

Tasks performed usually include: planning, formulating and implementing policies; managing daily operations and reviewing results; negotiating with suppliers, customers and other enterprises; planning and controlling the use of resources and the selection of staff; reporting to owners, if any; supervising other workers.

Occupations in this minor group are classified into the following unit groups:

1311   General managers in agriculture, hunting, forestry and fishing

1312   General managers in manufacturing

1313   General managers in construction

1314   General managers in wholesale and retail trade

1315   General managers of restaurants and hotels

---

[1] See footnote 2 at beginning of Major group 1.

1316   General managers in transport, storage and communications

1317   General managers of business services

1318   General managers in personal care, cleaning, and related services

1319   General managers not elsewhere classified

Note
    The unit groups defined in this minor group classify jobs of *General managers* found in nine broad areas of economic activity. To define these areas in more detail, the following references can be made to the *International standard classification of all economic activities (ISIC)*, issued by the United Nations Secretariat ST/ESA/STAT/SER.M/4/REV.3/ADD.2, New York, 1988.

– Unit group 1311 refers to the jobs of *General managers* found in enterprises classified in ISIC tabulation category A *Agriculture, hunting, and forestry,* and B *Fishing.*

– Unit group 1312 refers to the jobs of *General managers* found in enterprises classified in ISIC tabulation category C *Mining and quarrying,* D *Manufacturing* and Unit group E *Electricity, gas and water supply.*

– Unit group 1313 refers to the jobs of *General managers* found in enterprises classified in ISIC tabulation category F *Construction.*

– Unit group 1314 refers to the jobs of *General managers* found in enterprises classified in ISIC tabulation category G *Wholesale and retail trade; Repair of motor vehicles, motor cycles and personal and household goods.*

– Unit group 1315 refers to the jobs of *General managers* found in enterprises classified in ISIC tabulation category H *Hotels and Restaurants.*

– Unit group 1316 refers to the jobs of *General managers* found in enterprises classified in ISIC tabulation category I *Transport, storage and communication.*

– Unit group 1317 refers to the jobs of *General managers* found in enterprises classified in ISIC tabulation categories J *Financing intermediation* and K *Real estate, renting and business activities.*

– Unit group 1318 refers to the jobs of *General managers* found in enterprises classified in ISIC divisions 90, *Sewage and refuse disposal, sanitation and similar activities,* and 93 *Other service activities,* and in tabulation category P *Private households with employed persons.*

– Unit group 1319 refers to the jobs of *General managers* found in enterprises classified in ISIC tabulation categories M *Education,* and N *Health and social work,* and in division 92 *Recreational, cultural and sporting activities.*

1311   GENERAL MANAGERS IN AGRICULTURE, HUNTING, FORESTRY AND FISHING

    General managers in agriculture, hunting, forestry and fishing head small agricultural farms or hunting, forestry or fishing businesses and, on their own behalf or on behalf of the proprietor, plan, direct and co-ordinate the activities of the business, with the assistance of no more than one other manager and some non-managerial help.

    Tasks include –
(a)   planning and implementing policies;
(b)   making budgetary estimates;
(c)   negotiating with suppliers and customers and with other organisations;
(d)   planning and controlling the use of resources and hiring workers;
(e)   managing daily operations;
(f)   reporting to owners, if any;
(g)   performing related tasks;
(h)   supervising other workers.

Examples of the occupations classified here:
  ▪ General manager, agriculture
  ▪ General manager, fishing
  ▪ General manager, forestry
  ▪ General manager, hunting

Some related occupations classified elsewhere:
  ▪ Department manager, production and operations/agriculture – 1221
  ▪ Farmer, field crop – 6111

- Farmer, livestock – 6121
- Managing director, enterprise/agriculture – 1210

1312 GENERAL MANAGERS IN MANUFACTURING

General managers in manufacturing head small manufacturing businesses and, on their own behalf or on behalf of the proprietor, plan, direct and co-ordinate the activities of the business, with the assistance of no more than one other manager and some non-managerial help.

Tasks include –
(a) planning and implementing policies;
(b) making budgetary estimates;
(c) negotiating with suppliers and customers and with other organisations;
(d) planning and controlling the use of resources and hiring workers;
(e) managing daily operations;
(f) reporting to owners, if any;
(g) performing related tasks;
(h) supervising other workers.

Examples of the occupations classified here:
- General manager, manufacturing

Some related occupations classified elsewhere:
- Department manager, production and operations/manufacturing – 1222
- Managing director, enterprise/manufacturing – 1210

1313 GENERAL MANAGERS IN CONSTRUCTION

General managers in construction head small construction businesses and, on their own behalf or on behalf of the proprietor, plan, direct and co-ordinate the activities of the business, with the assistance of no more than one other manager and some non-managerial help.

Tasks include –
(a) planning and implementing policies;
(b) making budgetary estimates;
(c) negotiating with suppliers and customers and with other organisations;
(d) planning and controlling the use of resources and hiring workers;
(e) managing daily operations;
(f) reporting to owners, if any;
(g) performing related tasks;
(h) supervising other workers.

Examples of the occupations classified here:
- General manager, construction

Some related occupations classified elsewhere:
- Department manager, production and operations/construction – 1223
- Managing director, enterprise/construction – 1210

1314 GENERAL MANAGERS IN WHOLESALE AND RETAIL TRADE

General managers in wholesale and retail trade head small wholesale or retail businesses and, on their own behalf or on behalf of the proprietor, plan, direct and co-ordinate the activities of the business, with the assistance of no more than one other manager and some non-managerial help.

Tasks include –
(a) planning and implementing policies;
(b) making budgetary estimates;
(c) negotiating with suppliers and customers and with other organisations;
(d) planning and controlling the use of resources and hiring workers;
(e) managing daily operations;
(f) reporting to owners, if any;
(g) performing related tasks;
(h) supervising other workers.

Examples of the occupations classified here:
- General manager, retail trade
- General manager, wholesale trade

Some related occupations classified elsewhere:
- Department manager, production and operations/retail trade – 1224
- Managing director, enterprise/wholesale trade – 1210

1

1315 GENERAL MANAGERS OF RESTAURANTS AND HOTELS

General managers of restaurants and hotels head small restaurant or hotel businesses and, on their own behalf or on behalf of the proprietor, plan, direct and co-ordinate the activities of the business, with the assistance of no more than one other manager and some non-managerial help.

Tasks include –
(a) planning and implementing policies;
(b) making budgetary estimates;
(c) negotiating with suppliers and customers and with other organisations;
(d) planning and controlling the use of resources and hiring workers;
(e) managing daily operations;
(f) reporting to owners, if any;
(g) performing related tasks;
(h) supervising other workers.

Examples of the occupations classified here:
- General manager, hotel
- General manager, restaurant

Some related occupations classified elsewhere:
- Department manager, production and operations/restaurant – 1225
- Managing director, enterprise/hotel – 1210

1316 GENERAL MANAGERS IN TRANSPORT, STORAGE AND COMMUNICATIONS

General managers in transport, storage and communications head small transport, storage or communications businesses and, on their own behalf or on behalf of the proprietor, plan, direct and co-ordinate the activities of the business, with the assistance of no more than one other manager and some non-managerial help.

Tasks include –
(a) planning and implementing policies;
(b) making budgetary estimates;
(c) negotiating with suppliers and customers and with other organisations;
(d) planning and controlling the use of resources and hiring workers;
(e) managing daily operations;
(f) reporting to owners, if any;
(g) performing related tasks;
(h) supervising other workers.

Examples of the occupations classified here:
- General manager, communications
- General manager, storage
- General manager, transport

Some related occupations classified elsewhere:
- Department manager, production and operations/communications – 1226
- Department manager, production and operations/storage – 1226
- Managing director, enterprise/transport – 1210

1317 GENERAL MANAGERS OF BUSINESS SERVICES

General managers of business services head small firms providing various business services and, on their own behalf or on behalf of the proprietor, plan, direct and co-ordinate the activities of the enterprise with the assistance of no more than one other manager and some non-managerial help.

Tasks include –
(a) planning and implementing policies;
(b) making budgetary estimates;
(c) negotiating with suppliers and customers and with other organisations;
(d) planning and controlling the use of resources and hiring workers;
(e) managing daily operations;
(f) reporting to owners, if any;
(g) performing related tasks;
(h) supervising other workers.

Examples of the occupations classified here:
- General manager, business services

Some related occupations classified elsewhere:
- Department manager, production and operations/business services – 1227
- Managing director, enterprise/business services – 1210

1318 GENERAL MANAGERS IN PERSONAL CARE, CLEANING AND RELATED SERVICES

General managers in personal care, cleaning and related services head small businesses providing personal care, cleaning and related services and, on their own behalf or on behalf of the proprietor, plan, direct and co-ordinate the activities of the business, with the assistance of no more than one other manager and some non-managerial help.

Tasks include –
(a) planning and implementing policies;
(b) making budgetary estimates;
(c) negotiating with suppliers and customers and with other organisations;
(d) planning and controlling the use of resources and hiring workers;
(e) managing daily operations;
(f) reporting to owners, if any;
(g) performing related tasks;
(h) supervising other workers.

Examples of the occupations classified here:
- General manager, cleaning
- General manager, personal care

Some related occupations classified elsewhere:
- Department manager, production and operations/cleaning – 1228
- Department manager, production and operations/personal care – 1228
- Managing director, enterprise/cleaning – 1210

1319 GENERAL MANAGERS NOT ELSEWHERE CLASSIFIED

This unit group covers general managers not elsewhere classified in Minor group 131, *General managers*.

For instance, here should be classified those who head small businesses in the fields of education, health, or recreational, cultural or sporting activities and, on their own behalf or on behalf of the proprietor, plan, direct and co-ordinate the activities of the business, with the assistance of no more than one other manager and some non-managerial help.

In such cases tasks would include –
(a) planning and implementing policies;
(b) making budgetary estimates;
(c) negotiating with suppliers and customers and with other organisations;
(d) planning and controlling the use of resources and hiring workers;
(e) managing daily operations;
(f) reporting to owners, if any;
(g) performing related tasks;
(h) supervising other workers.

Examples of the occupations classified here:
- General manager, education
- General manager, health
- General manager, recreation
- General manager, travel agency

Some related occupations classified elsewhere:
- Dean – 1229
- Department manager, production and operations/recreation – 1229
- Managing director, enterprise/education – 1210
- Managing director, enterprise/health – 1210

MAJOR GROUP **2**
PROFESSIONALS

Professionals increase the existing stock of knowledge, apply scientific or artistic concepts and theories, teach about the foregoing in a systematic manner, or engage in any combination of these three activities. Most occupations in this major group require skills at the fourth ISCO skill level.

Tasks performed by professionals usually include: conducting analysis and research, and developing concepts, theories and operational methods, and advising on or applying existing knowledge related to physical sciences including mathematics, engineering and technology, and to life sciences including the medical profession, as well as to social sciences and humanities; teaching the theory and practice of one or more disciplines at different educational levels; teaching and educating handicapped persons; providing various business, legal and social services; creating and performing works of art; providing spiritual guidance; preparing scientific papers and reports. Supervision of other workers may be included.

It should be noted that, depending on the specific tasks and degree of responsibility in executing them, as well as on the national educational and training requirements, it may be appropriate to classify some of the occupations that are identified here into Major group 3, *Technicians and associate professionals*. Suchlike cases are to be found in particular among *teaching occupations*, *nursing occupations* and *social services occupations*.

Occupations in this major group are classified into the following sub-major groups:

21 Physical, mathematical and engineering science professionals

22 Life science and health professionals

23 Teaching professionals

24 Other professionals

SUB-MAJOR GROUP **21**
PHYSICAL, MATHEMATICAL AND ENGINEERING SCIENCE PROFESSIONALS

Physical, mathematical and engineering science professionals conduct research, improve or develop concepts, theories and operational methods, or apply scientific knowledge relating to fields such as physics, astronomy, meteorology, chemistry,

2

geophysics, geology, mathematics, statistics, computing, architecture, engineering, and technology.

Tasks performed by workers in this sub-major group usually include: conducting research, enlarging, advising on or applying scientific knowledge obtained through the study of structures and properties of physical matter and phenomena, chemical characteristics and processes of various substances, materials and products, and of mathematical, statistical and computing concepts and methods; advising on, designing and directing construction of buildings, towns and traffic systems, or civil engineering and industrial structures, as well as machines and other equipment, and advising on and applying mining methods, and ensuring their optimum use; surveying land and sea and making maps; studying and advising on technological aspects of particular materials, products and processes, and on efficiency of production and work organisation; preparing scientific papers and reports. Supervision of other workers may be included.

Occupations in this sub-major group are classified into the following minor groups:

211 Physicists, chemists and related professionals

212 Mathematicians, statisticians and related professionals

213 Computing professionals

214 Architects, engineers and related professionals

MINOR GROUP 211
PHYSICISTS, CHEMISTS AND RELATED PROFESSIONALS

Physicists, chemists and related professionals conduct research, improve or develop concepts, theories and operational methods, or apply scientific knowledge relating to physics, astronomy, meteorology, chemistry, geology and geophysics.

Tasks performed usually include: enlarging scientific knowledge through research and experiments related to mechanics, thermodynamics, optics, sonics, electricity, magnetism, electronics, nuclear physics, astronomy, various branches of chemistry, as well as to atmospheric conditions, or the physical nature of the earth, and advising on or applying this knowledge in such fields as manufacturing, agriculture, medicine, navigation, space exploration, oil, gas, water and mineral exploitation, telecommunications and other services, or civil engineering; preparing scientific papers and reports. Supervision of other workers may be included.

Occupations in this minor group are classified into the following unit groups:

2111 Physicists and astronomers

2112 Meteorologists

2113 Chemists

2114 Geologists and geophysicists

2111 PHYSICISTS AND ASTRONOMERS

Physicists and astronomers conduct research, improve or develop concepts, theories and operational methods, or apply scientific knowledge relating to physics and astronomy in industrial, medical, military or other fields.

Tasks include –

(a) conducting research, and improving or developing concepts, theories and operational methods related to physics and astronomy;

(b) conducting experiments, tests and analyses in fields such as mechanics, thermodynamics, optics, sonics, electricity, magnetism, electronics and nuclear physics, or astronomy;

(c) conducting experiments, tests and analyses of the structure and properties of matter in solid state and its behaviour under temperature, pressure, stress and other conditions;

(d) evaluating results of investigations and experiments and expressing conclusions, mainly using mathematical techniques and models;

(e) developing or improving industrial, medical, military and other practical applications of the principles and techniques of physics or astronomy;

(f) observing, analysing and interpreting celestial phenomena and developing methods and techniques to be used in fields such as navigation or space exploration;

(g) preparing scientific papers and reports;

(h) performing related tasks;

(i) supervising other workers.

Examples of the occupations classified here:

- Astronomer
- Physicist

2112 METEOROLOGISTS

Meteorologists conduct research, improve or develop concepts, theories and operational methods related to the composition, structure and dynamics of the atmosphere, and prepare detailed or long-term weather forecasts used in aviation, shipping, agriculture and other areas and for the information of the general public.

Tasks include –

(a) conducting research and improving or developing concepts, theories and operational methods related to the composition, structure and dynamics of the atmosphere;

(b) investigating direction and speed of air movements, pressures, temperatures, humidity and other phenomena such as cloud formation and precipitation, electrical disturbances or solar radiation;

(c) studying data collected from weather stations, preparing detailed or long-term weather maps and forecasts used in aviation, shipping, agriculture and other areas and for the information of the general public;

(d) conducting experiments in fog dispersal, rain-making and other types of weather control;

(e) preparing scientific papers and reports;

(f) performing related tasks;

(g) supervising other workers.

Examples of the occupations classified here:

- Climatologist
- Forecaster, weather
- Meteorologist

2113 CHEMISTS

Chemists conduct research, improve or develop concepts, theories and operational methods, or apply scientific knowledge relating to chemistry, mainly to test, develop and improve materials, and industrial products and processes.

Tasks include –

(a) conducting research and improving or developing concepts, theories and operational methods related to chemistry;

(b) conducting experiments, tests and analyses to investigate chemical composition and energy and chemical changes in various natural, artificial or synthetic substances, materials and products;

(c) evaluating results of investigations and experiments and deriving conclusions;

(d) developing or improving pharmaceutical and other industrial materials, products and processes;

2

(e) developing quality control procedures for manufacturers or users;

(f) preparing scientific papers and reports;

(g) performing related tasks;

(h) supervising other workers.

Examples of the occupations classified here:

- Chemist
- Chemist, pharmaceutical

Some related occupations classified elsewhere:

- Biochemist – 2212
- Pharmacist – 2224
- Pharmacologist – 2212

2114   GEOLOGISTS AND GEOPHYSICISTS

Geologists and geophysicists conduct research, improve or develop concepts, theories and operational methods, or apply scientific knowledge relating to geology and geophysics in such fields as oil, gas and mineral exploitation, water conservation, civil engineering, telecommunications and navigation.

Tasks include –

(a) conducting research and improving or developing concepts, theories and operational methods related to geology and geophysics;

(b) studying composition and structure of the earth's crust, examining rocks, minerals, fossil remains, etc., to determine processes affecting the development of the earth, trace evolution of past life and establish nature and chronology of geological formations;

(c) interpreting research data and preparing geological reports, maps, charts and diagrams;

(d) applying results of research to assess development potential of mineral, gas and oil deposits and underground water resources;

(e) applying geological knowledge to problems encountered in civil engineering projects such as the construction of dams, bridges, tunnels and large buildings;

(f) investigating and measuring seismic, gravitational, electrical, thermal and magnetic forces affecting the earth;

(g) investigating and measuring optical and acoustic phenomena in the atmosphere;

(h) estimating weight, size and mass of the earth and composition and structure of its interior, and studying the nature and activity of volcanoes, glaciers and earthquakes;

(i) charting the earth's magnetic field and applying this and other collected data for purposes of broadcasting and navigation;

(j) studying and measuring physical properties of seas and the atmosphere and their inter-relationship, such as the exchange of thermal energy;

(k) locating and determining the nature and extent of oil, gas and mineral deposits and of ground-water resources, using seismological, gravimetric, magnetic, electrical or radiometric methods;

(l) preparing scientific papers and reports;

(m) performing related tasks;

(n) supervising other workers.

Examples of the occupations classified here:

- Geologist
- Geophysicist

MINOR GROUP 212
MATHEMATICIANS, STATISTICIANS AND RELATED PROFESSIONALS

Mathematicians, statisticians and related professionals conduct research, improve or develop mathematical, actuarial or statistical concepts, theories and operational methods and techniques, and apply this knowledge to a wide range of tasks in such fields as engineering, business or medicine as well as in other areas of natural, social or life sciences.

Tasks performed usually include: conducting research in fundamental mathematics and advising on or applying mathematical, actuarial and statistical principles and techniques; dealing with, and advising on, actuarial matters, including design of insurance and pension schemes; planning, designing and conducting statistical collections; evaluating, organising, processing, interpreting and analysing statistical data; preparing scientific papers and reports. Supervision of other workers may be included.

Occupations in this minor group are classified into the following unit groups:

2121 Mathematicians and related professionals
2122 Statisticians

2121 MATHEMATICIANS AND RELATED PROFESSIONALS

Mathematicians and related professionals conduct research and improve or develop mathematical and actuarial concepts, theories and operational methods and techniques and advise on or engage in their practical application in such fields as engineering, business or medicine as well as in other areas of natural, social or life sciences.

Tasks include –

(a) studying, improving and developing mathematical and actuarial theories and techniques;

(b) advising on or applying mathematical principles, models and techniques to a wide range of tasks in the fields of engineering, agronomy and medicine, as well as in other areas of natural, social or life sciences;

(c) conducting logical analyses of management problems, especially in terms of input-output effectiveness, and formulating mathematical models of each problem usually for programming and solution by computer;

(d) designing and putting into operation pension schemes and life, health, social and other types of insurance systems;

(e) preparing scientific papers and reports;

(f) performing related tasks;

(g) supervising other workers.

Examples of the occupations classified here:
- Actuary
- Analyst, operations research
- Mathematician, applied mathematics
- Mathematician, pure mathematics

Some related occupations classified elsewhere:
- Assistant, actuarial – 3434
- Assistant, mathematical – 3434
- Clerk, actuarial – 4122
- Statistician, mathematical – 2122

2122 STATISTICIANS

Statisticians conduct research, improve or develop mathematical and other aspects of statistical concepts, theories and operational methods and techniques, and advise on or engage in their practical application, in such fields as business or medicine as well as in other areas of natural, social or life sciences.

Tasks include –

(a) studying, improving and developing statistical theories and methodologies;

(b) planning and organising surveys and other statistical collections, and designing questionnaires;

(c) evaluating, processing, analysing, and interpreting statistical data and preparing them for publication;

(d) advising on or applying various data collection methods and statistical methods and techniques, and determining reliability of findings, especially in such fields as business or medicine as well as in other areas of natural, social or life sciences;

(e) preparing scientific papers and reports;

2

(f) performing related tasks;
(g) supervising other workers.

Examples of the occupations classified here:

- Demographer
- Statistician

- Statistician, applied statistics
- Statistician, mathematical

Some related occupations classified elsewhere:

- Assistant, statistical − 3434
- Clerk, statistical − 4122

MINOR GROUP 213
COMPUTING PROFESSIONALS

Computing professionals conduct research, plan, develop and improve computer-based information systems, software and related concepts, develop principles and operational methods as well as maintain data dictionary and management systems of databases to ensure integrity and security of data.

Tasks performed usually include: conducting research into the theoretical aspects of and operational methods for the use of computers, such as computer architecture and design, data structures and databases, algorithms, artificial intelligence, computer languages, data communication and robotics; evaluating, planning and designing hardware and software configurations for specific applications; designing, writing, testing and maintaining computer programs; preparing scientific papers and technical reports, documentation and manuals. Supervision of other workers may be included.

Occupations in this minor group are classified into the following unit groups:

2131   Computer systems designers and analysts

2132   Computer programmers

2139   Computing professionals not elsewhere classified

2131   COMPUTER SYSTEMS DESIGNERS AND ANALYSTS

Computer systems designers and analysts conduct research, improve or develop computing concepts and operational methods, and advise on or engage in their practical application.

Tasks include −

(a) researching into the principles and operational methods of computers and computer-based systems for information communication and processing, planning, design, process control and production; development and maintenance of computer software, as well as data structures and databases,

algorithms, artificial intelligence and robotics;

(b) maintaining data dictionary and management systems of databases to ensure validity and safety of data;

(c) contributing to and keeping up with technical developments of computers, peripherals, computing methods and software, their potential and limitations;

(d) analysing computer users' requirements, by consultation, to determine hardware and software configurations and development needs and preparing cost-benefit analyses;

(e) writing programming specifications and preparing technical reports and instruction manuals specifying methods of operation and maintenance of the computer hardware and software configurations;

(f) designing, writing, maintaining and updating software which controls the overall functioning of computers and which links hardware and computer applications software;

(g) designing and implementing communication networks between different computer installations;

(h) developing improved methods and instruments, including computer languages, for writing, documenting and maintaining computer software;

(i) preparing scientific papers and reports;

(j) performing related tasks;

(k) supervising other workers.

Examples of the occupations classified here:

- Analyst, communications/computers
- Analyst, database/computers
- Analyst, systems/computers
- Database administrator
- Designer, systems/computers
- Engineer, computer systems

Some related occupations classified elsewhere:

- Engineer, computer applications – 2139
- Technician, computer – 3121

2132 COMPUTER PROGRAMMERS

Computer programmers write, test and maintain computer programs to meet the needs of users of computer systems.

Tasks include –

(a) studying program intent, output requirements, nature and sources of input data, internal checks and other controls required in consultation with *Computer systems designers and analysts* and subject-matter specialists;

(b) preparing detailed logical workflow charts and diagrams and establishing sequence of steps for data input and computer processing operations;

(c) writing and providing detailed documentation of computer programs in a machine code, assembler, or high-level language such as PL/1, COBOL, FORTRAN, PASCAL, BASIC or C, based when necessary on specifications provided by *Computer systems designers and analysts*, and testing programs to eliminate errors;

(d) maintaining computer programs and their documentation to take account of changed input or output specifications or hardware configurations;

(e) performing related tasks;

(f) supervising other workers.

Examples of the occupations classified here:

- Programmer
- Programmer, communications
- Programmer, database

2139 COMPUTING PROFESSIONALS NOT ELSEWHERE CLASSIFIED

This unit group covers computing professionals not classified elsewhere in Minor group 213, *Computing professionals*.

For instance, here should be classified those who have a general knowledge of both computer hardware and software.

In such cases tasks would include:

(a) designing and implementing computer software applications, and computer operating systems;

(b) maintaining and updating computer software applications, and computer operating systems;

(c) installing computers and performing diagnostics on computer hardware;

(d) performing related tasks;

(e) supervising other workers.

Examples of the occupations classified here:

- Engineer, computer applications

MINOR GROUP **214**
ARCHITECTS, ENGINEERS AND RELATED PROFESSIONALS

Architects, engineers and related professionals conduct research and improve or develop concepts, theories and operational methods, or apply existing knowledge in such fields as architecture and engineering, as well as in the field of technological and economic efficiency of production processes.

Tasks performed usually include: conducting research and advising on, designing, and directing the construction of buildings, towns, traffic and landscape systems, and advising on and directing their maintenance and repairs; or civil engineering and other industrial structures, or electrical and electronic products and systems, as well as machines, machinery and industrial plant; developing and applying commercial-scale chemical processes for the production of various substances and materials; developing and applying commercial-scale methods to extract water, oil, gas and other minerals from the earth, or metals from their ores, or to develop new materials; surveying land, sea and other areas and producing graphic, digital and pictorial representations; studying and advising on technological aspects of particular materials, products and processes and on efficiency of production and work organisation; preparing scientific papers and reports. Supervision of other workers may be included.

Occupations in this minor group are classified into the following unit groups:

2141   Architects, town and traffic planners

2142   Civil engineers

2143   Electrical engineers

2144   Electronics and telecommunications engineers

2145   Mechanical engineers

2146   Chemical engineers

2147   Mining engineers, metallurgists and related professionals

2148   Cartographers and surveyors

2149   Architects, engineers and related professionals not elsewhere classified

2141   ARCHITECTS, TOWN AND TRAFFIC PLANNERS

Architects, town and traffic planners conduct research and advise on and design residential, commercial and industrial buildings, layout of towns, landscapes and traffic systems, and plan and monitor their construction, maintenance and rehabilitation.

Tasks include –

(a) developing new or improved architectural theories and methods;

(b) inspecting sites, consulting with clients and making recommendations regarding style and other aspects of construction;

(c) designing buildings, preparing detailed drawings and plans for their construction and rehabilitation and making necessary contacts to ensure feasibility of projects regarding style, cost, timing, compliance with regulations, etc.;

(d) identifying and finding best solutions for problems regarding function and quality of interior environments of buildings and making necessary designs, drawings and plans;

(e) monitoring construction to ensure compliance with specifications;

(f) planning layout and co-ordinating development of urban areas;

(g) planning and designing the development of land areas for parks, schools, institutions, airports, roadways and related projects, and for commercial, industrial and residential sites;

(h) planning and advising on routing and control of road and other traffic for efficiency and safety;

(i) maintaining technical liaison and consultancy with other relevant specialists;

(j) preparing scientific papers and reports;

(k) performing related tasks;

(l) supervising other workers.

Examples of the occupations classified here:
- Architect, building
- Architect, interior
- Architect, landscape
- Planner, traffic
- Planner, urban

Some related occupations classified elsewhere:
- Decorator, interior − 3471
- Designer, decoration − 3471

2142 CIVIL ENGINEERS

Civil engineers conduct research and advise on, design, and direct construction, and manage the operation and maintenance of civil engineering structures, or study and advise on technological aspects of particular materials.

Tasks include −

(a) conducting research and developing new or improved theories and methods related to civil engineering;

(b) advising on and designing structures such as bridges, dams, docks, roads, airports, railways, canals, pipelines, waste-disposal and flood-control systems, and industrial and other large buildings;

(c) determining and specifying construction methods, materials and quality standards, and directing construction work;

(d) establishing control systems to ensure efficient functioning of structures as well as safety and environmental protection;

(e) locating and correcting malfunctions;

(f) organising and directing maintenance and repair of existing structures;

(g) studying and advising on technological aspects of particular materials;

(h) maintaining technical liaison and consultancy with other relevant specialists;

(i) preparing scientific papers and reports;

(j) performing related tasks;

(k) supervising other workers.

Examples of the occupations classified here:
- Engineer, civil
- Engineer, civil/aerodrome construction
- Engineer, civil/bridge construction
- Engineer, civil/building construction
- Engineer, civil/highway and street construction
- Technologist, building materials

2143 ELECTRICAL ENGINEERS

Electrical engineers conduct research and advise on, design, and direct construction of electrical systems, motors and equipment, and advise on and direct their functioning, maintenance and repairs, or study and advise on technological aspects of particular materials, products and processes.

Tasks include −

(a) advising on and designing systems for electrical power generation, transmission and distribution;

(b) advising on and designing systems for electrical motors, electrical traction and other equipment, or electrical domestic appliances;

(c) specifying electrical installation and application in industrial and other buildings and objects and if necessary directing some of the work;

(d) establishing control standards and procedures to ensure efficient functioning and safety of electrical generating and distribution systems, motors and equipment;

(e) locating and correcting malfunctions;

(f) organising and directing maintenance and repair of existing electrical systems, motors and equipment;

(g) studying and advising on technological aspects of particular materials, products or processes;

(h) maintaining technical liaison and consultancy with other relevant specialists;

(i) preparing scientific papers and reports;

(j) performing related tasks;

(k) supervising other workers.

Examples of the occupations classified here:

- Engineer, electrical
- Engineer, electrical/electric power generation
- Engineer, electrical/electromechanical equipment
- Technologist, engineering/electrical

2144   ELECTRONICS AND TELECOMMMUNICATIONS ENGINEERS

Electronics and telecommunications engineers conduct research and advise on, design, and direct construction of electronic systems and equipment, and advise on and direct their functioning, maintenance and repairs, or study and advise on technological aspects of particular materials, products or processes.

Tasks include –

(a) advising on and designing electronic devices, systems, motors and equipment such as computers or telecommunications equipment;

(b) specifying production or installation methods, materials and quality standards and directing production or installation work of electronic or telecommunications products and systems;

(c) establishing control standards and procedures to ensure efficient functioning and safety of electronic systems, motors and equipment;

(d) locating and correcting malfunctions;

(e) organising and directing maintenance and repair of existing electronic systems, motors and equipment;

(f) studying and advising on technological aspects of particular materials, products or processes;

(g) maintaining technical liaison and consultancy with other relevant specialists;

(h) preparing scientific papers and reports;

(i) performing related tasks;

(j) supervising other workers.

Examples of the occupations classified here:

- Engineer, electronics
- Engineer, telecommunications
- Engineer, telecommunications/radio
- Technologist, engineering/electronics
- Technologist, engineering/telecommunications

2145   MECHANICAL ENGINEERS

Mechanical engineers conduct research and advise on, design, and direct production of machines, machinery and industrial plant, equipment and systems, and advise on and direct their functioning, maintenance and repairs, or study and advise on technological aspects of particular materials, products or processes.

Tasks include –

(a) advising on and designing machinery and tools for manufacturing, mining, construction, agricultural work, and other industrial purposes;

(b) advising on and designing steam, internal combustion and other non-electric motors and engines used for propulsion of railway locomotives, road vehicles or aircraft, or for driving industrial or other machinery;

(c) advising on and designing ships' propulsion systems, power plant, heating and ventilation systems, steering gear, pumps, and other mechanical equipment;

(d) advising on and designing hulls and superstructures of ships and other vessels;

(e) advising on and designing airframes, undercarriages and other equipment for aircraft;

(f) advising on and designing road vehicle bodies, suspension systems, brakes and other components;

(g) advising on and designing heating, ventilation and refrigeration systems and equipment;

(h) advising on and designing mechanical plant and equipment for the release, control and utilisation of nuclear energy;

(i) advising on and designing non-electrical parts of apparatus or products such as word processors, computers, precision instruments, cameras and projectors, etc.;

(j) specifying and checking production or installation methods and work of agricultural and other machines, machinery, tools, motors, engines, industrial plant, equipment or systems;

(k) establishing control standards and procedures to ensure efficient functioning and safety of machines, machinery, tools, motors, engines, industrial plant, equipment, or systems;

(l) locating and correcting malfunctions;

(m) organising and directing maintenance and repair of existing machines, machinery, tools, motors, engines, industrial plant, equipment, or systems;

(n) studying and advising on technological aspects of particular materials, products or processes;

(o) maintaining technical liaison and consultancy with other relevant specialists;

(p) preparing scientific papers and reports;

(q) performing related tasks;

(r) supervising other workers.

Examples of the occupations classified here:

- Engineer, aeronautical
- Engineer, marine
- Engineer, mechanical
- Engineer, mechanical/agriculture
- Engineer, nuclear power
- Technologist, engineering/mechanical

Some related occupations classified elsewhere:

- Engineer, ship – 3141

2146 CHEMICAL ENGINEERS

Chemical engineers conduct research and develop, advise on and direct commercial-scale chemical processes and production of various substances and items such as crude oil, petroleum derivatives, food and drink products, medicaments, or synthetic materials, and direct maintenance and repair of industrial plant, or study and advise on technological aspects of particular materials, products or processes.

Tasks include –

(a) conducting research and advising on, and developing commercial-scale chemical processes to refine crude oil and other liquids or gases, and to produce substances and items such as petroleum derivatives, explosives, food and drink products, medicaments, or synthetic materials;

(b) specifying relevant aspects of the construction of chemical manufacturing plants;

(c) specifying production methods, materials and quality standards and ensuring that they conform to specifications;

(d) establishing control standards and procedures to ensure safety and efficiency of production operations;

(e) locating and correcting malfunctions;

(f) organising and directing maintenance and repair of existing equipment;

(g) studying and advising on technological aspects of particular materials, products or processes;

(h) maintaining technical liaison and consultancy with other relevant specialists;

(i) preparing scientific papers and reports;

(j) performing related tasks;

(k) supervising other workers.

Examples of the occupations classified here:

- Engineer, chemical
- Engineer, chemical process
- Engineer, chemical/petroleum and natural gas
- Technologist, food and drink
- Technologist, fuel

2147 MINING ENGINEERS, METALLURGISTS AND RELATED PROFESSIONALS

Mining engineers, metallurgists and related professionals conduct research, design and develop and maintain commercial-scale methods of extracting metals from their ores, or minerals, water, oil or gas from the earth and of developing new alloys, ceramic and other materials, or study and advise on technological aspects of particular materials, products or processes.

Tasks include –

(a) conducting research and advising on, designing and developing new or improved methods to deal with engineering aspects of mining and oil, gas or water extraction;

(b) determining most suitable methods of efficient mining and extraction, types of machinery to be used, planning layout and directing construction of shafts and tunnels;

(c) determining drilling site and devising methods of controlling the flow of water, oil or gas from wells;

(d) planning and directing storage, initial treatment and transportation of water, oil or gas;

(e) establishing safety standards and procedures and first-aid facilities, especially underground;

(f) conducting research, developing methods of extracting metals from their ores and advising on their application;

(g) investigating properties of metals and alloys, developing new alloys and advising on and supervising technical aspects of metal and alloy manufacture and processing;

(h) studying and advising on technological aspects of particular materials or processes;

(i) maintaining technical liaison and consultancy with other relevant specialists, in particular with geologists and geophysicists;

(j) preparing scientific papers and reports;

(k) performing related tasks;

(l) supervising other workers.

Examples of the occupations classified here:
- Engineer, mining
- Engineer, mining/coal
- Engineer, mining/metal
- Engineer, mining/petroleum and natural gas
- Metallurgist, extractive
- Technologist, extractive

2148 CARTOGRAPHERS AND SURVEYORS

Cartographers and surveyors apply surveying methods and techniques to determine the exact position of natural and constructed features and boundaries of land, seas, underground areas and celestial bodies, and prepare or revise digital, graphic and pictorial representations.

Tasks include –

(a) surveying, measuring and describing land surfaces for various purposes, including mapmaking, construction work or establishment of property boundaries;

(b) surveying mines, delineating underground surfaces, noting exact position of various features and making charts and maps with a view to controlling direction and extent of mining;

(c) surveying sea, river and lake beds, delineating underwater surfaces, noting exact position of various features and making charts and maps to be used in particular in determining navigable waters and channels and in planning construction of marine structures;

(d) planning and conducting aerial photographic surveys;

(e) analysing aerial and other photographs, remote sensing and surveying data to prepare and revise topographic maps and charts, utility maps and other thematic maps;

(f) studying and advising on technical, aesthetic and economic aspects of map production;

(g) maintaining technical liaison and consultancy with other relevant specialists;

(h) preparing scientific papers and reports;

(i) performing related tasks;

(j) supervising other workers.

Examples of the occupations classified here:

- Cartographer
- Photogrammetrist
- Surveyor, aerial
- Surveyor, hydrographic
- Surveyor, land
- Surveyor, mining

Some related occupations classified elsewhere:

- Surveyor, marine — 3115
- Surveyor, quantity — 2149

2149 ARCHITECTS, ENGINEERS AND RELATED PROFESSIONALS NOT ELSEWHERE CLASSIFIED

This unit group covers architects, engineers and related professionals not classified elsewhere in Minor group 214, *Architects, engineers and related professionals*.

For instance, here should be classified those who are engaged in conducting research, advising on or developing procedures concerning efficiency of production and work organisation, as well as those who perform quantity surveying and those who study and advise on technological aspects of particular materials, products and manufacturing processes.

In such cases tasks would include —

(a) consulting with management and supervisory personnel and advising on planning and production methods;

(b) consulting with management and supervisory personnel and advising on methods to promote the efficient, safe and economic utilisation of personnel, material and equipment;

(c) making recommendations regarding methods of work and sequence of operations and supervising their implementation;

(d) making recommendations and supervising time and motion aspects of work organisation;

(e) advising on most efficient layout of plant or establishment;

(f) identifying potential hazards and introducing safety procedures and devices;

(g) preparing and monitoring cost estimates and bills of quantities for architectural and construction projects;

(h) studying and advising on technological aspects of particular manufacturing processes, such as those related to glass, ceramics, textiles, leather products, wood, and printing;

(i) preparing scientific papers and reports;

(j) performing related tasks;

(k) supervising other workers.

Examples of the occupations classified here:

- Engineer, industrial efficiency
- Engineer, production
- Engineer, time and motion study
- Surveyor, quantity
- Technologist, textiles

SUB-MAJOR GROUP 22
LIFE SCIENCE AND HEALTH PROFESSIONALS

Life science and health professionals conduct research, improve or develop concepts, theories and operational methods, or apply scientific knowledge relating to fields such as biology, zoology, botany, ecology, physiology, biochemistry, microbiology, pharmacology, agronomy, and medicine.

Tasks performed by workers in this sub-major group usually include: conducting research, enlarging, advising on or applying scientific knowledge obtained through the study of all forms of human, animal and plant life, including specific organs, tissues, cells and micro-organisms and the effect of environmental factors, or drugs and other substances, on them; studying human, animal or plant illnesses, advising on and applying preventive, curative and nursing measures, or promoting health; preparing scientific papers and reports. Supervision of other workers may be included.

It should be noted that, depending on the specific tasks and degree of responsibility in executing them, as well as on the national educational and training requirements, it may be appropriate to classify some of the occupations that are identified here into Sub-major group 32, *Life science and health associate professionals*. This is particularly relevant to the occupations classified into Minor group 223, *Nursing and midwifery professionals*.

Occupations in this sub-major group are classified into the following minor groups:

221 Life science professionals

222 Health professionals (except nursing)

223 Nursing and midwifery professionals

MINOR GROUP **221**
LIFE SCIENCE PROFESSIONALS

Life science professionals conduct research, improve or develop concepts, theories and operational methods, or apply scientific knowledge relating to biology, microbiology, botany, zoology, ecology, anatomy, bacteriology, biochemistry, physiology, cytology, genetics, agronomy, pathology, or pharmacology.

Tasks performed usually include: conducting research and obtaining scientific knowledge through the study of all forms of human, animal and plant life, including specific organs, tissues, cells and micro-organisms and the effect of environmental factors, or drugs and other substances, on them; advising on or applying this knowledge in such fields as agriculture, pharmaceutical and other industries, or medicine; preparing scientific papers and reports. Supervision of other workers may be included.

Occupations in this minor group are classified into the following unit groups:

2211 Biologists, botanists, zoologists and related professionals

2212 Pharmacologists, pathologists and related professionals

2213 Agronomists and related professionals

2211 BIOLOGISTS, BOTANISTS, ZOOLOGISTS AND RELATED PROFESSIONALS

Biologists, botanists, zoologists and related professionals conduct research, improve or develop concepts, theories and operational methods, and apply scientific knowledge relating to biology, microbiology, bacteriology, cytology, genetics, zoology, botany and ecology, especially in the fields of medicine and agriculture.

Tasks include –

(a) conducting research, improving or developing concepts, theories and operational methods in their respective fields;

(b) conducting field and laboratory experiments concerning all forms of life by identifying and classifying human, animal, insect or plant specimens, and studying their origin, development, chemical and physical form, structure, composition, and life and reproductive processes;

(c) studying and conducting experiments concerning the structure, development and characteristics of micro-organisms such as bacteria or viruses;

(d) studying and conducting experiments concerning the factors involved in the origin, development and transmission of hereditary characteristics in human beings, animals or plants;

(e) studying all forms of plant life and developing practical applications of this knowledge in fields such as agriculture and medicine;

(f) studying all forms of animal life and developing practical applications of this knowledge in fields such as agriculture and medicine;

(g) studying and conducting experiments concerning the structure and functions of living cells, and the influence of physical and chemical factors upon normal and abnormal cells;

(h) studying inter-relationships of animal and plant life and the environmental factors involved, and giving professional advice to related disciplines;

(i) developing industrial, medical and other applications of knowledge in their respective fields;

(j) preparing scientific papers and reports;

(k) performing related tasks;

(l) supervising other workers.

Examples of the occupations classified here:

- Bacteriologist
- Biologist
- Botanist
- Ecologist
- Microbiologist
- Zoologist

2212 PHARMACOLOGISTS, PATHOLOGISTS AND RELATED PROFESSIONALS

Pharmacologists, pathologists and related professionals conduct research, improve or develop concepts, theories and operational methods, and apply scientific knowledge relating to anatomy, biochemistry, biophysics, physiology, pathology, or pharmacology, in such fields as medicine, agriculture or industry.

Tasks include –

(a) conducting research, improving or developing concepts, theories and operational methods in their respective fields;

(b) studying and conducting experiments concerning the form, structure and other anatomical characteristics of living organisms;

(c) studying and conducting experiments concerning the chemical composition and processes of living organisms;

(d) studying and conducting experiments concerning the life processes and functions of human, animal or plant organs, tissues, cells, glands and systems under normal and abnormal or exceptional conditions;

(e) studying and conducting experiments concerning the nature, causes and development of human, animal or plant diseases and disorders;

(f) studying and conducting experiments concerning the effects of drugs and other substances on the tissues, organs and physiological processes of human beings and animals, and improving existing or developing new drugs;

(g) developing industrial, medical and other applications of knowledge in their respective fields;

(h) preparing scientific papers and reports;

(i) performing related tasks;

(j) supervising other workers.

Examples of the occupations classified here:

- Anatomist
- Biochemist
- Biophysicist
- Pathologist
- Pharmacologist
- Physiologist

2213 AGRONOMISTS AND RELATED PROFESSIONALS

Agronomists and related professionals conduct research and improve or develop concepts, theories and operational methods, and apply scientific knowledge relating to crop and animal husbandry.

Tasks include –

(a) researching into field crops and grasses and developing new or improved cultivation methods;

(b) researching into horticultural crops and developing new or improved cultivation methods;

(c) researching into animal husbandry and developing new or improved breeding methods;

(d) researching into, and developing new or improved methods for tree propagation and culture, or planning and directing afforestation and exploitation of forest stands;

(e) researching into characteristics, use capability and productivity of soils and applying findings to development of improved agricultural, horticultural and forestry practices;

(f) researching into, and developing new or improved methods for wildlife conservation;

(g) researching into, and developing new or improved methods for economic exploitation of grazing lands;

(h) preparing scientific papers and reports;

(i) performing related tasks;

(j) supervising other workers.

Examples of the occupations classified here:

- Agronomist
- Animal scientist
- Forestry scientist
- Horticulturist
- Soil scientist

MINOR GROUP **222**
HEALTH PROFESSIONALS (EXCEPT NURSING)

Health professionals (except nursing) conduct research, improve or develop concepts, theories and operational methods, and apply scientific knowledge relating to medicine, dentistry, veterinary medicine, pharmacy, and promotion of health.

Tasks performed usually include: conducting research and obtaining scientific knowledge through the study of human and animal disorders and illnesses and ways of treating them; advising on or applying preventive and curative measures, or promoting health; preparing scientific papers and reports. Supervision of other workers may be included.

Occupations in this minor group are classified into the following unit groups:

2221 Medical doctors

2222 Dentists

2223 Veterinarians

2224 Pharmacists

2229 Health professionals (except nursing) not elsewhere classified

2221 MEDICAL DOCTORS

Medical doctors conduct research, improve or develop concepts, theories and operational methods, and apply preventive or curative measures.

Tasks include –

(a) conducting research into human disorders and illnesses and preventive or curative methods;
(b) conducting medical examinations and making diagnoses;
(c) prescribing and giving treatment for diagnosed illnesses, disorders or injuries;
(d) giving specialised medical or surgical treatment for particular types of illnesses, disorders or injuries;
(e) giving advice on and applying preventive medicine methods and treatments;
(f) participating in the development and implementation of public health laws and regulations for safeguarding and promoting the health of a community;
(g) preparing scientific papers and reports;
(h) performing related tasks;
(i) supervising other workers.

Examples of the occupations classified here:
- Doctor, medical
- Ophthalmologist
- Physician
- Psychiatrist
- Surgeon

2222 DENTISTS

Dentists conduct research, improve or develop concepts, theories and operational methods, and apply medical knowledge in the field of dentistry.

Tasks include –

(a) conducting research into dental and related disorders and illnesses and preventive or curative methods;
(b) making diagnoses, advising on and giving necessary dental treatment;
(c) giving surgical, medical and other forms of treatment for particular types of dental and oral diseases and disorders;
(d) participating in public action to maintain or improve standards of oral health and dental care;
(e) preparing scientific papers and reports;
(f) performing related tasks;
(g) supervising other workers.

Examples of the occupations classified here:
- Dentist
- Dentist, pedodontistry
- Surgeon, oral/dentistry

2223 VETERINARIANS

Veterinarians conduct research, improve or develop concepts, theories and operational methods, and apply medical knowledge in the veterinary field.

Tasks include –

(a) conducting research, improving or developing concepts, theories and operational methods;
(b) conducting examinations and diagnosing diseases or injuries of animals;
(c) administering surgical or medical veterinary treatment;
(d) testing dairy and other herds and inoculating animals against diseases;
(e) advising on care and breeding of animals;
(f) inspecting quality, purity and safety of food made wholly or partly from raw materials of animal origin intended for human consumption;
(g) assisting in epidemiological, radiological and other surveillance of animal health;
(h) preparing scientific papers and reports;
(i) performing related tasks;
(j) supervising other workers.

Examples of the occupations classified here:
- Veterinarian
- Veterinarian, epidemiology

2224 PHARMACISTS

Pharmacists apply pharmaceutical concepts and theories by preparing and dispensing or selling medicaments and drugs.

Tasks include –

(a) preparing and directing the preparation of medicaments according to prescriptions of medical, dental and veterinary practitioners, or established formulae;

(b) checking prescriptions to ensure that recommended dosages are not exceeded, and that instructions are understood by patient – or person administering the medicament – and advising on possible drug incompatibility;

(c) dispensing medicaments and drugs in hospitals or selling them in pharmacies;

(d) maintaining records, especially of narcotics, poisons and habit-forming drugs issued;

(e) testing drugs to determine identity, purity and strength;

(f) participating in the development of controls and regulations;

(g) preparing scientific papers and reports;

(h) performing related tasks;

(i) supervising other workers.

Examples of the occupations classified here:

- Pharmacist

Some related occupations classified elsewhere:

- Chemist, pharmaceutical – 2113

2229 HEALTH PROFESSIONALS (EXCEPT NURSING) NOT ELSEWHERE CLASSIFIED

This unit group covers health professionals (except nursing) not classified elsewhere in Minor group 222, *Health professionals (except nursing)*.

MINOR GROUP 223
NURSING AND MIDWIFERY PROFESSIONALS

Nursing and midwifery professionals apply medical concepts and principles relating to the delivery of babies and to nursing of the ill, injured or disabled, and of mothers and their newborn babies.

Tasks performed usually include: helping medical doctors in the practical application of preventive and curative measures and dealing with emergencies in their absence; providing professional nursing services, care and advice for the sick, injured, physically and mentally disabled and others in need of such care, and directing auxiliary nursing staff; delivering or assisting in the delivery of babies, and instructing mothers in baby care. Supervision of other workers may be included.

It should be noted that, depending on the specific tasks and degree of responsibility in executing them, as well as on the national educational and training requirements, it may be appropriate to classify some or all of the occupations that are identified here into Minor group 323, *Nursing and midwifery associate professionals*.

Occupations in this minor group are classified into the following unit group:

2230 Nursing and midwifery professionals

2230 NURSING AND MIDWIFERY PROFESSIONALS

Nursing and midwifery professionals assist medical doctors in their tasks, deal with emergencies in their absence, and provide professional nursing care for the sick, injured, physically and mentally disabled, and others in need of such care, or they deliver or assist in the delivery of babies, provide antenatal and post-natal care and instruct parents in baby care.

Tasks include –

(a) giving professional nursing care and treatment, either as curative or preventive measures, to ill, injured, disabled and other patients, and newborn babies and their mothers, in hospitals, clinics or other establishments;

(b) assisting medical doctors in their tasks, dealing with emergencies and giving first-aid treatment in their absence;

(c) administering medicine and drugs, applying surgical dressings and giving other forms of treatment prescribed by physicians;

(d) supervising and co-ordinating the work of nursing and other non-medical staff in operating theatres and assisting surgeons during operations;

(e) participating in preparations for physical and psychological treatment of mentally ill patients;

(f) participating in preparations for social adjustment, development and education of mentally or physically handicapped patients;

(g) giving professional nursing care to patients in their own homes;

(h) providing professional nursing services, care and advice within the community or at a workplace;

(i) specialising in consultant services to schools, industry and other organisations;

(j) checking on general health and progress of expectant mothers during pregnancy, and giving them professional advice and care;

(k) delivering babies in normal births and assisting doctors with difficult deliveries;

(l) attending mothers in the post-natal period to supervise their recovery, to check on babies' progress, and to instruct parents in baby care;

(m) advising on and administering birth control methods;

(n) performing related tasks;

(o) supervising other workers.

Examples of the occupations classified here:
- Matron
- Midwife, professional
- Nurse, professional
- Sister, nursing/professional

Some related occupations classified elsewhere:
- Aid, nursing/hospital – 5132
- Midwife, associate professional – 3232
- Nurse, associate professional – 3231

SUB-MAJOR GROUP 23
TEACHING PROFESSIONALS

Teaching professionals teach the theory and practice of one or more disciplines at different educational levels, conduct research and improve or develop concepts, theories and operational methods pertaining to their particular discipline, and prepare scholarly papers and books.

Tasks performed by workers in this sub-major group usually include: conducting classes, courses, or tutorials at a particular educational level, for educational or voca-

2

tional purposes, including private lessons; conducting adult literacy programmes; teaching and educating handicapped persons; designing and modifying curricula; inspecting and advising on teaching methods and aids; participating in decisions concerning the organisation of teaching and related activities at schools and universities; conducting research in their particular subjects to improve or develop concepts, theories or operational methods for application in industrial and other fields; preparing scholarly papers and books. Supervision of other workers may be included.

It should be noted that, depending on the specific tasks and degree of responsibility in executing them, as well as on the national educational and training requirements, it may be appropriate to classify some of the occupations that are identified here into Sub-major group 33, *Teaching associate professionals*. This is particularly relevant to the occupations classified into Minor groups 233, *Primary and pre-primary education teaching professionals*, and 234, *Special education teaching professionals*.

Occupations in this sub-major group are classified into the following minor groups:

231 College, university and higher education teaching professionals

232 Secondary education teaching professionals

233 Primary and pre-primary education teaching professionals

234 Special education teaching professionals

235 Other teaching professionals

MINOR GROUP **231**
COLLEGE, UNIVERSITY AND HIGHER EDUCATION TEACHING PROFESSIONALS

College, university and higher education teaching professionals teach their subjects at different levels after the termination of secondary education, conduct research and improve or develop concepts, theories and operational methods pertaining to their particular discipline, and prepare scholarly papers and books.

Tasks performed usually include: designing and modifying curricula; conducting courses, giving seminars and tutorials or delivering lectures; participating in decisions concerning the organisation of university teaching and related activities; conducting research in their particular subjects to improve or develop concepts, theories and operational methods for application in industrial and other fields; preparing scholarly papers and books. Supervision of other workers may be included.

Occupations in this minor group are classified into the following unit group:

2310 College, university and higher education teaching professionals

2310 COLLEGE, UNIVERSITY AND HIGHER EDUCATION TEACHING PROFESSIONALS

College, university and higher education teaching professionals teach their subjects at some or all levels after the termination of secondary education, conduct research and improve or develop concepts, theories and operational methods, and prepare scholarly papers and books.

Tasks include –

(a) designing and modifying curricula and preparing courses of study in accordance with requirements;

(b) delivering lectures and conducting tutorials, seminars and laboratory experiments;

(c) stimulating discussion and independent thought among students;

(d) supervising, where appropriate, experimental and practical work undertaken by students;

(e) administering, evaluating and marking examination papers and tests;

(f) directing research of post-graduate students or other members of department;

(g) researching into and developing concepts, theories and operational methods for application in industrial and other fields;

(h) preparing scholarly books, papers or articles;

(i) attending conferences and seminars;

(j) participating in decision-making processes concerning college or university departmental, budgetary and other policy matters;

(k) assisting with extra-curricular activities, such as debating societies;

(l) performing related tasks;

(m) supervising other workers.

Examples of the occupations classified here:
- Lecturer, college
- Lecturer, university
- Professor, college
- Professor, university
- Reader, university

Some related occupations classified elsewhere:
- Chancellor, university – 1210
- Dean – 1229
- Head, college faculty – 1229

MINOR GROUP 232
SECONDARY EDUCATION TEACHING PROFESSIONALS

Secondary education teaching professionals teach one or more subjects, for educational or vocational purposes, at some or all levels between the termination of primary education and the beginning of studies at colleges or universities.

Tasks performed usually include: designing and modifying curricula; conducting classes or giving courses in one or more subjects, for educational or vocational purposes, including private lessons; conducting adult literacy programmes; participating in decisions concerning the organisation of school teaching and related activities. Supervision of other workers may be included.

Occupations in this minor group are classified into the following unit group:

2320   Secondary education teaching professionals

2320 SECONDARY EDUCATION TEACHING PROFESSIONALS

Secondary education teaching professionals teach one or more subjects, for educational or vocational purposes, at some or all levels between the termination of primary education and the beginning of studies at colleges or universities.

Tasks include –

(a) designing and modifying curricula and preparing educational, as well as vocational, courses of study in accordance with requirements;

(b) giving lessons in their subjects and supervising pupils' class work and discipline;

(c) preparing, assigning and correcting exercises;

(d) administering and marking tests and examinations to evaluate pupils' progress;

(e) preparing reports about pupils' work and conferring with other teachers and parents;

(f) teaching reading, writing and other primary subjects to adults;

(g) participating at meetings concerning school's educational or organisational policies;

(h) organising or assisting with extra-curricular activities such as debating societies or hobby clubs;

(i) giving private lessons;

(j) performing related tasks;

(k) supervising other workers.

Examples of the occupations classified here:

- Teacher, secondary education
- Teacher, secondary education/adult literacy
- Teacher, secondary education/vocational training

Some related occupations classified elsewhere:

- Head teacher – 1229
- Inspector, school – 2352

MINOR GROUP **233**
PRIMARY AND PRE-PRIMARY EDUCATION TEACHING PROFESSIONALS

Primary and pre-primary education teaching professionals teach a range of subjects at the primary level of education and organise educational activities for children below primary school age.

Tasks performed usually include: preparing programme of learning and giving instruction in a range of subjects at the primary education level; planning and organising activities designed to facilitate children's development of language, physical and social skills; preparing reports. Supervision of other workers may be included.

It should be noted that, depending on the specific tasks and degree of responsibility in executing them, as well as on the national educational and training requirements, it may be appropriate to classify some or all of the occupations that are identified here into Minor groups 331, *Primary education teaching associate professionals* and 332, *Pre-primary education teaching associate professionals*.

Occupations in this minor group are classified into the following unit groups:

2331   Primary education teaching professionals

2332   Pre-primary education teaching professionals

2331 PRIMARY EDUCATION TEACHING PROFESSIONALS

Primary education teaching professionals teach a range of subjects at the primary education level.

Tasks include –
(a) preparing programme of learning and giving instruction in areas such as reading, writing, arithmetic and other subjects, within prescribed or recommended curriculum;
(b) preparing, administering and marking tests, projects and assignments to train pupils and to evaluate their progress, and giving remedial instruction if necessary;
(c) organising and supervising pupils' extra-curricular activities;
(d) encouraging personal development of pupils and discussing their progress with parents and head teacher;
(e) supervising pupils in classroom and other areas of school;
(f) preparing reports;
(g) performing related tasks;
(h) supervising other workers.

Examples of the occupations classified here:
- Teacher, primary education/professional

Some related occupations classified elsewhere:
- Head teacher – 1229
- Inspector, school – 2352
- Teacher, primary education/associate professional – 3310

2332 PRE-PRIMARY EDUCATION TEACHING PROFESSIONALS

Pre-primary education teaching professionals organise group and individual play and educational activities to support and promote physical, mental and social development of children below primary school age.

Tasks include –
(a) planning and organising activities designed to facilitate the children's development of physical and social skills;
(b) promoting language development through story-telling, role-play, songs, rhymes and informal conversations and discussions;
(c) observing children in order to evaluate and discuss progress and possible problems with parents;
(d) supervising children's activities to ensure safety and resolve conflicts;
(e) performing related tasks;
(f) supervising other workers.

Examples of the occupations classified here:
- Teacher, pre-primary education/professional

Some related occupations classified elsewhere:
- Teacher, pre-primary education/associate professional – 3320

MINOR GROUP 234
SPECIAL EDUCATION TEACHING PROFESSIONALS

Special education teaching professionals teach physically or mentally handicapped children, young persons or adults, or those with learning difficulties, at a given level of education.

Tasks performed usually include: adapting curriculum to suit the particular group of mentally or physically handicapped persons, or those with learning difficulties; teaching one or more subjects to, for instance, deaf or blind persons by using braille, lip-reading and other special aids and techniques; preparing reports. Supervision of other workers may be included.

It should be noted that, depending on the specific tasks and degree of responsibility in executing them, as well as on the national educational and training requirements, it may be appropriate to classify some or all of the occupations that are identified here into Minor group 333, *Special education teaching associate professionals*.

Occupations in this minor group are classified into the following unit group:

2340   Special education teaching professionals

2340   SPECIAL EDUCATION TEACHING PROFESSIONALS

Special education teaching professionals teach physically or mentally handicapped children, young persons, or adults, or those with learning difficulties, at a given level of education.

Tasks include –

(a) designing or modifying curricula and preparing lessons and activities in accordance with requirements;

(b) giving instruction using techniques or special aids – such as braille or lip-reading – appropriate to pupil's handicap and level, and supervising work in class;

(c) encouraging pupils to have confidence, helping them to discover and adopt methods which would compensate for limitations imposed by their handicap, and giving them a feeling of achievement;

(d) administering tests, evaluating and noting progress of each pupil and discus-

sing it with parents, head teacher, therapists, social workers, etc.;

(e) giving private instruction;

(f) preparing reports;

(g) performing related tasks;

(h) supervising other workers.

Examples of the occupations classified here:

- Teacher, remedial/professional
- Teacher, special education/for the blind (professional)
- Teacher, special education/for the mentally handicapped (professional)

Some related occupations classified elsewhere:

- Teacher, remedial/associate professional – 3330
- Teacher, special education/for the blind (associate professional) – 3330
- Teacher, special education/for the mentally handicapped (associate professional) – 3330

MINOR GROUP 235
OTHER TEACHING PROFESSIONALS

Other teaching professionals conduct research and develop or advise on teaching methods and aids, or review and examine teachers' work and the results achieved in applying a particular curriculum programme and suggest changes and improvements, if necessary.

Tasks performed usually include: carrying out research on current developments in curricula, teaching methods and other educational practices, including teaching aids, and advising on necessary changes and improvements; carrying out periodic inspection of teachers' work in the application of a particular curriculum programme and suggesting changes and improvements if necessary; preparing reports. Supervision of other workers may be included.

Occupations in this minor group are classified into the following unit groups:

2351   Education methods specialists

2352   School inspectors

2359   Other teaching professionals not elsewhere classified

2351   EDUCATION METHODS SPECIALISTS

Education methods specialists conduct research and develop or advise on teaching methods and aids.

Tasks include –
(a)   researching into current developments in curricula, teaching methods and other educational practices, and advising on necessary changes and possible improvements;
(b)   advising on contents of courses and methods of examination;
(c)   researching into audio-visual and other teaching aids and advising on, planning and organising their introduction in educational establishments;
(d)   preparing papers and reports;
(e)   performing related tasks;
(f)   supervising other workers.

Examples of the occupations classified here:
- Adviser, education methods
- Curricula developer
- Specialist, teaching aids

2352   SCHOOL INSPECTORS

School inspectors review and examine teachers' work and the results achieved in applying a particular curriculum programme and suggest changes and improvements, if necessary.

Tasks include –
(a)   inspecting schools periodically and conferring with the administration and teaching staff on questions relating to curricula, teaching methods, equipment and other matters;
(b)   visiting class-rooms to observe teaching techniques and to evaluate teachers' performance, and scholastic results obtained;
(c)   preparing reports and making recommendations to educational authorities concerning possible changes and improvements in curricula, teaching methods, and other matters;
(d)   performing related tasks;
(e)   supervising other workers.

Examples of the occupations classified here:
- Inspector, school

Some related occupations classified elsewhere:
- Head teacher – 1229

2359   OTHER TEACHING PROFESSIONALS NOT ELSEWHERE CLASSIFIED

This unit group covers teaching professionals not classified elsewhere in Minor group 235, *Other teaching professionals*.

2

SUB-MAJOR GROUP 24
OTHER PROFESSIONALS

Other professionals conduct research, improve or develop concepts, theories and operational methods, or apply knowledge relating to information dissemination and organisation of business, as well as to philosophy, law, psychology, politics, economics, history, religion, languages, sociology, other social sciences, and to arts and entertainment.

Tasks performed by workers in this sub-major group usually include: dealing with information dissemination and operational methods relating to organisation of business; application of the law; enlarging, advising on or applying knowledge obtained through the study of individual or group behaviour, language development, and philosophical, political, economic, juridical, educational, social, religious and other doctrines, concepts, theories, systems and organisations, from a current and historical perspective; conceiving and creating or performing works of art; preparing scholarly papers and reports. Supervision of other workers may be included.

It should be noted that, depending on the specific tasks and degree of responsibility in executing them, as well as on the national educational and training requirements, it may be appropriate to classify some of the occupations that are identified here into Sub-major group 34, *Other associate professionals*. This is particularly relevant to the occupations classified into Unit group 2446, *Social work professionals*.

Occupations in this sub-major group are classified into the following minor groups:

241   Business professionals

242   Legal professionals

243   Archivists, librarians and related information professionals

244   Social science and related professionals

245   Writers and creative or performing artists

246   Religious professionals

MINOR GROUP 241
BUSINESS PROFESSIONALS

Business professionals improve, advise on or apply operational methods relating to organisation of business.

Tasks performed usually include: studying, planning, advising on and executing accounting services, or services related to personnel policies and vocational guidance; dealing with other business matters such as marketing, advertising, public relations, application of rules concerning patents, or steps to be taken in setting up a business;

advising on principles of home economics. Supervision of other workers may be included.

Occupations in this minor group are classified into the following unit groups:

2411   Accountants

2412   Personnel and careers professionals

2419   Business professionals not elsewhere classified

2411   ACCOUNTANTS

Accountants advise on accounting matters and perform accountancy services or audits.

Tasks include –

(a) advising on, planning and installing budgetary, accounts controlling and other accounting policies and systems;

(b) preparing and certifying financial statements for presentation to management, shareholders and statutory or other bodies;

(c) preparing tax returns, advising on taxation problems and contesting disputed claims before tax officials;

(d) preparing or reporting on profit forecasts and budgets;

(e) conducting financial investigations in such matters as suspected fraud, insolvency and bankruptcy;

(f) auditing accounts and book-keeping records;

(g) performing related tasks;

(h) supervising other workers.

Examples of the occupations classified here:

- Accountant
- Accountant, chartered
- Auditor

Some related occupations classified elsewhere:

- Assistant, accounting – 3434
- Bookkeeper – 3433
- Clerk, accounts – 4121

2412   PERSONNEL AND CAREERS PROFESSIONALS

Personnel and careers professionals provide professional business services related to personnel policies such as employee recruitment or development, occupational analyses and vocational guidance.

Tasks include –

(a) advising on and performing personnel functions relating to employee recruitment, placement, training, promotion, compensation, and employee-management relations or other areas of personnel policy;

(b) studying and analysing jobs performed in an establishment by various means, including interviews with workers, supervisors and management, and writing detailed post, job and occupation descriptions from data obtained;

(c) preparing occupational information booklets or working on occupational classification systems;

(d) advising and working on the foregoing and other aspects of job and occupation analyses in such fields as personnel administration, manpower research and planning, training, or occupational information and vocational guidance;

(e) studying and advising individuals on employment opportunities, career choices and further education or training that may be desirable;

(f) performing related tasks;

(g) supervising other workers.

Examples of the occupations classified here:

- Adviser, careers
- Analyst, job
- Analyst, occupational
- Counsellor, vocational guidance

2419 BUSINESS PROFESSIONALS NOT ELSEWHERE CLASSIFIED

This unit group covers business professionals not classified elsewhere in Minor group 241, *Business professionals*.

For instance, here should be classified those who are engaged in studying, advising on and applying operational methods relating to various aspects of business undertakings, such as marketing, advertising, public relations, application of rules concerning patents, or steps to be taken in setting up and running a business, and home economics principles.

In such cases tasks would include –

(a) conducting research and determining or advising on existing level of sales for particular products or services, and assessing potential markets and future trends;

(b) planning, advising on or directing and co-ordinating production of advertising campaigns;

(c) studying, advising on and conducting public relations programmes with a view to improving the public's knowledge and understanding of the enterprise or establishment in question;

(d) giving advice concerning patents and assisting in preparing applications or examining applications submitted for registration, and writing reports setting out reasons for or against the granting of a patent;

(e) studying and advising on financial, legal, organisational, marketing and other aspects connected with setting up and running a business;

(f) studying, interpreting and informing about and advising on principles of home economics and management with a view to promoting welfare of families, as well as the consumption of household goods, or the promotion of new products;

(g) performing related tasks;

(h) supervising other workers.

Examples of the occupations classified here:

- Account executive, advertising
- Analyst, market research
- Home economist
- Officer, public relations
- Patent agent

Some related occupations classified elsewhere:

- Company secretary – 1231

MINOR GROUP 242
LEGAL PROFESSIONALS

Legal professionals conduct research on legal problems, draft laws and regulations, advise clients on legal aspects of problems, and plead cases or conduct prosecutions in courts of justice, or preside over judicial proceedings and pronounce judgement in courts of justice.

Tasks performed usually include: giving clients legal advice, undertaking legal business on clients' behalf, and conducting litigation when necessary; or presiding over judicial proceedings and pronouncing judgements in courts of justice. Supervision of other workers may be included.

Occupations in this minor group are classified into the following unit groups:

2421 Lawyers

2422 Judges

2429 Legal professionals not elsewhere classified

2421 LAWYERS

Lawyers give clients legal advice on a wide variety of subjects and plead cases or conduct prosecutions in courts of justice, or instruct barristers or advocates to plead in higher courts of justice.

Tasks include –

(a) conducting research on legal theories and principles and their relationship to specific laws or court judgements;

(b) drafting legislation and preparing government regulations based on existing laws;

(c) giving clients – including the Government – legal advice on a wide variety of subjects and undertaking legal business on clients' behalf;

(d) assisting clients to negotiate settlements in matters which involve legal disputes;

(e) examining the circumstances of disputes or reported crimes to ascertain facts and their legal implications;

(f) preparing pleadings or cases for plaintiff or defendant and conducting them in court;

(g) representing clients in the lower court or instructing barristers or advocates to plead in higher courts of justice;

(h) accepting briefs and pleading in the higher court;

(i) acting as prosecutor on behalf of the Government in criminal cases;

(j) drawing up legal documents;

(k) performing related tasks;

(l) supervising other workers.

Examples of the occupations classified here:
- Advocate
- Attorney
- Barrister
- Lawyer
- Prosecutor
- Solicitor

Some related occupations classified elsewhere:
- Clerk, conveyancing – 3432
- Clerk, law – 3432

2422 JUDGES

Judges hear and judge cases in courts of justice, instruct the jury on points of law, or pronounce judgement.

Tasks include –

(a) hearing and weighing arguments and evidence;

(b) ruling on questions of procedure;

(c) determining the rights and obligations of the parties involved, and, in cases tried by jury, instructing jury members on points of law;

(d) pronouncing judgement;

(e) performing related tasks;

(f) supervising other workers.

Examples of the occupations classified here:
- Chief justice
- Judge
- Magistrate

Some related occupations classified elsewhere:
- Clerk, court – 3432

2429 LEGAL PROFESSIONALS NOT ELSEWHERE CLASSIFIED

This unit group covers legal professionals not classified elsewhere in Minor group 242, *Legal professionals*.

For instance, here should be classified those who perform legal functions other than pleading or prosecuting cases or presiding over judicial proceedings.

In such cases tasks would include –

(a) giving advice on legal aspects of various personal, business and administrative problems;

(b) drawing up legal documents and contracts;

(c) arranging property transfers;

(d) determining, by inquest, the causes of any death not obviously due to natural causes;

(e) performing related tasks;

(f) supervising other workers.

Examples of the occupations classified here:
- Coroner
- Jurist, except lawyer or judge
- Notary

MINOR GROUP **243**
ARCHIVISTS, LIBRARIANS AND RELATED INFORMATION PROFESSIONALS

Archivists, librarians and related information professionals develop and maintain the collections of archives, libraries, museums, art galleries, and similar establishments.

Tasks performed usually include: conducting research, appraising or developing and organising the contents of archives and artifacts of historical, cultural and artistic interest, and ensuring their safe-keeping and preservation; organising the collections of, and exhibitions at, museums, art galleries and similar establishments; developing and maintaining the systematic collection of recorded and published material and making it available to users in libraries and related institutions; preparing scholarly papers and reports. Supervision of other workers may be included.

Occupations in this minor group are classified into the following unit groups:

2431   Archivists and curators

2432   Librarians and related information professionals

2431   ARCHIVISTS AND CURATORS

Archivists and curators conduct research, collect, appraise and ensure the safekeeping and preservation of the contents of archives and artifacts of historical, cultural and artistic interest, and of art and other objects and organise exhibitions at museums and art galleries.

Tasks include –

(a)   researching into, appraising, and developing, organising and preserving historically significant and valuable documents such as government papers, private papers, photographs, sound recordings and films;

(b)   directing or carrying out the preparation of indexes, bibliographies, microfilm copies and other reference aids to the collected material and making them available to users;

(c)   researching into the origin, distribution and use of materials and objects of cultural and historical interest;

(d)   organising, developing and maintaining collections of artistic, cultural, scientific or historically significant items in museums or art galleries;

(e)   directing or undertaking classification and cataloguing of museum and art gallery collections and organising exhibitions;

(f)   preparing scholarly papers and reports;
(g)   performing related tasks;
(h)   supervising other workers.

Examples of the occupations classified here:
- Archivist
- Curator, art gallery
- Curator, museum

2432   LIBRARIANS AND RELATED INFORMATION PROFESSIONALS

Librarians and related information professionals collect and store recorded or published material, and retrieve and provide information as requested.

Tasks include –

(a)   organising, developing and maintaining a systematic collection of books, periodicals and other printed or audio-visually recorded material;

(b)   selecting and recommending acquisitions of books and other printed or audio-visually recorded material;

(c)   organising, classifying and cataloguing library material;

(d)   organising and administering loan systems and information networks;

(e) retrieving material and providing information to business and other users based on the collection itself or on library and information-network systems;

(f) conducting research and analysing or modifying library and information services in accordance with changes in users' needs;

(g) preparing scholarly papers and reports;

(h) performing related tasks;

(i) supervising other workers.

Examples of the occupations classified here:

- Information scientist, business services
- Information scientist, technical information
- Librarian

MINOR GROUP 244
SOCIAL SCIENCE AND RELATED PROFESSIONALS

Social science and related professionals conduct research, improve or develop concepts, theories and operational methods, or apply knowledge relating to philosophy, politics, economics, sociology, anthropology, history, philology, languages, psychology, and other social sciences, or they provide social services to meet the needs of individuals and families in a community.

Tasks performed usually include: formulating and applying solutions to present or projected economic, political or social problems; researching into and analysing past events and activities and tracing the origin and evolution of the human race; studying the origin and development of languages, or translating or interpreting them; studying mental processes and behaviour of individuals and groups; providing social services; preparing scholarly papers and reports. Supervision of other workers may be included.

It should be noted that, depending on the specific tasks and degree of responsibility in executing them, as well as on the national educational and training requirements, it may be appropriate to classify some of the occupations that are identified here into Minor group 346, *Social work associate professionals*. This is particularly relevant to the occupations classified into Unit group 2446, *Social work professionals*.

Occupations in this minor group are classified into the following unit groups:

2441 Economists

2442 Sociologists, anthropologists and related professionals

2443 Philosophers, historians and political scientists

2444 Philologists, translators and interpreters

2445 Psychologists

2446 Social work professionals

2

2441 ECONOMISTS

Economists conduct research to improve or develop economic concepts, theories and operational methods used to understand and describe the behaviour of national and international markets for goods, services and labour, and advise on or apply the knowledge to draw up economic policies and to formulate solutions to present or projected economic problems.

Tasks include –

(a) studying, advising on, or dealing with various economic aspects, such as production and marketing methods, national and international trade trends, monetary, fiscal and pricing policies, employment, income, productivity and consumption;

(b) compiling, analysing and interpreting economic data using economic theory and a variety of statistical and other techniques;

(c) advising on economic policy and course of action to be followed in the light of past, present and projected economic factors and trends;

(d) preparing scholarly papers and reports;

(e) performing related tasks;

(f) supervising other workers.

Examples of the occupations classified here:

- Econometrician
- Economist

2442 SOCIOLOGISTS, ANTHROPOLOGISTS AND RELATED PROFESSIONALS

Sociologists, anthropologists and related professionals investigate and describe the social structure of societies, the origin and evolution of humanity, and the interdependence between environmental conditions and human activities, and make the knowledge obtained available as a basis for policy decisions.

Tasks include –

(a) conducting research on the origin, development, structure, social patterns, organisations and inter-relationships of human society;

(b) tracing the origin and evolution of humanity through the study of changing characteristics and cultural and social institutions;

(c) tracing the development of humanity through the material remains of its past, such as dwellings, temples, tools, pottery, coins, weapons, or sculpture;

(d) studying physical and climatic aspects of areas and regions, and correlating these findings with the economic, social and cultural activities;

(e) advising on the practical application of these findings in the formulation of economic and social policies for population groups and regions, and for the development of markets;

(f) preparing scholarly papers and reports;

(g) performing related tasks;

(h) supervising other workers.

Examples of the occupations classified here:

- Anthropologist
- Archaeologist
- Ethnologist
- Geographer
- Sociologist

2443 PHILOSOPHERS, HISTORIANS AND POLITICAL SCIENTISTS

Philosophers, historians and political scientists work, mostly by reasoning, in the field of epistemology, metaphysics or ethics. They conduct research and describe past events and activities, including the development of social and economic structures, or cultural and political institutions and movements, and make the knowledge obtained available as a basis for political, diplomatic and related policies.

Tasks include –

(a) researching, mostly by reasoning, into the general causes, principles and meanings of the world, human actions, experience and existence, and interpreting and developing philosophical concepts and theories;

(b) consulting and comparing primary sources, such as original or contemporary records of past events, and secondary sources such as archaeological or anthropological findings;

(c) extracting relevant material, checking its authenticity, and researching into and describing the history of a particular period, country or region, or a particular facet – for example economic, social or political – of its history;

(d) conducting research in such fields as political philosophy, or past and present theory and practice of political systems, institutions or behaviour;

(e) observing contemporary political institutions and collecting data on them from various sources, including interviews with government and political party officials and other relevant persons;

(f) presenting findings and conclusions for publication or use by government, political parties or other organisations and interested persons;

(g) preparing scholarly papers and reports;

(h) performing related tasks;

(i) supervising other workers.

Examples of the occupations classified here:

- Historian
- Philosopher
- Political scientist

2444 PHILOLOGISTS, TRANSLATORS AND INTERPRETERS

Philologists, translators and interpreters study the origin, development and structure of languages, and translate or interpret from one language into another.

Tasks include –

(a) studying relationships between ancient parent languages and modern language groups, tracing the origin and evolution of words, grammar and language forms, and presenting findings;

(b) advising on or preparing language classification systems, grammars, dictionaries and similar materials;

(c) translating from one language into another and ensuring that the correct meaning of the original is retained, that legal, technical or scientific works are correctly rendered, and that the phraseology and terminology of the spirit and style of literary works are conveyed as far as possible;

(d) develop methods for the use of compu-

ters and other instruments to improve productivity and quality of translations;

(e) interpreting from one language into another, in particular at conferences, meetings and similar occasions, and ensuring that the correct meaning and, as far as possible, the spirit of the original are transmitted;

(f) preparing scholarly papers and reports;

(g) performing related tasks;

(h) supervising other workers.

Examples of the occupations classified here:

- Interpreter
- Lexicographer
- Philologist
- Translator

Some related occupations classified elsewhere:

- Editor – 2451

2445 PSYCHOLOGISTS

Psychologists research into and study mental processes and behaviour of human beings as individuals or in groups, and apply this knowledge to promote personal, social, educational or occupational adjustment and development.

Tasks include –

(a) planning and carrying out tests to measure mental, physical and other characteristics such as intelligence, abilities, aptitudes, potentialities, etc., interpreting and evaluating results, and providing advice;

(b) analysing the effect of heredity, social, occupational and other factors on individual thought and behaviour;

(c) conducting counselling or therapeutic interviews with individuals and groups, and providing follow-up services;

(d) maintaining required contacts, such as those with family members, educational authorities or employers, and recommending possible solutions to, and treatment of, problems;

(e) studying psychological factors in the diagnosis, treatment and prevention of mental illnesses and emotional or personality disorders, and conferring with related professionals;

(f) preparing scholarly papers and reports;
(g) performing related tasks;
(h) supervising other workers.

Examples of the occupations classified here:

- Psychologist

2446 SOCIAL WORK PROFESSIONALS

Social work professionals provide guidance to clients in social and related matters to enable them to find and use resources to overcome difficulties and achieve particular goals.

Tasks include –

(a) helping individuals and families with personal and social problems;

(b) collecting information relevant to clients' needs and advising them on their rights and obligations;

(c) analysing the client's situation and presenting alternative approaches to resolving problems;

(d) compiling case records or reports for courts and other legal proceedings;

(e) planning, evaluating, improving and developing welfare services;

(f) working to prevent development of delinquency or to achieve rehabilitation of delinquents by organising and supervising social, recreational and educational activities in youth clubs, community centres and similar organisations, or by other means;

(g) helping physically or mentally handicapped persons to obtain adequate treatment and improve their ability to function in society;

(h) planning, organising or providing home-help services;

(i) performing related tasks;

(j) supervising other workers.

Examples of the occupations classified here:

- Social worker, professional
- Social worker, professional/enterprise
- Welfare worker, professional

Some related occupations classified elsewhere:

- Social worker, associate professional – 3460
- Social worker, associate professional/enterprise – 3460
- Welfare worker, associate professional – 3460

MINOR GROUP 245
WRITERS AND CREATIVE OR PERFORMING ARTISTS

Writers and creative or performing artists conceive and create or perform literary, dramatic, musical and other works of art.

Tasks performed usually include: writing literary works; appraising merits of literary and other works of art; collecting information about current affairs and writing about them; sculpting, painting, engraving, or creating cartoons; restoring paintings; composing music; dancing or acting in dramatic productions or directing such productions. Supervision of other workers may be included.

Occupations in this minor group are classified into the following unit groups:

2451 Authors, journalists and other writers

2452 Sculptors, painters and related artists

2453 Composers, musicians and singers

2454 Choreographers and dancers

2455 Film, stage and related actors and directors

2451 AUTHORS, JOURNALISTS AND OTHER WRITERS

Authors, journalists and other writers write literary works for publication or presentation in dramatic form, appraise merits of artistic productions, or literary and other works of art, or write and edit news, stories and commentaries.

Tasks include –

(a) conceiving and writing literary works for publication or presentation in dramatic form;

(b) writing scripts and continuities and preparing programmes for stage, film, radio and television productions;

(c) appraising and writing about merits of literary, musical and other works of art, and about artistic performances;

(d) collecting, reporting and commenting on news and current affairs for publication in newspapers and periodicals, or for broadcasting by radio or television;

(e) interviewing politicians and other public figures at press conferences and on other occasions, including individual interviews recorded for radio or television;

(f) writing editorials and selecting, revising, arranging and editing submitted articles and other material for publication in newspapers and periodicals;

(g) appraising manuscripts submitted for publication in book form, making recommendations thereon and editing or supervising editing of the material;

(h) writing advertising copy promoting particular products or services;

(i) selecting, assembling and preparing publicity material about business or other organisations for issue through press, radio, television and other media;

(j) designing and writing brochures, handbooks and similar technical publications;

(k) performing related tasks;

(l) supervising other workers.

Examples of the occupations classified here:
- Author
- Copywriter, advertising
- Critic
- Editor
- Journalist
- Writer, technical

2452 SCULPTORS, PAINTERS AND RELATED ARTISTS

Sculptors, painters and related artists create and execute works of art by sculpting, painting, drawing, creating cartoons, engraving or using related techniques.

Tasks include –

(a) creating representational or abstract three-dimensional or relief forms by shaping and combining materials such as wood, stone, clay or metal;

(b) creating representational or abstract drawings and paintings using pencils, ink, chalk, oil paints, water colours or through the application of other techniques;

(c) creating drawings and engraving or etching them on metal, wood, or other materials;

(d) creating cartoons to depict persons and events, often in caricature;

(e) creating and executing designs and illustrations for books, magazines, advertising and similar purposes;

(f) restoring damaged, soiled and faded paintings and other art objects;

(g) painting miniatures;

(h) performing related tasks;

(i) supervising other workers.

Examples of the occupations classified here:
- Artist, commercial
- Cartoonist
- Engraver-etcher, artistic
- Painter, portrait
- Restorer, picture
- Sculptor

Some related occupations classified elsewhere:
- Designer, industrial products – 3471

2453 COMPOSERS, MUSICIANS AND SINGERS

Composers, musicians and singers compose and adapt musical works and conduct or participate in performances of them.

Tasks include –

(a) conceiving and writing musical compositions;
(b) adapting or arranging music for particular instrumental groups, instruments or occasions;
(c) conducting instrumental or vocal groups;
(d) playing one or more musical instruments as a soloist or as a member of an orchestra;
(e) singing as soloists or members of vocal groups;
(f) performing related tasks;
(g) supervising other workers.

Examples of the occupations classified here:
- Composer, music
- Conductor, orchestra
- Conductor, vocal group
- Instrumentalist
- Orchestrator
- Singer, opera

Some related occupations classified elsewhere:
- Band leader – 3473
- Musician, street – 3473
- Singer, street – 3473

2454 CHOREOGRAPHERS AND DANCERS

Choreographers and dancers conceive and create or perform dances.

Tasks include –

(a) conceiving and creating dances, which often convey a story, theme, idea or mood, by a pattern of steps, movements and gestures;
(b) performing dances as a soloist, with a partner or as a member of a dancing group;

(c) performing related tasks;
(d) supervising other workers.

Examples of the occupations classified here:
- Choreographer
- Dancer, ballet

Some related occupations classified elsewhere:
- Dancer, night-club – 3473

2455 FILM, STAGE AND RELATED ACTORS AND DIRECTORS

Film, stage and related actors and directors act in, or direct, motion pictures, television or radio productions and stage shows.

Tasks include –

(a) learning lines and cues and playing parts in dramatic productions on stage, television, radio or in motion pictures;
(b) telling stories or reading literary works aloud to educate or entertain listeners;
(c) studying scripts to determine artistic interpretation, instructing actors on acting methods, and directing all aspects of dramatic productions on stage, television, radio or in motion pictures, including choice of actors, and final decisions concerning costumes, set designs, sound or lighting effects;
(d) performing related tasks;
(e) supervising other workers.

Examples of the occupations classified here:
- Actor
- Director, motion picture
- Director, stage
- Story-teller, radio or television

Some related occupations classified elsewhere:
- Clown – 3474
- Impresario – 1229
- Producer, theatre – 1229
- Stage manager, 1229

MINOR GROUP **246**
RELIGIOUS PROFESSIONALS

Religious professionals function as perpetrators of the sacred traditions, practices and beliefs and celebrate or administer at the rituals of initiation, preside over ritual reenactments of creative, redemptive or salvatory events, and offer sacrifices to the gods or to one God.

Tasks performed usually include: perpetuating sacred traditions, practices and beliefs; conducting religious services, rites and ceremonies; undertaking various administrative and social duties within the framework of a particular religious organisation; providing spiritual and moral guidance in accordance with the religion professed; preparing religious sermons and preachings. Supervision of other workers may be included.

Occupations in this minor group are classified into the following unit group:

2460   Religious professionals

2460   RELIGIOUS PROFESSIONALS

Religious professionals function as perpetrators of the sacred traditions, practices and beliefs and celebrate or administer at the rituals of initiation, preside over ritual reenactments of creative, redemptive or salvatory events, and offer sacrifices to the gods or to one God.

Tasks include –

(a) perpetuating sacred traditions, practices and beliefs;

(d) conducting religious services, rites and ceremonies;

(c) undertaking various administrative and social duties, including attending committees and meetings of religious organisations;

(d) providing spiritual and moral guidance in accordance with the religion professed;

(e) propagating religious doctrines in own country or abroad;

(f) preparing religious sermons and preachings;

(g) performing related tasks;

(h) supervising other workers.

Examples of the occupations classified here:
- Bonze
- Imam
- Minister, religion
- Monk, professional
- Nun, professional
- Poojari
- Priest
- Rabbi

Some related occupations classified elsewhere:
- Monk, associate professional – 3480
- Nun, associate professional – 3480
- Preacher, lay – 3480

MAJOR GROUP **3**
TECHNICIANS AND ASSOCIATE PROFESSIONALS

Technicians and associate professionals perform mostly technical and related tasks connected with research and the application of scientific or artistic concepts and operational methods, and government or business regulations, and teach at certain educational levels. Most occupations in this major group require skills at the third ISCO skill level.

Tasks performed by technicians and associate professionals usually include: undertaking and carrying out technical work connected with research and the application of concepts and operational methods in the fields of physical sciences including engineering and technology, life sciences including the medical profession, and social sciences and humanities. Tasks also include: teaching children at primary and pre-primary levels; teaching and educating handicapped persons; initiating and carrying out various technical services related to trade, finance, administration, including administration of a number of government laws and regulations, and to social work; providing artistic and sports entertainment; executing some religious tasks. Supervision of other workers may be included.

Technicians and associate professionals may receive guidance from *Senior government officials*, *Managers* or *Professionals*.

It should be noted that, depending on the specific tasks and degree of responsibility in executing them, as well as on the national educational and training requirements, it may be appropriate to classify some of the occupations that are identified here into Major group 2, *Professionals*. Examples are to be found in particular among *teaching occupations*, *nursing occupations* and *social services occupations*.

Occupations in this major group are classified into the following sub-major groups:

31 Physical and engineering science associate professionals

32 Life science and health associate professionals

33 Teaching associate professionals

34 Other associate professionals

3

SUB-MAJOR GROUP **31**
PHYSICAL AND ENGINEERING SCIENCE ASSOCIATE PROFESSIONALS

Physical and engineering science associate professionals perform technical tasks connected with research and the application of concepts and operational methods in the field of physical science, as well as computing and engineering, or they control and operate technical equipment, fly aircraft, navigate ships, and investigate safety aspects of manufacturing and other processes and products.

Tasks performed by workers in this sub-major group usually include: undertaking and carrying out technical work in the field of physical science, as well as computing and engineering; controlling and operating optical, electronic and related equipment and systems; flying aircraft and navigating ships; inspecting application of safety standards and procedures relating to structures, equipment, processes and products. They may receive guidance from *Senior government officials*, *Managers* or *Professionals*. Supervision of other workers may be included.

Occupations in this sub-major group are classified into the following minor groups:

311   Physical and engineering science technicians

312   Computer associate professionals

313   Optical and electronic equipment operators

314   Ship and aircraft controllers and technicians

315   Safety and quality inspectors

MINOR GROUP **311**
PHYSICAL AND ENGINEERING SCIENCE TECHNICIANS

Physical and engineering science technicians perform technical tasks related to research and the practical application of concepts, principles and operational methods particular to physical sciences including such areas as engineering, technical drawing or economic efficiency of production processes.

Tasks performed usually include: undertaking and carrying out technical work related to chemistry, physics, geology, meteorology, or astronomy, as well as to engineering, technical drawing, and economic efficiency of production processes. They may receive guidance from *Managers* or *Professionals*. Supervision of other workers may be included.

Occupations in this minor group are classified into the following unit groups:

3111   Chemical and physical science technicians

3112   Civil engineering technicians

3113   **Electrical engineering technicians**

3114   **Electronics and telecommunications engineering technicians**

3115   **Mechanical engineering technicians**

3116   **Chemical engineering technicians**

3117   **Mining and metallurgical technicians**

3118   **Draughtspersons**

3119   **Physical and engineering science technicians not elsewhere classified**

3111 CHEMICAL AND PHYSICAL SCIENCE TECHNICIANS

Chemical and physical science technicians perform technical tasks connected with research in chemistry, physics, geology, geophysics, meteorology and astronomy, as well as with the development of industrial, medical, military and other practical applications of research results.

Tasks include –

(a) collecting samples and preparing materials and equipment for experiments, tests and analyses;

(b) assisting with the design of and performing experiments, tests and analyses;

(c) preparing detailed estimates of quantities and costs of materials and labour required for projects, according to the specifications given;

(d) applying technical knowledge in order to identify and solve problems arising in the course of work;

(e) organising maintenance and repairs of research equipment;

(f) performing related tasks;

(g) supervising other workers.

Examples of the occupations classified here:

- Technician, chemistry
- Technician, geology
- Technician, meteorology
- Technician, physics

3112 CIVIL ENGINEERING TECHNICIANS

Civil engineering technicians perform technical tasks connected with civil engineering research, as well as with the design, construction, operation, maintenance and repair of buildings and other structures, such as water supply and sewage systems, bridges, roads, dams and airports.

Tasks include –

(a) performing or helping with field and laboratory tests of soils and construction materials;

(b) providing technical assistance connected with the construction of buildings and other structures, and with surveys or the preparation of survey reports;

(c) representing building architects and civil engineers on construction sites to ensure compliance with design specifications and maintenance of desired standards of materials and work;

(d) applying technical knowledge of building and civil engineering principles and practices in order to identify and solve problems arising in the course of their work;

(e) assisting with the preparation of detailed estimates of quantities and costs of materials and labour required for projects, according to the specifications given;

(f) organising maintenance and repairs;

(g) performing related tasks;

(h) supervising other workers.

3

Examples of the occupations classified here:

- Clerk of works
- Technician, engineering/civil
- Technician, surveying

Some related occupations classified elsewhere:

- Surveyor, marine − 3115
- Surveyor, quantity − 2149

3113 ELECTRICAL ENGINEERING TECHNICIANS

Electrical engineering technicians perform technical tasks connected with electrical engineering research, as well as with the design, manufacture, assembly, construction, operation, maintenance and repair of electrical equipment, facilities and distribution systems.

Tasks include −

(a) providing technical assistance connected with research and the development of electrical equipment and facilities, or testing prototypes;

(b) designing and preparing blueprints of electrical installations and circuitry according to the specifications given;

(c) preparing detailed estimates of quantities and costs of materials and labour required for manufacture and installation according to the specifications given;

(d) providing technical supervision of the manufacture, installation, utilisation, maintenance and repair of electrical systems and equipment to ensure satisfactory performance and compliance with specifications and regulations;

(e) applying technical knowledge of electrical engineering principles and practices in order to identify and solve problems arising in the course of their work;

(f) performing related tasks;

(g) supervising other workers.

Examples of the occupations classified here:

- Technician, engineering/electrical
- Technician, engineering/electrical (electric power transmission)

Some related occupations classified elsewhere:

- Assembler, electrical equipment − 8282
- Mechanic, electrical − 7241

3114 ELECTRONICS AND TELECOMMUNICATIONS ENGINEERING TECHNICIANS

Electronics and telecommunications engineering technicians perform technical tasks connected with electronic and telecommunications engineering research, as well as with the design, manufacture, assembly, construction, operation, maintenance and repair of electronic equipment and electronic and electromechanical telecommunications systems.

Tasks include −

(a) providing technical assistance connected with research and the development of electronic and telecommunications equipment, or testing prototypes;

(b) designing and preparing blueprints of electronic circuitry according to the specifications given;

(c) preparing detailed estimates of quantities and costs of materials and labour required for the manufacture and installation of electronic and telecommunications equipment, according to the specifications given;

(d) providing technical supervision of the manufacture, utilisation, maintenance and repair of electronic equipment and telecommunications systems to ensure satisfactory performance and compliance with specifications and regulations;

(e) applying technical knowledge of electronic and telecommunications engineering principles and practices in order to identify and solve problems arising in the course of their work;

(f) performing related tasks;

(g) supervising other workers.

Examples of the occupations classified here:

- Technician, engineering/electronics
- Technician, engineering/telecommunications

Some related occupations classified elsewhere:
- Assembler, electronic equipment – 8283
- Mechanic, electronics – 7243

3115 MECHANICAL ENGINEERING TECHNICIANS

Mechanical engineering technicians perform technical tasks connected with mechanical engineering research, as well as with the design, manufacture, assembly, construction, operation, maintenance and repair of machines and mechanical installations and facilities.

Tasks include –

(a) providing technical assistance connected with research and the development of machines and mechanical installations, facilities and components, or testing prototypes;

(b) designing and preparing layouts of machines and mechanical installations, facilities and components according to the specifications given;

(c) preparing detailed estimates of quantities and costs of materials and labour required for manufacture and installation according to the specifications given;

(d) providing technical supervision of manufacture, utilisation, maintenance and repair of machines and mechanical installations, facilities and components to ensure satisfactory performance and compliance with specifications and regulations;

(e) applying technical knowledge of machinery and mechanical engineering principles and practices in order to identify and solve problems arising in the course of their work;

(f) developing and monitoring the implementation of safety standards and procedures for marine survey work in relation to ships' hulls, equipment and cargoes;

(g) co-ordinating and supervising activities of workers engaged in dry-docking vessels for cleaning, painting and repair;

(h) performing related tasks;

(i) supervising other workers.

Examples of the occupations classified here:
- Technician, engineering/aeronautics
- Technician, engineering/marine
- Technician, engineering/mechanical
- Technician, engineering/nuclear power

Some related occupations classified elsewhere:
- Assembler, mechanical machinery – 8281
- Mechanic, industrial machinery – 7233

3116 CHEMICAL ENGINEERING TECHNICIANS

Chemical engineering technicians perform technical tasks connected with chemical engineering research, as well as with the design, manufacture, construction, operation, maintenance and repair of chemical plant.

Tasks include –

(a) providing technical assistance connected with research and the development of industrial chemical processes, plant and equipment, or testing prototypes;

(b) designing and preparing layouts of chemical plant according to the specifications given;

(c) preparing detailed estimates of quantities and costs of materials and labour required for manufacture and installation according to the specifications given;

(d) providing technical supervision of the construction, installation, operation, maintenance and repair of chemical plant to ensure satisfactory performance and compliance with specifications and regulations;

(e) applying technical knowledge of chemical engineering principles and practices in order to identify and solve problems arising in the course of their work;

(f) providing technical assistance regarding technological aspects of particular materials, products and processes;

(g) performing related tasks;

(h) supervising other workers.

3

Examples of the occupations classified here:

- Technician, engineering/chemical
- Technician, engineering/chemical process
- Technician, engineering/petroleum

Some related occupations classified elsewhere:

- Kiln-operator, chemical and related processes − 8152
- Machine-operator, blending/chemical and related processes − 8151

3117 MINING AND METALLURGICAL TECHNICIANS

Mining and metallurgical technicians perform technical tasks connected with metallurgical research to develop improved methods of extracting solid minerals, oil and gas, as well as with the design, construction, operation, maintenance and repair of mines and mine installations, systems for transporting and storing oil and natural gas, and plant for extracting metals from their ores and refining metal.

Tasks include −

(a) providing technical assistance connected with research and the development of processes to determine the properties of metal and new alloys, or of improved methods for the extraction of solid minerals, oil and natural gas, and for transporting and storing oil and natural gas, or testing prototypes;

(b) providing technical assistance in geological and topographical surveys, and in the design and layout of oil, natural gas and mineral ore extraction and transport systems, and processing and refining plant for minerals and metals;

(c) preparing detailed estimates of quantities and costs of materials and labour required for mineral, oil and natural gas exploration, extraction and transport projects and plant, and for processing and mineral refining plant according to the specifications given;

(d) providing technical supervision of the construction, installation, operation, maintenance and repair of mineral ore, oil and natural gas exploration, extraction, transport and storage installations

and mineral processing plant to ensure satisfactory performance and compliance with specifications and regulations;

(e) applying technical knowledge of mining, of oil and natural gas extraction, transport and storage, and of metallurgical principles and practices in order to identify and solve problems arising in the course of their work;

(f) performing related tasks;

(g) supervising other workers.

Examples of the occupations classified here:

- Technician, engineering/mining
- Technician, metallurgy/extractive

Some related occupations classified elsewhere:

- Machine-operator, drilling/mine − 8111
- Miner − 7111
- Quarrier − 7111

3118 DRAUGHTSPERSONS

Draughtspersons prepare technical drawings, maps and illustrations from sketches, measurements and other data, and copy drawings and paintings onto printing plates.

Tasks include −

(a) preparing and revising working drawings from sketches and specifications prepared by engineers and designers for the manufacture, installation and erection of machinery and equipment or for the construction, modification, maintenance and repair of buildings, dams, bridges, roads and other architectural and civil engineering projects;

(b) operating computer-assisted drawing equipment to create, modify and generate hard-copy and digital representations of working drawings;

(c) operating digitising table or similar equipment to transfer hard-copy representation of working drawings, maps and other curves to digital form;

(d) using stereo instruments to capture topographical data in analogue or digital form, and using these and other data to prepare and revise topographical, hydrographic, utility and other thematic maps;

(e) preparing and revising illustrations for reference works, brochures and technical manuals dealing with the assembly, installation, operation, maintenance and repair of machinery and other equipment and goods;

(f) copying drawings and paintings onto stone or metal plates for printing;

(g) performing related tasks;

(h) supervising other workers.

Examples of the occupations classified here:

- Draughtsperson
- Draughtsperson, architectural
- Draughtsperson, cartographical
- Draughtsperson, engineering/civil
- Illustrator, technical

3119 PHYSICAL AND ENGINEERING SCIENCE TECHNICIANS NOT ELSEWHERE CLASSIFIED

This unit group covers physical and engineering science technicians not classified elsewhere in Minor group 311, *Physical and engineering science technicians*.

For instance here should be classified those who assist engineers with production engineering matters, time and motion studies, or preparation of cost estimates and bills of quantities.

In such cases tasks would include –

(a) collecting data and providing technical assistance regarding:
- planning and production methods;
- efficient, safe and economic utilisation of personnel, material and equipment;
- methods of work and sequence of operations and supervision of their implementation;
- time and motion aspects of work organisation;
- efficient layout of plant or establishment;

(b) participating in the work concerning identification of potential hazards and introducing safety procedures and devices;

(c) collecting data and providing technical assistance regarding the preparation and monitoring of cost estimates and bills of quantities for construction and architectural projects;

(d) performing related tasks;

(e) supervising other workers.

Examples of the occupations classified here:

- Technician, engineering/industrial efficiency
- Technician, engineering/production
- Technician, engineering/time and motion study
- Technician, quantity surveying

Some related occupations classified elsewhere:

- Engineer, production – 2149
- Engineer, time and motion study – 2149
- Surveyor, quantity – 2149

MINOR GROUP 312
COMPUTER ASSOCIATE PROFESSIONALS

Computer associate professionals provide assistance to users of micro-computers and standard software packages, control and operate computers and peripheral equipment and carry out limited programming tasks connected with the installation and maintenance of computer hardware and software.

Tasks performed usually include: assisting users of micro-computers and standard software systems at installation and when problems occur; installing new computer programs on particular hardware and operating systems configurations, and installing new peripheral units; making minor changes and adjustments to existing programs to update and maintain them; operating and controlling computers and peripheral equipment; organising computing jobs; keeping log of computing operations; performing back-up operations; activating industrial robots, programming them for specific functions and controlling their operation. They may receive guidance from *Managers* or *Professionals*. Supervision of other workers may be included.

Occupations in this minor group are classified into the following unit groups:

3121   Computer assistants

3122   Computer equipment operators

3123   Industrial robot controllers

3121   COMPUTER ASSISTANTS

Computer assistants provide assistance to users of micro-computers and standard software systems at installation and when problems occur, install new computer programs on particular hardware and operating systems configurations, install new peripheral units, and maintain and update existing programs by making minor changes and adjustments to them under the guidance of *Computing professionals*.

Tasks include –

(a)   assisting users of micro-computers and standard software systems at installation and when problems occur;

(b)   installing new computer programs on particular hardware and operating systems configurations;

(c)   installing new peripheral units and making necessary parameter adjustments in operating systems and drives;

(d)   installing, maintaining and updating computer programs by making minor changes and adjustments to them, under the guidance of *Computing professionals*;

(e)   maintaining and updating documentation of computer programs and installations;

(f)   applying knowledge of principles and practices in the area of programming and computing in order to identify and solve problems arising in the course of their work;

(g)   performing related tasks;

(h)   supervising other workers.

Examples of the occupations classified here:
- Assistant, computer/programming
- Assistant, computer/systems analysis
- Assistant, computer/users' services

Some related occupations classified elsewhere:
- Mechanic, electronics/computer – 7243
- Technician, engineering/electronics – 3114

3122   COMPUTER EQUIPMENT OPERATORS

Computer equipment operators operate and control peripheral and related computer equipment used for recording, storing, transmitting and processing digital data and for displaying data as letters, numbers or graphs on screen, paper or film.

Tasks include –

(a)   operating and controlling peripheral and related computer equipment which is used to record, store, transmit and process digital data and to display data as letters, numbers or graphs on screen, paper or film, as requested by users;

(b)   organising computing jobs as specified by users to ensure timely, safe and efficient execution;

(c)   mounting magnetic tapes and disks as needed for processing or recording data in machine-readable form and keeping library of disks and tapes;

(d)   keeping log of computing operations;

(e) performing back-up operations according to regular procedures;

(f) applying knowledge of principles and practices of computers and peripheral equipment in order to identify and solve problems arising in the course of their use and making minor repairs and adjustments;

(g) performing related tasks;

(h) supervising other workers.

Examples of the occupations classified here:

- Operator, computer peripheral equipment
- Operator, computer peripheral equipment/high-speed printer

Some related occupations classified elsewhere:

- Mechanic, electronics/computer – 7243
- Technician, engineering/electronics – 3114

3123 INDUSTRIAL ROBOT CONTROLLERS

Industrial robot controllers activate industrial robots, programme or reprogramme them for specific functions, control their operation, and provide basic maintenance and on-the-spot adjustments.

Tasks include –

(a) programming or reprogramming industrial robots for specific functions within their range of capabilities;

(b) activating industrial robots;

(c) controlling and ensuring the smooth functioning of industrial robots;

(d) trying, by careful and systematic control, to foresee and, if possible, to prevent malfunctioning of industrial robots;

(e) providing on-the-spot adjustments of the robot mechanism;

(f) performing related tasks;

(g) supervising other workers.

Examples of the occupations classified here:

- Controller, robot

Some related occupations classified elsewhere:

- Engineer, robotics – 2149
- Operator, robot – 8172
- Technician, engineering/electronics – 3114

MINOR GROUP 313
OPTICAL AND ELECTRONIC EQUIPMENT OPERATORS

Optical and electronic equipment operators take photographs, control motion picture and video cameras and other equipment to record and edit images and sound, control broadcasting and telecommunications equipment and systems, as well as technical equipment used for medical diagnosis or treatment.

Tasks performed usually include: taking photographs; controlling motion picture and video cameras and other equipment to record and edit images and sound; controlling technical functioning of radio and television broadcasting equipment and telecommunications systems; controlling technical equipment used to diagnose or treat illnesses and disorders.

Occupations in this minor group are classified into the following unit groups:

3131 Photographers and image and sound recording equipment operators

3132 Broadcasting and telecommunications equipment operators

3133 Medical equipment operators

3139 Optical and electronic equipment operators not elsewhere classified

3131 PHOTOGRAPHERS AND IMAGE AND SOUND RECORDING EQUIPMENT OPERATORS

Photographers and image and sound recording equipment operators take photographs, control motion picture and video cameras and other equipment to record and edit images and sound.

Tasks include –

(a) taking photographs for advertising, or other commercial, industrial or scientific purposes and to illustrate stories and articles in newspapers, magazines and other publications;

(b) taking portrait photographs of persons and groups of persons;

(c) setting and operating motion picture, video, microscopic and other specialised cameras, including those for aerial photography, to record images;

(d) controlling equipment to record sound for motion pictures, video tapes, gramophone records, audio tapes, digital discs, direct broadcasting or other purposes;

(e) controlling equipment to edit and mix image and sound recordings to ensure satisfactory quality and to create special image and sound effects;

(f) applying knowledge of principles and practices of image and sound recording and editing in order to identify and solve problems arising in the course of their work;

(g) performing related tasks;

(h) supervising other workers.

Examples of the occupations classified here:

- Operator, camera/motion picture
- Operator, recording equipment/sound
- Operator, studio equipment/television
- Photographer

Some related occupations classified elsewhere:

- Mechanic, electronics – 7243
- Photographer, photogravure – 7343
- Photolithographer – 7343
- Repairer, photographic equipment – 7311

3132 BROADCASTING AND TELECOMMUNICATIONS EQUIPMENT OPERATORS

Broadcasting and telecommunications equipment operators control technical functioning of equipment for transmitting radio and television broadcasts of pre-recorded or live images and sounds, as well as other types of telecommunications signals on land and sea or in aircraft.

Tasks include –

(a) controlling transmitting and broadcasting systems and satellite systems for radio and television programmes;

(b) controlling radio communications systems, satellite services and multiplex systems on land and sea and in aircraft;

(c) controlling cinema projection equipment;

(d) applying knowledge of principles and practices of broadcasting, telecommunications terminals and transmission systems, in order to identify and solve problems arising in the course of their work and maintain equipment;

(e) keeping logs of operations;

(f) performing related tasks;

(g) supervising other workers.

Examples of the occupations classified here:

- Operator, broadcasting equipment/radio
- Operator, telecommunications equipment
- Operator, transmitting equipment/television

Some related occupations classified else-where:

- Mechanic, electronics − 7243
- Technician, engineering/telecommuni-cations − 3114

3133 MEDICAL EQUIPMENT OPERATORS

Medical equipment operators control technical equipment used to diagnose or treat illnesses and disorders.

Tasks include −

(a) controlling technical equipment used to diagnose illnesses and disorders of the nervous system and organs, or in radio-graphy or anaesthetics;

(b) applying knowledge of technical equip-ment and some principles and practices of medicine in order to identify and solve problems arising in the course of their work and maintain equipment;

(c) performing related tasks;

(d) supervising other workers.

Examples of the occupations classified here:

- Operator, electrocardiograph equip-ment
- Operator, medical X-ray equipment
- Operator, scanning equipment

Some related occupations classified else-where:

- Mechanic, electronics − 7243

3139 OPTICAL AND ELECTRONIC EQUIPMENT OPERATORS NOT ELSEWHERE CLASSIFIED

This unit group covers optical and elec-tronic equipment operators not classified elsewhere in Minor group 313, *Optical and electronic equipment operators*.

MINOR GROUP 314
SHIP AND AIRCRAFT CONTROLLERS AND TECHNICIANS

Ship and aircraft controllers and technicians command and navigate ships and aircraft and perform technical functions to ensure safe and efficient movement and operations.

Tasks performed usually include: controlling the operation of mechanical, electrical and electronic equipment on board ship or on aircraft, commanding and navigating ships or aircraft or directing the movements of ships or aircraft.

Occupations in this minor group are classified into the following unit groups:

3141 **Ships' engineers**

3142 **Ships' deck officers and pilots**

3143 **Aircraft pilots and related associate professionals**

3144 **Air traffic controllers**

3145 **Air traffic safety technicians**

3

3141 SHIPS' ENGINEERS

Ships' engineers control and participate in the operation, maintenance and repair of mechanical, electrical and electronic equipment and machinery on board ship, or perform related supporting functions on shore.

Tasks include –

(a) controlling and participating in the operation, maintenance and repair of mechanical, electrical and electronic equipment and machinery on board ship;

(b) ordering fuel and other engine-room department stores and maintaining record of operations;

(c) performing technical supervision of the installation, maintenance and repair of ship's machinery and equipment to ensure compliance with specifications and regulations;

(d) applying knowledge of principles and practices relating to ship's machinery and equipment in order to identify and solve problems arising in the course of their work;

(e) performing related tasks;

(f) supervising other workers.

Examples of the occupations classified here:
- Engineer, ship

Some related occupations classified elsewhere:
- Engineer, marine – 2145

3142 SHIPS' DECK OFFICERS AND PILOTS

Ships' deck officers and pilots command and navigate ships and similar vessels, and perform related functions on shore.

Tasks include –

(a) commanding and navigating ship or similar vessel at sea or on inland waterways;

(b) controlling and participating in deck and bridge-watch activities;

(c) navigating vessels into and out of ports and through channels, straits and other waters where special knowledge is required;

(d) ensuring safe loading and unloading of cargo and observance of safety regulations and procedures by crew and passengers;

(e) performing technical supervision of maintenance and repair of ship to ensure compliance with specifications and regulations;

(f) applying knowledge of principles and practices relating to ship's operation and navigation in order to identify and solve problems arising in the course of their work;

(g) ordering ship's stores and recruiting crew as required and maintaining record of operations;

(h) performing related tasks;

(i) supervising other workers.

Examples of the occupations classified here:
- Captain, ship/sea
- Pilot, ship
- Skipper, yacht

Some related occupations classified elsewhere:
- Sailor – 8340

3143 AIRCRAFT PILOTS AND RELATED ASSOCIATE PROFESSIONALS

Aircraft pilots and related associate professionals control the operation of mechanical, electrical and electronic equipment, in order to navigate aircraft for transporting passengers, mail and freight and perform related pre-flight and in-flight tasks.

Tasks include –

(a) flying and navigating aircraft in accordance with established control and operating procedures;

(b) preparing and submitting flight plan or examining standard flight plan;

(c) controlling the operation of mechanical, electrical and electronic equipment and ensuring that all instruments and controls work properly;

(d) applying knowledge of principles and practices of flying in order to identify and solve problems arising in the course of their work;

(e) performing related tasks;
(f) supervising other workers.

Examples of the occupations classified here:

- Engineer, flight
- Navigator, flight
- Pilot, aircraft

Some related occupations classified elsewhere:

- Instructor, flying − 3340

3144 AIR TRAFFIC CONTROLLERS

Air traffic controllers direct aircraft movements in airspace and on the ground, using radio, radar and lighting systems, and provide information relevant to the operation of aircraft.

Tasks include −

(a) directing and controlling aircraft approaching and leaving airport and their movement on the ground;
(b) directing and controlling aircraft operating in designated airspace sector;
(c) examining and approving flight plans;
(d) informing flight crew and operations staff about weather conditions, operational facilities, flight plans and air traffic;
(e) applying knowledge of principles and practices of air traffic control in order to identify and solve problems arising in the course of their work;
(f) initiating and organising emergency, search and rescue services and procedures;
(g) performing related tasks;
(h) supervising other workers.

Examples of the occupations classified here:

- Controller, air traffic

3145 AIR TRAFFIC SAFETY TECHNICIANS

Air traffic safety technicians perform technical tasks concerning the design, installation, operation, maintenance and repair of air traffic control and air navigation systems.

Tasks include −

(a) carrying out technical duties related to development work concerning electronic and electromechanical equipment of air navigation systems, and testing prototypes;
(b) providing technical help in the design and layout of specific interface circuitry of air navigation and aircraft detection tracking systems;
(c) contributing to the preparation of cost estimates and technical and training specifications for air traffic control and safety equipment;
(d) assisting with the technical supervision of construction, installation and operation of ground-based air navigation equipment and its maintenance and repair to ensure that standards and recommendations are met;
(e) applying knowledge of air traffic safety engineering principles and practices in order to identify and solve problems arising in the course of their work;
(f) modifying existing ground-based air navigation equipment to adapt it to new air traffic control procedures;
(g) controlling and calibrating the ground-based air navigation instruments to ensure maximum accuracy and safety of flight, take-off and landing operations;
(h) performing related tasks;
(i) supervising other workers.

Examples of the occupations classified here:

- Technician, air traffic safety

Some related occupations classified elsewhere:

- Aeromechanic − 7232

3

Safety and quality inspectors, on behalf of the government or industrial and other enterprises, examine the implementation of rules and regulations relating to fire prevention and other hazards, occupational safety, protection of health and the environment, safety of production processes, and goods and services produced, used or sold, as well as those relating to the quality standards and specifications of manufacturers.

Tasks performed usually include: ensuring that buildings and other structures comply with approved building plans, grading and zoning laws and fire regulations; advising on and inspecting fire-prevention systems; investigating fire sites to determine the cause of fire; inspecting industrial and other enterprises on the grounds of occupational safety, and safety of production processes, as well as of goods produced, used or sold; ensuring compliance with health and environment protection rules and regulations; ensuring compliance with the quality standards and specifications of manufacturers. Supervision of other workers may be included.

Occupations in this minor group are classified into the following unit groups:

3151   Building and fire inspectors

3152   Safety, health and quality inspectors

3151   BUILDING AND FIRE INSPECTORS

Building and fire inspectors, on behalf of the government or industrial and other enterprises, inspect new and existing houses, industrial plant, hotels and other buildings and structures to ensure compliance with building, grading and zoning laws and with approved plans, specifications and standards, or inspect fire-prevention systems and investigate fire sites to determine cause of fire.

Tasks include –

(a) advising those erecting buildings and other structures on the implementation of building, grading and zoning laws, as well as other rules concerning quality and safety of buildings;

(b) inspecting buildings and structures during and after construction to ensure that they comply with building, grading, zoning and safety laws and approved plans, specifications and standards, as well as with other rules concerning quality and safety of buildings;

(c) inspecting existing buildings and structures to determine whether lack of proper maintenance, housing violations or hazardous conditions exist;

(d) inspecting industrial plant, hotels, cinemas and other buildings and structures to detect fire hazards and advise on how they can be removed;

(e) advising on the installation of fire detectors and sprinkler systems and the use of materials in the construction of buildings and means of transportation to reduce risk of fire and extent of damage and danger if fire occurs;

(f) investigating fire sites to determine cause of fire;

(g) performing related tasks;

(h) supervising other workers.

Examples of the occupations classified here:

- Inspector, building
- Inspector, fire
- Specialist, fire prevention

Some related occupations classified elsewhere:

- Fire-fighter – 5161

3152 SAFETY, HEALTH AND QUALITY INSPECTORS

Safety, health and quality inspectors, on behalf of the government or industrial and other enterprises, inspect places of work on the grounds of occupational safety, and safety of production processes, or of goods produced, used or sold, and ensure compliance with health and environment protection rules and regulations, as well as with the quality standards and specifications of manufacturers.

Tasks include –

(a) advising employers' and workers' representatives on the implementation of government and other rules and regulations concerning occupational safety and the working environment;

(b) inspecting places of work to ensure that the working environment, machinery and equipment conform to government and other rules, regulations and standards;

(c) inspecting places of work and, by interviews, observations and other means, obtaining facts about work practices and accidents to determine compliance with safety rules and regulations;

(d) inspecting areas of production, processing, transport, handling, storage and sale of products to ensure conformity with government and other rules, regulations and standards;

(e) inspecting finished products or parts for conformity with manufacturers' specifications and standards;

(f) advising enterprises and the general public on the implementation of government and other rules and regulations concerning hygiene, sanitation, purity and grading of primary products, food, drugs, cosmetics and similar goods;

(g) advising producers, operators and those maintaining and repairing aircraft, cars and other vehicles on the implementation of government and other rules and regulations concerning technical standards and conditions of vehicles;

(h) inspecting vehicles and places authorised to maintain and repair vehicles to ensure that they conform to technical standards and government and other regulations;

(i) inspecting establishments to ensure that they conform to government and other rules and regulations concerning emission of pollutants and disposal of dangerous wastes;

(j) performing related tasks;

(k) supervising other workers.

Examples of the occupations classified here:
- Inspector, occupational safety
- Inspector, quality/products
- Inspector, safety and health/consumer protection
- Inspector, safety and health/pollution

Some related occupations classified elsewhere:
- Inspector, sanitary – 3222
- Inspector, wage – 3449

SUB-MAJOR GROUP 32
LIFE SCIENCE AND HEALTH ASSOCIATE PROFESSIONALS

Life science and health associate professionals perform technical tasks connected with research and the practical application of concepts, theories, principles and operational methods particular to life sciences, including agriculture, forestry, sanitation, medicine, veterinary medicine, pharmacy and related fields, and provide nursing, midwifery, traditional medicine and faith-healing care.

Tasks performed by workers in this sub-major group usually include: undertaking and carrying out research and technical work pertaining to life sciences, including agriculture, forestry, sanitation, medicine, veterinary medicine, pharmacy and related fields; providing help with nursing, midwifery, traditional medicine and faith-healing care. They may receive guidance from *Life science and health professionals*. Supervision of other workers may be included.

It should be noted that depending on the specific tasks and degree of responsibility in executing them, as well as on the national educational and training requirements, it may be appropriate to classify some of the occupations that are identified here into Sub-major group 22, *Life science and health professionals*. This is particularly relevant to the occupations classified into Minor group 323, *Nursing and midwifery associate professionals*.

Occupations in this sub-major group are classified into the following minor groups:

321 Life science technicians and related associate professionals

322 Modern health associate professionals (except nursing)

323 Nursing and midwifery associate professionals

324 Traditional medicine practitioners and faith healers

MINOR GROUP 321
LIFE SCIENCE TECHNICIANS AND RELATED ASSOCIATE PROFESSIONALS

Life science technicians and related associate professionals perform technical tasks related to research and the practical application of concepts, principles and operational methods particular to life sciences, such as biology, botany, zoology, bacteriology and biochemistry, as well as to agriculture, agronomy and forestry.

Tasks performed usually include: undertaking and carrying out technical work connected either with research in the field of life sciences, or with the application of their concepts, principles and operational methods, especially in the areas of medicine, agriculture or pharmaceutical manufacture.

Occupations in this minor group are classified into the following unit groups:

3211 Life science technicians

3212 Agronomy and forestry technicians

3213 Farming and forestry advisers

3211 LIFE SCIENCE TECHNICIANS

Life science technicians perform technical tasks connected with research in biology or other life sciences, as well as with the development of industrial, agricultural, medical, public health and other practical applications of research results.

Tasks include –
(a) preparing materials and equipment for experiments, tests and analyses;
(b) collecting and preparing specimens such as plant, animal or human cells, and tissues, parts or organs for experiments, tests and analyses;
(c) assisting with and performing experiments, tests and analyses in their field of specialisation;
(d) collecting data and estimating quantities and costs of materials and labour required for projects;
(e) applying knowledge of scientific principles and practices in order to identify and solve problems arising in the course of their work;
(f) organising maintenance and repairs of research equipment;
(g) performing related tasks;
(h) supervising other workers.

Examples of the occupations classified here:
- Technician, bacteriology
- Technician, biochemistry
- Technician, blood-bank
- Technician, pharmacology
- Technician, serology
- Technician, zoology

3212 AGRONOMY AND FORESTRY TECHNICIANS

Agronomy and forestry technicians perform technical tasks connected with research in agronomy and forestry, as well as with the development of agricultural and forestry applications of research results.

Tasks include –
(a) preparing materials and equipment for experiments, tests and analyses;
(b) collecting and preparing specimens such as plant or animal cells, tissues or parts or animal organs for experiments, tests and analyses;
(c) assisting with and performing experiments, tests and analyses in their field of specialisation;
(d) analysing samples of seeds for quality, purity and germination rating;
(e) collecting data and estimating quantities and costs of materials and labour required for projects;
(f) applying knowledge of scientific principles and practices in order to identify and solve problems arising in the course of their work;
(g) organising maintenance and repairs of research equipment;
(h) performing related tasks;
(i) supervising other workers.

Examples of the occupations classified here:
- Technician, agronomy
- Technician, forestry
- Technician, soil science

Some related occupations classified elsewhere:
- Adviser, farming – 3213
- Adviser, forestry – 3213
- Assistant, veterinary/artificial insemination – 3227
- Farm demonstrator – 3213

3213 FARMING AND FORESTRY ADVISERS

Farming and forestry advisers provide technical assistance and advice on farming and forestry methods and problems.

Tasks include –
(a) keeping abreast of relevant farming or forestry methods and techniques;
(b) advising on ways of raising quality of output, increasing yield and measures to increase efficiency of operations and to conserve natural assets and the environment;
(c) advising on measures to deal with problems such as soil erosion or pest infestations;
(d) collecting data and estimating quantities and costs of materials and labour required for projects;

(e) organising demonstrations, giving lectures and distributing material to promote adoption of improved practices and techniques;

(f) applying knowledge of scientific principles and practices in order to identify and solve problems arising in the course of their work;

(g) performing related tasks;

(h) supervising other workers.

Examples of the occupations classified here:

- Adviser, farming
- Adviser, forestry
- Farm demonstrator

Some related occupations classified elsewhere:

- Technician, agronomy − 3212
- Technician, forestry − 3212

MINOR GROUP 322
MODERN HEALTH ASSOCIATE PROFESSIONALS (EXCEPT NURSING)

Modern health associate professionals (except nursing) perform technical tasks related to research and the practical application of concepts, principles and operational methods in the fields of medicine, veterinary medicine, dentistry, pharmacy, sanitation, promotion of health and related disciplines.

Tasks performed usually include: carrying out of a limited number of advisory and diagnostic duties including both preventive and curative medical, dental or veterinary work; advising on action to improve hygienic and sanitary conditions; developing and applying nutritional methods and diets; examining eyes and prescribing glasses or contact lenses; advising on prevention and treating disorders of bones and muscular systems; assisting in dispensing and preparing medicaments and other pharmaceutical products; applying homeopathic treatment or treating speech and other impediments. They may work under the guidance of *Health professionals (except nursing)*. Supervision of other workers may be included.

Occupations in this minor group are classified into the following unit groups:

3221 Medical assistants

3222 Sanitarians

3223 Dieticians and nutritionists

3224 Optometrists and opticians

3225 Dental assistants

3226 Physiotherapists and related associate professionals

3227 Veterinary assistants

3228 Pharmaceutical assistants

3229 Modern health associate professionals (except nursing) not elsewhere classified

3221 MEDICAL ASSISTANTS

Medical assistants carry out advisory, diagnostic, preventive and curative medical tasks, more limited in scope and complexity than those carried out by *Medical doctors*. They work independently or with the guidance and supervision of *Medical doctors* in institutions or in the field as part of the public health service, and may work mainly with diseases and disorders common in their region, or mainly apply specific types of treatment.

Tasks include –

(a) advising communities and individuals on birth control, hygiene, diet and other preventive medical measures;

(b) conducting medical examinations to make diagnoses, or refer more difficult cases to *Medical doctors* if possible;

(c) prescribing medicine and giving treatment for diagnosed illnesses, disorders or injuries;

(d) performing simple surgical operations;

(e) performing related tasks;

(f) supervising other workers.

Examples of the occupations classified here:
- Assistant, medical

3222 SANITARIANS

Sanitarians provide technical assistance and advice on measures to restore or improve sanitary conditions, and supervise their implementation.

Tasks include –

(a) inspecting and giving advice on environmental sanitary problems and techniques;

(b) initiating action to maintain or improve hygienic quality and prevent pollution of water, air, food or soil;

(c) promoting preventive and corrective measures such as control of disease-carrying organisms and of harmful substances in the air, hygienic food handling, proper disposal of waste and cleaning of public places;

(d) organising demonstrations, giving lectures and distributing material to promote adoption of improved practices and techniques;

(e) collecting data and estimating quantities and costs of materials and labour required for projects;

(f) applying knowledge of hygiene and sanitation principles and practices in order to identify and solve problems arising in the course of their work;

(g) performing related tasks;

(h) supervising other workers.

Examples of the occupations classified here:
- Inspector, sanitary
- Sanitarian

Some related occupations classified elsewhere:
- Inspector, safety and health – 3152
- Inspector, safety and health/industrial waste-processing – 3152
- Inspector, safety and health/pollution – 3152

3223 DIETICIANS AND NUTRITIONISTS

Dieticians and nutritionists conduct research and improve or develop concepts and operational methods concerning the preparation and application of diets for general and therapeutic purposes.

Tasks include –

(a) developing nutritional methods and diets and testing them;

(b) planning and directing the preparation of therapeutic and other diets for individuals, groups in hospitals, or workers in particular sectors;

(c) participating in programmes for nutrition education and nutrition rehabilitation activities;

(d) advising on nutrition aspects of community food issues and health programmes;

(e) keeping up with knowledge in related fields and maintaining contacts with appropriate professionals;

(f) giving talks and lectures on diet and nutrition;

(g) performing related tasks;

(h) supervising other workers.

Examples of the occupations classified here:
- Consultant, dietetic/food processing
- Dietician
- Nutritionist

3224 OPTOMETRISTS AND OPTICIANS

Optometrists and opticians prescribe and fit glasses and contact lenses and advise on their use or the use of other visual aids, as well as on proper lighting for work and reading.

Tasks include –

(a) examining eyes and prescribing glasses, contact lenses or other treatment to improve vision, referring cases which may require medical treatment to *Medical doctors*;

(b) advising on the proper use of glasses and contact lenses, appropriate lighting for work or reading and other visual aids;

(c) fitting prescribed lenses into frames and fitting frames or contact lenses to customers;

(d) performing related tasks;

(e) supervising other workers.

Examples of the occupations classified here:
- Optician, dispensing
- Optician, ophthalmic
- Optometrist

Some related occupations classified elsewhere:
- Ophthalmologist – 2221

3225 DENTAL ASSISTANTS

Dental assistants carry out advisory, diagnostic, preventive and curative dental tasks, more limited in scope and complexity than those carried out by *Dentists*, and they assist *Dentists* by preparing and taking care of instruments and other equipment, preparing materials and helping patients prepare for examination and treatment.

Tasks include –

(a) advising communities and individuals on dental hygiene, diet and other preventive dental measures;

(b) conducting dental examinations to make diagnoses and refer more difficult cases to *Dentists* when needed;

(c) cleaning teeth, preparing cavities and placing fillings;

(d) performing certain types of prosthetic work and some surgical procedures;

(e) preparing and taking care of dental instruments and equipment;

(f) preparing dental materials;

(g) helping patients prepare for examination or treatment;

(h) performing related tasks;

(i) supervising other workers.

Examples of the occupations classified here:
- Assistant, dental
- Assistant, dental/school service
- Hygienist, dental

Some related occupations classified elsewhere:
- Aid, dental – 5132
- Mechanic, dental – 7311

3226 PHYSIOTHERAPISTS AND RELATED ASSOCIATE PROFESSIONALS

Physiotherapists and related associate professionals treat disorders of bones, muscles and parts of the circulatory or the nervous system by manipulative methods, and ultrasound, heating, laser or similar techniques, or apply physiotherapy and related therapies as part of the treatment for the physically disabled, mentally ill or unbalanced.

Tasks include –

(a) advising communities and individuals on correct body postures, for work or otherwise, to avoid injuries and strain and to strengthen muscles;

(b) conducting examinations to make diagnoses of disorders of bones, muscles and parts of the circulatory or the nervous system to determine proper treatment or refer to *Medical doctors*, if necessary;

(c) treating disorders of bones, muscles and parts of the circulatory or the nervous system by manipulative methods,

and the use of ultrasound, heating, laser or similar techniques;

(d) massaging client or patient to improve circulation, soothe or stimulate nerves, facilitate elimination of waste matter, stretch contracted tendons and produce other therapeutic effects;

(e) examining body deformities and disorders to determine and write specifications for artificial limbs or other appliances, helping to fit them and explaining their use;

(f) applying physiotherapy and related techniques as part of the treatment of the mentally ill or unbalanced;

(g) performing related tasks;

(h) supervising other workers.

Examples of the occupations classified here:

- Chiropractor
- Physiotherapist
- Podiatrist

Some related occupations classified elsewhere:

- Therapist, occupational − 3229

3227 VETERINARY ASSISTANTS

Veterinary assistants carry out advisory, diagnostic, preventive and curative veterinary tasks, more limited in scope and complexity than those carried out by *Veterinarians*, and they assist *Veterinarians* by preparing and taking care of instruments and other equipment, preparing materials and getting animals ready for examination and treatment.

Tasks include −

(a) advising communities and individuals on the treatment of animals and their diseases and injuries;

(b) conducting examinations of animals to make diagnoses or refer more difficult cases to *Veterinarians* when needed;

(c) treating ill or injured animals, especially for common diseases and disorders;

(d) preparing and taking care of instruments and materials used in the treatment of animals;

(e) carrying out technical tasks connected with artificial insemination of animals;

(f) getting animals ready for examination or treatment and holding them during treatment, when necessary;

(g) performing related tasks;

(h) supervising other workers.

Examples of the occupations classified here:

- Assistant, veterinary
- Assistant, veterinary/artificial insemination
- Vaccinator, veterinary

Some related occupations classified elsewhere:

- Aid, veterinary − 5139

3228 PHARMACEUTICAL ASSISTANTS

Pharmaceutical assistants dispense and prepare medicaments, lotions and mixtures under the guidance of *Pharmacists*, in pharmacies, hospitals and dispensaries.

Tasks include −

(a) preparing medicaments and other pharmaceutical compounds under the guidance of *Pharmacists*;

(b) dispensing medicines and drugs and giving written and oral instructions on their use, as prescribed by *Medical doctors*, *Veterinarians* or other authorised workers;

(c) cleaning and preparing equipment and containers used to prepare and dispense medicine and pharmaceutical compounds;

(d) performing related tasks;

(e) supervising other workers.

Examples of the occupations classified here:

- Assistant, pharmaceutical

Some related occupations classified elsewhere:

- Aid, pharmacy − 5139

3229   MODERN HEALTH ASSOCIATE PROFESSIONALS (EXCEPT NURSING) NOT ELSEWHERE CLASSIFIED

This unit group covers modern health associate professionals (except nursing) not classified elsewhere in Minor group 322, *Modern health associate professionals (except nursing)*.

For instance, here should be classified those who practise homoeopathy, plan and carry out therapeutical activities to help the mentally unbalanced, ill, or physically handicapped, deal with speech impediments, provide eye exercises as remedial treatment, or deal with orientation problems of the blind.

In such cases tasks would include –

(a)   treating a particular illness by giving the patient infinitesimal doses of the bodies which provoke similar illnesses;

(b)   planning or carrying out therapeutic activities connected with education, vocational training or recreation in order to help the mentally unbalanced, ill, or physically handicapped;

(c)   dealing with pronunciation defects;

(d)   correcting sonority of language pronunciation;

(e)   applying remedial treatment to the eye muscles by means of eye exercises;

(f)   treating orientation problems of the blind;

(g)   performing related tasks;

(h)   supervising other workers.

Examples of the occupations classified here:
- Homeopath
- Orthoepist
- Orthophonist
- Therapist, occupational

MINOR GROUP 323
NURSING AND MIDWIFERY ASSOCIATE PROFESSIONALS

Nursing and midwifery associate professionals apply medical concepts and principles relating to the delivery of babies and to nursing of the ill, injured or disabled, and of mothers and their newborn babies.

Tasks performed usually include: helping medical doctors, or nursing and midwifery professionals, in the practical application of preventive and curative measures, and dealing with emergencies in their absence; providing nursing services, care and advice for the sick, injured, physically and mentally disabled and others in need of such care; delivering or assisting in the delivery of babies, and instructing mothers in baby care. Supervision of other workers may be included.

It should be noted that depending on the specific tasks and degree of responsibility in executing them, as well as on the national educational and training requirements, it may be appropriate to classify some or all of the occupations that are identified here into Minor group 223, *Nursing and midwifery professionals*.

Occupations in this minor group are classified into the following unit groups:

3231   Nursing associate professionals

3232   Midwifery associate professionals

3231 NURSING ASSOCIATE PROFESSIONALS

Nursing associate professionals provide nursing care for the sick, injured, and others in need of such care, and, in the absence of medical doctors or professional nurses, deal with emergencies.

Tasks include –

(a) providing nursing care, treatment and advice to the ill, injured, disabled, and others in need of such care;

(b) assisting medical doctors and professional nurses in their tasks, administering medicine and drugs, applying surgical dressings and giving other forms of treatment under instructions from physicians or professional nurses;

(c) assisting in giving first-aid treatment in emergencies;

(d) assisting in preparations for physical and psychiatric treatment of mentally ill patients;

(e) assisting in preparations for social adjustment, development and education of mentally or physically handicapped patients;

(f) providing nursing care to patients in their homes;

(g) providing nursing services, care and advice within a community or at a workplace;

(h) performing related tasks;

(i) supervising other workers.

Examples of the occupations classified here:

- Nurse, associate professional

Some related occupations classified elsewhere:

- Aid, nursing/hospital – 5132
- Nurse, professional – 2230

3232 MIDWIFERY ASSOCIATE PROFESSIONALS

Midwifery associate professionals deliver or assist doctors or midwifery professionals in the delivery of babies, provide antenatal and post-natal care and instruct parents in baby care.

Tasks include –

(a) advising expectant mothers on appropriate diet, exercises and behaviour to ease pregnancy and childbirth, and noting their general health and progress;

(b) delivering babies, or, more often, assisting doctors or midwifery professionals in deliveries;

(c) attending mothers in the post-natal period to supervise their recovery, to check on babies' progress, and to instruct parents in baby care;

(d) advising on and administering birth control methods;

(e) performing related tasks;

(f) supervising other workers.

Examples of the occupations classified here:

- Midwife, associate professional

Some related occupations classified elsewhere:

- Midwife, professional – 2230

MINOR GROUP 324
TRADITIONAL MEDICINE PRACTITIONERS AND FAITH HEALERS

Traditional medicine practitioners and faith healers advise on methods to preserve or improve health and treat human mental and physical illness by techniques traditionally used in the community and believed to cure through assisting and stimulating nature, or by power of faith and spiritual advice.

Tasks performed usually include: advising clients on proper behaviour and diet to preserve or regain mental and physical health and strength; treating patients by applying traditional techniques which cure through assisting or stimulating nature; endeavouring to cure sickness by mental influence, suggestion, and power of faith. Supervision of other workers may be included.

Occupations in this minor group are classified into the following unit groups:

3241 Traditional medicine practitioners

3242 Faith healers

3241 TRADITIONAL MEDICINE PRACTITIONERS

Traditional medicine practitioners treat human mental and physical sickness by herbs, medicinal plants and other techniques traditionally used in the community, and believed to cure and heal by assisting or stimulating nature, and advise on methods to preserve or improve health and well-being.

Tasks include –

(a) treating sickness and injuries using herbs, medicinal plants, insects, and other traditional techniques used in the community believed to cure and heal by assisting or stimulating nature;

(b) advising community and individuals on proper diet and behaviour to preserve or improve health and well-being;

(c) performing related tasks;

(d) supervising other workers.

Examples of the occupations classified here:

- Healer, drugless treatment
- Healer, herbal
- Healer, village
- Naturopath

3242 FAITH HEALERS

Faith healers endeavour to cure human mental and physical illness by mental influence and suggestion, power of faith and spiritual advice.

Tasks include –

(a) endeavouring to cure human mental and physical ailments by power of faith;

(b) advising community and individuals on proper behaviour and faith to preserve or improve health and well-being;

(c) performing related tasks;

(d) supervising other workers.

Examples of the occupations classified here:

- Faith healer

SUB-MAJOR GROUP 33
TEACHING ASSOCIATE PROFESSIONALS

Teaching associate professionals teach a range of subjects at the primary and pre-primary education levels, organise educational activities especially for children below primary school age, or teach physically or mentally handicapped children, young persons or adults, or those with learning difficulties.

Tasks performed by workers in this sub-major group usually include: preparing programme of learning and giving instruction in a range of subjects at the pre-primary and primary education levels; planning and organising activities designed to facilitate children's development of language, or physical and social skills; adapting curriculum to suit the particular group of mentally or physically handicapped persons, or those with learning difficulties, and teaching them using braille, lip-reading and other special aids and techniques; engage in other teaching activities including teaching how to fly aircraft or drive motor vehicles or other engines. Supervision of other workers may be included.

It should be noted that, depending on the specific tasks and degree of responsibility in executing them, as well as on the national educational and training requirements, it may be appropriate to classify some of the occupations that are identified here into Sub-major group 23, *Teaching professionals*. This is relevant to the occupations classified into Minor groups 331, *Primary education teaching associate professionals*, 332, *Pre-primary education teaching associate professionals*, and 333, *Special education teaching associate professionals*.

Occupations in this sub-major group are classified into the following minor groups:

331 Primary education teaching associate professionals

332 Pre-primary education teaching associate professionals

333 Special education teaching associate professionals

334 Other teaching associate professionals

MINOR GROUP **331**
PRIMARY EDUCATION TEACHING ASSOCIATE PROFESSIONALS

Primary education teaching associate professionals teach a range of subjects at the primary education level.

Tasks performed usually include: preparing programme of learning, giving instruction in a range of subjects at the primary education level, and organising some educational activities; preparing reports. Supervision of other workers may be included.

It should be noted that, depending on the specific tasks and degree of responsibility in executing them, as well as on the national educational and training requirements, it may be appropriate to classify some or all of the occupations that are identified here into Minor group 233, *Primary and pre-primary education teaching professionals*.

Occupations in this minor group are classified into the following unit group:

3310 Primary education teaching associate professionals

3310 PRIMARY EDUCATION TEACHING ASSOCIATE PROFESSIONALS

Primary education teaching associate professionals teach a range of subjects at the primary education level.

Tasks performed usually include: preparing programme of learning, giving instruction in a range of subjects at the primary education level, and organising some educational activities; preparing reports. Supervision of other workers may be included.

Tasks include –

(a) preparing programme of learning and giving instruction in areas such as reading, writing, and arithmetic, within prescribed or recommended curriculum;

(b) preparing, administering and marking tests, projects and assignments to train pupils and to evaluate their progress, and giving remedial instruction if necessary;

(c) organising and supervising pupils' extra-curricular activities;

(d) encouraging personal development of pupils and discussing their progress with parents and head teacher;

(e) supervising pupils in classroom and other areas of school;

(f) preparing reports;

(g) performing related tasks;

(h) supervising other workers.

Examples of the occupations classified here:
- Teacher, primary education/associate professional

Some related occupations classified elsewhere:
- Head teacher – 1229
- Inspector, school – 2352
- Teacher, primary education/professional – 2331

MINOR GROUP 332
PRE-PRIMARY EDUCATION TEACHING ASSOCIATE PROFESSIONALS

Pre-primary education teaching associate professionals organise educational activities for children below primary school age.

Tasks performed usually include: planning and organising activities designed to facilitate children's development of language, or physical and social skills. Supervision of other workers may be included.

It should be noted that, depending on the specific tasks and degree of responsibility in executing them, as well as on the national educational and training requirements, it may be appropriate to classify some or all of the occupations that are identified here into Minor group 233, *Primary and pre-primary education teaching professionals*.

Occupations in this minor group are classified into the following unit group:

3320 Pre-primary education teaching associate professionals

3320 PRE-PRIMARY EDUCATION TEACHING ASSOCIATE PROFESSIONALS

Pre-primary education teaching associate professionals organise group and individual play and education activities to support and promote physical, mental and social development of children below primary school age.

Tasks include –

(a) planning and organising activities designed to facilitate the children's development of physical and social skills;

(b) promoting language development through story-telling, role-play, songs, rhymes and informal conversations and discussions;

(c) observing children in order to evaluate and discuss progress and possible problems with parents;

(d) supervising children's activities to ensure safety and resolve conflicts;

(e) performing related tasks;

(f) supervising other workers.

Examples of the occupations classified here:

- Teacher, nursery/associate professional

- Teacher, pre-primary education/associate professional

Some related occupations classified elsewhere:

- Teacher, pre-primary education/professional − 2332

MINOR GROUP 333
SPECIAL EDUCATION TEACHING ASSOCIATE PROFESSIONALS

Special education teaching associate professionals teach physically or mentally handicapped children, young persons or adults, or those with learning difficulties, at a given level of education.

Tasks performed usually include: adapting curriculum to suit the particular group of mentally or physically handicapped persons, or those with learning difficulties; teaching one or more subjects to, for instance, deaf or blind persons by using braille, lip-reading and other special aids and techniques; preparing reports. Supervision of other workers may be included.

It should be noted that, depending on the specific tasks and degree of responsibility in executing them, as well as on the national educational and training requirements, it may be appropriate to classify some or all of the occupations that are identified here into Minor group 234, *Special education teaching professionals*.

Occupations in this minor group are classified into the following unit group:

3330 Special education teaching associate professionals

3330 SPECIAL EDUCATION TEACHING ASSOCIATE PROFESSIONALS

Special education teaching associate professionals teach physically or mentally handicapped children, young persons or adults, or those with learning difficulties, at a given level of education.

Tasks include –

(a) designing or modifying curricula and preparing lessons and activities in accordance with requirements;

(b) giving instruction using techniques or special aids − such as braille or lip-reading − appropriate to pupil's handicap and level, and supervising work in class;

(c) encouraging pupils to have confidence, helping them to discover and adopt methods which would compensate for limitations imposed by their handicap, and giving them a feeling of achievement;

(d) administering tests, evaluating and noting progress of each pupil and discussing it with parents, head teacher, therapists, social workers, etc.;

(e) giving private instruction;

(f) preparing reports;

(g) performing related tasks;

(h) supervising other workers.

Examples of the occupations classified here:

- Teacher, remedial/associate professional
- Teacher, special education/for the blind (associate professional)
- Teacher, special education/for the mentally handicapped (associate professional)

Some related occupations classified elsewhere:

- Teacher, remedial/professional – 2340
- Teacher, special education/for the blind (professional) – 2340
- Teacher, special education/for the mentally handicapped (professional) – 2340

MINOR GROUP 334
OTHER TEACHING ASSOCIATE PROFESSIONALS

Other teaching associate professionals engage in teaching activities other than those connected with primary, pre-primary and special education school levels.

Tasks performed may include teaching how to fly aircraft, or how to drive motor vehicles, or railway and other engines. Supervision of other workers may be included.

It should be noted that, depending on the specific tasks and degree of responsibility in executing them, as well as on the national educational and training requirements, it may be appropriate to classify some or all of the occupations that are identified here into Unit group 2359, *Other teaching professionals not elsewhere classified*.

Occupations in this minor group are classified into the following unit group:

3340   Other teaching associate professionals

3340   OTHER TEACHING ASSOCIATE PROFESSIONALS

Other teaching associate professionals engage in other teaching activities than those connected with primary and pre-primary school level. They may, for instance, teach how to fly aircraft, or how to drive motor vehicles, or railway and other engines.

Tasks include –

(a) explaining uses and operations of flying/driving controls;

(b) accompanying pupils on training flights/drives and demonstrating relevant tasks;

(c) explaining flying/driving regulations and laws;

(d) performing related tasks;

(e) supervising other workers.

Examples of the occupations classified here:

- Instructor, driving
- Instructor, flying

SUB-MAJOR GROUP **34**
OTHER ASSOCIATE PROFESSIONALS

Other associate professionals perform technical tasks connected with the practical application of knowledge relating to finance and sales, or business enterprise administration, bookkeeping, legal, statistical and other services, government activities relating to customs, travel, tax, welfare, job placement, licensing, the police force, as well as with social work, entertainment, sport, and religion.

Tasks performed by workers in this sub-major group usually include: undertaking specialised business in the field of securities, insurance or property; organising travel; engaging in the wholesale trade of technical and other goods; acting as appraisers, valuers or auctioneers; providing business services as agents, trade brokers or labour contractors; engaging in enterprise administration, bookkeeping, legal, statistical and other services; executing government work related to various fields such as border control, customs, travel, tax, welfare, job placement, licensing, the police force; performing social work; designing products, and creating interior decorating schemes; performing in the fields of entertainment and sport; executing some religious tasks. They may receive guidance from *Senior government officials*, *Managers* or *Professionals*. Supervision of other workers may be included.

It should be noted that, depending on the specific tasks and degree of responsibility in executing them, as well as on the national educational and training requirements, it may be appropriate to classify some of the occupations that are identified here into Sub-major group 24, *Other professionals*. This is particularly relevant to the occupations classified into Minor group 346, *Social work associate professionals*.

Occupations in this sub-major group are classified into the following minor groups:

341 Finance and sales associate professionals

342 Business services agents and trade brokers

343 Administrative associate professionals

344 Customs, tax and related government associate professionals

345 Police inspectors and detectives

346 Social work associate professionals

347 Artistic, entertainment and sports associate professionals

348 Religious associate professionals

MINOR GROUP **341**
FINANCE AND SALES ASSOCIATE PROFESSIONALS

Finance and sales associate professionals buy and sell financial instruments, different types of insurance, real estate, travel and other business services, deal on the foreign exchange, act as wholesale representatives or as buyers on behalf of organisations, or they appraise the value of commodities, real estate and other properties, and sell these by auction.

Tasks performed usually include: analysing market trends for financial instruments, the foreign exchange, commodities and real estate and buying or selling on behalf of clients or on their own behalf; advising on and selling insurance coverage; ensuring proper recording of transfers of financial instruments and ownership of real estate; organising and advising on travel arrangements and selling tours; selling various goods on a wholesale basis on behalf of producer or importer, including technical installations and equipment; buying goods or services on behalf of organisations; appraising the value of commodities, real estate or other property, or selling by auction. They may receive guidance from *Managers* or *Professionals*. Supervision of other workers may be included.

Occupations in this minor group are classified into the following unit groups:

3411 **Securities and finance dealers and brokers**

3412 **Insurance representatives**

3413 **Estate agents**

3414 **Travel consultants and organisers**

3415 **Technical and commercial sales representatives**

3416 **Buyers**

3417 **Appraisers, valuers and auctioneers**

3419 **Finance and sales associate professionals not elsewhere classified**

3411 SECURITIES AND FINANCE DEALERS AND BROKERS

Securities and finance dealers and brokers buy and sell securities, stocks, bonds and other financial instruments, and deal on the foreign exchange on spot or on futures markets, on behalf of their own company or for customers on a commission basis and recommend transactions to clients or senior management.

Tasks include –

(a) obtaining information about the financial circumstances of customers and companies in which investments may be made;

(b) analysing market trends for securities, bonds, stocks and other financial instruments, including foreign exchange;

(c) informing prospective customers about market conditions and prospects;

(d) advising on and participating in the negotiation of terms for, and organisation of, loans and placement of stocks and bonds in the financial market to raise capital for customers;

(e) recording and transmitting buy and sell orders for securities, stocks, bonds or other financial instruments and for foreign exchange for future or immediate delivery;

(f) performing related tasks;

(g) supervising other workers.

Examples of the occupations classified here:
- Broker, foreign exchange
- Broker, securities
- Broker, stocks and shares

Some related occupations classified elsewhere:
- Clerk, securities − 4122

3412 INSURANCE REPRESENTATIVES

Insurance representatives advise on and sell life, accident, automobile, liability, endowment, fire, marine and other types of insurance to new and established clients.

Tasks include −

(a) obtaining information about customers' circumstances necessary to determine appropriate type of insurance and conditions;

(b) negotiating with customers to determine type and degree of risk for which insurance is derived, extent of coverage and terms of payment;

(c) negotiating and placing reinsurance contracts;

(d) advising on, negotiating terms for and placing insurance contracts for large or special types of projects, installations or risks;

(e) performing related tasks;

(f) supervising other workers.

Examples of the occupations classified here:
- Agent, insurance
- Insurance broker
- Underwriter, insurance

Some related occupations classified elsewhere:
- Assessor, insurance − 3417
- Clerk, insurance − 3432

3413 ESTATE AGENTS

Estate agents arrange the sale, purchase, rental and lease of real property, usually on behalf of clients and on a commission basis.

Tasks include −

(a) obtaining information about properties to be sold or leased, the circumstances of their owner and the needs of prospective buyers or tenants;

(b) showing properties to be sold or leased to prospective buyers or tenants and explaining terms of sale or conditions of rent or lease;

(c) arranging signing of lease agreements and transfer of property rights;

(d) collecting rent and bond monies on behalf of owner and inspecting properties before, during and after tenancies;

(e) performing related tasks;

(f) supervising other workers.

Examples of the occupations classified here:
- Agent, estate
- Realtor
- Salesperson, property

Some related occupations classified elsewhere:
- Clerk, mortgage − 4122

3414 TRAVEL CONSULTANTS AND ORGANISERS

Travel consultants and organisers plan itineraries and schedule travel accommodation for customers, and organise or sell complete group travel tours for business or vacation.

Tasks include −

(a) obtaining information about availability, cost and convenience of different types of transport and accommodation, ascertaining customers' requirements and advising them on travel arrangements;

(b) making and confirming travel and hotel reservations, giving customers tickets and vouchers and receiving payments;

(c) organising complete group tours for business or vacation travel and selling them to groups or individuals;

(d) helping customers in obtaining necessary certificates and travel documents;

(e) performing related tasks;

(f) supervising other workers.

Examples of the occupations classified here:
- Consultant, travel
- Organiser, travel

Some related occupations classified elsewhere:
- Clerk, ticket issuing/travel — 4221
- Clerk, travel agency — 4221
- General manager, travel agency — 1319

3415 TECHNICAL AND COMMERCIAL SALES REPRESENTATIVES

Technical and commercial sales representatives sell various goods on a wholesale basis including installations, equipment and technical products and related services, and provide specialised information as required.

Tasks include —

(a) soliciting orders and selling goods to retail, industrial, wholesale and other establishments;

(b) selling technical equipment, supplies and related services to business establishments or individuals;

(c) providing prospective customers with general and specialised information about the characteristics and functions of the equipment, and demonstrating its use;

(d) reporting customers' reactions and requirements to manufacturers;

(e) performing related tasks;

(f) supervising other workers.

Examples of the occupations classified here:
- Adviser, after-sales service
- Canvasser
- Commercial traveller
- Salesperson, technical

Some related occupations classified elsewhere:
- Salesperson, retail establishment — 5220

3416 BUYERS

Buyers buy goods and services on behalf of industrial, commercial or other enterprises and organisations.

Tasks include —

(a) negotiating and contracting for the purchase of equipment, raw materials, products and supplies for industrial plant, utilities, government units or other establishments and the purchasing of merchandise for resale;

(b) obtaining information about requirements and stock, and determining quantity and quality to be purchased, costs, delivery dates and other contract conditions;

(c) performing related tasks;

(d) supervising other workers.

Examples of the occupations classified here:
- Buyer
- Buyer, merchandise/retail trade
- Buyer, merchandise/wholesale trade

3417 APPRAISERS, VALUERS AND AUCTIONEERS

Appraisers, valuers and auctioneers value property and various goods and assess losses covered by insurance policies, or sell objects, properties and goods by auction.

Tasks include —

(a) determining the quality or value of raw materials, real estate, industrial equipment, personal and household effects, works of art, gems and other objects offered for sale or to be insured;

(b) assessing the extent of damage or loss and liabilities of insurance companies and underwriters for losses covered by insurance policies;

(c) selling by auction various kinds of property, cars, commodities, livestock, art, jewellery and other objects;

(d) performing related tasks;

(e) supervising other workers.

Examples of the occupations classified here:

- Appraiser
- Assessor, claims
- Assessor, insurance
- Auctioneer
- Inspector, claims
- Valuer

3419 FINANCE AND SALES ASSOCIATE PROFESSIONALS NOT ELSEWHERE CLASSIFIED

This unit group covers finance and sales associate professionals not classified elsewhere in Minor group 341, *Finance and sales associate professionals*.

MINOR GROUP 342
BUSINESS SERVICES AGENTS AND TRADE BROKERS

Business services agents and trade brokers establish necessary contacts between buyers and sellers, buy and sell commodities usually in bulk, carry out customs clearance procedures and ensure that insurance and export/import licences are in order, match jobseekers with vacancies known to government placement offices, find workers for vacant posts on a commission basis, or contract labour for particular projects, and sell various other business services.

Tasks performed usually include: buying and selling commodities in bulk; carrying out customs clearance procedures and ensuring that insurance and export/import licences are in order; matching jobseekers with vacancies known to government placement offices, or advising on training schemes; finding workers for various posts or contracting labour for particular projects at the request of enterprises and other, including government, institutions; finding places for jobseekers on a commission basis; establishing business contacts; selling business services such as advertising space in the media, transport services and other facilities, or credit and other business information; arranging contracts for performances of entertainers and artists, as well as for the publication of books, production of plays, recording and sale of music. They may receive guidance from *Managers* or *Professionals*. Supervision of other workers may be included.

Occupations in this minor group are classified into the following unit groups:

3421 Trade brokers

3422 Clearing and forwarding agents

3423 Employment agents and labour contractors

3429 Business services agents and trade brokers not elsewhere classified

3421 TRADE BROKERS

Trade brokers buy and sell commodities, usually in bulk, at auctions of the spot or futures markets.

Tasks include –

(a) establishing contact between buyers and sellers of commodities;

(b) discussing buying or selling requirements of client and giving advice accordingly;

(c) arranging for the production of auction catalogues, fixing reserve prices, attending auctions of the spot or futures markets and bidding on behalf of client;

(d) negotiating purchase/sale by private treaty of goods not sold at auction;

(e) obtaining cargo space, and fixing and collecting freight charges from client;

(f) performing related tasks;

(g) supervising other workers.

Examples of the occupations classified here:
- Broker, commodity
- Broker, shipping
- Broker, trade

3422 CLEARING AND FORWARDING AGENTS

Clearing and forwarding agents carry out customs clearing procedures and ensure that insurance, export/import licences and other formalities are in order.

Tasks include –

(a) carrying out customs clearing procedures for exports or imports;

(b) ensuring that insurance is in order;

(c) ensuring that export/import licences and other formalities are in order;

(d) signing and issuing bills of lading;

(e) performing related tasks;

(f) supervising other workers.

Examples of the occupations classified here:
- Agent, clearing
- Agent, forwarding
- Agent, shipping

3423 EMPLOYMENT AGENTS AND LABOUR CONTRACTORS

Employment agents and labour contractors match jobseekers with vacancies, find workers for employers and contract labour for particular projects at the request of enterprises and other, including government, institutions, or find places for jobseekers for a commission.

Tasks include –

(a) matching jobseeker with vacancies known to government job placement offices, or advising on training schemes;

(b) finding workers for vacant posts against a commission from the employer or worker;

(c) discussing with enterprises/organisations the needed skills and other characteristics of the workers to be employed or contracted;

(d) finding workers with appropriate skills, etc., and undertaking the necessary formalities according to national or international regulations and requirements;

(e) ensuring that the employment contracts meet legal requirements and signing them;

(f) performing related tasks;

(g) supervising other workers.

Examples of the occupations classified here:
- Agent, employment
- Contractor, labour
- Officer, job placement

3429 BUSINESS SERVICES AGENTS AND TRADE BROKERS NOT ELSEWHERE CLASSIFIED

This unit group covers business services agents and trade brokers not classified elsewhere in Minor group 342, *Business services agents and trade brokers*.

For instance, here should be classified those who establish business contacts, sell business services such as advertising space in the media, transport services, and other facilities, credit and other business information, arrange contracts for performances of athletes, entertainers and artists, as well as for the publication of books, the production of plays, or the recording, performing and sale of music.

In such cases tasks would include –

(a) obtaining information about services to be sold and needs of prospective buyers;

(b) negotiating contracts on behalf of seller or buyer and explaining terms of sale and payment to client;

(c) signing agreements on behalf of seller or buyer and ensuring that contract is honoured;

(d) making sure that the business service purchased is made available to the buyer in the agreed form at the agreed time;

(e) performing related tasks;

(f) supervising other workers.

Examples of the occupations classified here:

- Agent, literary
- Agent, musical performance
- Agent, sports
- Agent, theatrical
- Salesperson, business services/advertising

MINOR GROUP **343** ADMINISTRATIVE ASSOCIATE PROFESSIONALS

Administrative associate professionals implement and support the communication, documentation and internal managerial co-ordination activities of an organisational unit and organise the flow of information among different organisational units.

Tasks performed usually include: implementing and supporting the communication, documentation and internal managerial co-ordination activities of an organisational unit to assist the head of unit and other staff; making verbatim reports of proceedings; examining and summarising legal records and documents; maintaining complete records of financial transactions; collecting, processing and presenting mathematical, statistical and actuarial data. They may receive guidance from *Managers* or *Professionals*. Supervision of other workers may be included.

Occupations in this minor group are classified into the following unit groups:

3431 Administrative secretaries and related associate professionals

3432 Legal and related business associate professionals

3433 Bookkeepers

3434 Statistical, mathematical and related associate professionals

3439 Administrative associate professionals not elsewhere classified

3

3431 ADMINISTRATIVE SECRETARIES AND RELATED ASSOCIATE PROFESSIONALS

Administrative secretaries and related associate professionals implement and support the communication, documentation and internal managerial co-ordination activities of an organisational unit to assist the head of unit and other members of staff, and make verbatim reports of proceedings.

Tasks include –

(a) drafting administrative correspondence and minutes;

(b) obtaining, proposing and monitoring deadlines and follow-up dates;

(c) screening requests for meetings, scheduling and organising meetings and travel arrangements for the head of unit and other members of staff;

(d) assisting in the preparation of budgets, monitoring of expenditures, drafting of contracts and purchasing or acquisition orders;

(e) assisting the head of unit and other staff with inquiries of an administrative or organisational nature;

(f) assisting the head of unit in organising and hosting hospitality functions for outside visitors or members of staff;

(g) making verbatim reports of proceedings in legislative assemblies, courts of law or other places in shorthand or by other means;

(h) writing and answering business or technical letters and other similar correspondence;

(i) performing related tasks;

(j) supervising other workers.

Examples of the occupations classified here:
- Administrative secretary
- Assistant, correspondence
- Verbatim reporter

Some related occupations classified elsewhere:
- Secretary – 4115

3432 LEGAL AND RELATED BUSINESS ASSOCIATE PROFESSIONALS

Legal and related business associate professionals assist *Corporate managers*, *General managers*, and *Legal Professionals*, as well as various business professionals in connection with legal matters, including those related to insurance contracts, granting of loans and other financial transactions.

Tasks include –

(a) examining, or making arrangements for examining, legal records and other relevant documents;

(b) preparing papers summarising legal positions, or setting out conditions of loans or insurance;

(c) advising clients and agents on legal or technical matters relating to their particular cases;

(d) preparing documents relating to transfer of real estate, stocks or other matters requiring formal registration;

(e) checking validity of documents and forwarding them to company's share register;

(f) performing related tasks;

(g) supervising other workers.

Examples of the occupations classified here:
- Bailiff
- Clerk, conveyancing
- Clerk, court
- Clerk, judge's
- Clerk, law

3433 BOOKKEEPERS

Bookkeepers maintain complete records of financial transactions of an undertaking and verify accuracy of documents and records relating to such transactions.

Tasks include –

(a) maintaining complete records of all financial transactions of an undertaking according to general bookkeeping principles, with guidance from *Accountants*;

(b) verifying accuracy of documents and records relating to payments, receipts and other financial transactions;

(c) preparing financial statements and reports for specified periods;

(d) applying knowledge of bookkeeping principles and practices in order to identify and solve problems arising in the course of their work;

(e) performing related tasks;

(f) supervising other workers.

Examples of the occupations classified here:

- Bookkeeper

Some related occupations classified elsewhere:

- Accountant — 2411
- Clerk, bookkeeping — 4121

3434 STATISTICAL, MATHEMATICAL AND RELATED ASSOCIATE PROFESSIONALS

Statistical, mathematical and related associate professionals assist in planning the collection, processing and presentation of mathematical, statistical or actuarial data and in carrying out these operations, usually working under the guidance of *Mathematicians and related professionals*, or *Statisticians*.

Tasks include —

(a) assisting in planning and performing mathematical, actuarial, statistical, accounting and related calculations;

(b) preparing detailed estimates of quantities and costs of materials and labour required for statistical census and survey operations;

(c) performing technical tasks connected with establishing, maintaining and using registers and sampling frames for census and survey operations;

(d) performing technical tasks connected with data collection and quality control operations in censuses and surveys;

(e) using standard computer software packages to perform mathematical, actuarial statistical accounting and related calculations;

(f) preparing mathematical, actuarial, statistical, accounting and other results for presentation in graphical or tabular form;

(g) applying knowledge of mathematical, actuarial, statistical, accounting and related principles and practices in order to identify and solve problems arising in the course of their work;

(h) performing related tasks;

(i) supervising other workers.

Examples of the occupations classified here:

- Assistant, accounting
- Assistant, actuarial
- Assistant, mathematical
- Assistant, statistical

Some related occupations classified elsewhere:

- Actuary — 2121
- Clerk, statistical — 4122
- Mathematician, actuarial science — 2121
- Statistician — 2122

3439 ADMINISTRATIVE ASSOCIATE PROFESSIONALS NOT ELSEWHERE CLASSIFIED

This unit group covers administrative associate professionals not classified elsewhere in Minor group 343, *Administrative associate professionals*.

For instance, here should be classified those who act as administrative consular officials, undertake executive secretarial duties for departmental heads or official committees, analyse files and other sources of information and write reports for responsible administrators, giving relevant information and some advice on policy questions, departmental programmes, administrative problems and other matters.

In such cases tasks would include:

(a) acting as administrative consular official;

(b) undertaking executive secretarial duties for departmental heads;

(c) undertaking executive secretarial duties for official committees;

(d) analysing files and other sources of information, and writing reports for responsible administrators;

(e) performing related tasks;

(f) supervising other workers.

Examples of the occupations classified here:

- Executive secretary, committee

- Executive secretary, government administration
- Official, consular

MINOR GROUP 344
CUSTOMS, TAX AND RELATED GOVERNMENT ASSOCIATE PROFESSIONALS

Customs, tax and related government associate professionals enforce or apply relevant government rules and regulations relating to national borders, taxes, social benefits, and provide or examine applications for licences or authorisations in connection with travel, exports and imports of goods, establish a business, erection of buildings and other activities subject to government regulations.

Tasks performed usually include: patrolling national borders and checking persons and vehicles, travel and transport documents and goods transported across the border to ensure enforcement of government rules and regulations; examining tax returns to determine taxes payable by persons and businesses; examining and deciding on applications for social benefits, examining and deciding on applications for government authorisations and licences necessary to travel, export or import goods, erect buildings, establish a business or undertake other activities subject to government regulations; monitoring the application of price, wage or weights and measures regulations. They may receive guidance from *Senior government officials* or *Managers*. Supervision of other workers may be included.

Occupations in this minor group are classified into the following unit groups:

3441 Customs and border inspectors

3442 Government tax and excise officials

3443 Government social benefits officials

3444 Government licensing officials

3449 Customs, tax and related government associate professionals not elsewhere classified

3441 CUSTOMS AND BORDER INSPECTORS

Customs and border inspectors check persons and vehicles crossing national borders to enforce relevant government rules and regulations.

Tasks include –

(a) patrolling national borders and coastal waters to stop persons from illegally

entering or leaving the country and from illegally importing or exporting currency or goods;

(b) checking travel documents of persons crossing national borders to ensure that they have the necessary authorisations and certificates;

(c) inspecting the luggage of persons crossing national borders to ensure that it conforms to government rules and

regulations concerning import or export of goods and currencies;

(d) checking transport documents and freight of vehicles crossing national borders to ensure conformity with government rules and regulations concerning goods in transit and the import and export of goods, and to verify that necessary payments have been made;

(e) when necessary, testifying in a court of law about the circumstances and results of investigations carried out;

(f) performing related tasks;

(g) supervising other workers.

Examples of the occupations classified here:
- Inspector, border
- Inspector, customs
- Officer, passport checking

3442 GOVERNMENT TAX AND EXCISE OFFICIALS

Government tax and excise officials examine tax returns, bills of sale and other documents to determine the type and amount of taxes, duties and other types of fees to be paid by individuals or businesses, referring exceptional or important cases to *Senior government officials* or *Managers*.

Tasks include –

(a) advising organisations, enterprises and the general public on the proper understanding of government laws, rules and regulations concerning the determination and payment of taxes, duties and other government fees, and on the public's rights and obligations;

(b) examining tax returns, bills of sale and other relevant documents to determine type and amount of taxes, duties and other types of fees to be paid;

(c) performing related tasks;

(d) supervising other workers.

Examples of the occupations classified here:
- Officer, excise
- Officer, tax

3443 GOVERNMENT SOCIAL BENEFITS OFFICIALS

Government social benefits officials examine applications for benefits, in cash or in kind, to determine eligibility and amount of benefit, referring exceptional or important cases to *Senior government officials* or *Managers*.

Tasks include –

(a) advising individuals and organisations on the proper understanding of government laws, rules and regulations concerning government benefits and the determination and disbursement of payments, as well as on the public's rights and obligations;

(b) examining applications and other relevant documents to determine type and amount of benefit which individuals should receive;

(c) performing related tasks;

(d) supervising other workers.

Examples of the occupations classified here:
- Officer, pensions
- Officer, social benefits
- Officer, social security claims

3444 GOVERNMENT LICENSING OFFICIALS

Government licensing officials examine applications for licences to export or import goods, set up a business, build a house or other structures, or to obtain a passport, and determine whether applications for licences or passports are to be approved and whether specific conditions are to be attached to the licence, referring exceptional or important cases to *Senior government officials* or *Managers*.

Tasks include –

(a) advising individuals on the proper understanding of government laws and regulations concerning the type of licence required and the conditions attached to such licences, and on the public's rights and obligations;

(b) examining applications and relevant documents and determining whether a licence can be granted and the conditions which should be attached;

(c) examining applications and approving the issue of passports;

(d) performing related tasks;

(e) supervising other workers.

Examples of the occupations classified here:

- Officer, licensing
- Officer, passport issuing

3449 CUSTOMS, TAX, AND RELATED GOVERNMENT ASSOCIATE PROFESSIONALS NOT ELSEWHERE CLASSIFIED

This unit group covers customs, tax and related government associate professionals not classified elsewhere in Minor group 344, *Customs, tax and related government associate professionals*.

For instance, here should be classified those who examine places of business to ensure the use of correct weights and measures in trade and monitor the application of price or wage regulations, referring exceptional or important cases to *Senior government officials* or *Managers*.

In such cases tasks would include –

(a) examining places of business to ensure the use of correct weights and measures in trade;

(b) monitoring price regulations;

(c) monitoring wage regulations;

(d) performing related tasks;

(e) supervising other workers.

Examples of the occupations classified here:

- Inspector, price
- Inspector, sanitary
- Inspector, wage
- Inspector, weights and measures

Some related occupations classified elsewhere:

- Inspector, occupational safety – 3152
- Inspector, quality/products – 3152

MINOR GROUP 345
POLICE INSPECTORS AND DETECTIVES

Police inspectors and detectives investigate crimes committed and try to obtain information about persons and establishments which may be used in crime prevention.

Tasks performed usually include: investigating facts and circumstances relating to crimes committed in order to identify culprits; collecting information about persons or establishments usually with the aim of preventing a crime; investigating suspicious behaviour in enterprises, shops and other public places; making arrests, if authorised; testifying in courts of law. Supervision of other workers may be included.

Occupations in this minor group are classified into the following unit group:

3450 Police inspectors and detectives

3450 POLICE INSPECTORS AND DETECTIVES

Police inspectors and detectives investigate facts and circumstances relating to crimes committed and obtain information not readily available or apparent concerning establishments or the circumstances and behaviour of persons, mostly in order to prevent crimes.

Tasks include –

(a) establishing contacts and sources of information about crimes planned or

committed, in order to prevent crimes or identify culprits;

(b) investigating events and circumstances suspected of being criminal in nature to obtain evidence and identify the perpetrators;

(c) establishing contacts and sources of information not readily available or apparent concerning establishments or the circumstances and behaviour of persons, usually with the aim of preventing a crime;

(d) investigating possible cases of theft of goods, money or information from business establishments and of other possible cases of unlawful behaviour by customers or employees;

(e) investigating establishments or other circumstances and behaviour of persons on behalf of legal authorities or clients;

(f) making arrests or assisting in making arrests, if authorised;

(g) testifying in court of law or reporting to superiors or clients about circumstances and results of investigations;

(h) performing related tasks;

(i) supervising other workers.

Examples of the occupations classified here:

- Agent, inquiry/police
- Detective
- Inspector, police

Some related occupations classified elsewhere:

- Inspector-general, police − 1120
- Commissioner, police − 1120
- Police officer − 5162

MINOR GROUP 346
SOCIAL WORK ASSOCIATE PROFESSIONALS

Social work associate professionals provide guidance to clients in social and related matters to enable them to find and use resources to overcome difficulties and achieve particular goals.

Tasks performed usually include: helping individuals and families with personal and social problems; working to prevent development of delinquency or to achieve rehabilitation by organising and supervising social activities of individuals and groups; helping physically or mentally handicapped persons to obtain adequate treatment and improve their ability to function in society.

It should be noted that, depending on the specific tasks and degree of responsibility in executing them, as well as on the national educational and training requirements, it may be appropriate to classify some of the occupations that are identified here into Unit Group 2446 *Social work professionals*.

Occupations in this minor group are classified into the following unit group:

3460   Social work associate professionals

3460 SOCIAL WORK ASSOCIATE PROFESSIONALS

Social work associate professionals provide guidance to clients in social and related matters to enable them to find and use resources to overcome difficulties and achieve particular goals.

Tasks include –

(a) helping individuals and families with personal and social problems;

(b) collecting information relevant to clients' needs and advising them on their rights and obligations;

(c) analysing the client's situation and presenting alternative approaches to resolving problems;

(d) compiling case records or reports for courts and other legal proceedings;

(e) planning, evaluating, improving and developing welfare services;

(f) working to prevent development of delinquency or to achieve rehabilitation of delinquents by organising and supervising social, recreational and educational activities in youth clubs, community centres and similar organisations, or by other means;

(g) helping physically or mentally handicapped persons to obtain adequate treatment and improve their ability to function in society;

(h) planning, organising or providing home-help services;

(i) performing related tasks;

(j) supervising other workers.

Examples of the occupations classified here:
- Social worker, associate professional
- Social worker, associate professional/enterprise
- Welfare worker, associate professional

Some related occupations classified elsewhere:
- Social worker, professional – 2446
- Social worker, professional/enterprise – 2446
- Welfare worker, professional – 2446

MINOR GROUP 347
ARTISTIC, ENTERTAINMENT AND SPORTS ASSOCIATE PROFESSIONALS

Artistic, entertainment and sports associate professionals design products or decorate interiors, present information through the media, entertain audiences by performing spectacular, amusing or exciting acts on stage, in the streets or in circuses, or participate in sports competitions and in some cases train or direct those who perform such activities.

Tasks performed usually include: designing products, creating interior decorating schemes; presenting information through the media; entertaining audiences by performing on stage, or in the streets; performing amusing antics, tricks of illusion, or difficult and spectacular acrobatics; participating in sports competitions. Supervision of other workers may be included.

Occupations in this minor group are classified into the following unit groups:

3471 Decorators and commercial designers

3472 Radio, television and other announcers

3473 Street, night-club and related musicians, singers and dancers

3474 Clowns, magicians, acrobats and related associate professionals

3475 Athletes, sportspersons and related associate professionals

3471 DECORATORS AND COMMERCIAL DESIGNERS

Decorators and commercial designers apply artistic techniques to product design, interior decoration and sales promotion.

Tasks include –
(a) designing industrial and commercial products, including new types and styles of clothing and accessories, and endeavouring to harmonise aesthetic considerations with technical and other requirements;
(b) creating interior decorating schemes and planning furnishings for homes, public buildings, ships and other places;
(c) designing and painting stage scenery;
(d) tatooing decorative designs on client's skin;
(e) creating and executing artistic effects for use in show windows and other display areas;
(f) performing related tasks;
(g) supervising other workers.

Examples of the occupations classified here:
- Decorator, display
- Decorator, interior
- Designer, fashion
- Designer, industrial products
- Tattooist

Some related occupations classified elsewhere:
- Architect, interior – 2141
- Artist, commercial – 2452

3472 RADIO, TELEVISION AND OTHER ANNOUNCERS

Radio, television and other announcers read news bulletins, conduct interviews, and make other announcements or introductions on radio, television or in theatres and other establishments.

Tasks include –
(a) reading news bulletins and making other announcements on radio or television;
(b) introducing performing artists or persons being interviewed, and making related announcements on radio, television, or in theatres, night-clubs and other establishments;
(c) interviewing persons in public, especially on radio and television;
(d) performing related tasks;
(e) supervising other workers.

Examples of the occupations classified here:
- Announcer, radio
- Announcer, television
- Compere
- Interviewer, media
- Newscaster

3473 STREET, NIGHT-CLUB AND RELATED MUSICIANS, SINGERS AND DANCERS

Street, night-club and related musicians, singers and dancers perform music, or sing or dance on the streets, in night-clubs, circuses and related places.

Tasks include –
(a) playing one or more musical instruments as a soloist, or as a member of a popular music orchestra of circus, or other bands;
(b) singing popular arias as a soloist, or as a member of vocal groups in night-clubs, or on the streets;
(c) performing dances as a soloist, with a partner or as a member of dancing groups, in places such as circuses, night-clubs or on the streets;

(d) performing related tasks;
(e) supervising other workers.

Examples of the occupations classified here:
- Band leader
- Dancer, night-club
- Musician, night-club
- Singer, street

Some related occupations classified elsewhere:
- Conductor, orchestra – 2453
- Dancer, ballet – 2454
- Instrumentalist – 2453
- Singer, choir – 2453

3474 CLOWNS, MAGICIANS, ACROBATS AND RELATED ASSOCIATE PROFESSIONALS

Clowns, magicians, acrobats and related associate professionals entertain audiences in circuses and other places by performing a variety of acts.

Tasks include –
(a) performing amusing antics and telling funny stories;
(b) performing tricks of illusion and sleight of hand, and feats of hypnotism;
(c) performing difficult and spectacular acrobatics, and gymnastic or juggling feats;
(d) training and performing with animals;
(e) performing related tasks;
(f) supervising other workers.

Examples of the occupations classified here:
- Acrobat
- Aerialist
- Clown
- Hypnotist
- Magician

3475 ATHLETES, SPORTSPERSONS AND RELATED ASSOCIATE PROFESSIONALS

Athletes, sportspersons and related associate professionals participate in competitive sporting events, conduct sports training, compile rules concerning sporting events, and control the progress of these events.

Tasks include –
(a) participating in competitive sporting events;
(b) conducting sports training to develop ability in and knowledge of the sport;
(c) compiling rules concerning the conduct of sporting competitions, and controlling the progress of these events;
(d) performing related tasks;
(e) supervising other workers.

Examples of the occupations classified here:
- Athlete
- Boxer
- Coach, sports
- Official, sports
- Wrestler

MINOR GROUP 348
RELIGIOUS ASSOCIATE PROFESSIONALS

Religious associate professionals participate in the practice of religious works, or devote their lives to contemplative prayer or meditation, or preach and propagate the teachings of their particular religion.

Tasks performed usually include: participating in the practice of religious works; devoting their lives to contemplative prayer or meditation; and preaching and propagating the teachings of their particular religion. Supervision of other workers may be included.

Occupations in this minor group are classified into the following unit group:

3480   Religious associate professionals

3480   RELIGIOUS ASSOCIATE PROFESSIONALS

Religious associate professionals undertake religious works, devote their lives to contemplative prayer or meditation, and preach and propagate the teachings of their particular religion.

Tasks include –
(a)   undertaking religious works;
(b)   living as a member of a separate community, and observing its rules and practices;
(c)   devoting their lives to contemplative prayer or meditation;
(d)   preaching and propagating the teachings of a particular religious faith;
(e)   performing related tasks;
(f)   supervising other workers.

Examples of the occupations classified here:
- Monk, associate professional
- Nun, associate professional
- Preacher, lay

Some related occupations classified elsewhere:
- Bonze – 2460
- Imam – 2460
- Minister, religion – 2460
- Monk, professional – 2460
- Nun, professional – 2460
- Poojari – 2460
- Priest – 2460
- Rabbi – 2460

MAJOR GROUP 4
CLERKS

Clerks record, organise, store, compute and retrieve information related to the work in question, and perform a number of clerical duties especially in connection with money-handling operations, travel arrangements, requests for information, and appointments. Most occupations in this major group require skills at the second ISCO skill level.

Tasks performed by clerks usually include: stenography, typing, and operating word processors and other office machines; entering data into computers; carrying out secretarial duties; recording and computing numerical data; keeping records relating to stocks, production and transport; keeping records relating to passenger and freight transport; carrying out clerical duties in libraries; filing documents; carrying out duties in connection with mail services; preparing and checking material for printing; writing on behalf of illiterate persons; performing money-handling operations; dealing with travel arrangements; supplying information requested by clients and making appointments; operating a telephone switchboard. Supervision of other workers may be included.

Occupations in this major group are classified into the following sub-major groups:

41   Office clerks

42   Customer services clerks

SUB-MAJOR GROUP 41
OFFICE CLERKS

Office clerks record, organise, store and retrieve information related to the work in question and compute financial, statistical, and other numerical data.

Tasks performed by workers in this sub-major group usually include: stenography and typing; operating word-processors or data entry, calculating, bookkeeping and similar office machines; carrying out secretarial duties; recording and computing accounting, bookkeeping, statistical, actuarial, financial and other numerical data; keeping records of production schedules, level of stocks and timely delivery of goods; keeping records of operational aspects and co-ordinating the timing of passenger and freight transport; carrying out clerical duties in libraries; filing documents; carrying out duties in connection with mail services; preparing and checking material for printing; writing on behalf of illiterate persons; performing a wide range of general clerical duties. Supervision of other workers may be included.

4

Occupations in this sub-major group are classified into the following minor groups:

411   Secretaries and keyboard-operating clerks

412   Numerical clerks

413   Material-recording and transport clerks

414   Library, mail and related clerks

419   Other office clerks

MINOR GROUP **411**
SECRETARIES AND KEYBOARD-OPERATING CLERKS

Secretaries and keyboard-operating clerks record oral or written information on paper or in machine-readable form, operate bookkeeping and calculating machines, edit and transcribe correspondence and documents to conform to office standards, and perform other secretarial duties.

Tasks performed usually include: recording dictated and other matter in shorthand; typing it on paper or using word processors or teleprinters; entering various data into electronic equipment or in the form of perforations on cards or special tapes; operating bookkeeping and calculating machines; editing and transcribing correspondence and documents to conform to office standards; performing various secretarial duties. Supervision of other workers may be included.

Occupations in this minor group are classified into the following unit groups:

4111   Stenographers and typists

4112   Word-processor and related operators

4113   Data entry operators

4114   Calculating-machine operators

4115   Secretaries

4111   STENOGRAPHERS AND TYPISTS

Stenographers and typists record oral or written matter in shorthand and, using typewriters, produce documents on paper.

Tasks include –

(a)   taking dictation and recording other matter in shorthand;

(b)   making transcripts in typewritten form;

(c)   performing limited clerical duties, such as filing or using photocopying machines;

(d)   performing related tasks;

(e)   supervising other workers.

Examples of the occupations classified here:

■ Typist

■ Typist, stenography

Some related occupations classified elsewhere:
- Secretary, typing – 4115
- Verbatim reporter – 3431

4112 WORD-PROCESSOR AND RELATED OPERATORS

Word-processor and related operators type, edit, and print various documents using word-processing equipment, or send and receive messages and facsimiles by means of a teleprinter, telefax or similar machines.

Tasks include –
(a) typing correspondence, business forms and other documents into word-processing machines;
(b) planning and executing layout and format, if not pre-set;
(c) altering, rearranging and editing typed text;
(d) operating printer, usually linked to the word processor;
(e) sending and receiving messages or facsimiles by means of a teleprinter, telefax or similar machines;
(f) performing limited clerical duties;
(g) performing related tasks;
(h) supervising other workers.

Examples of the occupations classified here:
- Clerk, telefax
- Clerk, teleprinter
- Clerk, telex
- Clerk, word processing

4113 DATA ENTRY OPERATORS

Data entry operators enter numerical and other data into electronic equipment for processing and transmission, or enter data on cards and tapes, using punching machines.

Tasks include –
(a) entering numerical and other data from source material into computer-compatible storage and processing devices;
(b) entering data from source material in the form of perforations on cards or paper tapes;
(c) correcting entered data, if needed;
(d) performing related tasks;
(e) supervising other workers.

Examples of the occupations classified here:
- Clerk, data entry/computer
- Clerk, data entry/converter (card-to-tape)
- Clerk, data entry/electronic mail
- Clerk, data entry/punching machine (card and tape)

4114 CALCULATING-MACHINE OPERATORS

Calculating-machine operators operate bookkeeping and calculating machines.

Tasks include –
(a) operating bookkeeping machines to make records of business transactions;
(b) operating electrical or manual machines to make arithmetical calculations;
(c) performing related tasks;
(d) supervising other workers.

Examples of the occupations classified here:
- Clerk, accounting machine
- Clerk, adding machine
- Clerk, bookkeeping machine
- Clerk, calculating machine

4115 SECRETARIES

Secretaries use typewriters or word-processing equipment to check and transcribe correspondence and other documents, deal with incoming and outgoing mail, screen requests for meetings or appointments, record and screen leave and other staff entitlements, organise and supervise filing systems, and deal with routine correspondence on their own initiative.

Tasks include –
(a) checking and transcribing correspondence, minutes and reports from dictation or written drafts to conform to office standards, using typewriter or word-processing equipment;
(b) dealing with incoming or outgoing mail;
(c) scanning, recording and distributing mail, correspondence and documents;

4

(d) screening requests for meetings or appointments and helping to organise meetings;

(e) screening and recording leave and other staff-members' entitlements;

(f) organising and supervising filing systems;

(g) dealing with routine correspondence on their own initiative;

(h) performing related tasks;

(i) supervising other workers.

Examples of the occupations classified here:
- Secretary
- Secretary, stenography/typing
- Secretary, typing
- Secretary, word-processing

Some related occupations classified elsewhere:
- Assistant, correspondence − 3431
- Secretary, administrative − 3431

MINOR GROUP **412**
NUMERICAL CLERKS

Numerical clerks obtain, compile and compute accounting, bookkeeping, statistical, financial and other numerical data, and take charge of cash transactions incidental to business matters.

Tasks performed usually include: helping with accounting and bookkeeping records and computations; calculating unit production costs; calculating wages and in some cases preparing wage packets and paying wages; taking charge of cash transactions incidental to the business; obtaining, compiling and computing statistical or actuarial data; performing clerical tasks relating to the financial transactions of a bank or similar establishment. Supervision of other workers may be included.

Occupations in this minor group are classified into the following unit groups:

> **4121   Accounting and bookkeeping clerks**
>
> **4122   Statistical and finance clerks**

4121   ACCOUNTING AND BOOK-KEEPING CLERKS

Accounting and bookkeeping clerks help with accounting and bookkeeping records and computations, wages and production costs computations as well as with cash payments.

Tasks include –

(a) making entries in accounting and bookkeeping records;

(b) making necessary calculations;

(c) performing other limited accounting and bookkeeping functions;

(d) calculating from existing records production costs per unit;

(e) calculating wages due from records of hours worked, or work performed by individual employees;

(f) taking charge of cash and keeping records of cash transactions incidental to the business; may prepare wage packets and pay wages;

(g) performing related tasks;

(h) supervising other workers.

Examples of the occupations included here:
- Clerk, accounts
- Clerk, bookkeeping
- Clerk, cost computing
- Clerk, wages

Some related occupations classified else-where:

- Assistant, accounting – 3434
- Bookkeeper – 3433

4122 STATISTICAL AND FINANCE CLERKS

Statistical and finance clerks obtain, compile and compute statistical or actuarial data or perform clerical tasks relating to the transactions of a bank and other financial establishments.

Tasks include –

(a) obtaining and compiling statistical or actuarial data based on routine or special sources of information;

(b) calculating totals, averages, percentages and other details and presenting them in the required tabular form;

(c) preparing financial documents, and calculating interest or brokerage charges and stamp duties payable;

(d) maintaining records of bonds, shares and other securities bought or sold on behalf of clients or employer;

(e) performing related tasks;

(f) supervising other workers.

Examples of the occupations classified here:

- Clerk, actuarial
- Clerk, brokerage
- Clerk, finance
- Clerk, securities
- Clerk, statistical
- Clerk, tax

Some related occupations classified else-where:

- Assistant, statistical – 3434
- Broker, stocks and shares – 3411
- Broker, trade – 3421

MINOR GROUP 413
MATERIAL-RECORDING AND TRANSPORT CLERKS

Material-recording and transport clerks keep records of goods produced, purchased, stocked, dispatched, and of materials needed at specified production dates, or keep records of operational aspects and co-ordinate the timing of passenger and freight transport.

Tasks performed usually include: recording produced, stocked, ordered and dispatched goods; recording production materials received, put into stock or issued; computing quantities of the production materials required at specified dates and helping with preparation and checking of production operation schedules; keeping records of operational aspects and co-ordinating the timing of passenger and freight transport. Supervision of other workers may be included.

Occupations in this minor group are classified into the following unit groups:

4131 Stock clerks

4132 Production clerks

4133 Transport clerks

4

4131 STOCK CLERKS

Stock clerks maintain records of goods produced and production materials received, weighed, issued, dispatched or put into stock.

Tasks include –

(a) arranging and controlling receipt and dispatch of goods and keeping relevant records;

(b) maintaining stock records, verifying issue of goods, estimating needs and making requisitions of new stocks;

(c) receiving, storing and issuing tools, spare parts, or various equipment and maintaining relevant records;

(d) weighing goods received, issued, produced, or dispatched and maintaining relevant records;

(e) compiling inventories of furniture and other items received for storage;

(f) performing related tasks;

(g) supervising other workers.

Examples of the occupations classified here:
- Clerk, freight/dispatching
- Clerk, freight/receiving
- Clerk, stock/records
- Clerk, stock/storeroom
- Clerk, weighing

4132 PRODUCTION CLERKS

Production clerks compute quantities of materials required at specified dates for the production programme and prepare and check production operation schedules.

Tasks include –

(a) computing quantities, qualities and types of materials required by production programme;

(b) preparing production requirements schedules, ensuring that materials are available when needed, and keeping relevant records;

(c) preparing or assisting in the preparation of production operation schedules on the basis of customers' orders and production capacity and performance;

(d) verifying stocks, arranging deliveries and investigating delays;

(e) performing related tasks;

(f) supervising other workers.

Examples of the occupations classified here:
- Clerk, order/materials
- Clerk, planning/materials
- Clerk, production planning
- Clerk, schedule/materials

4133 TRANSPORT CLERKS

Transport clerks keep records of operational aspects and co-ordinate the timing of train, road and air passenger and freight transport, and prepare reports for management.

Tasks include –

(a) keeping records of operational aspects, and co-ordinating the timing of passenger and freight transport;

(b) directing train routings within a division or zone of a railway system and keeping related records;

(c) directing, controlling and keeping records of freight handling at a railway yard;

(d) co-ordinating and keeping records of operational activities concerning road transport, such as allocation and scheduling of vehicles and drivers, loading and unloading of vehicles and storage of goods in transit;

(e) co-ordinating and keeping records of operational activities concerning air transport of passengers and freight, such as passenger lists and freight manifests;

(f) preparing reports for management;

(g) performing related tasks;

(h) supervising other workers.

Examples of the occupations classified here:
- Controller, clerical/air transport service
- Controller, clerical/railway service
- Controller, clerical/road transport service
- Dispatcher, clerical/boat
- Dispatcher, clerical/bus
- Dispatcher, clerical/train
- Dispatcher, clerical/truck

MINOR GROUP **414**
LIBRARY, MAIL AND RELATED CLERKS

Library, mail and related clerks perform clerical duties in libraries and post offices, file documents, prepare data for processing, check material for printing and write on behalf of illiterate persons.

Tasks performed usually include: recording information regarding acquisition, issue and return of books; classifying and filing various documents and other records; sorting, recording and delivering mail from post offices, as well as from or within an enterprise; coding; correcting proofs; performing a number of miscellaneous clerical duties; writing on behalf of illiterate persons. Supervision of other workers may be included.

Occupations in this minor group are classified into the following unit groups:

> **4141   Library and filing clerks**
>
> **4142   Mail carriers and sorting clerks**
>
> **4143   Coding, proof-reading, and related clerks**
>
> **4144   Scribes and related workers**

4141   LIBRARY AND FILING CLERKS

Library and filing clerks maintain library services or perform duties related to the filing and classification of records.

Tasks include –

(a) maintaining library records relating to the acquisition, issue and return of books and other publications;

(b) photocopying or reproducing documents and other records;

(c) classifying and systematically filing papers, documents and other records;

(d) performing related tasks;

(e) supervising other workers.

Examples of the occupations classified here:
- Clerk, filing
- Clerk, library

4142   MAIL CARRIERS AND SORTING CLERKS

Mail carriers and sorting clerks perform sorting, recording, delivery and other duties in connection with mail services from post offices or related organisations, as well as from or within an establishment.

Tasks include –

(a) performing mail-handling duties in public post offices;

(b) sorting and delivering mail to private houses and elsewhere;

(c) sorting and keeping simple records of incoming and outgoing correspondence and dispatching outgoing mail in various establishments;

(d) performing related tasks;

(e) supervising other workers.

Examples of the occupations classified here:
- Clerk, mail/dispatch
- Clerk, mail/sorting
- Post carrier
- Postman
- Postwoman

4143   CODING, PROOF-READING, AND RELATED CLERKS

Coding, proof-reading, and related clerks convert information into codes, verify and correct proofs, and perform a number of miscellaneous clerical duties.

Tasks include –

(a) converting information into codes and classifying information by codes for data-processing purposes;

(b) comparing proofs of texts and related material prepared for printing with original material, correcting errors and marking texts for printer according to the established rules;

(c) sorting forms and marking them with identification numbers;

(d) sorting documents for filing or to collate sets of pages;

(e) addressing circulars and envelopes by hand;

(f) performing related tasks;

(g) supervising other workers.

Examples of the occupations classified here:

- Clerk, coding
- Proof-reader, clerical

4144   SCRIBES AND RELATED WORKERS

Scribes and related workers write letters and complete forms on behalf of illiterate persons.

Tasks include –

(a) reading letters and other written matter to illiterate persons and providing necessary interpretation and information;

(b) writing letters and completing forms on behalf of illiterate persons;

(c) offering advice to individuals and interpreting and helping with the completion of government and other official forms;

(d) performing related tasks;

(e) supervising other workers.

Examples of the occupations classified here:

- Scribe

MINOR GROUP 419
OTHER OFFICE CLERKS

Other office clerks perform a wide range of general clerical duties, mostly connected with the keeping of various office records.

Tasks performed usually include: keeping address lists; keeping mailing lists; keeping personnel or any other office records; or performing clerical services such as filing, photocopying, or mimeographing. Supervision of other workers may be included.

Occupations in this minor group are classified into the following unit group:

4190   Other office clerks

4190   OTHER OFFICE CLERKS

Other office clerks perform a wide range of general clerical duties mostly connected with the keeping of various office records.

Tasks include –

(a) keeping personnel records of all the organisation's employees, showing name, address, and other details;

(b) keeping personnel records of employees' leave and other information;

(c) preparing and maintaining the organisation's address and telephone lists;

(d) preparing and maintaining the organisation's mailing lists;

(e) performing related tasks;

(f) supervising other workers.

Examples of the occupations classified here:

- Clerk, compilation/directory
- Clerk, list/addresses
- Clerk, records/personnel

SUB-MAJOR GROUP 42
CUSTOMER SERVICES CLERKS

Customer services clerks deal directly with clients in connection with money-handling operations, travel arrangements, requests for information, appointments, and by operating telephone switchboards.

Tasks performed by workers in this sub-major group usually include: performing money-handling operations in banks, post-offices, betting and gambling establishments, or as payments for goods and services bought or pledged; dealing with travel arrangements; supplying information requested by clients and making appointments; operating a telephone switchboard. Supervision of other workers may be included.

Occupations in this sub-major group are classified into the following minor groups:

421   Cashiers, tellers and related clerks

422   Client information clerks

MINOR GROUP 421
CASHIERS, TELLERS AND RELATED CLERKS

Cashiers, tellers and related clerks perform money-handling operations in stores and other establishments, including those related to betting or gambling, pawning and debt-collecting.

Tasks performed usually include: receiving payments from clients for goods and services bought; dealing with clients of banks or post offices in connection with money operations or postal services; receiving and paying off bets on results of sporting events; conducting gambling games; lending money against articles deposited or other securities; collecting debts and other payments. Supervision of other workers may be included.

Occupations in this minor group are classified into the following unit groups:

4211   Cashiers and ticket clerks

4212   Tellers and other counter clerks

4213   Bookmakers and croupiers

4214   Pawnbrokers and money-lenders

4215   Debt-collectors and related workers

4211 CASHIERS AND TICKET CLERKS

Cashiers and ticket clerks receive, directly from clients, payments for goods or services bought in establishments such as stores and ticket offices, or they pay out cash in banks and related organisations.

Tasks include –

(a) receiving and verifying cash, cheque or credit-card payments in stores, ticket offices, or similar establishments;

(b) giving change and issuing receipts;

(c) issuing tickets at ticket offices, and taking corresponding payments;

(d) paying out cash, mostly in banks, against written orders, credit notes, or resulting from currency exchanges, and obtaining receipts;

(e) keeping records and reconciling them with cash balance;

(f) receiving incoming cash of an establishment, checking it against sales slips and other documents, and preparing it for deposit at bank;

(g) paying out wages to establishments' personnel;

(h) operating cash register;

(i) performing related tasks;

(j) supervising other workers.

Examples of the occupations classified here:
- Cashier, bank
- Cashier, store
- Clerk, ticket issuing/except travel

4212 TELLERS AND OTHER COUNTER CLERKS

Tellers and other counter clerks deal directly with clients of banks or post offices in connection with receiving, changing and paying out money, or providing mail services.

Tasks include –

(a) receiving money or cheques from clients;

(b) paying out money to clients;

(c) paying bills and making money transfers on clients' behalf;

(d) crediting and debiting clients' accounts;

(e) changing money from one currency to another, as requested by clients;

(f) making records of all transactions and reconciling them with cash balance;

(g) receiving mail, selling postage stamps and conducting other post office counter business such as bill payments, money transfers and related business;

(h) performing related tasks;

(i) supervising other workers.

Examples of the occupations classified here:
- Clerk, post office counter
- Money changer
- Teller, bank

4213 BOOKMAKERS AND CROUPIERS

Bookmakers and croupiers determine odds and receive and pay off bets on results of sporting or other events, or conduct games of chance in gambling establishments.

Tasks include –

(a) determining risks to decide odds and to hedge or refuse bets;

(b) preparing and issuing lists of approximate odds;

(c) distributing cards, rolling dice or spinning a roulette wheel;

(d) explaining and interpreting operating rules of a gambling establishment;

(e) announcing winning numbers, paying winners and collecting payments from losers;

(f) performing related tasks;

(g) supervising other workers.

Examples of the occupations classified here:
- Bookmaker
- Croupier

4214 PAWNBROKERS AND MONEY-LENDERS

Pawnbrokers and money-lenders lend money against articles deposited as pledges, or against property or other security.

Tasks include –

(a) evaluating articles offered as pledges, calculating interest, and lending money;

(b) returning articles when the loan is paid or, in the event of non-payment, selling pledged articles;

(c) lending money as personal loans against success of future harvest and other similar undertakings;

(d) performing related tasks;

(e) supervising other workers.

Examples of the occupations classified here:

- Money-lender
- Pawnbroker

4215 DEBT-COLLECTORS AND RELATED WORKERS

Debt-collectors and related workers collect payments and perform clerical duties associated with these collections.

Tasks include –

(a) telephoning or writing to customers to collect money or arrange for later payments;

(b) tracing addresses of customers and paying visits to collect debts;

(c) noting amounts collected;

(d) recommending legal action when payment cannot be otherwise obtained;

(e) asking for and collecting charity payments;

(f) performing related tasks;

(g) supervising other workers.

Examples of the occupations classified here:

- Collector, charity
- Collector, debt

MINOR GROUP 422
CLIENT INFORMATION CLERKS

Client information clerks deal directly with clients in connection with travel arrangements, various types of information requested, appointments to be made, including those for hospitals, medical and dental surgeries, as well as incoming or requested telephone calls.

Tasks performed usually include: preparing itineraries and making travel and hotel reservations for clients; receiving clients or patients, providing relevant information and making appointments on behalf of various establishments, including hospitals, medical or dental surgeries; operating a telephone switchboard. Supervision of other workers may be included.

Occupations in this minor group are classified into the following unit groups:

4221 Travel agency and related clerks

4222 Receptionists and information clerks

4223 Telephone switchboard operators

4

4221 TRAVEL AGENCY AND RELATED CLERKS

Travel agency and related clerks supply information, arrange travel itineraries and obtain necessary reservations.

Tasks include –
(a) advising customer on itineraries and method of travel;
(b) preparing itineraries;
(c) making necessary reservations;
(d) issuing tickets, vouchers and other documents;
(e) obtaining visas, if necessary;
(f) preparing bills and receiving payments;
(g) performing related tasks;
(h) supervising other workers.

Examples of the occupations classified here:
- Clerk, ticket issuing/travel
- Clerk, travel/airlines
- Clerk, travel agency

Some related occupations classified elsewhere:
- Clerk, ticket issuing/except travel – 4211
- Consultant, travel – 3414
- Department manager, production and operations/travel agency – 1229
- General manager, travel agency – 1319
- Organiser, travel – 3414

4222 RECEPTIONISTS AND INFORMATION CLERKS

Receptionists and information clerks receive clients or patients, provide information and make appointments on behalf of various establishments including hospitals, medical or dental surgeries.

Tasks include –
(a) receiving clients or patients, noting inquiries and providing relevant information;
(b) making appointments for clients or patients;
(c) dealing with telephone requests for information or appointments;
(d) directing clients or patients to appropriate location or person;
(e) making reservations and arranging registration for hotel guests or patients, as well as keeping records, or presenting bills on departure;
(f) supplying information pamphlets, brochures or forms;
(g) performing related tasks;
(h) supervising other workers.

Examples of the occupations classified here:
- Clerk, information
- Receptionist
- Receptionist, dental
- Receptionist, hotel
- Receptionist, medical

4223 TELEPHONE SWITCHBOARD OPERATORS

Telephone switchboard operators operate a telephone switchboard or a section thereof, and deal with local or long-distance calls, and various telephone inquiries.

Tasks include –
(a) establishing contact between caller and person called;
(b) making connections for outgoing calls, and routing long-distance calls;
(c) recording charges;
(d) dealing with telephone inquiries and recording messages;
(e) performing related tasks;
(f) supervising other workers.

Examples of the occupations classified here:
- Switchboard-operator, telephone

MAJOR GROUP 5
SERVICE WORKERS AND SHOP AND MARKET SALES WORKERS

Service workers and shop and market sales workers provide personal and protective services related to travel, housekeeping, catering, personal care, or protection against fire and unlawful acts, or they pose as models for artistic creation and display, or demonstrate and sell goods in wholesale or retail shops and similar establishments, as well as at stalls and on markets. Most occupations in this major group require skills at the second ISCO skill level.

Tasks performed by service workers and shop and market sales workers usually include: organisation and provision of services during travel; housekeeping; preparation and serving of food and beverages; child care; rudimentary nursing and related care at homes or in institutions; personal care, such as hairdressing or beauty treatment; companionship; astrology and fortune-telling; embalming; funeral arrangements; protection of individuals and property against fire and unlawful acts and enforcement of law and order; posing as models for advertising, artistic creation and display of goods; selling goods in wholesale or retail establishments, as well as at stalls and on markets; demonstrating goods to potential customers. Supervision of other workers may be included.

Occupations in this major group are classified into the following sub-major groups:

51   Personal and protective services workers

52   Models, salespersons and demonstrators

SUB-MAJOR GROUP 51
PERSONAL AND PROTECTIVE SERVICES WORKERS

Personal and protective services workers provide personal and protective services related to travel, housekeeping, catering, personal care, or protection against fire and unlawful acts.

Tasks performed by workers in this sub-major group usually include: organisation and provision of services during travel; housekeeping; preparation and serving of food and beverages; child care; rudimentary nursing and related care at homes or in institutions; personal care, such as hairdressing or beauty treatment; companionship; astrology

5

and fortune-telling; embalming; funeral arrangements; protection of individuals and property against fire and unlawful acts and enforcement of law and order. Supervision of other workers may be included.

Occupations in this sub-major group are classified into the following minor groups:

511 Travel attendants and related workers

512 Housekeeping and restaurant services workers

513 Personal care and related workers

514 Other personal services workers

515 Astrologers, fortune-tellers and related workers

516 Protective services workers

MINOR GROUP **511**
TRAVEL ATTENDANTS AND RELATED WORKERS

Travel attendants and related workers provide various personal services in connection with travelling by aircraft, train, ship, bus or other vehicle, and escorting individuals and groups on travel tours, sightseeing visits and excursions.

Tasks performed usually include: ensuring the comfort and safety of passengers; serving food and refreshments; providing necessary or requested information and answering various questions in connection with the journey; collecting or issuing tickets on board public transport; accompanying individuals or groups on sightseeing tours or excursions and describing points of interest; providing other guide services. Supervision of other workers may be included.

Occupations in this minor group are classified into the following unit groups:

5111 Travel attendants and travel stewards

5112 Transport conductors

5113 Travel guides

5111 TRAVEL ATTENDANTS AND TRAVEL STEWARDS

Travel attendants and travel stewards render personal services to ensure the comfort and safety of passengers, serve meals and beverages, or plan and co-ordinate housekeeping and social activities on ships.

Tasks include –

(a) greeting passengers entering aircraft, conducting them to their seats, ensuring that seat-belts are fastened and "no smoking" and similar signs are obeyed;

(b) explaining the use of safety equipment such as lifebelts and oxygen masks;

(c) distributing reading material, head-phones, blankets and similar items, and answering passengers' inquiries;

(d) serving pre-prepared meals as well as beverages;

(e) selling duty-free goods;

(f) administering minor medical aid to passengers in need;

(g) taking appropriate action in case of emergencies or accidents;

(h) taking care of passengers at airports;

(i) taking care of general needs and comfort of ship's passengers, including keeping cabins tidy and serving meals in them, on request;

(j) performing related tasks;

(k) supervising other workers.

Examples of the occupations classified here:

- Attendant, airport
- Attendant, flight
- Steward, ship

5112 TRANSPORT CONDUCTORS

Transport conductors collect or issue tickets and take care of safety and comfort on trains, trams, buses and other public transport vehicles.

Tasks include –

(a) collecting or issuing tickets, passes or fares, or checking the validity of tickets issued previously;

(b) taking care of sleeping-car on a passenger train, including the checking of passengers' tickets, their safety and information requests;

(c) ensuring that safety regulations are respected;

(d) giving information to passengers, especially about stops and connections;

(e) co-operating with the driver in maintaining time schedules;

(f) taking appropriate action in case of emergencies or accidents;

(g) performing related tasks;

(h) supervising other workers.

Examples of the occupations classified here:

- Conductor, bus
- Conductor, cable car
- Conductor, train
- Conductor, tram

5113 TRAVEL GUIDES

Travel guides accompany individuals or groups on sightseeing tours or excursions, describe points of interest and provide other guide services.

Tasks include –

(a) escorting tourists and looking after their comfort;

(b) accompanying tourists on sightseeing tours and describing points of interest;

(c) accompanying tourists to museums and exhibitions and giving information on exhibits;

(d) guiding groups through factories and similar establishments and giving relevant information;

(e) conducting excursions such as mountain climbing, hunting or fishing;

(f) performing related tasks;

(g) supervising other workers.

Examples of the occupations classified here:

- Guide, art gallery
- Guide, travel
- Guide, travel/game park
- Guide, travel/safari
- Guide, travel/sightseeing

MINOR GROUP **512**
HOUSEKEEPING AND RESTAURANT SERVICES WORKERS

Housekeeping and restaurant services workers organise, supervise and carry out housekeeping functions in commercial establishments, institutions or private households, or perform various kinds of work related to the preparation and cooking of meals and the serving of food and beverages in various commercial establishments, institutions, private households, ships or passenger trains.

Tasks performed usually include: engaging, training and discharging domestic staff; organising and conducting the work of domestic staff; taking care of general welfare and suitable conduct of individuals in institutions; controlling the purchase, storage and issue of supplies; preparing and cooking foodstuffs; serving food and beverages. Supervision of other workers may be included.

Occupations in this minor group are classified into the following unit groups:

5121 Housekeepers and related workers

5122 Cooks

5123 Waiters, waitresses and bartenders

5121 HOUSEKEEPERS AND RELATED WORKERS

Housekeepers and related workers organise, supervise and carry out housekeeping functions in hotels, clubs, boarding schools and other enterprises and institutions and in private households.

Tasks include –
(a) engaging, training, discharging, organising and supervising workers employed as domestic staff;
(b) purchasing or controlling the purchase of supplies;
(c) controlling storage and issue of supplies;
(d) supervising general welfare and conduct of individuals in institutions;
(e) assisting in cases of minor injury or illness by performing tasks such as taking temperature, giving medicine, putting on bandages;
(f) performing related tasks;
(g) supervising other workers.

Examples of the occupations classified here:
- Housekeeper

- Matron, housekeeping
- Steward, house

5122 COOKS

Cooks plan, organise, prepare and cook foodstuffs in hotels, restaurants and other public eating places, on board ships, on passenger trains and in private households.

Tasks include –
(a) planning meals, preparing and cooking foodstuffs;
(b) planning, supervising and co-ordinating work in the kitchen;
(c) performing related tasks;
(d) supervising other workers.

Examples of the occupations classified here:
- Cook
- Cook, head

5123 WAITERS, WAITRESSES AND BARTENDERS

Waiters, waitresses and bartenders serve food and beverages in commercially-operated dining and drinking places, clubs, institutions and canteens, on board ships and on passenger trains.

Tasks include –

(a) serving food and beverages;

(b) advising on the choice of wines and serving them;

(c) serving alcoholic and non-alcoholic drinks at a bar;

(d) performing related tasks;

(e) supervising other workers.

Examples of the occupations classified here:

- Bartender
- Waiter
- Waiter, head
- Waitress
- Waitress, wine

MINOR GROUP 513
PERSONAL CARE AND RELATED WORKERS

Personal care and related workers provide child care and help in looking after schoolchildren, perform various tasks in order to assist medical and nursing professionals and associate professionals in their duties at hospitals and other institutions, provide home-based personal care, or help veterinary, pharmaceutical or other professionals in their tasks.

Tasks performed usually include: taking care of employers' children and helping teachers by taking care of children at lunch or other school breaks or outings; providing rudimentary nursing and related care in hospitals and similar institutions, or to patients at home; helping veterinary and pharmaceutical professionals in their duties. Supervision of other workers may be included.

Occupations in this minor group are classified into the following unit groups:

5131   Child-care workers

5132   Institution-based personal care workers

5133   Home-based personal care workers

5139   Personal care and related workers not elsewhere classified

5131   CHILD-CARE WORKERS

Child-care workers take care of employers' children and oversee their daily activities, or engage in helping teachers to look after schoolchildren.

Tasks include –

(a) assisting children to bath, dress and feed themselves;

(b) taking children to and from school or outdoors for recreation;

(c) playing games with children, or entertaining children by reading or storytelling;

(d) maintaining order in children's bedrooms and playrooms;

(e) taking care of schoolchildren at lunch or other school breaks;

(f) taking care of schoolchildren on excursions, museum visits and similar outings;

(g) performing related tasks;

(h) supervising other workers.

Examples of the occupations classified here:

- Governess, children
- Nanny

5132 INSTITUTION-BASED PERSONAL CARE WORKERS

Institution-based personal care workers perform simple tasks to assist medical, nursing, midwifery and dental professionals or associate professionals in their duties.

Tasks include –

(a) preparing patients for examination or treatment;

(b) changing bed-linen and helping patients with their toilet;

(c) providing hot-water bottles and other comforts for patients;

(d) serving and collecting food trays and feeding patients needing help;

(e) sterilising surgical and other instruments and equipment;

(f) assisting dentists by adjusting lights and passing tools and materials as requested;

(g) performing related tasks;

(h) supervising other workers.

Examples of the occupations classified here:

- Aid, dental
- Aid, nursing/clinic
- Aid, nursing/hospital
- Ambulance man
- Ambulance woman

Some related occupations classified elsewhere:

- Aid, nursing/home − 5133
- Nurse, associate professional − 3231
- Nurse, professional − 2230

5133 HOME-BASED PERSONAL CARE WORKERS

Home-based personal care workers attend to various personal needs and in general provide personal care for persons in need of such care at their own homes because of physical or mental illness or disability or because of impairment due to old age.

Tasks include –

(a) assisting persons in getting into and out of bed and making the appropriate change in dress;

(b) changing bed-linen and helping persons with their bath and toilet;

(c) serving food – prepared by them or others – and feeding persons needing help;

(d) giving or ensuring that persons take the necessary medicaments;

(e) watching for any sign of deterioration in the person's health and informing the relevant medical doctor or social services;

(f) performing related tasks;

(g) supervising other workers.

Examples of the occupations classified here:

- Aid, nursing/home

Some related occupations classified elsewhere:

- Aid, nursing/clinic − 5132
- Nurse, associate professional − 3231
- Nurse, professional − 2230
- Social worker, associate professional − 3460
- Social worker, professional − 2446

5139 PERSONAL CARE AND RELATED WORKERS NOT ELSEWHERE CLASSIFIED

This unit group covers personal care and related workers not classified elsewhere in Minor group 513, *Personal care and related workers*.

For instance, here should be classified those who are engaged in helping veterinary or pharmaceutical professionals or associate professionals in performing their tasks.

In such cases tasks would include –

(a) bathing and feeding animals;

(b) leading or carrying animals to treatment room and holding them during treatment;

(c) cleaning and sterilising veterinary surgical instruments;

(d) labelling drugs, chemicals and other pharmaceutical preparations and replenishing stock on shelves;

(e) sterilising bottles, beakers and other equipment;

(f) performing related tasks;

(g) supervising other workers.

Examples of the occupations classified here:

- Aid, pharmacy
- Aid, veterinary

MINOR GROUP **514**
OTHER PERSONAL SERVICES WORKERS

Other personal services workers perform various tasks in order to improve the appearance of individuals, provide companionship or look after the wardrobe and other personal effects of employers, or provide embalming and funeral services.

Tasks performed usually include: cutting and dressing hair; shaving and trimming beards; giving beauty treatment and applying cosmetics and make-up; shaping and polishing finger- and toe-nails and treating minor ailments of the human foot; attending to clients taking baths and administering elementary massage; providing services as companions or valets; providing embalming and funeral services. Supervision of other workers may be included.

Occupations in this minor group are classified into the following unit groups:

5141   Hairdressers, barbers, beauticians and related workers

5142   Companions and valets

5143   Undertakers and embalmers

5149   Other personal services workers not elsewhere classified

5141   HAIRDRESSERS, BARBERS, BEAUTICIANS AND RELATED WORKERS

Hairdressers, barbers, beauticians and related workers cut and dress hair, shave and trim beards, give beauty treatment, apply cosmetics and make-up and give other kinds of treatment to individuals in order to improve their appearance.

Tasks include –

(a) cutting, washing, tinting and waving hair;

(b) cutting and washing hair and shaving or trimming beards;

(c) giving scalp treatment;

(d) fitting wigs according to customers' requirements;

(e) cleaning and applying creams, lotions and related products to face and parts of body;

(f) giving facial and body massage;

(g) applying make-up to clients of a beauty parlour;

(h) applying make-up to actors and other performers;

(i) cleaning, shaping and polishing finger- and toe-nails and treating minor ailments of the human foot such as corns, calluses or deformed toe-nails;

(j) attending to clients taking baths and administering elementary massage;

(k) performing related tasks;

(l) supervising other workers.

5

Examples of the occupations classified here:
- Attendant, bath
- Barber
- Beautician
- Chiropodist
- Hairdresser
- Manicurist

5142 COMPANIONS AND VALETS

Companions and valets provide companionship and attend to various personal needs of the employer.

Tasks include –
(a) providing companionship to employer by accompanying him/her to various places, reading, conversing and participating in activities such as sports;
(b) assisting in entertaining visitors in employer's home;
(c) keeping wardrobe and personal effects of the employer in good order;
(d) performing related tasks;
(e) supervising other workers.

Examples of the occupations classified here:
- Companion
- Valet

Some related occupations classified elsewhere:
- Escort, social – 5149
- Partner, dancing – 5149

5143 UNDERTAKERS AND EMBALMERS

Undertakers and embalmers perform various tasks in the disposal of dead human bodies.

Tasks include –
(a) making arrangements for, and conducting, funerals, cremations and burials;
(b) embalming human bodies to retard or arrest the process of decay;
(c) performing related tasks;
(d) supervising other workers.

Examples of the occupations classified here:
- Embalmer
- Undertaker

5149 OTHER PERSONAL SERVICES WORKERS NOT ELSEWHERE CLASSIFIED

This unit group covers personal services workers not classified elsewhere in Minor group 514, *Other personal services workers.*

For instance, here should be classified those who undertake to be dancing partners or social escorts, or perform duties of club or night-club hostesses or hosts.

In such cases tasks would include –
(a) accompanying clients to restaurants and other outings;
(b) acting as a dancing partner;
(c) welcoming clients to a night-club and ensuring that they are entertained well;
(d) performing related tasks;
(e) supervising other workers.

Examples of the occupations classified here:
- Escort, social
- Host, club
- Hostess, club
- Partner, dancing

Some related occupations classified elsewhere:
- Companion – 5142

MINOR GROUP **515**
ASTROLOGERS, FORTUNE-TELLERS AND RELATED WORKERS

Astrologers, fortune-tellers and related workers predict future events in persons' lives by practising astrology or by other techniques and give warnings and advice on possible courses of action.

Tasks performed usually include: making forecasts of future events based on the position of stars and planets at specified times or on characteristics of clients' palms, samples of playing cards drawn at random, position of tea leaves or coffee remnants in a cup and similar techniques.

Occupations in this minor group are classified into the following unit groups:

> **5151   Astrologers and related workers**
>
> **5152   Fortune-tellers, palmists and related workers**

5151   ASTROLOGERS AND RELATED WORKERS

Astrologers and related workers predict future events in persons' lives by practising astrology or related techniques and give warnings and advice on possible courses of action.

Tasks include –

(a) casting horoscopes of individuals at birth or later to recount past and forecast future events and conditions of their lives;

(b) determining auspicious times for various human activities such as inaugurations, marriages, journeys and religious and other ceremonies;

(c) studying the influence of the constellation of stars and of other phenomena on a person's life and situation;

(d) advising individuals on precautions to be taken to avoid evil influences;

(e) performing related tasks;

(f) supervising other workers.

Examples of the occupations classified here:
- Astrologer

5152   FORTUNE-TELLERS, PALMISTS AND RELATED WORKERS

Fortune-tellers, palmists and related workers recount past and forecast future events on the basis of the characteristics of clients' palms, samples of playing cards drawn at random or other factors.

Tasks include –

(a) interpreting characteristics of clients' palms, samples of playing cards, position of tea leaves or coffee remnants in a cup, shapes and patterns of bones of dead animals, etc.;

(b) forecasting future events on the basis of these interpretations;

(c) giving warnings and advice on possible courses of action;

(d) performing related tasks;

(e) supervising other workers.

Examples of the occupations classified here:
- Fortune-teller
- Numerologist
- Palmist

5

PROTECTIVE SERVICES WORKERS

Protective services workers protect individuals and property against fire and other hazards, maintain law and order and enforce laws and regulations.

Tasks performed usually include: preventing, fighting and extinguishing fires, rescuing persons and salvaging property and goods during and after fires and major accidents; maintaining law and order, protecting persons and property from hazards and unlawful acts and arresting persons for contraventions of the law; directing traffic and assuming authority in the event of accidents; watching over and maintaining discipline among inmates of prisons, reformatories or penitentiaries. Supervision of other workers may be included.

Occupations in this minor group are classified into the following unit groups:

5161 Fire-fighters

5162 Police officers

5163 Prison guards

5169 Protective services workers not elsewhere classified

5161 FIRE-FIGHTERS

Fire-fighters prevent, fight and try to extinguish fires, rescue persons and salvage property and goods during and after fires and major accidents.

Tasks include –

(a) preventing, fighting and extinguishing fires;

(b) fighting special types of fires and using special equipment in industrial establishments;

(c) preventing and extinguishing fires in crashed or damaged aircraft and rescuing crew and passengers;

(d) rescuing persons and salvaging property and goods during and after fires and major accidents;

(e) preventing or limiting the spread of dangerous substances in case of fires or accidents;

(f) performing related tasks;

(g) supervising other workers.

Examples of the occupations classified here:
- Fire-fighter
- Fire-fighter, aircraft accidents

- Fire-fighter, forest
- Salvageman, fire
- Salvagewoman, fire

Some related occupations classified elsewhere:
- Inspector, fire – 3151
- Investigator, fire – 3151
- Specialist, fire prevention – 3151

5162 POLICE OFFICERS

Police officers maintain law and order and enforce laws and regulations.

Tasks include –

(a) maintaining law and order;

(b) protecting persons and property from hazards and unlawful acts;

(c) arresting persons for contraventions of the law;

(d) directing traffic and assuming authority in the event of accidents;

(e) performing related tasks;

(f) supervising other workers.

Examples of the occupations classified here:

- Constable
- Patrolman, police
- Patrolwoman, police
- Police officer

Some related occupations classified elsewhere:

- Chief constable, police – 1120
- Commissioner, police – 1120
- Inspector-general, police – 1120

5163 PRISON GUARDS

Prison guards watch over and maintain discipline among inmates of prisons, reformatories or penitentiaries.

Tasks include –

(a) searching arriving prisoners, putting their valuables in safekeeping, escorting prisoners to cells and locking them in;

(b) making periodic inspection tours of cells;

(c) supervising prisoners at work, meals, or during walks and patrolling prison areas to prevent escape;

(d) performing related tasks;

(e) supervising other workers.

Examples of the occupations classified here:

- Guard, prison

5169 PROTECTIVE SERVICES WORKERS NOT ELSEWHERE CLASSIFIED

This unit group covers protective services workers not classified elsewhere in Minor group 516, *Protective services workers.*

For instance, here should be classified those who patrol buildings and areas to prevent illegal entry, theft, violence and other unlawful acts, and who, if necessary, use force to prevent such acts and apprehend perpetrators, as well as those who act as bodyguards, life-guards or game-wardens.

In such cases tasks would include –

(a) patrolling buildings and areas to prevent theft, violence, infractions of rules or other irregularities;

(b) if necessary, exercising the right to use force and to apprehend perpetrators;

(c) performing the duties of a bodyguard;

(d) patrolling beaches and swimming pools to prevent accidents and to rescue bathers from drowning;

(e) patrolling natural reserves, game parks, forest areas and enclosures to prevent theft and killing of game;

(f) performing related tasks;

(g) supervising other workers.

Examples of the occupations classified here:

- Bodyguard
- Game-warden
- Life-guard
- Patrolman, security
- Patrolwoman, security

Some related occupations classified elsewhere:

- Doorkeeper – 9152
- Guard, museum – 9152
- Watchman – 9152
- Watchwoman – 9152

SUB-MAJOR GROUP 52
MODELS, SALESPERSONS AND DEMONSTRATORS

Models, salespersons and demonstrators pose as models for artistic creation and display, or demonstrate and sell goods in wholesale or retail shops and similar establishments, as well as at stalls and on markets.

5

Tasks performed by workers in this sub-major group usually include the following: posing as models for advertising, artistic creation and display of goods; selling goods in wholesale or retail establishments, or at stalls usually placed at particular places and on markets; demonstrating goods to potential customers. Supervision of other workers may be included.

Occupations in this sub-major group are classified into the following minor groups:

521   Fashion and other models

522   Shop salespersons and demonstrators

523   Stall and market salespersons

MINOR GROUP 521
FASHION AND OTHER MODELS

Fashion and other models wear and display clothing and other items for sale or pose as models for advertising or for artistic creation.

Tasks performed usually include: putting on clothes and various accessories to display them for customers in showrooms of manufacturers, wholesalers, retailers or at special fashion-shows; posing as models for artistic photography, sculpture or painting; posing as models for photography or films in the field of advertising. Supervision of other workers may be included.

Occupations in this minor group are classified into the following unit group:

5210   Fashion and other models

5210   FASHION AND OTHER MODELS

Fashion and other models wear and display clothing and other items for sale or pose as models for advertising or for artistic creation.

Tasks include –

(a) dressing in sample apparel of new or current styles or of type wanted by customer;

(b) walking, turning and otherwise demonstrating style and other characteristics to best advantage;

(c) posing as model for artistic photography, sculpture or painting;

(d) posing as model for photography or films in the field of advertising;

(e) performing related tasks;

(f) supervising other workers.

Examples of the occupations classified here:
- Model, advertising
- Model, artist's
- Model, fashion

MINOR GROUP **522**
SHOP SALESPERSONS AND DEMONSTRATORS

Shop salespersons and demonstrators sell goods in wholesale or retail establishments and demonstrate and explain functions and qualities of these goods.

Tasks performed usually include: selling goods in wholesale establishments to retailers or large-scale consumers; selling goods to customers of retail establishments; demonstrating and explaining qualities and functions of these goods. Supervision of other workers may be included.

Occupations in this minor group are classified into the following unit group:

5220   Shop salespersons and demonstrators

5220   SHOP SALESPERSONS AND DEMONSTRATORS

Shop salespersons and demonstrators demonstrate and sell goods in wholesale establishments to retailers and large-scale consumers or to customers in retail establishments.

Tasks include –
(a) moving goods to be sold from storage area to sales area and placing them on display;
(b) ascertaining nature and quality of the product desired by the customer;
(c) assisting customer in making a choice;
(d) quoting prices, credit terms and discounts;
(e) packing and arranging delivery of goods, if necessary;
(f) writing bill, invoice, docket or receipt;
(g) verifying cashier's receipt, if necessary;
(h) giving demonstrations of articles on sale in order to inform customers about their characteristics and mode of use, as well as to stimulate buying interest;
(i) performing related tasks;
(j) supervising other workers.

Examples of the occupations classified here:
- Demonstrator
- Salesperson, retail establishment
- Salesperson, wholesale establishment

Some related occupations classified elsewhere:
- Salesperson, kiosk – 5230
- Salesperson, market – 5230
- Salesperson, street stall – 5230

MINOR GROUP **523**
STALL AND MARKET SALESPERSONS

Stall and market salespersons sell various goods such as leather or textile craft products, wood carvings, embroidery, lace, or newspapers, periodicals, postcards, cigarettes, chocolates and ice-creams, at stalls which are usually placed, by licence, at particular places in streets or other open spaces, or they sell fruit, vegetables and other, mostly perishable, foodstuffs on markets.

Tasks performed usually include: buying and then selling the above-mentioned or other similar goods at stalls usually grouped at particular places in streets or other open spaces by permission of the relevant local authorities; selling fruit, vegetables and other, mostly perishable, foodstuffs on markets. Supervision of other workers may be included.

Occupations in this minor group are classified into the following unit group:

5230 Stall and market salespersons

5230 STALL AND MARKET SALESPERSONS

Stall and market salespersons sell various goods such as leather or textile craft-products, wood carvings, embroidery, lace, or newspapers, periodicals, postcards, cigarettes, chocolates and ice-creams, at stalls usually grouped at particular places in streets or other open spaces by permission of the relevant local authorities, or they sell fruit, vegetables and other, mostly perishable, foodstuffs on markets.

Tasks include –

(a) obtaining, from the local authorities, permission to set up a stand at a particular place in streets or other open spaces;

(b) buying or contracting a regular supply of various goods to be sold such as leather or textile craft products, wood carvings, embroidery or lace, displaying them on stands and selling them;

(c) buying or contracting a regular supply of newspapers, periodicals, postcards, cigarettes, chocolates and ice-creams and selling them at kiosks;

(d) buying from wholesale markets, or directly from farmers, fresh fruit and vegetables or other, mostly perishable, foodstuffs and selling them on markets;

(e) loading and unloading goods for sale;

(f) receiving payment;

(g) keeping accounts;

(h) performing related tasks;

(i) supervising other workers.

Examples of the occupations classified here:
- Salesperson, kiosk
- Salesperson, market
- Salesperson, street stall

Some related occupations classified elsewhere:
- Vendor, refreshments/cinema – 9111
- Vendor, street/food – 9111
- Vendor, street/non-food products – 9112

MAJOR GROUP **6**
SKILLED AGRICULTURAL AND FISHERY WORKERS

Skilled agricultural and fishery workers grow and harvest field or tree and shrub crops, gather wild fruits and plants, breed, tend or hunt animals, produce a variety of animal husbandry products, cultivate, conserve and exploit forests, breed or catch fish and cultivate or gather other forms of aquatic life in order to provide food, shelter and income for themselves and their households. Most occupations in this major group require skills at the second ISCO skill level.

Tasks performed by skilled agricultural and fishery workers usually include: preparing the soil; sowing, planting, spraying, fertilising and harvesting field crops; growing fruit and other tree and shrub crops; growing garden vegetables and horticultural products; gathering wild fruits and plants; breeding, raising, tending or hunting animals mainly to obtain meat, milk, hair, fur, skin, sericultural, apiarian or other products; cultivating, conserving and exploiting forests; breeding or catching fish; cultivating or gathering other forms of aquatic life; storing and carrying out some basic processing of their produce; selling their products to purchasers, marketing organisations or at markets. Supervision of other workers may be included.

Occupations in this major group are classified into the following sub-major groups:

61   Market-oriented skilled agricultural and fishery workers

62   Subsistence agricultural and fishery workers

Note
The division between the two sub-major groups in this major group, namely 61, *Market-oriented skilled agricultural and fishery workers,* and 62, *Subsistence agricultural and fishery workers,* should reflect differences in the degree of market orientation which are correlated with differences in organisation of work, quality control, use of commercial or high-yield seeds and fodder, use of traditional or modern techniques, irrigation, formal credit arrangements and degree and type of marketing arrangements for the products. Subsistence agricultural and fishery workers may market a part of their produce to obtain cash for purchasing basic goods, paying taxes, etc., but, as a rule, they do not have any of the advantages that go with formal credit or marketing arrangements.

Workers in agriculture and fishing with mainly managerial tasks should be classified into one of the following unit groups: 1210, *Directors and chief executives;* 1221, *Production and operations department managers in agriculture, hunting, forestry and fishing;* or 1311, *General managers in agriculture, hunting, forestry and fishing.* Workers who mainly operate agricultural and forestry machinery should be classified into Minor group 833, *Agricultural and other mobile-plant operators.* Workers with simple and routine tasks – such as helpers and labourers – which mainly entail the use of hand-held tools and some physical effort, and which require little or no previous experience and understanding of the work and only limited initiative or judgement, should be classified into Minor group 921, *Agricultural, fishery and related labourers.*

6

SUB-MAJOR GROUP **61**
MARKET-ORIENTED SKILLED AGRICULTURAL AND FISHERY WORKERS

Market-oriented skilled agricultural and fishery workers plan and carry out the necessary operations to grow and harvest field or tree and shrub crops, gather wild fruits and plants, breed, tend or hunt animals, produce a variety of animal husbandry products, cultivate, conserve and exploit forests, breed or catch fish and cultivate or gather other forms of aquatic life, for sale or delivery on a regular basis to wholesale buyers, marketing organisations or at markets.

Tasks performed by workers in this sub-major group usually include: preparing the soil; sowing, planting, spraying, fertilising and harvesting field crops; growing fruit and other tree and shrub crops; growing garden vegetables and horticultural products; growing or gathering wild fruits, medicinal and other plants; raising, breeding, tending or hunting animals mainly to obtain meat, milk, hair, fur, skin, sericultural, apiarian or other products; cultivating, conserving and exploiting forests; breeding and raising fish or catching them; cultivating or gathering other forms of aquatic life; storing and carrying out some basic processing of their produce; selling their products to purchasers, marketing organisations or at markets. Supervision of other workers may be included.

Occupations in this sub-major group are classified into the following minor groups:

611   Market gardeners and crop growers

612   Market-oriented animal producers and related workers

613   Market-oriented crop and animal producers

614   Forestry and related workers

615   Fishery workers, hunters and trappers

Note

Workers in agriculture and fishing with mainly managerial tasks should be classified into one of the following unit groups: 1210, *Directors and chief executives;* 1221, *Production and operations department managers in agriculture, hunting, forestry and fishing;* or 1311, *General managers in agriculture, hunting, forestry and fishing.* Workers who mainly operate agricultural and forestry machinery should be classified into Minor group 833, *Agricultural and other mobile plant operators.* Workers with simple and routine tasks — such as helpers and labourers — which mainly entail the use of hand-held tools and some physical effort, and which require little or no previous experience and understanding of the work and only limited initiative or judgement, should be classified into Minor group 921, *Agricultural, fishery and related labourers.*

MINOR GROUP **611**
MARKET GARDENERS AND CROP GROWERS

Market gardeners and crop growers plan and carry out the necessary operations to grow and harvest field crops, to grow fruit and other tree and shrub crops, to grow garden vegetables and medicinal and other plants, and to produce horticultural and horticultural nurseries products, for sale or delivery on a regular basis to wholesale buyers, marketing organisations or at markets.

Tasks performed usually include: determining kinds and amounts of field, tree and shrub crops to be grown, as well as vegetables and horticultural products, including those of horticultural nurseries; purchasing seeds, bulbs and fertiliser; renting or investing in land and land improvements, buildings, working animals, equipment and machinery; preparing land, sowing, planting, cultivating and harvesting various crops; tending working animals and maintaining farm buildings, machinery and equipment; producing saplings, bulbs and seeds; storing and carrying out some basic processing of their produce; delivering or marketing farm products. Supervision of other workers may be included.

Occupations in this minor group are classified into the following unit groups:

6111 Field crop and vegetable growers

6112 Tree and shrub crop growers

6113 Gardeners, horticultural and nursery growers

6114 Mixed-crop growers

Note

Workers in agriculture and fishing with mainly managerial tasks should be classified into one of the following unit groups: 1210, *Directors and chief executives*; 1221, *Production and operations department managers in agriculture, hunting, forestry and fishing;* or 1311, *General managers in agriculture, hunting forestry and fishing.* Workers who mainly operate agricultural and forestry machinery should be classified into Minor group 833, *Agricultural and other mobile plant operators.* Workers with simple and routine tasks – such as helpers and labourers – which mainly entail the use of hand-held tools and some physical effort, and which require little or no previous experience and understanding of the work and only limited initiative or judgement, should be classified into Minor group 921, *Agricultural, fishery and related labourers.*

6111 FIELD CROP AND VEGETABLE GROWERS

Field crop and vegetable growers plan and carry out the necessary operations to grow and harvest various types of field crops such as wheat and other cereals, rice, beetroot, sugar-cane, ground-nuts, tobacco, reeds or other field crops and potatoes, cabbages or other field vegetables, for sale or delivery on a regular basis to wholesale buyers, marketing organisations or at markets.

Tasks include –

(a) determining kinds and amounts of crops to be grown;

(b) purchasing seeds, fertiliser and other supplies;

(c) renting or investing in land and land improvements, buildings, working animals, equipment and machinery;

(d) performing farm operations such as land preparation, sowing, planting, cultivating and harvesting crops and field vegetables;

(e) storing and carrying out some basic processing of their produce;

(f) tending working animals and maintaining farm buildings, machinery and equipment;

(g) delivering or marketing farm products;

(h) performing related tasks;

(i) supervising other workers.

6

Examples of the occupations classified here:

- Farm worker, skilled/field crops
- Farmer, cereal
- Farmer, cotton
- Farmer, field crop
- Farmer, rice
- Farmer, sugar-cane

Some related occupations classified elsewhere:

- Department manager, production and operations/agriculture – 1221
- General manager, agriculture – 1311
- Labourer, farm – 9211
- Managing director, enterprise/agriculture – 1210
- Operator, agricultural machinery – 8331

6112 TREE AND SHRUB CROP GROWERS

Tree and shrub crop growers plan and carry out the necessary operations to grow and harvest trees and shrubs, such as fruit and nut trees, tea and coffee bushes, grape vines, berry-bearing bushes, cocoa trees and rubber trees and to collect sap, for sale or delivery on a regular basis to wholesale buyers, marketing organisations or at markets.

Tasks include –

(a) determining kinds and amounts of crops to be grown;
(b) purchasing seeds, fertiliser and other supplies;
(c) renting or investing in land and land improvements, buildings, working animals, equipment and machinery;
(d) performing farm operations such as land preparation, sowing, planting and tending trees or bushes, collecting sap and harvesting crops;
(e) storing and carrying out some basic processing of their produce;
(f) tending working animals and maintaining farm buildings, machinery and equipment;
(g) delivering or marketing farm products;
(h) performing related tasks;
(i) supervising other workers.

Examples of the occupations classified here:

- Farm worker, skilled/shrub crop
- Farmer, fruit
- Farmer, rubber
- Farmer, tea
- Farmer, vineyard

Some related occupations classified elsewhere:

- Department manager, production and operations/agriculture – 1221
- General manager, agriculture – 1311
- Labourer, farm – 9211
- Managing director, enterprise/agriculture – 1210
- Operator, agricultural machinery – 8331

6113 GARDENERS, HORTICULTURAL AND NURSERY GROWERS

Gardeners, horticultural and nursery growers plan and carry out the necessary operations to grow vegetables by intensive cultivation techniques, to cultivate trees, shrubs, flowers and other plants, and to produce saplings, bulbs and seeds, for sale or delivery on a regular basis to wholesale buyers, marketing organisations or at markets.

Tasks include –

(a) determining kinds and amounts of vegetables, horticultural and nursery products to be grown;
(b) purchasing seeds, bulbs, fertiliser and other supplies;
(c) renting or investing in land and land improvements, buildings, working animals, equipment and machinery;
(d) performing farm operations such as land preparation, sowing, growing vegetables by intensive cultivation, cultivating flowers, trees or bushes and harvesting crops;
(e) producing saplings, bulbs and seeds;
(f) cultivating flowers, trees, shrubs and other plants in parks or public or private gardens;
(g) growing plants for exhibition or medicinal purposes;
(h) delivering or marketing products;

(i) storing and carrying out some basic processing of their produce;

(j) tending working animals and maintaining buildings, machinery and equipment;

(k) performing related tasks;

(l) supervising other workers.

Examples of the occupations classified here:

- Cultivator, mushroom
- Farm worker, skilled/nursery
- Gardener
- Grower, horticultural nursery
- Horticultural grower

Some related occupations classified elsewhere:

- Department manager, production and operations/agriculture − 1221
- General manager, agriculture − 1311
- Labourer, farm − 9211
- Managing director, enterprise/agriculture − 1210
- Operator, agricultural machinery − 8331

6114 MIXED-CROP GROWERS

Mixed-crop growers plan and carry out the necessary operations to grow and harvest specific combinations of field crops, field vegetables, tree and shrub crops, and garden, horticultural and nursery products, for sale or delivery on a regular basis to wholesale buyers, marketing organisations or at markets.

Tasks include −

(a) determining kinds and amounts of crops to be grown;

(b) purchasing seeds, fertiliser and other supplies;

(c) renting or investing in land and land improvements, buildings, working animals, equipment and machinery;

(d) performing farm operations such as land preparation, sowing, planting and tending trees or bushes and cultivating and harvesting crops;

(e) growing vegetables by intensive cultivation, and producing saplings, bulbs and seeds;

(f) cultivating flowers, trees, shrubs and other plants for parks or public or private gardens;

(g) growing plants for exhibition or medicinal purposes;

(h) storing and carrying out some basic processing of their produce;

(i) tending working animals and maintaining buildings, machinery and equipment;

(j) delivering or marketing products;

(k) performing related tasks;

(l) supervising other workers.

Examples of the occupations classified here:

- Farm worker, skilled/mixed crop
- Farmer, mixed crop

Some related occupations classified elsewhere:

- Department manager, production and operations/agriculture − 1221
- General manager, agriculture − 1311
- Labourer, farm − 9211
- Managing director, enterprise/agriculture − 1210
- Operator, agricultural machinery − 8331

MINOR GROUP 612
MARKET-ORIENTED ANIMAL PRODUCERS AND RELATED WORKERS

Market-oriented animal producers and related workers plan and carry out the necessary operations to breed, raise and tend livestock such as cattle, sheep, pigs, goats, horses or other animals, including birds, reptiles, fur-producing animals, poultry, game, and to produce a variety of animal husbandry products, for sale or delivery on a regular basis to wholesale buyers, marketing organisations or at markets.

6

Tasks performed usually include: determining kinds and amounts of livestock, poultry, game, birds, reptiles, bees, silkworms and other animals to be raised; purchasing animals, producing and purchasing fodder and other supplies; renting or investing in grazing land and land improvements, buildings, machinery, livestock and other animals; performing farm operations such as breeding and raising livestock, poultry, etc., and producing various animal husbandry products; storing and carrying out some basic processing of their produce; maintaining farm buildings, machinery and equipment; delivering or marketing farm products. Supervision of other workers may be included.

Occupations in this minor group are classified into the following unit groups:

    6121   Dairy and livestock producers

    6122   Poultry producers

    6123   Apiarists and sericulturists

    6124   Mixed-animal producers

    6129   Market-oriented animal producers and related workers not elsewhere classified

Note

Workers in animal production and breeding with mainly managerial tasks should be classified into one of the following unit groups: 1210, *Directors and chief executives;* 1221, *Production and operations department managers in agriculture, hunting, forestry and fishing;* or 1311, *General managers in agriculture, hunting, forestry and fishing.* Workers who mainly operate agricultural and forestry machinery should be classified into Minor group 833, *Agricultural and other mobile plant operators.* Workers with simple and routine tasks – such as helpers and labourers – which mainly entail the use of hand-held tools and some physical effort, and which require little or no previous experience and understanding of the work and only limited initiative or judgement, should be classified into Minor group 921, *Agricultural, fishery and related labourers.*

6121 DAIRY AND LIVESTOCK PRODUCERS

Dairy and livestock producers plan and carry out the necessary operations to breed, raise and tend livestock such as cattle, sheep, pigs, goats, horses, dogs or cats to be used as working, sporting, or pet animals, as well as for meat, milk, hair, hides and other products, for sale or delivery on a regular basis to wholesale buyers, marketing organisations or at markets.

Tasks include –

(a) determining kinds and amounts of livestock and livestock products to be produced;

(b) purchasing animals, producing and purchasing fodder and other supplies;

(c) renting or investing in grazing land, buildings, equipment and machinery;

(d) breeding, raising and tending livestock;

(e) milking animals and shearing sheep;

(f) killing and skinning animals, and preparing animals or animal products for market;

(g) storing and carrying out some basic processing of their produce;

(h) maintaining farm buildings, machinery and equipment;

(i) delivering or marketing farm products;

(j) performing related tasks;

(k) supervising other workers.

Examples of the occupations classified here:
- Breeder, cat
- Breeder, dog
- Farm worker, skilled/livestock
- Farmer, dairy
- Farmer, horse raising
- Farmer, livestock
- Farmer, sheep
- Farmer, sheep/astrakhan

Some related occupations classified elsewhere:
- Department manager, production and operations/agriculture − 1221
- General manager, agriculture − 1311
- Labourer, farm − 9211
- Managing director, enterprise/agriculture − 1210

6122   POULTRY PRODUCERS

Poultry producers plan and carry out the necessary operations to breed, raise and tend poultry for sale or delivery of eggs, meat or feathers on a regular basis to wholesale buyers, marketing organisations or at markets.

Tasks include −
(a) determining kinds and amounts of poultry and poultry products to be produced;
(b) purchasing chicks, growing and purchasing food and other supplies;
(c) renting or investing in buildings, equipment and machinery;
(d) breeding, raising and tending poultry, and collecting eggs;
(e) killing, dressing and packing poultry for shipment;
(f) storing and carrying out some basic processing of their produce;
(g) maintaining farm buildings, machinery and equipment;
(h) delivering or marketing farm products;
(i) performing related tasks;
(j) supervising other workers.

Examples of the occupations classified here:
- Farm worker, skilled/poultry
- Farmer, poultry

Some related occupations classified elsewhere:
- Department manager, production and operations/agriculture − 1221
- General manager, agriculture − 1311
- Labourer, farm − 9211
- Managing director, enterprise/agriculture − 1210

6123   APIARISTS AND SERICULTURISTS

Apiarists and sericulturists plan and carry out the necessary operations to breed, raise and tend insects such as honey bees, silkworms or other species, for sale or delivery of honey, beeswax, silk cocoons, etc., on a regular basis to wholesale buyers, marketing organisations or at markets.

Tasks include −
(a) determining kinds and amounts of insect products to be produced;
(b) purchasing insects, growing or purchasing food and other supplies;
(c) renting or investing in buildings, equipment and machinery;
(d) breeding, raising and tending insects and collecting their products;
(e) storing and carrying out some basic processing of their produce;
(f) maintaining buildings, machinery and equipment;
(g) delivering or marketing products;
(h) performing related tasks;
(i) supervising other workers.

Examples of the occupations classified here:
- Apiarist
- Apiary worker, skilled
- Sericulturist

Some related occupations classified elsewhere:
- Department manager, production and operations/agriculture − 1221
- General manager, agriculture − 1311
- Labourer, farm − 9211
- Managing director, enterprise/agriculture − 1210

6124 MIXED-ANIMAL PRODUCERS

Mixed-animal producers plan and carry out the necessary operations to breed, raise and tend different types of livestock, such as cattle, sheep, pigs, goats and horses, as well as poultry, and to produce apiarian and sericultural products, for sale or delivery on a regular basis to wholesale buyers, marketing organisations or at markets.

Tasks include –
- (a) deciding on the specific combinations of mixed-animal husbandry;
- (b) determining kinds and amounts of livestock and livestock products, poultry and poultry products, and apiarian and sericultural products to be produced;
- (c) purchasing animals, producing and purchasing fodder, other kinds of food and supplies;
- (d) renting or investing in grazing land, buildings, equipment and machinery;
- (e) breeding, raising and tending the particular combination of livestock, poultry and/or insects;
- (f) milking animals and shearing sheep;
- (g) killing and skinning animals, and preparing animals or animal products for market;
- (h) collecting eggs, honey and other produce;
- (i) storing and carrying out some basic processing of their produce;
- (j) maintaining farm buildings, machinery and equipment;
- (k) delivering or marketing farm products;
- (l) performing related tasks;
- (m) supervising other workers.

Examples of the occupations classified here:
- Farm worker, skilled/mixed-animal husbandry
- Farmer, mixed-animal husbandry

Some related occupations classified elsewhere:
- Department manager, production and operations/agriculture – 1221
- General manager, agriculture – 1311
- Labourer, farm – 9211
- Managing director, enterprise/agriculture – 1210

6129 MARKET-ORIENTED ANIMAL PRODUCERS AND RELATED WORKERS NOT ELSEWHERE CLASSIFIED

This unit group covers market-oriented animal producers and related workers not classified elsewhere in Minor group 612, *Market-oriented animal producers and related workers*.

For instance, here should be classified those who are engaged in breeding, raising and tending wild mammals, game birds and other birds, snails, non-domesticated fur-giving animals, snakes and other reptiles, as well as various insects and animals used for laboratory tests, for sale or delivery on a regular basis to wholesale buyers, marketing organisations, zoos and circuses, or at markets. Here should also be classified those who look after or train animals in animal reserves, stables, zoos, circuses, research organisations, animal homes, and similar institutions.

In such cases tasks would include –
- (a) buying or setting up necessary buildings, open or sheltered space, equipment, etc., and maintaining them;
- (b) determining kinds and amounts of animals to be raised;
- (c) purchasing animals, growing or purchasing food and other supplies;
- (d) breeding, raising, feeding and tending animals;
- (e) killing and skinning animals, and preparing animals or animal products for market;
- (f) storing and carrying out some basic processing of their produce;
- (g) protecting animals, especially in animal reserves;
- (h) training animals for racing, circus performances and the like;
- (i) delivering or marketing products;
- (j) performing related tasks;
- (k) supervising other workers.

Examples of the occupations classified here:
- Breeder, bird
- Breeder, game bird
- Breeder, laboratory animal/mice
- Breeder, lion

- Breeder, snail
- Farmer, fur/non-domesticated animals
- Keeper, animal reserve
- Keeper, zoo

Some related occupations classified elsewhere:
- Game-warden − 5169

MINOR GROUP 613
MARKET-ORIENTED CROP AND ANIMAL PRODUCERS

Market-oriented crop and animal producers plan and carry out the necessary operations for mixed farming of the kind that produces a combination of both crops and animals and related products, for delivery or sale on a regular basis to wholesale buyers, marketing organisations or at markets.

Tasks performed usually include: determining kinds and amounts of field, tree and other crops to be grown and animals to be raised; purchasing seeds, fertiliser, fodder and other supplies; renting or investing in arable or grazing land, animals, buildings and machinery; performing farm operations such as land preparation, sowing, cultivating and harvesting crops; breeding, raising and tending animals, and producing various animal husbandry products; maintaining farm buildings, machinery and equipment; storing and carrying out some basic processing of their produce; delivering or marketing farm products. Supervision of other workers may be included.

Occupations in this minor group are classified into the following unit group:

6130 Market-oriented crop and animal producers

Note

Workers in agriculture and fishing with mainly managerial tasks should be classified into one of the following unit groups: 1210, *Directors and chief executives;* 1221, *Production and operations department managers in agriculture, hunting, forestry and fishing;* or 1311, *General managers in agriculture, hunting, forestry and fishing.* Workers who mainly operate agricultural and forestry machinery should be classified into Minor group 833, *Agricultural and other mobile plant operators.* Workers with simple and routine tasks − such as helpers and labourers − which mainly entail the use of hand-held tools and some physical effort, and which require little or no previous experience and understanding of the work and only limited initiative or judgement, should be classified into Minor group 921, *Agricultural, fishery and related labourers.*

6130 MARKET-ORIENTED CROP AND ANIMAL PRODUCERS

Market-oriented crop and animal producers plan and carry out the necessary operations to grow and harvest field, tree and various other crops, as well as to breed, raise and tend animals and to produce a variety of animal husbandry products, for sale or delivery on a regular basis to wholesale buyers, marketing organisations or at markets.

Tasks include −

(a) determining kinds and amounts of crops to be grown and animals to be raised;

(b) purchasing seeds, fertiliser, and other supplies;

(c) renting or investing in land and land improvements, buildings, machinery, livestock and other animals;

6

(d) performing operations such as land preparation, sowing, planting, cultivating and harvesting crops;

(e) producing or buying fodder and other food supplies;

(f) breeding, raising and tending animals;

(g) killing and skinning animals, and preparing animals or animal products for market;

(h) storing and carrying out some basic processing of their produce;

(i) maintaining farm buildings, machinery and equipment;

(j) delivering or marketing farm products;

(k) performing related tasks;

(l) supervising other workers.

Examples of the occupations classified here:

- Farm worker, skilled/mixed farming
- Farmer, mixed farming

Some related occupations classified elsewhere:

- Department manager, production and operations/agriculture − 1221
- General manager, agriculture − 1311
- Labourer, farm − 9211
- Managing director, enterprise/agriculture − 1210

MINOR GROUP 614
FORESTRY AND RELATED WORKERS

Forestry and related workers plan and carry out the necessary operations to cultivate, conserve and exploit forests, for sale or delivery of forestry products on a regular basis to wholesale buyers, marketing organisations or at markets.

Tasks performed usually include: establishing and caring for forest stands; locating trees to be felled and estimating volume of timber; felling trees and sawing them into logs; trimming and topping trees; shaping rough wooden products from logs at felling site; stacking logs, loading them in chutes or floating them down rivers; operating a simple kiln or digester to convert wood into charcoal or extract crude turpentine from wood; keeping watch to detect forest fires and participating in fire-fighting operations. Supervision of other workers may be included.

Occupations in this minor group are classified into the following unit groups:

6141   Forestry workers and loggers

6142   Charcoal burners and related workers

Note

Workers in agriculture and fishing with mainly managerial tasks should be classified into one of the following unit groups: 1210, *Directors and chief executives;* 1221, *Production and operations department managers in agriculture, hunting, forestry and fishing;* or 1311, *General managers in agriculture, hunting, forestry and fishing.* Workers who mainly operate agricultural and forestry machinery should be classified into Minor group 833, *Agricultural and other mobile-plant operators.* Workers with simple and routine tasks − such as helpers and labourers − which mainly entail the use of hand-held tools and some physical effort, and which require little or no previous experience and understanding of the work and only limited initiative or judgement, should be classified into Minor group 921, *Agricultural, fishery and related labourers.*

6141 FORESTRY WORKERS AND LOGGERS

Forestry workers and loggers carry out the necessary operations to cultivate, conserve and exploit forests, for sale or delivery of forestry products on a regular basis to wholesale buyers, marketing organisations or at markets.

Tasks include –

(a) establishing and caring for forest stands;
(b) locating trees to be felled and estimating volume of timber;
(c) trimming, topping and felling trees and sawing them into logs;
(d) shaping rough wooden products from logs at felling site;
(e) stacking logs, loading them in chutes or floating them down rivers;
(f) keeping watch to detect forest fires and participating in firefighting operations;
(g) delivering or marketing forestry products;
(h) performing related tasks;
(i) supervising other workers.

Examples of the occupations classified here:
- Climber, logging
- Cruiser, timber
- Feller-bucker, tree
- Forestry worker, skilled
- Logger

Some related occupations classified elsewhere:
- Department manager, production and operations/forestry – 1221
- General manager, forestry – 1311
- Labourer, forestry – 9212
- Managing director, enterprise/forestry – 1210
- Operator, forestry machinery – 8331

6142 CHARCOAL BURNERS AND RELATED WORKERS

Charcoal burners and related workers carry out the necessary operations to convert wood into charcoal or to extract crude turpentine from wood, using traditional techniques.

Tasks include –

(a) operating a simple kiln to convert wood into charcoal by a slow-burning process;
(b) operating a simple digester or still at the tree-felling site to obtain or distil crude wood turpentine;
(c) performing related tasks;
(d) supervising other workers.

Examples of the occupations classified here:
- Burner, charcoal
- Forestry worker, skilled/wood distillation (traditional techniques)

MINOR GROUP 615
FISHERY WORKERS, HUNTERS AND TRAPPERS

Fishery workers, hunters and trappers catch, breed and cultivate fish and other forms of aquatic life, or hunt and trap mammals, birds and reptiles, for sale or delivery, on a regular basis, of the animals or animal products to wholesale buyers, marketing organisations or at markets.

Tasks performed usually include: preparing nets and other fishing gear and equipment; operating fishing vessels to, from and at fishing grounds; baiting, setting and hauling in fishing gear; cleaning, freezing, icing or salting catch on- or offshore; breeding, raising and cultivating fish, oysters, mussels, or other forms of aquatic life; hunting or trapping mammals, birds or reptiles. Supervision of other workers may be included.

6

Occupations in this minor group are classified into the following unit groups:

6151   Aquatic-life cultivation workers

6152   Inland and coastal waters fishery workers

6153   Deep-sea fishery workers

6154   Hunters and trappers

Note
Workers in agriculture and fishing with mainly managerial tasks should be classified into one of the following unit groups: 1210, *Directors and chief executives;* 1221, *Production and operations department managers in agriculture, hunting, forestry and fishing;* or 1311, *General managers in agriculture, hunting, forestry and fishing.* Workers who mainly operate agricultural and forestry machinery should be classified into Minor group 833, *Agricultural and other mobile plant operators.* Workers with simple and routine tasks – such as helpers and labourers – which mainly entail the use of hand-held tools and some physical effort, and which require little or no previous experience and understanding of the work and only limited initiative or judgement, should be classified into Minor group 921, *Agricultural, fishery and related labourers.*

6151   AQUATIC-LIFE CULTIVATION WORKERS

Aquatic-life cultivation workers breed and raise fish and cultivate mussels, oysters and other forms of aquatic life, for sale or delivery on a regular basis to wholesale buyers, marketing organisations or at markets.

Tasks include –
(a)   renting or investing in buildings, equipment and machinery;
(b)   purchasing food and other supplies;
(c)   breeding, raising and cultivating fish, mussels, oysters and other forms of aquatic life;
(d)   killing and preparing fish and other products for shipment;
(e)   cleaning, freezing, icing or salting catch on- or offshore;
(f)   maintaining buildings, machinery and equipment;
(g)   delivering or marketing products;
(h)   performing related tasks;
(i)   supervising other workers.

Examples of the occupations classified here:
- Cultivator, algae
- Cultivator, pearl
- Farm worker, skilled/fish
- Farm worker, skilled/seafood
- Farmer, fish
- Farmer, oyster
- Farmer, seafood

Some related occupations classified elsewhere:
- Department manager, production and operations/fishing – 1221
- General manager, fishing – 1311
- Labourer, fishery – 9213
- Managing director, enterprise/fishing – 1210

6152   INLAND AND COASTAL WATERS FISHERY WORKERS

Inland and coastal waters fishery workers, alone or as members of fishing-vessel crews, catch fish or gather other forms of aquatic life in inland or coastal waters, for sale or delivery on a regular basis to wholesale buyers, marketing organisations or at markets.

Tasks include –
(a)   preparing and repairing nets and other fishing gear and equipment;
(b)   operating fishing vessels to, from and at fishing grounds;
(c)   baiting, setting and hauling in fishing gear;
(d)   gathering different forms of aquatic life from shores and shallow waters;
(e)   cleaning, freezing, icing or salting catch on- or offshore;
(f)   delivering or marketing products;
(g)   performing related tasks;
(h)   supervising other workers.

Examples of the occupations classified here:
- Diver, oyster
- Diver, sponge
- Fisherman, coastal waters
- Fisherwoman, inland waters

Some related occupations classified elsewhere:
- Department manager, production and operations/fishing – 1221
- General manager, fishing – 1311
- Labourer, fishery – 9213
- Managing director, enterprise/fishing – 1210

6153   DEEP-SEA FISHERY WORKERS

Deep-sea fishery workers, as members of fishing vessel crews, catch deep-sea fish, for sale or delivery on a regular basis to wholesale buyers, marketing organisations or at markets.

Tasks include –
(a) preparing and repairing nets and other fishing gear and equipment;
(b) operating fishing vessels to, from and at fishing grounds;
(c) baiting, setting and hauling in fishing gear;
(d) cleaning, freezing, icing or salting catch on- or offshore;
(e) delivering or marketing catch;
(f) performing related tasks;
(g) supervising other workers.

Examples of the occupations classified here:
- Fisherman, deep-sea
- Fisherwoman, deep-sea

Some related occupations classified elsewhere:
- Department manager, production and operations/fishing – 1221

- General manager, fishing – 1311
- Labourer, fishery – 9213
- Managing director, enterprise/fishing – 1210

6154   HUNTERS AND TRAPPERS

Hunters and trappers catch and kill mammals, birds or reptiles mainly for meat, skin, feathers and other products, for sale or delivery on a regular basis to wholesale buyers, marketing organisations or at markets.

Tasks include –
(a) setting traps to catch mammals, birds or reptiles;
(b) killing trapped or free mammals, birds or reptiles with firearms or other weapons;
(c) skinning and otherwise treating killed mammals, birds or reptiles to obtain desired products for sale or delivery;
(d) delivering or selling trapped live mammals, birds or reptiles;
(e) repairing and maintaining equipment;
(f) performing related tasks;
(g) supervising other workers.

Examples of the occupations classified here:
- Hunter, seal
- Hunter, whale
- Trapper, fur

Some related occupations classified elsewhere:
- Department manager, production and operations/hunting – 1221
- General manager, hunting – 1311
- Labourer, hunting – 9213
- Labourer, trapping – 9213
- Managing director, enterprise/hunting – 1210

SUB-MAJOR GROUP **62**
SUBSISTENCE AGRICULTURAL AND FISHERY WORKERS

Subsistence agricultural and fishery workers grow and harvest field or tree and shrub crops, grow vegetables and fruit, tend or hunt animals, gather wild fruits and plants, catch fish and gather other forms of aquatic life in order to provide food, shelter and a minimum of cash income for themselves and their households.

Tasks performed by workers in this sub-major group usually include: preparing the soil; sowing, planting, tending and harvesting field crops; growing vegetables; growing and gathering fruit and other tree and shrub crops; gathering wild fruits, medicinal and other plants; tending, feeding or hunting animals mainly to obtain meat, milk, hair, skin or other products; gathering firewood; fetching water; breeding or catching fish and cultivating or gathering other forms of aquatic life; building shelters and making simple tools, clothes and utensils for use by the household; storing and carrying out some basic processing of their produce; selling some products at local markets.

It should be noted that the necessary skills — an understanding of the natural environment and the crops and animals worked with, as well as manual strength and dexterity — are usually acquired by working from childhood with other members of the household to produce the necessities for subsisting.

Occupations in this sub-major group are classified into the following minor group:

621 Subsistence agricultural and fishery workers

MINOR GROUP **621**
SUBSISTENCE AGRICULTURAL AND FISHERY WORKERS

Subsistence agricultural and fishery workers grow and harvest field or tree and shrub crops, grow vegetables and fruit, tend or hunt animals, gather wild fruits and plants, catch fish and gather other forms of aquatic life in order to provide food, shelter and a minimum of cash income for themselves and their households.

Tasks performed usually include: preparing the soil; sowing, planting, tending and harvesting field crops; growing vegetables, plants, fruit and other tree and shrub crops; gathering wild fruits, medicinal and other plants; tending, feeding or hunting animals mainly to obtain meat, milk, hair, skin or other products; fetching water; gathering firewood; catching fish and gathering other forms of aquatic life; building shelters and making simple tools, clothes and utensils for use by the household; storing and carrying out some basic processing of their produce; selling some products at local markets.

Occupations in this minor group are classified into the following unit group:

6210 Subsistence agricultural and fishery workers

Note

Further subdivision of Minor group 621, *Subsistence agricultural and fishery workers,* should reflect differences in required skills due to factors such as differences in climate and other natural conditions.

6210 SUBSISTENCE AGRICULTURAL AND FISHERY WORKERS

Subsistence agricultural and fishery workers grow and harvest field or tree and shrub crops, grow vegetables and fruit, gather wild fruits, medicinal and other plants, tend or hunt animals, catch fish and gather various forms of aquatic life in order to provide food, shelter and a minimum of cash income for themselves and their households.

Tasks include –

(a) preparing the soil, sowing, planting, tending and harvesting field crops;
(b) growing vegetables, fruit and other tree and shrub crops;
(c) gathering wild fruits, medicinal and other plants;
(d) tending, feeding or hunting animals mainly to obtain meat, milk, hair, skin or other products;
(e) fetching water and gathering firewood;
(f) catching fish and gathering other forms of aquatic life;
(g) storing or carrying out some basic processing of their produce;
(h) building shelters and making simple tools, clothes and utensils for use by the household;
(i) selling some products at local markets;
(j) performing related tasks.

Examples of the occupations classified here:

- Farm worker, skilled/subsistence farming
- Farmer, subsistence farming

Some related occupations classified elsewhere:

- Labourer, farm – 9211
- Labourer, fishery – 9213

MAJOR GROUP **7**
CRAFT AND RELATED TRADES WORKERS

Craft and related trades workers apply their specific knowledge and skills in the fields of mining and construction, form metal, erect metal structures, set machine tools, or make, fit, maintain and repair machinery, equipment or tools, carry out printing work as well as produce or process foodstuffs, textiles, or wooden, metal and other articles, including handicraft goods.

The work is carried out by hand and by hand-powered and other tools which are used to reduce the amount of physical effort and time required for specific tasks, as well as to improve the quality of the products. The tasks call for an understanding of all stages of the production process, the materials and tools used, and the nature and purpose of the final product. Most occupations in this major group require skills at the second ISCO skill level.

Tasks performed by craft and related trades workers usually include: extracting and working solid minerals; constructing, maintaining and repairing buildings and other structures; casting, welding and shaping metal; installing and erecting heavy metal structures, tackle and related equipment; making machinery, tools, equipment, and other metal articles; setting for operators, or setting and operating various machine tools; fitting, maintaining and repairing industrial machinery, including engines and vehicles, as well as electrical and electronic instruments and other equipment; making precision instruments, jewellery, household and other precious-metal articles, pottery, glass and related products; producing handicrafts; executing printing work; producing and processing foodstuffs and various articles made of wood, textiles, leather and related materials. Supervision of other workers may be included.

Occupations in this major group are classified into the following sub-major groups:

71 Extraction and building trades workers

72 Metal, machinery and related trades workers

73 Precision, handicraft, printing and related trades workers

74 Other craft and related trades workers

Note

Occupations are classified into Major group 8, *Plant and machine operators and assemblers,* if the tasks call mainly for experience with and an understanding of the machinery operated and monitored.

Occupations are classified into Major group 9, *Elementary occupations,* if the tasks are of a simple and routine nature, mainly entail the use of hand-held tools, some physical effort, little or no previous experience and understanding of the work, and limited initiative or judgement.

7

SUB-MAJOR GROUP **71**
EXTRACTION AND BUILDING TRADES WORKERS

Extraction and building trades workers extract and work solid minerals from underground or surface mines or quarries, shape and finish stone for building and other purposes, or construct, maintain and repair buildings and other structures.

The work is carried out by hand and by hand-powered and other tools which are used to reduce the amount of physical effort and time required for specific tasks, as well as to improve the quality of the products. The tasks call for an understanding of the work organisation, the materials and tools used, and the nature and purpose of the final product.

Tasks performed by workers in this sub-major group usually include: extracting and working solid minerals from underground or surface mines or quarries; cutting and shaping stone for building and other purposes; constructing, maintaining and repairing buildings and other structures; applying paint to buildings and other structures, as well as to various products such as vehicles, or various manufactured articles, or covering interior walls with wallpaper or fabric; cleaning chimneys and exterior surfaces of buildings and other structures. Supervision of other workers may be included.

Occupations in this sub-major group are classified into the following minor groups:

> **711 Miners, shotfirers, stone cutters and carvers**
> **712 Building frame and related trades workers**
> **713 Building finishers and related trades workers**
> **714 Painters, building structure cleaners and related trades workers**

Note

Occupations are classified into Major group 8, *Plant and machine operators and assemblers,* if the tasks call mainly for experience with and an understanding of the machinery operated and monitored.

Occupations are classified into Major group 9, *Elementary occupations,* if the tasks are of a simple and routine nature, mainly entail the use of hand-held tools, some physical effort, little or no previous experience and understanding of the work, and limited initiative or judgement.

MINOR GROUP **711**
MINERS, SHOTFIRERS, STONE CUTTERS AND CARVERS

Miners, shotfirers, stone cutters and carvers extract solid minerals from underground or surface mines or quarries, charge and detonate explosives, or cut and shape stone for building and other purposes.

Tasks performed usually include: extracting solid minerals from underground or surface mines or quarries; charging and detonating explosives in mines, quarries, building sites and other places; cutting and shaping stone for building and other purposes. Supervision of other workers may be included.

Occupations in this minor group are classified into the following unit groups:

7111   Miners and quarry workers

7112   Shotfirers and blasters

7113   Stone splitters, cutters and carvers

Note

Occupations are classified into Major group 8, *Plant and machine operators and assemblers,* if the tasks call mainly for experience with and an understanding of the machinery operated and monitored.

Occupations are classified into Major group 9, *Elementary occupations,* if the tasks are of a simple and routine nature, mainly entail the use of hand-held tools, some physical effort, little or no previous experience and understanding of the work, and limited initiative or judgement.

7111   MINERS AND QUARRY WORKERS

Miners and quarry workers extract solid minerals from underground or surface mines or quarries.

Tasks include –
(a) extracting coal, ores and other solid minerals from underground or surface mines;
(b) extracting granite, limestone, slate, flint or other kinds of rocks from quarries;
(c) setting and operating machines which cut channels or drill blasting holes into the open face of mines or quarries;
(d) cutting, fitting and installing wood or steel props, pillars and arches to support walls and roof of underground workings;
(e) collecting samples of coal or ore for laboratory analysis;
(f) extracting chalk, clay, gravel or sand from open pits;
(g) performing related tasks;
(h) supervising other workers.

Examples of the occupations classified here:
- Miner
- Quarrier

Some related occupations classified elsewhere:
- Machine-operator, drilling/mine – 8111
- Machine-operator, mining/continuous – 8111

7112   SHOTFIRERS AND BLASTERS

Shotfirers and blasters determine location and force of explosions required, charge and detonate explosives to fragment or dislodge coal, ores, rock or other solid minerals in mines or quarries, or to clear building sites and similar places.

Tasks include –
(a) ensuring observance of workplace safety procedures and regulations;
(b) determining location of explosions required and giving instructions on holes to be drilled;
(c) deciding on force required and placing correct quantity of explosives, and preparing blasting site;
(d) firing blasting-charge in mines or quarries;
(e) performing related tasks;
(f) supervising other workers.

Examples of the occupations classified here:

- Blaster
- Shotfirer,

7113 STONE SPLITTERS, CUTTERS AND CARVERS

Stone splitters, cutters and carvers break quarried stone into slabs or blocks, or by using hand or hand-powered tools cut, shape and finish stone for building, ornamental, monumental and other purposes.

Tasks include –

(a) driving wedges into quarried stone to break it into slabs or blocks;

(b) selecting and grading slabs and blocks of granite, marble, and other stone;

(c) cutting, shaping and finishing building and monumental stone such as granite or marble by using hand or hand-powered tools;

(d) making patterns and marking shapes on stone for subsequent sawing, planing, drilling and other dressing and cutting operations;

(e) cutting and carving characters, figures or designs on stone blocks used for monuments or memorials;

(f) setting stone in the erection of monuments and memorials;

(g) cutting and carving characters, figures or designs on stone used for decorative facings on buildings;

(h) performing related tasks;

(i) supervising other workers.

Examples of the occupations classified here:

- Carver, stone
- Cutter, stone
- Mason, monument
- Splitter, stone

Some related occupations classified elsewhere:

- Machine-operator, carving/stone products – 8212
- Machine-operator, cutting/stone products – 8212
- Machine-operator, splitting/stone – 8112
- Sculptor – 2452
- Stonemason, construction – 7122

MINOR GROUP 712
BUILDING FRAME AND RELATED TRADES WORKERS

Building frame and related trades workers construct, maintain and repair foundations, walls and other main parts of buildings and other constructions, both internally and externally.

Tasks performed usually include: erecting and repairing small and large buildings and other structures by using traditional building techniques and materials such as bamboo, hay, straw or mud; erecting and repairing foundations, walls and structures of brick, stone and similar materials; erecting reinforced concrete frameworks and structures and finishing cement surfaces; erecting and repairing various types of wooden structures and fittings; performing miscellaneous construction and building maintenance tasks. Supervision of other workers may be included.

Occupations in this minor group are classified into the following unit groups:

7121 Builders, traditional materials

7122 Bricklayers and stonemasons

7123 Concrete placers, concrete finishers and related workers

7124   Carpenters and joiners

7129   Building frame and related trades workers not elsewhere classified

Note

Occupations are classified into Major group 8, *Plant and machine operators and assemblers,* if the tasks call mainly for experience with and an understanding of the machinery operated and monitored.

Occupations are classified into Major group 9, *Elementary occupations,* if the tasks are of a simple and routine nature, mainly entail the use of hand-held tools, some physical effort, little or no previous experience and understanding of the work, and limited initiative or judgement.

It should also be noted that workers who prepare, assemble and erect structural metal frameworks are classified into Unit group 7214, *Structural-metal preparers and erectors.*

7121   BUILDERS, TRADITIONAL MATERIALS

Builders, traditional materials erect, maintain and repair small and large buildings and other structures by using traditional building techniques and materials such as bamboo, hay, straw, reeds, mud, planks, poles or leaves.

Tasks include –

(a)   preparing ground for erecting building or other structures;

(b)   collecting necessary materials;

(c)   erecting structures to support roof, and building and covering walls with mud, straw or other materials;

(d)   fixing rafters to roof and covering with roofing material;

(e)   levelling floor to make it smooth and serviceable;

(f)   maintaining and repairing existing structures;

(g)   performing related tasks;

(h)   supervising other workers.

Examples of the occupations classified here:

- Housebuilder, traditional materials

7122   BRICKLAYERS AND STONEMASONS

Bricklayers and stonemasons erect and repair foundations, walls and structures of brick, stone and similar materials.

Tasks include –

(a)   laying stone, brick, hollow tile and similar building blocks to construct or repair walls, partitions, fireplaces and other structures such as smokestacks, furnaces, converters, kilns and ovens, piers and abutments;

(b)   laying walks, curbs and pavements of stone;

(c)   performing related tasks;

(d)   supervising other workers.

Examples of the occupations classified here:

- Bricklayer, construction
- Stonemason, construction

7123   CONCRETE PLACERS, CONCRETE FINISHERS AND RELATED WORKERS

Concrete placers, concrete finishers and related workers erect reinforced concrete frameworks and structures, make forms for moulding concrete, reinforce concrete surfaces, cement openings in walls or casings for wells, finish and repair cement surfaces and carry out terrazzo work.

Tasks include –

(a)   constructing and repairing reinforced concrete floors, walls, tanks, silos and other concrete structures;

(b)   making shuttering or assembling prefabricated forms for moulding concrete;

(c)   cementing openings in walls or casings for wells;

(d) finishing and smoothing surfaces of concrete structures;

(e) applying a durable, smooth surfacing composed of cement, sand pigment and marble particles to floors, known as a terrazzo finish;

(f) performing related tasks;

(g) supervising other workers.

Examples of the occupations classified here:
- Finisher, cement
- Placer, concrete
- Terrazzo worker

Some related occupations classified elsewhere:
- Machine-operator, finishing/concrete – 8212
- Operator, road surface laying machinery – 8332

7124 CARPENTERS AND JOINERS

Carpenters and joiners cut, shape, assemble, erect, maintain and repair various types of wooden structures and fittings.

Tasks include –

(a) making, altering and repairing structural and other woodwork at a work-bench and on a construction site;

(b) constructing, erecting and installing heavy-framed wooden structures on building sites;

(c) fitting, assembling and altering internal and external fixtures of buildings, such as walls, doors, door and window frames, facings and panelling;

(d) making, repairing and fitting scenic equipment for theatrical performances, motion picture or television productions;

(e) constructing, assembling, altering and repairing wooden fixtures and fittings in train coaches, aircraft, ships, boats, floats, pontoons and other vehicles;

(f) cutting, shaping, fitting and assembling wooden parts, mainly at a work-bench;

(g) performing related tasks;

(h) supervising other workers.

Examples of the occupations classified here:
- Carpenter
- Joiner
- Shipwright, wood

Some related occupations classified elsewhere:
- Cabinet-maker – 7422
- Wheel-wright – 7422

7129 BUILDING FRAME AND RELATED TRADES WORKERS NOT ELSEWHERE CLASSIFIED

This unit group covers building frame and related trades workers not classified elsewhere in Minor group 712, *Building frame and related trades workers.*

For instance, here should be classified those who perform miscellaneous construction and building maintenance tasks.

In such cases tasks would include –

(a) performing miscellaneous construction and building maintenance work on structures such as office buildings, apartment houses, factories and similar establishments in good repair;

(b) performing construction, maintenance or repair work at unusual heights;

(c) erecting temporary metal or wooden scaffolding on building sites;

(d) demolishing buildings and other structures;

(e) performing related tasks;

(f) supervising other workers.

Examples of the occupations classified here:
- Demolition worker
- Housebuilder, non-traditional materials
- Scaffolder
- Steeplejack

Some related occupations classified elsewhere:
- Labourer, construction/buildings – 9313
- Labourer, demolition – 9313

MINOR GROUP **713**
BUILDING FINISHERS AND RELATED TRADES WORKERS

Building finishers and related trades workers cover, apply or install, maintain and repair roofs, floors, walls, insulation systems, glass in windows or other frames, as well as plumbing, piping and electrical systems in buildings and other constructions.

Tasks performed usually include: covering roof frameworks with one or more kinds of material; installing parquet and other kinds of flooring or covering floors and walls with tiles or mosaic panels; applying plaster to walls and ceilings; applying insulating material to walls, floors and ceilings; cutting, fitting and setting glass in windows and similar openings; installing plumbing and pipeline systems; installing electrical wiring and related equipment. Supervision of other workers may be included.

Occupations in this minor group are classified into the following unit groups:

7131   Roofers

7132   Floor layers and tile setters

7133   Plasterers

7134   Insulation workers

7135   Glaziers

7136   Plumbers and pipe fitters

7137   Building and related electricians

Note

Occupations are classified into Major group 8, *Plant and machine operators and assemblers,* if the tasks call mainly for experience with and an understanding of the machinery operated and monitored.

Occupations are classified into Major group 9, *Elementary occupations,* if the tasks are of a simple and routine nature, mainly entail the use of hand-held tools, some physical effort, little or no previous experience and understanding of the work, and limited initiative or judgement.

7131   ROOFERS

Roofers cover, maintain and repair roof frameworks with one or more kinds of material.

Tasks include –
(a) covering roof frameworks with slates and tiles, synthetic materials, asphalt, metal sheets, or thatching materials;
(b) performing related tasks;
(c) supervising other workers.

Examples of the occupations classified here:
- Roofer, asphalt
- Roofer, metal
- Roofer, slate
- Roofer, tile
- Thatcher

7132   FLOOR LAYERS AND TILE SETTERS

Floor layers and tile setters install, maintain and repair parquet and other kinds of flooring, or they cover floors, walls and other surfaces with tiles or mosaic panels for decorative or other purposes.

Tasks include –
(a) preparing floor areas for covering with parquet, tiles or other materials;
(b) assembling parquetry pieces or other materials and laying them on floors according to design and other specifications;
(c) preparing wall areas for covering with tiles or other materials for decorative or other purposes such as acoustical insulation;
(d) setting tiles and constructing and laying mosaic panels to walls, floors and other surfaces;
(e) performing related tasks;
(f) supervising other workers.

Examples of the occupations classified here:
- Parquetry worker
- Setter, marble
- Setter, tile

7133 PLASTERERS

Plasterers install and repair laths and apply plaster to walls and ceilings of buildings.

Tasks include –
(a) installing and repairing laths and applying one or more coats of plaster to interior walls and ceilings of buildings to produce finished surface;
(b) moulding and installing ornamental plaster panels and casting and trimming ornamental plaster cornices;
(c) applying protective and decorative covering of cement, plaster and similar materials to exterior building surfaces;
(d) making and installing decorative plaster fixtures of fibrous plaster;
(e) performing related tasks;
(f) supervising other workers.

Examples of the occupations classified here:
- Plasterer
- Plasterer, ornamental
- Plasterer, stucco

7134 INSULATION WORKERS

Insulation workers apply and repair insulating materials to buildings, boilers, pipes or refrigeration and air-conditioning equipment.

Tasks include –
(a) applying slabs and sheets of insulating or sound-absorbing materials to walls, floors and ceilings of buildings;
(b) blowing and packing insulating or sound-absorbing materials into cavities between walls, floors and ceilings of buildings with power-driven machines;
(c) applying insulating materials to exposed surfaces of equipment such as boilers, pipes and tanks;
(d) insulating refrigeration and air-conditioning equipment;
(e) performing related tasks;
(f) supervising other workers.

Examples of the occupations classified here:
- Insulation worker
- Insulation worker, acoustical
- Insulation worker, boiler and pipe
- Insulation worker, refrigeration and air-conditioning equipment.

Some related occupations classified elsewhere:
- Machine-operator, insulation – 8290

7135 GLAZIERS

Glaziers cut, fit and set glass in windows, doors, shop fronts and other frames.

Tasks include –
(a) selecting glass panes, cutting them to measure and fixing them in windows, doors and partitions of buildings;
(b) fastening glass panes in skylights;
(c) installing flat or curved glass in shop fronts, swing-doors, show-cases, portholes or other openings;
(d) cutting, assembling and installing pieces of glass in lead or copper framework to form decorative windows and panels;
(e) installing ordinary or shatter-proof glass panels in windows, doors and windscreens of vehicles;
(f) performing related tasks;
(g) supervising other workers.

Examples of the occupations classified here:
- Glazier
- Glazier, roofing
- Glazier, vehicle

7136 PLUMBERS AND PIPE FITTERS

Plumbers and pipe fitters assemble, fit, install and repair plumbing fixtures, or pipes and pipeline systems.

Tasks include –

(a) cutting, threading, bending, jointing, assembling, installing, maintaining and repairing pipes, fittings and fixtures of drainage, heating, water supply and sewerage systems;

(b) assembling, installing, maintaining and repairing pipeline systems in ships, aircraft, buildings, industrial plant, etc.;

(c) laying clay, concrete or cast-iron pipes in ditches to form sewers, drains or water mains, or for other purposes;

(d) performing related tasks;

(e) supervising other workers.

Examples of the occupations classified here:

- Fitter, pipe
- Layer, pipe
- Plumber

Some related occupations classified elsewhere:

- Machine-operator, pipe installation – 8290

7137 BUILDING AND RELATED ELECTRICIANS

Building and related electricians install, maintain and repair electrical wiring systems and related equipment.

Tasks include –

(a) installing, maintaining and repairing electrical wiring systems and related equipment in various buildings such as schools, hospitals, commercial establishments, residential buildings and other structures;

(b) installing, maintaining and repairing electrical equipment in theatres and radio or television studios;

(c) performing related tasks;

(d) supervising other workers.

Examples of the occupations classified here:

- Electrician
- Electrician, building repairs

Some related occupations classified elsewhere:

- Fitter, electrical – 7241
- Mechanic, electrical – 7241

MINOR GROUP 714
PAINTERS, BUILDING STRUCTURE CLEANERS AND RELATED TRADES WORKERS

Painters, building structure cleaners and related trades workers prepare surfaces, apply paint and similar materials to buildings and other structures, vehicles, or various manufactured articles, cover interior walls and ceilings with wallpaper, clean chimneys and exterior surfaces of buildings and other structures.

Tasks performed usually include: preparing surfaces and applying paint and similar materials to buildings and other structures; applying paint or varnish to vehicles or various manufactured articles, usually with a hand-spraying device; covering interior walls and ceilings with wallpaper, silk or other fabrics; cleaning chimneys; cleaning exterior surfaces of buildings and other structures. Supervision of other workers may be included.

7

Occupations in this minor group are classified into the following unit groups:

7141   Painters and related workers

7142   Varnishers and related painters

7143   Building structure cleaners

Note

Occupations are classified into Major group 8, *Plant and machine operators and assemblers,* if the tasks call mainly for experience with and an understanding of the machinery operated and monitored.

Occupations are classified into Major group 9, *Elementary occupations,* if the tasks are of a simple and routine nature, mainly entail the use of hand-held tools, some physical effort, little or no previous experience and understanding of the work, and limited initiative or judgement.

7141   PAINTERS AND RELATED WORKERS

Painters and related workers prepare surfaces of buildings and other structures for painting, apply protective and decorative coats of paint or similar materials or cover interior walls and ceilings of buildings with wallpaper, silk or other fabrics.

Tasks include –
(a) cleaning and preparing walls and other surfaces of buildings for painting or wallpapering;
(b) applying or spraying paint, varnish, shellac and similar materials to surfaces, fixtures and fittings of buildings;
(c) measuring and mounting wallpaper, silk or other fabrics on interior walls and ceilings of buildings and ships;
(d) applying or spraying paint, red lead, bituminous emulsion and similar materials to ships' hulls and metal structures, steel frameworks of buildings, bridges and metal constructions;
(e) performing related tasks;
(f) supervising other workers in this group.

Examples of the occupations classified here:
- Painter, building
- Paperhanger

7142   VARNISHERS AND RELATED PAINTERS

Varnishers and related painters paint vehicles such as cars, buses or trucks, or apply protective coats of enamel or varnish on metal, wooden and other manufactured articles, usually with a hand-spraying device.

Tasks include –
(a) painting cars, buses, trucks and other vehicles, and applying varnish and other protective coatings;
(b) applying paint as well as protective coatings of enamel or varnish on metal, wooden and other manufactured products, usually with a hand-spraying device;
(c) performing related tasks;
(d) supervising other workers.

Examples of the occupations classified here:
- Painter, manufactured articles
- Painter, vehicle
- Varnisher, manufactured articles

Some related occupations classified elsewhere:
- Machine-operator, painting/metal – 8223
- Machine-operator, painting/wood – 8240
- Painter, building – 7141
- Painter, decorative – 7324

7143   BUILDING STRUCTURE CLEANERS

Building structure cleaners remove soot from chimneys, or clean exterior surfaces of buildings and other structures.

Tasks include –
(a) removing soot from flues, chimneys and connecting pipes;
(b) cleaning exterior surfaces of stone, brick, metal or similar materials by means of chemicals, of a jet of steam or sand applied under great pressure;
(c) performing related tasks;
(d) supervising other workers.

Examples of the occupations classified here:
- Chimney sweep
- Cleaner, building exteriors
- Sandblaster, building exteriors

SUB-MAJOR GROUP 72
METAL, MACHINERY AND RELATED TRADES WORKERS

Metal, machinery and related trades workers cast, weld, forge and, by other methods, form metal, erect, maintain and repair heavy metal structures, engage in machine-tool setting as well as in fitting, maintaining and repairing machinery, including engines, vehicles, electrical and electronic equipment, or they produce tools and various non-precious-metal articles.

The work is carried out by hand and by hand-powered and other tools which are used to reduce the amount of physical effort and time required for specific tasks, as well as to improve the quality of the products. The tasks call for an understanding of the work organisation, the materials and tools used, and the nature and purpose of the final product.

Tasks performed by workers in this sub-major group usually include: making moulds and cores for casting metal; casting, welding and shaping metal; installing, erecting, maintaining and repairing heavy metal structures, tackle and related equipment; forging and forming steel and other non-precious metals to make and repair machinery, tools, equipment and other articles; setting for operators or setting and operating various machine tools; fitting, maintaining and repairing industrial machinery, including engines and vehicles, as well as electrical and electronic instruments and other equipment. Supervision of other workers may be included.

Occupations in this sub-major group are classified into the following minor groups:

721 Metal moulders, welders, sheet-metal workers, structural-metal preparers and related trades workers

722 Blacksmiths, tool-makers and related trades workers

723 Machinery mechanics and fitters

724 Electrical and electronic equipment mechanics and fitters

Note

Occupations are classified into Major group 8, *Plant and machine operators and assemblers,* if the tasks call mainly for experience with and an understanding of the machinery operated and monitored.

Occupations are classified into Major group 9, *Elementary occupations,* if the tasks are of a simple and routine nature, mainly entail the use of hand-held tools, some physical effort, little or no previous experience and understanding of the work, and limited initiative or judgement.

7

METAL MOULDERS, WELDERS, SHEET-METAL WORKERS, STRUCTURAL-METAL PREPARERS AND RELATED TRADES WORKERS

Metal moulders, welders, sheet-metal workers, structural-metal preparers and related trades workers make moulds and cores for casting metal, weld and cut metal parts, make and repair articles of sheet metal, install, erect, maintain and repair heavy metal structures, tackle, cable-cars and related equipment, or carry out similar work under water.

Tasks performed usually include: making moulds and cores for casting metal; casting, welding and shaping metal parts; making and repairing articles of sheet metal such as sheet steel, copper, tin or brass; installing, erecting, maintaining and repairing heavy metal structures, as well as tackle, cable cars and related equipment; carrying out similar work under water. Supervision of other workers may be included.

Occupations in this minor group are classified into the following unit groups:

7211 Metal moulders and coremakers

7212 Welders and flamecutters

7213 Sheet-metal workers

7214 Structural-metal preparers and erectors

7215 Riggers and cable splicers

7216 Underwater workers

Note

Occupations are classified into Major group 8, *Plant and machine operators and assemblers,* if the tasks call mainly for experience with and an understanding of the machinery operated and monitored.

Occupations are classified into Major group 9, *Elementary occupations,* if the tasks are of a simple and routine nature, mainly entail the use of hand-held tools, some physical effort, little or no previous experience and understanding of the work and limited initiative or judgement.

7211 METAL MOULDERS AND COREMAKERS

Metal moulders and coremakers make moulds and cores for casting metal.

Tasks include –

(a) making moulds by hand or by using auxiliary machines on a bench for small metal castings, or on the foundry floor or in a pit for large castings;

(b) making cores for use in metal moulds;

(c) performing related tasks;

(d) supervising other workers.

Examples of the occupations classified here:
- Coremaker, metal
- Moulder, metal castings

Some related occupations classified elsewhere:
- Machine-operator, coremaking/metal – 8211

7212 WELDERS AND FLAMECUTTERS

Welders and flamecutters weld and cut metal parts using gas flame, or an electric arc and other sources of heat to melt and cut, or to melt and fuse metal.

Tasks include –

(a) welding metal parts using gas flame, or an electric arc, thermite compound or other methods;
(b) operating resistance-welding machines;
(c) using blowtorch to make and repair lead linings, pipes, floors and other lead fixtures;
(d) brazing metal parts together;
(e) cutting metal pieces using gas flame or an electric arc;
(f) joining metal parts by hand soldering;
(g) performing related tasks;
(h) supervising other workers.

Examples of the occupations classified here:
- Brazier
- Flamecutter
- Welder

7213   SHEET-METAL WORKERS

Sheet-metal workers make, install and repair articles and parts of articles of sheet metal such as sheet steel, copper, tin, brass, aluminium, zinc or galvanised iron.

Tasks include –

(a) marking sheet metal for cutting and shaping;
(b) making and repairing household utensils and other articles in tin, copper and light alloys, or ornamental articles and fittings;
(c) making and repairing boilers, tanks, vats and similar containers;
(d) installing and repairing sheet-metal parts of vehicles and aircraft;
(e) performing related tasks;
(f) supervising other workers.

Examples of the occupations classified here:
- Boilersmith
- Coppersmith
- Sheet-metal worker
- Tinsmith

7214   STRUCTURAL-METAL PREPARERS AND ERECTORS

Structural-metal preparers and erectors shape, assemble and erect heavy metal girders and plates to form structures and frameworks.

Tasks include –

(a) marking metal members as a guide when drilling, cutting, and shaping them for use in buildings, ships and other structures;
(b) drilling, cutting and shaping structural steel in a workshop;
(c) erecting steel members for buildings, bridges and other constructions;
(d) assembling and erecting the framework and other metal parts of ships' structures;
(e) shaping and fitting structural-steel plates of ships under construction or repair;
(f) riveting structural-metal members by hand, machine or pneumatic riveter;
(g) performing related tasks;
(h) supervising other workers.

Examples of the occupations classified here:
- Erector, structural metal
- Preparer, structural metal
- Riveter

Some related occupations classified elsewhere:
- Machine-operator, rivet production – 8211

7215   RIGGERS AND CABLE SPLICERS

Riggers and cable splicers erect tackle for lifting and hauling, or install and maintain cables, ropes and wires on construction sites, oil- and gas-well drilling sites, or in ships, aircraft, and other places.

Tasks include –

(a) setting up various types of cages, funicular railways, aerial cableways, moving platforms, lifting tackle and other hoisting equipment for moving passengers, workers, materials, machinery and other heavy objects in mountainous areas, across deep gorges or fiords, about workshops, shipyards, or other locations;

(b) joining, repairing and fitting attachments to wires, hemp ropes and cables;

(c) installing and repairing ropes, wires and cables on ships and aircraft;

(d) working as member of crew erecting and repairing derricks for drilling water, gas- and oil-wells and installing cables, hoisting and drilling equipment;

(e) working as member of cable crew fitting and installing wire cables in the construction of suspension bridges;

(f) performing related tasks;

(g) supervising other workers.

Examples of the occupations classified here:

- Rigger
- Rigger, ship
- Splicer, cable and rope

Some related occupations classified elsewhere:

- Machine-operator, splicing/cable and rope – 8290

7216 UNDERWATER WORKERS

Underwater workers work under water, dressed in scuba gear or diving suit, to inspect, install, repair, and remove equipment and structures.

Tasks include –

(a) working under water to lay and repair bridges, piers and harbour-wall foundations;

(b) inspecting for suspected damage and making minor repairs to ships' hulls and underwater installations;

(c) reporting on condition of wrecked ships;

(d) removing underwater obstructions;

(e) drilling holes for underwater blasting;

(f) performing various underwater tasks connected with salvage work or recovering dead bodies;

(g) performing related tasks;

(h) supervising other workers.

Examples of the occupations classified here:

- Frogman, salvage
- Underwater worker

MINOR GROUP 722
BLACKSMITHS, TOOL-MAKERS AND RELATED TRADES WORKERS

Blacksmiths, tool-makers and related trades workers hammer and forge bars, rods or ingots of iron, steel and other metals to make and repair various kinds of tools, equipment and other articles, set for operators or set and operate various machine tools, and polish and sharpen metal surfaces.

Tasks performed usually include: hammering and forging iron, steel and other metals to make and repair various kinds of tools, equipment and other articles; setting for operators or setting and operating various machine tools working to fine tolerances; polishing and sharpening metal surfaces and tools. Supervision of other workers may be included.

Occupations in this minor group are classified into the following unit groups:

7221 Blacksmiths, hammer-smiths and forging-press workers

7222 Tool-makers and related workers

7223 Machine-tool setters and setter-operators
7224 Metal wheel-grinders, polishers and tool sharpeners

Note

Occupations are classified into Major group 8, *Plant and machine operators and assemblers,* if the tasks call mainly for experience with and an understanding of the machinery operated and monitored.

Occupations are classified into Major group 9, *Elementary occupations,* if the tasks are of a simple and routine nature, mainly entail the use of hand-held tools, some physical effort, little or no previous experience and understanding of the work, and limited initiative or judgement.

7221 BLACKSMITHS, HAMMER-SMITHS AND FORGING-PRESS WORKERS

Blacksmiths, hammer-smiths and forging-press workers draw wire, hammer and forge bars, rods, ingots and plates of iron, steel or other metals to make and repair various kinds of tools, metal articles, pieces of equipment, agricultural and related implements.

Tasks include –
(a) heating metal in forge furnace and manufacturing and repairing articles by drawing, bending, cutting, hammering metal on an anvil, punching, shearing, joining and hardening or tempering;
(b) shaping heated metal into forgings on power hammer equipped with open dies;
(c) operating closed-die drop hammer to forge metal articles;
(d) operating a power-press machine equipped with closed dies to forge metal articles;
(e) drawing wire;
(f) performing related tasks;
(g) supervising other workers.

Examples of the occupations classified here:
- Blacksmith
- Drop-hammer worker
- Forging-press worker
- Hammer-smith

Some related occupations classified elsewhere:
- Machine-operator, casting/metal – 8122
- Machine-operator, machine-tool – 8211

7222 TOOL-MAKERS AND RELATED WORKERS

Tool-makers and related workers make and repair tools, sports guns, locks, dies, patterns and other metal articles, as well as make engines or machinery components, and parts thereof, using hand and machine tools to work metal to fine tolerances.

Tasks include –
(a) making, maintaining and repairing dies, jigs, gauges and fixtures, using hand tools and various kinds of machine tools;
(b) making engines or machinery components, and parts thereof;
(c) fitting and assembling parts to make and repair jigs, fixtures and gauges;
(d) repairing and modifying sports guns and other small arms;
(e) making, fitting, assembling, repairing and installing lock parts and locks;
(f) making and repairing metal patterns for preparation of foundry moulds;
(g) laying out lines and reference points on metal stock to guide other workers who cut, turn, mill, grind or otherwise shape metal;
(h) performing related tasks;
(i) supervising other workers.

Examples of the occupations classified here:
- Gunsmith
- Locksmith
- Toolmaker

Some related occupations classified elsewhere:
- Machine-operator, tool production – 8211

7

7223 MACHINE-TOOL SETTERS AND SETTER-OPERATORS

Machine-tool setters and setter-operators set for operators, or set and operate, various machine tools working to fine tolerances.

Tasks include –

(a) setting one or more types of machine tools for operators to produce metal articles in standardised series;

(b) setting and operating a variety of machine tools;

(c) setting and operating particular types of metalworking machines, such as lathe, milling, planing, boring, drilling, grinding or honing machines, including multipurpose numerically controlled metalworking machines;

(d) performing similar tasks when machining plastics and other metal substitutes;

(e) performing related tasks;

(f) supervising other workers.

Examples of the occupations classified here:
- Setter, machine tool
- Setter-operator, drilling machine/metalworking
- Setter-operator, grinding machine/metalworking
- Setter-operator, lathe/metalworking

Some related occupations classified elsewhere:
- Machine-operator, drilling/metal – 8211
- Machine-operator, grinding/metal – 8211
- Machine-operator, machine tool – 8211

7224 METAL WHEEL-GRINDERS, POLISHERS AND TOOL SHARPENERS

Metal wheel-grinders, polishers and tool sharpeners grind and polish metal surfaces and sharpen tools.

Tasks include –

(a) operating fixed or portable buffing and polishing machines;

(b) sharpening cutting tools and instruments using grinding wheel or mechanically operated grinding machines;

(c) repairing, adjusting and sharpening saw blades and metal teeth of cylinders in textile carding machines;

(d) performing related tasks;

(e) supervising other workers.

Examples of the occupations classified here:
- Finisher, metal
- Grinder, tool
- Polisher, metal
- Sharpener, knife

Some related occupations classified elsewhere:
- Machine-operator, finishing/metal – 8223
- Machine-operator, polishing/metal – 8223

MINOR GROUP 723
MACHINERY MECHANICS AND FITTERS

Machinery mechanics and fitters fit, install, maintain and repair engines, vehicles, agricultural or industrial machinery, and mechanical equipment.

Tasks performed usually include: fitting, installing, maintaining and repairing engines, vehicles, agricultural or industrial machinery, and mechanical equipment. Supervision of other workers may be included.

Occupations in this minor group are classified into the following unit groups:

7231 Motor vehicle mechanics and fitters

7232 Aircraft engine mechanics and fitters

7233 Agricultural- or industrial-machinery mechanics and fitters

Note

Occupations are classified into Major group 8, *Plant and machine operators and assemblers,* if the tasks call mainly for experience with and an understanding of the machinery operated and monitored.

Occupations are classified into Major group 9, *Elementary occupations,* if the tasks are of a simple and routine nature, mainly entail the use of hand-held tools, some physical effort, little or no previous experience and understanding of the work and limited initiative or judgement.

7231 MOTOR VEHICLE MECHANICS AND FITTERS

Motor vehicle mechanics and fitters fit, install, maintain, service and repair engines and the mechanical and related equipment of motor cycles, passenger cars and delivery trucks and other motor vehicles.

Tasks include –
(a) fitting, examining, testing and servicing motor vehicle engines;
(b) replacing engine components or complete engines;
(c) fitting, examining, adjusting, dismantling, rebuilding and replacing defective parts of motor vehicles;
(d) installing or adjusting motors and brakes, and adjusting steering or other parts of motor vehicles;
(e) performing related tasks;
(f) supervising other workers.

Examples of the occupations classified here:
- Fitter, engine/motor-vehicle
- Mechanic, garage
- Mechanic, motor-vehicle

Some related occupations classified elsewhere:
- Assembler, engine/motor-vehicles – 8281

7232 AIRCRAFT ENGINE MECHANICS AND FITTERS

Aircraft engine mechanics and fitters fit, service, repair and overhaul aircraft engines.

Tasks include –
(a) fitting, examining, testing and servicing aircraft engines;
(b) replacing engine components or complete engines;
(c) performing related tasks;
(d) supervising other workers.

Examples of the occupations classified here:
- Fitter, engine/aircraft
- Mechanic, engine/aircraft

Some related occupations classified elsewhere:
- Assembler, engine/aircraft – 8281

7233 AGRICULTURAL- OR INDUSTRIAL-MACHINERY MECHANICS AND FITTERS

Agricultural- or industrial-machinery mechanics and fitters fit, install, examine, service and repair engines (except motor vehicle and aircraft engines), agricultural or industrial machinery and mechanical equipment.

Tasks include –
(a) fitting, installing, examining, servicing and repairing engines (except motor

vehicle and aircraft engines), agricultural or industrial machinery and mechanical equipment;

(b) oiling and greasing stationary engines, machinery and vehicles;

(c) inspecting and testing new machinery and mechanical equipment for conformity with standards and specifications;

(d) performing related tasks;

(e) supervising other workers.

Examples of the occupations classified here:
- Fitter, engine/marine
- Fitter, mining machinery
- Fitter, textile machinery
- Mechanic, construction machinery
- Mechanic, farm machinery

Some related occupations classified elsewhere:
- Assembler, textile machinery − 8281

MINOR GROUP 724
ELECTRICAL AND ELECTRONIC EQUIPMENT MECHANICS AND FITTERS

Electrical and electronic equipment mechanics and fitters fit, adjust, install and repair electrical and electronic equipment such as computer hardware, sound and image recording and telecommunications systems, and construct, install and repair electrical lines and joint cables.

Tasks performed usually include: fitting, adjusting and repairing electrical machinery and equipment; fitting, adjusting, servicing and repairing computer hardware and other electronic products; servicing and repairing radio, television and hi-fi sound equipment; installing, servicing and repairing telegraph and telephone equipment; installing and repairing electrical lines and jointing cables. Supervision of other workers may be included.

Occupations in this minor group are classified into the following unit groups:

7241 Electrical mechanics and fitters

7242 Electronics fitters

7243 Electronics mechanics and servicers

7244 Telegraph and telephone installers and servicers

7245 Electrical line installers, repairers and cable jointers

Note

Occupations are classified into Major group 8, *Plant and machine operators and assemblers,* if the tasks call mainly for experience with and an understanding of the machinery operated and monitored.

Occupations are classified into Major group 9, *Elementary occupations,* if the tasks are of a simple and routine nature, mainly entail the use of hand-held tools, some physical effort, little or no previous experience and understanding of the work and limited initiative or judgement.

7241 ELECTRICAL MECHANICS AND FITTERS

Electrical mechanics and fitters fit, adjust, install and repair electrical machinery and other electrical apparatus and equipment in buildings, factories, workshops, or other places.

Tasks include –

(a) fitting, adjusting and repairing various kinds of electrical machinery and motors, generators, switchgear and control apparatus, instruments, or electrical parts of elevators and related equipment;

(b) fitting, adjusting and repairing electrical parts in domestic appliances, industrial machines and other appliances, or electrical apparatus in aircraft, ships and vehicles;

(c) inspecting and testing manufactured electrical products;

(d) performing related tasks;

(e) supervising other workers.

Examples of the occupations classified here:
- Builder, armature
- Fitter, electrical/generator
- Mechanic, electrical

Some related occupations classified elsewhere:
- Assembler, electrical equipment – 8282

7242 ELECTRONICS FITTERS

Electronics fitters fit and adjust computer hardware, as well as sound and image recording and transmitting telecommunications and other electronic equipment.

Tasks include –

(a) fitting and adjusting computer hardware, sound and image recorders and transmitters, radar equipment, electronic components of musical instruments, medical or industrial equipment and signalling systems;

(b) inspecting and testing manufactured electronic products;

(c) performing related tasks;

(d) supervising other workers.

Examples of the occupations classified here:
- Fitter, electronics/computer equipment
- Fitter, electronics/telecommunications equipment

Some related occupations classified elsewhere:
- Assembler, electronic equipment – 8283

7243 ELECTRONICS MECHANICS AND SERVICERS

Electronics mechanics and servicers service and repair radio and television equipment, tape recorders, video cassette recorders, and other audio-visual equipment.

Tasks include –

(a) examining radio or television equipment, tape recorders, video cassette recorders, and other audio-visual equipment, replacing defective parts and making adjustments and repairs;

(b) performing related tasks;

(c) supervising other workers.

Examples of the occupations classified here:
- Erector, radio aerial
- Mechanic, electronics/audio-visual equipment
- Servicer, electronics equipment

7244 TELEGRAPH AND TELEPHONE INSTALLERS AND SERVICERS

Telegraph and telephone installers and servicers install, service and repair telephone and telegraph equipment in central sites or individual locations.

Tasks include –

(a) installing, servicing and repairing telephone and telegraph equipment in central sites or individual locations;

(b) performing related tasks;

(c) supervising other workers.

Examples of the occupations classified here:
- Installer, telephone
- Mechanic, telegraph
- Servicer, telephone

Some related occupations classified elsewhere:
- Fitter, electronics/telecommunications equipment – 7242

7245 ELECTRICAL LINE INSTALLERS, REPAIRERS AND CABLE JOINTERS

Electrical line installers, repairers and cable jointers install and repair electrical lines and joint cables.

Tasks include –

(a) installing and repairing overhead and underground electrical power and electrical traction lines;

(b) installing and repairing overhead and underground telephone and telegraph lines;

(c) making joints in overhead and underground cables;

(d) performing related tasks;

(e) supervising other workers.

Examples of the occupations classified here:
- Cable worker, telegraph
- Jointer, cable/electric
- Line worker/electric power

Some related occupations classified elsewhere:
- Machine-operator, electrical line installation – 8290

SUB-MAJOR GROUP 73
PRECISION, HANDICRAFT, PRINTING AND RELATED TRADES WORKERS

Precision, handicraft, printing and related trades workers make and repair precision instruments, musical instruments, various articles such as jewellery, precious metalware, ceramics, porcelainware and glassware, as well as handicrafts made of wood or textile, leather or related materials, or they perform printing or book-binding tasks.

The work is carried out by hand and by hand-powered and other tools which are used to reduce the amount of physical effort and time required for specific tasks, as well as to improve the quality of the products. The tasks call for an understanding of the work organisation, the materials and tools used, and the nature and purpose of the final product.

Tasks performed by workers in this sub-major group usually include: making and repairing nautical, meteorological, optical and other precision instruments and equipment; making and repairing musical instruments; making jewellery and precious metalware; making pottery, porcelainware, ceramics and glassware; painting and decorating various articles; producing handicraft articles in wood or textile, leather and related materials; performing printing or book-binding tasks. Supervision of other workers may be included.

Occupations in this sub-major group are classified into the following minor groups:

731 Precision workers in metal and related materials

732 Potters, glass-makers and related trades workers

733 Handicraft workers in wood, textile, leather and related materials

734 Printing and related trades workers

Note

Occupations are classified into Major group 8, *Plant and machine operators and assemblers,* if the tasks call mainly for experience with and an understanding of the machinery operated and monitored.

Occupations are classified into Major group 9, *Elementary occupations,* if the tasks are of a simple and routine nature, mainly entail the use of hand-held tools, some physical effort, little or no previous experience and understanding of the work, and limited initiative or judgement.

MINOR GROUP 731
PRECISION WORKERS IN METAL AND RELATED MATERIALS

Precision workers in metal and related materials make and repair precision instruments, musical instruments, jewellery and other articles of precious metals.

Tasks performed usually include: making and repairing watches, clocks, nautical, meteorological, optical, surgical, dental, othopaedic and other precision instruments and equipment; making and repairing musical instruments; cutting or setting gems, and making and repairing jewellery and precious metalware. Supervision of other workers may be included.

Occupations in this minor group are classified into the following unit groups:

> **7311   Precision-instrument makers and repairers**
>
> **7312   Musical-instrument makers and tuners**
>
> **7313   Jewellery and precious-metal workers**

Note

Occupations are classified into Major group 8, *Plant and machine operators and assemblers,* if the tasks call mainly for experience with and understanding of the machinery operated and monitored.

Occupations are classified into Major group 9, *Elementary occupations,* if the tasks are of a simple and routine nature, mainly entail the use of hand-held tools, some physical effort, little or no previous experience and understanding of the work, and limited initiative or judgement.

7311   PRECISION-INSTRUMENT MAKERS AND REPAIRERS

Precision-instrument makers and repairers make and repair mechanical watches, clocks, nautical, meteorological, optical, surgical, dental, orthopaedic and other precision instruments and equipment.

Tasks include –

(a)   making, adjusting and repairing mechanical watches and clocks;

(b)   making, adjusting and repairing nautical and meteorological instruments and equipment;

(c)   making, adjusting and repairing optical instruments;

(d) making, adjusting and repairing surgical instruments and other medical equipment;

(e) making and repairing medical, orthopaedic and dental appliances and prostheses;

(f) performing related tasks;

(g) supervising other workers.

Examples of the occupations classified here:
- Maker, instrument/meteorological
- Maker, instrument/surgical
- Maker, orthopaedic appliance
- Maker, watch

Some related occupations classified elsewhere:
- Assembler, watch – 8283
- Machine-operator, machine-tool – 8211

7312 MUSICAL-INSTRUMENT MAKERS AND TUNERS

Musical-instrument makers and tuners make, repair and tune stringed, wind or percussion instruments with hand or power tools.

Tasks include –

(a) making and repairing accordions, stringed and wind instruments;

(b) building and repairing organs and making parts for such organs;

(c) making instrumental parts of pianos and assembling and repairing such pianos;

(d) tuning organs, pianos and other instruments;

(e) making and repairing other musical instruments;

(f) performing related tasks;

(g) supervising other workers.

Examples of the occupations classified here:
- Maker, instrument/musical (brass)
- Maker, instrument/musical (string)
- Maker, instrument/musical (woodwind)
- Tuner, musical instrument

7313 JEWELLERY AND PRECIOUS-METAL WORKERS

Jewellery and precious-metal workers make and repair jewellery and precious metalware, cut and set gems and engrave designs on jewellery and precious metal articles.

Tasks include –

(a) casting jewellery and other non-ferrous metal articles by hand;

(b) making complete jewellery articles such as rings, brooches and bracelets;

(c) cutting and polishing gems and setting them in jewellery articles;

(d) making and repairing precious metalware;

(e) rolling and beating precious metals;

(f) engraving letters and designs on jewellery and precious metalware;

(g) performing related tasks;

(h) supervising other workers.

Examples of the occupations classified here:
- Enameller, jewellery
- Goldsmith
- Jeweller
- Setter, gem
- Silversmith

MINOR GROUP **732**
POTTERS, GLASS-MAKERS AND RELATED TRADES WORKERS

Potters, glass-makers and related trades workers make bricks, tiles, pottery, porcelainware and glassware, engrave and etch designs on glass articles, and paint or decorate glass, ceramics and related articles and signs.

Tasks performed usually include: making abrasive wheels, pottery, porcelainware, bricks and tiles; making glassware; engraving and etching designs on glass articles; decorating glass and ceramic articles; applying decorative coatings of paint and similar materials to various articles, or applying letters and designs to signs. Supervision of other workers may be included.

Occupations in this minor group are classified into the following unit groups:

> **7321 Abrasive wheel formers, potters and related workers**
>
> **7322 Glass-makers, cutters, grinders and finishers**
>
> **7323 Glass engravers and etchers**
>
> **7324 Glass, ceramics and related decorative painters**

Note

Occupations are classified into Major group 8, *Plant and machine operators and assemblers,* if the tasks call mainly for experience with and an understanding of the machinery operated and monitored.

Occupations are classified into Major group 9, *Elementary occupations,* if the tasks are of a simple and routine nature, mainly entail the use of hand-held tools, some physical effort, little or no previous experience and understanding of the work, and limited initiative or judgement.

7321 ABRASIVE WHEEL FORMERS, POTTERS AND RELATED WORKERS

Abrasive wheel formers, potters and related workers make pottery, porcelainware, bricks, tiles and abrasive wheels.

Tasks include –
(a) making articles of pottery and porcelain;
(b) making clay or plaster-of-Paris moulds;
(c) forming articles on potter's wheel with hands, or using interior or exterior moulding shapes and shaping tools;
(d) forming articles by casting semi-liquid clay in plaster-of-Paris moulds;
(e) forming bricks and tiles into special shapes by hand;
(f) making articles by pressing plastic clay into moulds by hand;
(g) operating screw-press or hydraulic press to make products from clay dust;
(h) operating a machine which extrudes moist clay for further processing;
(i) forming abrasive wheels by moulding and pressing abrasive mixture;
(j) performing related tasks;
(k) supervising other workers.

Examples of the occupations classified here:
- Caster, pottery and porcelain
- Modeller, pottery and porcelain
- Potter

Some related occupations classified elsewhere:
- Kiln operator, brick and tile – 8131
- Kiln operator, pottery and porcelain – 8131

7322 GLASS-MAKERS, CUTTERS, GRINDERS AND FINISHERS

Glass-makers, cutters, grinders and finishers blow, mould, press and roll shapes from molten glass and cut, grind and polish glass.

Tasks include –

(a) shaping molten glass by means of blow-pipe, hand moulding, heating and bending;

(b) heating, moulding and pressing optical glass to make lens blanks;

(c) grinding and polishing lens blanks;

(d) grinding and bevelling edges of glass;

(e) cutting sheet glass with hand tools and sawing prisms and other shapes from optical glass blocks;

(f) performing related tasks;

(g) supervising other workers.

Examples of the occupations classified here:
- Blower, glass
- Cutter, glass
- Finisher, glass
- Grinder, glass

Some related occupations classified elsewhere:
- Furnace-operator, glass production – 8131

7323 GLASS ENGRAVERS AND ETCHERS

Glass engravers and etchers engrave and etch designs on glass articles.

Tasks include –

(a) engraving monograms and ornamental designs on glassware;

(b) etching decorative designs, calibration markings and other figures on glass articles;

(c) performing related tasks;

(d) supervising other workers.

Examples of the occupations classified here:
- Cutter, crystal glass
- Engraver, glass
- Etcher, glass

7324 GLASS, CERAMICS AND RELATED DECORATIVE PAINTERS

Glass, ceramics and related decorative painters decorate articles made of wood, metal, textiles, glass, ceramics and other materials, and plan, lay out and paint letters and designs to make signs.

Tasks include –

(a) painting designs on articles with a brush, by spraying, or by transferring designs using stencils, transfers, rubber stamps and other means;

(b) applying, for decorative purposes, paint, glaze, enamel, stain, varnish, lacquer and similar materials on articles by spraying or dipping;

(c) coating mirror glass with silver solutions;

(d) laying out and painting letters and designs to make signs;

(e) performing related tasks;

(f) supervising other workers.

Examples of the occupations classified here:
- Enameller, glass
- Painter, decorative
- Sign-writer

Some related occupations classified elsewhere:
- Machine-operator, painting/ceramics – 8131
- Machine-operator, painting/glass – 8131
- Painter, building – 7141
- Painter, manufactured articles – 7142
- Painter, vehicle – 7142

MINOR GROUP **733**
HANDICRAFT WORKERS IN WOOD, TEXTILE, LEATHER AND RELATED MATERIALS

Handicraft workers in wood, textile, leather and related materials apply traditional techniques to produce various articles for personal or household use, as well as for decorative purposes.

Tasks performed usually include: preparing wood, straw, rattan, reeds, bone, stone, shells and other materials; carving, moulding, assembling, painting and decorating various articles; weaving, knitting, embroidering, lace-making; producing traditional footwear; producing handbags, belts and other accessories. Supervision of other workers may be included.

Occupations in this minor group are classified into the following unit groups:

7331 Handicraft workers in wood and related materials

7332 Handicraft workers in textile, leather and related materials

Note

Occupations are classified into Major group 8, *Plant and machine operators and assemblers,* if the tasks call mainly for experience with and an understanding of the machinery operated and monitored.

Occupations are classified into Major group 9, *Elementary occupations,* if the tasks are of a simple and routine nature, mainly entail the use of hand-held tools, some physical effort, little or no previous experience and understanding of the work, and limited initiative or judgement.

7331 HANDICRAFT WORKERS IN WOOD AND RELATED MATERIALS

Handicraft workers in wood and related materials apply traditional techniques to prepare wood, straw, rattan, reeds, stone, clay, shells, and other materials, and carve, mould, assemble, weave, or paint and decorate various articles for personal or household use, or for decorative purposes.

Tasks include –
(a) preparing wood, straw, rattan, reeds, stone, shells, or similar materials;
(b) carving, assembling, weaving, painting and decorating various articles for personal or household use such as salad bowls, serving-spoons, cutting-boards, trays, vases, jugs, baskets, straw hats, straw mats and similar objects;
(c) carving, assembling, weaving and painting various decorative articles such as statues and other sculptures, chess pieces, jewellery, and similar objects;

(d) performing related tasks;
(e) supervising other workers.

Examples of the occupations classified here:
- Handicraft worker, reed weaving
- Handicraft worker, stone articles
- Handicraft worker, wooden articles

Some related occupations classified elsewhere:
- Maker, brush – 7424
- Machine-operator, carving/stone products – 8212
- Machine-operator, wood products – 8240

7332 HANDICRAFT WORKERS IN TEXTILE, LEATHER AND RELATED MATERIALS

Handicraft workers in textile, leather and related materials apply traditional techniques and patterns to produce woven fabrics, knitted, embroidered, woven and other garments and articles for household use, as well as traditional footwear, handbags, belts and other accessories.

Tasks include –

(a) spinning and dyeing with natural dye-stuffs, wool, cotton and other fibres;

(b) lace-making and weaving, knitting, or embroidering various garments and articles for household use;

(c) preparing and dyeing hides with natural dyestuffs and making traditional footwear or handbags, belts and other accessories;

(d) performing related tasks;

(e) supervising other workers.

Examples of the occupations classified here:
- Handicraft worker, carpets
- Handicraft worker, leather
- Handicraft worker, textiles

Some related occupations classified elsewhere:
- Machine-operator, weaving/fabrics – 8262
- Weaver, cloth – 7432

MINOR GROUP 734
PRINTING AND RELATED TRADES WORKERS

Printing and related trades workers set and arrange printing type or copy by hand or by electronic keyboarding or other machines, make printing plates from typographically or electronically set-up type or copy, engrave lithographic stones, printing plates and rollers, make and print with silk-screens, print on paper and other materials, or bind and finish books.

Tasks performed usually include: setting and arranging printing type or copy by hand or by electronic keyboarding or other machines; making printing plates from typographically or electronically set-up type or copy; engraving lithographic stones, printing plates, rollers, dies and blocks; making and printing with silk-screens; printing on paper and other materials; binding covers to books and performing book-finishing operations. Supervision of other workers may be included.

Occupations in this minor group are classified into the following unit groups:

7341 Compositors, typesetters and related workers

7342 Stereotypers and electrotypers

7343 Printing engravers and etchers

7344 Photographic and related workers

7345 Bookbinders and related workers

7346 Silk-screen, block and textile printers

Note

Occupations are classified into Major group 8, *Plant and machine operators and assemblers,* if the tasks call mainly for experience with and an understanding of the machinery operated and monitored.

Occupations are classified into Major group 9, *Elementary occupations,* if the tasks are of a simple and routine nature, mainly entail the use of hand-held tools, some physical effort, little or no previous experience and understanding of the work, and limited initiative or judgement.

7341 COMPOSITORS, TYPESETTERS AND RELATED WORKERS

Compositors, typesetters and related workers set and arrange printing type by hand or machine.

Tasks include –
(a) setting type by hand and printing copies with simple machines;
(b) operating linotype, monotype and type-casting machines;
(c) arranging set-up of type and spacing material and illustration blocks to make pages;
(d) arranging pages in sequence for printing;
(e) operating electronic keyboarding machines which enable characters to be converted into film, sensitised tape or paper for subsequent photo plate-making;
(f) performing related tasks;
(g) supervising other workers.

Examples of the occupations classified here:
- Compositor, printing
- Printer
- Typesetter

Some related occupations classified elsewhere:
- Press-operator, printing/cylinder – 8251

7342 STEREOTYPERS AND ELECTROTYPERS

Stereotypers and electrotypers make printing plates from set-up type by stereotyping and electroplating processes.

Tasks include –
(a) making moulds of set-up type with papier mâché, wax or other materials;
(b) making printing plates by casting metal in moulds of papier mâché or other material bearing impression of type, or by putting lead alloy backing on copper shell made by electroplating moulds to reproduce type;
(c) performing related tasks;
(d) supervising other workers.

Examples of the occupations classified here:
- Electrotyper
- Stereotyper

7343 PRINTING ENGRAVERS AND ETCHERS

Printing engravers and etchers engrave lithographic stones and printing plates, rollers, dies and blocks by various processes.

Tasks include –
(a) cutting designs through film applied to surface of lithographic stones;
(b) engraving steel and copper plates, rollers, dies or wood, rubber and linoleum blocks by hand;
(c) engraving metal plates and rollers by machine;
(d) transferring designs from lithographic stone to metal plates;
(e) performing all or several tasks in preparing printing plates by photogravure process;
(f) etching metal plates or rollers with acid and retouching;
(g) performing related tasks;
(h) supervising other workers.

Examples of the occupations classified here:
- Engraver, printing/lithographic stone
- Engraver, printing/metal plate
- Etcher, printing/metal plate
- Photo-engraver

Some related occupations classified elsewhere:
- Designer, graphic – 3471

7344 PHOTOGRAPHIC AND RELATED WORKERS

Photographic and related workers develop and process photographic film and make prints or slides.

Tasks include –
(a) processing black and white or colour film and plates to obtain negatives or transparent positives;
(b) printing black and white or colour photographs;

(c) performing related tasks;

(d) supervising other workers.

Examples of the occupations classified here:

- Darkroom worker, film developing/colour photography
- Developer, film/colour

Some related occupations classified elsewhere:

- Machine-operator, film developing — 8224

7345 BOOKBINDERS AND RELATED WORKERS

Bookbinders and related workers bind covers to books and perform book-finishing operations.

Tasks include –

(a) binding books and periodicals by hand;

(b) setting and operating bookbinding machines;

(c) embossing designs or titles on books by hand or machine;

(d) performing related tasks;

(e) supervising other workers.

Examples of the occupations classified here:

- Bookbinder
- Embosser, book

Some related occupations classified elsewhere:

- Machine-operator, bookbinding — 8252

7346 SILK-SCREEN, BLOCK AND TEXTILE PRINTERS

Silk-screen, block and textile printers cut stencils for use in silk-screen printing and print on paper, metal, textiles and other materials with silk-screens, blocks of rubber, wood or other materials, or engraved printing rollers.

Tasks include –

(a) cutting stencils for silk-screen printing;

(b) printing on paper, metal, textiles and other materials by silk-screen process;

(c) printing designs and patterns on cloth or wallpaper with engraved blocks or machines equipped with engraved rollers;

(d) performing related tasks;

(e) supervising other workers.

Examples of the occupations classified here:

- Cutter, stencil/silk-screen
- Printer, block
- Printer, silk-screen
- Printer, textile

SUB-MAJOR GROUP 74
OTHER CRAFT AND RELATED TRADES WORKERS

Other craft and related trades workers treat and process agricultural and fisheries raw materials into food and other products, and produce and repair goods made of wood, textiles, fur, leather, or other materials.

The work is carried out by hand and by hand-powered and other tools which are used to reduce the amount of physical effort and time required for specific tasks, as well as to improve the quality of the products. The tasks call for an understanding of the work organisation, the materials and tools used, and the nature and purpose of the final product.

Tasks performed by this sub-major group usually include: treating and processing meat, fish, grain, fruit, vegetables and related materials into foodstuffs, and tobacco into tobacco products; tasting and grading food products and beverages; treating and processing natural fibres, skins and hides; making and repairing furniture and other goods made of wood; preparing hides, skins and pelts for further use; making and repairing textiles, garments, hats, shoes and related products. Supervision of other workers may be included.

Occupations in this sub-major group are classified into the following minor groups:

741   Food processing and related trades workers

742   Wood treaters, cabinet-makers and related trades workers

743   Textile, garment and related trades workers

744   Pelt, leather and shoemaking trades workers

Note

Occupations are classified into Major group 8, *Plant and machine operators and assemblers,* if the tasks call mainly for experience with and an understanding of the machinery operated and monitored.

Occupations are classified into Major group 9, *Elementary occupations,* if the tasks are of a simple and routine nature, mainly entail the use of hand-held tools, some physical effort, little or no previous experience and understanding of the work, and limited initiative or judgement.

MINOR GROUP **741**
FOOD PROCESSING AND RELATED TRADES WORKERS

Food processing and related trades workers slaughter animals, kill fish, treat and prepare them and related food items for human and animal consumption, make various kinds of bread, cakes and other flour products, process and preserve fruit, vegetables and related foods, taste and grade various food products and beverages, or prepare tobacco and make tobacco products.

Tasks performed usually include: slaughtering animals; killing fish; treating meat and fish and preparing them and related food items; making various kinds of bread, cakes and other flour products; processing and preserving fruit, vegetables and related foods; tasting and grading various food products and beverages; preparing tobacco and making tobacco products. Supervision of other workers may be included.

Occupations in this minor group are classified into the following unit groups:

7411   Butchers, fishmongers and related food preparers

7412   Bakers, pastry-cooks and confectionery makers

7413   Dairy products makers

7414   Fruit, vegetable and related preservers

7415   Food and beverage tasters and graders

7416   Tobacco preparers and tobacco products makers

Note

Occupations are classified into Major group 8, *Plant and machine operators and assemblers,* if the tasks call mainly for experience with and an understanding of the machinery operated and monitored.

Occupations are classified into Major group 9, *Elementary occupations,* if the tasks are of a simple and routine nature, mainly entail the use of hand-held tools, some physical effort, little or no previous experience and understanding of the work, and limited initiative or judgement.

7411 BUTCHERS, FISHMONGERS AND RELATED FOOD PREPARERS

Butchers, fishmongers and related food preparers slaughter animals, kill fish, clean, cut and dress meat and fish and prepare related food items or preserve meat, fish and other foods and food products by drying, salting or smoking.

Tasks include –
(a) slaughtering animals or killing fish;
(b) flaying and trimming carcasses;
(c) cutting and dressing meat and fish for sale or further processing;
(d) preparing ingredients and making sausages and similar products using simple chopping, mixing and shaping machines;
(e) curing meat, fish and other foods;
(f) operating smokehouses or ovens to smoke meat, fish and other foodstuffs;
(g) cooking or in other ways preparing meat, fish and related food items for sale;
(h) performing related tasks;
(i) supervising other workers.

Examples of the occupations classified here:
- Butcher
- Fishmonger

Some related occupations classified elsewhere:
- Machine operator, meat processing – 8271
- Machine operator, fish processing – 8271

7412 BAKERS, PASTRY-COOKS AND CONFECTIONERY MAKERS

Bakers, pastry-cooks and confectionery makers make various kinds of bread, cakes, and other flour products, as well as handmade chocolate and sugar confectionery.

Tasks include –
(a) making bread, cakes, biscuits, pastries, pies and other flour products;
(b) making handmade confectionery from mixtures of sugar, chocolate and other ingredients with the help of tools and some machines;
(c) performing related tasks;
(d) supervising other workers.

Examples of the occupations classified here:
- Baker
- Confectioner
- Maker, chocolate
- Pastry-cook

Some related occupations classified elsewhere:
- Cook – 5122
- Machine-operator, bakery products – 8274
- Machine-operator, bread production – 8274
- Machine-operator, chocolate production – 8274

7413 DAIRY PRODUCTS MAKERS

Dairy products makers process butter and various types of cheese, cream or other dairy products.

Tasks include –
(a) boiling milk, separating cream from milk, churning cream into butter;
(b) curdling milk, heating curd until it reaches desired firmness, draining curd and finally placing cheese into moulds to press it into shape;
(c) performing related tasks;
(d) supervising other workers.

Examples of the occupations classified here:
- Maker, butter
- Maker, cheese

Some related occupations classified else-where:
- Machine-operator, dairy products – 8272
- Machine-operator, milk processing – 8272

7414   FRUIT, VEGETABLE AND RELATED PRESERVERS

Fruit, vegetable and related preservers process or preserve fruit, nuts and related foods in various ways including cooking, drying, salting, or juice or oil extraction.

Tasks include –
(a) extracting juices from various fruits;
(b) extracting oils from oil-bearing seeds, nuts or fruits;
(c) cooking, salting or drying fruit, vegetables and related foods;
(d) performing related tasks;
(e) supervising other workers.

Examples of the occupations classified here:
- Expeller, oil
- Preserver, fruit
- Preserver, vegetable

Some related occupations classified else-where:
- Machine-operator, canning/fruit – 8275
- Machine-operator, canning/vegetables – 8275

7415   FOOD AND BEVERAGE TASTERS AND GRADERS

Food and beverage tasters and graders inspect, taste and grade various types of agricultural products, food and beverages.

Tasks include –
(a) inspecting, testing and tasting agricultural products, food and beverages at various stages of processing to determine quality and grade into appropriate class;
(b) performing related tasks;
(c) supervising other workers.

Examples of the occupations classified here:
- Grader, food
- Taster, food
- Taster, liquor
- Taster, wine

7416   TOBACCO PREPARERS AND TOBACCO PRODUCTS MAKERS

Tobacco preparers and tobacco products makers prepare tobacco leaves and make various tobacco products.

Tasks include –
(a) grading cured tobacco leaves by type, quality and locality where grown;
(b) mixing tobacco leaves according to formula to obtain a blend of distinct flavour;
(c) tending vacuum container which moistens tobacco for further processing;
(d) removing midribs and stalks from tobacco leaves and shredding tobacco;
(e) making cigars, cigarettes, snuff and other tobacco products by hand or with simple machines;
(f) performing related tasks;
(g) supervising other workers.

Examples of the occupations classified here:
- Grader, tobacco
- Maker, cigar
- Maker, cigarette

Some related occupations classified else-where:
- Machine-operator, cigar production – 8279
- Machine-operator, cigarette production – 8279

7

MINOR GROUP 742
WOOD TREATERS, CABINET-MAKERS AND RELATED TRADES WORKERS

Wood treaters, cabinet-makers, and related trades workers season and preserve wood and wooden items, make and repair wooden furniture, wooden fittings, patterns and models, by using tools and woodworking machines; set or set and operate woodworking machines, make wicker furniture and related articles, and decorate and repair wooden articles and wooden parts of goods.

Tasks performed usually include: seasoning and preserving wood; making, decorating and repairing wooden furniture; making, decorating and repairing parts of or entire wooden vehicles, wooden models, patterns, and various articles such as pipes, wooden skis, shoes, or sports goods; setting or setting and operating woodworking machines such as those for precision sawing, shaping or carving; making wicker furniture, baskets and similar items, or brooms and brushes. Supervision of other workers may be included.

Occupations in this minor group are classified into the following unit groups:

7421 Wood treaters

7422 Cabinet-makers and related workers

7423 Woodworking-machine setters and setter-operators

7424 Basketry weavers, brush makers and related workers

Note

Occupations are classified into Major group 8, *Plant and machine operators and assemblers,* if the tasks call mainly for experience with and an understanding of the machinery operated and monitored.

Occupations are classified into Major group 9, *Elementary occupations,* if the tasks are of a simple and routine nature, mainly entail the use of hand-held tools, some physical effort, little or no previous experience and understanding of the work, and limited initiative or judgement.

7421 WOOD TREATERS

Wood treaters season and preserve wood.

Tasks include –

(a) operating steam-heated kilns to season wood;

(b) treating wood with chemicals to protect it against decay or parasites;

(c) performing related tasks;

(d) supervising other workers.

Examples of the occupations classified here:

■ Wood seasoner
■ Wood treater

Some related occupations classified elsewhere:

■ Machine-operator, treating/wood – 8141

7422 CABINET-MAKERS AND RELATED WORKERS

Cabinet-makers and related workers, by using tools and woodworking machines, make, decorate and repair wooden furniture, wheels or other wooden parts of vehicles, wooden fittings, patterns, models and other items such as pipes, wooden skis, shoes, or sports racquets and sticks.

Tasks include –

(a) making and repairing wooden articles, such as cabinets and other furniture, using woodworking machines and hand tools;

(b) making and repairing wooden vehicles, wheels or other wooden parts of vehicles;

(c) making and repairing wooden articles, such as patterns, scale models and mock-ups, casks, tobacco pipes, wooden skis, shoes or sports racquets or sticks;

(d) decorating furniture and fixtures by inlaying wood, applying veneer and carving designs;

(e) finishing surfaces of wooden articles or furniture;

(f) performing related tasks;

(g) supervising other workers.

Examples of the occupations classified here:

- Cabinet-maker
- Cart-wright
- Wheel-wright

Some related occupations classified elsewhere:

- Carpenter – 7124
- Joiner – 7124
- Machine-operator, furniture production – 8240

7423 WOODWORKING-MACHINE SETTERS AND SETTER-OPERATORS

Woodworking-machine setters and setter-operators set or set and operate woodworking machines, such as precision sawing, shaping, planing, boring, turning and woodcarving machines.

Tasks include –

(a) setting and adjusting various kinds of machines for operation by others;

(b) setting and operating one or several types of woodworking machines;

(c) performing related tasks;

(d) supervising other workers.

Examples of the occupations classified here:

- Sawyer, precision woodworking
- Setter, woodworking machine
- Setter-operator, woodworking machine
- Turner, wood

Some related occupations classified elsewhere:

- Machine-operator, woodworking – 8240
- Setter-operator, metalworking machine – 7223

7424 BASKETRY WEAVERS, BRUSH MAKERS AND RELATED WORKERS

Basketry weavers, brush makers and related workers make wicker furniture, brushes and brooms and weave baskets.

Tasks include –

(a) making wicker furniture from peeled and softened rattan, reeds, rushes, willow branches and similar materials;

(b) making various kinds of baskets by interlacing osier, rattan, reeds, rushes or similar materials;

(c) selecting and preparing brush materials, such as bristles, nylon, fibres and wire, and setting them in brush base;

(d) selecting and preparing materials, such as broom corn, bass and whisker fibre, and fastening them to broom handles;

(e) performing related tasks;

(f) supervising other workers.

Examples of the occupations classified here:

- Maker, basket
- Maker, brush
- Maker, furniture/wicker

Some related occupations classified elsewhere:

- Handicraft worker, wooden articles – 7331
- Machine-operator, woodworking – 8240

MINOR GROUP **743**
TEXTILE, GARMENT AND RELATED TRADES WORKERS

Textile, garment and related trades workers prepare natural textile fibres, threads and yarns, and make fabrics by weaving, knitting and other means, make and repair garments and other textile and fur articles, or they upholster furniture.

Tasks performed usually include: preparing natural textile fibres, spinning, doubling, twisting and winding threads and yarns; making fabrics by weaving, knitting and other techniques; making tailored garments; participating in the manufacture of ready-to-wear garments; making, altering and repairing articles made of fur; making patterns and marking and cutting textiles and similar materials; sewing textiles and similar materials by hand or hand-operated machines; upholstering furniture and making mattresses. Supervision of other workers may be included.

Occupations in this minor group are classified into the following unit groups:

> **7431 Fibre preparers**
>
> **7432 Weavers, knitters and related workers**
>
> **7433 Tailors, dressmakers and hatters**
>
> **7434 Furriers and related workers**
>
> **7435 Textile, leather and related pattern-makers and cutters**
>
> **7436 Sewers, embroiderers and related workers**
>
> **7437 Upholsterers and related workers**

Note

Occupations are classified into Major group 8, *Plant and machine operators and assemblers,* if the tasks call mainly for experience with and an understanding of the machinery operated and monitored.

Occupations are classified into Major group 9, *Elementary occupations,* if the tasks are of a simple and routine nature, mainly entail the use of hand-held tools, some physical effort, little or no previous experience and understanding of the work, and limited initiative or judgement.

7431 FIBRE PREPARERS

Fibre preparers prepare wool, cotton, flax, jute, hemp and other natural textile fibres for spinning and winding.

Tasks include –
(a) grading and classifying natural textile fibres;
(b) washing wool fibres;
(c) cleaning and fluffing textile fibres;
(d) forming fibres into sliver, combing them, combining sliver into sliver laps or forming sliver into rove;

(e) performing related tasks;
(f) supervising other workers.

Examples of the occupations classified here:
- Comber, fibre/textiles
- Drawer, fibre/textiles
- Rover, fibre/textiles

Some related occupations classified elsewhere:
- Machine-operator, combing/textile fibres – 8261

7432 WEAVERS, KNITTERS AND RELATED WORKERS

Weavers, knitters and related workers spin and wind yarn by hand, weave materials on hand looms, make carpets by using a knotting technique, knit garment fabrics by hand or hand-operated machine or perform similar manufacturing tasks by hand or hand-operated machine.

Tasks include –
(a) spinning and winding yarn by hand;
(b) drawing warp threads into loom by hand;
(c) weaving plain or figured cloth, tapestry, lace, carpet or other fabrics on hand looms;
(d) making carpets by using a knotting technique;
(e) knitting garments and other articles on hand-operated machine or by hand;
(f) crocheting or making braid by hand;
(g) making nets by hand;
(h) performing related tasks;
(i) supervising other workers.

Examples of the occupations classified here:
- Knitter
- Spinner, thread and yarn
- Threader, loom
- Weaver, carpet
- Weaver, cloth

Some related occupations classified elsewhere:
- Handicraft worker, textiles – 7332
- Machine-operator, knitting – 8262
- Machine-operator, weaving – 8262

7433 TAILORS, DRESSMAKERS AND HATTERS

Tailors, dressmakers and hatters make suits, dresses and other garments from textile fabrics, leather or any other material except fur, carry out alterations and repairs, or make hats, or participate in the manufacture of ready-to-wear garments.

Tasks include –
(a) making overcoats, suits, skirts, shirts, blouses, lingerie, corsetry and similar garments often to clients' individual requirements;
(b) participating in the manufacture of ready-to-wear clothing;
(c) making hats;
(d) altering, restyling and repairing garments;
(e) making and caring for costumes used in theatrical, television and motion picture productions;
(f) performing related tasks;
(g) supervising other workers.

Examples of the occupations classified here:
- Dressmaker
- Milliner
- Tailor

Some related occupations classified elsewhere:
- Handicraft worker, textiles – 7332
- Machine-operator, sewing – 8263

7434 FURRIERS AND RELATED WORKERS

Furriers and related workers make, alter, repair and restyle garments and other articles made of fur, or participate in the manufacture of ready-to-wear fur garments.

Tasks include –
(a) choosing, stretching and trimming dressed furs to conform to the chosen pattern outline of fur garments or other articles;
(b) making coats, jackets and other fur garments and articles;
(c) participation in the manufacture of ready-to-wear fur clothing;
(d) reclaiming furs or skins from old coats, gluing fabric to interior of fur coats and trimming blocked fur garments;
(e) altering, restyling and repairing fur garments and other fur articles;
(f) performing related tasks;
(g) supervising other workers.

Examples of the occupations classified here:
- Furrier

Some related occupations classified elsewhere:
- Machine-operator, sewing/fur − 8263

7435 TEXTILE, LEATHER AND RELATED PATTERN-MAKERS AND CUTTERS

Textile, leather and related pattern-makers and cutters make patterns and mark and cut textile, leather and other materials in the manufacture of garments, gloves and miscellaneous products.

Tasks include −
(a) drawing and cutting out patterns for making suits, dresses, shirts, blouses, gloves, hats and caps and other garments;
(b) making outlines of patterns on cloth, light leathers or other materials to guide cutting;
(c) cutting material according to pattern outline for making up garments, gloves and related items;
(d) performing pattern-making, marking and cutting tasks in the manufacture of other products such as soft furnishings, canvas goods and umbrellas;
(e) performing related tasks;
(f) supervising other workers.

Examples of the occupations classified here:
- Cutter, garment
- Cutter, glove
- Pattern-maker, fur
- Pattern-maker, garment

Some related occupations classified elsewhere:
- Machine-operator, pattern-making/textiles − 8269

7436 SEWERS, EMBROIDERERS AND RELATED WORKERS

Sewers, embroiderers and related workers sew together, repair and decorate garments, gloves and other products of textile, fur, leather and other materials by hand or by using simple sewing machines, and perform various related tasks.

Tasks include −
(a) performing various sewing tasks in making, altering and repairing articles of textile, leather and other materials;
(b) embroidering decorative designs on garments or materials;
(c) sewing sails, tents, awnings and similar articles;
(d) assembling and covering umbrellas;
(e) performing related tasks;
(f) supervising other workers.

Examples of the occupations classified here:
- Embroiderer
- Maker, umbrella
- Sewer

Some related occupations classified elsewhere:
- Dressmaker − 7433
- Handicraft worker, textiles − 7332
- Machine-operator, sewing − 8263

7437 UPHOLSTERERS AND RELATED WORKERS

Upholsterers and related workers upholster furniture, make mattresses, or make and install interior decorations of textile, leather and similar materials.

Tasks include −
(a) installing, arranging and securing springs, padding and covering material to furniture frames;
(b) fitting and installing covers and cushioning for seats and other furnishings on vehicles, such as motor cars, railways coaches and aircraft;
(c) making mattresses;
(d) fitting and installing soft furnishings and interior decorations of textile, leather and similar materials;
(e) performing related tasks;
(f) supervising other workers.

Examples of the occupations classified here:
- Maker, mattress
- Upholsterer, furniture
- Upholsterer, vehicle

MINOR GROUP **744**
PELT, LEATHER AND SHOEMAKING TRADES WORKERS

Pelt, leather and shoemaking trades workers prepare fur- and wool-bearing pelts for further use, make leather from hides and skins, make and repair footwear and other articles made of natural or synthetic leather with the exception of garments, hats and gloves, or make various other articles from leather and similar materials.

Tasks performed usually include: preparing fur- and wool-bearing pelts for making garments and other products by hand or by using simple tools; making leather from hides and skins; making and repairing footwear and other articles made from leather and similar materials, with the exception of garments, hats and gloves. Supervision of other workers may be included.

Occupations in this minor group are classified into the following unit groups:

> **7441   Pelt dressers, tanners and fellmongers**
>
> **7442   Shoe-makers and related workers**

Note

Occupations are classified into Major group 8, *Plant and machine operators and assemblers,* if the tasks call mainly for experience with and an understanding of the machinery operated and monitored.

Occupations are classified into Major group 9, *Elementary occupations,* if the tasks are of a simple and routine nature, mainly entail the use of hand-held tools, some physical effort, little or no previous experience and understanding of the work, and limited initiative or judgement.

7441   PELT DRESSERS, TANNERS AND FELLMONGERS

Pelt dressers, tanners and fellmongers prepare fur- and wool-bearing pelts for making garments and other products, and make leather from hides and skins.

Tasks include –

(a) sorting and grading pelts, hides and skins;

(b) removing flesh and fat from pelts before curing;

(c) removing flesh and hair from hides;

(d) removing long, coarse hair from pelts and trimming underlying hair to even length;

(e) operating machine to split hides edge-ways;

(f) treating hides to convert them into leather;

(g) applying dyes to fur pelts;

(h) dressing and applying dyes and stains to leather;

(i) stretching and smoothing dressed pelts;

(j) performing related tasks;

(k) supervising other workers.

Examples of the occupations classified here:

- Fellmonger
- Grader, pelt
- Tanner

Some related occupations classified elsewhere:

- Machine-operator, tanning – 8265

7442   SHOE-MAKERS AND RELATED WORKERS

Shoe-makers and related workers make and repair standard or special footwear and,

7

except for leather garments, hats and gloves, make natural or synthetic leather articles, such as luggage, handbags, and belts, or participate in the manufacture of shoes and related goods.

Tasks include –

(a) making patterns to guide the cutting of shoe parts;

(b) cutting out, preparing and fitting together shoe parts;

(c) sewing shoe parts together;

(d) making standard or orthopaedic footwear to individual requirements;

(e) making other special types of footwear to order;

(f) examining and finishing footwear;

(g) repairing footwear;

(h) making and repairing articles such as saddles and harnesses for animals, luggage, handbags, brief-cases, leather bags and other accessories;

(i) cutting out, shaping and padding parts for making leather articles;

(j) sewing and stitching leather parts by hand or machine;

(k) performing related tasks;

(l) supervising other workers.

Examples of the occupations classified here:

- Cobbler
- Saddler
- Shoe-maker

Some related occupations classified elsewhere:

- Machine-operator, shoe production – 8266

MAJOR GROUP **8**
PLANT AND MACHINE OPERATORS AND ASSEMBLERS

Plant and machine operators and assemblers operate and monitor industrial and agricultural machinery and equipment on the spot or by remote control, drive and operate trains, motor vehicles and mobile machinery and equipment, or assemble products from component parts according to strict specifications and procedures.

The work mainly calls for experience with and an understanding of industrial and agricultural machinery and equipment as well as an ability to cope with machine-paced operations and to adapt to technological innovations. Most occupations in this major group require skills at the second ISCO skill level.

Tasks performed by plant and machine operators and assemblers usually include: operating and monitoring mining or other industrial machinery and equipment for processing metal, minerals, glass, ceramics, wood, paper, or chemicals, as well as operating and monitoring water-treating or electrical-power-generating installations, and related plant; operating and monitoring machinery and equipment used to produce articles made of metal, minerals, chemicals, rubber, plastics, wood, paper, textiles, fur, or leather, and which process foodstuffs and related products; operating printing and bookbinding machines; driving and operating trains and motor vehicles; driving, operating and monitoring mobile industrial and agricultural machinery and equipment; assembling products from component parts according to strict specifications and procedures. Supervision of other workers may be included.

Occupations in this major group are classified into the following sub-major groups:

81 Stationary-plant and related operators

82 Machine operators and assemblers

83 Drivers and mobile-plant operators

Note

Occupations are classified into Major group 7, *Craft and related trades workers* if the tasks are carried out by hand and by hand-powered and other tools and call for an understanding of the work organisation, the materials and tools used, and the nature and purpose of the final product.

Occupations are classified into Major group 9, *Elementary occupations* if the tasks are of a simple and routine nature, mainly entail the use of hand-held tools, some physical effort, little or no previous experience and understanding of the work, and limited initiative or judgement.

8

SUB-MAJOR GROUP **81**
STATIONARY-PLANT AND RELATED OPERATORS

Stationary-plant and related operators operate and monitor, on the spot or by remote control, industrial plant for mining or for the processing of metal, minerals, glass, ceramics, wood, paper, chemicals, or water-treating, electrical-power-generating and other purposes, as well as automated and semi-automated assembling processes and industrial robots.

The work mainly calls for experience with and an understanding of the industrial plant which is being operated and monitored. Ability to cope with machine-paced operations and to adapt to innovations in machinery and equipment is often required.

Tasks performed by workers in this sub-major group usually include: operating and monitoring industrial plant for mining or for the processing of metal, minerals, glass, ceramics, wood, paper, chemicals, or water-treating, electrical-power-generating and other purposes; operating and monitoring automated or semi-automated assembly lines as well as industrial robots. Supervision of other workers may be included.

Occupations in this sub-major group are classified into the following minor groups:

811   Mining- and mineral-processing-plant operators

812   Metal-processing-plant operators

813   Glass, ceramics and related plant operators

814   Wood-processing- and papermaking-plant operators

815   Chemical-processing-plant operators

816   Power-production and related plant operators

817   Automated-assembly-line and industrial-robot operators

Note

Occupations are classified into Major group 7, *Craft and related trades workers* if the tasks are carried out by hand and by hand-powered and other tools and call for an understanding of the work organisation, the materials and tools used, and the nature and purpose of the final product.

Occupations are classified into Major group 9, *Elementary occupations* if the tasks are of a simple and routine nature, mainly entail the use of hand-held tools, some physical effort, little or no previous experience and understanding of the work, and limited initiative or judgement.

MINOR GROUP **811**
MINING- AND MINERAL-PROCESSING-PLANT OPERATORS

Mining- and mineral-processing-plant operators operate and monitor plant for cutting channels in a mine workface, for processing mineral ore and stone, or for the drilling and sinking of wells.

Tasks performed usually include: operating and monitoring machinery and equipment used for continuous mining or for drilling holes or cutting channels in a mine or quarry workface; operating and monitoring machinery and equipment used for processing mineral ore and stone, as well as for the drilling and sinking of wells. Supervision of other workers may be included.

Occupations in this minor group are classified into the following unit groups:

> **8111 Mining-plant operators**
>
> **8112 Mineral-ore- and stone-processing-plant operators**
>
> **8113 Well drillers and borers and related workers**

Note
Occupations are classified into Major group 7, *Craft and related trades workers* if the tasks are carried out by hand and by hand-powered and other tools and call for an understanding of the work organisation, the materials and tools used, and the nature and purpose of the final product.

Occupations are classified into Major group 9, *Elementary occupations* if the tasks are of a simple and routine nature, mainly entail the use of hand-held tools, some physical effort, little or no previous experience and understanding of the work, and limited initiative or judgement.

8111 MINING-PLANT OPERATORS

Mining-plant operators operate and monitor machinery and equipment which cut channels in a mine or quarry workface or drill holes for blasting, or they operate continuous-mining machines.

Tasks include –
(a) operating and monitoring machinery for cutting channels in a mine or quarry workface or for drilling blasting holes in mines or quarries;
(b) operating and monitoring continuous-mining machines;
(c) performing related tasks;
(d) supervising other workers.

Examples of the occupations classified here:
- Machine-operator, cutting/mine
- Machine-operator, drilling/mine
- Machine-operator, mining/continuous

Some related occupations classified elsewhere:
- Miner – 7111
- Quarrier – 7111
- Shotfirer – 7112

8112 MINERAL-ORE- AND STONE-PROCESSING-PLANT OPERATORS

Mineral-ore- and stone-processing-plant operators operate and monitor machinery and equipment for processing mineral ore and stone.

Tasks include –
(a) operating and monitoring equipment which crushes and breaks lumps of minerals and stones to required size;
(b) operating and monitoring washing, separating, leaching, precipitating, fil-

tering, extracting and combining equipment to wash mineral ores in order to remove waste material;

(c) combining mineral ores with solvents to facilitate further processing;

(d) separating metal or mineral concentrates from ore or alluvial deposits by thickening, flotation, gravity separation, filtration, or magnetic or electrostatic separation;

(e) performing related tasks;

(f) supervising other workers.

Examples of the occupations classified here:

- Floatation worker, minerals
- Machine-operator, crushing/mineral ore
- Machine-operator, milling/minerals
- Machine-operator, stone processing

Some related occupations classified elsewhere:

- Cutter, stone − 7113
- Splitter, stone − 7113

8113 WELL DRILLERS AND BORERS AND RELATED WORKERS

Well drillers and borers and related workers erect and operate drilling machinery and equipment and perform related tasks in the sinking and operation of wells.

Tasks include –

(a) preparing and operating derrick pipe-handling devices and slush pumps;

(b) operating rotary- or percussion-drilling machinery and equipment to drill oil or gas wells;

(c) cleaning and servicing oil or gas wells and replacing pumping rods, casings and tubings;

(d) setting up and operating drilling machinery and equipment to drill wells or bores other than for oil or gas;

(e) performing related tasks;

(f) supervising other workers.

Examples of the occupations classified here:

- Operator, boring equipment/wells
- Operator, derrick/oil and gas wells
- Operator, drilling equipment/wells

MINOR GROUP 812
METAL-PROCESSING-PLANT OPERATORS

Metal-processing-plant operators operate and monitor ore-smelting, metal-converting and refining furnaces, metal-rolling mills, metal-heat-treating- or metal-extrusion plant.

Tasks performed usually include: operating and monitoring furnaces for ore-smelting, melting, refining, converting or reheating metal, as well as plant for rolling, extruding or shaping metal. Supervision of other workers may be included.

Occupations in this minor group are classified into the following unit groups:

8121 Ore and metal furnace operators

8122 Metal melters, casters and rolling-mill operators

8123 Metal-heat-treating-plant operators

8124 Metal drawers and extruders

8121 ORE AND METAL FURNACE OPERATORS

Ore and metal furnace operators operate and monitor ore-smelting, metal-converting and refining furnaces.

Tasks include –

(a) operating and monitoring blast furnaces to smelt ores for the production of ferrous or non-ferrous metals;

(b) operating and monitoring furnaces to convert or refine pig-iron or scrap-metal to produce steel;

(c) operating and monitoring furnaces to convert or refine non-ferrous metals;

(d) performing related tasks;

(e) supervising other workers.

Examples of the occupations classified here:
- Furnace-operator, converting/non-ferrous metals
- Furnace-operator, refining/steel (open-hearth furnace)
- Furnace-operator, smelting/metal (blast furnace)

8122 METAL MELTERS, CASTERS AND ROLLING-MILL OPERATORS

Metal melters, casters and rolling-mill operators operate and monitor rolling mills to roll metal, or furnaces to melt or reheat metal, or machines to cast metal.

Tasks include –

(a) operating and monitoring furnaces to melt ferrous and non-ferrous metal for casting;

(b) operating and monitoring furnaces to reheat stock metal forms prior to forging, power-pressing, rolling and further processing;

(c) operating and monitoring rolling mills to shape hot or cold steel into shapes for further processing, or into final shapes;

(d) operating and monitoring rolling mills to reduce or form hot or cold non-ferrous metal to specified shapes, such as plate, sheet or foil;

(e) operating and monitoring rolls to form seamless tubes and pipes from billets which have been pierced longitudinally;

(f) pouring molten metal into moulds and operating and monitoring casting machines;

(g) performing related tasks;

(h) supervising other workers.

Examples of the occupations classified here:
- Furnace-operator, melting/metal
- Machine-operator, casting/metal
- Operator, rolling mill/non-ferrous metal

8123 METAL-HEAT-TREATING-PLANT OPERATORS

Metal-heat-treating-plant operators operate and monitor plant altering the physical properties of metal objects by heating, cooling and chemical treatment.

Tasks include –

(a) operating and monitoring furnaces which heat and cool metal objects to relieve internal stresses, restore ductility and refine grain structure;

(b) operating and monitoring furnaces which harden steel objects;

(c) operating and monitoring plant which imparts a hard skin and tough, ductile core to steel objects by treating them with chemicals, heating and quenching or cooling them;

(d) operating and monitoring furnaces which reheat hardened steel objects to

relieve stresses and to impart tough-
ness;

(e) performing related tasks;

(f) supervising other workers.

Examples of the occupations classified here:

- Annealer
- Furnace-operator, hardening/metal
- Furnace-operator, heat-treating/metal

8124 METAL DRAWERS AND EXTRUDERS

Metal drawers and extruders operate and monitor machinery and equipment which draw and extrude metals to make wire, tubes and similar products.

Tasks include –

(a) operating and monitoring wire-drawing machines;

(b) operating and monitoring machines to draw seamless metal tubing;

(c) operating and monitoring extrusion presses to make metal rods, bars and seamless tubing;

(d) performing related tasks;

(e) supervising other workers.

Examples of the occupations classified here:

- Machine-operator, drawing/wire
- Machine-operator, extruding/metal

Some related occupations classified elsewhere:

- Drawer, wire – 7221

MINOR GROUP 813
GLASS, CERAMICS AND RELATED PLANT OPERATORS

Glass, ceramics and related plant operators operate and monitor kilns, furnaces and other machinery and equipment used in the manufacture of glass as well as ceramic products.

Tasks performed usually include: operating and monitoring kilns, furnaces and other machinery and equipment used for making glass as well as ceramic products. Supervision of other workers may be included.

Occupations in this minor group are classified into the following unit groups:

8131 Glass and ceramics kiln and related machine operators

8139 Glass, ceramics and related plant operators not elsewhere classified

Note
Occupations are classified into Major group 7, *Craft and related trades workers* if the tasks are carried out by hand and by hand-powered and other tools and call for an understanding of the work organisation, the materials and tools used, and the nature and purpose of the final product.

Occupations are classified into Major group 7, *Elementary occupations* if the tasks are of a simple and routine nature, mainly entail the use of hand-held tools, some physical effort, little or no previous experience and understanding of the work, and limited initiative or judgement.

8131 GLASS AND CERAMICS KILN AND RELATED MACHINE OPERATORS

Glass and ceramics kiln and related machine operators operate and monitor kilns, furnaces and other machinery and equipment used in the manufacture of glass, ceramics, porcelain or bricks.

Tasks include –

(a) operating and monitoring glass-making furnaces;

(b) operating and monitoring glass-annealing furnaces to prevent or remove internal stresses;

(c) operating and monitoring tempering furnaces to toughen glass;

(d) operating and monitoring machines which shape glass articles by blowing or pressure-moulding;

(e) operating and monitoring machines which draw or roll molten glass to a continuous sheet of flat glass;

(f) operating and monitoring floating-glass production plant;

(g) operating and monitoring machines which polish and level plate-glass surfaces;

(h) operating and monitoring machines which make glass rods and tubes from molten glass by drawing or drawing and blowing;

(i) operating and monitoring kilns which bake pottery and porcelainware or which fix glazing and decoration by re-baking;

(j) operating and monitoring kilns which bake bricks and tiles;

(k) performing related tasks;

(l) supervising other workers.

Examples of the occupations classified here:
- Furnace-operator, glass production
- Kiln-operator, brick and tile
- Kiln-operator, pottery and porcelain
- Machine-operator, blowing/glass

Some related occupations classified elsewhere:
- Blower, glass – 7322
- Cutter, glass – 7322
- Moulder, brick and tile – 7321

8139 GLASS, CERAMICS AND RELATED PLANT OPERATORS NOT ELSEWHERE CLASSIFIED

This unit group covers glass and ceramics plant operators not classified elsewhere in Minor group 813, *Glass and ceramics plant operators*.

For instance, here should be classified those who are engaged in operating and monitoring machinery and equipment used to mix ingredients for glass-making or for the preparation of clay, glaze and abrasives, or which extrude molten glass in order to form fibreglass filaments.

In such cases tasks would include –

(a) operating and monitoring machines which mix ingredients for glass-making;

(b) operating and monitoring machines which prepare clay for the production of ceramics and bricks;

(c) operating and monitoring machines for making glaze or abrasives;

(d) operating and monitoring machines which extrude molten glass to form fibreglass filaments;

(e) performing related tasks;

(f) supervising other workers.

Examples of the occupations classified here:
- Machine-operator, mixing/clay
- Machine-operator, mixing/glass

MINOR GROUP **814**
WOOD-PROCESSING- AND PAPERMAKING-PLANT OPERATORS

Wood-processing- and papermaking-plant operators operate and monitor machinery and equipment which saw, cut and grind wood in preparation for further use, convert wood and other materials into pulp, and make paper from pulp.

Tasks performed usually include: operating and monitoring machinery and equipment which process wood for further use, convert wood and other materials into pulp, and make paper from pulp. Supervision of other workers may be included.

Occupations in this minor group are classified into the following unit groups:

8141   Wood-processing-plant operators

8142   Paper-pulp plant operators

8143   Papermaking-plant operators

Note
Occupations are classified into Major group 7, *Craft and related trades workers* if the tasks are carried out by hand and by hand-powered and other tools and call for an understanding of the work organisation, the materials and tools used, and the nature and purpose of the final product.

Occupations are classified into Major group 9, *Elementary occupations* if the tasks are of a simple and routine nature, mainly entail the use of hand-held tools, some physical effort, little or no previous experience and understanding of the work, and limited initiative or judgement.

8141   WOOD-PROCESSING-PLANT OPERATORS

Wood-processing-plant operators operate and monitor machinery and equipment for sawing wood, cutting veneer and making plywood, and otherwise prepare wood for further use.

Tasks include –
(a) operating and monitoring log in-feed and conveyor systems;
(b) operating and monitoring head saws, resaws and multiblade saws to saw logs, cants, flitches, slabs or wings and remove rough edges from sawn timber;
(c) operating and monitoring machines which cut veneer;
(d) operating and monitoring plywood core-laying machines and hot-plate plywood presses;
(e) performing related tasks;
(f) supervising other workers.

Examples of the occupations classified here:
- Operator, band-saw
- Operator, sawmill
- Operator, wood-processing plant
- Press-operator, plywood

Some related occupations classified elsewhere:
- Wood seasoner – 7421
- Wood treater – 7421

8142   PAPER-PULP PLANT OPERATORS

Paper-pulp plant operators operate and monitor machinery and equipment which converts materials such as wood, rags, esparto, straw, scrap-pulp and paper into stock for use in papermaking.

Tasks include –

(a) operating and monitoring chipper and grinding machines which reduce logs to pulp;

(b) operating and monitoring digesters which produce pulp from materials such as wood, rags, esparto, straw or scrap-pulp and scrap paper;

(c) operating and monitoring machines which bleach wood pulp, rags, esparto, straw or scrap-pulp and scrap paper;

(d) operating and monitoring machines which mix, beat and hydrate pulp and other ingredients to prepare stuff for making paper;

(e) performing related tasks;

(f) supervising other workers.

Examples of the occupations classified here:

- Machine-operator, grinding/wood
- Operator, chipper/paper pulp
- Operator, paper-pulp plant

8143 PAPERMAKING-PLANT OPERATORS

Papermaking-plant operators operate and monitor machinery and equipment which makes paper, paper board and sheet pulp from pulp stock.

Tasks include –

(a) operating and monitoring section of papermaking machinery and equipment in which wet pulp is formed into paper or in which paper is dried, calendered, wound, slit and rewound;

(b) operating and monitoring supercalenders used to impart gloss and finish to surface of paper;

(c) operating and monitoring machinery and equipment used to glaze or impregnate paper with coating mixture;

(d) performing related tasks;

(e) supervising other workers.

Examples of the occupations classified here:

- Operator, papermaking plant
- Operator, supercalender

MINOR GROUP 815
CHEMICAL-PROCESSING-PLANT OPERATORS

Chemical-processing-plant operators operate and monitor machinery and equipment which process chemicals and related materials to obtain products with desirable properties.

Tasks performed usually include: operating and monitoring machinery and equipment for processing chemicals by crushing, heating, mixing, distilling or filtering to obtain products with desirable properties, or plant for treating petroleum and petroleum-based products. Supervision of other workers may be included.

Occupations in this minor group are classified into the following unit groups:

8151 Crushing-, grinding- and chemical-mixing-machinery operators

8152 Chemical-heat-treating-plant operators

8153 Chemical-filtering- and separating-equipment operators

8154 Chemical-still and reactor operators (except petroleum and natural gas)

8155 Petroleum- and natural-gas-refining-plant operators

8159 Chemical-processing-plant operators not elsewhere classified

Note

Occupations are classified into Major group 7, *Craft and related trades workers* if the tasks are carried out by hand and by hand-powered and other tools and call for an understanding of the work organisation, the materials and tools used, and the nature and purpose of the final product.

Occupations are classified into Major group 9, *Elementary occupations* if the tasks are of a simple and routine nature, mainly entail the use of hand-held tools, some physical effort, little or no previous experience and understanding of the work, and limited initiative or judgement.

8151 CRUSHING-, GRINDING- AND CHEMICAL-MIXING-MACHINERY OPERATORS

Crushing-, grinding- and chemical-mixing-machinery operators operate and monitor machinery which crushes, grinds, mixes and blends chemicals and other materials used in chemical and related processes.

Tasks include –
(a) operating and monitoring mills and crushing machines which reduce solid chemicals and related materials to suitable size for further processing;
(b) operating and monitoring machines in which solids or liquids used in chemical and related processes are mixed or blended;
(c) performing related tasks;
(d) supervising other workers.

Examples of the occupations classified here:
- Machine-operator, crushing/chemical and related processes
- Machine-operator, mixing/chemical and related processes
- Operator, mill/chemical and related processes

8152 CHEMICAL-HEAT-TREATING-PLANT OPERATORS

Chemical-heat-treating-plant operators operate and monitor machinery and equipment which cook, roast and provide other types of heat treatment in chemical and related processes.

Tasks include –
(a) operating and monitoring machinery and equipment which cook materials in order to purify, mix or compound them, give them special properties or effect chemical changes in them;
(b) operating and monitoring ovens, kilns or similar devices which heat substances in order to dry them, give them special properties or effect chemical changes in them;
(c) operating and monitoring driers for the processing of chemicals and related materials;
(d) performing related tasks;
(e) supervising other workers.

Examples of the occupations classified here:
- Kiln-operator, chemical and related processes
- Operator, cement production plant
- Operator, roasting equipment/chemical and related processes

8153 CHEMICAL-FILTERING- AND SEPARATING-EQUIPMENT OPERATORS

Chemical-filtering- and separating-equipment operators operate and monitor machines and equipment which filter and separate chemicals and related materials.

Tasks include –
(a) operating and monitoring equipment in which solutions are forced, under pressure, through a filtering unit;
(b) operating and monitoring equipment in which solutions are vacuum-drawn through filtering media fitted to a rotating drum;

(c) operating and monitoring machines which separate substances by centrifugal force;

(d) operating and monitoring equipment which removes sediment and water from crude oil;

(e) performing related tasks;

(f) supervising other workers.

Examples of the occupations classified here:

- Operator, separator/chemical and related processes
- Operator, treating equipment/crude oil
- Filter-press operator, chemical and related materials

8154 CHEMICAL-STILL AND REACTOR OPERATORS (EXCEPT PETROLEUM AND NATURAL GAS)

Still and reactor operators (except petroleum and natural gas) operate and monitor equipment which distils and refines chemicals, except petroleum.

Tasks include –

(a) operating and monitoring equipment in which crude liquid chemicals are treated to refine or separate them into their chemical constituents;

(b) operating and monitoring equipment which performs a sequence of operations in a chemical reaction process;

(c) operating and monitoring evaporation tanks, vacuum pans or similar devices to concentrate solutions and suspensions;

(d) performing related tasks;

(e) supervising other workers.

Examples of the occupations classified here:

- Operator, converter/chemical processes (except petroleum and natural gas)
- Operator, reactor/chemical processes (except petroleum and natural gas)
- Operator, still/turpentine

8155 PETROLEUM- AND NATURAL-GAS-REFINING-PLANT OPERATORS

Petroleum- and natural-gas-refining-plant operators operate and monitor plant which refines, distils and treats petroleum, petroleum-based products and by-products, or natural gas.

Tasks include –

(a) operating and monitoring plant which removes sulphur from petroleum and petroleum-based products, and by-products;

(b) operating and monitoring pumps which circulate petroleum products or water and chemical solutions through refinery;

(c) operating and monitoring stills which distil or refine petroleum products;

(d) operating and monitoring machines which blend petrol with chemicals and other additives;

(e) operating and monitoring machines which refine or otherwise treat natural gas;

(f) performing related tasks;

(g) supervising other workers.

Examples of the occupations classified here:

- Operator, blender/petroleum and natural gas refining (ethyl)
- Operator, paraffin plant
- Operator, still/petroleum and natural gas refining

8159 CHEMICAL-PROCESSING-PLANT OPERATORS NOT ELSEWHERE CLASSIFIED

This unit group covers chemical-processing-plant operators not classified elsewhere in Minor group 815, *Chemical-processing-plant operators.*

For instance, here should be classified those who are engaged in operating and monitoring machinery and equipment which treat chemical solutions with bleaching reagents, produce coke or gas from coal, extrude and form natural or synthetic polymers into synthetic fibres, produce fertilisers, or extract and process radioactive materials.

In such cases tasks would include –

(a) operating and monitoring plant which treats chemical solutions with bleaching reagents;

(b) operating and monitoring plant which produces coke or gas from coal;

(c) operating and monitoring plant which extrudes or forms natural or synthetic polymers into synthetic fibres;

(d) operating and monitoring fertiliser plant equipment;

(e) operating and monitoring plant which separates and extracts radioactive materials from their ores or processes such materials;

(f) performing related tasks;

(g) supervising other workers.

Examples of the occupations classified here:
- Operator, coke production plant
- Operator, fertiliser plant
- Operator, synthetic-fibre production plant

MINOR GROUP 816
POWER-PRODUCTION AND RELATED PLANT OPERATORS

Power-production and related plant operators operate and monitor machinery and equipment in an electrical-power-generating plant, and water-treatment, incinerator and related plant, and operate and maintain ships' and other types of steam-engines, as well as boilers.

Tasks performed usually include: operating and monitoring machinery and equipment for producing electric power; operating and monitoring steam-engines and boilers and other stationary machinery and equipment such as incinerators or water-treatment plant and pumping stations. Supervision of other workers may be included.

Occupations in this minor group are classified into the following unit groups:

8161   Power-production plant operators

8162   Steam-engine and boiler operators

8163   Incinerator, water-treatment and related plant operators

Note
Occupations are classified into Major group 7, *Craft and related trades workers* if the tasks are carried out by hand and by hand-powered and other tools and call for an understanding of the work organisation, the materials and tools used, and the nature and purpose of the final product.

Occupations are classified into Major group 9, *Elementary occupations* if the tasks are of a simple and routine nature, mainly entail the use of hand-held tools, some physical effort, little or no previous experience and understanding of the work, and limited initiative or judgement.

8161   POWER-PRODUCTION PLANT OPERATORS

Power-production plant operators operate and monitor machinery and equipment which produce electric or other power and control its distribution.

Tasks include –

(a) operating and monitoring coal-, oil- or natural-gas-fired steam-power-generating plant;

(b) operating and monitoring nuclear-fuelled steam-power-generating plant;

(c) operating and monitoring hydroelectric-power-generating stations;

(d) operating and monitoring other power-generating plant, such as solar, tidal, geo-thermal or wind energy;

(e) controlling power output and distribution of electricity from power stations;

(f) performing related tasks;

(g) supervising other workers.

Examples of the occupations classified here:

- Operator, electric power plant
- Operator, hydroelectric power plant
- Operator, nuclear power plant
- Operator, solar power plant

8162 STEAM-ENGINE AND BOILER OPERATORS

Steam-engine and boiler operators operate and monitor steam-engines and boilers on land and at sea.

Tasks include –

(a) operating and monitoring coal- or oil-fired steam-engines or boilers on land and at sea;

(b) performing related tasks;

(c) supervising other workers.

Examples of the occupations classified here:

- Operator, boiler/ship
- Operator, steam engine

8163 INCINERATOR, WATER-TREATMENT AND RELATED PLANT OPERATORS

Incinerator, water-treatment and related plant operators operate and monitor various types of plant, such as incinerators, water-treatment plant, air and gas compressors, pumping stations, refrigeration or heating and ventilation systems.

Tasks include –

(a) operating and monitoring incinerator machinery and equipment which burn garbage or other waste materials;

(b) operating and monitoring machinery and equipment which purify and clarify water for human consumption or use and later disposal into natural water systems;

(c) operating and monitoring air and gas compressors;

(d) operating and monitoring pumping stations for transferring liquids, gases, semi-liquids and powdered substances from one location to another;

(e) operating and monitoring refrigeration systems for cool or cold storage, or industrial processes;

(f) operating and monitoring heating and ventilation systems;

(g) performing related tasks;

(h) supervising other workers.

Examples of the occupations classified here:

- Operator, incinerator/refuse disposal
- Operator, pumping-station/water
- Operator, water purification plant

MINOR GROUP **817**
AUTOMATED-ASSEMBLY-LINE AND INDUSTRIAL-ROBOT OPERATORS

Automated-assembly-line and industrial-robot operators operate and monitor automated or semi-automated assembly lines as well as industrial robots.

Tasks performed usually include: operating and monitoring automated or semi-automated assembly lines as well as industrial robots.

Occupations in this minor group are classified into the following unit groups:

8171 Automated-assembly-line operators

8172 Industrial-robot operators

Note

Occupations are classified into Major group 7, *Craft and related trades workers* if the tasks are carried out by hand and by hand-powered and other tools and call for an understanding of the work organisation, the materials and tools used, and the nature and purpose of the final product.

Occupations are classified into Major group 9, *Elementary occupations* if the tasks are of a simple and routine nature, mainly entail the use of hand-held tools, some physical effort, little or no previous experience and understanding of the work, and limited initiative or judgement.

8171 AUTOMATED-ASSEMBLY-LINE OPERATORS

Automated-assembly-line operators operate and monitor automated or semi-automated assembly lines.

Tasks include –
(a) operating and monitoring automated or semi-automated assembly lines;
(b) performing related tasks;
(c) supervising other workers.

Examples of the occupations classified here:

Operator, assembly-line/automated.

8172 INDUSTRIAL-ROBOT OPERATORS

Industrial-robot operators load and unload industrial robots and perform related tasks.

Tasks include –
(a) operating and monitoring industrial robots;
(b) performing related tasks;
(c) supervising other workers.

Examples of the occupations classified here:

- Operator, robot

Some related occupations classified elsewhere:

- Controller, robot – 3123

SUB-MAJOR GROUP 82
MACHINE OPERATORS AND ASSEMBLERS

Machine operators and assemblers operate and monitor industrial machines, on the spot or by remote control, or they assemble products from parts according to strict specifications and procedures.

The work mainly calls for experience with and an understanding of the industrial machinery and equipment which is being operated and monitored. Ability to cope with machine-paced operations and to adapt to technological innovations is often required.

Tasks performed by workers in this sub-major group usually include: operating and monitoring machines which produce goods made of metal, minerals, chemicals, rubber, plastics, wood, paper, textiles, fur and leather, and which process foodstuffs and related products; operating printing and bookbinding machines; operating product-packing and labelling machines; assembling products from component parts according to strict specifications and procedures. Supervision of other workers may be included.

Occupations in this sub-major group are classified into the following minor groups:

821   Metal- and mineral-products machine operators

822   Chemical-products machine operators

823   Rubber- and plastic-products machine operators

824   Wood-products machine operators

825   Printing-, binding- and paper-products machine operators

826   Textile-, fur- and leather-products machine operators

827   Food and related products machine operators

828   Assemblers

829   Other machine operators and assemblers

Note

Occupations are classified into Major group 7, *Craft and related trades workers* if the tasks are carried out by hand and by hand-powered and other tools and call for an understanding of the work organisation, the materials and tools used and the nature and purpose of the final product.

Occupations are classified into Major group 9, *Elementary occupations* if the tasks are of a simple and routine nature, mainly entail the use of hand-held tools, some physical effort, little or no previous experience and understanding of the work, and limited initiative or judgement.

MINOR GROUP 821
METAL- AND MINERAL-PRODUCTS MACHINE OPERATORS

Metal- and mineral-products machine operators operate and monitor metalworking machines, or make products composed primarily of non-metallic mineral materials.

Tasks performed usually include: operating and monitoring metalworking machines such as lathes, power shears, and boring, grinding and metal-sawing machine tools, or machines to extrude, mould, mix, grind and cut various pre-cast cement, concrete and stone products. Supervision of other workers may be included.

Occupations in this minor group are classified into the following unit groups:

8211   Machine-tool operators

8212   Cement and other mineral products machine operators

8

Occupations are classified into Major group 7, *Craft and related trade workers* if the tasks are carried out by hand and by hand-powered and other tools and call for an understanding of the work organisation, the materials and tools used, and the nature and purpose of the final product.

Occupations are classified into Major group 9, *Elementary occupations* if the tasks are of a simple and routine nature, mainly entail the use of hand-held tools, some physical effort, little or no previous experience and understanding of the work, and limited initiative or judgement.

8211 MACHINE-TOOL OPERATORS

Machine-tool operators operate and monitor automatic or semi-automatic metal-working machines which perform repetitive work and are set up by machine-tool setters.

Tasks include –

(a) operating and monitoring one or more machine tools such as lathes, stamping presses, power shears, metal-bending, milling, planing, boring, drilling, grinding, honing or metal-sawing machines which may be numerically controlled or linked by an automatic-transfer machine;

(b) performing related tasks;

(c) supervising other workers.

Examples of the occupations classified here:

- Lathe-operator, capstan/metalworking
- Machine-operator, boring/metal
- Machine-operator, machine tool

Some related occupations classified elsewhere:

- Setter, machine-tool – 7223
- Setter-operator, machine-tool – 7223

8212 CEMENT AND OTHER MINERAL PRODUCTS MACHINE OPERATORS

Cement and other mineral products machine operators operate and monitor extrusion, moulding, mixing, grinding and cutting machines which manufacture and finish various pre-cast concrete and stone products, or which make cast stone for building purposes.

Tasks include –

(a) operating and monitoring extrusion, moulding, grinding and cutting machines which manufacture and finish various pre-cast concrete and stone products, such as flagstones, fencing posts, moulded pipe sections and trench liners, walling and partition slabs, building components, cable conduits, fume and dust extraction conduits;

(b) operating and monitoring machines which mix sand, gravel, cement and water to make concrete;

(c) performing related tasks;

(d) supervising other workers.

Examples of the occupations classified here:

- Machine-operator, cast-concrete products
- Machine-operator, cast-stone products

Some related occupations classified elsewhere:

- Kiln-operator, cement production – 8152
- Machine-operator, stone processing – 8112

MINOR GROUP **822**
CHEMICAL-PRODUCTS MACHINE OPERATORS

Chemical-products machine operators operate and monitor machines which process a variety of chemicals and other ingredients to produce pharmaceuticals, toiletries, explosives, photographic or other chemical products, or to finish, plate and coat metal articles.

Tasks performed usually include: operating and monitoring machines which mould, filter, ferment, mix, blend and otherwise process chemicals and other materials to give them the desired properties for further industrial production, or to make finished products; operating and monitoring machines which finish, plate and coat metal products. Supervision of other workers may be included.

Occupations in this minor group are classified into the following unit groups:

8221 Pharmaceutical- and toiletry-products machine operators

8222 Ammunition- and explosive-products machine operators

8223 Metal finishing-, plating- and coating-machine operators

8224 Photographic-products machine operators

8229 Chemical-products machine operators not elsewhere classified

Note
Occupations are classified into Major group 7, *Craft and related trades workers,* if the tasks are carried out by hand and by hand-powered and other tools and call for an understanding of the work organisation, the materials and tools used and the nature and purpose of the final product.

Occupations are classified into Major group 9, *Elementary occupations* if the tasks are of a simple and routine nature, mainly entail the use of hand-held tools, some physical effort, little or no previous experience and understanding of the work, and limited initiative or judgement.

8221 PHARMACEUTICAL- AND TOILETRY-PRODUCTS MACHINE OPERATORS

Pharmaceutical- and toiletry-products machine operators operate and monitor machines which process a variety of chemicals and other ingredients used in the production of pharmaceuticals and toiletries.

Tasks include –

(a) operating and monitoring machines for moulding, filtering, fermenting, heating, mixing, grinding, filling and sealing materials used in the production of pharmaceuticals, toiletries, detergents and related products;

(b) operating controls to regulate temperature, pressure, flow and speed of operation;

(c) cleaning and disinfecting equipment;

(d) performing related tasks;

(e) supervising other workers.

Examples of the occupations classified here:
- Machine-operator, detergent production
- Machine-operator, pharmaceutical products
- Machine-operator, toiletries production

8222 AMMUNITION- AND EXPLOSIVE-PRODUCTS MACHINE OPERATORS

Ammunition- and explosive-products machine operators operate and monitor machines which process a variety of chemicals and other ingredients in the production of ammunition and explosives.

Tasks include –

(a) operating and monitoring machines which mix, blend and otherwise process chemicals to produce explosive substances such as nitrocellulose, gelignite and various types of propellants;

(b) operating and monitoring machines which make fuses for explosives and pyrotechnics;

(c) operating and monitoring machines which assemble and load shells, bombs, rockets, mines and similar devices;

(d) performing related tasks;

(e) supervising other workers.

Examples of the occupations classified here:

- Machine-operator, ammunition products
- Machine-operator, explosives production
- Machine-operator, match production

8223 METAL FINISHING-, PLATING- AND COATING-MACHINE OPERATORS

Metal finishing-, plating- and coating-machine operators operate and monitor equipment which finishes, plates and coats metal articles or parts, in order to give them improved resistance to corrosion and abrasion, for decorative purposes, or to impart electrical or magnetic properties.

Tasks include –

(a) operating and monitoring equipment which cleans metal articles in preparation for electroplating, galvanising, enamelling or similar processes;

(b) operating and monitoring electroplating equipment;

(c) operating and monitoring hot-dip equipment used to coat iron and steel products;

(d) operating and monitoring machines which automatically coat wire with non-ferrous metal;

(e) operating and monitoring equipment used to spray molten metal or other substances on metal products to provide a protective or decorative coating or to build up worn or damaged surfaces;

(f) operating and monitoring equipment used to impart a rust-resistant finish to metal articles by treating them with chemicals and heating them;

(g) performing related tasks;

(h) supervising other workers.

Examples of the occupations classified here:

- Machine-operator, coating/metal
- Machine-operator, finishing/metal
- Machine-operator, plating/metal

8224 PHOTOGRAPHIC-PRODUCTS MACHINE OPERATORS

Photographic-products machine operators operate and monitor equipment which makes photographic film and paper, and which processes exposed photographic film and makes prints.

Tasks include –

(a) operating and monitoring equipment which makes photographic film and paper;

(b) operating and monitoring machines for coating and backing photographic plates;

(c) operating and monitoring equipment which processes colour and black-and-white films and plates to obtain negatives or transparent positives;

(d) operating and monitoring equipment which prints black-and-white or colour photographs or which enlarges or reduces photographs;

(e) performing related tasks;

(f) supervising other workers.

Examples of the occupations classified here:

- Machine-operator, developing/photography
- Machine-operator, enlarging/photography

- Machine-operator, photographic-film production
- Machine-operator, printing/photography (colour)

Some related occupations classified elsewhere:

- Developer, film/colour – 7344
- Enlarger, photograph – 7344
- Printer, photograph – 7344

8229 CHEMICAL-PRODUCTS MACHINE OPERATORS NOT ELSEWHERE CLASSIFIED

This unit group covers chemical-products machine operators not classified elsewhere in Minor group 822, *Chemical-products machine operators.*

For instance here should be classified those who operate and monitor machines which produce chemical-based products such as linoleum, candles, halogen gases and related items.

In such cases tasks would include –

(a) operating and monitoring machines which make linoleum, candles, halogen gases and related chemical products;

(b) performing related tasks;

(c) supervising other workers.

Examples of the occupations classified here:

- Machine-operator, candle production
- Machine-operator, halogen gas production
- Machine-operator, linoleum production

MINOR GROUP 823
RUBBER- AND PLASTIC-PRODUCTS MACHINE OPERATORS

Rubber- and plastic-products machine operators operate and monitor machines which knead and blend rubber and rubber compounds, and produce various components and products from natural and synthetic rubber and plastics.

Tasks performed usually include: operating and monitoring machines which knead and blend rubber and rubber compounds, and produce various components and products from natural and synthetic rubber and plastics. Supervision of other workers may be included.

Occupations in this minor group are classified into the following unit groups:

8231 Rubber-products machine operators

8232 Plastic-products machine operators

Note
Occupations are classified into Major group 7, *Craft and related trades workers* if the tasks are carried out by hand and by hand-powered and other tools and call for an understanding of the work organisation, the materials and tools used, and the nature and purpose of the final product.

Occupations are classified into Major group 9, *Elementary occupations* if the tasks are of a simple and routine nature, mainly entail the use of hand-held tools, some physical effort, little or no previous experience and understanding of the work, and limited initiative or judgement.

8231 RUBBER-PRODUCTS MACHINE OPERATORS

Rubber-products machine operators operate and monitor machines which knead and blend rubber and rubber compounds, and produce various components and products, from natural and synthetic rubber, such as moulded footwear, domestic articles, insulating materials, industrial accessories, or tyres for bicycles, automobiles, tractors, aircraft and other vehicles.

Tasks include –

(a) operating and monitoring machines which knead, mix and blend rubber and rubber compounds for further processing;

(b) operating and monitoring machines which produce sheets of rubber or rubberised fabric by a rolling process;

(c) operating and monitoring machines which extrude compounded rubber or shape vulcanised rubber by moulding;

(d) operating and monitoring machines which build up tires on a form, vulcanise tires and mould or rebuild used tires;

(e) performing related tasks;

(f) supervising other workers.

Examples of the occupations classified here:

- Machine-operator, extruding/rubber
- Machine-operator, milling/rubber
- Machine-operator, tyre production

8232 PLASTIC-PRODUCTS MACHINE OPERATORS

Plastic-products machine operators operate and monitor machines which knead and blend compounds to obtain plastic materials and which make various plastic components and articles.

Tasks include –

(a) operating and monitoring machines which knead and blend compounds to obtain plastic materials;

(b) operating and monitoring machines which shape plastic materials by moulding, extrusion, cutting and other means;

(c) operating and monitoring machines which laminate plastics and plastic-impregnated materials;

(d) performing related tasks;

(e) supervising other workers.

Examples of the occupations classified here:

- Machine-operator, extruding/plastics
- Machine-operator, moulding/plastics
- Machine-operator, plastics production

MINOR GROUP 824
WOOD-PRODUCTS MACHINE OPERATORS

Wood-products machine operators operate and monitor automatic and semi-automatic woodworking machines which perform repetitive work and are always set up by woodworking-machine setters.

Tasks performed usually include: operating and monitoring woodworking machines for sawing, shaping, boring, planing, turning or carving wood. Supervision of other workers may be included.

Occupations in this minor group are classified into the following unit group:

8240 Wood-products machine operators

Note
Occupations are classified into Major group 7, *Craft and related trades workers* if the tasks are carried out by hand and by hand-powered and other tools and call for an understanding of the work organisation, the materials and tools used, and the nature and purpose of the final product.

Occupations are classified into Major group 9, *Elementary occupations* if the tasks are of a simple and routine nature, mainly entail the use of hand-held tools, some physical effort, little or no previous experience and understanding of the work, and limited initiative or judgement.

8240 WOOD-PRODUCTS MACHINE OPERATORS

Wood-products machine operators operate and monitor automatic or semi-automatic woodworking machines which perform repetitive work and are always set up by woodworking-machine setters.

Tasks include –

(a) operating and monitoring one or more previously set up machines for sawing, shaping, boring, planing, turning or carving wood;

(b) performing related tasks;
(c) supervising other workers.

Examples of the occupations classified here:
- Machine-operator, carving/wood
- Machine-operator, furniture production
- Machine-operator, wood products

Some related occupations classified elsewhere:
- Setter, woodworking machine − 7423
- Setter-operator, woodworking machine − 7423

MINOR GROUP 825
PRINTING-, BINDING- AND PAPER-PRODUCTS MACHINE OPERATORS

Printing-, binding- and paper-products machine operators operate and monitor various types of printing and copying machines, or machines which bind and emboss books or which produce various articles from paper, paperboard and similar materials.

Tasks performed usually include: operating and monitoring various types of printing and copying machines, or machines which bind and emboss books or which produce various articles from paper, paperboard and similar materials. Supervision of other workers may be included.

Occupations in this minor group are classified into the following unit groups:

8251 Printing-machine operators

8252 Bookbinding-machine operators

8253 Paper-products machine operators

8

Note
Occupations are classified into Major group 7, *Craft and related trades workers* if the tasks are carried out by hand and by hand-powered and other tools and call for an understanding of the work organisation, the materials and tools used, and the nature and purpose of the final product.

Occupations are classified into Major group 9, *Elementary occupations* if the tasks are of a simple and routine nature, mainly entail the use of hand-held tools, some physical effort, little or no previous experience and understanding of the work, and limited initiative or judgement.

8251 PRINTING-MACHINE OPERATORS

Printing-machine operators operate and monitor various types of machines which print on paper, tin plate and other materials.

Tasks include –

(a) operating and monitoring cylinder, platen, rotary, offset, direct lithographic, rotogravure, and wallpaper-printing presses;

(b) performing related tasks;

(c) supervising other workers.

Examples of the occupations classified here:
- Press-operator, printing/cylinder
- Press-operator, printing/offset
- Press-operator, printing/rotary

Some related occupations classified elsewhere:
- Compositor, printing – 7341
- Printer – 7341
- Typesetter – 7341

8252 BOOKBINDING-MACHINE OPERATORS

Bookbinding-machine operators operate and monitor machines which bind and emboss books.

Tasks include –

(a) operating and monitoring bookbinding machines;

(b) operating and monitoring pressing machines which emboss designs and titles on book covers;

(c) performing related tasks;

(d) supervising other workers.

Examples of the occupations classified here:
- Machine-operator, bookbinding
- Machine-operator, embossing/books

Some related occupations classified elsewhere:
- Bookbinder – 7345
- Embosser, book – 7345

8253 PAPER-PRODUCTS MACHINE OPERATORS

Paper-products machine operators operate and monitor machines which produce boxes, envelopes, bags and other goods from paper, paperboard, cardboard, cellophane and similar materials.

Tasks include –

(a) operating and monitoring machines which glue paper to cardboard, cut it to the required length or cut and crease cardboard or paperboard to form box blanks;

(b) operating and monitoring pressing machines which form drinking cups or other containers from paper, paperboard or cardboard;

(c) operating and monitoring machines which cut, fold and glue paper to make envelopes and paper bags, or which form bags from other materials;

(d) performing related tasks;

(e) supervising other workers.

Examples of the occupations classified here:
- Machine-operator, cardboard products
- Machine-operator, envelope and paper bag production
- Machine-operator, paper box production
- Machine-operator, paper products

MINOR GROUP 826
TEXTILE-, FUR- AND LEATHER-PRODUCTS MACHINE OPERATORS

Textile-, fur- and leather-products machine operators operate and monitor machines which prepare fibres and yarns, or hides and pelts, and manufacture or dry-clean textiles, or fur and leather articles.

Tasks performed usually include: operating and monitoring machines which prepare fibres and spin and wind yarn and thread; weave and knit; manufacture machine-made garments from various materials; bleach, dye and clean textile garments; prepare hides, skins, pelts or fur to make leather; or make footwear and related products. Supervision of other workers may be included.

Occupations in this minor group are classified into the following unit groups:

8261 Fibre-preparing, spinning- and winding-machine operators

8262 Weaving- and knitting-machine operators

8263 Sewing-machine operators

8264 Bleaching-, dyeing- and cleaning-machine operators

8265 Fur- and leather-preparing-machine operators

8266 Shoemaking- and related machine operators

8269 Textile-, fur- and leather-products machine operators not elsewhere classified

Note
Occupations are classified into Major group 7, *Craft and related trades workers* if the tasks are carried out by hand and by hand-powered and other tools and call for an understanding of the work organisation, the materials and tools used, and the nature and purpose of the final product.

Occupations are classified into Major group 9, *Elementary occupations* if the tasks are of a simple and routine nature, mainly entail the use of hand-held tools, some physical effort, little or no previous experience and understanding of the work, and limited initiative or judgement.

8261 FIBRE-PREPARING, SPINNING- AND WINDING-MACHINE OPERATORS

Fibre-preparing, spinning- and winding-machine operators operate and monitor machines which prepare fibres, and spin, double, twist and wind yarn and thread.

Tasks include –
(a) operating and monitoring machines which combine textile fibres into uniform blends;
(b) operating and monitoring machines which clean and fluff textile fibres, transform them into sliver, comb them into sliver for first drawing, combine slivers into sliver lap or sliver laps into ribbon lap, combine several slivers into one attenuated strand of regular quality and weight;
(c) operating and monitoring machines which transform sliver into roving;
(d) operating and monitoring machines which spin thread and yarn from roving, wind two or more threads onto bobbin, twist two or more strands of yarn or thread into single heavier and stronger strand, or wind yarn or thread from one package to another;

(e) performing related tasks;
(f) supervising other workers.

Examples of the occupations classified here:
- Machine-operator, fibre preparing
- Machine-operator, spinning/thread and yarn
- Machine-operator, twisting/thread and yarn
- Machine-operator, winding/thread and yarn

Some related occupations classified elsewhere:
- Spinner − 7432

8262 WEAVING- AND KNITTING-MACHINE OPERATORS

Weaving- and knitting-machine operators operate and monitor weaving and knitting machines and related equipment used to produce materials and fabrics.

Tasks include −
(a) operating and monitoring machines used to weave or knit plain or figured cloth, tapestry, lace, carpets, garments, hosiery or other fabrics or articles;
(b) performing related tasks;
(c) supervising other workers.

Examples of the occupations classified here:
- Machine-operator, knitting
- Machine-operator, net production
- Machine-operator, weaving
- Machine-operator, weaving/carpets

Some related occupations classified elsewhere:
- Knitter − 7432
- Weaver, carpet − 7432
- Weaver, cloth − 7432

8263 SEWING-MACHINE OPERATORS

Sewing-machine operators operate and monitor sewing machines to make textile, fur or leather garments or embroider ornamental designs on garments or other materials.

Tasks include −
(a) operating and monitoring standard or specialised single- or multiple-needle sewing machines to make or repair garments, gloves and miscellaneous products in textiles, fur or leather;
(b) operating and monitoring standard or specialised single- or multiple-needle sewing machines to embroider ornamental designs on textiles or other materials;
(c) performing related tasks;
(d) supervising other workers.

Examples of the occupations classified here:
- Machine-operator, sewing
- Machine-operator, sewing/embroidery
- Machine-operator, sewing/textile products

Some related occupations classified elsewhere:
- Embroiderer − 7436
- Furrier − 7434
- Handicraft worker, textiles − 7332
- Tailor − 7433

8264 BLEACHING-, DYEING- AND CLEANING-MACHINE OPERATORS

Bleaching-, dyeing- and cleaning-machine operators operate and monitor machines which bleach, dye, wash and otherwise treat fibres, yarn, or cloth or dry-clean textile, fur and leather articles.

Tasks include −
(a) operating and monitoring machines which treat textile products to make them lighter in colour or to give them a specific colour;
(b) operating and monitoring machines which wash or dry-clean textile, fur or leather products to remove dirt, impurities, excess chemicals or natural gum;
(c) operating and monitoring machines which shrink cloth or strengthen the weave by interlocking the fibres;
(d) operating and monitoring machines which impregnate textiles with chemicals to render them waterproof;
(e) operating and monitoring machines which treat silk to give it body and weight;

(f) operating and monitoring machines which press, stretch, or impart lustre, or other type of finish to textiles;

(g) performing related tasks;

(h) supervising other workers.

Examples of the occupations classified here:

- Machine-operator, dry-cleaning
- Machine-operator, dyeing/textile fibres
- Machine-operator, laundering
- Machine-operator, pressing/laundry

Some related occupations classified elsewhere:

- Launderer, hand − 9133
- Presser, hand − 9133

8265 FUR- AND LEATHER-PREPARING-MACHINE OPERATORS

Fur- and leather-preparing-machine operators operate and monitor various machines which prepare leather or treat fur- or wool-bearing pelts.

Tasks include −

(a) operating and monitoring machines which remove flesh and fat from pelts before curing;

(b) operating and monitoring machines which remove long coarse hair from fur pelts, trim hair to even length, and dye, stretch and smooth dressed pelts;

(c) operating and monitoring machines which separate residual wool from skins, or flesh and hair from hides, and which split hides;

(d) operating and monitoring machines which treat hides and skins in solutions and apply finishing product to convert them into leather;

(e) operating and monitoring machines which apply dyes and stains to leather;

(f) performing related tasks;

(g) supervising other workers.

Examples of the occupations classified here:

- Machine-operator, dehairing/hide
- Machine-operator, staining/leather
- Machine-operator, tanning

Some related occupations classified elsewhere:

- Dyer, pelt − 7441
- Tanner − 7441

8266 SHOEMAKING- AND RELATED MACHINE OPERATORS

Shoemaking- and related machine operators operate and monitor machines which produce and repair standard or special footwear, handbags and other accessories, mainly made of leather.

Tasks include −

(a) operating and monitoring machines which mark patterns and cut shoe parts;

(b) operating and monitoring machines which sew shoe parts together, or edge, polish, or apply ornaments and perform finishing tasks;

(c) operating and monitoring machines which produce luggage, handbags, belts and other accessories, as well as other items such as saddles, collars or harnesses;

(d) performing related tasks;

(e) supervising other workers.

Examples of the occupations classified here:

- Machine-operator, footwear production

Some related occupations classified elsewhere:

- Cobbler − 7442
- Handicraft worker, leather − 7332

8269 TEXTILE-, FUR- AND LEATHER-PRODUCTS MACHINE OPERATORS NOT ELSEWHERE CLASSIFIED

This unit group covers textile-, fur- and leather-products machine operators not classified elsewhere in Minor group 826, *Textile-, fur- and leather-products machine operators.*

For instance, here should be classified those who are engaged in operating and monitoring machines which make hats or miscellaneous articles such as braids or other trim-mings.

In such cases tasks would include –

(a) operating and monitoring machines which form and make hats out of tex-tiles, fur or leather;

(b) operating and monitoring machines which make miscellaneous articles such as braids or other trimmings;

(c) performing related tasks;

(d) supervising other workers.

Examples of the occupations classified here:

- Machine-operator, braid production
- Machine-operator, hat making
- Machine-operator, pattern making/tex-tiles

Some related occupations classified else-where:

- Milliner – 7433
- Pattern-maker, garment – 7435

MINOR GROUP **827**
FOOD AND RELATED PRODUCTS MACHINE OPERATORS

Food and related products machine operators operate and monitor machines which process foodstuffs and manufacture food and related products for human and animal consumption.

Tasks performed usually include: operating and monitoring machines for slaughter-ing animals and cutting carcasses and fish into pieces for storage or sale; manufactur-ing meat and fish products; processing milk and cream and manufacturing dairy products; crushing and grinding grain, spices or similar foodstuffs, making bread, pasta and related products; processing fruit, nuts and vegetables; processing and refining sugar; processing tea, coffee and cocoa, or producing beer, wine, spirits and other beverages, or tobacco products. Supervision of other workers may be included.

Occupations in this minor group are classified into the following unit groups:

8271 **Meat- and fish-processing-machine operators**

8272 **Dairy-products machine operators**

8273 **Grain- and spice-milling-machine operators**

8274 **Baked-goods, cereal and chocolate-products machine operators**

8275 **Fruit-, vegetable- and nut-processing-machine operators**

8276 **Sugar production machine operators**

8277 **Tea-, coffee-, and cocoa-processing-machine operators**

8278 **Brewers, wine and other beverage machine operators**

8279 **Tobacco production machine operators**

8

Note
Occupations are classified into Major group 7, *Craft and related trades workers* if the tasks are carried out by hand and by hand-powered and other tools and call for an understanding of the work organisation, the materials and tools used, and the nature and purpose of the final product.

Occupations are classified into Major group 9, *Elementary occupations* if the tasks are of a simple and routine nature, mainly entail the use of hand-held tools, some physical effort, little or no previous experience and understanding of the work, and limited initiative or judgement.

8271 MEAT- AND FISH-PROCESSING-MACHINE OPERATORS

Meat- and fish-processing-machine operators operate and monitor machines used to slaughter animals, trim carcasses, prepare standard meat or fish cuts, and manufacture meat and fish products.

Tasks include –
(a) operating and monitoring machines used to slaughter animals and to cut carcasses or fish into standard pieces;
(b) operating and monitoring machines used to mince and mix meat or fish;
(c) operating and monitoring machines used to process meat and fish and manufacture various meat and fish products, such as sausages, smoked meat or smoked fish;
(d) operating and monitoring machines used to produce canned or frozen meat and fish dishes;
(e) performing related tasks;
(f) supervising other workers.

Examples of the occupations classified here:
- Machine-operator, fish processing
- Machine-operator, meat processing

Some related occupations classified elsewhere:
- Butcher – 7411
- Fishmonger – 7411

8272 DAIRY-PRODUCTS MACHINE OPERATORS

Dairy-products machine operators operate and monitor machines which process milk and cream and make dairy products.

Tasks include –
(a) operating and monitoring machines which pasteurise, homogenise and heat-treat milk and cream;
(b) operating and monitoring machines which make condensed or powdered milk;
(c) operating and monitoring machines which make butter, cheese and other milk or milk-based products;
(d) performing related tasks;
(e) supervising other workers.

Examples of the occupations classified here:
- Machine-operator, dairy products
- Machine-operator, pasteurising/milk

Some related occupations classified elsewhere:
- Maker, butter – 7413
- Maker, cheese – 7413

8273 GRAIN- AND SPICE-MILLING-MACHINE OPERATORS

Grain- and spice-milling-machine operators operate and monitor machinery used to crush, grind, blend and otherwise process grain, spices and related foodstuffs for human or animal consumption.

Tasks include –
(a) operating and monitoring machinery used for the production of flour, meal and animal feed and for processing rice;
(b) operating and monitoring milling machines used for grinding grain and spices;
(c) performing related tasks;
(d) supervising other workers.

Examples of the occupations classified here:

- Machine-operator, milling/grain
- Machine-operator, milling/rice
- Machine-operator, milling/spices

8274 BAKED-GOODS, CEREAL AND CHOCOLATE-PRODUCTS MACHINE OPERATORS

Baked-goods, cereal and chocolate-products machine operators operate and monitor mixing, blending, shaping and baking machines which produce cereals, bread, pastry, pasta, chocolate and related products from flour, cocoa and other ingredients.

Tasks include –
- *(a)* operating and monitoring machines which mix and blend flour with other ingredients to prepare dough for the production of bread, pastries, pasta and related products;
- *(b)* operating and monitoring machines which extrude and shape dough for the production of bread, pastries, pasta and related products;
- *(c)* operating and monitoring ovens used for baking bread, pastries, pasta and related products;
- *(d)* operating and monitoring machines used for making cereals;
- *(e)* operating and monitoring machines used for making chocolate and confectionery;
- *(f)* performing related tasks;
- *(g)* supervising other workers.

Examples of the occupations classified here:

- Machine-operator, bread production
- Machine-operator, chocolate production
- Machine-operator, confectionery production
- Machine-operator, pastry production

Some related occupations classified elsewhere:

- Baker – 7412
- Maker, chocolate – 7412

8275 FRUIT-, VEGETABLE- AND NUT-PROCESSING-MACHINE OPERATORS

Fruit-, vegetable- and nut-processing-machine operators operate and monitor machines which extract juice from fruit and vegetables or oil from oil-bearing seeds, nuts and fruit, and which process fruit, vegetables and nuts by drying, cooking, canning or freezing.

Tasks include –
- *(a)* operating and monitoring machines which extract juice from fruit and vegetables by heating or pressing;
- *(b)* operating and monitoring machines which extract and refine oil from oil-bearing seeds, nuts and fruit;
- *(c)* operating and monitoring machines which make margarine and similar products from animal and vegetable oils;
- *(d)* operating and monitoring machines which prepare fruit, vegetables and nuts for further processing;
- *(e)* operating and monitoring machines which dry, cook, can, freeze or otherwise process fruit, vegetables and nuts;
- *(f)* performing related tasks;
- *(g)* supervising other workers.

Examples of the occupations classified here:

- Machine-operator, fruit processing
- Machine-operator, vegetable processing
- Press-operator, edible oils

Some related occupations classified elsewhere:

- Expeller, oil – 7414
- Machine-operator, soft-drinks production – 8278
- Preserver, fruit – 7414
- Preserver, vegetable – 7414

8276 SUGAR PRODUCTION MACHINE OPERATORS

Sugar production machine operators operate and monitor machines which process sugar-cane and sugar-beet and produce refined sugar.

Tasks include –

(a) operating and monitoring machines which crush sugar-cane or extract liquor from sugar-beet;

(b) operating and monitoring tanks used to purify sugar liquor or produce sugar crystals from hot sugar liquor;

(c) operating and monitoring machines which refine sugar-beet or sugar-cane by a continuous process;

(d) operating and monitoring machines which extract and refine sugar juices from maple, palm and other vegetable sources;

(e) operating and monitoring machines which process honey;

(f) performing related tasks;

(g) supervising other workers.

Examples of the occupations classified here:

- Machine-operator, sugar production

8277 TEA-, COFFEE- AND COCOA-PROCESSING-MACHINE OPERATORS

Tea-, coffee- and cocoa-processing-machine operators operate and monitor machines to blend and prepare tea leaves, coffee or cocoa beans and chicory roots.

Tasks include –

(a) operating and monitoring machines used to dry tea leaves, roll withered leaves or dry rolled leaves, and blend various grades of tea;

(b) operating and monitoring machines used to cut coffee or cocoa berries and remove and wash off pulp, peel off husk from beans, and cure and blend beans;

(c) operating and monitoring machines which roast blended coffee or cocoa beans or chicory roots;

(d) operating and monitoring machines which crush tea or grind coffee, cocoa or chicory;

(e) performing related tasks;

(f) supervising other workers.

Examples of the occupations classified here:

- Machine-operator, cocoa-bean processing

- Machine-operator, coffee-bean processing

- Machine-operator, tea-leaf processing

8278 BREWERS, WINE AND OTHER BEVERAGE MACHINE OPERATORS

Brewers, wine and other beverage machine operators operate and monitor machines which mix, press, or malt and ferment grains and fruit to make malt liquors, wine and other alcoholic or non-alcoholic beverages, except fruit and vegetable juices.

Tasks include –

(a) operating and monitoring machines which process barley and other grains used in making distilled and malt liquors, and controlling the fermentation process;

(b) operating and monitoring machines which process grapes and other fruit used in making wines, and controlling the fermentation process;

(c) operating and monitoring stills which increase or reduce the alcohol content of alcoholic beverages;

(d) operating and monitoring machines which blend wines and liquors to obtain desired tastes and flavours;

(e) operating and monitoring machines which make non-alcoholic beverages, except fruit and vegetable juices;

(f) performing related tasks;

(g) supervising other workers.

Examples of the occupations classified here:

- Brewer
- Machine-operator, malting/spirits
- Machine-operator, soft-drinks production

Some related occupations classified elsewhere:

- Machine-operator, fruit juice production – 8275
- Taster, wine – 7415

8279 TOBACCO PRODUCTION MACHINE OPERATORS

Tobacco production machine operators operate and monitor machines which process tobacco and make cigarettes and other tobacco products.

Tasks include –

(a) operating and monitoring machines which process tobacco in preparation for manufacturing cigarettes and other tobacco products;

(b) operating and monitoring machines which produce cigarettes and other tobacco products;

(c) performing related tasks;

(d) supervising other workers.

Examples of the occupations classified here:
- Machine-operator, cigar production
- Machine-operator, cigarette production
- Machine-operator, tobacco processing

Some related occupations classified elsewhere:
- Grader, tobacco – 7416
- Maker, cigar – 7416

MINOR GROUP 828
ASSEMBLERS

Assemblers assemble components into products according to strictly laid down procedures. The products worked on may be moved from one worker to the next along assembly lines.

Tasks performed usually include: assembling components into various types of products according to strictly laid down procedures.

Occupations in this minor group are classified into the following unit groups:

8281 Mechanical-machinery assemblers

8282 Electrical-equipment assemblers

8283 Electronic-equipment assemblers

8284 Metal-, rubber- and plastic-products assemblers

8285 Wood and related products assemblers

8286 Paperboard, textile and related products assemblers

Note

Occupations are classified into Major group 7, *Craft and related trades workers* if the tasks are carried out by hand and by hand-powered and other tools and call for an understanding of the work organisation, the materials and tools used, and the nature and purpose of the final product.

Occupations are classified into Major group 9, *Elementary occupations* if the tasks are of a simple and routine nature, mainly entail the use of hand-held tools, some physical effort, little or no previous experience and understanding of the work, and limited initiative or judgement.

8281 MECHANICAL-MACHINERY ASSEMBLERS

Mechanical-machinery assemblers assemble the components or parts of mechanical machinery, according to strictly laid down procedures.

Tasks include –
(a) assembling the components or parts of mechanical machinery, engines and vehicles, according to strictly laid down procedures;
(b) performing related tasks;
(c) supervising other workers.

Examples of the occupations classified here:
- Assembler, aircraft
- Assembler, mechanical machinery
- Assembler, vehicle

Some related occupations classified elsewhere:
- Operator, assembly-line/automated – 8171

8282 ELECTRICAL-EQUIPMENT ASSEMBLERS

Electrical-equipment assemblers assemble the components or parts of electrical equipment, according to strictly laid down procedures.

Tasks include –
(a) assembling the components or parts of electrical equipment, according to strictly laid down procedures;
(b) performing related tasks;
(c) supervising other workers.

Examples of the occupations classified here:
- Assembler, electrical equipment

8283 ELECTRONIC-EQUIPMENT ASSEMBLERS

Electronic-equipment assemblers assemble the components or parts of electronic equipment, according to strictly laid down procedures.

Tasks include –
(a) assembling the components or parts of electronic equipment, according to strictly laid down procedures;
(b) performing related tasks;
(c) supervising other workers.

Examples of the occupations classified here:
- Assembler, electronic equipment

8284 METAL-, RUBBER- AND PLASTIC-PRODUCTS ASSEMBLERS

Metal-, rubber- and plastic-products assemblers perform limited, specialised tasks in assembling the metal, rubber or plastic components or parts of various types of products such as toys, sports articles, bicycles, etc., according to strictly laid down procedures.

Tasks include –
(a) assembling the metal, rubber or plastic components or parts of various types of products, according to strictly laid down procedures;
(b) performing related tasks;
(c) supervising other workers.

Examples of the occupations classified here:
- Assembler, metal products
- Assembler, plastic products
- Assembler, rubber products

8285 WOOD AND RELATED PRODUCTS ASSEMBLERS

Wood and related products assemblers assemble the components or parts made from wood or related materials, of various types of products, according to strictly laid down procedures.

Tasks include –
(a) assembling the components or parts made from wood or related materials, of various types of products, according to strictly laid down procedures;
(b) performing related tasks;
(c) supervising other workers.

Examples of the occupations classified here:

- Assembler, wood products

8286 PAPERBOARD, TEXTILE AND RELATED PRODUCTS ASSEMBLERS

Paperboard, textile and related products assemblers assemble the components or parts made from paperboard, textile, leather and related materials, of various types of products, according to strictly laid down procedures.

Tasks include –

(a) assembling the components or parts made from paperboard, textile, leather and related materials, of various types of products, according to strictly laid down procedures;

(b) attaching metal, plastic or other fittings;

(c) performing related tasks;

(d) supervising other workers.

Examples of the occupations classified here:

- Assembler, leather products
- Assembler, paperboard products
- Assembler, textile products

MINOR GROUP 829
OTHER MACHINE OPERATORS AND ASSEMBLERS

Other machine operators and assemblers operate and monitor machines which pack, label, and, if needed, add revenue stamps to products, packages and containers, or assemble, according to strictly laid down procedures, products whose component parts are made of a wide range of materials.

Tasks performed usually include: operating and monitoring machines which pack, label and, if needed, add revenue stamps to products, packages and containers; assembling, according to strictly laid down procedures, products whose components are made of a wide range of materials. Supervision of other workers may be included.

Occupations in this minor group are classified into the following unit group:

8290 Other machine operators and assemblers

Note

Occupations are classified into Major group 7, *Craft and related trades workers,* if the tasks are carried out by hand and by hand-powered and other tools and call for an understanding of the work organisation, the materials and tools used, and the nature and purpose of the final product.

Occupations are classified into Major group 9, *Elementary occupations* if the tasks are of a simple and routine nature, mainly entail the use of hand-held tools, some physical effort, little or no previous experience and understanding of the work, and limited initiative or judgement.

8290 OTHER MACHINE OPERATORS AND ASSEMBLERS

Other machine operators and assemblers operate and monitor machines which pack, label and, if needed, add revenue stamps to products, packages and containers, or assemble, according to strictly laid down procedures, products whose component parts are made of a wide range of materials.

Tasks include –

(a) operating and monitoring machines which wrap and pack various products, including liquid ones, for storage or shipment;

(b) operating and monitoring machines which, by gluing or other methods, label products, packages and various containers, or add revenue stamps;

(c) assembling, according to strictly laid down procedures, products whose component parts are made of a very wide range of materials;

(d) performing related tasks;

(e) supervising other workers.

Examples of the occupations classified here:

- Assembler, composite products
- Machine-operator, labelling
- Machine-operator, packing

Some related occupations classified elsewhere:

- Packer, hand – 9322

SUB-MAJOR GROUP 83
DRIVERS AND MOBILE-PLANT OPERATORS

Drivers and mobile-plant operators drive and tend trains and motor vehicles, or drive, operate and monitor mobile industrial and agricultural machinery and equipment, or execute deck duties on board ship and other water-borne craft.

The work mainly calls for experience with and an understanding of the machinery and equipment which is being operated and monitored. Ability to cope with machine-paced operations and to adapt to technological innovations is often required.

Tasks performed by workers in this sub-major group usually include: driving and tending trains and motor vehicles; driving, operating and monitoring mobile industrial and agricultural machinery and equipment; carrying out deck duties on board ship and other water-borne craft. Supervision of other workers may be included.

Occupations in this minor group are classified into the following unit groups:

831 Locomotive-engine drivers and related workers

832 Motor-vehicle drivers

833 Agricultural and other mobile-plant operators

834 Ships' deck crews and related workers

8

MINOR GROUP **831**
LOCOMOTIVE-ENGINE DRIVERS AND RELATED WORKERS

Locomotive-engine drivers and related workers drive locomotive engines to transport freight or passengers, manœuvre railway coaches or operate railway signals.

Tasks performed usually include: driving railway engines, operating railway signals, switching rolling stock and making up trains in railway yards. Supervision of other workers may be included.

Occupations in this minor group are classified into the following unit groups:

8311   Locomotive-engine drivers

8312   Railway brakers, signallers and shunters

8311   LOCOMOTIVE-ENGINE DRIVERS

Locomotive-engine drivers drive, or assist in driving, locomotive engines to transport passengers and freight.

Tasks include –

(a) driving or assisting in driving a steam, electric or diesel-electric locomotive engine;

(b) driving an underground or elevated passenger train;

(c) driving a locomotive to haul carriages underground or on the surface of a mine or quarry;

(d) performing related tasks;

(e) supervising other workers.

Examples of the occupations classified here:

- Driver, engine/mine
- Driver, locomotive
- Driver, train

8312   RAILWAY BRAKERS, SIGNALLERS AND SHUNTERS

Railway brakers, signallers and shunters take charge of and safeguard railway freight trains during runs, control the movement of railway traffic by operating signals, switch rolling stock and make up trains in railway yards, make up trains for hauling in mines and control their movement.

Tasks include –

(a) taking charge of and safeguarding freight train during run;

(b) controlling flow of railway traffic over section of line by operating signals and switches from control panel or signal box;

(c) switching and coupling rolling stock in railway yards and sidings in accordance with orders about loading, unloading and make-up of trains;

(d) making up trains for hauling by locomotive or cable and directing their movement along haulageways in a mine or quarry;

(e) performing related tasks;

(f) supervising other workers.

Examples of the occupations classified here:
- Braker, railway
- Shunter, railway
- Signaller, railway

MINOR GROUP 832
MOTOR-VEHICLE DRIVERS

Motor-vehicle drivers drive and tend motor vehicles to transport materials, goods and passengers.

Tasks performed usually include: driving and tending motorcycles, cars, taxis, trams and buses, heavy trucks, lorries and vans, in order to transport materials, goods, and passengers. Supervision of other workers may be included.

Occupations in this minor group are classified into the following unit groups:

8321 Motor-cycle drivers

8322 Car, taxi and van drivers

8323 Bus and tram drivers

8324 Heavy-truck and lorry drivers

Note
Occupations are classified into Major group 7, *Craft and related trades workers,* if the tasks are carried out by hand and by hand-powered and other tools and call for an understanding of the work organisation, the materials and tools used, and the nature and purpose of the final product.

Occupations are classified into Major group 9, *Elementary occupations* if the tasks are of a simple and routine nature, mainly entail the use of hand-held tools, some physical effort, little or no previous experience and understanding of the work, and limited initiative or judgement.

8321 MOTOR-CYCLE DRIVERS

Motor-cycle drivers drive and tend motor cycles or motorised tricycles equipped to transport materials, goods or passengers.

Tasks include –

(a) driving and tending motor cycle or motorised tricycle to transport materials, goods and passengers;

(b) performing related tasks;

(c) supervising other workers.

Examples of the occupations classified here:
- Dispatch rider
- Motor-cyclist

Some related occupations classified elsewhere:
- Driver, pedal vehicle – 9331

8

8322 CAR, TAXI AND VAN DRIVERS

Car, taxi and van drivers drive and tend motor cars and vans to transport passengers, mail or goods.

Tasks include –
(a) driving and tending passenger cars or taxis;
(b) driving and tending cars, vans or small trucks to deliver mail or goods;
(c) performing related tasks;
(d) supervising other workers.

Examples of the occupations classified here:
- Driver, car
- Driver, taxi
- Driver, van

8323 BUS AND TRAM DRIVERS

Bus and tram drivers drive and tend buses or street tramcars to transport passengers, mail or goods.

Tasks include –
(a) driving and tending motor bus, trolley bus or motor coach to transport local or long-distance passengers, mail or goods;
(b) driving and tending street tramcar transporting passengers;

(c) performing related tasks;
(d) supervising other workers.

Examples of the occupations classified here:
- Driver, bus
- Driver, tram

8324 HEAVY-TRUCK AND LORRY DRIVERS

Heavy-truck and lorry drivers drive and tend heavy motor vehicles to transport goods, liquids and heavy materials over short or long distances.

Tasks include –
(a) driving and tending a heavy motor vehicle, such as a lorry with or without trailer or a dump-truck, to transport goods, liquids or heavy materials over short or long distances;
(b) performing related tasks;
(c) supervising other workers.

Examples of the occupations classified here:
- Driver, truck/heavy
- Operator, shuttle-car/mine

MINOR GROUP 833
AGRICULTURAL AND OTHER MOBILE-PLANT OPERATORS

Agricultural and other mobile-plant operators drive, tend, operate and monitor agricultural and other machinery and equipment for handling materials and heavy objects.

Tasks performed usually include: driving, tending, operating and monitoring tractors and other specialised machinery in agricultural use, or earth-moving, hoisting, lifting and related equipment. Supervision of other workers may be included.

Occupations in this minor group are classified into the following unit groups:

8331 Motorised farm and forestry plant operators

8332 Earth-moving- and related plant operators

8333 Crane, hoist and related plant operators

8334 Lifting-truck operators

Note

Occupations are classified into Major group 7, *Craft and related trades workers,* if the tasks are carried out by hand and by hand-powered and other tools and call for an understanding of the work organisation, the materials and tools used, and the nature and purpose of the final product.

Occupations are classified into Major group 9, *Elementary occupations* if the tasks are of a simple and routine nature, mainly entail the use of hand-held tools, some physical effort, little or no previous experience and understanding of the work, and limited initiative or judgement.

8331 MOTORISED FARM AND FORESTRY PLANT OPERATORS

Motorised farm and forestry plant operators drive, tend, operate and monitor one or more types of motorised, mobile machinery or equipment used in farming or forestry operations.

Tasks include –
(a) driving and tending tractor or self-propelled ploughing, planting, harvesting, baling or other special-purpose farm machinery, or similar tractor-drawn equipment;
(b) driving and tending tractor or self-propelled clearing, planting, harvesting, timber-carrying or other special-purpose forestry machinery;
(c) performing related tasks;
(d) supervising other workers.

Examples of the occupations classified here:
- Driver, timber carrier
- Driver, tractor
- Operator, harvester
- Operator, motorised farm equipment

8332 EARTH-MOVING- AND RELATED PLANT OPERATORS

Earth-moving- and related plant operators operate and monitor machines to excavate, grade, level and compact earth or similar materials and lay surfaces of asphalt and concrete.

Tasks include –
(a) operating and monitoring excavating machines, equipped with moveable shovel, grab-bucket or dragline bucket, to excavate and move earth, rock, sand, gravel or similar materials, or to tear down buildings or other structures;

(b) operating and monitoring machines for digging trenches for sewers, drainage, water, oil, gas or similar pipelines;
(c) operating and monitoring machines equipped with concave steel blade to move, distribute and level earth, sand, snow and other materials;
(d) operating and monitoring equipment to remove sand, gravel and mud from bottom of body of water;
(e) operating and monitoring machines for hammering wooden, concrete or steel piles into ground;
(f) operating and monitoring power roller to compact and smooth layers of materials in making roads, pavements and similar work;
(g) operating and monitoring machines which spread and smooth concrete or bituminous or tar preparations to construct roadways, roads or similar work;
(h) performing related tasks;
(i) supervising other workers.

Examples of the occupations classified here:
- Operator, bulldozer
- Operator, excavator
- Operator, pile-driver
- Operator, road-roller

8333 CRANE, HOIST AND RELATED PLANT OPERATORS

Crane, hoist and related plant operators operate and monitor cranes and other hoisting equipment.

Tasks include –
(a) operating and monitoring mobile or stationary cranes with mobile or fixed jib or boom;
(b) operating and monitoring equipment for hoisting, lowering or raising men and

materials on construction site or in mine;

(c) operating and monitoring ski-lifts and similar equipment;

(d) operating and monitoring machinery used to haul ferry or barge with goods, passengers and vehicles across short stretches of water;

(e) operating and monitoring machinery to open and close bridge for the passage of road and water traffic;

(f) performing related tasks;

(g) supervising other workers.

Examples of the occupations classified here:

- Operator, crane
- Operator, hoist

8334   LIFTING-TRUCK OPERATORS

Lifting-truck operators drive, operate and monitor lifting-truck or similar vehicle to transport, lift and stack pallets with goods.

Tasks include –

(a) operating and monitoring lifting-truck and similar equipment to load and unload, transport, lift and stack goods and pallets in terminals, harbours, warehouses, factories and other establishments;

(b) performing related tasks;

(c) supervising other workers.

Examples of the occupations classified here:

- Operator, truck/fork-lift

MINOR GROUP 834
SHIPS' DECK CREWS AND RELATED WORKERS

Ships' deck crews and related workers carry out deck duties on board ship and similar duties on board other water-borne craft.

Tasks performed usually include: standing look-out watches at sea and in harbour, steering ship according to instructions, and cleaning, painting and maintaining ship and its deck equipment as required. Supervision of other workers may be included.

Occupations in this minor group are classified into the following unit group:

8340   Ships' deck crews and related workers

8340   SHIPS' DECK CREWS AND RELATED WORKERS

Ship's deck crews and related workers carry out deck duties on board ship and similar duties on board other water-borne craft.

Tasks include –

(a) standing look-out watches at sea and when entering or leaving harbour or other narrow waters;

(b) steering ship according to instructions;

(c) handling mooring lines on board;

(d) maintaining and, in some cases, operating ship's equipment, cargo gear, rigging, life-saving and fire-fighting appliances;

(e) performing deck and hull cleaning, scraping, painting and other maintenance duties as required;

(f) performing related tasks;

(g) supervising other workers.

Examples of the occupations classified here:

- Boatswain
- Sailor
- Seaman, able
- Seawoman, able

MAJOR GROUP 9
ELEMENTARY OCCUPATIONS

Elementary occupations consist of simple and routine tasks which mainly require the use of hand-held tools and often some physical effort. Most occupations in this major group require skills at the first ISCO skill level.

Tasks performed by workers in elementary occupations usually include: selling goods in streets and public places, or from door to door; providing various street services; cleaning, washing, pressing; taking care of apartment houses, hotels, offices and other buildings; washing windows and other glass surfaces of buildings; delivering messages or goods; carrying luggage; doorkeeping and property watching; stocking vending machines or reading and emptying meters; collecting garbage; sweeping streets and similar places; performing various simple farming, fishing, hunting or trapping tasks; performing simple tasks connected with mining, construction and manufacturing including product-sorting and simple hand-assembling of components; packing by hand; freight handling; pedalling or hand-guiding vehicles to transport passengers and goods; driving animal-drawn vehicles or machinery. Supervision of other workers may be included.

Occupations in this major group are classified into the following sub-major groups:

91   Sales and services elementary occupations

92   Agricultural, fishery and related labourers

93   Labourers in mining, construction, manufacturing and transport

---

SUB-MAJOR GROUP 91
SALES AND SERVICES ELEMENTARY OCCUPATIONS

Sales and services elementary occupations mainly consist of tasks connected with street or door-to-door sales or services, or cleaning, property watching and caretaking, delivering goods and messages or carrying luggage.

Tasks performed by workers in this sub-major group usually include: selling goods in streets and public places, or from door to door; providing various street services; cleaning, washing, pressing, sweeping or garbage collecting; doorkeeping, property watching and building caretaking; washing windows or other glass surfaces; ushering; delivering messages or goods; stocking vending machines or reading and emptying meters; carrying luggage. Supervision of other workers may be included.

Occupations in this sub-major group are classified into the following minor groups:

911   Street vendors and related workers

912   Shoe cleaning and other street services elementary occupations

913   Domestic and related helpers, cleaners and launderers

914   Building caretakers, window and related cleaners

915   Messengers, porters, doorkeepers and related workers

916   Garbage collectors and related labourers

MINOR GROUP 911
STREET VENDORS AND RELATED WORKERS

Street vendors and related workers sell food and other goods in streets and public places, or from door to door, or by telephone.

Tasks performed usually include: preparing and selling, or selling previously prepared, foodstuffs, drinks or other goods, in streets and other public places; selling goods for establishments by going from door to door, or by telephone. Supervision of other workers may be included.

Occupations in this minor group are classified into the following unit groups:

9111   Street food vendors

9112   Street vendors, non-food products

9113   Door-to-door and telephone salespersons

9111   STREET FOOD VENDORS

Street food vendors prepare and sell, or sell previously prepared, hot or cold foods, vegetables, fruit, ice-cream and various drinks, in streets and public places such as stations, cinemas, or theatres.

Tasks include –
(a) obtaining food and drinks for sale;
(b) preparing, either beforehand or on the spot, food and drinks for sale;
(c) loading and unloading push-cart or truck, to bring food and drinks to the desired place in the street, or to public places such as stations or cinemas;
(d) displaying food and drinks;
(e) receiving payment on the spot;
(f) performing related tasks;
(g) supervising other workers.

Examples of the occupations classified here:

- Vendor, refreshments/cinema
- Vendor, refreshments/theatre
- Vendor, street/food

Some related occupations classified elsewhere:

- Salesperson, market − 5230
- Salesperson, street stall − 5230
- Vendor, street/non-food products − 9112

9112 STREET VENDORS, NON-FOOD PRODUCTS

Street vendors, non-food products sell various goods in streets and public places such as stations, cinemas or theatres.

Tasks include −

(a) buying or making various items for sale;
(b) loading and unloading push-cart, bicycle, truck or other vehicle, to transport goods to the streets or public places such as stations or cinemas;
(c) displaying goods;
(d) approaching customer and selling newspapers or similar goods;
(e) receiving payment on the spot;
(f) performing related tasks;
(g) supervising other workers.

Examples of the occupations classified here:

- Hawker
- Pedlar

- Vendor, theatre programme
- Vendor, street/non-food products

Some related occupations classified elsewhere:

- Salesperson, market − 5230
- Salesperson, street stall − 5230
- Vendor, street/food − 9111

9113 DOOR-TO-DOOR AND TELEPHONE SALESPERSONS

Door-to-door and telephone salespersons solicit business for an establishment, particularly from households, by going from door to door or by telephoning.

Tasks include −

(a) giving details of various goods or services and of the firm's terms of sale either by going from door to door or by telephoning;
(b) demonstrating goods by pointing to their main characteristics or showing how they work;
(c) taking notes of orders received and forwarding them to the firm;
(d) distributing advertising literature or leaving samples;
(e) collecting payment of instalments, if necessary;
(f) performing related tasks;
(g) supervising other workers.

Examples of the occupations classified here:

- Salesperson, door-to-door
- Salesperson, telephone

MINOR GROUP 912
SHOE CLEANING AND OTHER STREET SERVICES ELEMENTARY OCCUPATIONS

Shoe cleaning and other street services elementary occupations consist of providing various on-the-spot street services such as cleaning shoes, washing car windows, or running errands.

Tasks performed usually include: cleaning shoes in the street and other public places; washing car windows in the street; running errands. Supervision of other workers may be included.

Occupations in this minor group are classified into the following unit group:

9120 Shoe cleaning and other street services elementary occupations

9120 SHOE CLEANING AND OTHER STREET SERVICES ELEMENTARY OCCUPATIONS

Shoe cleaning and other street services elementary occupations usually include cleaning shoes, washing car windows, running errands and providing other on-the-spot street services.

Tasks include –
(a) obtaining the materials necessary to perform cleaning services;
(b) cleaning and polishing shoes;
(c) cleaning and polishing car windows;
(d) running errands;
(e) receiving immediate payment;
(f) performing related tasks;
(g) supervising other workers.

Examples of the occupations classified here:
- Errand boy
- Shoe-polisher
- Washer, hand/street (car windows)

MINOR GROUP 913
DOMESTIC AND RELATED HELPERS, CLEANERS AND LAUNDERERS

Domestic and related helpers, cleaners and launderers perform various tasks in private households, hotels, offices, hospitals and other establishments, as well as in aircraft, trains, coaches, trams, and similar vehicles, in order to keep the interiors and fixtures clean, or they do hand-laundering and pressing.

Tasks performed usually include: sweeping or vacuum-cleaning, taking care of linen, washing and polishing floors, furniture and other objects, or bed-making; helping with various kitchen work or, in private households, cooking and serving meals; performing the tasks of hand-launderers and pressers. Supervision of other workers may be included.

Occupations in this minor group are classified into the following unit groups:

9131 Domestic helpers and cleaners

9132 Helpers and cleaners in offices, hotels and other establishments

9133 Hand-launderers and pressers

9131 DOMESTIC HELPERS AND CLEANERS

Domestic helpers and cleaners sweep, vacuum-clean, wash and polish, take care of household linen, purchase household supplies, prepare food, serve meals and perform various other domestic duties.

Tasks include –

(a) sweeping, vacuum-cleaning, polishing and washing floors and furniture, or washing windows and other fixtures;

(b) washing, ironing and mending linen and other textiles;

(c) washing dishes;

(d) preparing, cooking and serving meals and refreshments;

(e) purchasing food and various other household supplies;

(f) performing related tasks;

(g) supervising other workers.

Examples of the occupations classified here:
- Charworker, domestic
- Cleaner, domestic

Some related occupations classified elsewhere:
- Cleaner, hotel – 9132
- Housekeeper – 5121
- Launderer, hand – 9133
- Sweeper, street – 9162

9132 HELPERS AND CLEANERS IN OFFICES, HOTELS AND OTHER ESTABLISHMENTS

Helpers and cleaners in offices, hotels and other establishments perform various cleaning tasks in order to keep clean and tidy the interiors and fixtures of hotels, offices and other establishments, as well as of aircraft, trains, buses and similar vehicles.

Tasks include –

(a) sweeping or vacuum-cleaning, washing and polishing floors, furniture and other fixtures in buildings, coaches, buses, trams, trains and aircraft;

(b) making beds, cleaning bathrooms, supplying towels, soap and related items;

(c) cleaning kitchens and generally helping with kitchen work, including dishwashing;

(d) performing related tasks;

(e) supervising other workers.

Examples of the occupations classified here:
- Cleaner, aircraft
- Cleaner, hotel
- Cleaner, office
- Washer, hand/dishes

Some related occupations classified elsewhere:
- Caretaker, building – 9141
- Cleaner, domestic – 9131
- Housekeeper – 5121
- Sweeper, street – 9162

9133 HAND-LAUNDERERS AND PRESSERS

Hand-launderers and pressers launder, press or dry-clean linen and other textiles by hand.

Tasks include –

(a) laundering and pressing linen, clothing, fabrics and similar articles by hand in a laundry or other establishment;

(b) cleaning, by hand and with chemical solutions, clothing, fabrics, leather goods and similar articles, in a dry-cleaning or other establishment;

(c) performing related tasks;

(d) supervising other workers.

Examples of the occupations classified here:
- Dry-cleaner, hand
- Launderer, hand
- Presser, hand

Some related occupations classified elsewhere:
- Machine-operator, dry-cleaning – 8264
- Machine-operator, pressing/laundry – 8264
- Machine-operator, washing/laundry – 8264

9

MINOR GROUP **914**
BUILDING CARETAKERS, WINDOW AND RELATED CLEANERS

Building caretakers, window and related cleaners take care of apartment houses, hotels, offices, churches and other buildings and maintain them in a clean and orderly condition.

Tasks performed usually include: looking after, and participating in the cleaning, simple repair and maintenance of apartment houses, hotels, offices, churches and other buildings; regulating conduct of tenants and other users of the buildings in such matters as noise abatement or misuse of property; providing small services to absent tenants, such as accepting deliveries on their behalf or providing requested information to callers; cleaning windows, showcases and other glass surfaces of buildings, or vehicles. Supervision of other workers may be included.

Occupations in this minor group are classified into the following unit groups:

9141   Building caretakers

9142   Vehicle, window and related cleaners

9141   BUILDING CARETAKERS

Building caretakers take care of apartment houses, hotels, offices, churches and other buildings and maintain them in a clean and orderly condition.

Tasks include –
(a) participating in cleaning, simple repairs and maintenance of building interiors;
(b) tending furnaces and boilers to ensure provision of heat and hot water;
(c) regulating conduct of tenants and visitors in such matters as noise abatement or misuse of property;
(d) providing small services to absent tenants such as accepting deliveries on their behalf or providing requested information to callers;
(e) performing related tasks;
(f) supervising other workers.

Examples of the occupations classified here:
- Caretaker, building/cleaning
- Concierge, building
- Janitor
- Sexton

9142   VEHICLE, WINDOW AND RELATED CLEANERS

Vehicle, window and related cleaners clean windows, showcases or other glass surfaces of buildings, or vehicles.

Tasks include –
(a) cleaning, washing and polishing cars and other vehicles, by hand or machine;
(b) washing windows or other glass surfaces with water or various solutions, drying and polishing them;
(c) performing related tasks;
(d) supervising other workers.

Examples of the occupations classified here:
- Cleaner, window
- Washer, hand/vehicle

MESSENGERS, PORTERS, DOORKEEPERS AND RELATED WORKERS

Messengers, porters, doorkeepers and related workers deliver messages or goods, carry luggage, attend parking places and watch private and public properties to prevent illegal entry, theft or fire, perform ushering duties, or collect vending-machine money, or read electricity, gas or water meters.

Tasks performed usually include: delivering messages, packages and other items within an establishment or between establishments, to households or other places; carrying luggage especially at hotels, stations or airports; doorkeeping or watching properties; performing ushering duties; stocking vending machines and collecting money from them or from parking meters and other coin boxes ; reading electricity, gas or water meters. Supervision of other workers may be included.

Occupations in this minor group are classified into the following unit groups:

9151 Messengers, package and luggage porters and deliverers

9152 Doorkeepers, watchpersons and related workers

9153 Vending-machine money collectors, meter readers and related workers

9151 MESSENGERS, PACKAGE AND LUGGAGE PORTERS AND DELIVERERS

Messengers, package and luggage porters and deliverers carry and deliver messages, packages and other items within an establishment or between establishments, to households and elsewhere, or carry luggage especially at hotels, stations and airports.

Tasks include –
(a) delivering messages, packages and other items within an establishment or between establishments, or elsewhere;
(b) performing the duties of a post-runner;
(c) delivering various goods to and from enterprises, shops, households and other places;
(d) carrying and delivering luggage at hotels, stations, airports, and elsewhere;
(e) performing related tasks;
(f) supervising other workers.

Examples of the occupations classified here:
- Deliverer, hand/newspapers

- Messenger
- Porter, luggage
- Post-runner

Some related occupations classified elsewhere:
- Postman – 4142
- Postwoman – 4142

9152 DOORKEEPERS, WATCHPERSONS AND RELATED WORKERS

Doorkeepers, watchpersons and related workers undertake doorkeeping duties in apartment houses and other buildings, attend parking places, watch houses and other properties to prevent illegal entry or theft and detect fire or other hazards, collect tickets, or perform ushering duties.

Tasks include –
(a) doorkeeping in hotels and helping guests, especially on their arrival and departure, with luggage, keys, or information about directions, etc.;
(b) doorkeeping in apartment houses and other buildings, checking the right-of-

entry of callers and giving them requested information;

(c) watching houses and other properties
to prevent illegal entry or theft, fire or
other hazards;

(d) ushering people into courtrooms, sporting places and similar establishments;

(e) collecting tickets in cinemas, theatres,
circuses and related places;

(f) taking charge of cloakrooms or lava-
tories in public places;

(g) attending parking places;

(h) performing related tasks;

(i) supervising other workers.

**Examples of the occupations classified
here:**
- Attendant, cloakroom
- Collector, ticket
- Concierge, hotel desk
- Doorkeeper
- Guard, museum
- Porter, hotel
- Watchman
- Watchwoman

**Some related occupations classified else-
where:**
- Bodyguard − 5169
- Concierge, building − 9141

- Game-warden − 5169
- Patrolman, security − 5169
- Patrolwoman, security − 5169
- Porter, luggage − 9151

9153 VENDING-MACHINE MONEY COLLECTORS, METER READERS AND RELATED WORKERS

Vending-machine money collectors, meter readers and related workers stock vending
machines and collect money from them or
from parking meters and other coin-boxes,
or read electricity, gas or water meters.

Tasks include −

(a) filling storage areas of vending
machines and collecting money from
their containers;

(b) collecting money from parking meters
and similar coin-boxes;

(c) reading electricity, gas or water meters
and recording consumption;

(d) performing related tasks;

(e) supervising other workers.

**Examples of the occupations classified
here:**
- Collector, vending machine
- Meter reader

MINOR GROUP 916
GARBAGE COLLECTORS AND RELATED LABOURERS

Garbage collectors and related labourers collect garbage from buildings, yards,
streets and other public places, or keep streets and other public places clean, or
perform odd jobs for private households or establishments.

Tasks performed usually include: collecting, loading and unloading garbage;
sweeping streets, parks and other public places; unloading coal or wood and putting it
into the cellars of households or establishments; chopping firewood; carrying water;
beating dust out of carpets, and performing other odd-job tasks. Supervision of other
workers may be included.

Occupations in this minor group are classified into the following unit groups:

9161 Garbage collectors

9162 Sweepers and related labourers

9161 GARBAGE COLLECTORS

Garbage collectors collect and remove garbage from buildings, yards, streets and other public places.

Tasks include –

(a) collecting garbage by putting it into bigger containers;

(b) collecting garbage and loading it onto a vehicle;

(c) performing related tasks;

(d) supervising other workers.

Examples of the occupations classified here:

- Collector, refuse
- Dustman
- Dustwoman

9162 SWEEPERS AND RELATED LABOURERS

Sweepers and related labourers sweep and clean streets, parks, airports, stations and other public places or perform odd jobs.

Tasks include –

(a) sweeping streets, parks, airports, stations and similar public places;

(b) unloading coal or wood and putting it into cellars of private households or establishments;

(c) chopping and stacking wood;

(d) carrying water;

(e) shovelling snow;

(f) beating dust out of carpets by using a carpet-beater;

(g) performing related tasks;

(h) supervising other workers.

Examples of the occupations classified here:

- Odd-job person
- Sweeper, park
- Sweeper, street

SUB-MAJOR GROUP 92
AGRICULTURAL, FISHERY AND RELATED LABOURERS

Agricultural, fishery and related labourers mainly perform simple and routine farming, forestry, fishing, hunting or trapping tasks, requiring the use of simple hand-held tools and very often considerable physical effort.

Tasks performed by labourers in this sub-major group usually include: digging, shovelling, loading, unloading, stacking, raking, pitching; spreading manure or fertilizers; watering and weeding; picking fruit, vegetables and various plants; feeding animals; cleaning animal quarters and farm ground; clearing forest ground and undergrowth; cleaning sea-bed and performing other simple tasks connected with aquatic cultivation; gathering seaweed, clams and other mollusca; performing simple tasks connected with hunting and trapping. Supervision of other workers may be included.

Occupations in this sub-major group are classified into the following minor group:

921 Agricultural, fishery and related labourers

MINOR GROUP 921
AGRICULTURAL, FISHERY AND RELATED LABOURERS

Agricultural, fishery and related labourers mainly perform simple and routine farming, forestry, fishing, hunting or trapping tasks, requiring the use of simple hand-held tools and very often considerable physical effort.

Tasks performed usually include: digging, shovelling, loading, unloading, stacking, raking, pitching; spreading manure or fertilizers; watering and weeding; picking fruit, vegetables and various plants; feeding animals; cleaning animal quarters and farm yards; clearing undergrowth in forest stands; cleaning sea-bed and performing other simple tasks connected with aquatic cultivation; gathering seaweed, sea mosses, clams and other mollusca; digging holes, keeping watch and performing other simple tasks connected with hunting and trapping. Supervision of other workers may be included.

Occupations in this minor group are classified into the following unit groups:

9211   Farm-hands and labourers

9212   Forestry labourers

9213   Fishery, hunting and trapping labourers

9211   FARM-HANDS AND LABOURERS

Farm-hands and labourers help with farm work by performing a variety of simple farming tasks.

Tasks include –
(a) digging and shovelling to clear ditches or for other purposes;
(b) loading, unloading various crops and other materials;
(c) raking, pitching and stacking hay;
(d) watering and weeding;
(e) picking fruit, vegetables and various plants;
(f) helping with planting, harvesting and general farmwork;
(g) feeding, watering, and cleaning animals and keeping their quarters clean;
(h) performing related tasks;
(i) supervising other workers.

Examples of the occupations classified here:
- Labourer, farm
- Picker, fruit

Some related occupations classified elsewhere:
- Shepherd – 6121
- Farm worker, skilled/field crops – 6111
- Farm worker, skilled/livestock – 6121

9212   FORESTRY LABOURERS

Forestry labourers help with work in natural forests or in forestry plantations by performing a variety of simple forestry tasks.

Tasks include –
(a) digging holes for tree planting;
(b) stacking logs and timber;
(c) clearing undergrowth in forest stands;
(d) performing related tasks;
(e) supervising other workers.

Examples of the occupations classified here:
- Labourer, forestry

Some related occupations classified elsewhere:
- Forestry worker, skilled – 6141

9213 FISHERY, HUNTING AND TRAPPING LABOURERS

Fishery, hunting and trapping labourers, by performing a variety of simple tasks, help with work connected with fish and seafood cultivation, or with hunting and trapping.

Tasks include –

(a) cleaning the sea-bed and feeding fish and mollusca that are being cultivated;

(b) gathering seaweed, sea mosses, clams and other mollusca;

(c) digging pits and holes, setting traps, keeping watch and performing other simple tasks connected with hunting and trapping;

(d) performing related tasks;

(e) supervising other workers.

Examples of the occupations classified here:
- Labourer, fishery
- Labourer, hunting
- Labourer, trapping

Some related occupations classified elsewhere:
- Hunter – 6154
- Trapper, fur – 6154
- Fishery worker, skilled/pisciculture – 6151

SUB-MAJOR GROUP 93
LABOURERS IN MINING, CONSTRUCTION, MANUFACTURING AND TRANSPORT

Labourers in mining, construction, manufacturing and transport mainly perform simple and routine tasks in connection with mining, construction, manufacturing and transport, requiring the use of simple hand-held tools and very often considerable physical effort.

Tasks performed by labourers in this sub-major group usually include: digging, shovelling, lifting, moving, carrying, clearing, loading, unloading; cleaning disused workings in mines and quarries; spreading gravel, carrying bricks, and performing similar tasks in the construction of roads, dams, or buildings; working on demolition sites; carrying out simple tasks in manufacturing, including product-sorting and simple hand-assembling of components, where it is not necessary to follow strictly laid-down rules; packing by hand; freight handling; pedalling or hand-guiding vehicles to transport passengers and goods. Supervision of other workers may be included.

Occupations in this sub-major group are classified into the following minor groups:

931 Mining and construction labourers

932 Manufacturing labourers

933 Transport labourers and freight handlers

9

MINING AND CONSTRUCTION LABOURERS

Mining and construction labourers perform simple and routine tasks connected with mining or construction, requiring the use of simple hand-held tools and very often considerable physical effort.

Tasks performed usually include: digging, shovelling, lifting, moving, carrying, clearing, loading and unloading; clearing disused workings in mines and quarries; digging out chalk, clay, gravel or sand from open pits; working on demolition sites; spreading gravel, carrying bricks or performing similar tasks in the construction of roads, dams, or buildings. Supervision of other workers may be included.

Occupations in this minor group are classified into the following unit groups:

9311   Mining and quarrying labourers

9312   Construction and maintenance labourers: roads, dams and similar constructions

9313   Building construction labourers

9311   MINING AND QUARRYING LABOURERS

Mining and quarrying labourers perform simple and routine tasks in connection with mining or quarrying.

Tasks include –

(a)   removing wood and steel supports from disused workings in mines and quarries;

(b)   digging out chalk, clay, gravel or sand from open pits;

(c)   clearing various obstructions as instructed;

(d)   performing related tasks;

(e)   supervising other workers.

Examples of the occupations classified here:
- Labourer, digging/quarry
- Labourer, mining

Some related occupations classified elsewhere:
- Miner – 7111
- Quarrier – 7111

9312   CONSTRUCTION AND MAINTENANCE LABOURERS: ROADS, DAMS AND SIMILAR CONSTRUCTIONS

Construction and maintenance labourers perform simple and routine tasks in connection with the building and maintenance of roads, dams and similar constructions.

Tasks include –

(a)   digging and filling holes and trenches, spreading gravel and related materials and performing other tasks related to the building and maintenance of railway tracks and roads;

(b)   carrying bricks and mortar to bricklayer or helping in other ways in the building of dams and similar constructions;

(c)   performing related tasks;

(d)   supervising other workers.

Examples of the occupations classified here:
- Labourer, construction
- Labourer, maintenance/dams

9313 BUILDING CONSTRUCTION LABOURERS

Building construction labourers perform simple and routine tasks in connection with various aspects of building construction work.

Tasks include –

(a) cleaning used building bricks and doing other simple work on demolition sites;

(b) clearing various obstructions as instructed;

(c) carrying bricks and mortar to bricklayer on construction site;

(d) performing related tasks;

(e) supervising other workers.

Examples of the occupations classified here:
- Labourer, construction/buildings
- Labourer, demolition

Some related occupations classified elsewhere:
- Bricklayer, construction – 7122
- Builder, house/traditional materials – 7121
- Demolition worker – 7129

MINOR GROUP 932 MANUFACTURING LABOURERS

Manufacturing labourers perform simple and routine tasks connected with manufacturing which require the use of simple hand-held tools and very often considerable physical effort, or they undertake product-sorting and simple hand-assembling of components.

Tasks performed usually include: simple hand-assembling of components; lifting, carrying, loading, unloading or washing raw materials or products in manufacturing establishments; packing by hand. Supervision of other workers may be included.

Occupations in this minor group are classified into the following unit groups:

9321 Assembling labourers

9322 Hand packers and other manufacturing labourers

9321 ASSEMBLING LABOURERS

Assembling labourers undertake product-sorting or simple hand-assembling of components.

Tasks include –

(a) carrying out manual sorting of products or components;

(b) carrying out simple assembling of components;

(c) performing related tasks;

(d) supervising other workers.

Examples of the occupations classified here:
- Bottle sorter
- Labourer, assembling

Some related occupations classified elsewhere:
- Assembler, electrical equipment – 8282
- Assembler, electronic equipment – 8283
- Assembler, leather products – 8286
- Assembler, rubber products – 8284
- Assembler, vehicle – 8281
- Assembler, wood products – 8285

9

9322 HAND PACKERS AND OTHER MANUFACTURING LABOURERS

Hand packers and other manufacturing labourers pack materials or products by hand and perform a variety of simple routine tasks connected with manufacturing.

Tasks include –

(a) packing materials or products by hand in boxes, bags, cartons, crates, kegs and other containers for shipment or storage;

(b) moving, lifting, carrying, loading, unloading or washing raw materials or products, in various manufacturing industries or repair and maintenance establishments;

(c) performing related tasks;

(d) supervising other workers.

Examples of the occupations classified here:
- Labourer, manufacturing
- Packer, hand

Some related occupations classified elsewhere:
- Machine-operator, labelling – 8290
- Machine-operator, packing – 8290

MINOR GROUP 933
TRANSPORT LABOURERS AND FREIGHT HANDLERS

Transport labourers and freight handlers propel cycles and similar vehicles, drive animal-drawn vehicles, farm or other machinery, and carry out freight handling by hand.

Tasks performed usually include: propelling cycles and similar vehicles or driving animal-drawn vehicles to transport passengers and goods; driving animal-drawn machinery; freight-handling. Supervision of other workers may be included.

Occupations in this minor group are classified into the following unit groups:

9331 Hand or pedal vehicle drivers

9332 Drivers of animal-drawn vehicles and machinery

9333 Freight handlers

9331 HAND OR PEDAL VEHICLE DRIVERS

Hand or pedal vehicle drivers propel cycles and similar vehicles to transport passengers or goods.

Tasks include –

(a) loading or unloading goods, or assisting passengers in getting on or off a vehicle;

(b) moving vehicle in the desired direction with due regard to other traffic and traffic regulations;

(c) making minor repairs and keeping vehicle in good order;

(d) collecting fares or charges;

(e) performing related tasks;

(f) supervising other workers.

Examples of the occupations classified here:
- Driver, pedal vehicle
- Driver, rickshaw

Some related occupations classified elsewhere:
- Rider, motor cycle – 8321

9332 DRIVERS OF ANIMAL-DRAWN VEHICLES AND MACHINERY

Drivers of animal-drawn vehicles and machinery drive animal-drawn vehicles to transport passengers or goods, as well as animal-drawn machinery usually in connection with farming.

Tasks include –
(a) harnessing animals and hitching them to vehicles or machinery;
(b) loading or unloading goods, or assisting passengers in getting on or off a vehicle;
(c) driving animals in the desired direction with due regard to other traffic and traffic regulations;
(d) collecting fares or charges;
(e) driving animals to haul wagons in mines or quarries;
(f) driving animals hitched to farm or other machinery;
(g) driving working elephants;
(h) making minor repairs and keeping vehicles in good order;
(i) performing related tasks;
(j) supervising other workers.

Examples of the occupations classified here:
- Driver, animal-drawn vehicle/road
- Driver, animal train
- Driver, elephant

Some related occupations classified elsewhere:
- Driver, car – 8322
- Driver, locomotive – 8311

9333 FREIGHT HANDLERS

Freight handlers carry out tasks such as packing, carrying, loading and unloading furniture and other household items, or loading and unloading ship and aircraft cargoes and other freight, or carrying and stacking goods in various warehouses.

Tasks include –
(a) packing office or household furniture, machines, appliances and related goods to be transported from one place to another;
(b) carrying goods to be loaded on or unloaded from vans, trucks, wagons, ships, or aircraft;
(c) loading and unloading grain, coal, sand and similar goods by placing them on conveyor-belts, pipes, etc.;
(d) connecting hoses between main shore installation pipes and tanks of barges, tankers and other ships to load and unload petroleum, liquefied gases and other liquids;
(e) carrying and stacking goods in warehouses and similar establishments;
(f) performing related tasks;
(g) supervising other workers.

Examples of the occupations classified here:
- Handler, freight

Some related occupations classified elsewhere:
- Operator, crane – 8333
- Operator, truck/lifting – 8334

MAJOR GROUP 0
ARMED FORCES

Members of the armed forces are those personnel who are currently serving in the armed forces, including auxiliary services, whether on a voluntary or compulsory basis, and who are not free to accept civilian employment. Included are regular members of the army, navy, air force and other military services, as well as conscripts enrolled for military training or other service for a specified period, depending on national requirements. Excluded are persons in civilian employment of government establishments concerned with defence issues; police (other than military police); customs inspectors and members of border or other armed civilian services; persons who have been temporarily withdrawn from civilian life for a short period of military training or retraining, according to national requirements, and members of military reserves not currently on active service. Reference to a skill level has not been used in defining the scope of this major group.

Occupations in this major group are classified into the following sub-major, minor and unit groups:

01   **Armed forces**

011   **Armed forces**

0110   **Armed forces**

INDEXES

NOTES ON THE ISCO-88 INDEX OF OCCUPATIONAL TITLES

The index of the International Standard Classification of Occupations 1988 (ISCO-88) consists of a set of occupational titles and the corresponding codes. Each index entry has been given two codes: one identifying its unit group in ISCO-88 and the other its occupational category in ISCO-68. Three separate listings of the index are provided. The first is according to ISCO-88 numerical order, the second by ISCO-68 numerical order, while the third is in the form of an alphabetical list of occupational titles.

Index structure

Entries in the ISCO-88 index follow a strict ‹keyword›, ‹qualifiers› format to facilitate the search for an index title corresponding to a job or occupation. An index entry will usually have the following components:

1. *Keyword*: A keyword is usually one word which can, on its own, stand as an occupational title. For example, *Teacher, Engineer, Clerk* are all valid keywords. In a few cases, the keyword will comprise of more than one word. These are discussed in the section on "Special occupational titles" below.

2. *Primary qualifier*: This is usually a single word descriptor for the keyword. The primary qualifier designates the occupational title to a unique, or very narrow, range of occupations. A primary qualifier is separated from the keyword by a comma. Examples include: ‹Physicist, *atomic*›; ‹Farmer, *fruit*›; etc. In most cases it is possible to reverse the order of the keyword and primary qualifier, to read an occupational title. For example, ‹Physicist, atomic› can be read as ‹Atomic physicist›, ‹Driver, truck› as ‹Truck driver›, and so on.

3. *Secondary qualifier*: A secondary qualifier is a descriptor which provides additional information in cases where such information is necessary for the identification of a particular occupation. The secondary qualifier is separated from the primary qualifier by a solidus (slant line). Examples include: ‹Engineer, civil/*dredging*›; ‹Engineer, civil/*hydraulic*›; etc.

4. *Tertiary qualifier*: In a few instances, a tertiary (third) qualifier may be required. The tertiary qualifier is placed next to the secondary qualifier and enclosed in parentheses, such as in ‹Operator, generator/electric power *(steam)*›.

Special occupational titles

In a few special cases, the structure of the index entries differs from the general structure outlined above. In such instances, the keyword may consist of more than one word. It has been necessary to deviate from the index structure in the following cases:

(a) *Change of meaning*: In some instances, strict arrangement of an occupational title as a single-word keyword, followed by qualifiers, may lead to a change in meaning. The title ‹Home economist›, comprising two words, provides us with a good example. If the title were to be rearranged to read ‹Economist, home›, the meaning of the title would be changed, since a home economist is not an economist in the accepted sense of the word and should therefore not be given the keyword ‹Economist›. The keyword here is ‹Home economist›, comprising two words. Other examples include ‹Political scientist›; ‹Inspector-general›; etc.

(b) *Multiple function occupations :* Certain occupational titles describe more than one main task. An example is the job of both setting and operating a machine. The index entry for the occupation has the keyword ‹Setter-operator› where the two components are separated by a dash. The sequence of the components depends on common usage and the relative importance of the two functions to the overall occupation, or on the sequence of implementation of the two functions. Examples include ‹Engraver-etcher›; ‹Cutter-polisher›, and so on.

(c) *Loss of clarity :* In some cases, rearrangement in the strict ‹single-word keyword, qualifiers› format would result in a lack of clarity in the occupational title. For this reason, the following main exceptions have been made:

Heads of enterprises and organisations have been designated the keywords: *Chief executive, Director-general* and *Managing director.*

Managers have been designated the keywords: *Department manager* (those who manage a department of an enterprise or organisation), and *General manager*.

High-ranking officials in public or private organisations have been designated the keyword *Senior official*.

Titles with the word *worker* require the use of a double-word keyword. The first part of the keyword describes the specialisation of the job. The second word is *worker.* Examples include: ‹Social worker›, ‹Welfare worker›, ‹Farm worker›, ‹Timbering worker›, ‹Terrazzo worker›, ‹Sheet-metal worker›.

In other cases, certain keywords have been avoided in order to conform to the conceptual side of the classification. The keyword *Supervisor* has not been used, as supervising occupations, if not managerial, are classified together with the jobs whose tasks they supervise. No keyword has been used for *coaching occupations* when concerned with on-the-job training as they are classified with the occupations whose workers they instruct in particular trades, crafts or machine-operating tasks. The keyword, *Working proprietor,* has not been used, as ISCO-88, unlike its predecessor, does not take into consideration whether a worker is a working proprietor or not.

(d) *Too many qualifiers :* An exception to the general rules was made for operators. In order to maintain a single-word keyword *Operator,* it would have been necessary to use three, or even four qualifiers in many instances. To avoid this, the major types of operators have been given the separate keywords, *Furnace-operator, Kiln-operator, Lathe-operator, Machine-operator* and *Press-operator.* All other operators, including plant and equipment operators appear under the keyword *Operator;* for example, ‹Operator, barge›. The primary qualifier of occupational titles for furnace, kiln, lathe, machine and press operators is a description of the function of the machine, or a description of the products being manufactured; examples include ‹Furnace-operator, annealing/glass›, ‹Kiln-operator, brick and tile/oven kiln›, ‹Lathe-operator, stoneworking›, ‹Machine-operator, drilling/metal›,

‹Machine-operator, sugar production› and ‹Press-operator, baling›. Conversely, for the single-word keyword *Operator*, the primary qualifier is a description of the type of equipment used; examples include: ‹Operator, medical X-ray equipment› and ‹Operator, truck/lifting›.

Use of the index

The ISCO-88 index is intended to be used to identify the correct ISCO-88 (and ISCO-68) group for a particular job or occupation, based on the occupational title and/or a description of main tasks and duties. The following steps are involved, when using the index to find the correct code for an occupational title or description.

1. Determine the words which are most likely to point to the corresponding occupational title listed in the index. For example, in the response, ‹Worker at a steel factory, operating a furnace for converting steel›, the four most important words are ‹operating›, ‹furnace›, ‹converting› and ‹steel›.

2. Determine the keyword. In the above example, the keyword is *Furnace-operator.*

3. Examine the entries in the index, for the keyword determined in step 2. In the example given, these entries include:

. . . .

. . . .

8152 Furnace-operator, chemical and related processes
8121 Furnace-operator, converting/non-ferrous metal
8121 Furnace-operator, converting/steel (bessemer furnace)
8121 Furnace-operator, converting/steel (oxygen furnace)

. . . .

. . . .

4. Select a matching index entry based on the qualifiers. In the above list, the matching entry is either the third or the fourth entry. As both entries belong to the same unit group, 8121 is the correct ISCO-88 code.

Note on the recasting of the ISCO-68 index

When using the ISCO-88 index it should be remembered that the index represents a recasting of titles found in the "Expanded alphabetical list of titles" in ISCO-68. This rearrangement has carried over several of the shortcomings of the ISCO-68 index. The main deficiency arises from uneven coverage of different occupational sectors. For example, almost half of the occupations in the ISCO-88 index occur in manufacturing or related sectors. In addition many new activities which have developed during the past 20 years are sparsely represented. One good example is the silicon-chip industry. This recently developed industry is represented by only one index entry, ‹Machine-operator, silicon-chip production›, which was incorporated into the ISCO-88 index. It is hoped that the future inclusion of occupational titles from updated national sources (see page 5 of the introduction) will help to resolve this and other similar problems.

Index of occupational titles according to ISCO-88 numerical order

1110	2-01.10	Chancellor, government
1110	2-01.10	Chief whip
1110	2-01.10	Congressman
1110	2-01.10	Congresswoman
1110	2-01.10	Councillor, city
1110	2-01.10	Councillor, government
1110	2-01.10	Governor, commonwealth
1110	2-01.10	Governor, state
1110	2-01.10	Mayor
1110	2-01.10	Member, parliament
1110	2-01.10	Minister, government
1110	2-01.10	Minister, government/junior
1110	2-01.10	Official, legislative
1110	2-01.10	Parliamentarian
1110	2-01.10	President, government
1110	2-01.10	Prime minister
1110	2-01.10	Secretary, government/legislative
1110	2-01.10	Secretary, state
1110	2-01.10	Senator
1110	2-01.10	Speaker
1120	2-02.10	Administrator, city
1120	2-02.10	Administrator, government
1120	2-02.10	Administrator, intergovernmental organisation
1120	2-02.10	Ambassador
1120	2-02.10	Chief constable, police
1120	2-02.10	Commissioner, civil service
1120	2-02.10	Commissioner, fire
1120	2-02.10	Commissioner, inland revenue
1120	2-02.10	Commissioner, police
1120	2-02.10	Consul-general
1120	2-02.10	Diplomatic representative, embassy
1120	2-02.10	Director-general, government administration/regional
1120	2-02.10	Director-general, government department
1120	2-02.10	Director-general, intergovernmental organisation
1120	2-02.10	Governor, prison
1120	2-02.10	Head, chancery
1120	2-02.10	Head, government department
1120	2-02.10	High commissioner, government
1120	2-02.10	Inspector-general, police
1120	2-02.10	Paymaster-general, government

1120	2-02.10	Postmaster-general, government
1120	2-02.10	Registrar-general, government
1120	2-02.10	Representative, diplomatic
1120	2-02.10	Secretary, embassy
1120	2-02.10	Secretary, government/non-legislative
1120	2-02.10	Secretary-general, government administration
1120	2-02.10	Secretary-general, government administration/deputy
1120	2-02.10	Senior official, government
1120	2-02.10	Under-secretary, government
1130	2-01.10	Chief, village
1130	2-01.10	Head, village
1141	2-11.10	Chairperson, political party
1141	2-11.10	Leader, political party
1141	2-11.10	President, political party
1141	2-11.10	Secretary-general, political party
1141	2-11.10	Senior official, political party
1142	2-11.10	Director-general, employers' organisation
1142	2-11.10	Leader, trade union
1142	2-11.10	President, employers' organisation
1142	2-11.10	Secretary-general, employers' organisation
1142	2-11.10	Secretary-general, trade union
1142	2-11.10	Senior official, employers' organisation
1142	2-11.10	Senior official, trade union
1143	2-11.10	Secretary-general, environment protection organisation
1143	2-11.10	Secretary-general, human rights organisation
1143	2-11.10	Secretary-general, humanitarian organisation
1143	2-11.10	Secretary-general, Red Crescent organisation
1143	2-11.10	Secretary-general, Red Cross organisation
1143	2-11.10	Secretary-general, special-interest organisation
1143	2-11.10	Secretary-general, wild life protection organisation

1210	2-11.10	Director-general, enterprise/travel agency
1210	2-11.10	Director-general, enterprise/wholesale trade
1210	2-11.10	Director-general, organisation
1210	2-11.10	Director-general, organisation/cultural activities
1210	2-11.10	Director-general, organisation/education
1210	2-11.10	Director-general, organisation/extra-territorial organisations
1210	2-11.10	Director-general, organisation/fishing
1210	2-11.10	Director-general, organisation/forestry
1210	2-11.10	Director-general, organisation/health
1210	2-11.10	Director-general, organisation/public administration
1210	2-11.10	Director-general, organisation/recreation
1210	2-11.10	Director-general, organisation/social work
1210	2-11.10	Director-general, organisation/sporting activities
1210	2-11.10	Managing director, enterprise
1210	2-11.10	Managing director, enterprise/agriculture
1210	2-11.10	Managing director, enterprise/business services
1210	2-11.10	Managing director, enterprise/cleaning
1210	2-11.10	Managing director, enterprise/communications
1210	2-11.10	Managing director, enterprise/construction
1210	2-11.10	Managing director, enterprise/cultural activities
1210	2-11.10	Managing director, enterprise/education
1210	2-11.10	Managing director, enterprise/fishing
1210	2-11.10	Managing director, enterprise/forestry
1210	2-11.10	Managing director, enterprise/health
1210	2-11.10	Managing director, enterprise/hotel
1210	2-11.10	Managing director, enterprise/hunting
1210	2-11.10	Managing director, enterprise/manufacturing
1210	2-11.10	Managing director, enterprise/personal care
1210	2-11.10	Managing director, enterprise/recreation
1210	2-11.10	Managing director, enterprise/restaurant
1210	2-11.10	Managing director, enterprise/retail trade
1210	2-11.10	Managing director, enterprise/social work
1210	2-11.10	Managing director, enterprise/sporting activities
1210	2-11.10	Managing director, enterprise/storage
1210	2-11.10	Managing director, enterprise/transport
1210	2-11.10	Managing director, enterprise/travel agency
1210	2-11.10	Managing director, enterprise/wholesale trade
1210	2-11.10	Managing director, organisation
1210	2-11.10	Managing director, organisation/cultural activities
1210	2-11.10	Managing director, organisation/education
1210	2-11.10	Managing director, organisation/extra-territorial organisations
1210	2-11.10	Managing director, organisation/fishing
1210	2-11.10	Managing director, organisation/forestry
1210	2-11.10	Managing director, organisation/health
1210	2-11.10	Managing director, organisation/public administration
1210	2-11.10	Managing director, organisation/recreation
1210	2-11.10	Managing director, organisation/social work
1210	2-11.10	Managing director, organisation/sporting activities
1210	2-11.10	President, enterprise
1210	2-11.10	President, organisation
1210	2-11.10	Principal, college
1210	2-11.10	Principal, university
1221	6-00.20	Department manager, production and operations/agriculture
1221	2-12.10	Department manager, production and operations/fishing
1221	2-12.10	Department manager, production and operations/forestry
1221	2-12.10	Department manager, production and operations/hunting
1222	2-12.10	Department manager, production and operations/manufacturing
1223	2-12.10	Department manager, production and operations/construction

1235	2-19.90	Department manager, distribution
1235	2-19.90	Department manager, purchasing
1235	2-19.90	Department manager, supplies
1235	2-19.90	Department manager, warehouse
1236	2-19.90	Department manager, computing services
1237	2-19.20	Department manager, research and development
1311	6-00.20	General manager, agriculture
1311	6-00.20	General manager, fishing
1311	6-00.20	General manager, forestry
1311	6-00.20	General manager, hunting
1312	2-11.10	General manager, manufacturing
1313	2-11.10	General manager, construction
1314	4-00.30	General manager, retail trade
1314	4-00.30	General manager, retail trade/chain store
1314	4-00.30	General manager, retail trade/ discount store
1314	4-00.30	General manager, retail trade/mail-order store
1314	4-00.30	General manager, retail trade/self-service store
1314	4-00.30	General manager, retail trade/shop
1314	4-00.20	General manager, wholesale trade
1314	4-10.20	General manager, wholesale trade/ export
1314	4-10.20	General manager, wholesale trade/ import
1314	4-10.30	Merchant, retail trade
1314	4-10.20	Merchant, wholesale trade
1314	4-10.30	Retailer
1314	4-10.30	Shopkeeper
1314	4-10.20	Wholesaler
1315	5-10.50	Barkeeper
1315	5-00.90	General manager, boarding-house
1315	5-00.90	General manager, cafe
1315	5-00.90	General manager, camping site
1315	5-00.90	General manager, canteen
1315	5-10.90	General manager, caravan park
1315	5-10.40	General manager, guest-house
1315	5-00.90	General manager, hostel
1315	5-10.20	General manager, hotel
1315	5-10.20	General manager, inn
1315	5-10.90	General manager, lodging-house
1315	5-00.20	General manager, motel
1315	5-00.90	General manager, refreshment-room
1315	5-00.30	General manager, restaurant
1315	5-10.90	General manager, self-service restaurant
1315	5-10.50	General manager, snack-bar
1315	5-10.20	Innkeeper
1315	5-10.30	Restaurateur
1316	2-11.10	General manager, communications
1316	2-11.10	General manager, storage
1316	2-11.10	General manager, transport
1317	2-11.10	General manager, business services
1318	2-11.10	General manager, cleaning
1318	2-11.10	General manager, personal care
1319	2-11.10	General manager, cultural activities
1319	2-11.10	General manager, education
1319	2-11.10	General manager, health
1319	2-11.10	General manager, recreation
1319	2-11.10	General manager, social work
1319	2-11.10	General manager, sporting activities
1319	2-11.10	General manager, travel agency
1319	2-11.10	Travel agent
2111	0-12.20	Aerodynamicist
2111	0-12.10	Astronomer
2111	0-13.50	Astronomer, radio
2111	0-13.50	Astrophysicist
2111	0-12.20	Ballistician
2111	0-12.20	Hydrodynamicist
2111	0-12.10	Physicist
2111	0-12.50	Physicist, acoustics
2111	0-13.50	Physicist, astronomy
2111	0-12.80	Physicist, atomic
2111	0-12.20	Physicist, ballistics
2111	0-12.60	Physicist, electricity and magnetism
2111	0-12.70	Physicist, electronics
2111	0-12.30	Physicist, heat
2111	0-12.20	Physicist, hydrodynamics
2111	0-12.40	Physicist, light
2111	0-12.20	Physicist, mechanics
2111	0-12.80	Physicist, molecular
2111	0-12.80	Physicist, nuclear
2111	0-12.50	Physicist, optics
2111	0-12.20	Physicist, rheology
2111	0-12.90	Physicist, solid-state
2111	0-12.50	Physicist, sound
2111	0-12.90	Physicist, theoretical
2111	0-12.30	Physicist, thermodynamics

2211	0-52.50	Bacteriologist, industrial
2211	0-52.50	Bacteriologist, medical
2211	0-52.50	Bacteriologist, pharmaceutical
2211	0-52.50	Bacteriologist, soil
2211	0-52.50	Bacteriologist, veterinary
2211	0-51.10	Biologist
2211	0-51.90	Biologist, fresh-water
2211	0-51.90	Biologist, marine
2211	0-51.90	Biologist, molecular
2211	0-51.20	Botanist
2211	0-51.20	Botanist, ecology
2211	0-51.20	Botanist, economic
2211	0-51.20	Botanist, histology
2211	0-51.20	Botanist, mycology
2211	0-51.20	Botanist, soil
2211	0-51.20	Botanist, taxonomy
2211	0-51.90	Cytologist
2211	0-52.90	Cytologist, animal
2211	0-52.90	Cytologist, plant
2211	0-51.90	Ecologist
2211	0-51.30	Ecologist, animal
2211	0-51.20	Ecologist, plant
2211	0-51.30	Embryologist
2211	0-52.90	Engineer, genetics
2211	0-51.30	Entomologist
2211	0-52.90	Geneticist
2211	0-52.90	Geneticist, animal
2211	0-52.90	Geneticist, plant
2211	0-51.90	Histologist
2211	0-51.30	Histologist, animal
2211	0-51.20	Histologist, plant
2211	0-51.90	Hydrobiologist
2211	0-51.30	Ichthyologist
2211	0-51.90	Immunologist
2211	0-51.30	Mammalogist
2211	0-52.50	Microbiologist
2211	0-51.20	Mycologist
2211	0-51.30	Ornithologist
2211	0-51.30	Parasitologist
2211	0-51.30	Pisciculturist
2211	0-51.90	Taxonomist
2211	0-51.30	Taxonomist, animal
2211	0-51.20	Taxonomist, plant
2211	0-51.30	Zoologist
2211	0-51.30	Zoologist, ecology
2211	0-51.30	Zoologist, embryology
2211	0-51.30	Zoologist, entomology
2211	0-51.30	Zoologist, histology
2211	0-51.30	Zoologist, ichthyology
2211	0-51.30	Zoologist, mammalogy
2211	0-51.30	Zoologist, ornithology
2211	0-51.30	Zoologist, parasitology
2211	0-51.30	Zoologist, pisciculture
2211	0-51.30	Zoologist, taxonomy
2212	0-52.20	Anatomist
2212	0-52.30	Biochemist
2212	0-52.90	Biophysicist
2212	0-52.40	Endocrinologist
2212	0-52.40	Epidemiologist
2212	0-52.60	Histopathologist
2212	0-52.60	Neuropathologist
2212	0-52.60	Pathologist
2212	0-52.65	Pathologist, animal
2212	0-52.60	Pathologist, clinical
2212	0-52.60	Pathologist, forensic
2212	0-52.60	Pathologist, histopathology
2212	0-52.60	Pathologist, medical
2212	0-52.60	Pathologist, neuropathology
2212	0-52.90	Pathologist, plant
2212	0-52.60	Pathologist, surgical
2212	0-52.65	Pathologist, veterinary
2212	0-52.70	Pharmacologist
2212	0-52.70	Pharmacologist, toxicology
2212	0-52.40	Physiologist
2212	0-52.40	Physiologist, animal
2212	0-52.40	Physiologist, endocrinology
2212	0-52.40	Physiologist, epidemiology
2212	0-52.40	Physiologist, neurology
2212	0-52.40	Physiologist, plant
2212	0-52.70	Toxicologist
2213	0-53.20	Agricultural scientist
2213	0-53.20	Agronomist
2213	0-52.80	Animal scientist
2213	0-53.30	Arboriculturist
2213	0-53.20	Crop research scientist
2213	0-53.30	Floriculturist
2213	0-53.40	Forestry scientist
2213	0-53.30	Horticulturist
2213	0-53.30	Olericulturist
2213	0-53.30	Pomologist
2213	0-53.40	Silviculturist
2213	0-53.50	Soil scientist
2221	0-61.20	Anaesthetist
2221	0-61.20	Cardiologist
2221	0-61.90	Consultant, medical insurance
2221	0-61.20	Dermatologist
2221	0-61.05	Doctor, medical
2221	0-61.20	Doctor, medical/anaesthetics
2221	0-61.20	Doctor, medical/cardiology
2221	0-61.20	Doctor, medical/dermatology
2221	0-61.20	Doctor, medical/gynaecology
2221	0-61.90	Doctor, medical/medical insurance consultancy

2310	1-31.20	Teacher, post-secondary education/biochemistry
2310	1-31.30	Teacher, post-secondary education/biology
2310	1-31.30	Teacher, post-secondary education/botany
2310	1-31.45	Teacher, post-secondary education/business management
2310	1-31.20	Teacher, post-secondary education/chemistry
2310	1-31.75	Teacher, post-secondary education/chiropractic
2310	1-31.45	Teacher, post-secondary education/commerce
2310	1-31.40	Teacher, post-secondary education/community development
2310	1-31.90	Teacher, post-secondary education/computer science
2310	1-31.80	Teacher, post-secondary education/construction technology
2310	1-31.90	Teacher, post-secondary education/dancing
2310	1-31.65	Teacher, post-secondary education/demography
2310	1-31.30	Teacher, post-secondary education/dentistry
2310	1-31.75	Teacher, post-secondary education/dietetics
2310	1-31.90	Teacher, post-secondary education/drama
2310	1-31.45	Teacher, post-secondary education/economics
2310	1-31.55	Teacher, post-secondary education/education
2310	1-31.25	Teacher, post-secondary education/engineering
2310	1-31.25	Teacher, post-secondary education/engineering (chemical)
2310	1-31.25	Teacher, post-secondary education/engineering (civil)
2310	1-31.25	Teacher, post-secondary education/engineering (electrical)
2310	1-31.25	Teacher, post-secondary education/engineering (electronics)
2310	1-31.25	Teacher, post-secondary education/engineering (mechanical)
2310	1-31.80	Teacher, post-secondary education/engineering (technology)
2310	1-31.25	Teacher, post-secondary education/engineering (telecommunications)
2310	1-31.30	Teacher, post-secondary education/entomology
2310	1-31.90	Teacher, post-secondary education/family planning
2310	1-31.60	Teacher, post-secondary education/fishery
2310	1-31.90	Teacher, post-secondary education/food technology
2310	1-31.90	Teacher, post-secondary education/forensic science
2310	1-31.60	Teacher, post-secondary education/forestry
2310	1-31.20	Teacher, post-secondary education/geodesy
2310	1-31.65	Teacher, post-secondary education/geography
2310	1-31.20	Teacher, post-secondary education/geology
2310	1-31.20	Teacher, post-secondary education/geophysics
2310	1-31.65	Teacher, post-secondary education/government
2310	1-31.65	Teacher, post-secondary education/history
2310	1-31.90	Teacher, post-secondary education/home economics
2310	1-31.60	Teacher, post-secondary education/horticulture
2310	1-31.60	Teacher, post-secondary education/husbandry
2310	1-31.80	Teacher, post-secondary education/industrial arts
2310	1-31.80	Teacher, post-secondary education/industrial design
2310	1-31.80	Teacher, post-secondary education/industrial technology
2310	1-31.65	Teacher, post-secondary education/international affairs
2310	1-31.70	Teacher, post-secondary education/journalism
2310	1-31.70	Teacher, post-secondary education/languages
2310	1-31.50	Teacher, post-secondary education/law
2310	1-31.90	Teacher, post-secondary education/librarianship
2310	1-31.30	Teacher, post-secondary education/life sciences
2310	1-31.70	Teacher, post-secondary education/linguistics
2310	1-31.70	Teacher, post-secondary education/literature
2310	1-31.45	Teacher, post-secondary education/management
2310	1-31.90	Teacher, post-secondary education/marketing
2310	1-31.40	Teacher, post-secondary education/mathematics

2320	1-32.60	Teacher, secondary education/ commercial subjects
2320	1-32.80	Teacher, secondary education/ computer science
2320	1-32.50	Teacher, secondary education/ dancing
2320	1-32.75	Teacher, secondary education/ domestic science
2320	1-32.50	Teacher, secondary education/ drama
2320	1-32.40	Teacher, secondary education/ economics
2320	1-32.80	Teacher, secondary education/ engineering
2320	1-32.50	Teacher, secondary education/fine arts
2320	1-32.40	Teacher, secondary education/ geography
2320	1-32.30	Teacher, secondary education/ geology
2320	1-32.40	Teacher, secondary education/ government
2320	1-32.80	Teacher, secondary education/ handicrafts and crafts
2320	1-32.40	Teacher, secondary education/ history
2320	1-32.15	Teacher, secondary education/ language
2320	1-32.15	Teacher, secondary education/ languages and literature
2320	1-32.30	Teacher, secondary education/life sciences
2320	1-32.15	Teacher, secondary education/ linguistics
2320	1-32.15	Teacher, secondary education/ literature
2320	1-32.20	Teacher, secondary education/ mathematics
2320	1-32.80	Teacher, secondary education/ metalwork
2320	1-32.50	Teacher, secondary education/ music
2320	1-32.30	Teacher, secondary education/ natural science
2320	1-32.75	Teacher, secondary education/ nursing
2320	1-32.90	Teacher, secondary education/ pedagogy
2320	1-32.90	Teacher, secondary education/ philosophy
2320	1-32.80	Teacher, secondary education/ photography
2320	1-32.90	Teacher, secondary education/ physical education
2320	1-32.30	Teacher, secondary education/ physics
2320	1-32.80	Teacher, secondary education/ printing
2320	1-32.40	Teacher, secondary education/ religion
2320	1-32.50	Teacher, secondary education/ sculpture
2320	1-32.60	Teacher, secondary education/ secretarial subjects
2320	1-32.40	Teacher, secondary education/ social studies
2320	1-32.40	Teacher, secondary education/ sociology
2320	1-32.80	Teacher, secondary education/ stonemasonry
2320	1-32.80	Teacher, secondary education/ technical drawing
2320	1-32.80	Teacher, secondary education/ technical education
2320	1-32.60	Teacher, secondary education/ typing
2320	1-32.80	Teacher, secondary education/ vocational training
2320	1-32.80	Teacher, secondary education/ woodwork
2320	1-32.30	Teacher, secondary education/ zoology
2331	1-33.90	Teacher, primary education/ professional
2331	1-33.90	Teacher, primary education/ reading (professional)
2331	1-33.90	Teacher, primary education/writing (professional)
2332	1-34.90	Teacher, kindergarten/professional
2332	1-34.20	Teacher, nursery/professional
2332	1-34.20	Teacher, pre-primary education/ professional
2340	1-35.90	Teacher, remedial/professional
2340	1-35.20	Teacher, special education/for the blind (professional)
2340	1-35.30	Teacher, special education/for the deaf (professional)
2340	1-35.90	Teacher, special education/for the dumb (professional)
2340	1-35.40	Teacher, special education/for the mentally handicapped (professional)
2340	1-35.90	Teacher, special education/for the physically handicapped (professional)
2340	1-35.90	Teacher, special education/ remedial (professional)
2351	1-39.20	Adviser, education
2351	1-39.20	Adviser, education methods

ISCO-88

2442	1-92.40	Ethnologist
2442	1-92.50	Geographer
2442	1-92.50	Geographer, economic
2442	1-92.50	Geographer, physical
2442	1-92.50	Geographer, political
2442	1-92.20	Penologist
2442	1-92.20	Social pathologist
2442	1-92.20	Sociologist
2442	1-92.20	Sociologist, criminology
2442	1-92.20	Sociologist, industrial
2442	1-92.20	Sociologist, penology
2442	1-92.20	Sociologist, social pathology
2443	1-92.90	Genealogist
2443	1-92.60	Historian
2443	1-92.60	Historian, economic
2443	1-92.60	Historian, political
2443	1-92.60	Historian, social
2443	1-92.70	Philosopher
2443	1-92.70	Philosopher, political
2443	1-92.70	Political scientist
2444	1-95.20	Etymologist
2444	1-95.20	Graphologist
2444	1-95.40	Interpreter
2444	1-95.20	Lexicographer
2444	1-95.20	Linguist
2444	1-95.20	Morphologist
2444	1-95.20	Philologist
2444	1-95.20	Philologist, etymology
2444	1-95.20	Philologist, graphology
2444	1-95.20	Philologist, lexicography
2444	1-95.20	Philologist, linguistics
2444	1-95.20	Philologist, morphology
2444	1-95.20	Philologist, phonology
2444	1-95.20	Philologist, semantics
2444	1-95.20	Phonologist
2444	1-95.20	Semasiologist
2444	1-95.30	Translator
2445	1-92.30	Psychologist
2445	1-92.30	Psychologist, clinical
2445	1-92.30	Psychologist, educational
2445	1-92.30	Psychologist, experimental
2445	1-92.30	Psychologist, industrial
2445	1-92.30	Psychologist, occupational
2445	1-92.30	Psychologist, social
2446	1-93.20	Almoner, professional
2446	1-93.20	Caseworker, professional
2446	1-93.20	Caseworker, professional/child welfare
2446	1-93.20	Caseworker, professional/family welfare
2446	1-93.20	Caseworker, professional/social welfare
2446	1-93.20	Housefather, professional
2446	1-93.40	Housemaster, professional/ approved school
2446	1-93.20	Housemother, professional
2446	1-93.40	Parole officer, professional
2446	1-93.40	Probation officer, professional
2446	1-93.10	Social worker, professional
2446	1-93.30	Social worker, professional/ community centre
2446	1-93.30	Social worker, professional/cultural centre
2446	1-93.40	Social worker, professional/ delinquency
2446	1-93.10	Social worker, professional/ enterprise
2446	1-93.90	Social worker, professional/family planning
2446	1-93.90	Social worker, professional/home-help service
2446	1-93.20	Social worker, professional/ medical
2446	1-93.40	Social worker, professional/ probation
2446	1-93.50	Social worker, professional/ psychiatric
2446	1-93.30	Warden, community centre/ professional
2446	1-93.40	Warden, probation home/ professional
2446	1-93.20	Welfare worker, professional
2446	1-93.50	Welfare worker, professional/ mental health
2446	1-93.20	Welfare worker, professional/moral welfare
2446	1-93.20	Welfare worker, professional/ prison
2446	1-93.90	Welfare worker, professional/the deaf
2446	1-93.90	Welfare worker, professional/the physically handicapped
2451	1-51.20	Author
2451	1-51.20	Biographer
2451	1-59.15	Columnist
2451	1-59.90	Commentator, extempore
2451	1-59.35	Commentator, news
2451	1-59.90	Commentator, sports
2451	1-59.50	Copywriter, advertising
2451	1-59.60	Copywriter, publicity
2451	1-59.65	Copywriter, technical
2451	1-59.15	Correspondent, media
2451	1-51.30	Critic
2451	1-51.30	Critic, art

2453	1-71.45	Soprano
2453	1-71.45	Tenor
2453	1-71.30	Transcriber, music
2453	1-71.40	Trombonist
2453	1-71.40	Trumpeter
2453	1-71.40	Violinist
2454	1-72.20	Arranger, ballet
2454	1-72.30	Ballerina
2454	1-72.20	Choreographer
2454	1-72.30	Dancer, ballet
2454	1-72.30	Dancer, ballroom
2455	1-73.20	Actor
2455	1-73.20	Actor, character
2455	1-73.20	Actor, comic
2455	1-73.20	Actor, dramatic
2455	1-73.20	Actor, film
2455	1-73.40	Director, motion picture
2455	1-73.40	Director, radio
2455	1-73.30	Director, stage
2455	1-73.40	Director, television
2455	1-73.30	Director, theatrical
2455	1-73.90	Impersonator
2455	1-73.50	Story-teller
2455	1-73.50	Story-teller, radio or television
2460	1-41.20	Archbishop
2460	1-41.20	Bishop
2460	1-41.20	Bonze
2460	1-41.20	Chaplain
2460	1-41.20	Curate
2460	1-41.20	Imam
2460	1-41.20	Minister, religion
2460	1-41.30	Missionary
2460	1-41.20	Monk, professional
2460	1-41.20	Nun, professional
2460	1-41.20	Pastor
2460	1-41.20	Poojari
2460	1-41.20	Priest
2460	1-41.20	Rabbi
2460	1-41.20	Rector, religion
2460	1-41.20	Talapoin
2460	1-49.90	Theologian
2460	1-41.20	Vicar
3111	0-14.90	Technician, astronomy
3111	0-14.20	Technician, chemistry
3111	0-14.90	Technician, geology
3111	0-14.90	Technician, geophysics
3111	0-14.90	Technician, meteorology
3111	0-14.90	Technician, oceanography
3111	0-14.30	Technician, physics
3112	0-33.40	Clerk of works
3112	0-33.20	Estimator, engineering/civil
3112	0-33.10	Technician, engineering/civil
3112	0-33.90	Technician, engineering/civil (construction)
3112	0-33.90	Technician, engineering/civil (dredging)
3112	0-33.90	Technician, engineering/civil (hydraulics)
3112	0-33.90	Technician, engineering/civil (hydrology)
3112	0-33.90	Technician, engineering/civil (irrigation)
3112	0-33.90	Technician, engineering/civil (public health)
3112	0-33.90	Technician, engineering/civil (sanitary)
3112	0-33.90	Technician, engineering/civil (soil mechanics)
3112	0-33.90	Technician, engineering/civil (structural)
3112	0-33.30	Technician, surveying
3113	0-34.90	Estimator, engineering/electrical
3113	0-34.05	Technician, engineering/electrical
3113	0-34.90	Technician, engineering/electrical (electric illumination)
3113	0-34.90	Technician, engineering/electrical (electric power distribution)
3113	0-34.90	Technician, engineering/electrical (electric power transmission)
3113	0-34.90	Technician, engineering/electrical (electric traction)
3113	0-34.20	Technician, engineering/electrical (high voltage)
3113	0-34.90	Technician, engineering/electrical systems
3114	0-34.90	Estimator, engineering/electronics
3114	0-34.90	Technician, engineering/aerospace
3114	0-34.10	Technician, engineering/ electronics
3114	0-34.90	Technician, engineering/ electronics (computer hardware design)
3114	0-34.90	Technician, engineering/ electronics (information engineering)
3114	0-34.90	Technician, engineering/ electronics (instrumentation)
3114	0-34.90	Technician, engineering/ electronics (semiconductors)
3114	0-34.30	Technician, engineering/ telecommunications
3114	0-34.90	Technician, engineering/ telecommunications (aerospace)

3114	0-34.90	Technician, engineering/telecommunications (radar)
3114	0-34.90	Technician, engineering/telecommunications (radio)
3114	0-34.90	Technician, engineering/telecommunications (signal systems)
3114	0-34.90	Technician, engineering/telecommunications (telegraph)
3114	0-34.90	Technician, engineering/telecommunications (telephone)
3114	0-34.90	Technician, engineering/telecommunications (television)
3115	9-89.20	Dockmaster, dry dock
3115	9-89.20	Dockmaster, graving dock
3115	0-35.90	Estimator, engineering/mechanical
3115	0-35.90	Surveyor, marine
3115	0-35.30	Technician, engineering/aeronautics
3115	0-35.20	Technician, engineering/marine
3115	0-35.10	Technician, engineering/mechanical
3115	0-35.30	Technician, engineering/mechanical (aeronautics)
3115	0-35.90	Technician, engineering/mechanical (agriculture)
3115	0-35.50	Technician, engineering/mechanical (air-conditioning)
3115	0-35.90	Technician, engineering/mechanical (automotive)
3115	0-35.20	Technician, engineering/mechanical (diesel)
3115	0-35.20	Technician, engineering/mechanical (gas turbine)
3115	0-35.50	Technician, engineering/mechanical (heating, ventilation and refrigeration)
3115	0-35.90	Technician, engineering/mechanical (industrial machinery and tools)
3115	0-35.90	Technician, engineering/mechanical (instruments)
3115	0-35.20	Technician, engineering/mechanical (internal combustion)
3115	0-35.20	Technician, engineering/mechanical (jet engine)
3115	0-35.20	Technician, engineering/mechanical (locomotive engine)
3115	0-35.90	Technician, engineering/mechanical (lubrication)
3115	0-35.90	Technician, engineering/mechanical (marine)
3115	0-35.20	Technician, engineering/mechanical (motor)
3115	0-35.90	Technician, engineering/mechanical (naval)
3115	0-35.90	Technician, engineering/mechanical (nuclear power)
3115	0-35.50	Technician, engineering/mechanical (refrigeration)
3115	0-35.90	Technician, engineering/mechanical (ship construction)
3115	0-35.20	Technician, engineering/motor and engine
3115	0-35.90	Technician, engineering/naval
3115	0-35.90	Technician, engineering/nuclear power
3116	0-36.90	Estimator, engineering/chemical
3116	0-36.90	Technician, engineering/chemical
3116	0-36.90	Technician, engineering/chemical process
3116	0-36.90	Technician, engineering/natural gas production and distribution
3116	0-36.20	Technician, engineering/petroleum
3117	7-13.70	Acidiser, oil and gas well
3117	7-13.50	Cementer, oil and gas wells
3117	7-13.90	Shooter, oil and gas wells
3117	0-38.10	Technician, engineering/mining
3117	0-38.90	Technician, engineering/mining (coal)
3117	0-38.90	Technician, engineering/mining (diamonds)
3117	0-38.90	Technician, engineering/mining (metal)
3117	0-38.20	Technician, engineering/mining (petroleum and natural gas)
3117	0-37.90	Technician, metallurgy/assaying
3117	0-37.20	Technician, metallurgy/extractive
3117	0-37.30	Technician, metallurgy/foundry
3117	0-37.30	Technician, metallurgy/physical
3117	0-37.90	Technician, metallurgy/radioactive minerals
3117	7-13.70	Treater, well acidising
3118	0-32.10	Draughtsperson
3118	0-32.50	Draughtsperson, architectural
3118	0-32.60	Draughtsperson, cartographical
3118	0-32.20	Draughtsperson, die
3118	0-32.10	Draughtsperson, engineering
3118	0-32.40	Draughtsperson, engineering/civil
3118	0-32.30	Draughtsperson, engineering/electrical
3118	0-32.30	Draughtsperson, engineering/electronics
3118	0-32.90	Draughtsperson, engineering/heating and ventilation systems
3118	0-32.20	Draughtsperson, engineering/marine

3118	0-32.20	Draughtsperson, engineering/mechanical
3118	0-32.40	Draughtsperson, engineering/structural
3118	0-32.20	Draughtsperson, engineering/aeronautical
3118	0-32.90	Draughtsperson, geological
3118	0-32.20	Draughtsperson, jig and tool
3118	0-32.80	Draughtsperson, lithographic
3118	0-32.70	Draughtsperson, technical
3118	0-32.60	Draughtsperson, topographical
3118	0-32.70	Illustrator, engineering
3118	0-32.70	Illustrator, technical
3119	0-39.30	Technician, engineering/industrial efficiency
3119	0-39.20	Technician, engineering/industrial layout
3119	0-39.20	Technician, engineering/methods
3119	0-39.20	Technician, engineering/planning
3119	0-39.20	Technician, engineering/production
3119	0-39.90	Technician, engineering/safety
3119	0-39.90	Technician, engineering/systems (except computers)
3119	0-39.30	Technician, engineering/time and motion study
3119	0-39.90	Technician, engineering/value
3119	0-39.30	Technician, engineering/work study
3119	0-39.90	Technician, quantity surveying
3121	0-34.90	Assistant, computer/communications
3121	0-34.90	Assistant, computer/database analysis
3121	0-34.90	Assistant, computer/engineering
3121	0-34.90	Assistant, computer/programming
3121	0-34.90	Assistant, computer/systems analysis
3121	0-34.90	Assistant, computer/systems design
3121	0-34.90	Assistant, computer/users' services
3121	0-34.90	Technician, computer
3121	0-34.90	Technician, engineering/systems (computers)
3122	3-42.20	Operator, computer peripheral equipment
3122	3-42.20	Operator, computer peripheral equipment/console
3122	3-42.90	Operator, computer peripheral equipment/high-speed printer

3123	0-39.90	Controller, robot
3123	0-35.90	Technician, robot
3131	1-63.50	Assistant, motion picture
3131	1-63.60	Cameraman, motion picture
3131	1-63.60	Camerawoman, motion picture
3131	1-63.60	Cinematographer
3131	8-62.90	Editor, sound/motion picture
3131	1-63.90	Microphotographer
3131	8-61.30	Operator, audio equipment/radio
3131	8-61.30	Operator, audio equipment/television
3131	1-63.60	Operator, camera/cinematography
3131	1-63.60	Operator, camera/motion picture
3131	1-63.70	Operator, camera/television
3131	8-62.90	Operator, dubbing equipment
3131	8-62.30	Operator, microphone
3131	8-62.20	Operator, recording equipment/discs
3131	8-62.20	Operator, recording equipment/sound
3131	8-62.90	Operator, recording equipment/sound mixing
3131	8-62.20	Operator, recording equipment/tape
3131	8-61.30	Operator, recording equipment/video
3131	8-62.20	Operator, recording equipment/wire
3131	8-61.30	Operator, studio equipment/radio
3131	8-61.30	Operator, studio equipment/television
3131	1-63.10	Photographer
3131	1-63.30	Photographer, advertising
3131	1-63.90	Photographer, aerial
3131	1-63.90	Photographer, architecture
3131	1-63.30	Photographer, commercial
3131	1-63.90	Photographer, commercial illustration
3131	1-63.30	Photographer, fashion
3131	1-63.30	Photographer, industrial
3131	1-63.90	Photographer, medical
3131	1-63.90	Photographer, microphotography
3131	1-63.40	Photographer, news
3131	1-63.90	Photographer, police
3131	1-63.20	Photographer, portrait
3131	1-63.40	Photographer, press
3131	1-63.90	Photographer, scientific
3131	8-62.90	Sound mixer
3131	8-62.90	Technician, sound-effects
3131	8-62.90	Technician, sound-testing
3131	8-62.20	Technician, sound/studio (radio)
3131	8-62.20	Technician, sound/studio (television)

3132	3-80.50	Officer, ship/radio
3132	8-61.90	Operator, broadcasting equipment/field
3132	8-61.30	Operator, broadcasting equipment/radio
3132	8-61.30	Operator, broadcasting equipment/telecine
3132	8-61.30	Operator, broadcasting equipment/television
3132	8-61.90	Operator, broadcasting equipment/television
3132	8-61.30	Operator, broadcasting equipment/video
3132	8-61.30	Operator, control-room equipment/radio
3132	8-61.30	Operator, control-room equipment/television
3132	3-80.40	Operator, morse code
3132	8-62.30	Operator, public address equipment
3132	3-80.60	Operator, radio equipment/flight
3132	3-80.30	Operator, radio equipment/land-based
3132	3-80.50	Operator, radio equipment/sea-based
3132	3-59.75	Operator, telecommunications equipment
3132	3-80.40	Operator, telegraphic equipment
3132	8-61.20	Operator, transmitting equipment/radio
3132	8-61.20	Operator, transmitting equipment/television
3132	8-62.40	Projectionist, cinema
3132	3-80.40	Telegrapher
3133	0-79.90	Operator, audiometric equipment
3133	0-79.90	Operator, electrocardiograph equipment
3133	0-79.90	Operator, electroencephalograph equipment
3133	0-77.10	Operator, medical X-ray equipment
3133	0-77.10	Operator, medical radiography equipment
3133	0-77.90	Operator, scanning equipment
3133	3-42.90	Operator, scanning equipment/optical
3141	0-43.15	Chief engineer, ship
3141	0-43.20	Engineer, ship
3141	0-43.20	Engineer, ship
3141	0-43.20	Engineer, ship/first
3141	0-43.20	Engineer, ship/second
3141	0-43.20	Engineer, ship/third
3141	0-43.20	Engineer, ship/fourth
3141	0-43.30	Superintendent, marine/technical
3142	0-42.50	Captain, port
3142	0-42.20	Captain, ship/inland waterways
3142	0-42.15	Captain, ship/sea
3142	0-42.20	Master, ship/inland waterways
3142	0-42.15	Master, ship/sea
3142	0-42.30	Officer, ship/deck
3142	0-42.30	Officer, ship/navigation
3142	0-42.90	Pilot, hovercraft
3142	0-42.40	Pilot, ship
3142	0-42.30	Shipmate
3142	0-42.90	Skipper, yacht
3142	0-42.50	Superintendent, marine/deck
3143	0-41.20	Captain, aircraft
3143	0-41.50	Engineer, flight
3143	0-41.40	Navigator, flight
3143	0-41.30	Pilot, aircraft
3143	0-41.20	Pilot, helicopter
3143	0-41.20	Pilot, seaplane
3143	0-41.30	Pilot, test
3143	0-41.30	Test pilot, aircraft
3144	3-59.60	Controller, air traffic
3144	3-59.60	Operator, air-traffic control equipment
3145	3-59.50	Technician, air traffic safety
3151	5-81.90	Fire investigator
3151	5-89.90	Inspector, building
3151	5-81.20	Inspector, fire
3151	5-81.20	Specialist, fire prevention
3152	7-54.70	Examiner, cloth
3152	7-54.70	Examiner, fabrics
3152	3-10.10	Inspector, occupational safety
3152	9-49.80	Inspector, product safety
3152	9-49.80	Inspector, quality
3152	8-59.20	Inspector, quality/electrical products
3152	8-59.20	Inspector, quality/electronic products
3152	7-54.70	Inspector, quality/fabrics
3152	9-49.80	Inspector, quality/industrial processes
3152	8-49.85	Inspector, quality/mechanical products
3152	9-49.80	Inspector, quality/products
3152	9-49.80	Inspector, quality/services
3152	3-10.10	Inspector, safety and health
3152	1-93.90	Inspector, safety and health/child care
3152	3-10.10	Inspector, safety and health/consumer protection

3152	3-10.10	Inspector, safety and health/electricity
3152	3-10.10	Inspector, safety and health/establishments
3152	3-10.10	Inspector, safety and health/factories
3152	3-10.10	Inspector, safety and health/industrial waste-processing
3152	3-10.10	Inspector, safety and health/labour
3152	3-10.10	Inspector, safety and health/pollution
3152	3-10.10	Inspector, safety and health/shops
3152	3-10.10	Inspector, safety and health/vehicles
3152	3-10.10	Inspector, safety and health/working conditions
3152	9-49.80	Inspector, vehicles/technical standards inspection
3152	9-49.80	Quality inspector
3152	8-59.20	Quality inspector, electrical products
3152	8-59.20	Quality inspector, electronic products
3152	8-59.85	Quality inspector, mechanical products
3152	9-49.80	Quality inspector, processes
3152	9-49.80	Quality inspector, products
3152	9-49.80	Quality inspector, services
3211	9-49.20	Taxidermist
3211	0-54.20	Technician, anatomy
3211	0-54.20	Technician, bacteriology
3211	0-54.20	Technician, biochemistry
3211	0-54.20	Technician, biology
3211	0-54.20	Technician, biophysics
3211	0-54.30	Technician, blood-bank
3211	0-54.20	Technician, botany
3211	0-54.30	Technician, cytology
3211	0-54.20	Technician, ecology
3211	0-54.20	Technician, genetics
3211	0-54.30	Technician, haematology
3211	0-54.30	Technician, histology
3211	0-54.30	Technician, medical science
3211	0-54.20	Technician, pathology
3211	0-54.20	Technician, pharmacology
3211	0-54.20	Technician, physiology
3211	0-54.30	Technician, serology
3211	0-54.30	Technician, tissue
3211	0-54.20	Technician, zoology
3212	0-54.90	Technician, agronomy
3212	0-54.90	Technician, arboriculture
3212	0-54.90	Technician, crop research
3212	0-54.90	Technician, floriculture
3212	0-54.90	Technician, forestry
3212	0-54.90	Technician, horticulture
3212	0-54.90	Technician, olericulture
3212	0-54.90	Technician, pomology
3212	0-54.90	Technician, silviculture
3212	0-54.90	Technician, soil science
3213	0-53.60	Adviser, agricultural
3213	0-53.60	Adviser, farming
3213	0-53.60	Adviser, forestry
3213	0-53.60	Farm demonstrator
3221	0-62.10	Assistant, medical
3221	0-62.10	Assistant, medical/family planning
3222	0-79.40	Inspector, sanitary
3222	0-79.40	Sanitarian
3223	0-69.90	Consultant, dietetic/food processing
3223	0-69.10	Dietician
3223	0-69.10	Dietician, therapeutic
3223	0-69.20	Nutritionist
3224	0-75.30	Optician, dispensing
3224	0-75.20	Optician, ophthalmic
3224	0-75.20	Optometrist
3225	0-64.20	Assistant, dental
3225	0-64.30	Assistant, dental/school service
3225	0-64.20	Auxiliary, dental
3225	0-64.40	Hygienist, dental
3225	0-64.40	Hygienist, oral
3225	0-64.40	Prophylactician
3226	0-79.30	Chiropractor
3226	0-76.20	Electrotherapist
3226	0-79.50	Fitter, artificial limb
3226	0-79.90	Gymnast, remedial
3226	0-76.40	Masseur
3226	0-76.40	Masseuse
3226	0-79.20	Osteopath, lay
3226	0-76.20	Physiotherapist
3226	0-79.90	Podiatrist
3226	0-79.50	Technician, orthopaedic
3226	0-79.50	Technician, prosthetic
3226	0-76.20	Therapist, physical
3226	0-76.30	Therapist, recreational
3227	0-66.10	Assistant, veterinary
3227	0-66.10	Assistant, veterinary/artificial insemination
3227	0-66.10	Vaccinator, veterinary

3228	0-68.10	Assistant, pharmaceutical
3229	0-79.90	Homeopath
3229	0-79.90	Orthoepist
3229	0-79.90	Orthophonist
3229	0-75.20	Orthoptist
3229	0-79.90	Practitioner, homeopathic
3229	0-79.90	Therapist, occupational
3229	0-79.90	Therapist, orientation of the blind
3229	0-79.90	Therapist, speech
3231	0-72.10	Nurse, associate professional
3231	0-71.20	Nurse, associate professional/ anaesthetics
3231	0-71.10	Nurse, associate professional/ charge
3231	0-71.10	Nurse, associate professional/ clinic
3231	0-71.90	Nurse, associate professional/ consultant
3231	0-71.10	Nurse, associate professional/ district
3231	0-71.40	Nurse, associate professional/ industrial
3231	0-71.20	Nurse, associate professional/ maternity
3231	0-71.20	Nurse, associate professional/ obstetrics
3231	0-71.40	Nurse, associate professional/ occupational health
3231	0-71.20	Nurse, associate professional/ orthopaedic
3231	0-71.20	Nurse, associate professional/ pediatric
3231	0-71.20	Nurse, associate professional/ psychiatric
3231	0-71.90	Nurse, associate professional/ school
3231	0-71.10	Officer, principal nursing/associate professional
3231	0-71.10	Sister, nursing/associate professional
3232	0-74.10	Midwife, associate professional
3232	0-73.10	Midwife, associate professional/ district
3241	0-79.90	Healer, drugless treatment
3241	0-79.90	Healer, herbal
3241	0-79.90	Healer, village
3241	0-79.90	Naturopath
3242	1-49.20	Faith healer
3242	1-49.20	Healer, faith
3310	1-33.20	Teacher, primary education/ associate professional
3310	1-33.90	Teacher, primary education/ reading (associate professional)
3310	1-33.90	Teacher, primary education/writing (associate professional)
3320	1-34.90	Teacher, kindergarten/associate professional
3320	1-34.20	Teacher, nursery/associate professional
3320	1-34.20	Teacher, pre-primary education/ associate professional
3330	1-35.90	Teacher, remedial/associate professional
3330	1-35.20	Teacher, special education/for the blind (associate professional)
3330	1-35.30	Teacher, special education/for the deaf (associate professional)
3330	1-35.90	Teacher, special education/for the dumb (associate professional)
3330	1-35.40	Teacher, special education/for the mentally handicapped (associate professional)
3330	1-35.90	Teacher, special education/for the physically handicapped (associate professional)
3330	1-35.90	Teacher, special education/ remedial (associate professional)
3340	9-85.90	Instructor, driving
3340	0-41.60	Instructor, flying
3340	1-80.30	Instructor, sailing
3340	0-41.60	Pilot, check
3411	4-41.40	Broker, foreign exchange
3411	4-41.40	Broker, investment
3411	4-41.40	Broker, securities
3411	4-41.40	Broker, stocks and shares
3411	4-41.90	Jobber, stock
3411	4-41.40	Salesperson, bond
3411	4-41.40	Salesperson, securities
3411	4-41.40	Sharebroker
3411	4-41.40	Stockbroker
3412	4-41.90	Agent, group insurance
3412	4-41.20	Agent, insurance
3412	4-41.20	Broker, insurance
3412	4-41.20	Insurance broker
3412	1-99.50	Underwriter
3412	1-99.50	Underwriter, insurance
3413	4-41.30	Agent, estate
3413	4-41.30	Agent, house

3413	4-41.30	Agent, property
3413	4-41.30	Realtor
3413	4-41.30	Salesperson, property
3413	4-41.30	Salesperson, real-estate
3414	1-99.90	Consultant, travel
3414	1-99.90	Organiser, travel
3415	4-31.30	Adviser, after-sales service
3415	4-32.20	Agent, sales/commercial
3415	4-31.20	Agent, sales/engineering
3415	4-32.30	Agent, sales/manufacturing
3415	4-31.20	Agent, sales/technical
3415	4-32.20	Canvasser
3415	4-32.20	Commercial traveller
3415	4-32.20	Representative, sales/commercial
3415	4-31.20	Representative, sales/engineering
3415	4-32.30	Representative, sales/ manufacturing
3415	4-31.20	Representative, sales/technical
3415	4-32.20	Salesperson, commercial
3415	4-31.20	Salesperson, engineering
3415	4-32.30	Salesperson, manufacturing
3415	4-31.20	Salesperson, technical
3415	4-32.20	Salesperson, travelling
3416	4-22.30	Agent, procurement
3416	4-22.30	Agent, purchasing
3416	4-22.20	Buyer
3416	4-22.20	Buyer, merchandise/retail trade
3416	4-22.20	Buyer, merchandise/wholesale trade
3416	4-22.30	Buyer, supplies
3416	4-22.20	Purchaser, merchandise
3416	4-22.20	Purchaser, merchandise/retail trade
3416	4-22.20	Purchaser, merchandise/wholesale trade
3417	4-43.30	Adjuster, claims
3417	4-43.30	Adjuster, claims/insurance
3417	4-43.30	Appraiser
3417	4-43.30	Assessor, claims
3417	4-43.30	Assessor, insurance
3417	4-43.30	Assessor, loss
3417	4-43.20	Auctioneer
3417	4-43.30	Inspector, claims
3417	4-43.30	Inspector, insurance claims
3417	4-43.30	Valuer
3421	4-10.20	Broker, commodity
3421	4-10.20	Broker, shipping
3421	4-10.20	Broker, trade
3422	1-99.90	Agent, clearing
3422	1-99.90	Agent, forwarding
3422	1-99.90	Agent, shipping
3423	1-99.90	Agent, employment
3423	1-99.90	Contractor, labour
3423	1-99.90	Officer, job placement
3423	1-99.90	Officer, youth employment
3423	1-99.90	Youth employment officer
3429	1-99.90	Agent, literary
3429	1-99.90	Agent, musical performance
3429	1-99.90	Agent, sports
3429	1-99.90	Agent, theatrical
3429	1-99.90	Promoter, sports
3429	4-42.20	Representative, business services
3429	4-42.30	Representative, business services/ advertising
3429	4-42.20	Representative, business services/ advertising space
3429	4-42.20	Salesperson, business services
3429	4-42.30	Salesperson, business services/ advertising
3429	4-42.30	Salesperson, business services/ advertising space
3431	3-21.20	Administrative secretary
3431	3-93.20	Assistant, correspondence
3431	3-21.30	Reporter, administrative/court
3431	3-21.30	Reporter, administrative/verbatim
3431	3-21.20	Secretary, administrative
3431	3-21.30	Verbatim reporter
3432	3-93.90	Assistant, bank
3432	3-93.40	Assistant, barrister's
3432	3-93.50	Assistant, broker's
3432	3-93.50	Assistant, insurance/adjustment
3432	3-93.50	Assistant, insurance/claims
3432	3-93.50	Assistant, insurance/policy
3432	3-93.40	Assistant, legal
3432	3-93.40	Assistant, solicitor's
3432	5-89.90	Bailiff
3432	3-93.40	Clerk, conveyancing
3432	3-93.40	Clerk, court
3432	3-93.50	Clerk, insurance
3432	3-93.40	Clerk, judge's
3432	3-93.40	Clerk, law
3432	3-93.40	Clerk, probate
3433	3-31.10	Bookkeeper
3433	3-31.10	Bookkeeper, ledger
3434	0-84.90	Assistant, accounting
3434	0-84.90	Assistant, actuarial

3471	1-62.50	Decorator, display
3471	1-62.50	Decorator, display/windows
3471	1-62.30	Decorator, interior
3471	1-62.30	Decorator, motion picture set
3471	1-62.90	Designer, armorial
3471	1-62.40	Designer, commercial products
3471	1-62.30	Designer, decoration
3471	1-62.50	Designer, display
3471	1-62.50	Designer, display/windows
3471	1-62.40	Designer, dress
3471	1-62.50	Designer, exhibition
3471	1-62.40	Designer, fashion
3471	1-62.40	Designer, furniture
3471	1-62.20	Designer, graphic
3471	1-62.40	Designer, industrial products
3471	1-62.30	Designer, interior decoration
3471	1-62.40	Designer, jewellery
3471	1-62.40	Designer, package
3471	1-62.20	Designer, poster
3471	1-62.90	Designer, scenery
3471	1-62.90	Designer, stage set
3471	1-62.40	Designer, textile
3471	1-62.20	Designer, typographical
3471	1-62.20	Illustrator, advertising
3471	1-62.20	Illustrator, book
3471	1-62.90	Tattooist
3472	1-79.20	Announcer, news
3472	1-79.20	Announcer, radio
3472	1-79.20	Announcer, television
3472	1-79.30	Compere
3472	1-79.30	Disc jockey
3472	1-79.20	Interviewer, media
3472	1-79.20	Newscaster
3473	1-71.35	Band leader
3473	1-71.35	Bandmaster
3473	1-71.35	Conductor, band
3473	1-72.30	Dancer, chorus
3473	1-72.30	Dancer, night-club
3473	1-72.30	Dancer, tap
3473	1-71.40	Musician, night-club
3473	1-71.40	Musician, street
3473	1-71.40	Singer, night-club
3473	1-71.45	Singer, street
3474	1-75.40	Acrobat
3474	1-75.50	Aerialist
3474	1-75.90	Artist, high-wire
3474	1-79.90	Artist, strip-tease
3474	1-75.90	Artist, tight-rope
3474	1-75.50	Artist, trapeze
3474	1-75.20	Clown
3474	1-75.20	Comic, circus
3474	1-75.30	Conjuror
3474	1-75.40	Contortionist
3474	1-79.90	Hypnotist
3474	1-75.30	Illusionist
3474	1-79.90	Imitator
3474	1-79.90	Imitator, animal noise
3474	1-75.90	Juggler
3474	1-75.30	Magician
3474	1-75.30	Prestidigitator
3474	1-79.90	Puppeteer
3474	1-79.90	Tamer, wild animal
3474	1-75.90	Trainer, wild animal
3474	1-75.40	Tumbler
3474	1-79.90	Ventriloquist
3475	1-80.20	Athlete
3475	1-80.20	Boxer
3475	1-80.30	Coach, athletic
3475	1-80.30	Coach, games
3475	1-80.30	Coach, sports
3475	1-80.20	Cycle racer
3475	1-80.20	Driver, motor racing
3475	1-80.90	Instructor, billiards
3475	1-80.90	Instructor, bridge
3475	1-80.90	Instructor, chess
3475	1-80.30	Instructor, sports
3475	1-80.20	Jockey
3475	1-80.40	Judge, sports
3475	1-80.40	Official, sports
3475	1-80.20	Player, sports
3475	1-80.20	Racer, cycle
3475	1-80.40	Referee, sports
3475	1-80.20	Sportsman, professional
3475	1-80.20	Sportwoman, professional
3475	1-80.30	Trainer, boxing
3475	1-80.30	Trainer, golf
3475	1-80.30	Trainer, martial arts
3475	1-80.50	Trainer, physical
3475	1-80.30	Trainer, sports
3475	1-80.30	Trainer, wrestling
3475	1-80.30	Trainer, yoga
3475	1-80.40	Umpire, sports
3475	1-80.20	Wrestler
3480	1-41.40	Evangelist
3480	1-41.40	Lay preacher
3480	1-49.90	Lay worker
3480	1-41.40	Monk, associate professional
3480	1-41.40	Nun, associate professional
3480	1-49.90	Parish worker
3480	1-41.40	Preacher, lay
3480	1-41.40	Religious worker
3480	1-41.40	Salvationist

4111	3-21.90	Clerk, justowriting
4111	3-21.40	Clerk, typing
4111	3-21.10	Justowriter
4111	3-21.10	Stenographer
4111	3-21.10	Stenographer, typing
4111	3-21.40	Typist
4111	3-21.40	Typist, clerical
4111	3-21.40	Typist, copy
4111	3-21.40	Typist, invoice
4111	3-21.90	Typist, perforator
4111	3-21.10	Typist, shorthand
4111	3-21.40	Typist, statistical
4111	3-21.10	Typist, stenography
4111	3-21.90	Typist, varityping
4111	3-21.90	Varitypist
4112	3-21.50	Clerk, telefax
4112	3-21.50	Clerk, telegraph
4112	3-21.50	Clerk, teleprinter
4112	3-21.50	Clerk, telex
4112	3-21.40	Clerk, word processing
4112	3-21.50	Teletypist
4113	3-42.20	Clerk, data entry
4113	3-42.20	Clerk, data entry/computer
4113	3-42.90	Clerk, data entry/converter (card-to-tape)
4113	3-42.30	Clerk, data entry/converter (tape-to-card)
4113	3-42.30	Clerk, data entry/converter (tape-to-page)
4113	3-42.20	Clerk, data entry/electronic mail
4113	3-22.20	Clerk, data entry/punching machine (card and tape)
4113	3-22.20	Clerk, data entry/punching machine (keys)
4113	3-42.30	Clerk, data entry/sorting machine
4113	3-42.30	Clerk, data entry/tabulating machine
4114	3-41.20	Clerk, accounting machine
4114	3-41.30	Clerk, adding machine
4114	3-41.20	Clerk, bookkeeping machine
4114	3-41.30	Clerk, calculating machine
4114	3-41.30	Clerk, comptometer
4114	3-41.30	Clerk, computing machine
4114	3-41.20	Clerk, invoicing machine
4114	3-41.20	Clerk, posting machine
4115	3-21.20	Secretary
4115	3-21.20	Secretary, stenography
4115	3-21.20	Secretary, stenography/typing
4115	3-21.20	Secretary, typing
4115	3-21.20	Secretary, word processing
4121	3-31.90	Clerk, auction
4121	3-31.90	Clerk, audit
4121	3-31.20	Clerk, bookkeeping
4121	3-31.20	Clerk, bookkeeping/accounts
4121	3-31.20	Clerk, bookkeeping/discount
4121	3-31.20	Clerk, bookkeeping/interest accrual
4121	3-39.20	Clerk, cost computing
4121	3-39.20	Clerk, estimating
4121	3-39.90	Clerk, invoice
4121	3-31.20	Clerk, ledger
4121	3-31.20	Clerk, office cash
4121	3-39.30	Clerk, payroll
4121	3-39.30	Clerk, salaries
4121	3-39.30	Clerk, wages
4122	3-99.20	Clerk, actuarial
4122	3-39.40	Clerk, adjustment
4122	3-39.40	Clerk, bond
4122	3-39.40	Clerk, brokerage
4122	3-39.40	Clerk, collateral
4122	3-39.40	Clerk, credit
4122	3-39.40	Clerk, finance
4122	3-39.40	Clerk, investment
4122	3-39.40	Clerk, mortgage
4122	3-39.40	Clerk, rating
4122	3-39.40	Clerk, securities
4122	3-99.20	Clerk, statistical
4122	3-39.40	Clerk, tax
4131	3-91.40	Attendant, tool crib
4131	3-91.90	Clerk, depository/furniture
4131	3-91.20	Clerk, freight
4131	3-91.20	Clerk, freight/dispatching
4131	3-91.20	Clerk, freight/inward
4131	3-91.20	Clerk, freight/receiving
4131	3-91.20	Clerk, freight/routing
4131	3-91.20	Clerk, freight/shipping
4131	3-91.20	Clerk, freight/traffic
4131	3-91.30	Clerk, stock
4131	3-91.30	Clerk, stock/control
4131	3-91.30	Clerk, stock/control (inventory)
4131	3-91.30	Clerk, stock/control (records)
4131	3-91.30	Clerk, stock/records
4131	3-91.40	Clerk, stock/storeroom
4131	3-91.40	Clerk, supply
4131	3-91.40	Clerk, warehouse
4131	3-91.50	Clerk, weighing
4131	3-91.50	Clerk, weighing/scale
4131	3-91.50	Clerk, weighing/tally
4131	3-91.40	Storekeeper
4132	3-92.20	Clerk, order/materials
4132	3-92.20	Clerk, planning/materials

4132	3-92.30	Clerk, production planning
4132	3-92.30	Clerk, production planning/ coordination
4132	3-92.30	Clerk, production planning/ schedule
4132	3-92.20	Clerk, schedule/materials
4133	3-59.70	Clerk, air transport operations
4133	3-59.70	Clerk, dispatch/air transport
4133	3-59.70	Clerk, flight operations
4133	3-59.35	Clerk, goods/railway
4133	3-99.90	Clerk, transport
4133	3-59.50	Controller, clerical/air transport service
4133	3-59.50	Controller, clerical/airline traffic
4133	3-59.20	Controller, clerical/railway service
4133	3-59.25	Controller, clerical/railway service (freight)
4133	3-59.40	Controller, clerical/road transport service
4133	3-59.25	Controller, clerical/train
4133	3-59.70	Dispatcher, clerical/aircraft
4133	3-59.90	Dispatcher, clerical/boat
4133	3-59.40	Dispatcher, clerical/bus
4133	3-59.90	Dispatcher, clerical/gas pipelines
4133	3-59.90	Dispatcher, clerical/oil pipelines
4133	3-59.25	Dispatcher, clerical/railway
4133	3-59.40	Dispatcher, clerical/road transport (*except bus and truck)
4133	3-59.25	Dispatcher, clerical/train
4133	3-59.40	Dispatcher, clerical/truck
4133	3-59.90	Float master
4133	3-59.30	Inspector, clerical/railway transport service
4133	3-59.45	Inspector, clerical/road transport service
4133	3-59.90	Superintendent, clerical/barge
4133	3-59.90	Superintendent, clerical/cargo
4133	3-59.90	Superintendent, clerical/ferry
4133	3-59.90	Superintendent, clerical/quay
4133	3-59.20	Superintendent, clerical/railway depot
4133	3-59.40	Superintendent, clerical/road transport depot
4133	3-59.40	Superintendent, clerical/road transport traffic
4133	3-59.90	Superintendent, clerical/water transport terminal
4133	3-59.90	Superintendent, clerical/wharf
4133	3-59.90	Wharfinger
4133	3-59.35	Yardmaster, railway
4141	3-95.20	Clerk, book-loan
4141	3-95.30	Clerk, classification
4141	3-99.50	Clerk, document duplication
4141	3-95.30	Clerk, filing
4141	3-95.30	Clerk, index
4141	3-95.20	Clerk, library
4141	3-95.20	Clerk, library/acquisitions
4141	3-99.50	Clerk, photocopying
4141	3-99.50	Clerk, reproduction processes/ office
4141	3-99.50	Mimeographer
4142	3-70.90	Clerk, mail/dispatch
4142	3-70.20	Clerk, mail/sorting
4142	3-59.80	Controller, clerical/mail
4142	3-59.80	Controller, clerical/mail depot
4142	3-59.80	Controller, clerical/postal service
4142	5-91.20	Courrier, travel
4142	3-70.30	Mailman
4142	3-70.30	Mailwoman
4142	3-70.30	Post carrier
4142	3-70.30	Postman
4142	3-70.30	Postwoman
4143	3-99.30	Clerk, coding
4143	3-99.30	Clerk, coding/data-processing
4143	3-99.30	Clerk, coding/statistics
4143	3-99.90	Clerk, document-sorting machine
4143	3-99.90	Clerk, franking machine
4143	3-93.90	Clerk, listing
4143	3-99.40	Clerk, proof reading
4143	3-99.40	Clerk, proof reading/printing
4143	3-99.90	Clerk, scripts
4143	3-99.30	Coder, clerical
4143	3-99.30	Coder, clerical/data-processing
4143	3-99.30	Coder, clerical/statistics
4143	3-99.40	Proof-reader, clerical
4144	3-99.90	Clerk, form filling assistance
4144	3-93.90	Public writer
4144	3-93.90	Scribe
4190	3-99.50	Clerk, addressing machine
4190	3-93.30	Clerk, compilation/directory
4190	3-93.90	Clerk, list/addresses
4190	3-99.90	Clerk, list/mail
4190	3-93.30	Clerk, records/personnel
4190	3-93.30	Compiler, clerical/directory
4190	3-39.90	Timekeeper
4211	3-31.60	Cashier, bank
4211	3-31.60	Cashier, booking-office
4211	3-31.60	Cashier, box-office
4211	3-31.60	Cashier, cash desk
4211	3-31.60	Cashier, check-out/self-service store
4211	3-31.30	Cashier, office

4211	3-31.60	Cashier, restaurant
4211	3-31.60	Cashier, store
4211	3-31.90	Clerk, bookmaking
4211	3-31.30	Clerk, cash-accounting
4211	3-31.60	Clerk, ticket issuing/except travel
4211	3-31.60	Clerk, toll collection
4212	3-39.90	Cashier, change-booth
4212	3-31.50	Cashier, currency exchange
4212	3-31.70	Clerk, post office counter
4212	3-31.50	Money changer
4212	3-31.40	Teller, bank
4213	5-99.20	Bookmaker
4213	5-99.20	Bookmaker, betting pool
4213	5-99.20	Bookmaker, pari-mutuel system
4213	5-99.20	Bookmaker, ticket writing
4213	5-99.20	Bookmaker, totalisator
4213	5-99.30	Croupier
4213	5-99.30	Croupier, gambling-table
4214	4-90.20	Money-lender
4214	4-90.20	Pawnbroker
4215	3-39.90	Clerk, bills
4215	3-39.90	Collector, charity
4215	3-39.90	Collector, debt
4215	3-39.90	Collector, payment
4215	3-39.90	Collector, rent
4221	3-31.60	Clerk, ticket issuing/travel
4221	3-94.40	Clerk, travel
4221	3-94.40	Clerk, travel /airlines
4221	3-94.40	Clerk, travel /railway
4221	3-94.40	Clerk, travel agency
4221	3-94.40	Clerk, travel agency/bookings
4221	3-94.40	Clerk, travel agency/reservations
4222	3-94.90	Clerk, appointments
4222	3-94.90	Clerk, information
4222	3-94.90	Clerk, inquiries
4222	3-94.10	Receptionist
4222	3-94.30	Receptionist, dental
4222	3-94.20	Receptionist, hotel
4222	3-94.30	Receptionist, medical
4223	3-80.20	Switchboard-operator, telephone
4223	3-80.20	Telephonist
5111	5-99.70	Attendant, airport
5111	5-99.70	Attendant, flight
5111	5-99.70	Attendant, ship's cabin
5111	5-20.50	Chief steward, ship
5111	5-20.50	Chief stewardess, ship
5111	5-99.70	Purser, aircraft
5111	5-40.60	Steward, ship
5111	5-40.60	Steward, ship/cabin
5111	5-40.60	Stewardess, ship
5111	5-40.60	Stewardess, ship/cabin
5112	3-60.40	Conductor, bus
5112	3-60.90	Conductor, cable car
5112	3-60.90	Conductor, ferryboat
5112	3-60.90	Conductor, hovercraft
5112	3-60.30	Conductor, pullman car
5112	3-60.30	Conductor, sleeping car
5112	3-60.20	Conductor, train
5112	3-60.40	Conductor, tram
5112	3-60.40	Conductor, trolley-bus
5112	3-60.20	Guard, railway
5113	5-91.30	Guide, art gallery
5113	5-91.30	Guide, museum
5113	5-91.20	Guide, travel
5113	5-91.90	Guide, travel/alpine
5113	5-91.30	Guide, travel/art gallery
5113	5-40.90	Guide, travel/bus
5113	5-91.90	Guide, travel/fishing
5113	5-91.90	Guide, travel/game park
5113	5-91.90	Guide, travel/hunting
5113	5-91.90	Guide, travel/industrial establishment
5113	5-91.30	Guide, travel/museum
5113	5-91.90	Guide, travel/safari
5113	5-91.30	Guide, travel/sightseeing
5121	5-20.90	Butler
5121	5-20.40	Chief steward, hotel
5121	5-20.40	Chief stewardess, hotel
5121	5-20.20	Housekeeper
5121	5-20.20	Housekeeper, executive
5121	5-20.60	Matron, housekeeping
5121	5-20.40	Steward, hotel
5121	5-20.40	Steward, house
5121	5-20.40	Stewardess, hotel
5121	5-20.40	Stewardess, house
5121	5-20.90	Warden, camp
5121	5-20.90	Warden, dormitory
5122	5-31.20	Chef de cuisine
5122	5-31.30	Cook
5122	5-31.20	Cook, head
5122	7-74.90	Cook, preserving
5122	5-31.30	Cook, restaurant
5122	5-31.50	Cook, ship
5122	5-31.50	Cook, ship's mess

ISCO-88

5122	5-31.90	Cook, special diets
5122	5-31.30	Cook, vegetable
5122	5-31.90	Cook, work camp
5123	5-32.90	Attendant, canteen
5123	5-32.90	Attendant, restaurant seating
5123	5-32.50	Bartender
5123	5-32.20	Maitre d'hotel
5123	5-32.10	Steward, mess
5123	5-32.10	Steward, ship/dining saloon
5123	5-32.30	Steward, ship/mess
5123	5-32.40	Steward, wine
5123	5-32.10	Stewardess, mess
5123	5-32.10	Stewardess, ship/dining saloon
5123	5-32.30	Stewardess, ship/mess
5123	5-32.40	Stewardess, ship/wine
5123	5-32.10	Waiter
5123	5-32.30	Waiter, banquet
5123	5-32.30	Waiter, formal
5123	5-32.20	Waiter, head
5123	5-32.10	Waiter, railway dining car
5123	5-32.40	Waiter, wine
5123	5-32.10	Waitress
5123	5-32.30	Waitress, banquet
5123	5-32.30	Waitress, formal
5123	5-32.20	Waitress, head
5123	5-32.10	Waitress, railway dining car
5123	5-32.40	Waitress, wine
5131	5-40.35	Attendant, schoolchildren
5131	5-40.35	Governess, children
5131	5-40.35	Nanny
5131	5-40.35	Nursemaid
5132	5-99.40	Aid, dental
5132	5-99.40	Aid, nursing/clinic
5132	5-99.40	Aid, nursing/hospital
5132	5-99.40	Ambulance man
5132	5-99.40	Ambulance woman
5132	5-99.40	Attendant, dental
5132	5-99.40	Attendant, first-aid
5132	5-99.40	Attendant, hospital
5132	5-99.40	Attendant, nursing/except home
5132	5-99.40	Orderly
5133	5-99.40	Aid, nursing/home
5133	5-99.40	Attendant, nursing/home
5139	5-99.50	Aid, pharmacy
5139	5-99.60	Aid, veterinary
5141	5-70.70	Attendant, bath
5141	5-70.70	Attendant, bath/hot-room

5141	5-70.70	Attendant, bath/sauna
5141	5-70.70	Attendant, bath/turkish
5141	5-70.30	Barber
5141	5-70.40	Beautician
5141	5-70.60	Beautician, make-up/stage
5141	5-70.20	Beautician, make-up/studio
5141	0-79.90	Chiropodist
5141	5-70.40	Cosmetologist
5141	5-70.90	Dresser, wig/stage
5141	5-70.30	Hairdresser
5141	5-70.30	Hairdresser, men
5141	5-70.20	Hairdresser, women
5141	5-70.60	Make-up artist, stage
5141	5-70.60	Make-up artist, studio
5141	5-70.50	Manicurist
5141	5-70.90	Trichologist
5142	5-40.40	Companion
5142	5-40.40	Companion, lady's
5142	5-40.30	Companion, man's
5142	5-40.30	Maid, lady's
5142	5-40.30	Maid, personal
5142	5-40.30	Manservant
5142	5-40.30	Valet
5142	5-40.90	Valet, hotel
5142	5-40.30	Valet, personal
5143	5-92.90	Attendant, funeral
5143	5-92.90	Attendant, undertaker's
5143	5-92.30	Embalmer
5143	5-92.10	Funeral director
5143	5-92.20	Mortician
5143	5-92.20	Undertaker
5149	5-99.90	Escort, social
5149	5-99.90	Host, club
5149	5-99.90	Hostess, club
5149	5-99.90	Partner, dancing
5151	1-99.60	Astrologer
5152	1-99.60	Fortune-teller
5152	1-99.60	Numerologist
5152	1-99.60	Palmist
5161	5-81.10	Fire-fighter
5161	5-81.40	Fire-fighter, aircraft accidents
5161	6-32.50	Fire-fighter, forest
5161	6-32.50	Patrolman, forest fire
5161	5-81.10	Patrolwoman, forest fire
5161	5-81.30	Salvageman, fire
5161	5-81.30	Salvagewoman, fire

5162	5-82.20	Constable	6111	6-22.90	Farm worker, skilled/jute
5162	5-82.40	Guard, police force	6111	6-22.20	Farm worker, skilled/potato
5162	5-82.20	Patrolman, police	6111	6-22.50	Farm worker, skilled/rice
5162	5-82.20	Patrolwoman, police	6111	6-22.20	Farm worker, skilled/sugar-beet
5162	5-82.20	Police officer	6111	6-22.60	Farm worker, skilled/sugar-cane
5162	5-82.20	Police officer, harbour	6111	6-22.90	Farm worker, skilled/tobacco
5162	5-82.20	Police officer, river	6111	6-22.20	Farm worker, skilled/vegetables
5162	5-82.20	Police officer, traffic	6111	6-22.30	Farm worker, skilled/wheat
			6111	6-12.20	Farmer, alfalfa
5163	5-89.30	Gaoler	6111	6-12.20	Farmer, cereal
5163	5-89.30	Guard, prison	6111	6-12.20	Farmer, corn
5163	5-89.30	Warden, prison	6111	6-12.20	Farmer, cotton
5163	5-89.30	Warder, prison	6111	6-12.20	Farmer, field crop
			6111	6-12.20	Farmer, field vegetable
5169	5-89.90	Bodyguard	6111	6-12.20	Farmer, flax
5169	5-89.90	Coastguard	6111	6-12.20	Farmer, grain
5169	6-49.90	Game-warden	6111	6-12.20	Farmer, groundnut
5169	5-89.90	Guard, beach	6111	6-12.20	Farmer, jute
5169	5-82.40	Guard, security	6111	6-12.20	Farmer, maize
5169	5-89.90	Life-guard	6111	6-12.20	Farmer, rice
5169	5-89.90	Patrolman, beach	6111	6-12.20	Farmer, sisal
5169	5-89.40	Patrolman, security	6111	6-12.20	Farmer, soya-bean
5169	5-89.90	Patrolwoman, beach	6111	6-12.20	Farmer, sugar-beet
5169	5-89.40	Patrolwoman, security	6111	6-12.20	Farmer, sugar-cane
5169	6-49.90	Warden, bird sanctuary	6111	6-12.20	Farmer, tobacco
5169	5-89.90	Warden, traffic	6111	6-12.20	Farmer, vegetable
5169	6-49.90	Warden, wild life	6111	6-12.20	Farmer, wheat
			6111	6-12.20	Grower, field crop
5210	4-51.40	Mannequin	6111	6-12.20	Grower, field vegetable
5210	4-51.90	Model, advertising	6111	6-12.20	Grower, soya-bean
5210	5-99.90	Model, artist's	6111	6-12.20	Grower, sugar-beet
5210	4-51.40	Model, clothing display	6111	6-29.50	Irrigation worker, skilled
5210	4-51.40	Model, fashion	6111	6-12.20	Planter, cotton
			6111	6-12.20	Planter, sugar-cane
5220	4-51.90	Assistant, shop/orders	6111	6-12.20	Planter, tobacco
5220	4-51.90	Attendant, petrol pump			
5220	4-51.90	Attendant, service station/ automobiles	6112	6-23.90	Budder-grafter, fruit tree
5220	4-51.30	Attendant, shop	6112	6-23.90	Farm worker, skilled/cocoa
5220	4-51.50	Demonstrator	6112	6-23.90	Farm worker, skilled/coffee
5220	4-51.30	Salesperson, retail establishment	6112	6-23.20	Farm worker, skilled/fruit
5220	4-51.30	Salesperson, shop	6112	6-23.20	Farm worker, skilled/grove
5220	4-51.20	Salesperson, wholesale establishment	6112	6-23.90	Farm worker, skilled/hops
			6112	6-23.20	Farm worker, skilled/orchard
			6112	6-23.50	Farm worker, skilled/rubber
5230	4-51.30	Salesperson, kiosk	6112	6-23.20	Farm worker, skilled/shrub crop
5230	4-51.30	Salesperson, market	6112	6-23.40	Farm worker, skilled/tea
5230	4-51.30	Salesperson, street stall	6112	6-23.20	Farm worker, skilled/tree crop
			6112	6-23.30	Farm worker, skilled/vineyard
6111	6-22.40	Farm worker, skilled/cotton	6112	6-12.30	Farmer, cocoa
6111	6-12.20	Farm worker, skilled/field crops	6112	6-12.30	Farmer, coconut
6111	6-22.90	Farm worker, skilled/flax	6112	6-12.30	Farmer, coffee
6111	6-22.90	Farm worker, skilled/groundnut	6112	6-12.30	Farmer, copra
6111	6-29.50	Farm worker, skilled/irrigation	6112	6-12.30	Farmer, fruit

6112	6-12.30	Farmer, hop
6112	6-12.30	Farmer, nut
6112	6-12.30	Farmer, orchard
6112	6-23.30	Farmer, rubber
6112	6-12.30	Farmer, rubber plantation
6112	6-12.30	Farmer, shrub crop
6112	6-23.30	Farmer, tea
6112	6-12.30	Farmer, tea plantation
6112	6-12.30	Farmer, tree crop
6112	6-23.30	Farmer, vineyard
6112	6-12.30	Farmer, viniculture
6112	6-23.90	Grafter, fruit tree
6112	6-12.30	Grower, cocoa
6112	6-12.30	Grower, coconut
6112	6-12.30	Grower, coffee
6112	6-12.30	Grower, rubber
6112	6-12.30	Grower, shrub crop
6112	6-12.20	Grower, tree crop
6112	6-23.50	Plantation worker, skilled/rubber
6112	6-23.10	Plantation worker, skilled/shrub crop
6112	6-23.40	Plantation worker, skilled/tea
6112	6-23.10	Plantation worker, skilled/tree crop
6112	6-12.30	Planter, copra
6112	6-12.30	Planter, tea
6112	6-23.90	Pruner, fruit trees
6112	6-23.90	Pruner, shrub crops
6112	6-29.40	Tapper, maple syrup
6112	6-29.40	Tapper, pine resin
6112	6-23.90	Tapper, rubber tree
6112	6-29.40	Tapper, toddy
6112	6-12.30	Viniculturist
6112	6-12.30	Winegrower
6113	6-27.30	Budder-grafter, shrubs
6113	6-29.90	Cultivator, mushroom
6113	6-29.90	Farm worker, skilled/mushroom
6113	6-27.30	Farm worker, skilled/nursery
6113	6-27.40	Gardener
6113	6-12.70	Gardener, greenhouse
6113	6-27.40	Gardener, jobbing
6113	6-29.60	Gardener, park
6113	6-27.30	Gardener, seed propagation
6113	6-27.30	Greenhouse worker, skilled
6113	6-29.60	Greenkeeper
6113	6-29.60	Groundsman
6113	6-29.60	Groundswoman
6113	6-12.70	Grower, carnation
6113	6-12.70	Grower, flower
6113	6-12.70	Grower, horticultural nursery
6113	6-12.70	Grower, market gardening
6113	6-12.90	Grower, mushroom
6113	6-12.70	Grower, nursery
6113	6-12.70	Grower, nursery/bulbs
6113	6-12.70	Grower, nursery/seeds
6113	6-12.90	Grower, nursery/spices
6113	6-12.70	Grower, nursery/vegetables
6113	6-12.90	Grower, osier
6113	6-12.90	Grower, reed
6113	6-12.70	Grower, rose
6113	6-12.70	Grower, tulip
6113	6-12.70	Horticultural grower
6113	6-27.30	Horticultural worker, skilled
6113	6-27.20	Market gardener
6113	6-27.20	Market gardening worker, skilled
6113	6-12.70	Nurseryman
6113	6-12.70	Nurserywoman
6114	6-11.10	Farm worker, skilled/mixed crop
6114	6-11.10	Farmer, mixed crop
6121	6-24.40	Breeder, cat
6121	6-12.40	Breeder, cattle
6121	6-24.40	Breeder, dog
6121	6-12.40	Breeder, stud
6121	6-24.20	Farm worker, skilled/cattle
6121	6-25.10	Farm worker, skilled/dairy
6121	6-24.50	Farm worker, skilled/domestic fur-bearing animals
6121	6-24.10	Farm worker, skilled/livestock
6121	6-24.40	Farm worker, skilled/pig
6121	6-24.30	Farm worker, skilled/sheep
6121	6-12.40	Farmer, cattle
6121	6-12.50	Farmer, dairy
6121	6-12.40	Farmer, fur/domestic animals
6121	6-12.40	Farmer, horse breeding
6121	6-12.40	Farmer, horse raising
6121	6-12.40	Farmer, livestock
6121	6-12.50	Farmer, milk
6121	6-24.90	Farmer, pelt
6121	6-12.40	Farmer, pig
6121	6-12.40	Farmer, ranch
6121	6-24.40	Farmer, sheep
6121	6-12.40	Farmer, sheep raising
6121	6-24.40	Farmer, sheep/astrakhan
6121	6-12.40	Farmer, stud breeding
6121	6-12.40	Grazier
6121	6-24.90	Kennel worker, skilled
6121	6-12.40	Raiser, cattle
6121	6-12.40	Raiser, pig
6121	6-12.40	Raiser, sheep
6121	6-12.40	Rancher, cattle
6121	6-24.90	Shearer, sheep
6121	6-24.30	Shepherd
6122	6-12.60	Breeder, poultry
6122	6-26.10	Farm worker, skilled/poultry

6122	6-12.60	Farmer, battery
6122	6-12.60	Farmer, chicken
6122	6-12.60	Farmer, duck
6122	6-12.60	Farmer, egg production
6122	6-12.60	Farmer, goose
6122	6-12.60	Farmer, poultry/hatching and breeding
6122	6-12.60	Farmer, turkey
6122	6-12.60	Hatcher-breeder, poultry
6122	6-26.20	Hatchery worker, skilled/poultry
6122	6-26.20	Operator, incubator
6123	6-12.90	Apiarist
6123	6-29.20	Apiary worker, skilled
6123	6-29.20	Beekeeper
6123	6-29.20	Beekeeping worker, skilled
6123	6-12.90	Farmer, apiary
6123	6-12.90	Farmer, beekeeping
6123	6-12.90	Farmer, sericulture
6123	6-12.90	Farmer, silkworm raising
6123	6-12.90	Raiser, silkworm
6123	6-29.30	Sericultural worker, skilled
6123	6-12.90	Sericulturist
6124	6-24.10	Farm worker, skilled/mixed-animal husbandry
6124	6-12.90	Farmer, mixed-animal husbandry
6129	6-12.90	Breeder, bird
6129	6-12.90	Breeder, game bird
6129	6-12.90	Breeder, laboratory animal
6129	6-12.90	Breeder, laboratory animal/mice
6129	6-12.90	Breeder, lion
6129	6-12.90	Breeder, reindeer
6129	6-12.90	Breeder, reptile
6129	6-12.90	Breeder, reptile/snake
6129	6-12.90	Breeder, snail
6129	6-24.50	Farm worker, skilled/non-domesticated fur-bearing animals
6129	6-24.90	Farm worker, skilled/ostrich
6129	6-24.50	Farmer, fur/non-domesticated animals
6129	6-49.90	Gamekeeper
6129	6-24.90	Horse-breaker
6129	6-49.90	Keeper, animal reserve
6129	6-12.90	Keeper, aviary
6129	6-12.90	Keeper, kennel
6129	6-24.90	Keeper, zoo
6129	6-49.90	Laboratory worker, skilled/animals
6129	6-12.90	Raiser, laboratory animal
6129	6-12.90	Raiser, ostrich
6129	6-24.90	Trainer, dog
6129	6-24.90	Trainer, horse-breaking
6129	6-24.90	Trainer, racehorse

6129	6-24.90	Zoo keeper
6129	6-49.90	Zoo worker, skilled
6130	6-21.05	Farm worker, skilled/mixed farming
6130	6-11.10	Farmer, mixed farming
6141	6-31.40	Assembler, raft
6141	6-31.20	Bucker, logging
6141	6-31.30	Climber, logging
6141	6-31.20	Cross-cutter, logging
6141	6-32.40	Cruiser, timber
6141	6-31.90	Cutter, pole and pile
6141	6-31.90	Cutter, railway tie
6141	6-31.90	Cutter, sleeper
6141	6-31.20	Cutter, timber/forestry
6141	6-31.40	Driver, raft/logging
6141	6-31.20	Feller, logging
6141	6-31.20	Feller-bucker, tree
6141	6-32.20	Forester
6141	6-32.30	Forestry worker, skilled
6141	6-32.30	Forestry worker, skilled/afforestation
6141	6-31.30	High climber, logging
6141	6-31.10	Logger
6141	6-31.10	Lumberjack
6141	6-31.40	Maker, log-raft
6141	6-32.90	Marker, timber
6141	6-32.90	Marker, tree
6141	6-32.90	Planter, forestry
6141	6-32.90	Pruner-trimmer, forestry
6141	6-32.90	Ranger, forest
6141	6-31.40	Rider, timber
6141	6-31.90	Scaler, log
6141	6-32.90	Stripper, cork bark
6141	6-31.30	Topper, logging
6141	6-31.90	Woodcutter, forest
6141	6-32.30	Woodman
6141	6-32.30	Woodwoman
6142	7-49.30	Burner, charcoal
6142	7-44.60	Forestry worker, skilled/charcoal burning (traditional techniques)
6142	7-44.60	Forestry worker, skilled/wood distillation (traditional techniques)
6151	6-49.90	Cultivator, algae
6151	6-49.90	Cultivator, pearl
6151	6-49.20	Farm worker, skilled/fish
6151	6-49.30	Farm worker, skilled/oyster
6151	6-49.90	Farm worker, skilled/seafood
6151	6-49.20	Farmer, fish
6151	6-49.30	Farmer, oyster
6151	6-49.20	Farmer, seafood
6151	6-49.20	Fishery worker, skilled/pisciculture

6151	6-49.20	Hatcher, fish
6151	6-49.20	Hatchery worker, skilled/fish
6152	6-49.90	Diver, oyster
6152	6-49.90	Diver, pearl
6152	6-49.90	Diver, sponge
6152	6-41.30	Fisherman, coastal waters
6152	6-41.30	Fisherman, inland waters
6152	6-41.30	Fisherwoman, coastal waters
6152	6-41.30	Fisherwoman, inland waters
6152	6-41.30	Fishery worker, skilled/coastal waters
6152	6-41.30	Fishery worker, skilled/inland
6152	6-49.90	Sponge hooker
6153	6-41.20	Crewman, drifter
6153	6-41.20	Crewman, trawler
6153	6-41.20	Crewwoman, drifter
6153	6-41.20	Crewwoman, trawler
6153	6-41.20	Fisherman, deep-sea
6153	6-41.20	Fisherwoman, deep-sea
6153	6-41.20	Fishery worker, skilled/deep-sea
6154	6-49.40	Crewman, whaling vessel
6154	6-49.40	Crewwoman, whaling vessel
6154	6-49.50	Fisherman, seal
6154	6-49.40	Fisherwoman, seal
6154	6-49.40	Flenser, whale
6154	6-49.90	Game beater
6154	6-49.40	Harpooner, whale
6154	6-49.60	Hunter
6154	6-49.50	Hunter, seal
6154	6-49.50	Hunter, whale
6154	6-49.40	Stripper, blubber
6154	6-49.60	Trapper, fur
6154	6-49.60	Trapper-hunter, fur
6210	6-11.10	Farm worker, skilled/subsistence farming
6210	6-11.10	Farmer, subsistence farming
7111	7-11.60	Bolter, roof/mine
7111	7-11.90	Clipper, mine
7111	7-11.90	Drawer, prop/mine
7111	7-11.90	Drawer, prop/quarry
7111	7-11.90	Drawer, timber/mine
7111	7-11.90	Drawer, timber/quarry
7111	7-11.05	Miner
7111	7-11.90	Miner, hydraulic/placer mining
7111	7-11.05	Miner, surface
7111	7-11.05	Miner, underground
7111	7-11.60	Piler, mine

7111	7-11.10	Quarrier
7111	7-11.90	Robber, timber/mine
7111	7-11.90	Sampler, core
7111	7-11.70	Sampler, mine
7111	7-11.90	Sampler, quarry
7111	7-11.60	Timbering worker, mine
7111	7-11.60	Timbering worker, quarry
7111	7-11.60	Timbering worker, underground
7112	7-11.50	Blaster
7112	7-11.50	Shotfirer
7113	8-20.70	Carver, stone
7113	8-20.80	Carver-setter, monument
7113	8-20.60	Cutter, stone
7113	8-20.60	Cutter, stone/lettering
7113	8-20.20	Cutter-finisher, stone
7113	8-20.20	Dresser, stone
7113	8-20.90	Driller, stone
7113	8-20.20	Finisher, stone
7113	8-20.30	Grader, stone
7113	8-20.20	Grinder, slate
7113	8-20.20	Grinder, stone
7113	8-20.80	Mason, monument
7113	8-20.20	Planer, stone
7113	8-20.20	Polisher, granite
7113	8-20.20	Polisher, marble
7113	8-20.20	Polisher, slate
7113	8-20.20	Polisher, stone
7113	8-20.90	Sandblaster, stonecutting
7113	8-20.20	Sawyer, stone
7113	8-20.50	Setter-operator, lathe/stone
7113	8-20.90	Shotblaster, stonecutting
7113	7-12.20	Splitter, stone
7113	8-20.40	Stonework layout worker
7113	8-20.40	Stoneworker
7113	8-20.50	Tuner, stone
7121	9-59.10	Builder, house/traditional materials
7121	9-59.10	Housebuilder, traditional materials
7122	9-51.25	Bricklayer, chimney
7122	9-51.20	Bricklayer, construction
7122	9-51.30	Bricklayer, firebrick
7122	9-51.30	Bricklayer, furnace lining
7122	9-51.90	Bricklayer, ingot mould lining
7122	9-51.30	Bricklayer, kiln
7122	9-51.30	Bricklayer, oven
7122	9-51.25	Builder, chimney
7122	9-51.30	Firebrick layer
7122	9-51.60	Paviour
7122	9-51.40	Stonemason, construction
7122	9-51.40	Stonemason, facings

7135	9-57.30	Glazier, roofing
7135	9-57.50	Glazier, stained-glass
7135	9-57.20	Glazier, structural
7135	9-57.60	Glazier, vehicle
7135	9-57.50	Setter, artistic/glass
7135	9-57.20	Setter, glass/buildings
7136	9-59.55	Digger, well
7136	8-71.10	Fitter, pipe
7136	8-71.40	Fitter, pipe/aircraft
7136	8-71.20	Fitter, pipe/gas
7136	8-71.30	Fitter, pipe/marine
7136	8-71.10	Fitter, pipe/sewerage
7136	8-71.90	Fitter, pipe/steam
7136	8-71.10	Fitter, pipe/ventilation
7136	8-71.10	Fitter, pipe/water supply
7136	8-71.40	Fitter, tube/aircraft
7136	9-59.50	Jointer, pipe-laying
7136	9-59.50	Layer, pipe
7136	9-59.50	Layer-jointer, mains pipes
7136	9-59.50	Pipeline worker
7136	8-71.05	Plumber
7136	8-71.90	Plumber, chemical
7136	8-71.30	Plumber, ship
7136	9-59.55	Sinker, well
7137	8-55.10	Electrician
7137	8-55.20	Electrician, building
7137	8-55.60	Electrician, building maintenance
7137	8-55.70	Electrician, building repairs
7137	8-55.20	Electrician, building/electrical installation
7137	8-55.60	Electrician, building/electrical maintenance
7137	8-55.90	Electrician, mine
7137	8-55.90	Electrician, neon-lighting
7137	8-55.50	Electrician, stage and studio
7137	8-55.50	Electrician, theatre
7141	9-31.20	Brush-painter, construction
7141	9-31.20	Outside painter, construction
7141	9-31.20	Painter, building
7141	9-31.20	Painter, construction
7141	9-31.20	Painter, house
7141	9-31.90	Painter, motion picture set
7141	9-31.20	Painter, outside/construction
7141	9-31.30	Painter, ship's hull
7141	9-31.90	Painter, stage scenery
7141	9-31.30	Painter, structural steel
7141	9-31.20	Painter-decorator, buildings
7141	9-59.25	Painter-decorator, wallcarpeting
7141	9-59.25	Painter-decorator, wallcovering
7141	9-59.25	Painter-decorator, wallpapering

7141	9-59.25	Paperhanger
7141	9-31.20	Spray-painter, construction
7141	9-59.25	Wallpaper hanger
7141	9-31.90	Whitewasher
7142	9-39.60	Painter, automobile
7142	9-39.10	Painter, manufactured articles
7142	9-39.90	Painter, metal
7142	9-39.60	Painter, vehicle
7142	7-28.50	Sprayer, metal
7142	9-39.10	Varnisher, manufactured articles
7142	9-39.90	Varnisher, metal
7142	9-39.60	Varnisher, vehicle
7143	5-52.40	Chimney sweep
7143	9-59.75	Cleaner, building exteriors
7143	5-52.40	Cleaner, chimney flue
7143	5-99.90	Exterminator
7143	9-59.75	Sandblaster, building exteriors
7143	5-52.40	Sweep, chimney
7211	7-25.50	Coremaker, metal
7211	7-24.20	Ladler, metal
7211	7-25.10	Moulder, metal castings
7211	7-25.20	Moulder, metal castings/bench
7211	7-25.30	Moulder, metal castings/floor and pit
7211	7-25.30	Moulder, metal castings/pit
7211	7-25.20	Moulder, metal castings/stump
7211	7-25.20	Moulder, metal castings/tub
7212	8-72.45	Brazier
7212	8-72.45	Brazier, flame
7212	8-72.90	Brazier, furnace
7212	8-72.45	Brazier, induction
7212	8-72.40	Burner, lead
7212	8-72.50	Flamecutter
7212	8-72.90	Setter-operator, soldering
7212	8-72.90	Setter-operator, soldering/jewellery
7212	8-72.90	Setter-operator, soldering/metal
7212	8-72.60	Solderer
7212	8-72.90	Solderer, dip
7212	8-72.90	Solderer, furnace
7212	8-72.90	Solderer, torch
7212	8-72.10	Welder
7212	8-72.15	Welder, acetylene
7212	8-72.35	Welder, butt
7212	8-72.35	Welder, contact
7212	8-72.20	Welder, electric arc
7212	8-72.35	Welder, flash
7212	8-72.15	Welder, gas
7212	8-72.10	Welder, gas and electric
7212	8-72.15	Welder, oxy-acetylene

7212	8-72.35	Welder, resistance
7212	8-72.35	Welder, seam
7212	8-72.35	Welder, spot
7212	8-72.30	Welder, thermite
7213	8-73.80	Beater, aircraft panel
7213	8-73.70	Beater, vehicle panel
7213	8-73.50	Boilersmith
7213	8-73.30	Coppersmith
7213	8-73.50	Maker, boiler
7213	8-73.20	Marker, sheet metal
7213	8-73.10	Sheet-metal worker
7213	8-73.80	Sheet-metal worker, aircraft
7213	8-73.30	Sheet-metal worker, copper
7213	8-73.90	Sheet-metal worker, furniture
7213	8-73.60	Sheet-metal worker, ornamental
7213	8-73.40	Sheet-metal worker, tin
7213	8-73.80	Sheet-metal worker, vehicles
7213	8-73.40	Tinsmith
7214	8-74.90	Bender, metal plate
7214	8-74.40	Erector, constructional steel
7214	8-74.50	Erector, ship beam and frame
7214	8-74.10	Erector, structural metal
7214	8-74.20	Loftsman, structural metal
7214	8-74.20	Loftswoman, structural metal
7214	8-74.20	Marker, structural metal
7214	8-74.55	Plater, ship
7214	8-74.10	Preparer, structural metal
7214	8-74.60	Riveter
7214	8-74.70	Riveter, pneumatic
7214	8-74.50	Shipwright, metal
7214	8-74.30	Structural steel worker, workshop
7215	9-72.60	Cable worker, bridge
7215	9-72.60	Cable worker, suspension bridge
7215	9-72.05	Rigger
7215	9-72.40	Rigger, aircraft
7215	9-72.05	Rigger, hoisting equipment
7215	9-72.20	Rigger, hoisting equipment/ construction
7215	9-72.50	Rigger, oil and gas well
7215	9-72.90	Rigger, railway cable
7215	9-72.30	Rigger, ship
7215	9-72.90	Rigger, ski-lift
7215	9-72.60	Spinner-squeezer, cable
7215	9-72.60	Spinner-squeezer, wire
7215	9-72.10	Splicer, cable and rope
7216	9-59.60	Diver, salvage
7216	5-89.90	Frogman, salvage
7216	5-89.90	Frogwoman, salvage
7216	9-59.60	Underwater worker

7221	8-31.10	Blacksmith
7221	7-24.20	Caster, metal
7221	7-27.20	Drawer, wire
7221	8-31.90	Driver, forge hammer
7221	8-31.20	Drop forger
7221	8-31.30	Drop-hammer worker
7221	8-31.10	Farrier
7221	8-31.40	Forging-press worker
7221	8-39.50	Former, metal
7221	8-31.20	Hammer-smith
7221	8-31.20	Hammer-smith, forge
7221	8-31.40	Press-operator, forging/metal
7221	8-31.10	Smith, agricultural implement
7221	8-31.10	Smith, anvil
7221	8-31.40	Smith, bulldozer
7221	8-31.10	Toolsmith
7222	8-32.90	Finisher, die
7222	8-39.20	Gunsmith
7222	8-39.30	Locksmith
7222	8-32.30	Maker, gauge
7222	8-32.30	Maker, jig-gauge
7222	8-32.20	Maker, press tool
7222	8-32.20	Maker, tap-die
7222	8-32.90	Maker, template
7222	8-32.20	Maker, tool
7222	8-32.20	Maker, tool and die
7222	8-32.90	Maker, tool/diamond-pointed
7222	8-32.50	Marker, metal
7222	8-32.40	Pattern-maker, metal foundry
7222	8-32.20	Toolmaker
7223	8-34.60	Borer, metal
7223	8-34.60	Driller, metal
7223	9-49.90	Maker, toy/metal
7223	8-33.05	Setter, machine tool
7223	8-33.05	Setter, metalworking machine
7223	8-33.05	Setter, metalworking machine
7223	8-33.50	Setter-operator, boring machine/ metalworking
7223	8-33.90	Setter-operator, cutting machine/ metalworking
7223	8-33.90	Setter-operator, die-sinking machine/metalworking
7223	8-33.60	Setter-operator, drilling machine/ metalworking
7223	7-27.50	Setter-operator, extruding machine/metalworking
7223	8-33.70	Setter-operator, grinding machine/ metalworking
7223	8-33.80	Setter-operator, honing machine/ metalworking
7223	8-33.90	Setter-operator, lapping machine/ metalworking

7223	8-33.20	Setter-operator, lathe/ metalworking
7223	8-33.10	Setter-operator, machine tool
7223	8-33.10	Setter-operator, metalworking machine
7223	8-33.30	Setter-operator, milling machine/ metalworking
7223	8-33.85	Setter-operator, numerical control machine/metalworking
7223	8-33.40	Setter-operator, planing machine/ metalworking
7223	8-33.70	Setter-operator, precision-grinding machine/metalworking
7223	8-33.60	Setter-operator, reaming machine/ metalworking
7223	8-33.90	Setter-operator, routing machine/ metalworking
7223	8-33.90	Setter-operator, shaping machine/ metalworking
7223	8-39.40	Spinner, metal
7223	8-39.40	Spinner, sheet-metal
7223	9-49.90	Toymaker, metal
7223	8-33.20	Turner
7224	7-29.20	Bluer, metal
7224	8-35.90	Buffer, metal
7224	8-35.20	Burnisher, metal
7224	7-29.40	Cleaner, metal
7224	7-29.30	Finisher, cast metal articles
7224	8-35.20	Finisher, metal
7224	8-35.30	Grinder, machine tool
7224	8-35.30	Grinder, metal
7224	8-35.60	Grinder, textile carding machine
7224	8-35.40	Grinder, tool
7224	8-35.90	Polisher, metal
7224	8-35.90	Polisher, metal/emery polishing
7224	8-35.90	Polisher, metal/mirror-finish
7224	8-35.90	Polisher, metal/sand polishing
7224	8-35.50	Repairer, saw
7224	8-35.40	Sharpener, cutting instruments
7224	8-35.90	Sharpener, itinerant
7224	8-35.40	Sharpener, knife
7224	8-35.50	Sharpener, saw
7224	8-35.40	Sharpener, tool
7224	8-35.30	Wheel-grinder, metal
7231	8-41.15	Fitter, engine/motor-vehicle
7231	8-43.20	Mechanic, automobile
7231	8-43.90	Mechanic, automobile transmission
7231	8-43.90	Mechanic, bus
7231	8-43.20	Mechanic, engine/diesel (motor vehicle)
7231	8-43.20	Mechanic, engine/motor vehicle
7231	8-43.20	Mechanic, garage
7231	8-43.40	Mechanic, motor cycle
7231	8-43.30	Mechanic, motor truck
7231	8-43.20	Mechanic, motor vehicle
7231	8-43.90	Mechanic, motor-vehicle transmission
7231	8-43.90	Mechanic, tractor
7231	8-43.30	Mechanic, truck
7231	8-49.75	Repairer, bicycle
7231	8-43.90	Repairer, motor vehicle
7231	8-49.75	Repairer, pedal cycle
7231	8-43.90	Tuner, engine-driving
7231	8-43.90	Tuner, vehicle engine
7232	8-44.10	Aeromechanic
7232	8-41.85	Erector, metal airframe
7232	8-41.20	Fitter, engine/aircraft
7232	8-41.85	Fitter-assembler, airframe
7232	8-44.20	Mechanic, engine/aircraft
7232	8-44.10	Repairer, engine/aircraft
7233	8-41.80	Erector, refrigeration and air-conditioning equipment
7233	8-41.75	Erector-installer, agricultural machinery
7233	8-41.75	Erector-installer, industrial machinery
7233	8-41.60	Fitter, agricultural machinery
7233	8-41.65	Fitter, earth-moving equipment
7233	8-41.25	Fitter, engine/marine
7233	8-41.90	Fitter, engine/steam
7233	8-41.05	Fitter, industrial machinery
7233	8-41.35	Fitter, machine-tool
7233	8-41.35	Fitter, metalworking machinery
7233	8-41.40	Fitter, mining machinery
7233	8-41.70	Fitter, office machinery
7233	8-49.70	Fitter, plant maintenance
7233	8-41.45	Fitter, printing machinery
7233	8-41.50	Fitter, textile machinery
7233	8-41.30	Fitter, turbine
7233	8-41.55	Fitter, woodworking machinery
7233	8-49.55	Mechanic, agricultural machinery
7233	8-41.80	Mechanic, air-conditioning equipment
7233	8-49.60	Mechanic, construction machinery
7233	8-49.60	Mechanic, earth-moving equipment
7233	8-49.20	Mechanic, engine/diesel (except motor vehicle)
7233	8-49.15	Mechanic, engine/steam
7233	8-49.55	Mechanic, farm machinery
7233	8-49.10	Mechanic, industrial machinery
7233	8-49.30	Mechanic, machine tool
7233	8-49.35	Mechanic, mining machinery

7233	8-49.70	Mechanic, plant maintenance
7233	8-49.40	Mechanic, printing machinery
7233	8-41.80	Mechanic, refrigeration and air-conditioning equipment
7233	8-41.80	Mechanic, refrigeration equipment
7233	8-49.90	Mechanic, ship
7233	8-49.45	Mechanic, textile machinery
7233	8-49.25	Mechanic, turbine
7233	8-49.65	Mechanic, typewriter
7233	8-49.50	Mechanic, woodworking machinery
7233	8-49.70	Millwright
7233	8-49.80	Oiler and greaser
7233	9-82.30	Oiler and greaser, ship
7241	8-51.90	Builder, armature
7241	8-51.90	Builder, commutator
7241	8-55.30	Electrician, aircraft
7241	8-55.40	Electrician, locomotive
7241	8-55.40	Electrician, motor vehicle
7241	8-55.35	Electrician, ship
7241	8-55.40	Electrician, tram
7241	8-55.40	Electrician, vehicle
7241	8-51.20	Fitter, dynamo
7241	8-51.10	Fitter, electrical
7241	8-51.40	Fitter, electrical/control apparatus
7241	8-51.60	Fitter, electrical/elevator and related equipment
7241	8-51.20	Fitter, electrical/generator
7241	8-51.50	Fitter, electrical/instruments
7241	8-51.20	Fitter, electrical/magneto
7241	8-51.20	Fitter, electrical/motor
7241	8-51.90	Fitter, electrical/refrigeration and air-conditioning
7241	8-51.40	Fitter, electrical/rheostat
7241	8-51.90	Fitter, electrical/signalling equipment
7241	8-51.40	Fitter, electrical/switchgear
7241	8-51.30	Fitter, electrical/transformer
7241	8-55.70	Mechanic, electrical
7241	8-55.70	Repairer, electrical equipment
7241	8-55.70	Servicer, electrical equipment
7242	8-52.10	Fitter, electronics
7242	8-52.20	Fitter, electronics/audio-visual equipment
7242	8-52.40	Fitter, electronics/computer equipment
7242	8-52.40	Fitter, electronics/data-processing equipment
7242	8-52.50	Fitter, electronics/industrial equipment
7242	8-52.90	Fitter, electronics/instruments
7242	8-52.30	Fitter, electronics/medical equipment
7242	8-52.90	Fitter, electronics/meteorological equipment
7242	8-52.10	Fitter, electronics/prototype
7242	8-52.20	Fitter, electronics/radar
7242	8-52.20	Fitter, electronics/radio
7242	8-52.60	Fitter, electronics/signalling equipment
7242	8-52.60	Fitter, electronics/signalling systems
7242	8-52.20	Fitter, electronics/telecommunications equipment
7242	8-52.20	Fitter, electronics/television
7243	8-54.90	Erector, radio aerial
7243	8-54.90	Erector, television aerial
7243	8-52.10	Mechanic, electronics
7243	8-49.65	Mechanic, electronics/accounting-machine
7243	8-54.20	Mechanic, electronics/audio-visual equipment
7243	8-49.65	Mechanic, electronics/business machine
7243	8-49.65	Mechanic, electronics/calculating machine
7243	8-52.40	Mechanic, electronics/computer
7243	8-49.65	Mechanic, electronics/office machine
7243	8-54.20	Mechanic, electronics/radio
7243	8-54.20	Mechanic, electronics/television
7243	8-52.10	Repairer, electronics equipment
7243	8-54.20	Repairer, electronics equipment/audio-visual
7243	8-54.20	Repairer, electronics equipment/radio
7243	8-54.20	Repairer, electronics equipment/television
7243	8-52.10	Servicer, electronics equipment
7243	8-54.20	Servicer, electronics equipment/audio-visual
7243	8-54.20	Servicer, electronics equipment/radio
7243	8-54.20	Servicer, electronics equipment/television
7244	8-56.20	Installer, telegraph
7244	8-56.20	Installer, telephone
7244	8-56.30	Mechanic, telegraph
7244	8-56.30	Mechanic, telephone
7244	8-56.30	Servicer, telegraph
7244	8-56.30	Servicer, telephone
7245	8-57.20	Cable worker, electric power/overhead cables
7245	8-57.90	Cable worker, electric power/underground cables

7245	8-57.30	Cable worker, electric traction/overhead cables
7245	8-57.40	Cable worker, telegraph
7245	8-57.40	Cable worker, telephone
7245	8-57.50	Jointer, cable
7245	8-57.50	Jointer, cable/electric
7245	8-57.50	Jointer, cable/telegraph
7245	8-57.50	Jointer, cable/telephone
7245	9-59.90	Layer, underground cable
7245	8-57.20	Line worker, electric power
7245	8-57.30	Line worker, electric traction
7245	8-57.40	Line worker, telegraph
7245	8-57.40	Line worker, telephone
7245	8-57.50	Plumber-jointer, electric cable
7245	8-57.20	Wire worker, electric power/overhead wires
7245	8-57.90	Wire worker, electric power/underground wires
7245	8-57.30	Wire worker, electric traction/overhead wires
7245	8-57.40	Wire worker, telegraph
7245	8-57.40	Wire worker, telephone
7311	8-42.30	Balancer, scale
7311	8-42.30	Calibrator, precision instrument
7311	8-42.45	Maker, artificial limb
7311	8-42.30	Maker, barometer
7311	8-42.45	Maker, brace/orthopaedic
7311	8-42.20	Maker, clock
7311	8-42.50	Maker, dental prosthesis
7311	8-42.90	Maker, instrument/dental
7311	8-42.30	Maker, instrument/meteorological
7311	8-42.30	Maker, instrument/nautical
7311	8-42.35	Maker, instrument/optical
7311	8-42.30	Maker, instrument/precision
7311	8-42.90	Maker, instrument/scientific
7311	8-42.90	Maker, instrument/surgical
7311	8-42.45	Maker, orthopaedic appliance
7311	8-42.40	Maker, photographic equipment
7311	8-42.40	Maker, precision instrument
7311	8-42.45	Maker, surgical appliance
7311	8-42.20	Maker, watch
7311	8-42.50	Mechanic, dental
7311	8-42.35	Repairer, camera
7311	8-42.25	Repairer, clock
7311	8-42.50	Repairer, dental prosthesis
7311	8-42.90	Repairer, instrument/dental
7311	8-42.35	Repairer, instrument/optical
7311	8-42.30	Repairer, instrument/precision
7311	8-42.90	Repairer, instrument/scientific
7311	8-42.90	Repairer, instrument/surgical
7311	8-42.45	Repairer, orthopaedic appliance
7311	8-42.90	Repairer, photographic equipment
7311	8-42.90	Repairer, surgical appliance
7311	8-42.25	Repairer, watch
7311	8-42.25	Watch adjuster
7312	9-41.60	Builder, organ
7312	9-41.50	Maker, accordion
7312	9-41.90	Maker, drum
7312	9-41.40	Maker, instrument/musical (brass)
7312	9-41.40	Maker, instrument/musical (metal wind)
7312	9-41.20	Maker, instrument/musical (string)
7312	9-41.30	Maker, instrument/musical (woodwind)
7312	9-41.60	Maker, organ
7312	9-41.60	Maker, organ/bellow
7312	9-41.60	Maker, organ/pipe
7312	9-41.70	Maker, piano
7312	9-41.50	Maker, piano accordion
7312	9-41.70	Maker, piano/key
7312	9-41.70	Maker, piano/sound-board
7312	9-41.20	Maker, violin
7312	9-41.90	Maker, xylophone
7312	9-41.90	Repairer, instrument/musical (percussion)
7312	9-41.20	Repairer, instrument/musical (string)
7312	9-41.40	Repairer, instrument/musical (wind)
7312	9-41.70	Stringer, piano
7312	9-41.30	Tone regulator, musical instruments
7312	9-41.80	Tuner, accordion
7312	9-41.80	Tuner, musical instrument
7312	9-41.80	Tuner, organ
7312	9-41.80	Tuner, piano
7312	9-41.80	Voicer, organ
7313	8-80.90	Caster, jewellery moulds
7313	8-80.90	Cutter, precious metal
7313	8-80.30	Cutter-polisher, gems
7313	8-80.30	Cutter-polisher, industrial diamonds
7313	8-80.30	Cutter-polisher, jewels
7313	8-80.90	Driller, precious metals
7313	8-80.90	Enameller, jewellery
7313	8-80.80	Engraver, jewellery
7313	8-80.70	Gold beater
7313	8-80.50	Goldsmith
7313	8-80.90	Hammer-smith, precious-metal articles
7313	8-80.10	Jeweller
7313	8-80.30	Lapidary
7313	7-24.90	Maker, jewellery
7313	8-80.90	Maker, precious-metal chain
7313	8-80.70	Maker, precious-metal leaf

7332	8-03.10	Handicraft worker, leather accessories
7332	7-54.30	Handicraft worker, textile weaving
7332	7-54.90	Handicraft worker, textiles
7341	9-21.20	Compositor, printing
7341	9-21.50	Imposer, printing
7341	9-21.30	Intertype operator
7341	9-22.90	Layer-on, printing press
7341	9-21.30	Linotyper
7341	9-21.90	Maker, braille plate
7341	9-21.90	Maker-up, photo-typesetting
7341	9-21.45	Maker-up, printing
7341	9-21.35	Monotyper
7341	9-21.55	Operator, desktop publishing equipment
7341	9-21.55	Photo type-setter, printing
7341	9-21.55	Photo-composer, printing
7341	9-21.10	Printer
7341	9-21.10	Printer, job
7341	9-21.90	Proof-presser
7341	9-21.40	Setter, printing machine
7341	9-21.40	Setter-operator, casting machine/printing type
7341	9-21.50	Stonehand, printing
7341	9-22.90	Taker-off, printing press
7341	9-21.20	Typesetter
7341	9-21.30	Typesetter, linotype
7341	9-21.55	Typesetter, photo-type
7341	9-21.30	Typographer
7342	9-23.30	Caster, electrotype
7342	9-23.20	Caster, stereotype
7342	9-23.30	Electrotyper
7342	9-23.30	Moulder, electrotype
7342	9-23.20	Moulder, stereotype
7342	9-23.20	Stereotyper
7343	9-25.20	Cameraman, photogravure
7343	9-25.90	Cameraman, xerography/offset printing
7343	9-25.20	Camerawoman, photogravure
7343	9-25.90	Camerawoman, xerography/offset printing
7343	9-24.30	Engraver, printing/linoleum block
7343	9-24.15	Engraver, printing/lithographic stone
7343	9-24.20	Engraver, printing/metal die
7343	9-24.20	Engraver, printing/metal plate
7343	9-24.40	Engraver, printing/metal roller
7343	9-24.90	Engraver, printing/music printing
7343	9-24.45	Engraver, printing/pantograph
7343	9-25.10	Engraver, printing/photogravure
7343	9-24.30	Engraver, printing/rubber block
7343	9-24.30	Engraver, printing/wood block
7343	9-24.60	Etcher, printing/metal engraving
7343	9-24.60	Etcher, printing/metal plate
7343	9-24.60	Etcher, printing/metal roller
7343	9-25.50	Etcher, printing/photogravure
7343	9-25.60	Finisher, photo-engraving/printing plates
7343	9-25.90	Grainer, photo-engraving/printing plates
7343	9-25.90	Grainer, photogravure/printing plates
7343	9-25.40	Maker, photogravure/printing plate
7343	9-24.90	Maker, stencil/printing plate
7343	9-25.90	Mounter, photo-engraving/printing plates
7343	9-25.90	Mounter, photogravure/printing
7343	9-25.10	Photo-engraver
7343	9-25.20	Photographer, photogravure
7343	9-25.20	Photolithographer
7343	9-24.45	Printer, pantograph
7343	9-25.90	Proofer, photogravure
7343	9-25.90	Prover, photo-engraving
7343	9-25.90	Prover, photogravure
7343	9-25.30	Retoucher, photogravure
7343	9-25.60	Retoucher, printing plates
7343	9-24.50	Transferrer, lithographic
7343	9-24.50	Transferrer, lithographic/direct
7343	9-24.50	Transferrer, lithographic/printing
7343	9-25.40	Transferrer, photo-mechanical/printing plates
7343	9-24.90	Tuscher, lithographic
7344	9-27.30	Darkroom worker, film developing/black and white photography
7344	9-27.20	Darkroom worker, film developing/colour photography
7344	9-27.50	Darkroom worker, photograph enlarging
7344	9-27.40	Darkroom worker, photograph printing
7344	9-27.30	Developer, film/black-and-white
7344	9-27.20	Developer, film/colour
7344	9-27.90	Developer, film/x-ray
7344	9-27.30	Developer, negative/black-and-white
7344	9-27.20	Developer, negative/colour
7344	9-27.30	Developer, photograph/black-and-white
7344	9-27.20	Developer, photograph/colour
7344	9-27.90	Developer, photographic plate
7344	9-27.30	Developer, positive/black-and-white
7344	9-27.20	Developer, positive/colour
7344	9-27.90	Developer, print
7344	9-27.50	Enlarger, photograph

7414	7-74.50	Pickler, fruit
7414	7-74.50	Pickler, vegetables
7414	7-74.90	Preserver, fruit
7414	7-79.90	Preserver, fruit juice
7414	7-74.90	Preserver, vegetable
7414	7-79.90	Preserver, vegetable juice
7415	7-74.90	Grader, food
7415	7-79.90	Grader, fruit
7415	7-73.90	Grader, meat
7415	7-79.90	Grader, oil
7415	7-74.90	Grader, vegetable
7415	7-77.20	Taster, coffee
7415	7-74.90	Taster, food
7415	7-74.90	Taster, juice
7415	7-78.60	Taster, liquor
7415	7-77.20	Taster, tea
7415	7-78.60	Taster, wine
7416	7-89.20	Blender, snuff
7416	7-81.30	Blender, tobacco
7416	7-81.30	Bulker, tobacco
7416	7-81.40	Conditioner, tobacco leaves
7416	7-81.70	Cutter, tobacco
7416	7-81.40	Dipper, tobacco
7416	7-89.20	Drier, snuff
7416	7-81.90	Drier, tobacco
7416	7-81.90	Dryer, tobacco
7416	7-81.90	Flavourer, tobacco
7416	7-81.20	Grader, tobacco
7416	7-89.20	Grinder, snuff
7416	7-82.20	Maker, cigar
7416	7-83.10	Maker, cigarette
7416	7-89.20	Maker, snuff
7416	7-89.90	Maker, tobacco cake
7416	7-89.90	Maker, tobacco plug
7416	7-89.20	Mixer, snuff
7416	7-81.30	Mixer, tobacco
7416	7-82.20	Moulder, cigar
7416	7-82.90	Presser, cigar
7416	7-82.20	Roller, cigar
7416	7-89.20	Screener, snuff
7416	7-82.90	Sorter, cigar
7416	7-81.50	Stemmer, tobacco
7416	7-81.90	Stover, tobacco
7416	7-81.50	Stripper, tobacco leaf
7416	7-81.40	Tobacco worker, conditioning
7416	7-81.70	Tobacco worker, cutting
7416	7-81.90	Tobacco worker, drying
7416	7-81.50	Tobacco worker, leaf stemming
7416	7-81.50	Tobacco worker, leaf stripping
7421	7-31.30	Dipper, wood treatment
7421	7-32.70	Grader, wood
7421	7-31.30	Impregnator, wood
7421	7-32.70	Wood grader
7421	7-31.90	Wood incising worker
7421	7-31.20	Wood seasoner
7421	7-31.30	Wood treater
7421	7-31.90	Woodworker, treating
7422	8-19.90	Bender, wood
7422	8-19.20	Builder, coach-body/wooden
7422	8-19.20	Builder, vehicle-body/wooden
7422	8-19.20	Builder, vehicle-frame/wooden
7422	8-11.20	Cabinet-maker
7422	8-19.25	Cart-wright
7422	8-19.45	Carver, wood
7422	8-19.30	Cooper
7422	8-19.55	Finisher, wooden furniture
7422	8-19.65	Inlayer, marquetry
7422	8-19.30	Maker, barrel
7422	8-11.20	Maker, cabinet
7422	8-19.30	Maker, cask
7422	8-11.90	Maker, chair
7422	8-11.90	Maker, clock case
7422	8-19.90	Maker, clog
7422	8-19.90	Maker, coffin
7422	9-42.50	Maker, furniture/cane
7422	8-11.90	Maker, instrument case
7422	8-19.90	Maker, ladder/wood
7422	8-19.40	Maker, model/wooden
7422	7-34.60	Maker, paper
7422	8-11.90	Maker, piano case
7422	8-19.90	Maker, picture frame
7422	8-19.60	Maker, pipe/smoking
7422	8-19.60	Maker, pipe/smoking (wood)
7422	8-19.90	Maker, sports equipment/wood
7422	8-19.30	Maker, tank/wooden
7422	8-19.90	Marker, woodworking
7422	8-19.35	Pattern-maker, wood patterns
7422	8-19.55	Stainer, wooden furniture
7422	8-12.90	Tenoner
7422	8-19.55	Varnisher, wooden furniture
7422	8-19.50	Veneer applier
7422	8-19.25	Wheel-wright
7423	8-12.90	Borer, wood
7423	8-12.20	Sawyer, precision woodworking
7423	8-12.20	Sawyer, wood
7423	8-12.05	Setter, woodworking machine
7423	8-12.80	Setter-operator, carving machine/ woodworking
7423	8-12.20	Setter-operator, fret-saw/ woodworking
7423	8-12.20	Setter-operator, jigsaw/ woodworking

7423	8-12.40	Setter-operator, lathe/ woodworking
7423	8-12.70	Setter-operator, planing machine/ woodworking
7423	8-12.60	Setter-operator, routing machine/ woodworking
7423	8-12.50	Setter-operator, shaping machine/ woodworking
7423	8-12.10	Setter-operator, woodworking machine
7423	8-12.30	Turner, wood
7423	8-12.30	Wood tuner
7423	8-12.30	Wood turner
7423	8-12.90	Woodworker, dovetailing
7423	8-12.90	Woodworker, dowelling
7423	8-12.90	Woodworker, morticing
7423	8-12.90	Woodworker, sanding
7423	8-12.90	Woodworker, tenoning
7424	7-54.90	Creeler
7424	9-42.20	Maker, basket
7424	9-42.40	Maker, broom
7424	9-42.30	Maker, brush
7424	9-49.90	Maker, footwear/raffia
7424	9-42.50	Maker, furniture/basket
7424	9-42.50	Maker, furniture/wicker
7424	9-49.90	Maker, toy/wooden
7424	9-42.20	Weaver, basket
7424	9-42.90	Weaver, straw
7431	7-56.15	Bleacher, fibre/textiles
7431	7-51.25	Blender, fibre/textiles
7431	7-51.35	Carder, fibre/textiles
7431	7-51.15	Classer, fibre/textiles
7431	7-51.45	Comber, fibre/textiles
7431	7-51.50	Drawer, fibre/textiles
7431	7-51.40	Fibre lapper, textiles
7431	7-51.15	Grader, fibre/textiles
7431	7-51.90	Opener, fibre/textiles
7431	7-51.30	Picker, fibre/textiles
7431	7-51.10	Preparer, fibre/textiles
7431	7-51.55	Rover, fibre/textiles
7431	7-51.20	Scourer, wool
7431	7-51.40	Sliver lapper
7431	7-51.90	Teaser, textiles
7431	7-51.90	Willeyer
7432	7-59.30	Crocheter
7432	7-54.20	Drawer-in, textile weaving
7432	7-53.20	Fixer, loom
7432	7-53.20	Fixer, loom/jacquard
7432	7-53.20	Fixer, loom/weaving
7432	7-55.40	Knitter
7432	7-55.40	Knitter, garments
7432	7-59.20	Maker, braid
7432	7-59.40	Maker, fishing net
7432	7-59.40	Maker, net
7432	7-59.40	Maker, safety net
7432	7-54.35	Maker, tapestry
7432	7-54.75	Repairer, fabrics
7432	7-55.40	Ribbon lapper
7432	7-53.30	Setter, knitting-machine
7432	7-53.20	Setter, loom
7432	7-52.20	Spinner, thread and yarn
7432	7-54.90	Stripper, bobbin
7432	7-54.20	Threader, loom
7432	7-54.90	Tufter, carpet weaving
7432	7-54.55	Weaver, carpet
7432	7-54.30	Weaver, cloth
7432	7-54.45	Weaver, jacquard
7432	7-54.35	Weaver, tapestry
7433	7-59.50	Coner, hat forms
7433	7-91.40	Dressmaker
7433	7-91.90	Dressmaker, theatrical
7433	7-91.90	Maker, blouse
7433	7-93.90	Maker, cap
7433	7-91.90	Maker, corset
7433	7-91.40	Maker, gown
7433	7-93.20	Maker, hat
7433	7-91.90	Maker, lingerie
7433	7-91.90	Maker, shirt
7433	9-49.90	Maker, wig
7433	7-93.20	Milliner
7433	7-91.10	Tailor
7433	7-91.90	Tailor, alteration
7433	7-91.20	Tailor, bespoke
7433	7-91.20	Tailor, garment/made-to-measure
7433	7-91.30	Tailor, garment/ready-to-wear
7433	7-91.90	Tailor, theatrical
7433	5-40.70	Wardrobe mistress, stage and studio
7434	7-92.50	Cutter, fur
7434	7-92.20	Fur tailor
7434	7-92.20	Furrier
7434	7-92.40	Grader, fur
7434	7-92.40	Matcher, fur
7434	7-92.60	Nailer, fur
7434	7-92.40	Sorter, fur
7434	7-92.90	Trimmer, fur
7435	7-94.50	Cutter, garment
7435	7-94.70	Cutter, glove
7435	7-94.90	Cutter, mattress
7435	7-94.90	Cutter, sail

7435	7-94.50	Cutter, tailor's
7435	7-94.90	Cutter, tent
7435	7-94.90	Cutter, umbrella
7435	7-94.90	Cutter, upholstery
7435	7-53.40	Jacquard design copyist
7435	7-94.40	Marker, garment
7435	7-94.30	Pattern-maker, caps
7435	7-92.30	Pattern-maker, fur
7435	7-94.20	Pattern-maker, garment
7435	7-94.90	Pattern-maker, gloves
7435	7-94.30	Pattern-maker, hats
7435	7-94.90	Pattern-maker, mattresses
7435	7-94.90	Pattern-maker, sails
7435	7-94.90	Pattern-maker, tents
7435	7-94.90	Pattern-maker, umbrellas
7435	7-94.90	Pattern-maker, upholstery
7436	7-95.60	Embroiderer
7436	7-99.90	Maker, artificial flower
7436	7-99.20	Maker, awning
7436	7-99.90	Maker, carpet
7436	7-99.20	Maker, sail, tent and awning
7436	7-99.20	Maker, tent
7436	9-49.40	Maker, toy/dolls and stuffed toys
7436	9-49.90	Maker, toy/soft toys
7436	9-49.40	Maker, toy/stuffed toys
7436	7-99.30	Maker, umbrella
7436	7-95.10	Seamstress
7436	7-95.10	Sewer
7436	8-02.50	Sewer, footwear
7436	7-95.40	Sewer, fur
7436	7-95.10	Sewer, garments
7436	7-95.90	Sewer, hat
7436	8-03.40	Sewer, leather
7436	7-95.90	Sewer, mattress
7436	7-95.90	Sewer, sail
7436	7-95.90	Sewer, tent
7436	7-95.10	Sewer, textile
7436	7-95.90	Sewer, upholstery
7437	7-96.90	Maker, bedding
7437	7-96.90	Maker, furniture/soft furnishing
7437	7-96.40	Maker, mattress
7437	7-96.90	Maker, quilt
7437	7-96.90	Maker, soft furnishing
7437	7-96.30	Upholsterer, aircraft
7437	7-96.30	Upholsterer, automobile
7437	7-96.20	Upholsterer, furniture
7437	7-96.30	Upholsterer, railway carriage
7437	7-96.90	Upholsterer, soft furnishing
7437	7-96.30	Upholsterer, vehicle
7441	7-61.90	Buffer, leather
7441	7-61.20	Classer, hide

7441	7-62.20	Classer, pelt
7441	7-61.20	Classer, skin
7441	7-61.50	Currier, leather
7441	7-61.30	Dehairer, hide
7441	7-62.10	Dresser, pelt
7441	7-61.90	Dyer, leather
7441	7-62.50	Dyer, pelt
7441	7-61.55	Dyer, vat/leather
7441	7-62.90	Dyer, vat/pelt
7441	7-61.90	Dyer-stainer
7441	7-61.55	Dyer-stainer, leather
7441	7-61.90	Dyer-stainer, spray
7441	7-61.25	Fellmonger
7441	7-62.60	Finisher, pelt
7441	7-61.30	Flesher, hide
7441	7-62.30	Flesher, pelt
7441	7-61.30	Flesher-dehairer, hide
7441	7-61.20	Grader, hide
7441	7-62.20	Grader, pelt
7441	7-61.20	Grader, skin
7441	7-62.90	Pickler, pelt
7441	7-62.40	Plucker-trimmer, pelt
7441	7-61.90	Polisher, leather
7441	7-62.40	Puller, pelt
7441	7-62.90	Shaver, fur
7441	7-61.40	Splitter, hide
7441	7-61.55	Stainer, leather
7441	7-61.90	Stretcher, leather
7441	7-62.60	Stretcher, pelt
7441	7-61.45	Tanner
7441	7-61.45	Tanner, hide
7441	7-61.45	Tanner, leather
7442	8-02.55	Burnisher, footwear/heels
7442	8-02.30	Burnisher, footwear/uppers
7442	8-02.30	Cementer, footwear/uppers
7442	8-02.40	Channeller, footwear/soles
7442	8-01.30	Cobbler
7442	8-02.25	Cutter, footwear
7442	8-02.20	Cutter, footwear/clicker
7442	8-03.30	Cutter, leather
7442	8-02.90	Eyeletter, footwear
7442	8-02.55	Finisher, footwear
7442	8-02.40	Fitter, footwear/soles
7442	8-02.30	Fitter, footwear/uppers
7442	8-02.30	Folder, footwear/uppers
7442	8-02.40	Grader, footwear/soles
7442	8-02.45	Laster, footwear
7442	8-01.10	Maker, footwear
7442	8-01.20	Maker, footwear/orthopaedic
7442	8-01.90	Maker, footwear/sport
7442	8-03.20	Maker, harness
7442	8-03.90	Maker, horse collar

7442	8-03.10	Maker, leather goods
7442	8-03.90	Maker, panel/saddlery
7442	8-03.20	Maker, saddle
7442	8-01.90	Maker, sports equipment/footwear
7442	8-01.20	Maker, surgical footwear
7442	8-03.90	Maker, whip
7442	8-02.15	Pattern-maker, footwear
7442	8-02.90	Polisher, footwear
7442	8-02.40	Preparer, footwear/soles
7442	8-02.30	Preparer, footwear/uppers
7442	8-02.35	Presser, footwear/soles
7442	8-01.30	Repairer, footwear
7442	8-01.30	Repairer, footwear
7442	8-02.40	Rounder, footwear
7442	8-03.20	Saddler
7442	8-01.10	Shoe-maker
7442	8-01.10	Shoe-maker, bespoke
7442	8-01.20	Shoe-maker, orthopaedic
7442	8-49.90	Shoe-maker, raffia
7442	8-01.90	Shoe-maker, sports
7442	8-02.30	Skiver, footwear
7442	8-02.90	Socker, footwear
7442	8-02.40	Sorter, footwear
7442	8-02.40	Splitter, footwear
7442	8-02.55	Stainer, footwear
7442	8-02.55	Taker-off, footwear finishing
7442	8-02.55	Trimmer, footwear finishing
8111	7-11.20	Machine-operator, channelling/mine
8111	7-11.20	Machine-operator, cutting/mine
8111	7-11.30	Machine-operator, drilling/mine
8111	7-11.30	Machine-operator, drilling/quarry
8111	7-11.40	Machine-operator, mining/continuous
8112	7-12.90	Cyanide worker, separation equipment
8112	7-12.60	Floatation worker, copper
8112	7-12.60	Floatation worker, minerals
8112	7-12.60	Floatation worker, molybdenum
8112	7-12.30	Machine-operator, crushing/coal
8112	7-12.30	Machine-operator, crushing/mineral ore
8112	7-12.30	Machine-operator, crushing/rock
8112	7-12.30	Machine-operator, crushing/stone
8112	8-20.20	Machine-operator, cutting/stone
8112	8-20.90	Machine-operator, drilling/stone
8112	8-20.20	Machine-operator, grinding/stone
8112	7-12.90	Machine-operator, magnetic ore processing
8112	7-12.40	Machine-operator, milling/minerals
8112	7-12.40	Machine-operator, milling/stone

8112	7-12.10	Machine-operator, mineral processing
8112	8-20.20	Machine-operator, planing/stone
8112	7-12.40	Machine-operator, pulverising/minerals
8112	8-20.20	Machine-operator, sawing/stone
8112	7-12.20	Machine-operator, splitting/stone
8112	7-12.10	Machine-operator, stone processing
8112	7-12.90	Machine-operator, washing/minerals
8112	7-12.80	Operator, breaker/gyratory
8112	7-12.80	Operator, cone/mine
8112	7-12.80	Operator, gravitation equipment/mine
8112	7-12.10	Operator, mineral-processing plant
8112	7-12.10	Operator, stone-processing plant
8112	7-12.70	Precipitator, gold
8112	7-12.70	Precipitator, silver
8112	7-12.50	Tender, jig
8113	7-13.80	Operator, boring equipment/wells
8113	7-13.20	Operator, derrick/oil and gas wells
8113	7-13.40	Operator, drilling equipment/cable (oil and gas wells)
8113	7-13.30	Operator, drilling equipment/rotary (oil and gas wells)
8113	7-13.80	Operator, drilling equipment/wells
8113	7-13.60	Operator, pulling equipment/oil and gas wells
8121	7-21.70	Furnace-operator, converting/non-ferrous metal
8121	7-21.10	Furnace-operator, converting/steel
8121	7-21.50	Furnace-operator, converting/steel (bessemer furnace)
8121	7-21.40	Furnace-operator, converting/steel (oxygen furnace)
8121	7-21.50	Furnace-operator, converting/steel (thomas furnace)
8121	7-21.90	Furnace-operator, puddling
8121	7-21.70	Furnace-operator, refining/non-ferrous metal
8121	7-21.10	Furnace-operator, refining/steel
8121	7-21.60	Furnace-operator, refining/steel (electric-arc furnace)
8121	7-21.30	Furnace-operator, refining/steel (open-hearth furnace)
8121	7-21.10	Furnace-operator, smelting/metal
8121	7-21.20	Furnace-operator, smelting/metal (blast furnace)
8122	7-23.20	Furnace-operator, melting/metal
8122	7-23.20	Furnace-operator, melting/metal (crucible furnace)

8122	7-23.30	Furnace-operator, melting/metal (cupola furnace)
8122	7-23.20	Furnace-operator, melting/metal (electric-arc furnace)
8122	7-23.20	Furnace-operator, melting/metal (open-hearth furnace)
8122	7-23.20	Furnace-operator, melting/metal (reverberatory furnace)
8122	7-23.40	Furnace-operator, reheating/metal
8122	7-24.30	Machine-operator, casting/ centrifugal (cylindrical metal products)
8122	7-24.50	Machine-operator, casting/ continuous rod (non-ferrous metal)
8122	7-24.40	Machine-operator, casting/die (non-ferrous metal)
8122	7-24.20	Machine-operator, casting/metal
8122	7-24.20	Machine-operator, pouring/metal
8122	7-22.70	Manipulator, rolling-mill
8122	7-24.20	Operator, ladle/metal pouring
8122	7-22.50	Operator, rolling-mill/non-ferrous metal
8122	7-22.60	Operator, rolling-mill/seamless pipe and tube
8122	7-22.40	Operator, rolling-mill/steel (cold-rolling)
8122	7-22.30	Operator, rolling-mill/steel (continuous)
8122	7-22.20	Operator, rolling-mill/steel (hot-rolling)
8123	7-26.20	Annealer
8123	7-26.20	Furnace-operator, annealing/metal
8123	7-26.40	Furnace-operator, case-hardening/ metal
8123	7-26.30	Furnace-operator, hardening/metal
8123	7-26.30	Furnace-operator, heat-treating/ metal
8123	7-26.90	Machine-operator, mixing/metal
8123	7-26.50	Machine-operator, tempering/ metal
8123	7-26.40	Nitrider
8123	7-26.40	Operator, carbonation equipment/ metal
8123	7-26.30	Operator, heat-treating plant/metal
8124	7-27.40	Machine-operator, drawing/metal
8124	7-27.40	Machine-operator, drawing/ seamless pipe
8124	7-27.40	Machine-operator, drawing/ seamless tube
8124	7-27.30	Machine-operator, drawing/wire
8124	7-27.50	Machine-operator, extruding/metal
8124	7-27.50	Press-operator, extruding/metal

8131	8-93.30	Furnace-operator, annealing/glass
8131	8-93.20	Furnace-operator, glass production
8131	8-93.30	Furnace-operator, lehr
8131	8-93.20	Furnace-operator, smelting/glass
8131	8-93.40	Furnace-operator, tempering/glass
8131	8-93.60	Kiln-operator, brick and tile
8131	8-93.60	Kiln-operator, brick and tile/dry kiln
8131	8-93.60	Kiln-operator, brick and tile/oven kiln
8131	8-93.60	Kiln-operator, brick and tile/retort kiln
8131	8-91.52	Kiln-operator, float-glass bath
8131	8-93.50	Kiln-operator, pottery and porcelain
8131	8-93.50	Kiln-operator, pottery and porcelain/biscuit kiln
8131	8-93.50	Kiln-operator, pottery and porcelain/dry kiln
8131	8-93.50	Kiln-operator, pottery and porcelain/glost kiln
8131	8-93.50	Kiln-operator, pottery and porcelain/oven kiln
8131	8-93.60	Kiln-operator, tile/biscuit kiln
8131	8-93.60	Kiln-operator, tile/glost kiln
8131	8-74.90	Machine-operator, bending/glass
8131	8-91.28	Machine-operator, blowing/glass
8131	8-91.28	Machine-operator, bottle production
8131	8-92.35	Machine-operator, casting/pottery and porcelain
8131	8-93.50	Machine-operator, ceramics production
8131	8-91.10	Machine-operator, cutting/glass
8131	8-91.40	Machine-operator, drawing/glass
8131	8-91.90	Machine-operator, drilling/glass
8131	8-92.90	Machine-operator, drilling/pottery
8131	8-94.20	Machine-operator, engraving/glass
8131	8-94.30	Machine-operator, etching/glass
8131	8-94.90	Machine-operator, finishing/glass
8131	8-93.10	Machine-operator, glass production
8131	8-93.10	Machine-operator, glass products
8131	8-91.76	Machine-operator, glass rod production
8131	8-91.76	Machine-operator, glass tube production
8131	8-91.10	Machine-operator, grinding/glass
8131	8-91.36	Machine-operator, moulding/glass
8131	8-95.50	Machine-operator, painting/ ceramics
8131	8-95.20	Machine-operator, painting/glass
8131	8-95.90	Machine-operator, plating/glass
8131	8-94.90	Machine-operator, polishing/glass
8131	8-91.72	Machine-operator, polishing/glass lens

8131	8-91.48	Machine-operator, polishing/plate-glass
8131	8-92.20	Machine-operator, pottery and porcelain production
8131	8-91.36	Machine-operator, pressing/glass
8131	8-91.44	Machine-operator, rolling/plate-glass
8131	8-93.40	Machine-operator, tempering/glass
8131	8-91.90	Operator, ladle/glass
8131	8-94.40	Operator, sandblasting equipment/glass
8139	8-99.50	Kiln-operator, frit
8139	8-99.40	Machine-operator, clay slips production
8139	8-99.70	Machine-operator, glass-fibre production
8139	8-99.50	Machine-operator, glaze production
8139	8-99.30	Machine-operator, grinding/clay
8139	8-99.50	Machine-operator, grinding/glaze
8139	8-99.60	Machine-operator, mixing/abrasives
8139	8-99.30	Machine-operator, mixing/clay
8139	8-99.20	Machine-operator, mixing/glass
8139	8-99.50	Machine-operator, mixing/glaze
8139	8.92.50	Operator, die-press/pottery and porcelain
8139	8-99.90	Operator, pug-mill/clay
8139	8.92.55	Press-operator, extruding/clay
8139	8-99.90	Press-operator, filtering/clay
8141	7-32.40	Lathe-operator, cutting/veneer
8141	7-32.10	Lathe-operator, cutting/wood
8141	7-32.10	Machine-operator, boring/wood
8141	7-32.40	Machine-operator, cutting/veneer
8141	7-32.40	Machine-operator, cutting/wood
8141	7-32.10	Machine-operator, drilling/wood
8141	7-32.10	Machine-operator, milling/wood
8141	7-32.10	Machine-operator, planing/wood
8141	7-32.50	Machine-operator, plywood core laying
8141	7-32.20	Machine-operator, sawing/wood
8141	7-31.20	Machine-operator, seasoning/wood
8141	7-32.90	Machine-operator, shaping/wood
8141	7-32.90	Machine-operator, shaving/wood
8141	7-32.90	Machine-operator, tempering/wood
8141	7-31.30	Machine-operator, treating/wood
8141	7-32.10	Machine-operator, wood processing
8141	7-32.30	Operator, band saw
8141	7-32.90	Operator, cut-off saw/barrel staves
8141	7-32.90	Operator, cut-off saw/log staves
8141	7-32.10	Operator, sawmill
8141	7-32.30	Operator, sawmill/band-saw
8141	7-32.10	Operator, wood-processing plant
8141	7-32.60	Press-operator, plywood
8141	7-32.60	Press-operator, veneer
8141	7-32.20	Sawyer, edge
8141	7-32.10	Sawyer, sawmill
8142	7-33.30	Machine-operator, chipping/wood
8142	7-33.20	Machine-operator, grinding/wood
8142	7-33.20	Machine-operator, pulping/wood
8142	7-33.60	Operator, beater/paper pulp
8142	7-33.50	Operator, bleacher/paper
8142	7-33.40	Operator, boiler/paper pulp
8142	7-33.30	Operator, chipper/paper pulp
8142	7-33.40	Operator, digester/paper pulp
8142	7-33.10	Operator, paper-pulp plant
8142	7-33.90	Operator, refinery/paper pulp
8142	7-33.90	Operator, screener/paper pulp
8143	7-34.10	Machine-operator, cardboard production
8143	7-34.50	Machine-operator, coating/paper
8143	7-34.10	Machine-operator, papermaking
8143	7-34.10	Machine-operator, papermaking/back end
8143	7-34.20	Machine-operator, papermaking/wet end
8143	7-34.90	Operator, combiner/paper production
8143	7-34.10	Operator, papermaking plant
8143	7-34.40	Operator, supercalender
8143	7-34.90	Press-operator, hardboard
8151	7-41.40	Machine-operator, blending/chemical and related processes
8151	7-41.40	Machine-operator, compounding/chemical and related processes
8151	7-41.20	Machine-operator, crushing/chemical and related processes
8151	7-41.30	Machine-operator, grinding/chemical and related processes
8151	7-41.30	Machine-operator, milling/chemical and related processes
8151	7-41.40	Machine-operator, mixing/chemical and related processes
8151	7-41.30	Machine-operator, pulverising/chemical and related processes
8151	7-41.30	Operator, mill/chemical and related processes
8152	7-42.40	Furnace-operator, chemical and related processes
8152	7-42.90	Kiln-operator, cement production

8152	7-42.40	Kiln-operator, chemical and related processes
8152	7-42.90	Operator, autoclave/chemical and related processes
8152	7-42.20	Operator, boiler/chemical and related processes
8152	7-42.40	Operator, burner/chemical and related processes
8152	7-42.40	Operator, calciner/chemical and related processes
8152	7-42.90	Operator, cement production plant
8152	7-42.40	Operator, chemical and related processing plant
8152	7-42.20	Operator, cooking equipment/chemical and related processes
8152	7-42.40	Operator, drier/chemical and related processes
8152	7-42.10	Operator, heat-treating-plant/chemical and related processes
8152	7-42.20	Operator, kettle/chemical and related processes
8152	7-42.40	Operator, oven/chemical and related processes
8152	7-42.40	Operator, retort/chemical and related processes
8152	7-42.30	Operator, roasting equipment/chemical and related processes
8152	7-42.90	Operator, spray-drier/chemical and related processes
8153	7-43.20	Filter-press operator, chemical and related materials
8153	7-43.40	Operator, centrifugal separator/chemical and related processes
8153	7-43.50	Operator, dehydrator/oilfield
8153	7-43.20	Operator, expeller/chemical and related materials
8153	7-43.90	Operator, extractor/chemical and related materials
8153	7-43.10	Operator, filter/chemical and related processes
8153	7-43.30	Operator, filter/rotary drum
8153	7-43.90	Operator, screener/chemical and related materials
8153	7-43.40	Operator, separator/chemical and related processes
8153	7-43.90	Operator, sifting equipment/chemical and related materials
8153	7-43.50	Operator, treating equipment/crude oil
8154	7-44.40	Operator, converter/chemical processes (except petroleum and natural gas)
8154	7-44.20	Operator, distiller/batch (chemical processes except petroleum and natural gas)

8154	7-44.30	Operator, distiller/continuous (chemical processes except petroleum and natural gas)
8154	7-44.90	Operator, distiller/turpentine
8154	7-44.50	Operator, evaporator/chemical processes (except petroleum and natural gas)
8154	7-44.60	Operator, extractor/wood distillation
8154	7-44.40	Operator, reactor-converter/chemical processes (except petroleum and natural gas)
8154	7-44.40	Operator, reactor/chemical processes (except petroleum and natural gas)
8154	7-44.20	Operator, still/batch (chemical processes except petroleum and natural gas)
8154	7-44.30	Operator, still/continuous (chemical processes except petroleum and natural gas)
8154	7-44.90	Operator, still/turpentine
8154	7-44.50	Operator, vacuum pan/chemical and related processes (except petroleum and natural gas)
8155	7-45.60	Operator, blender/petroleum and natural gas refining (ethyl)
8155	7-45.60	Operator, compounder/petroleum and natural gas refining
8155	7-45.50	Operator, control-panel/petroleum and natural gas refinery
8155	7-45.40	Operator, distiller/petroleum and natural gas refining
8155	7-45.70	Operator, paraffin plant
8155	7-45.30	Operator, pumping-station/petroleum and natural gas
8155	7-45.30	Operator, refinery/petroleum and natural gas
8155	7-45.30	Operator, still-pump/petroleum and natural gas refining
8155	7-45.40	Operator, still/petroleum and natural gas refining
8155	7-45.20	Operator, treater/desulphurisation (petroleum and natural gas refining)
8155	7-45.20	Operator, treater/petroleum and natural gas refining
8159	7-49.40	Hot cell technician
8159	7-49.30	Kiln-operator, charcoal production
8159	7-49.20	Kiln-operator, coke/retort kiln
8159	7-49.30	Machine-operator, charcoal production
8159	7-49.25	Machine-operator, coal gas production

8159	7-49.20	Machine-operator, coke production
8159	7-49.90	Machine-operator, fertiliser production
8159	7-49.35	Machine-operator, synthetic-fibre production
8159	7-49.15	Operator, bleacher/chemicals
8159	7-49.30	Operator, burner/charcoal production
8159	7-49.20	Operator, burner/coke production
8159	7-49.90	Operator, chemical processing plant/electric cells
8159	7-49.40	Operator, chemical processing plant/radioactive materials
8159	7-49.20	Operator, coke production plant
8159	7-49.90	Operator, fertiliser plant
8159	7-49.90	Operator, liquefaction plant/gases
8159	7-49.20	Operator, oven/coke production
8159	7-49.25	Operator, retort/coal gas
8159	7-49.90	Operator, rubber processing plant
8159	7-49.35	Operator, synthetic-fibre production plant
8159	7-49.40	Operator, treater/radioactive waste
8161	9-61.70	Dispatcher, load/electrical power station
8161	9-61.90	Operator, electric power plant
8161	9-61.90	Operator, gas plant/electric power generation
8161	9-61.10	Operator, generator/electric power
8161	9-61.30	Operator, generator/electric power (hydroelectric)
8161	9-61.20	Operator, generator/electric power (steam)
8161	9-61.90	Operator, geo-thermal power plant
8161	9-61.30	Operator, hydroelectric power plant
8161	9-61.90	Operator, natural gas plant/electric power generating
8161	9-61.40	Operator, nuclear power plant
8161	9-61.40	Operator, reactor/nuclear-power
8161	9-61.90	Operator, rectifier/electric current
8161	9-61.90	Operator, solar power plant
8161	9-61.20	Operator, steam power plant
8161	9-61.60	Operator, switchboard/electrical power station
8161	9-61.60	Operator, switchboard/power station generator
8161	9-61.90	Operator, tidal power plant
8161	9-61.50	Operator, turbine/electricity generation
8161	9-61.50	Operator, turbine/power station
8161	9-61.90	Operator, wind-energy plant/electric power generating

8162	9-69.30	Fireperson, boiler plant
8162	9-83.30	Fireperson, locomotive boiler
8162	9-82.20	Fireperson, ship
8162	9-69.30	Operator, boiler plant/steam
8162	9-83.30	Operator, boiler/locomotive
8162	9-82.20	Operator, boiler/ship
8162	9-69.30	Operator, steam engine
8162	9-82.20	Stoker, ship
8163	9-69.60	Furnace-operator, refuse disposal
8163	9-69.70	Machine-operator, ice production
8163	9-69.20	Operator, compressor/air
8163	9-69.25	Operator, compressor/gas
8163	9-69.70	Operator, cooling plant
8163	9-69.90	Operator, desilting basin
8163	9-69.50	Operator, filter/water
8163	9-69.70	Operator, freezer
8163	9-69.80	Operator, heating plant
8163	9-69.60	Operator, incinerator/refuse disposal
8163	9-69.40	Operator, pumping-station/water
8163	9-69.40	Operator, pumping-station/except petroleum and natural gas
8163	9-69.50	Operator, purification plant/water
8163	9-69.70	Operator, refrigeration system
8163	9-69.90	Operator, reservoir/water
8163	9-69.90	Operator, sewage plant
8163	9-69.50	Operator, treater/water
8163	9-69.80	Operator, ventilation equipment
8163	9-69.50	Operator, water purification plant
8163	9-69.50	Operator, water treatment plant
8163	9-69.90	Tender, water dam
8171	8-53.90	Machine-operator, automated assembly line
8171	8-53.90	Operator, assembly-line/automated
8172	0-39.90	Operator, robot
8211	8-34.20	Lathe-operator, capstan/metalworking
8211	8-34.20	Lathe-operator, centre/metalworking
8211	8-34.20	Lathe-operator, engine/metalworking
8211	8-34.20	Lathe-operator, metalworking
8211	8-34.20	Lathe-operator, turret/metalworking
8211	8-51.90	Machine-operator, armature production
8211	8-34.80	Machine-operator, automatic transfer/components
8211	8-39.70	Machine-operator, bending/metal

8211	8-73.50	Machine-operator, boiler production
8211	8-34.50	Machine-operator, boring/metal
8211	8-35.90	Machine-operator, buffing/metal
8211	8-35.20	Machine-operator, burnishing/metal
8211	8-39.90	Machine-operator, cable production
8211	8-42.20	Machine-operator, clock production
8211	8-51.90	Machine-operator, commutator production
8211	7-25.60	Machine-operator, core-blowing
8211	7-25.60	Machine-operator, coremaking/metal
8211	7-25.60	Machine-operator, coremaking/tube
8211	8-39.80	Machine-operator, cutting/metal
8211	8-34.60	Machine-operator, drilling/metal
8211	8-39.90	Machine-operator, engraving/metal
8211	9-24.60	Machine-operator, etching/metal
8211	8-72.55	Machine-operator, flamecutting/metal
8211	8-31.20	Machine-operator, forging/metal
8211	8-39.50	Machine-operator, forming/metal
8211	8-35.30	Machine-operator, grinding/machine-tool
8211	8-34.65	Machine-operator, grinding/metal
8211	8-35.40	Machine-operator, grinding/tool
8211	8-34.70	Machine-operator, honing/metal
8211	7-24.90	Machine-operator, jewellery production
8211	8-34.90	Machine-operator, lapping/metal
8211	8-34.10	Machine-operator, machine tool
8211	8-34.10	Machine-operator, metal products
8211	8-34.30	Machine-operator, milling/metal
8211	8-39.90	Machine-operator, minting/metal
8211	7-25.40	Machine-operator, moulding/metal
8211	8-39.90	Machine-operator, needle production
8211	8-39.90	Machine-operator, nut production/metal
8211	8-39.90	Machine-operator, pipe production
8211	8-34.40	Machine-operator, planing/metal
8211	8-34.65	Machine-operator, precision grinding/metal
8211	8-34.60	Machine-operator, reaming/metal
8211	8-39.90	Machine-operator, rivet production
8211	8-74.65	Machine-operator, riveting
8211	8-34.75	Machine-operator, sawing/metal
8211	8-34.90	Machine-operator, shaping/metal
8211	8-35.20	Machine-operator, sharpening/metal
8211	8-39.80	Machine-operator, shearing/metal
8211	8-39.40	Machine-operator, spinning/metal
8211	8-39.90	Machine-operator, sports equipment/metal
8211	8-32.20	Machine-operator, tool production
8211	9-49.90	Machine-operator, toy production/metal
8211	8-42.20	Machine-operator, watch production
8211	8-72.25	Machine-operator, welding/metal
8211	8-39.90	Machine-operator, wire goods production
8211	8-39.90	Machine-operator, wiring/electric
8211	8-34.10	Operator, machine-tool
8211	8-39.80	Operator, power-shear
8211	8-39.60	Press-operator, metal/except forging
8211	8-39.60	Press-operator, punching/metal
8211	8-39.60	Press-operator, stamping/metal
8212	8-20.50	Lathe-operator, stoneworking
8212	9-43.90	Machine-operator, abrasive-coatings production
8212	9-43.40	Machine-operator, artificial stone products
8212	9-43.30	Machine-operator, asbestos-cement products
8212	8-20.70	Machine-operator, carving/stone products
8212	9-43.20	Machine-operator, cast-concrete products
8212	9-43.40	Machine-operator, cast-stone products
8212	9-43.30	Machine-operator, cement products
8212	8-80.30	Machine-operator, cutting/industrial diamonds
8212	9-51.55	Machine-operator, cutting/mosiac
8212	8-20.50	Machine-operator, cutting/stone products
8212	8-20.90	Machine-operator, engraving/stone
8212	9-52.40	Machine-operator, finishing/concrete
8212	8-20.20	Machine-operator, finishing/stone
8212	8-80.10	Machine-operator, industrial-diamonds production
8212	8-20.10	Machine-operator, mineral products
8212	8-80.30	Machine-operator, polishing/industrial diamonds
8212	8-20.20	Machine-operator, polishing/stone
8212	8-20.10	Machine-operator, stone products
8212	9-74.75	Operator, concrete-mixing plant
8221	7-44.90	Machine-operator, detergent production

8221	7-44.90	Machine-operator, pharmaceutical products
8221	7-44.90	Machine-operator, toiletries production
8221	7-44.90	Operator, distilling equipment/ perfume
8221	7-44.90	Operator, granulation equipment/ pharmaceutical and toiletry products
8221	7-44.90	Operator, mouldbing equipment/ toiletries
8221	7-44.90	Operator, still/perfume
8222	9-49.90	Machine-operator, ammunition products
8222	9-49.90	Machine-operator, explosives production
8222	9-49.90	Machine-operator, fireworks production
8222	9-49.90	Machine-operator, match production
8223	7-28.90	Anodiser
8223	7-28.20	Electroplater
8223	7-29.30	Fettler
8223	7-29.20	Machine-operator, bluing/metal
8223	7-28.40	Machine-operator, coating/metal
8223	7-28.40	Machine-operator, coating/wire
8223	7-29.40	Machine-operator, degreasing/ metal
8223	7-28.30	Machine-operator, dipping/metal
8223	7-28.20	Machine-operator, electroplating/ metal
8223	7-29.30	Machine-operator, finishing/cast metal articles
8223	8-35.20	Machine-operator, finishing/metal
8223	7-28.30	Machine-operator, galvanising/ metal
8223	8-35.20	Machine-operator, laminating/ metal
8223	9-39.90	Machine-operator, painting/metal
8223	7-28.30	Machine-operator, plating/metal
8223	7-28.40	Machine-operator, plating/wire
8223	8-35.20	Machine-operator, polishing/metal
8223	7-28.20	Machine-operator, refining/metal
8223	7-29.30	Machine-operator, shotblasting/ metal
8223	7-28.50	Machine-operator, spraying/metal
8223	7-29.40	Operator, cleaning equipment/ metal
8223	7-29.30	Operator, sandblasting equipment/ metal
8223	7-28.90	Sherardiser
8224	9-27.90	Machine-operator, developing/ motion picture film
8224	9-27.30	Machine-operator, developing/ photography
8224	9-27.50	Machine-operator, enlarging/ photography
8224	9-27.30	Machine-operator, film developing
8224	9-49.70	Machine-operator, film paper production
8224	9-27.30	Machine-operator, photographic film developing
8224	9-49.70	Machine-operator, photographic film production
8224	9-49.70	Machine-operator, photographic paper production
8224	9-49.90	Machine-operator, photographic plate production
8224	9-27.10	Machine-operator, photographic products
8224	9-27.30	Machine-operator, printing/ photography (black and white)
8224	9-27.40	Machine-operator, printing/ photography (colour)
8229	9-49.60	Machine-operator, candle production
8229	7-49.90	Machine-operator, chlorine gas production
8229	7-49.90	Machine-operator, halogen gas production
8229	7-49.90	Machine-operator, hydrogen gas production
8229	7-49.90	Machine-operator, lead production
8229	9-49.30	Machine-operator, linoleum production
8229	9-49.90	Machine-operator, pencil production
8229	7-49.90	Machine-operator, washing/ chemical and related materials
8231	9-01.90	Machine-operator, coating/rubber
8231	9-01.20	Machine-operator, compounding/ rubber
8231	9-01.90	Machine-operator, embossing/ rubber
8231	9-01.20	Machine-operator, extruding/ rubber
8231	9-01.20	Machine-operator, milling/rubber
8231	9-01.35	Machine-operator, moulding/ rubber
8231	9-01.30	Machine-operator, moulding/tyres
8231	9-02.40	Machine-operator, rebuilding/tyres
8231	9-01.20	Machine-operator, rubber processing
8231	9-01.90	Machine-operator, rubber products
8231	9-49.50	Machine-operator, rubber stamp production

8231	9-02.90	Machine-operator, tyre production
8231	9-01.90	Machine-operator, vulcanising/rubber goods
8231	9-02.30	Machine-operator, vulcanising/tyres
8231	9-01.25	Operator, calender/rubber
8232	9-01.90	Machine-operator, buffing/plastics
8232	9-01.90	Machine-operator, carving/plastics
8232	9-01.90	Machine-operator, casting/plastic products
8232	9-01.55	Machine-operator, compression moulding/plastics
8232	9-01.90	Machine-operator, cutting/plastics
8232	9-01.90	Machine-operator, drilling/plastics
8232	9-01.90	Machine-operator, etching/plastics
8232	9-01.60	Machine-operator, extruding/plastics
8232	9-01.80	Machine-operator, fabrication/plastic products
8232	9-01.90	Machine-operator, finishing/plastics
8232	9-01.90	Machine-operator, grinding/plastics
8232	9-01.50	Machine-operator, injection moulding/plastics
8232	9-01.65	Machine-operator, laminating/plastics
8232	9-01.90	Machine-operator, moulding/plastics
8232	9-01.10	Machine-operator, plastic products
8232	9-01.10	Machine-operator, plastics production
8240	8-12.30	Lathe-operator, woodworking
8240	8-19.90	Machine-operator, bending/wood
8240	8-12.80	Machine-operator, carving/wood
8240	8-12.90	Machine-operator, engraving/wood
8240	8-12.90	Machine-operator, etching/wood
8240	8-12.90	Machine-operator, finishing/wood
8240	8-19.55	Machine-operator, furniture production
8240	8-19.90	Machine-operator, marking/wood
8240	9-39.90	Machine-operator, painting/wood
8240	8-12.90	Machine-operator, polishing/wood
8240	8-19.90	Machine-operator, sports equipment/wood
8240	9-49.90	Machine-operator, toy production/wood
8240	8-11.10	Machine-operator, wood products
8240	8-12.08	Machine-operator, woodworking
8251	9-21.40	Machine-operator, casting/printing type
8251	9-21.55	Machine-operator, photo-typesetting
8251	9-22.10	Machine-operator, printing
8251	9-22.90	Machine-operator, printing/textiles
8251	9-22.20	Operator, letterpress/cylinder
8251	9-22.25	Operator, letterpress/platen
8251	9-22.30	Operator, letterpress/rotary
8251	9-22.20	Press-operator, printing/cylinder
8251	9-22.50	Press-operator, printing/direct lithographic
8251	9-22.40	Press-operator, printing/offset
8251	9-22.40	Press-operator, printing/offset lithographic
8251	9-22.25	Press-operator, printing/platen
8251	9-22.30	Press-operator, printing/rotary
8251	9-22.60	Press-operator, printing/rotogravure
8251	9-22.70	Press-operator, printing/wallpaper
8252	9-26.30	Machine-operator, bookbinding
8252	9-26.50	Machine-operator, embossing/books
8253	9-10.90	Machine-operator, cardboard products
8253	9-10.80	Machine-operator, cellophane bag production
8253	9-10.50	Machine-operator, cutting/paper-boxes
8253	9-10.90	Machine-operator, embossing/paper
8253	9-10.70	Machine-operator, envelope and paper bag production
8253	9-10.50	Machine-operator, folding/paper boxes
8253	9-10.40	Machine-operator, lining/cardboard
8253	9-10.30	Machine-operator, paper box production
8253	9-10.10	Machine-operator, paper products
8253	9-10.10	Machine-operator, paperboard products
8253	9-10.80	Machine-operator, polythene bag production
8261	7-52.90	Baller, thread and yarn
8261	7-51.25	Machine-operator, blending/textile fibres
8261	7-51.45	Machine-operator, combing/textile fibres
8261	7-52.30	Machine-operator, doubling/thread and yarn
8261	7-51.50	Machine-operator, drawing-frame/textile fibres
8261	7-51.10	Machine-operator, fibre preparing
8261	7-51.40	Machine-operator, lapping/ribbon

8261	7-51.40	Machine-operator, lapping/sliver
8261	7-51.40	Machine-operator, lapping/textile fibres
8261	7-52.50	Machine-operator, reeling/thread and yarn
8261	7-51.55	Machine-operator, roving-frame/ textile fibres
8261	7-52.50	Machine-operator, skeining/thread and yarn
8261	7-49.35	Machine-operator, spinning/ synthetic fibre
8261	7-52.20	Machine-operator, spinning/thread and yarn
8261	7-52.50	Machine-operator, spooling/thread and yarn
8261	7-51.10	Machine-operator, textile fibre preparing
8261	7-52.40	Machine-operator, twining/thread and yarn
8261	7-52.40	Machine-operator, twisting/thread and yarn
8261	7-51.90	Machine-operator, washing/textile fibres
8261	7-52.50	Machine-operator, winding/thread and yarn
8262	7-53.50	Jacquard card cutter
8262	7-53.90	Jacquard card lacer
8262	7-99.90	Machine-operator, carpet production
8262	7-54.40	Machine-operator, cloth production
8262	7-59.35	Machine-operator, crocheting
8262	7-54.25	Machine-operator, drawing-in/ textile weaving
8262	7-95.70	Machine-operator, embroidery
8262	7-55.10	Machine-operator, knitting
8262	7-55.20	Machine-operator, knitting/ garment
8262	7-55.30	Machine-operator, knitting/hosiery
8262	7-54.50	Machine-operator, lace production
8262	7-54.65	Machine-operator, net production
8262	7-54.25	Machine-operator, threading/loom
8262	7-54.15	Machine-operator, warping/beam (textile weaving)
8262	7-54.40	Machine-operator, weaving
8262	7-54.60	Machine-operator, weaving/ carpets
8262	7-54.40	Machine-operator, weaving/fabrics
8262	7-54.45	Machine-operator, weaving/ jacquard
8262	7-54.50	Machine-operator, weaving/laces
8262	7-54.60	Operator, loom/carpet weaving
8262	7-54.45	Operator, loom/jacquard
8262	7-54.50	Operator, loom/lace production

8263	7-95.50	Machine-operator, sewing
8263	7-95.50	Machine-operator, sewing/ embroidery
8263	8-02.50	Machine-operator, sewing/ footwear
8263	7-95.50	Machine-operator, sewing/fur
8263	7-95.50	Machine-operator, sewing/ garments
8263	7-95.50	Machine-operator, sewing/hats
8263	8-03.50	Machine-operator, sewing/leather
8263	7-95.50	Machine-operator, sewing/textile products
8263	7-95.50	Machine-operator, sewing/ upholstery
8264	7-56.70	Calenderer, cloth
8264	5-60.90	Calenderer, laundry
8264	7-56.15	Machine-operator, bleaching/ textiles
8264	7-56.40	Machine-operator, degumming/ silk
8264	5-60.30	Machine-operator, dry-cleaning
8264	5-60.90	Machine-operator, drying/laundry
8264	7-56.90	Machine-operator, drying/textiles
8264	7-56.25	Machine-operator, dyeing/fabric
8264	7-56.30	Machine-operator, dyeing/ garments
8264	7-56.90	Machine-operator, dyeing/textile fibres
8264	7-56.20	Machine-operator, dyeing/yarn
8264	5-60.20	Machine-operator, laundering
8264	5-60.60	Machine-operator, laundry
8264	5-60.60	Machine-operator, pressing/ laundry
8264	7-56.50	Machine-operator, shrinking/ textiles
8264	7-56.65	Machine-operator, silk weighting
8264	7-56.35	Machine-operator, washing/cloth
8264	5-60.20	Machine-operator, washing/ laundry
8264	7-56.35	Machine-operator, washing/yarn
8264	7-56.60	Machine-operator, waterproofing/ cloth
8264	7-56.60	Machine-operator, waterproofing/ fabric
8264	7-56.60	Machine-operator, waterproofing/ textiles
8264	7-56.70	Operator, calender/textiles
8264	5-60.90	Operator, cleaning equipment/ carpets
8264	7-56.35	Operator, cleaning equipment/ cloth
8264	5-60.20	Operator, cleaning equipment/ laundry
8264	7-56.35	Operator, cleaning equipment/ textiles

8264	7-56.55	Operator, fulling-mill/textiles
8264	7-56.70	Press-operator, steam/textiles
8264	7-56.70	Press-operator, textile
8265	8-03.30	Machine-operator, cutting/leather
8265	7-61.35	Machine-operator, dehairing/hide
8265	7-62.60	Machine-operator, finishing/pelt
8265	7-61.35	Machine-operator, fleshing/hide
8265	7-62.30	Machine-operator, fleshing/pelt
8265	7-62.60	Machine-operator, fur preparing
8265	7-61.35	Machine-operator, hide processing
8265	7-61.50	Machine-operator, leather preparing
8265	7-59.45	Machine-operator, mixing/fur fibre
8265	7-62.60	Machine-operator, pelt processing
8265	7-61.55	Machine-operator, staining/leather
8265	7-61.45	Machine-operator, tanning
8265	7-61.90	Machine-operator, washing/hide
8266	8-01.10	Machine-operator, footwear production
8266	8-01.20	Machine-operator, footwear production/orthopaedic
8266	8-01.90	Machine-operator, footwear production/raffia
8266	8-01.90	Machine-operator, footwear production/sports
8266	8-01.10	Machine-operator, shoe production
8269	7-93.30	Blocker, hat
8269	7-93.30	Machine-operator, blocking/hats
8269	7-59.25	Machine-operator, braid production
8269	7-94.50	Machine-operator, cutting/garments
8269	7-94.50	Machine-operator, cutting/textiles
8269	7-59.50	Machine-operator, forming/felt hoods
8269	7-93.10	Machine-operator, hat making
8269	7-94.40	Machine-operator, mattress production
8269	7-94.10	Machine-operator, pattern-making/fur
8269	7-94.10	Machine-operator, pattern-making/leather
8269	7-94.10	Machine-operator, pattern-making/textiles
8271	7-74.15	Machine-operator, canning/fish
8271	7-74.15	Machine-operator, canning/meat
8271	7-74.50	Machine-operator, curing/meat
8271	7-79.40	Machine-operator, fish processing
8271	7-79.40	Machine-operator, fish products
8271	7-74.30	Machine-operator, freezing/fish
8271	7-74.30	Machine-operator, freezing/meat
8271	7-73.30	Machine-operator, meat processing
8271	7-73.90	Machine-operator, meat products
8271	7-74.15	Machine-operator, preserving/fish
8271	7-74.10	Machine-operator, preserving/meat
8271	7-74.20	Machine-operator, sterilising/fish
8271	7-74.20	Machine-operator, sterilising/meat
8271	7-73.90	Machine-operator, washing/carcasses
8271	7-74.20	Operator, autoclave/meat and fish
8272	7-75.10	Machine-operator, dairy products
8272	7-75.90	Machine-operator, freezing/dairy products
8272	7-75.90	Machine-operator, milk powder production
8272	7-75.90	Machine-operator, milk processing
8272	7-75.20	Machine-operator, pasteurising/dairy products
8272	7-75.20	Machine-operator, pasteurising/milk
8272	7-75.90	Operator, vacuum pan/condensed milk
8272	7-75.90	Salter, cheese
8273	7-71.90	Machine-operator, grain processing
8273	7-71.90	Machine-operator, hulling/grain
8273	7-71.90	Machine-operator, husking/grain
8273	7-71.20	Machine-operator, milling/grain
8273	7-71.90	Machine-operator, milling/mustard seeds
8273	7-71.30	Machine-operator, milling/rice
8273	7-71.40	Machine-operator, milling/spices
8273	7-71.20	Operator, rolling-mill/grain
8273	7-71.40	Operator, rolling-mill/spices
8274	7-76.90	Machine-operator, bakery products
8274	7-76.20	Machine-operator, bread production
8274	7-76.10	Machine-operator, cereal products
8274	7-76.50	Machine-operator, chocolate production
8274	7-76.30	Machine-operator, chocolate products
8274	7-76.50	Machine-operator, conching/chocolate
8274	7-76.60	Machine-operator, confectionery production
8274	7-76.40	Machine-operator, noodle production
8274	7-76.90	Machine-operator, pasta production

8274	7-76.30	Machine-operator, pastry production
8275	7-79.90	Machine-operator, blanching/edible nuts
8275	7-74.90	Machine-operator, canning/fruit
8275	7-74.90	Machine-operator, canning/vegetables
8275	7-74.40	Machine-operator, dehydrating/foodstuffs
8275	7-74.40	Machine-operator, drying/foodstuffs
8275	7-79.90	Machine-operator, edible nut processing
8275	7-79.20	Machine-operator, edible oil production
8275	7-74.30	Machine-operator, freezing/fruit
8275	7-74.30	Machine-operator, freezing/vegetables
8275	7-79.90	Machine-operator, fruit juice production
8275	7-74.90	Machine-operator, fruit processing
8275	7-79.90	Machine-operator, margarine processing
8275	7-79.20	Machine-operator, milling/oil-seed
8275	7-74.90	Machine-operator, preserving/fruit
8275	7-74.90	Machine-operator, preserving/vegetables
8275	7-79.25	Machine-operator, refining/oils and fats
8275	7-74.20	Machine-operator, sterilising/fruit
8275	7-74.20	Machine-operator, sterilising/vegetables
8275	7-79.90	Machine-operator, vegetable juice production
8275	7-74.90	Machine-operator, vegetable processing
8275	7-74.90	Machine-operator, washing/fruit
8275	7-74.90	Machine-operator, washing/vegetables
8275	7-74.20	Operator, autoclave/fruit and vegetables
8275	7-79.30	Operator, autoclave/oils and fats
8275	7-74.90	Operator, evaporation equipment/food essences
8275	7-79.30	Operator, hydrogenation equipment/oils and fats
8275	7-74.40	Operator, vacuum oven/foodstuffs
8275	7-74.90	Operator, vacuum pan/food essences
8275	7-79.20	Press-operator, edible oils
8275	7-78.80	Press-operator, fruit
8276	7-72.10	Machine-operator, refining/sugar
8276	7-72.60	Machine-operator, refining/sugar (continuous)
8276	7-72.10	Machine-operator, sugar production
8276	7-72.40	Operator, carbonation equipment/sugar refining
8276	7-72.50	Operator, crystallising equipment/sugar refining
8276	7-72.30	Operator, diffuser/beet sugar
8276	7-72.20	Operator, grinding equipment/sugar-cane
8277	7-77.30	Machine-operator, blending/coffee
8277	7-77.40	Machine-operator, blending/tea
8277	7-77.90	Machine-operator, cocoa-bean processing
8277	7-77.10	Machine-operator, coffee-bean processing
8277	7-77.10	Machine-operator, tea-leaf processing
8277	7-77.60	Operator, roasting equipment/cocoa-bean
8277	7-77.50	Operator, roasting equipment/coffee
8277	7-77.90	Winnower, cocoa-bean
8278	7-78.10	Brewer
8278	7-78.25	Kiln-operator, malting/spirits
8278	7-78.90	Machine-operator, blending/spirits
8278	7-78.90	Machine-operator, blending/wine
8278	7-78.10	Machine-operator, brewing/spirits
8278	7-44.90	Machine-operator, distilling/spirits
8278	7-78.90	Machine-operator, liqueur production
8278	7-78.20	Machine-operator, malting/spirits
8278	7-78.10	Machine-operator, soft-drinks production
8278	7-78.70	Machine-operator, vinegar making
8278	9-71.55	Machine-operator, washing/bottles
8278	7-78.20	Maltster
8278	7-78.30	Operator, cooking equipment/malt
8278	7-78.35	Operator, fermentation equipment/spirits
8278	7-78.20	Operator, germination equipment/malting (spirits)
8278	7-44.90	Operator, still/spirits
8278	7-78.50	Operator, winemaking plant
8278	7-78.20	Steeper, malting
8279	7-81.30	Machine-operator, blending/tobacco
8279	7-82.30	Machine-operator, cigar production
8279	7-83.20	Machine-operator, cigarette production
8279	7-81.70	Machine-operator, cutting/tobacco leaf

8279	7-81.60	Machine-operator, stripping/ tobacco-leaf
8279	7-81.10	Machine-operator, tobacco processing
8279	7-81.10	Machine-operator, tobacco products
8279	7-81.40	Operator, vacuum-conditioner/ tobacco processing
8281	8-41.60	Assembler, agricultural machinery
8281	8-41.20	Assembler, aircraft
8281	8-41.65	Assembler, earth-moving equipment
8281	8-41.20	Assembler, engine/aircraft
8281	8-41.15	Assembler, engine/internal combustion
8281	8-41.25	Assembler, engine/marine
8281	8-41.15	Assembler, engine/motor vehicles
8281	8-41.90	Assembler, engines/steam
8281	8-41.10	Assembler, industrial machinery
8281	8-41.35	Assembler, machine-tool
8281	8-41.10	Assembler, mechanical machinery
8281	8-49.90	Assembler, metal products
8281	8-41.40	Assembler, mining machinery
8281	8-41.45	Assembler, printing machinery
8281	8-41.50	Assembler, textile machinery
8281	8-41.30	Assembler, turbine
8281	8-41.10	Assembler, vehicle
8281	8-41.55	Assembler, woodworking machinery
8281	8-41.10	Machine-operator, assembly line/ vehicles
8281	8-41.10	Machine-operator, assembly-line/ aircraft
8281	8-73.80	Machine-operator, assembly-line/ except vehicles and aircraft
8281	9-39.90	Machine-operator, vehicle assembly
8282	8-53.90	Assembler, electrical components
8282	8-53.20	Assembler, electrical equipment
8282	8-53.40	Machine-operator, winding/ armature
8282	8-53.40	Machine-operator, winding/rotor coil
8282	8-53.40	Machine-operator, winding/stator coil
8282	8-53.40	Machine-operator, winding/ transformer coil
8283	8-53.30	Assembler, audio-visual equipment
8283	8-42.20	Assembler, chronometer
8283	8-42.20	Assembler, clock
8283	8-53.90	Assembler, electronic components
8283	8-53.30	Assembler, electronic equipment
8283	8-53.90	Assembler, hearing aid
8283	8-53.90	Assembler, microelectronics equipment
8283	8-41.70	Assembler, office machinery
8283	8-42.40	Assembler, precision instrument
8283	8-53.30	Assembler, radio
8283	8-53.30	Assembler, television
8283	8-42.20	Assembler, watch
8283	8-53.90	Machine-operator, winding/ filament
8284	8-73.90	Assembler, furniture/sheet-metal
8284	8-73.10	Assembler, metal products
8284	9-01.70	Assembler, plastic products
8284	9-01.40	Assembler, rubber products
8285	8-11.10	Assembler, furniture/wood and related materials
8285	8-11.10	Assembler, wood products
8286	8-03.60	Assembler, leather products
8286	9-10.10	Assembler, paperboard products
8286	7-99.90	Assembler, textile products
8290	8-53.30	Assembler, composite products
8290	9-71.55	Machine-operator, bottling
8290	9-71.60	Machine-operator, branding
8290	9-59.90	Machine-operator, cable installation
8290	9-71.55	Machine-operator, capping
8290	9-59.50	Machine-operator, drain installation
8290	9-59.90	Machine-operator, electrical line installation
8290	9-71.55	Machine-operator, filling/ containers
8290	9-56.30	Machine-operator, insulation
8290	9-71.60	Machine-operator, labelling
8290	9-71.60	Machine-operator, marking/goods
8290	9-71.55	Machine-operator, packing
8290	7-12.90	Machine-operator, pelletising
8290	9-59.50	Machine-operator, pipe installation
8290	9-71.55	Machine-operator, sealing
8290	8-53.90	Machine-operator, silicon chip production
8290	9-72.10	Machine-operator, splicing/cable and rope
8290	9-71.55	Machine-operator, wrapping
8290	9-39.90	Operator, marking equipment/ roads
8290	5-99.90	Operator, merry-go-round
8290	9-71.70	Press-operator, baling

8311	9-83.50	Driver, elevated train
8311	9-83.60	Driver, engine/mine
8311	9-83.60	Driver, engine/quarry
8311	9-83.20	Driver, locomotive
8311	9-83.60	Driver, locomotive/mine
8311	9-83.60	Driver, locomotive/quarry
8311	9-83.20	Driver, railway engine
8311	9-83.20	Driver, railway engine/mine
8311	9-83.20	Driver, railway engine/quarry
8311	9-83.90	Driver, shunting-engine
8311	9-83.20	Driver, train
8311	9-83.50	Driver, train/elevated
8311	9-83.50	Driver, train/underground
8311	9-83.50	Driver, underground train
8311	9-83.40	Driver-assistant, locomotive
8311	9-83.40	Driver-assistant, railway-engine
8311	9-83.40	Driver-assistant, train
8312	9-84.40	Braker, railway
8312	9-84.20	Braker, train/freight
8312	9-84.50	Braker, train/mine
8312	9-84.50	Braker, train/quarry
8312	9-84.40	Coupler, railway yard
8312	9-84.20	Guard, freight train
8312	9-84.20	Guard, goods train
8312	9-84.40	Shunter, railway
8312	9-84.30	Signaller, railway
8321	9-85.70	Dispatch rider
8321	9-85.70	Driver, dispatch
8321	9-85.70	Driver, motor cycle
8321	9-85.70	Driver, motor tricycle
8321	9-85.70	Driver, motor tricycle/goods
8321	9-85.70	Motor-cyclist
8321	9-85.70	Rider, dispatch
8321	9-85.70	Rider, motor cycle
8322	9-85.90	Chauffeur, motor-car
8322	9-85.90	Driver, ambulance
8322	9-85.30	Driver, cab
8322	9-85.90	Driver, car
8322	9-85.90	Driver, car-delivery
8322	9-85.90	Driver, mail van
8322	9-85.90	Driver, motor car
8322	9-85.90	Driver, postal van
8322	9-85.30	Driver, taxi
8322	9-85.30	Driver, taxi/motor-tricycle
8322	9-85.50	Driver, van
8323	9-85.40	Driver, bus
8323	9-85.40	Driver, motor bus
8323	9-85.20	Driver, streetcar
8323	9-85.20	Driver, tram

8323	9-85.20	Driver, tramcar
8323	9-85.40	Driver, trolley-bus
8324	9-79.30	Driver, dumper truck
8324	9-85.50	Driver, lorry
8324	9-85.60	Driver, tanker
8324	9-85.60	Driver, trailer-truck
8324	9-85.60	Driver, truck
8324	9-79.30	Driver, truck/dumper
8324	9-85.60	Driver, truck/heavy
8324	9-79.40	Operator, shuttle-car/mine
8324	9-79.40	Operator, shuttle-car/quarry
8331	9-79.50	Driver, lumber carrier
8331	9-79.50	Driver, timber carrier
8331	6-28.20	Driver, tractor
8331	6-28.20	Operator, agricultural machinery
8331	6-28.20	Operator, baler/farm
8331	6-28.20	Operator, combiner/agricultural
8331	8-32.90	Operator, forestry machinery
8331	6-28.20	Operator, harvester
8331	6-28.20	Operator, motorised farm equipment
8331	6-32.90	Operator, motorised forestry equipment
8331	6-28.20	Operator, thresher
8332	9-74.30	Driver, bulldozer
8332	9-74.25	Driver, digger/trench digging
8332	9-74.20	Driver, excavating machine
8332	9-74.45	Driver, road grader and scraper
8332	9-74.50	Driver, road roller
8332	9-74.50	Driver, steamroller
8332	9-74.60	Driver, tar-spreading machine
8332	9-74.25	Driver, trench-digging machine
8332	9-74.30	Operator, bulldozer
8332	9-74.25	Operator, digger/trench digging
8332	9-74.35	Operator, dredge
8332	9-74.90	Operator, drilling plant
8332	9-74.90	Operator, earth-boring machinery/ construction
8332	9-74.10	Operator, earth-moving equipment
8332	9-74.20	Operator, excavator
8332	9-74.45	Operator, grader and scraper/ construction
8332	9-74.60	Operator, paving machinery/ bituminous
8332	9-74.55	Operator, paving machinery/ concrete
8332	9-74.40	Operator, pile-driver
8332	9-74.60	Operator, road surface laying machinery
8332	9-74.50	Operator, road-roller
8332	9-74.20	Operator, shovel/mechanical

8332	9-74.60	Operator, spreader/asphalt
8332	9-74.55	Operator, spreader/concrete paving (construction)
8332	9-74.90	Operator, spreader/stone (construction)
8332	9-74.60	Operator, spreader/tar
8332	9-74.90	Operator, tamping machinery/ construction
8332	9-74.90	Operator, tunnelling machinery/ construction
8333	9-89.90	Attendant, dry dock
8333	9-73.45	Banksman, mine
8333	9-73.45	Bankswoman, mine
8333	9-73.40	Driver, cage/mine
8333	9-89.30	Lock-keeper, canal or port
8333	9-73.45	Onsetter, mine
8333	9-73.90	Operator, boat/derrick
8333	9-73.55	Operator, bridge
8333	9-73.55	Operator, bridge/bascule
8333	9-73.55	Operator, bridge/opening
8333	9-73.55	Operator, bridge/swing
8333	9-79.90	Operator, cable car
8333	9-73.45	Operator, cage/mine
8333	9-79.90	Operator, chair-lift
8333	9-79.90	Operator, conveyer
8333	9-73.10	Operator, crane
8333	9-73.20	Operator, crane/bridge
8333	9-73.30	Operator, crane/crawler
8333	9-73.90	Operator, crane/floating
8333	9-73.20	Operator, crane/gantry
8333	9-73.90	Operator, crane/locomotive
8333	9-73.30	Operator, crane/mobile
8333	9-73.90	Operator, crane/railway
8333	9-73.25	Operator, crane/stationary jib
8333	9-73.27	Operator, crane/tower
8333	9-73.30	Operator, crane/tractor
8333	9-73.50	Operator, donkey engine
8333	9-73.55	Operator, drawbridge
8333	9-79.90	Operator, elevator/material-handling
8333	9-73.10	Operator, hoist
8333	9-73.35	Operator, hoist/construction
8333	9-73.40	Operator, hoist/mine
8333	9-89.30	Operator, lock/canal or port
8333	9-79.90	Operator, ropeway/aerial
8333	9-89.90	Operator, sluice/dock
8333	9-73.50	Operator, winch
8333	9-89.90	Sluiceman, dock
8333	9-89.90	Sluicewoman, dock
8333	9-73.45	Tender, skip
8334	9-79.20	Operator, truck/fork-lift
8334	9-79.20	Operator, truck/industrial
8334	9-79.20	Operator, truck/lifting
8340	9-81.90	Boatman
8340	9-81.90	Boatman, ferry
8340	9-81.90	Boatman, motor
8340	9-81.90	Boatman, tug
8340	9-81.20	Boatswain
8340	9-81.90	Boatwoman
8340	9-81.90	Boatwoman, ferry
8340	9-81.90	Boatwoman, motor
8340	9-81.90	Boatwoman, tug
8340	9-81.90	Coxswain, lifeboat
8340	9-81.30	Crewman
8340	9-81.90	Crewman, dredger
8340	9-81.90	Crewman, yacht
8340	9-81.30	Crewwoman
8340	9-81.90	Crewwoman, dredger
8340	9-81.90	Crewwoman, yacht
8340	9-81.40	Deck hand, ship
8340	9-81.90	Hand, cable-ship
8340	9-81.40	Hand, deck
8340	9-89.40	Keeper, lighthouse
8340	9-81.90	Lifeboatman
8340	9-81.90	Lifeboatwoman
8340	9-81.90	Lighterman
8340	9-81.90	Lighterwoman
8340	9-89.40	Lighthouse keeper
8340	9-81.90	Lightshipman
8340	9-81.90	Lightshipwoman
8340	9-81.90	Operator, barge
8340	9-81.30	Sailor
8340	9-81.30	Seaman, able
8340	9-81.40	Seaman, ordinary
8340	9-81.30	Seawoman, able
8340	9-81.40	Seawoman, ordinary
8340	9-81.90	Waterman
8340	9-81.90	Waterwoman
9111	4-52.20	Vendor, fresh-water
9111	4-90.90	Vendor, refreshments
9111	4-90.90	Vendor, refreshments/cinema
9111	4-90.90	Vendor, refreshments/theatre
9111	4-52.20	Vendor, street/food
9112	4-52.20	Hawker
9112	4-52.40	Newsvendor
9112	4-52.20	Pedlar
9112	4-52.20	Tinker
9112	4-52.40	Vendor, newspapers
9112	4-52.20	Vendor, street/non-food products
9112	4-90.90	Vendor, theatre programme
9113	4-52.20	Roundsman, distribution/retail
9113	4-52.20	Roundswoman, distribution/retail

9113	4-52.30	Salesperson, door-to-door
9113	4-52.30	Salesperson, telephone
9120	5-99.90	Billposter
9120	3-70.40	Errand boy
9120	3-70.40	Errand girl
9120	5-99.90	Polisher, shoes
9120	5-99.90	Shiner, shoes
9120	5-99.90	Shoe-black
9120	5-99.90	Shoe-polisher
9120	5-99.90	Shoe-shiner
9120	9-99.10	Washer, hand/street (car windows)
9131	5-40.20	Charworker, domestic
9131	5-40.20	Cleaner, domestic
9131	5-40.20	Helper, domestic
9131	5-40.90	Helper, domestic/parlour
9131	5-40.90	Helper, kitchen/domestic
9131	5-40.20	Houseboy
9131	5-40.20	Housemaid
9132	5-40.50	Chambermaid
9132	5-52.20	Charworker, factory
9132	5-52.20	Charworker, hotel
9132	5-52.20	Charworker, office
9132	5-52.20	Charworker, restaurant
9132	5-52.90	Cleaner, aircraft
9132	5-52.90	Cleaner, bus
9132	9-99.10	Cleaner, factory
9132	5-52.20	Cleaner, hotel
9132	5-52.20	Cleaner, office
9132	5-52.20	Cleaner, restaurant
9132	5-52.90	Cleaner, train
9132	5-52.90	Hand, kitchen
9132	5-32.90	Helper, kitchen/non-domestic
9132	5-40.50	Maid, chamber
9132	9-99.10	Washer, hand/dishes
9133	5-60.40	Dry-cleaner, hand
9133	5-60.70	Ironer, hand
9133	5-60.10	Launderer, hand
9133	5-40.90	Maid, linen
9133	5-60.70	Presser, hand
9133	5-60.50	Spotter, dry-cleaning
9133	5-60.10	Washer, hand/laundry
9141	5-51.30	Caretaker, building
9141	5-51.30	Caretaker, building/cleaning
9141	5-51.20	Concierge, building
9141	5-51.20	Concierge, building/cleaning
9141	5-51.30	Janitor
9141	5-51.40	Sexton
9141	5-51.40	Verger

9142	9-99.10	Cleaner, vehicles
9142	5-52.30	Cleaner, window
9142	9-99.10	Washer, hand/vehicle
9151	5-99.90	Attendant, lift
9151	5-99.90	Bellboy
9151	5-99.90	Caddie, golf
9151	5-99.90	Cellarman
9151	5-99.90	Cellarwoman
9151	3-70.40	Deliverer, hand
9151	4-52.40	Deliverer, hand/newspapers
9151	3-70.40	Messenger
9151	3-70.40	Messenger boy
9151	3-70.40	Messenger girl
9151	3-70.40	Messenger, office
9151	3-70.40	Messenger, telegraph
9151	9-71.90	Porter, luggage
9151	3-70.40	Post-runner
9151	3-70.40	Runner post
9151	3-70.40	Runner, messages
9152	5-99.90	Attendant, amusement park
9152	5-99.90	Attendant, cloakroom
9152	5-99.90	Attendant, fairground
9152	5-99.90	Attendant, fun-fair
9152	5-99.90	Attendant, lavatory
9152	5-99.90	Attendant, parking lot
9152	5-99.90	Attendant, rest-room
9152	3-31.60	Collector, ticket
9152	5-40.55	Concierge, hotel desk
9152	5-99.90	Doorkeeper
9152	5-89.40	Guard, art gallery
9152	5-89.40	Guard, museum
9152	5-40.55	Porter, hotel
9152	5-99.90	Usher
9152	5-89.40	Watchman
9152	5-89.40	Watchman, night
9152	5-89.40	Watchwoman
9152	5-89.40	Watchwoman, night
9153	3-31.60	Collector, coin machine
9153	3-31.60	Collector, coin meter
9153	3-31.60	Collector, turnstile
9153	3-31.60	Collector, vending machine
9153	3-31.60	Collector, vending machine/money
9153	3-31.60	Collector, vending machine/tokens
9153	3-31.90	Meter reader
9161	9-99.10	Collector, garbage
9161	9-99.10	Collector, refuse
9161	9-99.10	Dustman
9161	9-99.10	Dustwoman

9162	9-99.10	Coalman
9162	9-99.10	Coalwoman
9162	9-99.10	Labourer, odd-jobbing
9162	9-99.10	Odd-job person
9162	9-99.10	Sweeper, factory
9162	9-99.10	Sweeper, house
9162	9-99.10	Sweeper, park
9162	9-99.10	Sweeper, street
9162	9-99.10	Sweeper, yard
9211	6-24.90	Cowboy
9211	6-24.90	Cowgirl
9211	6-24.20	Cowherd
9211	6-22.90	Cutter, sugar cane
9211	6-24.90	Drover, cattle
9211	6-24.90	Groom, stud
9211	6-21.05	Hand, farm
9211	6-23.20	Hand, farm/citrus fruit
9211	6-22.40	Hand, farm/cotton picking
9211	6-25.10	Hand, farm/dairy
9211	6-22.10	Hand, farm/field crops
9211	6-23.20	Hand, farm/fruit picking
9211	6-24.50	Hand, farm/fur-bearing animals
9211	6-24.10	Hand, farm/livestock
9211	6-25.90	Hand, farm/milch
9211	6-25.90	Hand, farm/milking
9211	6-23.20	Hand, farm/orchard
9211	6-29.30	Hand, farm/silk worms
9211	6-23.90	Hand, farm/tea plucking
9211	6-21.10	Hand, harvest
9211	6-22.90	Hand, harvest/field crops
9211	6-23.90	Hand, harvest/orchard
9211	6-24.20	Hand, ranch/cattle
9211	6-24.30	Hand, ranch/sheep
9211	6-21.10	Helper, farm
9211	6-24.20	Labourer, cattle station
9211	6-21.10	Labourer, farm
9211	6-21.10	Labourer, farm/casual
9211	6-22.40	Labourer, farm/cotton
9211	6-22.10	Labourer, farm/field crops
9211	6-21.10	Labourer, farm/migrant
9211	6-22.90	Labourer, farm/potato digging
9211	6-21.10	Labourer, farm/seasonal
9211	9-99.10	Labourer, roustabout
9211	6-12.40	Pastoralist
9211	6-22.90	Picker, cotton
9211	6-23.90	Picker, fruit
9211	6-23.90	Plucker, tea
9211	6-24.90	Stable lad
9211	6-24.20	Stockman, beef cattle
9211	6-24.10	Stockman, livestock
9211	6-24.30	Stockman, sheep
9211	6-24.20	Stockwoman, beef cattle

9211	6-24.10	Stockwoman, livestock
9211	6-24.30	Stockwoman, sheep
9212	9-99.10	Labourer, forestry
9212	9-99.10	Stump-grubber
9213	6-49.90	Beachcomber
9213	6-49.90	Gatherer, seaweed
9213	6-49.90	Gatherer, shellfish
9213	9-99.10	Labourer, fishery
9213	9-99.10	Labourer, hunting
9213	9-99.10	Labourer, trapping
9311	7-11.90	Labourer, digging/quarry
9311	7-11.90	Labourer, mining
9312	9-99.10	Labourer, construction
9312	9-99.10	Labourer, construction/dams
9312	9-99.10	Labourer, construction/roads
9312	9-99.10	Labourer, digging/ditch
9312	9-99.10	Labourer, digging/grave
9312	9-99.10	Labourer, digging/trench
9312	9-99.10	Labourer, maintenance
9312	9-99.10	Labourer, maintenance/dams
9312	9-99.10	Labourer, maintenance/roads
9312	9-99.10	Labourer, tube well
9312	9-99.10	Labourer, water well
9312	9-99.10	Land clearer
9312	9-99.10	Navvy
9312	9-99.10	Shoveller
9312	9-99.10	Trackman, railway
9312	9-99.10	Trackwoman, railway
9313	9-99.10	Handyman
9313	9-59.20	Handyman, building maintenance
9313	9-99.10	Handywoman
9313	9-59.20	Handywoman, building maintenance
9313	9-99.10	Hod carrier
9313	9-99.10	Labourer, construction/buildings
9313	9-99.10	Labourer, demolition
9313	9-99.10	Stacker, building construction
9321	9-99.10	Bottle sorter
9321	9-99.10	Labourer, assembling
9321	8-53.50	Winder, armature/hand
9321	8-53.50	Winder, coil/hand
9321	8-53.50	Winder, filament/hand
9321	8-53.50	Winder, rotor coil/hand
9321	8-53.50	Winder, stator coil/hand
9321	8-53.50	Winder, transformer coil/hand
9322	9-71.50	Bagger, hand
9322	9-71.50	Bottler, hand

9322	9-71.50	Crater, hand
9322	7-54.90	Doffer, cloth
9322	7-74.90	Hand, cannery
9322	7-54.90	Hand, shuttle
9322	9-71.60	Labeller, hand
9322	9-99.10	Labourer, manufacturing
9322	7-78.50	Labourer, wine production
9322	9-71.50	Packer, hand
9322	8-31.90	Striker, blacksmith's
9322	7-73.90	Washer, hand/carcass
9322	5-60.90	Washer, hand/cloth
9322	7-56.35	Washer, hand/fibre
9322	7-61.90	Washer, hand/hide
9322	9-99.10	Washer, hand/manufacturing process
9322	5-60.90	Washer, hand/yarn
9322	9-71.50	Wrapper, hand
9331	9-89.90	Berther, dock
9331	9-89.50	Bicyclist
9331	9-99.10	Driver, handtruck
9331	9-89.50	Driver, pedal vehicle
9331	9-89.90	Driver, rickshaw
9331	9-89.50	Driver, tricycle/non-motorised
9331	9-89.50	Rider, bicycle
9331	9-89.50	Rider, tricycle
9331	9-89.50	Tricyclist
9332	9-86.30	Driver, animal-drawn vehicle/mine
9332	9-86.30	Driver, animal-drawn vehicle/quarry
9332	9-86.20	Driver, animal-drawn vehicle/road
9332	9-86.90	Driver, animal train
9332	9-86.90	Driver, animal train/camel
9332	9-86.90	Driver, animal train/mule
9332	9-86.30	Driver, animal/mine
9332	9-86.30	Driver, animal/quarry
9332	9-86.90	Driver, elephant
9332	6-28.90	Driver, farm equipment/non-motorised
9332	9-86.90	Mahout
9333	9-71.20	Docker
9333	9-71.20	Freight handler
9333	9-71.90	Furniture mover
9333	9-71.20	Handler, freight
9333	9-71.35	Loader, aircraft
9333	9-71.40	Loader, boat
9333	9-71.40	Loader, boat/gases
9333	9-71.20	Loader, boat/liquids
9333	9-71.90	Loader, furniture
9333	9-71.30	Loader, railway vehicles
9333	9-71.30	Loader, road vehicles
9333	9-71.30	Loader, road vehicles/lorry
9333	9-71.30	Loader, road vehicles/truck
9333	9-71.20	Loader, ship
9333	9-71.40	Loader, ship/gases
9333	9-71.20	Loader, ship/liquids
9333	9-71.20	Longshoreman
9333	9-71.20	Longshorewoman
9333	9-71.45	Porter, cold-storage
9333	9-71.45	Porter, fish
9333	9-71.45	Porter, food market
9333	9-71.45	Porter, fruit
9333	9-71.30	Porter, goods-loading
9333	9-71.45	Porter, meat
9333	9-71.45	Porter, shop
9333	9-71.45	Porter, warehouse
9333	9-71.90	Remover, furniture
9333	9-71.90	Remover, household goods
9333	9-71.20	Stevedore

See Introduction, Supervisor
See Introduction, Teacher, private lessons
See Introduction, Working proprietor

Index of occupational titles according to ISCO-68 numerical order

0-11.10	2113	Chemist
0-11.20	2113	Chemist, detergents
0-11.20	2113	Chemist, dye
0-11.20	2113	Chemist, food
0-11.20	2113	Chemist, leather
0-11.20	2113	Chemist, organic
0-11.20	2113	Chemist, paint
0-11.20	2113	Chemist, petroleum
0-11.20	2113	Chemist, plastics
0-11.20	2113	Chemist, polymer
0-11.20	2113	Chemist, rubber
0-11.20	2113	Chemist, textile
0-11.30	2113	Chemist, glass
0-11.30	2113	Chemist, inorganic
0-11.30	2113	Chemist, metallurgical
0-11.40	2113	Chemist, corrosion
0-11.40	2113	Chemist, crystallography
0-11.40	2113	Chemist, nuclear
0-11.40	2113	Chemist, physical
0-11.40	2113	Crystallographer
0-11.50	2113	Chemist, analytical
0-11.50	2113	Chemist, quality control
0-11.90	2113	Chemist, pharmaceutical
0-11.90	2113	Pharmacist, industrial
0-12.10	2111	Astronomer
0-12.10	2111	Physicist
0-12.20	2111	Aerodynamicist
0-12.20	2111	Ballistician
0-12.20	2111	Hydrodynamicist
0-12.20	2111	Physicist, ballistics
0-12.20	2111	Physicist, hydrodynamics
0-12.20	2111	Physicist, mechanics
0-12.20	2111	Physicist, rheology
0-12.20	2111	Rheologist
0-12.30	2111	Physicist, heat
0-12.30	2111	Physicist, thermodynamics
0-12.30	2111	Thermodynamicist
0-12.40	2111	Physicist, light
0-12.50	2111	Physicist, acoustics
0-12.50	2111	Physicist, optics
0-12.50	2111	Physicist, sound
0-12.60	2111	Physicist, electricity and magnetism
0-12.70	2111	Physicist, electronics
0-12.80	2111	Physicist, atomic

0-12.80	2111	Physicist, molecular
0-12.80	2111	Physicist, nuclear
0-12.90	2111	Physicist, solid-state
0-12.90	2111	Physicist, theoretical
0-13.20	2114	Geodesist
0-13.20	2114	Geomagnetician
0-13.20	2114	Geomorphologist
0-13.20	2114	Geophysicist
0-13.20	2114	Geophysicist, geomagnetics
0-13.20	2114	Geophysicist, geomorphology
0-13.20	2114	Geophysicist, glaciology
0-13.20	2114	Geophysicist, hydrology
0-13.20	2114	Geophysicist, oceanography
0-13.20	2114	Geophysicist, seismology
0-13.20	2114	Geophysicist, volcanology
0-13.20	2114	Glaciologist
0-13.20	2114	Hydrologist
0-13.20	2114	Oceanographer, geophysical
0-13.20	2114	Seismologist
0-13.20	2114	Volcanologist
0-13.30	2114	Geologist
0-13.30	2114	Geologist, engineering
0-13.30	2114	Geologist, micropalaeontology
0-13.30	2114	Geologist, mining
0-13.30	2114	Geologist, oceanography
0-13.30	2114	Geologist, oil
0-13.30	2114	Geologist, palaeontology
0-13.30	2114	Geologist, petrology
0-13.30	2114	Geologist, stratigraphy
0-13.30	2114	Micropalaeontologist
0-13.30	2114	Oceanographer, geological
0-13.30	2114	Palaeontologist
0-13.30	2114	Petrologist
0-13.30	2114	Stratigrapher
0-13.40	2112	Climatologist
0-13.40	2112	Forecaster, weather
0-13.40	2112	Meteorologist
0-13.40	2112	Meteorologist, climatology
0-13.40	2112	Meteorologist, weather forecasting
0-13.50	2111	Astronomer, radio
0-13.50	2111	Astrophysicist
0-13.50	2111	Physicist, astronomy
0-13.90	2114	Mineralogist
0-14.20	3111	Technician, chemistry

0-24.20	2145	Engineer, mechanical/industrial machinery and tools
0-24.30	2145	Engineer, diesel
0-24.30	2145	Engineer, gas turbine
0-24.30	2145	Engineer, internal combustion engine
0-24.30	2145	Engineer, jet engine
0-24.30	2145	Engineer, locomotive engine
0-24.30	2145	Engineer, mechanical/diesel
0-24.30	2145	Engineer, mechanical/gas turbine
0-24.30	2145	Engineer, mechanical/motors and engines (except marine)
0-24.30	2145	Engineer, motor
0-24.40	2145	Engineer, marine
0-24.40	2145	Engineer, mechanical/motors and engines (marine)
0-24.50	2145	Architect, marine
0-24.50	2145	Architect, naval
0-24.50	2145	Engineer, mechanical/naval
0-24.50	2145	Engineer, mechanical/ship construction
0-24.50	2145	Engineer, naval
0-24.50	2145	Engineer, ship construction
0-24.60	2145	Designer, aircraft
0-24.60	2145	Engineer, aeronautical
0-24.60	2145	Engineer, mechanical/aeronautics
0-24.70	2145	Designer, motor-car
0-24.70	2145	Engineer, automotive
0-24.70	2145	Engineer, mechanical/automotive
0-24.80	2145	Engineer, air-conditioning
0-24.80	2145	Engineer, mechanical/air-conditioning
0-24.80	2145	Engineer, mechanical/heating, ventilation and refrigeration
0-24.80	2145	Engineer, mechanical/refrigeration
0-24.85	2145	Engineer, mechanical/nuclear power
0-24.85	2145	Engineer, nuclear power
0-24.90	2145	Engineer, cryogenic
0-24.90	2145	Engineer, lubrication
0-24.90	2145	Engineer, mechanical/instruments
0-24.90	2145	Technologist, engineering/mechanical
0-24.90	2145	Technologist, welding
0-25.10	2146	Engineer, chemical
0-25.10	2146	Technologist, engineering/chemical
0-25.20	2146	Engineer, chemical/petroleum and natural gas
0-25.20	2146	Engineer, petroleum
0-25.90	2146	Engineer, chemical process
0-25.90	2146	Engineer, natural gas production and distribution
0-25.90	2146	Technologist, chemical process
0-25.90	2146	Technologist, fuel
0-25.90	2146	Technologist, paint
0-25.90	2146	Technologist, plastics
0-25.90	2146	Technologist, polymer
0-25.90	2146	Technologist, rubber
0-25.90	2146	Technologist, tyre
0-26.20	2147	Metallurgist, extractive
0-26.30	2147	Assayer
0-26.30	2147	Metallurgist, foundry
0-26.30	2147	Metallurgist, physical
0-26.30	2147	Metallurgist-assayer
0-26.90	2147	Metallurgist, radioactive minerals
0-27.10	2147	Engineer, mining
0-27.20	2147	Engineer, mining/coal
0-27.30	2147	Engineer, mining/metal
0-27.40	2147	Engineer, mining/petroleum and natural gas
0-27.90	2147	Engineer, mining/diamonds
0-27.90	2147	Technologist, extractive
0-28.10	2149	Engineer, industrial efficiency
0-28.10	2149	Engineer, production
0-28.10	2419	Specialist, business efficiency
0-28.20	2419	Engineer, methods
0-28.20	2149	Engineer, planning
0-28.20	2419	Specialist, sales promotion methods
0-28.30	2149	Engineer, time and motion study
0-28.30	2149	Engineer, work study
0-28.90	2149	Engineer, cost evaluation
0-28.90	2149	Engineer, industrial
0-28.90	2149	Engineer, industrial layout
0-28.90	2149	Engineer, safety
0-29.20	2149	Technologist, ceramics
0-29.20	2149	Technologist, glass
0-29.30	2145	Engineer, mechanical/agriculture
0-29.40	2146	Technologist, brewing
0-29.40	2146	Technologist, fibre
0-29.40	2146	Technologist, food and drink
0-29.40	2146	Technologist, paper
0-29.50	2141	Engineer, traffic
0-29.50	2141	Planner, traffic
0-29.90	2149	Engineer, robotics
0-29.90	2149	Technologist, cement
0-29.90	2149	Technologist, leather
0-29.90	2149	Technologist, packaging
0-29.90	2149	Technologist, printing
0-29.90	2149	Technologist, textiles
0-29.90	2149	Technologist, wood

0-31.20	2148	Surveyor, cadastral
0-31.20	2148	Surveyor, geodesic
0-31.20	2148	Surveyor, land
0-31.20	2148	Surveyor, topographic
0-31.30	2148	Surveyor, mining
0-31.40	2148	Surveyor, hydrographic
0-31.50	2148	Photogrammetrist
0-31.90	2148	Surveyor, aerial
0-31.90	2148	Surveyor, photographic
0-32.10	3118	Draughtsperson
0-32.10	3118	Draughtsperson, engineering
0-32.20	3118	Draughtsperson, die
0-32.20	3118	Draughtsperson, engineering/ marine
0-32.20	3118	Draughtsperson, engineering/ mechanical
0-32.20	3118	Draughtsperson, engineering/ aeronautical
0-32.20	3118	Draughtsperson, jig and tool
0-32.30	3118	Draughtsperson, engineering/ electrical
0-32.30	3118	Draughtsperson, engineering/ electronics
0-32.40	3118	Draughtsperson, engineering/civil
0-32.40	3118	Draughtsperson, engineering/ structural
0-32.50	3118	Draughtsperson, architectural
0-32.60	2148	Cartographer
0-32.60	2148	Cartographer, marine
0-32.60	3118	Draughtsperson, cartographical
0-32.60	3118	Draughtsperson, topographical
0-32.60	2148	Map maker
0-32.70	3118	Draughtsperson, technical
0-32.70	3118	Illustrator, engineering
0-32.70	3118	Illustrator, technical
0-32.80	3118	Draughtsperson, lithographic
0-32.90	3118	Draughtsperson, engineering/ heating and ventilation systems
0-32.90	3118	Draughtsperson, geological
0-33.10	3112	Technician, engineering/civil
0-33.20	3112	Estimator, engineering/civil
0-33.20	2149	Surveyor, quantity
0-33.30	3112	Technician, surveying
0-33.40	3112	Clerk of works
0-33.90	3112	Technician, engineering/civil (construction)
0-33.90	3112	Technician, engineering/civil (dredging)
0-33.90	3112	Technician, engineering/civil (hydraulics)
0-33.90	3112	Technician, engineering/civil (hydrology)
0-33.90	3112	Technician, engineering/civil (irrigation)
0-33.90	3112	Technician, engineering/civil (public health)
0-33.90	3112	Technician, engineering/civil (sanitary)
0-33.90	3112	Technician, engineering/civil (soil mechanics)
0-33.90	3112	Technician, engineering/civil (structural)
0-34.05	3113	Technician, engineering/electrical
0-34.10	3114	Technician, engineering/ electronics
0-34.20	3113	Technician, engineering/electrical (high voltage)
0-34.30	3114	Technician, engineering/ telecommunications
0-34.90	3121	Assistant, computer/ communications
0-34.90	3121	Assistant, computer/database analysis
0-34.90	3121	Assistant, computer/engineering
0-34.90	3121	Assistant, computer/programming
0-34.90	3121	Assistant, computer/systems analysis
0-34.90	3121	Assistant, computer/systems design
0-34.90	3121	Assistant, computer/users' services
0-34.90	3113	Estimator, engineering/electrical
0-34.90	3114	Estimator, engineering/electronics
0-34.90	3121	Technician, computer
0-34.90	3114	Technician, engineering/aerospace
0-34.90	3113	Technician, engineering/electrical (electric illumination)
0-34.90	3113	Technician, engineering/electrical (electric power distribution)
0-34.90	3113	Technician, engineering/electrical (electric power transmission)
0-34.90	3113	Technician, engineering/electrical (electric traction)
0-34.90	3113	Technician, engineering/electrical systems
0-34.90	3114	Technician, engineering/ electronics (computer hardware design)
0-34.90	3114	Technician, engineering/ electronics (information engineering)
0-34.90	3114	Technician, engineering/ electronics (instrumentation)
0-34.90	3114	Technician, engineering/ electronics (semiconductors)
0-34.90	3121	Technician, engineering/systems (computers)

0-34.90	3114	Technician, engineering/telecommunications (aerospace)
0-34.90	3114	Technician, engineering/telecommunications (radar)
0-34.90	3114	Technician, engineering/telecommunications (radio)
0-34.90	3114	Technician, engineering/telecommunications (signal systems)
0-34.90	3114	Technician, engineering/telecommunications (telegraph)
0-34.90	3114	Technician, engineering/telecommunications (telephone)
0-34.90	3114	Technician, engineering/telecommunications (television)
0-35.10	3115	Technician, engineering/mechanical
0-35.20	3115	Technician, engineering/marine
0-35.20	3115	Technician, engineering/mechanical (diesel)
0-35.20	3115	Technician, engineering/mechanical (gas turbine)
0-35.20	3115	Technician, engineering/mechanical (internal combustion)
0-35.20	3115	Technician, engineering/mechanical (jet engine)
0-35.20	3115	Technician, engineering/mechanical (locomotive engine)
0-35.20	3115	Technician, engineering/mechanical (motor)
0-35.20	3115	Technician, engineering/motor and engine
0-35.30	3115	Technician, engineering/aeronautics
0-35.30	3115	Technician, engineering/mechanical (aeronautics)
0-35.50	3115	Technician, engineering/mechanical (air-conditioning)
0-35.50	3115	Technician, engineering/mechanical (heating, ventilation and refrigeration)
0-35.50	3115	Technician, engineering/mechanical (refrigeration)
0-35.90	3115	Estimator, engineering/mechanical
0-35.90	3115	Surveyor, marine
0-35.90	3115	Technician, engineering/mechanical (agriculture)
0-35.90	3115	Technician, engineering/mechanical (automotive)
0-35.90	3115	Technician, engineering/mechanical (industrial machinery and tools)
0-35.90	3115	Technician, engineering/mechanical (instruments)
0-35.90	3115	Technician, engineering/mechanical (lubrication)
0-35.90	3115	Technician, engineering/mechanical (marine)
0-35.90	3115	Technician, engineering/mechanical (naval)
0-35.90	3115	Technician, engineering/mechanical (nuclear power)
0-35.90	3115	Technician, engineering/mechanical (ship construction)
0-35.90	3115	Technician, engineering/naval
0-35.90	3115	Technician, engineering/nuclear power
0-35.90	3123	Technician, robot
0-36.20	3116	Technician, engineering/petroleum
0-36.90	3116	Estimator, engineering/chemical
0-36.90	3116	Technician, engineering/chemical
0-36.90	3116	Technician, engineering/chemical process
0-36.90	3116	Technician, engineering/natural gas production and distribution
0-37.20	3117	Technician, metallurgy/extractive
0-37.30	3117	Technician, metallurgy/foundry
0-37.30	3117	Technician, metallurgy/physical
0-37.90	3117	Technician, metallurgy/assaying
0-37.90	3117	Technician, metallurgy/radioactive minerals
0-38.10	3117	Technician, engineering/mining
0-38.20	3117	Technician, engineering/mining (petroleum and natural gas)
0-38.90	3117	Technician, engineering/mining (coal)
0-38.90	3117	Technician, engineering/mining (diamonds)
0-38.90	3117	Technician, engineering/mining (metal)
0-39.20	3119	Technician, engineering/industrial layout
0-39.20	3119	Technician, engineering/methods
0-39.20	3119	Technician, engineering/planning
0-39.20	3119	Technician, engineering/production
0-39.30	3119	Technician, engineering/industrial efficiency
0-39.30	3119	Technician, engineering/time and motion study
0-39.30	3119	Technician, engineering/work study
0-39.90	3123	Controller, robot
0-39.90	8172	Operator, robot
0-39.90	3119	Technician, engineering/safety
0-39.90	3119	Technician, engineering/systems (except computers)

ISCO-68

0-39.90	3119	Technician, engineering/value
0-39.90	3119	Technician, quantity surveying
0-41.20	3143	Captain, aircraft
0-41.20	3143	Pilot, helicopter
0-41.20	3143	Pilot, seaplane
0-41.30	3143	Pilot, aircraft
0-41.30	3143	Pilot, test
0-41.30	3143	Test pilot, aircraft
0-41.40	3143	Navigator, flight
0-41.50	3143	Engineer, flight
0-41.60	3340	Instructor, flying
0-41.60	3340	Pilot, check
0-42.15	3142	Captain, ship/sea
0-42.15	3142	Master, ship/sea
0-42.20	3142	Captain, ship/inland waterways
0-42.20	3142	Master, ship/inland waterways
0-42.30	3142	Officer, ship/deck
0-42.30	3142	Officer, ship/navigation
0-42.30	3142	Shipmate
0-42.40	3142	Pilot, ship
0-42.50	3142	Captain, port
0-42.50	3142	Superintendent, marine/deck
0-42.90	3142	Pilot, hovercraft
0-42.90	3142	Skipper, yacht
0-43.15	3141	Chief engineer, ship
0-43.20	3141	Engineer, ship
0-43.20	3141	Engineer, ship
0-43.20	3141	Engineer, ship/first
0-43.20	3141	Engineer, ship/second
0-43.20	3141	Engineer, ship/third
0-43.20	3141	Engineer, ship/fourth
0-43.30	3141	Superintendent, marine/technical
0-51.10	2211	Biologist
0-51.20	2211	Botanist
0-51.20	2211	Botanist, ecology
0-51.20	2211	Botanist, economic
0-51.20	2211	Botanist, histology
0-51.20	2211	Botanist, mycology
0-51.20	2211	Botanist, soil
0-51.20	2211	Botanist, taxonomy
0-51.20	2211	Ecologist, plant
0-51.20	2211	Histologist, plant
0-51.20	2211	Mycologist
0-51.20	2211	Taxonomist, plant
0-51.30	2211	Ecologist, animal
0-51.30	2211	Embryologist
0-51.30	2211	Entomologist
0-51.30	2211	Histologist, animal
0-51.30	2211	Ichthyologist
0-51.30	2211	Mammalogist
0-51.30	2211	Ornithologist
0-51.30	2211	Parasitologist
0-51.30	2211	Pisciculturist
0-51.30	2211	Taxonomist, animal
0-51.30	2211	Zoologist
0-51.30	2211	Zoologist, ecology
0-51.30	2211	Zoologist, embryology
0-51.30	2211	Zoologist, entomology
0-51.30	2211	Zoologist, histology
0-51.30	2211	Zoologist, ichthyology
0-51.30	2211	Zoologist, mammalogy
0-51.30	2211	Zoologist, ornithology
0-51.30	2211	Zoologist, parasitology
0-51.30	2211	Zoologist, pisciculture
0-51.30	2211	Zoologist, taxonomy
0-51.90	2211	Biologist, fresh-water
0-51.90	2211	Biologist, marine
0-51.90	2211	Biologist, molecular
0-51.90	2211	Cytologist
0-51.90	2211	Ecologist
0-51.90	2211	Histologist
0-51.90	2211	Hydrobiologist
0-51.90	2211	Immunologist
0-51.90	2211	Taxonomist
0-52.20	2212	Anatomist
0-52.30	2212	Biochemist
0-52.40	2221	Doctor, medical/neurology
0-52.40	2212	Endocrinologist
0-52.40	2212	Epidemiologist
0-52.40	2221	Neurologist
0-52.40	2212	Physiologist
0-52.40	2212	Physiologist, animal
0-52.40	2212	Physiologist, endocrinology
0-52.40	2212	Physiologist, epidemiology
0-52.40	2212	Physiologist, neurology
0-52.40	2212	Physiologist, plant
0-52.50	2211	Bacteriologist
0-52.50	2211	Bacteriologist, agricultural
0-52.50	2211	Bacteriologist, dairy
0-52.50	2211	Bacteriologist, fishery
0-52.50	2211	Bacteriologist, food
0-52.50	2211	Bacteriologist, industrial
0-52.50	2211	Bacteriologist, medical
0-52.50	2211	Bacteriologist, pharmaceutical
0-52.50	2211	Bacteriologist, soil
0-52.50	2211	Bacteriologist, veterinary
0-52.50	2211	Microbiologist
0-52.60	2212	Histopathologist
0-52.60	2212	Neuropathologist
0-52.60	2212	Pathologist
0-52.60	2212	Pathologist, clinical

0-52.60	2212	Pathologist, forensic
0-52.60	2212	Pathologist, histopathology
0-52.60	2212	Pathologist, medical
0-52.60	2212	Pathologist, neuropathology
0-52.60	2212	Pathologist, surgical
0-52.65	2212	Pathologist, animal
0-52.65	2212	Pathologist, veterinary
0-52.70	2212	Pharmacologist
0-52.70	2212	Pharmacologist, toxicology
0-52.70	2212	Toxicologist
0-52.80	2213	Animal scientist
0-52.90	2212	Biophysicist
0-52.90	2211	Cytologist, animal
0-52.90	2211	Cytologist, plant
0-52.90	2211	Engineer, genetics
0-52.90	2211	Geneticist
0-52.90	2211	Geneticist, animal
0-52.90	2211	Geneticist, plant
0-52.90	2212	Pathologist, plant
0-53.20	2213	Agricultural scientist
0-53.20	2213	Agronomist
0-53.20	2213	Crop research scientist
0-53.30	2213	Arboriculturist
0-53.30	2213	Floriculturist
0-53.30	2213	Horticulturist
0-53.30	2213	Olericulturist
0-53.30	2213	Pomologist
0-53.40	2213	Forestry scientist
0-53.40	2213	Silviculturist
0-53.50	2213	Soil scientist
0-53.60	3213	Adviser, agricultural
0-53.60	3213	Adviser, farming
0-53.60	3213	Adviser, forestry
0-53.60	3213	Farm demonstrator
0-54.20	3211	Technician, anatomy
0-54.20	3211	Technician, bacteriology
0-54.20	3211	Technician, biochemistry
0-54.20	3211	Technician, biology
0-54.20	3211	Technician, biophysics
0-54.20	3211	Technician, botany
0-54.20	3211	Technician, ecology
0-54.20	3211	Technician, genetics
0-54.20	3211	Technician, pathology
0-54.20	3211	Technician, pharmacology
0-54.20	3211	Technician, physiology
0-54.20	3211	Technician, zoology
0-54.30	3211	Technician, blood-bank
0-54.30	3211	Technician, cytology
0-54.30	3211	Technician, haematology
0-54.30	3211	Technician, histology
0-54.30	3211	Technician, medical science

0-54.30	3211	Technician, serology
0-54.30	3211	Technician, tissue
0-54.90	3212	Technician, agronomy
0-54.90	3212	Technician, arboriculture
0-54.90	3212	Technician, crop research
0-54.90	3212	Technician, floriculture
0-54.90	3212	Technician, forestry
0-54.90	3212	Technician, horticulture
0-54.90	3212	Technician, olericulture
0-54.90	3212	Technician, pomology
0-54.90	3212	Technician, silviculture
0-54.90	3212	Technician, soil science
0-61.05	2221	Doctor, medical
0-61.05	2221	Medical practitioner
0-61.05	2221	Physician
0-61.10	2221	Surgeon
0-61.20	2221	Anaesthetist
0-61.20	2221	Cardiologist
0-61.20	2221	Dermatologist
0-61.20	2221	Doctor, medical/anaesthetics
0-61.20	2221	Doctor, medical/cardiology
0-61.20	2221	Doctor, medical/dermatology
0-61.20	2221	Doctor, medical/gynaecology
0-61.20	2221	Doctor, medical/obstetrics
0-61.20	2221	Doctor, medical/ophthalmology
0-61.20	2221	Doctor, medical/osteopathy
0-61.20	2221	Doctor, medical/otolaryngology
0-61.20	2221	Doctor, medical/pediatrics
0-61.20	2221	Doctor, medical/psychiatry
0-61.20	2221	Doctor, medical/radiology
0-61.20	2221	Gynaecologist
0-61.20	2221	Obstetrician
0-61.20	2221	Ophthalmologist
0-61.20	2221	Otolaryngologist
0-61.20	2221	Pediatrician
0-61.20	2221	Psychiatrist
0-61.20	2221	Radiologist
0-61.30	2221	Neurosurgeon
0-61.30	2221	Surgeon, cardiology
0-61.30	2221	Surgeon, cardiothoracic
0-61.30	2221	Surgeon, neurosurgery
0-61.30	2221	Surgeon, orthopaedic
0-61.30	2221	Surgeon, osteopathic
0-61.30	2221	Surgeon, plastic
0-61.30	2221	Surgeon, thoracic
0-61.90	2221	Consultant, medical insurance
0-61.90	2221	Doctor, medical/medical insurance consultancy
0-62.10	3221	Assistant, medical
0-62.10	3221	Assistant, medical/family planning

0-63.10	2222	Dentist
0-63.20	2222	Dentist, oral surgery
0-63.20	2222	Dentist, orthodontistry
0-63.20	2222	Dentist, pedodontistry
0-63.20	2222	Dentist, peridontistry
0-63.20	2222	Dentist, prosthodontistry
0-63.20	2222	Orthodontist
0-63.20	2222	Pedodontist
0-63.20	2222	Periodontist
0-63.20	2222	Prosthodontist
0-63.20	2222	Surgeon, oral/dentistry
0-64.20	3225	Assistant, dental
0-64.20	3225	Auxiliary, dental
0-64.30	3225	Assistant, dental/school service
0-64.40	3225	Hygienist, dental
0-64.40	3225	Hygienist, oral
0-64.40	3225	Prophylactician
0-65.10	2223	Surgeon, veterinary
0-65.10	2223	Veterinarian
0-65.10	2223	Veterinarian, epidemiology
0-65.10	2223	Veterinarian, surgery
0-65.90	2223	Epidemiologist, veterinary
0-66.10	3227	Assistant, veterinary
0-66.10	3227	Assistant, veterinary/artificial insemination
0-66.10	3227	Vaccinator, veterinary
0-67.10	2224	Druggist
0-67.10	2224	Pharmacist
0-67.10	2224	Pharmacist, hospital
0-67.10	2224	Pharmacist, retail
0-68.10	3228	Assistant, pharmaceutical
0-69.10	3223	Dietician
0-69.10	3223	Dietician, therapeutic
0-69.20	3223	Nutritionist
0-69.90	3223	Consultant, dietetic/food processing
0-71.10	2230	Matron
0-71.10	3231	Nurse, associate professional/ charge
0-71.10	3231	Nurse, associate professional/ clinic
0-71.10	3231	Nurse, associate professional/ district
0-71.10	2230	Nurse, professional
0-71.10	2230	Nurse, professional/charge
0-71.10	2230	Nurse, professional/clinic
0-71.10	2230	Nurse, professional/district
0-71.10	3231	Officer, principal nursing/associate professional

0-71.10	2230	Officer, principal nursing/ professional
0-71.10	3231	Sister, nursing/associate professional
0-71.10	2230	Sister, nursing/professional
0-71.20	3231	Nurse, associate professional/ anaesthetics
0-71.20	3231	Nurse, associate professional/ maternity
0-71.20	3231	Nurse, associate professional/ obstetrics
0-71.20	3231	Nurse, associate professional/ orthopaedic
0-71.20	3231	Nurse, associate professional/ pediatric
0-71.20	3231	Nurse, associate professional/ psychiatric
0-71.20	2230	Nurse, professional/anaesthetics
0-71.20	2230	Nurse, professional/maternity
0-71.20	2230	Nurse, professional/obstetrics
0-71.20	2230	Nurse, professional/orthopaedic
0-71.20	2230	Nurse, professional/pediatric
0-71.20	2230	Nurse, professional/psychiatric
0-71.30	2230	Health visitor
0-71.40	3231	Nurse, associate professional/ industrial
0-71.40	3231	Nurse, associate professional/ occupational health
0-71.40	2230	Nurse, professional/industrial
0-71.40	2230	Nurse, professional/occupational health
0-71.90	3231	Nurse, associate professional/ consultant
0-71.90	3231	Nurse, associate professional/ school
0-71.90	2230	Nurse, professional/consultant
0-71.90	2230	Nurse, professional/school
0-72.10	3231	Nurse, associate professional
0-73.10	3232	Midwife, associate professional/ district
0-73.10	2230	Midwife, professional
0-73.10	2230	Midwife, professional/district
0-74.10	3232	Midwife, associate professional
0-75.20	3224	Optician, ophthalmic
0-75.20	3224	Optometrist
0-75.30	3224	Optician, dispensing
0-76.20	3226	Electrotherapist
0-76.20	3226	Physiotherapist
0-76.20	3226	Therapist, physical
0-76.30	3226	Therapist, recreational
0-76.40	3226	Masseur
0-76.40	3226	Masseuse

0-77.10	3133	Operator, medical X-ray equipment
0-77.10	3133	Operator, medical radiography equipment
0-77.90	3133	Operator, scanning equipment
0-79.20	2221	Osteopath
0-79.20	3226	Osteopath, lay
0-79.30	3226	Chiropractor
0-79.40	3222	Inspector, sanitary
0-79.40	3222	Sanitarian
0-79.50	3226	Fitter, artificial limb
0-79.50	3226	Technician, orthopaedic
0-79.50	3226	Technician, prosthetic
0-79.90	5141	Chiropodist
0-79.90	3226	Gymnast, remedial
0-79.90	3241	Healer, drugless treatment
0-79.90	3241	Healer, herbal
0-79.90	3241	Healer, village
0-79.90	3229	Homeopath
0-79.90	3241	Naturopath
0-79.90	3133	Operator, audiometric equipment
0-79.90	3133	Operator, electrocardiograph equipment
0-79.90	3133	Operator, electroencephalograph equipment
0-79.90	3229	Orthoepist
0-79.90	3229	Orthophonist
0-79.90	3229	Orthoptist
0-79.90	3226	Podiatrist
0-79.90	3229	Practitioner, homeopathic
0-79.90	3229	Therapist, occupational
0-79.90	3229	Therapist, orientation of the blind
0-79.90	3229	Therapist, speech
0-81.10	2122	Statistician
0-81.20	2122	Statistician, mathematical
0-81.30	2122	Biometrician
0-81.30	2122	Demographer
0-81.30	2122	Statistician, agricultural
0-81.30	2122	Statistician, applied statistics
0-81.30	2122	Statistician, biometrics
0-81.30	2122	Statistician, biostatistics
0-81.30	2122	Statistician, demography
0-81.30	2122	Statistician, economics
0-81.30	2122	Statistician, education
0-81.30	2122	Statistician, engineering
0-81.30	2122	Statistician, finance
0-81.30	2122	Statistician, health
0-81.30	2122	Statistician, opinion-polling
0-81.30	2122	Statistician, physical sciences
0-81.30	2122	Statistician, survey
0-82.20	2121	Mathematician, pure mathematics
0-82.30	2139	Engineer, computer applications
0-82.30	2121	Mathematician, applied mathematics
0-82.40	2121	Analyst, operations research
0-82.50	2121	Actuary
0-82.50	2121	Mathematician, actuarial science
0-83.10	2131	Analyst, systems/computers
0-83.10	2149	Analyst, systems/except computers
0-84.20	2131	Database administrator
0-84.20	2132	Programmer
0-84.20	2132	Programmer, communications
0-84.20	2132	Programmer, database
0-84.20	2132	Programmer, technical
0-84.90	3434	Assistant, accounting
0-84.90	3434	Assistant, actuarial
0-84.90	3434	Assistant, mathematical
0-84.90	3434	Assistant, statistical
0-90.10	2441	Econometrician
0-90.10	2441	Economist
0-90.10	2441	Economist, econometrics
0-90.20	2441	Economist, agricultural
0-90.20	2441	Economist, finance
0-90.20	2441	Economist, international trade
0-90.20	2441	Economist, labour
0-90.20	2441	Economist, price
0-90.20	2441	Economist, taxation
0-90.30	2419	Analyst, market research
1-10.10	2411	Accountant
1-10.10	2411	Accountant, chartered
1-10.10	2411	Accountant, company
1-10.10	2411	Accountant, municipal
1-10.10	2411	Accountant, public
1-10.20	2411	Accountant, auditing
1-10.20	2411	Auditor
1-10.90	2411	Accountant, cost
1-21.10	2421	Advocate
1-21.10	2421	Attorney
1-21.10	2421	Barrister
1-21.10	2421	Lawyer
1-21.10	2421	Lawyer, civil
1-21.10	2421	Lawyer, conveyancing
1-21.10	2421	Lawyer, criminal
1-21.10	2421	Lawyer, litigation
1-21.10	2421	Prosecutor
1-21.10	2421	Solicitor
1-22.10	2422	Chief justice
1-22.10	2422	Judge

ISCO-68

1-31.55	2310	Teacher, post-secondary education/education
1-31.55	2310	Teacher, post-secondary education/pedagogy
1-31.60	2310	Teacher, post-secondary education/agricultural science
1-31.60	2310	Teacher, post-secondary education/agronomy
1-31.60	2310	Teacher, post-secondary education/animal husbandry
1-31.60	2310	Teacher, post-secondary education/fishery
1-31.60	2310	Teacher, post-secondary education/forestry
1-31.60	2310	Teacher, post-secondary education/horticulture
1-31.60	2310	Teacher, post-secondary education/husbandry
1-31.60	2310	Teacher, post-secondary education/silviculture
1-31.65	2310	Teacher, post-secondary education/anthropology
1-31.65	2310	Teacher, post-secondary education/archaeology
1-31.65	2310	Teacher, post-secondary education/demography
1-31.65	2310	Teacher, post-secondary education/geography
1-31.65	2310	Teacher, post-secondary education/government
1-31.65	2310	Teacher, post-secondary education/history
1-31.65	2310	Teacher, post-secondary education/international affairs
1-31.65	2310	Teacher, post-secondary education/numismatics
1-31.65	2310	Teacher, post-secondary education/palaeography
1-31.65	2310	Teacher, post-secondary education/philosophy
1-31.65	2310	Teacher, post-secondary education/political science
1-31.65	2310	Teacher, post-secondary education/prehistory
1-31.65	2310	Teacher, post-secondary education/psychology
1-31.65	2310	Teacher, post-secondary education/religion
1-31.65	2310	Teacher, post-secondary education/social science
1-31.65	2310	Teacher, post-secondary education/sociology
1-31.65	2310	Teacher, post-secondary education/theology
1-31.70	2310	Teacher, post-secondary education/art criticism
1-31.70	2310	Teacher, post-secondary education/art history
1-31.70	2310	Teacher, post-secondary education/journalism
1-31.70	2310	Teacher, post-secondary education/languages
1-31.70	2310	Teacher, post-secondary education/linguistics
1-31.70	2310	Teacher, post-secondary education/literature
1-31.70	2310	Teacher, post-secondary education/philology
1-31.75	2310	Teacher, post-secondary education/chiropractic
1-31.75	2310	Teacher, post-secondary education/dietetics
1-31.75	2310	Teacher, post-secondary education/medical therapy
1-31.75	2310	Teacher, post-secondary education/nursing
1-31.75	2310	Teacher, post-secondary education/occupational therapy
1-31.75	2310	Teacher, post-secondary education/optometry
1-31.75	2310	Teacher, post-secondary education/osteopathy
1-31.75	2310	Teacher, post-secondary education/physiotherapy
1-31.75	2310	Teacher, post-secondary education/radiology
1-31.80	2310	Teacher, post-secondary education/construction technology
1-31.80	2310	Teacher, post-secondary education/engineering (technology)
1-31.80	2310	Teacher, post-secondary education/industrial arts
1-31.80	2310	Teacher, post-secondary education/industrial design
1-31.80	2310	Teacher, post-secondary education/industrial technology
1-31.80	2310	Teacher, post-secondary education/metallurgy
1-31.80	2310	Teacher, post-secondary education/mining technology
1-31.80	2310	Teacher, post-secondary education/textile technology
1-31.90	2310	Teacher, post-secondary education/advertising
1-31.90	2310	Teacher, post-secondary education/art
1-31.90	2310	Teacher, post-secondary education/computer science
1-31.90	2310	Teacher, post-secondary education/dancing
1-31.90	2310	Teacher, post-secondary education/drama

ISCO-68

1-62.20	3471	Designer, poster
1-62.20	3471	Designer, typographical
1-62.20	3471	Illustrator, advertising
1-62.20	3471	Illustrator, book
1-62.30	3471	Decorator, interior
1-62.30	3471	Decorator, motion picture set
1-62.30	3471	Designer, decoration
1-62.30	3471	Designer, interior decoration
1-62.40	2452	Artist, fashion creation
1-62.40	3471	Designer, commercial products
1-62.40	3471	Designer, dress
1-62.40	3471	Designer, fashion
1-62.40	3471	Designer, furniture
1-62.40	3471	Designer, industrial products
1-62.40	3471	Designer, jewellery
1-62.40	3471	Designer, package
1-62.40	3471	Designer, textile
1-62.50	3471	Decorator, display
1-62.50	3471	Decorator, display/windows
1-62.50	3471	Designer, display
1-62.50	3471	Designer, display/windows
1-62.50	3471	Designer, exhibition
1-62.90	3471	Designer, armorial
1-62.90	3471	Designer, scenery
1-62.90	3471	Designer, stage set
1-62.90	3471	Tattooist
1-63.10	3131	Photographer
1-63.20	3131	Photographer, portrait
1-63.30	3131	Photographer, advertising
1-63.30	3131	Photographer, commercial
1-63.30	3131	Photographer, fashion
1-63.30	3131	Photographer, industrial
1-63.40	3131	Photographer, news
1-63.40	3131	Photographer, press
1-63.50	3131	Assistant, motion picture
1-63.60	3131	Cameraman, motion picture
1-63.60	3131	Camerawoman, motion picture
1-63.60	3131	Cinematographer
1-63.60	3131	Operator, camera/cinematography
1-63.60	3131	Operator, camera/motion picture
1-63.70	3131	Operator, camera/television
1-63.90	3131	Microphotographer
1-63.90	3131	Photographer, aerial
1-63.90	3131	Photographer, architecture
1-63.90	3131	Photographer, commercial illustration
1-63.90	3131	Photographer, medical
1-63.90	3131	Photographer, microphotography
1-63.90	3131	Photographer, police
1-63.90	3131	Photographer, scientific
1-71.20	2453	Composer, music
1-71.20	2453	Musicologist

1-71.30	2453	Arranger, music
1-71.30	2453	Orchestrator
1-71.30	2453	Transcriber, music
1-71.35	3473	Band leader
1-71.35	3473	Bandmaster
1-71.35	3473	Conductor, band
1-71.35	2453	Conductor, orchestra
1-71.40	2453	Bassoonist
1-71.40	2453	Cellist
1-71.40	2453	Clarinettist
1-71.40	2453	Drummer
1-71.40	2453	Guitarist
1-71.40	2453	Harpist
1-71.40	2453	Instrumentalist
1-71.40	2453	Musician, instrumental
1-71.40	3473	Musician, night-club
1-71.40	3473	Musician, street
1-71.40	2453	Oboist
1-71.40	2453	Organist
1-71.40	2453	Percussionist
1-71.40	2453	Pianist
1-71.40	2453	Saxophonist
1-71.40	3473	Singer, night-club
1-71.40	2453	Sitar player
1-71.40	2453	Trombonist
1-71.40	2453	Trumpeter
1-71.40	2453	Violinist
1-71.45	2453	Baritone
1-71.45	2453	Contralto
1-71.45	2453	Mezzo-soprano
1-71.45	2453	Singer, bass
1-71.45	2453	Singer, choir
1-71.45	2453	Singer, concert
1-71.45	2453	Singer, jazz
1-71.45	2453	Singer, opera
1-71.45	2453	Singer, popular music
1-71.45	3473	Singer, street
1-71.45	2453	Soprano
1-71.45	2453	Tenor
1-71.50	2453	Choirmaster
1-71.50	2453	Chorus master
1-71.50	2453	Conductor, vocal group
1-71.90	1229	Director, musical
1-72.20	2454	Arranger, ballet
1-72.20	2454	Choreographer
1-72.30	2454	Ballerina
1-72.30	2454	Dancer, ballet
1-72.30	2454	Dancer, ballroom
1-72.30	3473	Dancer, chorus
1-72.30	3473	Dancer, night-club
1-72.30	3473	Dancer, tap

ISCO-68

1-92.30	2445	Psychologist, social
1-92.40	2442	Anthropologist
1-92.40	2442	Archaeologist
1-92.40	2442	Ethnologist
1-92.50	2442	Geographer
1-92.50	2442	Geographer, economic
1-92.50	2442	Geographer, physical
1-92.50	2442	Geographer, political
1-92.60	2443	Historian
1-92.60	2443	Historian, economic
1-92.60	2443	Historian, political
1-92.60	2443	Historian, social
1-92.70	2443	Philosopher
1-92.70	2443	Philosopher, political
1-92.70	2443	Political scientist
1-92.90	2443	Genealogist
1-93.10	3460	Social worker, associate professional
1-93.10	3460	Social worker, associate professional/enterprise
1-93.10	2446	Social worker, professional
1-93.10	2446	Social worker, professional/enterprise
1-93.20	3460	Almoner, associate professional
1-93.20	2446	Almoner, professional
1-93.20	3460	Caseworker, associate professional
1-93.20	3460	Caseworker, associate professional/child welfare
1-93.20	3460	Caseworker, associate professional/family welfare
1-93.20	3460	Caseworker, associate professional/social welfare
1-93.20	2446	Caseworker, professional
1-93.20	2446	Caseworker, professional/child welfare
1-93.20	2446	Caseworker, professional/family welfare
1-93.20	2446	Caseworker, professional/social welfare
1-93.20	3460	Housefather, associate professional
1-93.20	2446	Housefather, professional
1-93.20	3460	Housemother, associate professional
1-93.20	2446	Housemother, professional
1-93.20	3460	Social worker, associate professional/medical
1-93.20	2446	Social worker, professional/medical
1-93.20	3460	Welfare worker, associate professional
1-93.20	3460	Welfare worker, associate professional/moral welfare
1-93.20	3460	Welfare worker, associate professional/prison
1-93.20	2446	Welfare worker, professional
1-93.20	2446	Welfare worker, professional/moral welfare
1-93.20	2446	Welfare worker, professional/prison
1-93.30	3460	Social worker, associate professional/community centre
1-93.30	3460	Social worker, associate professional/cultural centre
1-93.30	2446	Social worker, professional/community centre
1-93.30	2446	Social worker, professional/cultural centre
1-93.30	3460	Warden, community centre/associate professional
1-93.30	2446	Warden, community centre/professional
1-93.40	1229	Headmaster
1-93.40	1229	Headmistress
1-93.40	3460	Housemaster, associate professional/approved school
1-93.40	2446	Housemaster, professional/approved school
1-93.40	3460	Parole officer, associate professional
1-93.40	2446	Parole officer, professional
1-93.40	3460	Probation officer, associate professional
1-93.40	2446	Probation officer, professional
1-93.40	3460	Social worker, associate professional/delinquency
1-93.40	3460	Social worker, associate professional/probation
1-93.40	2446	Social worker, professional/delinquency
1-93.40	2446	Social worker, professional/probation
1-93.40	3460	Warden, probation home/associate professional
1-93.40	2446	Warden, probation home/professional
1-93.50	3460	Social worker, associate professional/psychiatric
1-93.50	2446	Social worker, professional/psychiatric
1-93.50	3460	Welfare worker, associate professional/mental health
1-93.50	2446	Welfare worker, professional/mental health
1-93.90	3152	Inspector, safety and health/child care
1-93.90	3460	Social worker, associate professional/family planning
1-93.90	3460	Social worker, associate professional/home-help service

ISCO-68

2-02.10	1120	Diplomatic representative, embassy
2-02.10	1120	Director-general, government administration/regional
2-02.10	1120	Director-general, government department
2-02.10	1120	Director-general, intergovernmental organisation
2-02.10	1120	Governor, prison
2-02.10	1120	Head, chancery
2-02.10	1120	Head, government department
2-02.10	1120	High commissioner, government
2-02.10	1120	Inspector-general, police
2-02.10	1120	Paymaster-general, government
2-02.10	1120	Postmaster-general, government
2-02.10	1120	Registrar-general, government
2-02.10	1120	Representative, diplomatic
2-02.10	1120	Secretary, embassy
2-02.10	1120	Secretary, government/non-legislative
2-02.10	1120	Secretary-general, government administration
2-02.10	1120	Secretary-general, government administration/deputy
2-02.10	1120	Senior official, government
2-02.10	1120	Under-secretary, government
2-11.10	1210	Chairperson, enterprise
2-11.10	1210	Chairperson, organisation
2-11.10	1141	Chairperson, political party
2-11.10	1210	Chancellor, university
2-11.10	1210	Chief executive, enterprise
2-11.10	1210	Chief executive, enterprise/agriculture
2-11.10	1210	Chief executive, enterprise/business services
2-11.10	1210	Chief executive, enterprise/cleaning
2-11.10	1210	Chief executive, enterprise/communications
2-11.10	1210	Chief executive, enterprise/construction
2-11.10	1210	Chief executive, enterprise/cultural activities
2-11.10	1210	Chief executive, enterprise/education
2-11.10	1210	Chief executive, enterprise/fishing
2-11.10	1210	Chief executive, enterprise/forestry
2-11.10	1210	Chief executive, enterprise/health
2-11.10	1210	Chief executive, enterprise/hotel
2-11.10	1210	Chief executive, enterprise/hunting
2-11.10	1210	Chief executive, enterprise/manufacturing
2-11.10	1210	Chief executive, enterprise/personal care
2-11.10	1210	Chief executive, enterprise/recreation
2-11.10	1210	Chief executive, enterprise/restaurant
2-11.10	1210	Chief executive, enterprise/retail trade
2-11.10	1210	Chief executive, enterprise/social work
2-11.10	1210	Chief executive, enterprise/sporting activities
2-11.10	1210	Chief executive, enterprise/storage
2-11.10	1210	Chief executive, enterprise/transportation
2-11.10	1210	Chief executive, enterprise/travel agency
2-11.10	1210	Chief executive, enterprise/wholesale trade
2-11.10	1210	Chief executive, organisation
2-11.10	1210	Chief executive, organisation/cultural activities
2-11.10	1210	Chief executive, organisation/education
2-11.10	1210	Chief executive, organisation/extra-territorial organisations
2-11.10	1210	Chief executive, organisation/fishing
2-11.10	1210	Chief executive, organisation/forestry
2-11.10	1210	Chief executive, organisation/health
2-11.10	1210	Chief executive, organisation/public administration
2-11.10	1210	Chief executive, organisation/recreation
2-11.10	1210	Chief executive, organisation/social work
2-11.10	1210	Chief executive, organisation/sporting activities
2-11.10	1142	Director-general, employers' organisation
2-11.10	1210	Director-general, enterprise
2-11.10	1210	Director-general, enterprise/agriculture
2-11.10	1210	Director-general, enterprise/business services
2-11.10	1210	Director-general, enterprise/cleaning
2-11.10	1210	Director-general, enterprise/communications
2-11.10	1210	Director-general, enterprise/construction
2-11.10	1210	Director-general, enterprise/cultural activities
2-11.10	1210	Director-general, enterprise/education
2-11.10	1210	Director-general, enterprise/fishing

ISCO-68

2-11.10	1210	Director-general, enterprise/ forestry
2-11.10	1210	Director-general, enterprise/health
2-11.10	1210	Director-general, enterprise/hotel
2-11.10	1210	Director-general, enterprise/ hunting
2-11.10	1210	Director-general, enterprise/ manufacturing
2-11.10	1210	Director-general, enterprise/ personal care
2-11.10	1210	Director-general, enterprise/ recreation
2-11.10	1210	Director-general, enterprise/ restaurant
2-11.10	1210	Director-general, enterprise/retail trade
2-11.10	1210	Director-general, enterprise/social work
2-11.10	1210	Director-general, enterprise/ sporting activities
2-11.10	1210	Director-general, enterprise/ storage
2-11.10	1210	Director-general, enterprise/ transportation
2-11.10	1210	Director-general, enterprise/travel agency
2-11.10	1210	Director-general, enterprise/ wholesale trade
2-11.10	1210	Director-general, organisation
2-11.10	1210	Director-general, organisation/ cultural activities
2-11.10	1210	Director-general, organisation/ education
2-11.10	1210	Director-general, organisation/ extra-territorial organisations
2-11.10	1210	Director-general, organisation/ fishing
2-11.10	1210	Director-general, organisation/ forestry
2-11.10	1210	Director-general, organisation/ health
2-11.10	1210	Director-general, organisation/ public administration
2-11.10	1210	Director-general, organisation/ recreation
2-11.10	1210	Director-general, organisation/ social work
2-11.10	1210	Director-general, organisation/ sporting activities
2-11.10	1317	General manager, business services
2-11.10	1318	General manager, cleaning
2-11.10	1316	General manager, communications
2-11.10	1313	General manager, construction
2-11.10	1319	General manager, cultural activities
2-11.10	1319	General manager, education
2-11.10	1319	General manager, health
2-11.10	1312	General manager, manufacturing
2-11.10	1318	General manager, personal care
2-11.10	1319	General manager, recreation
2-11.10	1319	General manager, social work
2-11.10	1319	General manager, sporting activities
2-11.10	1316	General manager, storage
2-11.10	1316	General manager, transport
2-11.10	1319	General manager, travel agency
2-11.10	1141	Leader, political party
2-11.10	1142	Leader, trade union
2-11.10	1210	Managing director, enterprise
2-11.10	1210	Managing director, enterprise/ agriculture
2-11.10	1210	Managing director, enterprise/ business services
2-11.10	1210	Managing director, enterprise/ cleaning
2-11.10	1210	Managing director, enterprise/ communications
2-11.10	1210	Managing director, enterprise/ construction
2-11.10	1210	Managing director, enterprise/ cultural activities
2-11.10	1210	Managing director, enterprise/ education
2-11.10	1210	Managing director, enterprise/ fishing
2-11.10	1210	Managing director, enterprise/ forestry
2-11.10	1210	Managing director, enterprise/ health
2-11.10	1210	Managing director, enterprise/ hotel
2-11.10	1210	Managing director, enterprise/ hunting
2-11.10	1210	Managing director, enterprise/ manufacturing
2-11.10	1210	Managing director, enterprise/ personal care
2-11.10	1210	Managing director, enterprise/ recreation
2-11.10	1210	Managing director, enterprise/ restaurant
2-11.10	1210	Managing director, enterprise/retail trade
2-11.10	1210	Managing director, enterprise/ social work
2-11.10	1210	Managing director, enterprise/ sporting activities
2-11.10	1210	Managing director, enterprise/ storage
2-11.10	1210	Managing director, enterprise/ transport

ISCO-68

ISCO-68

3-91.20	4131	Clerk, freight/dispatching
3-91.20	4131	Clerk, freight/inward
3-91.20	4131	Clerk, freight/receiving
3-91.20	4131	Clerk, freight/routing
3-91.20	4131	Clerk, freight/shipping
3-91.20	4131	Clerk, freight/traffic
3-91.30	4131	Clerk, stock
3-91.30	4131	Clerk, stock/control
3-91.30	4131	Clerk, stock/control (inventory)
3-91.30	4131	Clerk, stock/control (records)
3-91.30	4131	Clerk, stock/records
3-91.40	4131	Attendant, tool crib
3-91.40	4131	Clerk, stock/storeroom
3-91.40	4131	Clerk, supply
3-91.40	4131	Clerk, warehouse
3-91.40	4131	Storekeeper
3-91.50	4131	Clerk, weighing
3-91.50	4131	Clerk, weighing/scale
3-91.50	4131	Clerk, weighing/tally
3-91.90	4131	Clerk, depository/furniture
3-92.20	4132	Clerk, order/materials
3-92.20	4132	Clerk, planning/materials
3-92.20	4132	Clerk, schedule/materials
3-92.30	4132	Clerk, production planning
3-92.30	4132	Clerk, production planning/ coordination
3-92.30	4132	Clerk, production planning/ schedule
3-93.20	3431	Assistant, correspondence
3-93.30	4190	Clerk, compilation/directory
3-93.30	4190	Clerk, records/personnel
3-93.30	4190	Compiler, clerical/directory
3-93.40	3432	Assistant, barrister's
3-93.40	3432	Assistant, legal
3-93.40	3432	Assistant, solicitor's
3-93.40	3432	Clerk, conveyancing
3-93.40	3432	Clerk, court
3-93.40	3432	Clerk, judge's
3-93.40	3432	Clerk, law
3-93.40	3432	Clerk, probate
3-93.50	3432	Assistant, broker's
3-93.50	3432	Assistant, insurance/adjustment
3-93.50	3432	Assistant, insurance/claims
3-93.50	3432	Assistant, insurance/policy
3-93.50	3432	Clerk, insurance
3-93.90	3432	Assistant, bank
3-93.90	4190	Clerk, list/addresses
3-93.90	4143	Clerk, listing
3-93.90	4144	Public writer
3-93.90	4144	Scribe
3-94.10	4222	Receptionist
3-94.20	4222	Receptionist, hotel
3-94.30	4222	Receptionist, dental
3-94.30	4222	Receptionist, medical
3-94.40	4221	Clerk, travel
3-94.40	4221	Clerk, travel /airlines
3-94.40	4221	Clerk, travel /railway
3-94.40	4221	Clerk, travel agency
3-94.40	4221	Clerk, travel agency/bookings
3-94.40	4221	Clerk, travel agency/reservations
3-94.90	4222	Clerk, appointments
3-94.90	4222	Clerk, information
3-94.90	4222	Clerk, inquiries
3-95.20	4141	Clerk, book-loan
3-95.20	4141	Clerk, library
3-95.20	4141	Clerk, library/acquisitions
3-95.30	4141	Clerk, classification
3-95.30	4141	Clerk, filing
3-95.30	4141	Clerk, index
3-99.20	4122	Clerk, actuarial
3-99.20	4122	Clerk, statistical
3-99.30	4143	Clerk, coding
3-99.30	4143	Clerk, coding/data-processing
3-99.30	4143	Clerk, coding/statistics
3-99.30	4143	Coder, clerical
3-99.30	4143	Coder, clerical/data-processing
3-99.30	4143	Coder, clerical/statistics
3-99.40	4143	Clerk, proof reading
3-99.40	4143	Clerk, proof reading/printing
3-99.40	2451	Proof-reader
3-99.40	4143	Proof-reader, clerical
3-99.50	4190	Clerk, addressing machine
3-99.50	4141	Clerk, document duplication
3-99.50	4141	Clerk, photocopying
3-99.50	4141	Clerk, reproduction processes/ office
3-99.50	4141	Mimeographer
3-99.90	4143	Clerk, document-sorting machine
3-99.90	4144	Clerk, form filling assistance
3-99.90	4143	Clerk, franking machine
3-99.90	4190	Clerk, list/mail
3-99.90	4143	Clerk, scripts
3-99.90	4133	Clerk, transport
4-00.20	1233	Department manager, marketing
4-00.20	1224	Department manager, production and operations/retail trade
4-00.20	1224	Department manager, production and operations/wholesale trade (export)
4-00.20	1314	General manager, wholesale trade

4-43.30	3417	Inspector, insurance claims
4-43.30	3417	Valuer
4-51.20	5220	Salesperson, wholesale establishment
4-51.30	5220	Attendant, shop
4-51.30	5230	Salesperson, kiosk
4-51.30	5230	Salesperson, market
4-51.30	5220	Salesperson, retail establishment
4-51.30	5220	Salesperson, shop
4-51.30	5230	Salesperson, street stall
4-51.40	5210	Mannequin
4-51.40	5210	Model, clothing display
4-51.40	5210	Model, fashion
4-51.50	5220	Demonstrator
4-51.90	5220	Assistant, shop/orders
4-51.90	5220	Attendant, petrol pump
4-51.90	5220	Attendant, service station/ automobiles
4-51.90	5210	Model, advertising
4-52.20	9112	Hawker
4-52.20	9112	Pedlar
4-52.20	9113	Roundsman, distribution/retail
4-52.20	9113	Roundswoman, distribution/retail
4-52.20	9112	Tinker
4-52.20	9111	Vendor, fresh-water
4-52.20	9111	Vendor, street/food
4-52.20	9112	Vendor, street/non-food products
4-52.30	9113	Salesperson, door-to-door
4-52.30	9113	Salesperson, telephone
4-52.40	9151	Deliverer, hand/newspapers
4-52.40	9112	Newsvendor
4-52.40	9112	Vendor, newspapers
4-90.20	4214	Money-lender
4-90.20	4214	Pawnbroker
4-90.90	9111	Vendor, refreshments
4-90.90	9111	Vendor, refreshments/cinema
4-90.90	9111	Vendor, refreshments/theatre
4-90.90	9112	Vendor, theatre programme
5-00.20	1225	Department manager, production and operations/hotel
5-00.20	1315	General manager, motel
5-00.30	1225	Department manager, production and operations/restaurant
5-00.30	1315	General manager, restaurant
5-00.40	1231	Purser, ship
5-00.90	1315	General manager, boarding-house
5-00.90	1315	General manager, cafe
5-00.90	1315	General manager, camping site
5-00.90	1315	General manager, canteen
5-00.90	1315	General manager, hostel
5-00.90	1315	General manager, refreshment-room
5-10.20	1315	General manager, hotel
5-10.20	1315	General manager, inn
5-10.20	1315	Innkeeper
5-10.30	1315	Restaurateur
5-10.40	1315	General manager, guest-house
5-10.50	1315	Barkeeper
5-10.50	1315	General manager, snack-bar
5-10.90	1315	General manager, caravan park
5-10.90	1315	General manager, lodging-house
5-10.90	1315	General manager, self-service restaurant
5-20.20	5121	Housekeeper
5-20.20	5121	Housekeeper, executive
5-20.40	5121	Chief steward, hotel
5-20.40	5121	Chief stewardess, hotel
5-20.40	5121	Steward, hotel
5-20.40	5121	Steward, house
5-20.40	5121	Stewardess, hotel
5-20.40	5121	Stewardess, house
5-20.50	5111	Chief steward, ship
5-20.50	5111	Chief stewardess, ship
5-20.60	5121	Matron, housekeeping
5-20.90	5121	Butler
5-20.90	5121	Warden, camp
5-20.90	5121	Warden, dormitory
5-31.20	5122	Chef de cuisine
5-31.20	5122	Cook, head
5-31.30	5122	Cook
5-31.30	5122	Cook, restaurant
5-31.30	5122	Cook, vegetable
5-31.40	7412	Pastry-cook
5-31.50	5122	Cook, ship
5-31.50	5122	Cook, ship's mess
5-31.90	5122	Cook, special diets
5-31.90	5122	Cook, work camp
5-32.10	5123	Steward, mess
5-32.10	5123	Steward, ship/dining saloon
5-32.10	5123	Stewardess, mess
5-32.10	5123	Stewardess, ship/dining saloon
5-32.10	5123	Waiter
5-32.10	5123	Waiter, railway dining car
5-32.10	5123	Waitress
5-32.10	5123	Waitress, railway dining car
5-32.20	5123	Maitre d'hotel
5-32.20	5123	Waiter, head
5-32.20	5123	Waitress, head
5-32.30	5123	Steward, ship/mess

ISCO-68

5-32.30	5123	Stewardess, ship/mess
5-32.30	5123	Waiter, banquet
5-32.30	5123	Waiter, formal
5-32.30	5123	Waitress, banquet
5-32.30	5123	Waitress, formal
5-32.40	5123	Steward, wine
5-32.40	5123	Stewardess, ship/wine
5-32.40	5123	Waiter, wine
5-32.40	5123	Waitress, wine
5-32.50	5123	Bartender
5-32.90	5123	Attendant, canteen
5-32.90	5123	Attendant, restaurant seating
5-32.90	9132	Helper, kitchen/non-domestic
5-40.20	9131	Charworker, domestic
5-40.20	9131	Cleaner, domestic
5-40.20	9131	Helper, domestic
5-40.20	9131	Houseboy
5-40.20	9131	Housemaid
5-40.30	5142	Companion, man's
5-40.30	5142	Maid, lady's
5-40.30	5142	Maid, personal
5-40.30	5142	Manservant
5-40.30	5142	Valet
5-40.30	5142	Valet, personal
5-40.35	5131	Attendant, schoolchildren
5-40.35	5131	Governess, children
5-40.35	5131	Nanny
5-40.35	5131	Nursemaid
5-40.40	5142	Companion
5-40.40	5142	Companion, lady's
5-40.50	9132	Chambermaid
5-40.50	9132	Maid, chamber
5-40.55	9152	Concierge, hotel desk
5-40.55	9152	Porter, hotel
5-40.60	5111	Steward, ship
5-40.60	5111	Steward, ship/cabin
5-40.60	5111	Stewardess, ship
5-40.60	5111	Stewardess, ship/cabin
5-40.70	7433	Wardrobe mistress, stage and studio
5-40.90	5113	Guide, travel/bus
5-40.90	9131	Helper, domestic/parlour
5-40.90	9131	Helper, kitchen/domestic
5-40.90	9133	Maid, linen
5-40.90	5142	Valet, hotel
5-51.20	9141	Concierge, building
5-51.20	9141	Concierge, building/cleaning
5-51.30	9141	Caretaker, building
5-51.30	9141	Caretaker, building/cleaning
5-51.30	9141	Janitor
5-51.40	9141	Sexton
5-51.40	9141	Verger
5-52.20	9132	Charworker, factory
5-52.20	9132	Charworker, hotel
5-52.20	9132	Charworker, office
5-52.20	9132	Charworker, restaurant
5-52.20	9132	Cleaner, hotel
5-52.20	9132	Cleaner, office
5-52.20	9132	Cleaner, restaurant
5-52.30	9142	Cleaner, window
5-52.40	7143	Chimney sweep
5-52.40	7143	Cleaner, chimney flue
5-52.40	7143	Sweep, chimney
5-52.90	9132	Cleaner, aircraft
5-52.90	9132	Cleaner, bus
5-52.90	9132	Cleaner, train
5-52.90	9132	Hand, kitchen
5-52.90	9132	Kitchen hand
5-60.10	9133	Launderer, hand
5-60.10	9133	Washer, hand/laundry
5-60.20	8264	Machine-operator, laundering
5-60.20	8264	Machine-operator, washing/laundry
5-60.20	8264	Operator, cleaning equipment/laundry
5-60.30	8264	Machine-operator, dry-cleaning
5-60.40	9133	Dry-cleaner, hand
5-60.50	9133	Spotter, dry-cleaning
5-60.60	8264	Machine-operator, laundry
5-60.60	8264	Machine-operator, pressing/laundry
5-60.70	9133	Ironer, hand
5-60.70	9133	Presser, hand
5-60.90	8264	Calenderer, laundry
5-60.90	8264	Machine-operator, drying/laundry
5-60.90	8264	Operator, cleaning equipment/carpets
5-60.90	9322	Washer, hand/cloth
5-60.90	9322	Washer, hand/yarn
5-70.20	5141	Beautician, make-up/studio
5-70.20	5141	Hairdresser, women
5-70.30	5141	Barber
5-70.30	5141	Hairdresser
5-70.30	5141	Hairdresser, men
5-70.40	5141	Beautician
5-70.40	5141	Cosmetologist
5-70.50	5141	Manicurist
5-70.60	5141	Beautician, make-up/stage
5-70.60	5141	Make-up artist, stage
5-70.60	5141	Make-up artist, studio
5-70.70	5141	Attendant, bath
5-70.70	5141	Attendant, bath/hot-room

ISCO-68

5-70.70	5141	Attendant, bath/sauna
5-70.70	5141	Attendant, bath/turkish
5-70.90	5141	Dresser, wig/stage
5-70.90	5141	Trichologist
5-81.10	5161	Fire-fighter
5-81.10	5161	Patrolwoman, forest fire
5-81.20	3151	Inspector, fire
5-81.20	3151	Specialist, fire prevention
5-81.30	5161	Salvageman, fire
5-81.30	5161	Salvagewoman, fire
5-81.40	5161	Fire-fighter, aircraft accidents
5-81.90	3151	Fire investigator
5-82.20	5162	Constable
5-82.20	5162	Patrolman, police
5-82.20	5162	Patrolwoman, police
5-82.20	5162	Police officer
5-82.20	5162	Police officer, harbour
5-82.20	5162	Police officer, river
5-82.20	5162	Police officer, traffic
5-82.30	3450	Agent, inquiry/police
5-82.30	3450	Detective
5-82.30	3450	Inspector, police
5-82.40	5162	Guard, police force
5-82.40	5169	Guard, security
5-89.20	3450	Detective, store
5-89.20	3450	Private detective
5-89.20	3450	Private investigator
5-89.30	5163	Gaoler
5-89.30	5163	Guard, prison
5-89.30	5163	Warden, prison
5-89.30	5163	Warder, prison
5-89.40	9152	Guard, art gallery
5-89.40	9152	Guard, museum
5-89.40	5169	Patrolman, security
5-89.40	5169	Patrolwoman, security
5-89.40	9152	Watchman
5-89.40	9152	Watchman, night
5-89.40	9152	Watchwoman
5-89.40	9152	Watchwoman, night
5-89.90	3432	Bailiff
5-89.90	5169	Bodyguard
5-89.90	5169	Coastguard
5-89.90	7216	Frogman, salvage
5-89.90	7216	Frogwoman, salvage
5-89.90	5169	Guard, beach
5-89.90	3151	Inspector, building
5-89.90	5169	Life-guard
5-89.90	5169	Patrolman, beach
5-89.90	5169	Patrolwoman, beach
5-89.90	5169	Warden, traffic
5-91.20	4142	Courrier, travel
5-91.20	5113	Guide, travel
5-91.30	5113	Guide, art gallery
5-91.30	5113	Guide, museum
5-91.30	5113	Guide, travel/art gallery
5-91.30	5113	Guide, travel/museum
5-91.30	5113	Guide, travel/sightseeing
5-91.90	5113	Guide, travel/alpine
5-91.90	5113	Guide, travel/fishing
5-91.90	5113	Guide, travel/game park
5-91.90	5113	Guide, travel/hunting
5-91.90	5113	Guide, travel/industrial establishment
5-91.90	5113	Guide, travel/safari
5-92.10	5143	Funeral director
5-92.20	5143	Mortician
5-92.20	5143	Undertaker
5-92.30	5143	Embalmer
5-92.90	5143	Attendant, funeral
5-92.90	5143	Attendant, undertaker's
5-99.20	4213	Bookmaker
5-99.20	4213	Bookmaker, betting pool
5-99.20	4213	Bookmaker, pari-mutuel system
5-99.20	4213	Bookmaker, ticket writing
5-99.20	4213	Bookmaker, totalisator
5-99.30	4213	Croupier
5-99.30	4213	Croupier, gambling-table
5-99.40	5132	Aid, dental
5-99.40	5132	Aid, nursing/clinic
5-99.40	5133	Aid, nursing/home
5-99.40	5132	Aid, nursing/hospital
5-99.40	5132	Ambulance man
5-99.40	5132	Ambulance woman
5-99.40	5132	Attendant, dental
5-99.40	5132	Attendant, first-aid
5-99.40	5132	Attendant, hospital
5-99.40	5133	Attendant, nursing/home
5-99.40	5132	Attendant, nursing/except home
5-99.40	5132	Orderly
5-99.50	5139	Aid, pharmacy
5-99.60	5139	Aid, veterinary
5-99.70	5111	Attendant, airport
5-99.70	5111	Attendant, flight
5-99.70	5111	Attendant, ship's cabin
5-99.70	5111	Purser, aircraft
5-99.90	9152	Attendant, amusement park
5-99.90	9152	Attendant, cloakroom
5-99.90	9152	Attendant, fairground
5-99.90	9152	Attendant, fun-fair
5-99.90	9152	Attendant, lavatory
5-99.90	9151	Attendant, lift

5-99.90	9152	Attendant, parking lot	6-12.20	6111	Farmer, tobacco
5-99.90	9152	Attendant, rest-room	6-12.20	6111	Farmer, vegetable
5-99.90	9151	Bellboy	6-12.20	6111	Farmer, wheat
5-99.90	9120	Billposter	6-12.20	6111	Grower, field crop
5-99.90	9151	Caddie, golf	6-12.20	6111	Grower, field vegetable
5-99.90	9151	Cellarman	6-12.20	6111	Grower, soya-bean
5-99.90	9151	Cellarwoman	6-12.20	6111	Grower, sugar-beet
5-99.90	9152	Doorkeeper	6-12.20	6112	Grower, tree crop
5-99.90	5149	Escort, social	6-12.20	6111	Planter, cotton
5-99.90	7143	Exterminator	6-12.20	6111	Planter, sugar-cane
5-99.90	5149	Host, club	6-12.20	6111	Planter, tobacco
5-99.90	5149	Hostess, club	6-12.30	6112	Farmer, cocoa
5-99.90	5210	Model, artist's	6-12.30	6112	Farmer, coconut
5-99.90	8290	Operator, merry-go-round	6-12.30	6112	Farmer, coffee
5-99.90	5149	Partner, dancing	6-12.30	6112	Farmer, copra
5-99.90	9120	Polisher, shoes	6-12.30	6112	Farmer, fruit
5-99.90	9120	Shiner, shoes	6-12.30	6112	Farmer, hop
5-99.90	9120	Shoe-black	6-12.30	6112	Farmer, nut
5-99.90	9120	Shoe-polisher	6-12.30	6112	Farmer, orchard
5-99.90	9120	Shoe-shiner	6-12.30	6112	Farmer, rubber plantation
5-99.90	9152	Usher	6-12.30	6112	Farmer, shrub crop
			6-12.30	6112	Farmer, tea plantation
6-00.20	1221	Department manager, production and operations/agriculture	6-12.30	6112	Farmer, tree crop
			6-12.30	6112	Farmer, viniculture
6-00.20	1311	General manager, agriculture	6-12.30	6112	Grower, cocoa
6-00.20	1311	General manager, fishing	6-12.30	6112	Grower, coconut
6-00.20	1311	General manager, forestry	6-12.30	6112	Grower, coffee
6-00.20	1311	General manager, hunting	6-12.30	6112	Grower, rubber
			6-12.30	6112	Grower, shrub crop
6-11.10	6114	Farm worker, skilled/mixed crop	6-12.30	6112	Planter, copra
6-11.10	6210	Farm worker, skilled/subsistence farming	6-12.30	6112	Planter, tea
			6-12.30	6112	Viniculturist
6-11.10	6114	Farmer, mixed crop	6-12.30	6112	Winegrower
6-11.10	6130	Farmer, mixed farming	6-12.40	6121	Breeder, cattle
6-11.10	6210	Farmer, subsistence farming	6-12.40	6121	Breeder, stud
			6-12.40	6121	Farmer, cattle
6-12.20	6111	Farm worker, skilled/field crops	6-12.40	6121	Farmer, fur/domestic animals
6-12.20	6111	Farmer, alfalfa	6-12.40	6121	Farmer, horse breeding
6-12.20	6111	Farmer, cereal	6-12.40	6121	Farmer, horse raising
6-12.20	6111	Farmer, corn	6-12.40	6121	Farmer, livestock
6-12.20	6111	Farmer, cotton	6-12.40	6121	Farmer, pig
6-12.20	6111	Farmer, field crop	6-12.40	6121	Farmer, ranch
6-12.20	6111	Farmer, field vegetable	6-12.40	6121	Farmer, sheep raising
6-12.20	6111	Farmer, flax	6-12.40	6121	Farmer, stud breeding
6-12.20	6111	Farmer, grain	6-12.40	6121	Grazier
6-12.20	6111	Farmer, groundnut	6-12.40	9211	Pastoralist
6-12.20	6111	Farmer, jute	6-12.40	6121	Raiser, cattle
6-12.20	6111	Farmer, maize	6-12.40	6121	Raiser, pig
6-12.20	6111	Farmer, rice	6-12.40	6121	Raiser, sheep
6-12.20	6111	Farmer, sisal	6-12.40	6121	Rancher, cattle
6-12.20	6111	Farmer, soya-bean	6-12.50	6121	Farmer, dairy
6-12.20	6111	Farmer, sugar-beet	6-12.50	6121	Farmer, milk
6-12.20	6111	Farmer, sugar-cane	6-12.60	6122	Breeder, poultry

6-12.60	6122	Farmer, battery
6-12.60	6122	Farmer, chicken
6-12.60	6122	Farmer, duck
6-12.60	6122	Farmer, egg production
6-12.60	6122	Farmer, goose
6-12.60	6122	Farmer, poultry/hatching and breeding
6-12.60	6122	Farmer, turkey
6-12.60	6122	Hatcher-breeder, poultry
6-12.70	6113	Gardener, greenhouse
6-12.70	6113	Grower, carnation
6-12.70	6113	Grower, flower
6-12.70	6113	Grower, horticultural nursery
6-12.70	6113	Grower, market gardening
6-12.70	6113	Grower, nursery
6-12.70	6113	Grower, nursery/bulbs
6-12.70	6113	Grower, nursery/seeds
6-12.70	6113	Grower, nursery/vegetables
6-12.70	6113	Grower, rose
6-12.70	6113	Grower, tulip
6-12.70	6113	Horticultural grower
6-12.70	6113	Nurseryman
6-12.70	6113	Nurserywoman
6-12.90	6123	Apiarist
6-12.90	6129	Breeder, bird
6-12.90	6129	Breeder, game bird
6-12.90	6129	Breeder, laboratory animal
6-12.90	6129	Breeder, laboratory animal/mice
6-12.90	6129	Breeder, lion
6-12.90	6129	Breeder, reindeer
6-12.90	6129	Breeder, reptile
6-12.90	6129	Breeder, reptile/snake
6-12.90	6129	Breeder, snail
6-12.90	6123	Farmer, apiary
6-12.90	6123	Farmer, beekeeping
6-12.90	6124	Farmer, mixed-animal husbandry
6-12.90	6123	Farmer, sericulture
6-12.90	6123	Farmer, silkworm raising
6-12.90	6113	Grower, mushroom
6-12.90	6113	Grower, nursery/spices
6-12.90	6113	Grower, osier
6-12.90	6113	Grower, reed
6-12.90	6129	Keeper, aviary
6-12.90	6129	Keeper, kennel
6-12.90	6129	Raiser, laboratory animal
6-12.90	6129	Raiser, ostrich
6-12.90	6123	Raiser, silkworm
6-12.90	6123	Sericulturist
6-21.05	6130	Farm worker, skilled/mixed farming
6-21.05	9211	Hand, farm
6-21.10	9211	Hand, harvest
6-21.10	9211	Helper, farm
6-21.10	9211	Labourer, farm
6-21.10	9211	Labourer, farm/casual
6-21.10	9211	Labourer, farm/migrant
6-21.10	9211	Labourer, farm/seasonal
6-22.10	9211	Hand, farm/field crops
6-22.10	9211	Labourer, farm/field crops
6-22.20	6111	Farm worker, skilled/potato
6-22.20	6111	Farm worker, skilled/sugar-beet
6-22.20	6111	Farm worker, skilled/vegetables
6-22.30	6111	Farm worker, skilled/wheat
6-22.40	6111	Farm worker, skilled/cotton
6-22.40	9211	Hand, farm/cotton picking
6-22.40	9211	Labourer, farm/cotton
6-22.50	6111	Farm worker, skilled/rice
6-22.60	6111	Farm worker, skilled/sugar-cane
6-22.90	9211	Cutter, sugar cane
6-22.90	6111	Farm worker, skilled/flax
6-22.90	6111	Farm worker, skilled/groundnut
6-22.90	6111	Farm worker, skilled/jute
6-22.90	6111	Farm worker, skilled/tobacco
6-22.90	9211	Hand, harvest/field crops
6-22.90	9211	Labourer, farm/potato digging
6-22.90	9211	Picker, cotton
6-23.10	6112	Plantation worker, skilled/shrub crop
6-23.10	6112	Plantation worker, skilled/tree crop
6-23.20	6112	Farm worker, skilled/fruit
6-23.20	6112	Farm worker, skilled/grove
6-23.20	6112	Farm worker, skilled/orchard
6-23.20	6112	Farm worker, skilled/shrub crop
6-23.20	6112	Farm worker, skilled/tree crop
6-23.20	9211	Hand, farm/citrus fruit
6-23.20	9211	Hand, farm/fruit picking
6-23.20	9211	Hand, farm/orchard
6-23.30	6112	Farm worker, skilled/vineyard
6-23.30	6112	Farmer, rubber
6-23.30	6112	Farmer, tea
6-23.30	6112	Farmer, vineyard
6-23.40	6112	Farm worker, skilled/tea
6-23.40	6112	Plantation worker, skilled/tea
6-23.50	6112	Farm worker, skilled/rubber
6-23.50	6112	Plantation worker, skilled/rubber
6-23.90	6112	Budder-grafter, fruit tree
6-23.90	6112	Farm worker, skilled/cocoa
6-23.90	6112	Farm worker, skilled/coffee
6-23.90	6112	Farm worker, skilled/hops
6-23.90	6112	Grafter, fruit tree
6-23.90	9211	Hand, farm/tea plucking
6-23.90	9211	Hand, harvest/orchard
6-23.90	9211	Picker, fruit
6-23.90	9211	Plucker, tea

6-23.90	6112	Pruner, fruit trees
6-23.90	6112	Pruner, shrub crops
6-23.90	6112	Tapper, rubber tree
6-24.10	6121	Farm worker, skilled/livestock
6-24.10	6124	Farm worker, skilled/mixed-animal husbandry
6-24.10	9211	Hand, farm/livestock
6-24.10	9211	Stockman, livestock
6-24.10	9211	Stockwoman, livestock
6-24.20	9211	Cowherd
6-24.20	6121	Farm worker, skilled/cattle
6-24.20	9211	Hand, ranch/cattle
6-24.20	9211	Labourer, cattle station
6-24.20	9211	Stockman, beef cattle
6-24.20	9211	Stockwoman, beef cattle
6-24.30	6121	Farm worker, skilled/sheep
6-24.30	9211	Hand, ranch/sheep
6-24.30	6121	Shepherd
6-24.30	9211	Stockman, sheep
6-24.30	9211	Stockwoman, sheep
6-24.40	6121	Breeder, cat
6-24.40	6121	Breeder, dog
6-24.40	6121	Farm worker, skilled/pig
6-24.40	6121	Farmer, sheep
6-24.40	6121	Farmer, sheep/astrakhan
6-24.50	6121	Farm worker, skilled/domestic fur-bearing animals
6-24.50	6129	Farm worker, skilled/non-domesticated fur-bearing animals
6-24.50	6129	Farmer, fur/non-domesticated animals
6-24.50	9211	Hand, farm/fur-bearing animals
6-24.90	9211	Cowboy
6-24.90	9211	Cowgirl
6-24.90	9211	Drover, cattle
6-24.90	6129	Farm worker, skilled/ostrich
6-24.90	6121	Farmer, pelt
6-24.90	9211	Groom, stud
6-24.90	6129	Horse-breaker
6-24.90	6129	Keeper, zoo
6-24.90	6121	Kennel worker, skilled
6-24.90	6121	Shearer, sheep
6-24.90	9211	Stable lad
6-24.90	6129	Trainer, dog
6-24.90	6129	Trainer, horse-breaking
6-24.90	6129	Trainer, racehorse
6-24.90	6129	Zoo keeper
6-25.10	6121	Farm worker, skilled/dairy
6-25.10	9211	Hand, farm/dairy
6-25.90	9211	Hand, farm/milch
6-25.90	9211	Hand, farm/milking

6-26.10	6122	Farm worker, skilled/poultry
6-26.20	6122	Hatchery worker, skilled/poultry
6-26.20	6122	Operator, incubator
6-27.20	6113	Market gardener
6-27.20	6113	Market gardening worker, skilled
6-27.30	6113	Budder-grafter, shrubs
6-27.30	6113	Farm worker, skilled/nursery
6-27.30	6113	Gardener, seed propagation
6-27.30	6113	Greenhouse worker, skilled
6-27.30	6113	Horticultural worker, skilled
6-27.40	6113	Gardener
6-27.40	6113	Gardener, jobbing
6-28.20	8331	Driver, tractor
6-28.20	8331	Operator, agricultural machinery
6-28.20	8331	Operator, baler/farm
6-28.20	8331	Operator, combiner/agricultural
6-28.20	8331	Operator, harvester
6-28.20	8331	Operator, motorised farm equipment
6-28.20	8331	Operator, thresher
6-28.90	9332	Driver, farm equipment/non-motorised
6-29.20	6123	Apiary worker, skilled
6-29.20	6123	Beekeeper
6-29.20	6123	Beekeeping worker, skilled
6-29.30	9211	Hand, farm/silk worms
6-29.30	6123	Sericultural worker, skilled
6-29.40	6112	Tapper, maple syrup
6-29.40	6112	Tapper, pine resin
6-29.40	6112	Tapper, toddy
6-29.50	6111	Farm worker, skilled/irrigation
6-29.50	6111	Irrigation worker, skilled
6-29.60	6113	Gardener, park
6-29.60	6113	Greenkeeper
6-29.60	6113	Groundsman
6-29.60	6113	Groundswoman
6-29.90	6113	Cultivator, mushroom
6-29.90	6113	Farm worker, skilled/mushroom
6-31.10	6141	Logger
6-31.10	6141	Lumberjack
6-31.20	6141	Bucker, logging
6-31.20	6141	Cross-cutter, logging
6-31.20	6141	Cutter, timber/forestry
6-31.20	6141	Feller, logging
6-31.20	6141	Feller-bucker, tree
6-31.30	6141	Climber, logging
6-31.30	6141	High climber, logging
6-31.30	6141	Topper, logging
6-31.40	6141	Assembler, raft

6-31.40	6141	Driver, raft/logging
6-31.40	6141	Maker, log-raft
6-31.40	6141	Rider, timber
6-31.90	6141	Cutter, pole and pile
6-31.90	6141	Cutter, railway tie
6-31.90	6141	Cutter, sleeper
6-31.90	6141	Scaler, log
6-31.90	6141	Woodcutter, forest
6-32.20	6141	Forester
6-32.30	6141	Forestry worker, skilled
6-32.30	6141	Forestry worker, skilled/ afforestation
6-32.30	6141	Woodman
6-32.30	6141	Woodwoman
6-32.40	6141	Cruiser, timber
6-32.50	5161	Fire-fighter, forest
6-32.50	5161	Patrolman, forest fire
6-32.90	6141	Marker, timber
6-32.90	6141	Marker, tree
6-32.90	8331	Operator, motorised forestry equipment
6-32.90	6141	Planter, forestry
6-32.90	6141	Pruner-trimmer, forestry
6-32.90	6141	Ranger, forest
6-32.90	6141	Stripper, cork bark
6-41.20	6153	Crewman, drifter
6-41.20	6153	Crewman, trawler
6-41.20	6153	Crewwoman, drifter
6-41.20	6153	Crewwoman, trawler
6-41.20	6153	Fisherman, deep-sea
6-41.20	6153	Fisherwoman, deep-sea
6-41.20	6153	Fishery worker, skilled/deep-sea
6-41.30	6152	Fisherman, coastal waters
6-41.30	6152	Fisherman, inland waters
6-41.30	6152	Fisherwoman, coastal waters
6-41.30	6152	Fisherwoman, inland waters
6-41.30	6152	Fishery worker, skilled/coastal waters
6-41.30	6152	Fishery worker, skilled/inland
6-49.20	6151	Farm worker, skilled/fish
6-49.20	6151	Farmer, fish
6-49.20	6151	Farmer, seafood
6-49.20	6151	Fishery worker, skilled/pisciculture
6-49.20	6151	Hatcher, fish
6-49.20	6151	Hatchery worker, skilled/fish
6-49.30	6151	Farm worker, skilled/oyster
6-49.30	6151	Farmer, oyster
6-49.40	6154	Crewman, whaling vessel
6-49.40	6154	Crewwoman, whaling vessel
6-49.40	6154	Fisherwoman, seal

6-49.40	6154	Flenser, whale
6-49.40	6154	Harpooner, whale
6-49.40	6154	Stripper, blubber
6-49.50	6154	Fisherman, seal
6-49.50	6154	Hunter, seal
6-49.50	6154	Hunter, whale
6-49.60	6154	Hunter
6-49.60	6154	Trapper, fur
6-49.60	6154	Trapper-hunter, fur
6-49.90	9213	Beachcomber
6-49.90	6151	Cultivator, algae
6-49.90	6151	Cultivator, pearl
6-49.90	6152	Diver, oyster
6-49.90	6152	Diver, pearl
6-49.90	6152	Diver, sponge
6-49.90	6151	Farm worker, skilled/seafood
6-49.90	6154	Game beater
6-49.90	5169	Game-warden
6-49.90	6129	Gamekeeper
6-49.90	9213	Gatherer, seaweed
6-49.90	9213	Gatherer, shellfish
6-49.90	6129	Keeper, animal reserve
6-49.90	6129	Laboratory worker, skilled/animals
6-49.90	6152	Sponge hooker
6-49.90	5169	Warden, bird sanctuary
6-49.90	5169	Warden, wild life
6-49.90	6129	Zoo worker, skilled
7-11.05	7111	Miner
7-11.05	7111	Miner, surface
7-11.05	7111	Miner, underground
7-11.10	7111	Quarrier
7-11.20	8111	Machine-operator, channelling/ mine
7-11.20	8111	Machine-operator, cutting/mine
7-11.30	8111	Machine-operator, drilling/mine
7-11.30	8111	Machine-operator, drilling/quarry
7-11.40	8111	Machine-operator, mining/ continuous
7-11.50	7112	Blaster
7-11.50	7112	Shotfirer
7-11.60	7111	Bolter, roof/mine
7-11.60	7111	Piler, mine
7-11.60	7111	Timbering worker, mine
7-11.60	7111	Timbering worker, quarry
7-11.60	7111	Timbering worker, underground
7-11.70	7111	Sampler, mine
7-11.90	7111	Clipper, mine
7-11.90	7111	Drawer, prop/mine
7-11.90	7111	Drawer, prop/quarry
7-11.90	7111	Drawer, timber/mine
7-11.90	7111	Drawer, timber/quarry
7-11.90	9311	Labourer, digging/quarry

7-11.90	9311	Labourer, mining
7-11.90	7111	Miner, hydraulic/placer mining
7-11.90	7111	Robber, timber/mine
7-11.90	7111	Sampler, core
7-11.90	7111	Sampler, quarry
7-12.10	8112	Machine-operator, mineral processing
7-12.10	8112	Machine-operator, stone processing
7-12.10	8112	Operator, mineral-processing plant
7-12.10	8112	Operator, stone-processing plant
7-12.20	8112	Machine-operator, splitting/stone
7-12.20	7113	Splitter, stone
7-12.30	8112	Machine-operator, crushing/coal
7-12.30	8112	Machine-operator, crushing/ mineral ore
7-12.30	8112	Machine-operator, crushing/rock
7-12.30	8112	Machine-operator, crushing/stone
7-12.40	8112	Machine-operator, milling/minerals
7-12.40	8112	Machine-operator, milling/stone
7-12.40	8112	Machine-operator, pulverising/ minerals
7-12.50	8112	Tender, jig
7-12.60	8112	Floatation worker, copper
7-12.60	8112	Floatation worker, minerals
7-12.60	8112	Floatation worker, molybdenum
7-12.70	8112	Precipitator, gold
7-12.70	8112	Precipitator, silver
7-12.80	8112	Operator, breaker/gyratory
7-12.80	8112	Operator, cone/mine
7-12.80	8112	Operator, gravitation equipment/ mine
7-12.90	8112	Cyanide worker, separation equipment
7-12.90	8112	Machine-operator, magnetic ore processing
7-12.90	8290	Machine-operator, pelletising
7-12.90	8112	Machine-operator, washing/ minerals
7-13.20	8113	Operator, derrick/oil and gas wells
7-13.30	8113	Operator, drilling equipment/rotary (oil and gas wells)
7-13.40	8113	Operator, drilling equipment/cable (oil and gas wells)
7-13.50	3117	Cementer, oil and gas wells
7-13.60	8113	Operator, pulling equipment/oil and gas wells
7-13.70	3117	Acidiser, oil and gas well
7-13.70	3117	Treater, well acidising
7-13.80	8113	Operator, boring equipment/wells
7-13.80	8113	Operator, drilling equipment/wells
7-13.90	3117	Shooter, oil and gas wells

7-21.10	8121	Furnace-operator, converting/steel
7-21.10	8121	Furnace-operator, refining/steel
7-21.10	8121	Furnace-operator, smelting/metal
7-21.20	8121	Furnace-operator, smelting/metal (blast furnace)
7-21.30	8121	Furnace-operator, refining/steel (open-hearth furnace)
7-21.40	8121	Furnace-operator, converting/steel (oxygen furnace)
7-21.50	8121	Furnace-operator, converting/steel (bessemer furnace)
7-21.50	8121	Furnace-operator, converting/steel (thomas furnace)
7-21.60	8121	Furnace-operator, refining/steel (electric-arc furnace)
7-21.70	8121	Furnace-operator, converting/non-ferrous metal
7-21.70	8121	Furnace-operator, refining/non-ferrous metal
7-21.90	8121	Furnace-operator, puddling
7-22.20	8122	Operator, rolling-mill/steel (hot-rolling)
7-22.30	8122	Operator, rolling-mill/steel (continuous)
7-22.40	8122	Operator, rolling-mill/steel (cold-rolling)
7-22.50	8122	Operator, rolling-mill/non-ferrous metal
7-22.60	8122	Operator, rolling-mill/seamless pipe and tube
7-22.70	8122	Manipulator, rolling-mill
7-23.20	8122	Furnace-operator, melting/metal
7-23.20	8122	Furnace-operator, melting/metal (crucible furnace)
7-23.20	8122	Furnace-operator, melting/metal (electric-arc furnace)
7-23.20	8122	Furnace-operator, melting/metal (open-hearth furnace)
7-23.20	8122	Furnace-operator, melting/metal (reverberatory furnace)
7-23.30	8122	Furnace-operator, melting/metal (cupola furnace)
7-23.40	8122	Furnace-operator, reheating/metal
7-24.20	7221	Caster, metal
7-24.20	7211	Ladler, metal
7-24.20	8122	Machine-operator, casting/metal
7-24.20	8122	Machine-operator, pouring/metal
7-24.20	8122	Operator, ladle/metal pouring
7-24.30	8122	Machine-operator, casting/ centrifugal (cylindrical metal products)
7-24.40	8122	Machine-operator, casting/die (non-ferrous metal)

7-24.50	8122	Machine-operator, casting/continuous rod (non-ferrous metal)
7-24.90	8211	Machine-operator, jewellery production
7-24.90	7313	Maker, jewellery
7-25.10	7211	Moulder, metal castings
7-25.20	7211	Moulder, metal castings/bench
7-25.20	7211	Moulder, metal castings/stump
7-25.20	7211	Moulder, metal castings/tub
7-25.30	7211	Moulder, metal castings/floor and pit
7-25.30	7211	Moulder, metal castings/pit
7-25.40	8211	Machine-operator, moulding/metal
7-25.50	7211	Coremaker, metal
7-25.60	8211	Machine-operator, core-blowing
7-25.60	8211	Machine-operator, coremaking/metal
7-25.60	8211	Machine-operator, coremaking/tube
7-26.20	8123	Annealer
7-26.20	8123	Furnace-operator, annealing/metal
7-26.30	8123	Furnace-operator, hardening/metal
7-26.30	8123	Furnace-operator, heat-treating/metal
7-26.30	8123	Operator, heat-treating plant/metal
7-26.40	8123	Furnace-operator, case-hardening/metal
7-26.40	8123	Nitrider
7-26.40	8123	Operator, carbonation equipment/metal
7-26.50	8123	Machine-operator, tempering/metal
7-26.90	8123	Machine-operator, mixing/metal
7-27.20	7221	Drawer, wire
7-27.30	8124	Machine-operator, drawing/wire
7-27.40	8124	Machine-operator, drawing/metal
7-27.40	8124	Machine-operator, drawing/seamless pipe
7-27.40	8124	Machine-operator, drawing/seamless tube
7-27.50	8124	Machine-operator, extruding/metal
7-27.50	8124	Press-operator, extruding/metal
7-27.50	7223	Setter-operator, extruding machine/metalworking
7-28.20	8223	Electroplater
7-28.20	8223	Machine-operator, electroplating/metal
7-28.20	8223	Machine-operator, refining/metal
7-28.30	8223	Machine-operator, dipping/metal
7-28.30	8223	Machine-operator, galvanising/metal
7-28.30	8223	Machine-operator, plating/metal
7-28.40	8223	Machine-operator, coating/metal
7-28.40	8223	Machine-operator, coating/wire
7-28.40	8223	Machine-operator, plating/wire
7-28.50	8223	Machine-operator, spraying/metal
7-28.50	7142	Sprayer, metal
7-28.90	8223	Anodiser
7-28.90	8223	Sherardiser
7-29.20	7224	Bluer, metal
7-29.20	8223	Machine-operator, bluing/metal
7-29.30	8223	Fettler
7-29.30	7224	Finisher, cast metal articles
7-29.30	8223	Machine-operator, finishing/cast metal articles
7-29.30	8223	Machine-operator, shotblasting/metal
7-29.30	8223	Operator, sandblasting equipment/metal
7-29.40	7224	Cleaner, metal
7-29.40	8223	Machine-operator, degreasing/metal
7-29.40	8223	Operator, cleaning equipment/metal
7-31.20	8141	Machine-operator, seasoning/wood
7-31.20	7421	Wood seasoner
7-31.30	7421	Dipper, wood treatment
7-31.30	7421	Impregnator, wood
7-31.30	8141	Machine-operator, treating/wood
7-31.30	7421	Wood treater
7-31.90	7421	Wood incising worker
7-31.90	7421	Woodworker, treating
7-32.10	8141	Lathe-operator, cutting/wood
7-32.10	8141	Machine-operator, boring/wood
7-32.10	8141	Machine-operator, drilling/wood
7-32.10	8141	Machine-operator, milling/wood
7-32.10	8141	Machine-operator, planing/wood
7-32.10	8141	Machine-operator, wood processing
7-32.10	8141	Operator, sawmill
7-32.10	8141	Operator, wood-processing plant
7-32.10	8141	Sawyer, sawmill
7-32.20	8141	Machine-operator, sawing/wood
7-32.20	8141	Sawyer, edge
7-32.30	8141	Operator, band saw
7-32.30	8141	Operator, sawmill/band-saw
7-32.40	8141	Lathe-operator, cutting/veneer
7-32.40	8141	Machine-operator, cutting/veneer
7-32.40	8141	Machine-operator, cutting/wood

ISCO-68

7-32.50	8141	Machine-operator, plywood core laying
7-32.60	8141	Press-operator, plywood
7-32.60	8141	Press-operator, veneer
7-32.70	7421	Grader, wood
7-32.70	7421	Wood grader
7-32.90	8141	Machine-operator, shaping/wood
7-32.90	8141	Machine-operator, shaving/wood
7-32.90	8141	Machine-operator, tempering/ wood
7-32.90	8141	Operator, cut-off saw/barrel staves
7-32.90	8141	Operator, cut-off saw/log staves
7-33.10	8142	Operator, paper-pulp plant
7-33.20	8142	Machine-operator, grinding/wood
7-33.20	8142	Machine-operator, pulping/wood
7-33.30	8142	Machine-operator, chipping/wood
7-33.30	8142	Operator, chipper/paper pulp
7-33.40	8142	Operator, boiler/paper pulp
7-33.40	8142	Operator, digester/paper pulp
7-33.50	8142	Operator, bleacher/paper
7-33.60	8142	Operator, beater/paper pulp
7-33.90	8142	Operator, refinery/paper pulp
7-33.90	8142	Operator, screener/paper pulp
7-34.10	8143	Machine-operator, cardboard production
7-34.10	8143	Machine-operator, papermaking
7-34.10	8143	Machine-operator, papermaking/ back end
7-34.10	8143	Operator, papermaking plant
7-34.20	8143	Machine-operator, papermaking/ wet end
7-34.40	8143	Operator, supercalender
7-34.50	8143	Machine-operator, coating/paper
7-34.60	7422	Maker, paper
7-34.90	8143	Operator, combiner/paper production
7-34.90	8143	Press-operator, hardboard
7-41.20	8151	Machine-operator, crushing/ chemical and related processes
7-41.30	8151	Machine-operator, grinding/ chemical and related processes
7-41.30	8151	Machine-operator, milling/ chemical and related processes
7-41.30	8151	Machine-operator, pulverising/ chemical and related processes
7-41.30	8151	Operator, mill/chemical and related processes
7-41.40	8151	Machine-operator, blending/ chemical and related processes
7-41.40	8151	Machine-operator, compounding/ chemical and related processes

7-41.40	8151	Machine-operator, mixing/ chemical and related processes
7-42.10	8152	Operator, heat-treating-plant/ chemical and related processes
7-42.20	8152	Operator, boiler/chemical and related processes
7-42.20	8152	Operator, cooking equipment/ chemical and related processes
7-42.20	8152	Operator, kettle/chemical and related processes
7-42.30	8152	Operator, roasting equipment/ chemical and related processes
7-42.40	8152	Furnace-operator, chemical and related processes
7-42.40	8152	Kiln-operator, chemical and related processes
7-42.40	8152	Operator, burner/chemical and related processes
7-42.40	8152	Operator, calciner/chemical and related processes
7-42.40	8152	Operator, chemical and related processing plant
7-42.40	8152	Operator, drier/chemical and related processes
7-42.40	8152	Operator, oven/chemical and related processes
7-42.40	8152	Operator, retort/chemical and related processes
7-42.90	8152	Kiln-operator, cement production
7-42.90	8152	Operator, autoclave/chemical and related processes
7-42.90	8152	Operator, cement production plant
7-42.90	8152	Operator, spray-drier/chemical and related processes
7-43.10	8153	Operator, filter/chemical and related processes
7-43.20	8153	Filter-press operator, chemical and related materials
7-43.20	8153	Operator, expeller/chemical and related materials
7-43.30	8153	Operator, filter/rotary drum
7-43.40	8153	Operator, centrifugal separator/ chemical and related processes
7-43.40	8153	Operator, separator/chemical and related processes
7-43.50	8153	Operator, dehydrator/oilfield
7-43.50	8153	Operator, treating equipment/ crude oil
7-43.90	8153	Operator, extractor/chemical and related materials
7-43.90	8153	Operator, screener/chemical and related materials
7-43.90	8153	Operator, sifting equipment/ chemical and related materials

7-44.20	8154	Operator, distiller/batch (chemical processes except petroleum and natural gas)
7-44.20	8154	Operator, still/batch (chemical processes except petroleum and natural gas)
7-44.30	8154	Operator, distiller/continuous (chemical processes except petroleum and natural gas)
7-44.30	8154	Operator, still/continuous (chemical processes except petroleum and natural gas)
7-44.40	8154	Operator, converter/chemical processes (except petroleum and natural gas)
7-44.40	8154	Operator, reactor-converter/chemical processes (except petroleum and natural gas)
7-44.40	8154	Operator, reactor/chemical processes (except petroleum and natural gas)
7-44.50	8154	Operator, evaporator/chemical processes (except petroleum and natural gas)
7-44.50	8154	Operator, vacuum pan/chemical and related processes (except petroleum and natural gas)
7-44.60	6142	Forestry worker, skilled/charcoal burning (traditional techniques)
7-44.60	6142	Forestry worker, skilled/wood distillation (traditional techniques)
7-44.60	8154	Operator, extractor/wood distillation
7-44.90	8221	Machine-operator, detergent production
7-44.90	8278	Machine-operator, distilling/spirits
7-44.90	8221	Machine-operator, pharmaceutical products
7-44.90	8221	Machine-operator, toiletries production
7-44.90	8154	Operator, distiller/turpentine
7-44.90	8221	Operator, distilling equipment/perfume
7-44.90	8221	Operator, granulation equipment/pharmaceutical and toiletry products
7-44.90	8221	Operator, moulding equipment/toiletries
7-44.90	8221	Operator, still/perfume
7-44.90	8278	Operator, still/spirits
7-44.90	8154	Operator, still/turpentine
7-45.20	8155	Operator, treater/desulphurisation (petroleum and natural gas refining)
7-45.20	8155	Operator, treater/petroleum and natural gas refining
7-45.30	8155	Operator, pumping-station/petroleum and natural gas
7-45.30	8155	Operator, refinery/petroleum and natural gas
7-45.30	8155	Operator, still-pump/petroleum and natural gas refining
7-45.40	8155	Operator, distiller/petroleum and natural gas refining
7-45.40	8155	Operator, still/petroleum and natural gas refining
7-45.50	8155	Operator, control-panel/petroleum and natural gas refinery
7-45.60	8155	Operator, blender/petroleum and natural gas refining (ethyl)
7-45.60	8155	Operator, compounder/petroleum and natural gas refining
7-45.70	8155	Operator, paraffin plant
7-49.15	8159	Operator, bleacher/chemicals
7-49.20	8159	Kiln-operator, coke/retort kiln
7-49.20	8159	Machine-operator, coke production
7-49.20	8159	Operator, burner/coke production
7-49.20	8159	Operator, coke production plant
7-49.20	8159	Operator, oven/coke production
7-49.25	8159	Machine-operator, coal gas production
7-49.25	8159	Operator, retort/coal gas
7-49.30	6142	Burner, charcoal
7-49.30	8159	Kiln-operator, charcoal production
7-49.30	8159	Machine-operator, charcoal production
7-49.30	8159	Operator, burner/charcoal production
7-49.35	8261	Machine-operator, spinning/synthetic fibre
7-49.35	8159	Machine-operator, synthetic-fibre production
7-49.35	8159	Operator, synthetic-fibre production plant
7-49.40	8159	Hot cell technician
7-49.40	8159	Operator, chemical processing plant/radioactive materials
7-49.40	8159	Operator, treater/radioactive waste
7-49.90	8229	Machine-operator, chlorine gas production
7-49.90	8159	Machine-operator, fertiliser production
7-49.90	8229	Machine-operator, halogen gas production
7-49.90	8229	Machine-operator, hydrogen gas production
7-49.90	8229	Machine-operator, lead production
7-49.90	8229	Machine-operator, washing/chemical and related materials

7-49.90	8159	Operator, chemical processing plant/electric cells
7-49.90	8159	Operator, fertiliser plant
7-49.90	8159	Operator, liquefaction plant/gases
7-49.90	8159	Operator, rubber processing plant
7-51.10	8261	Machine-operator, fibre preparing
7-51.10	8261	Machine-operator, textile fibre preparing
7-51.10	7431	Preparer, fibre/textiles
7-51.15	7431	Classer, fibre/textiles
7-51.15	7431	Grader, fibre/textiles
7-51.20	7431	Scourer, wool
7-51.25	7431	Blender, fibre/textiles
7-51.25	8261	Machine-operator, blending/textile fibres
7-51.30	7431	Picker, fibre/textiles
7-51.35	7431	Carder, fibre/textiles
7-51.40	7431	Fibre lapper, textiles
7-51.40	8261	Machine-operator, lapping/ribbon
7-51.40	8261	Machine-operator, lapping/sliver
7-51.40	8261	Machine-operator, lapping/textile fibres
7-51.40	7431	Sliver lapper
7-51.45	7431	Comber, fibre/textiles
7-51.45	8261	Machine-operator, combing/textile fibres
7-51.50	7431	Drawer, fibre/textiles
7-51.50	8261	Machine-operator, drawing-frame/textile fibres
7-51.55	8261	Machine-operator, roving-frame/textile fibres
7-51.55	7431	Rover, fibre/textiles
7-51.90	8261	Machine-operator, washing/textile fibres
7-51.90	7431	Opener, fibre/textiles
7-51.90	7431	Teaser, textiles
7-51.90	7431	Willeyer
7-52.20	8261	Machine-operator, spinning/thread and yarn
7-52.20	7432	Spinner, thread and yarn
7-52.30	8261	Machine-operator, doubling/thread and yarn
7-52.40	8261	Machine-operator, twining/thread and yarn
7-52.40	8261	Machine-operator, twisting/thread and yarn
7-52.50	8261	Machine-operator, reeling/thread and yarn
7-52.50	8261	Machine-operator, skeining/thread and yarn
7-52.50	8261	Machine-operator, spooling/thread and yarn
7-52.50	8261	Machine-operator, winding/thread and yarn
7-52.90	8261	Baller, thread and yarn
7-53.20	7432	Fixer, loom
7-53.20	7432	Fixer, loom/jacquard
7-53.20	7432	Fixer, loom/weaving
7-53.20	7432	Setter, loom
7-53.30	7432	Setter, knitting-machine
7-53.40	7435	Jacquard design copyist
7-53.50	8262	Jacquard card cutter
7-53.90	8262	Jacquard card lacer
7-54.15	8262	Machine-operator, warping/beam (textile weaving)
7-54.20	7432	Drawer-in, textile weaving
7-54.20	7432	Threader, loom
7-54.25	8262	Machine-operator, drawing-in/textile weaving
7-54.25	8262	Machine-operator, threading/loom
7-54.30	7332	Handicraft worker, textile weaving
7-54.30	7432	Weaver, cloth
7-54.35	7332	Handicraft worker, carpets
7-54.35	7432	Maker, tapestry
7-54.35	7432	Weaver, tapestry
7-54.40	8262	Machine-operator, cloth production
7-54.40	8262	Machine-operator, weaving
7-54.40	8262	Machine-operator, weaving/fabrics
7-54.45	8262	Machine-operator, weaving/jacquard
7-54.45	8262	Operator, loom/jacquard
7-54.45	7432	Weaver, jacquard
7-54.50	8262	Machine-operator, lace production
7-54.50	8262	Machine-operator, weaving/laces
7-54.50	8262	Operator, loom/lace production
7-54.55	7432	Weaver, carpet
7-54.60	8262	Machine-operator, weaving/carpets
7-54.60	8262	Operator, loom/carpet weaving
7-54.65	8262	Machine-operator, net production
7-54.70	3152	Examiner, cloth
7-54.70	3152	Examiner, fabrics
7-54.70	3152	Inspector, quality/fabrics
7-54.75	7432	Repairer, fabrics
7-54.90	7424	Creeler
7-54.90	9322	Doffer, cloth
7-54.90	9322	Hand, shuttle
7-54.90	7332	Handicraft worker, textiles
7-54.90	7432	Stripper, bobbin
7-54.90	7432	Tufter, carpet weaving
7-55.10	8262	Machine-operator, knitting
7-55.20	8262	Machine-operator, knitting/garment

7-55.30	8262	Machine-operator, knitting/hosiery
7-55.40	7432	Knitter
7-55.40	7432	Knitter, garments
7-55.40	7432	Ribbon lapper
7-55.50	7332	Handicraft worker, garment knitting
7-56.15	7431	Bleacher, fibre/textiles
7-56.15	8264	Machine-operator, bleaching/textiles
7-56.20	8264	Machine-operator, dyeing/yarn
7-56.25	8264	Machine-operator, dyeing/fabric
7-56.30	8264	Machine-operator, dyeing/garments
7-56.35	8264	Machine-operator, washing/cloth
7-56.35	8264	Machine-operator, washing/yarn
7-56.35	8264	Operator, cleaning equipment/cloth
7-56.35	8264	Operator, cleaning equipment/textiles
7-56.35	9322	Washer, hand/fibre
7-56.40	8264	Machine-operator, degumming/silk
7-56.50	8264	Machine-operator, shrinking/textiles
7-56.55	8264	Operator, fulling-mill/textiles
7-56.60	8264	Machine-operator, waterproofing/cloth
7-56.60	8264	Machine-operator, waterproofing/fabric
7-56.60	8264	Machine-operator, waterproofing/textiles
7-56.65	8264	Machine-operator, silk weighting
7-56.70	8264	Calenderer, cloth
7-56.70	8264	Operator, calender/textiles
7-56.70	8264	Press-operator, steam/textiles
7-56.70	8264	Press-operator, textile
7-56.90	8264	Machine-operator, drying/textiles
7-56.90	8264	Machine-operator, dyeing/textile fibres
7-59.20	7432	Maker, braid
7-59.25	8269	Machine-operator, braid production
7-59.30	7432	Crocheter
7-59.35	8262	Machine-operator, crocheting
7-59.40	7432	Maker, fishing net
7-59.40	7432	Maker, net
7-59.40	7432	Maker, safety net
7-59.45	8265	Machine-operator, mixing/fur fibre
7-59.50	7433	Coner, hat forms
7-59.50	8269	Machine-operator, forming/felt hoods
7-61.20	7441	Classer, hide
7-61.20	7441	Classer, skin
7-61.20	7441	Grader, hide
7-61.20	7441	Grader, skin
7-61.25	7441	Fellmonger
7-61.30	7441	Dehairer, hide
7-61.30	7441	Flesher, hide
7-61.30	7441	Flesher-dehairer, hide
7-61.35	8265	Machine-operator, dehairing/hide
7-61.35	8265	Machine-operator, fleshing/hide
7-61.35	8265	Machine-operator, hide processing
7-61.40	7441	Splitter, hide
7-61.45	8265	Machine-operator, tanning
7-61.45	7441	Tanner
7-61.45	7441	Tanner, hide
7-61.45	7441	Tanner, leather
7-61.50	7441	Currier, leather
7-61.50	8265	Machine-operator, leather preparing
7-61.55	7441	Dyer, vat/leather
7-61.55	7441	Dyer-stainer, leather
7-61.55	8265	Machine-operator, staining/leather
7-61.55	7441	Stainer, leather
7-61.90	7441	Buffer, leather
7-61.90	7441	Dyer, leather
7-61.90	7441	Dyer-stainer
7-61.90	7441	Dyer-stainer, spray
7-61.90	8265	Machine-operator, washing/hide
7-61.90	7441	Polisher, leather
7-61.90	7441	Stretcher, leather
7-61.90	9322	Washer, hand/hide
7-62.10	7441	Dresser, pelt
7-62.20	7441	Classer, pelt
7-62.20	7441	Grader, pelt
7-62.30	7441	Flesher, pelt
7-62.30	8265	Machine-operator, fleshing/pelt
7-62.40	7441	Plucker-trimmer, pelt
7-62.40	7441	Puller, pelt
7-62.50	7441	Dyer, pelt
7-62.60	7441	Finisher, pelt
7-62.60	8265	Machine-operator, finishing/pelt
7-62.60	8265	Machine-operator, fur preparing
7-62.60	8265	Machine-operator, pelt processing
7-62.60	7441	Stretcher, pelt
7-62.90	7441	Dyer, vat/pelt
7-62.90	7441	Pickler, pelt
7-62.90	7441	Shaver, fur
7-71.20	8273	Machine-operator, milling/grain
7-71.20	8273	Operator, rolling-mill/grain
7-71.30	8273	Machine-operator, milling/rice
7-71.40	8273	Machine-operator, milling/spices
7-71.40	8273	Operator, rolling-mill/spices

7-74.90	7414	Preserver, vegetable
7-74.90	7415	Taster, food
7-74.90	7415	Taster, juice
7-75.10	8272	Machine-operator, dairy products
7-75.10	7413	Maker, dairy products
7-75.20	8272	Machine-operator, pasteurising/dairy products
7-75.20	8272	Machine-operator, pasteurising/milk
7-75.30	7413	Maker, butter
7-75.30	7413	Maker, cheese
7-75.50	7413	Maker, ice-cream
7-75.90	8272	Machine-operator, freezing/dairy products
7-75.90	8272	Machine-operator, milk powder production
7-75.90	8272	Machine-operator, milk processing
7-75.90	8272	Operator, vacuum pan/condensed milk
7-75.90	8272	Salter, cheese
7-76.10	7412	Baker
7-76.10	8274	Machine-operator, cereal products
7-76.20	7412	Baker, bread
7-76.20	8274	Machine-operator, bread production
7-76.20	7412	Mixer, bread dough
7-76.20	7412	Oven worker, bread
7-76.20	7412	Table hand, bread
7-76.30	7412	Baker, pastry
7-76.30	8274	Machine-operator, chocolate products
7-76.30	8274	Machine-operator, pastry production
7-76.30	7412	Maker, pastry
7-76.30	7412	Maker, pie
7-76.30	7412	Maker, sponge cake
7-76.30	7412	Mixer, flour confectionery
7-76.30	7412	Mixer, pie paste
7-76.30	7412	Oven worker, flour confectionery
7-76.30	7412	Table hand, flour confectionery
7-76.40	8274	Machine-operator, noodle production
7-76.40	7412	Maker, noodle
7-76.40	7412	Presser, noodle extruding
7-76.50	7412	Concher, chocolate
7-76.50	7412	Confectioner
7-76.50	7412	Grinder, chocolate
7-76.50	8274	Machine-operator, chocolate production
7-76.50	8274	Machine-operator, conching/chocolate
7-76.50	7412	Maker, chocolate
7-76.50	7412	Mixer, chocolate
7-76.50	7412	Presser, chocolate production
7-76.50	7412	Refiner, chocolate
7-76.60	7412	Cutter, sugar confectionery
7-76.60	8274	Machine-operator, confectionery production
7-76.60	7412	Maker, confectionery
7-76.60	7412	Mixer, sugar confectionery
7-76.60	7412	Roller, sugar confectionery
7-76.90	7412	Baker, biscuit
7-76.90	7412	Dipper, sugar confectionery
7-76.90	8274	Machine-operator, bakery products
7-76.90	8274	Machine-operator, pasta production
7-76.90	7412	Maker, biscuit
7-76.90	7412	Maker, chewing-gum
7-76.90	7412	Moulder, chocolate
7-76.90	7412	Oven worker, biscuits
7-76.90	7412	Temperer, chocolate
7-77.10	8277	Machine-operator, coffee-bean processing
7-77.10	8277	Machine-operator, tea-leaf processing
7-77.20	7415	Taster, coffee
7-77.20	7415	Taster, tea
7-77.30	8277	Machine-operator, blending/coffee
7-77.40	8277	Machine-operator, blending/tea
7-77.50	8277	Operator, roasting equipment/coffee
7-77.60	8277	Operator, roasting equipment/cocoa-bean
7-77.90	8277	Machine-operator, cocoa-bean processing
7-77.90	8277	Winnower, cocoa-bean
7-78.10	8278	Brewer
7-78.10	8278	Machine-operator, brewing/spirits
7-78.10	8278	Machine-operator, soft-drinks production
7-78.20	8278	Machine-operator, malting/spirits
7-78.20	8278	Maltster
7-78.20	8278	Operator, germination equipment/malting (spirits)
7-78.20	8278	Steeper, malting
7-78.25	8278	Kiln-operator, malting/spirits
7-78.30	8278	Operator, cooking equipment/malt
7-78.35	8278	Operator, fermentation equipment/spirits
7-78.40	7412	Maker, yeast
7-78.50	9322	Labourer, wine production
7-78.50	8278	Operator, winemaking plant
7-78.60	7415	Taster, liquor

7-78.60	7415	Taster, wine
7-78.70	8278	Machine-operator, vinegar making
7-78.80	8275	Press-operator, fruit
7-78.90	8278	Machine-operator, blending/spirits
7-78.90	8278	Machine-operator, blending/wine
7-78.90	8278	Machine-operator, liqueur production
7-79.20	8275	Machine-operator, edible oil production
7-79.20	8275	Machine-operator, milling/oil-seed
7-79.20	8275	Press-operator, edible oils
7-79.25	8275	Machine-operator, refining/oils and fats
7-79.30	8275	Operator, autoclave/oils and fats
7-79.30	8275	Operator, hydrogenation equipment/oils and fats
7-79.40	7411	Boner, fish
7-79.40	7411	Cutter, fish
7-79.40	7411	Dresser, fish
7-79.40	7411	Filleter, fish
7-79.40	7411	Fishmonger
7-79.40	8271	Machine-operator, fish processing
7-79.40	8271	Machine-operator, fish products
7-79.90	7414	Expeller, oil
7-79.90	7415	Grader, fruit
7-79.90	7415	Grader, oil
7-79.90	8275	Machine-operator, blanching/edible nuts
7-79.90	8275	Machine-operator, edible nut processing
7-79.90	8275	Machine-operator, fruit juice production
7-79.90	8275	Machine-operator, margarine processing
7-79.90	8275	Machine-operator, vegetable juice production
7-79.90	7414	Maker, fruit juice
7-79.90	7414	Maker, vegetable juice
7-79.90	7414	Preserver, fruit juice
7-79.90	7414	Preserver, vegetable juice
7-81.10	8279	Machine-operator, tobacco processing
7-81.10	8279	Machine-operator, tobacco products
7-81.20	7416	Grader, tobacco
7-81.30	7416	Blender, tobacco
7-81.30	7416	Bulker, tobacco
7-81.30	8279	Machine-operator, blending/tobacco
7-81.30	7416	Mixer, tobacco
7-81.40	7416	Conditioner, tobacco leaves
7-81.40	7416	Dipper, tobacco

7-81.40	8279	Operator, vacuum-conditioner/tobacco processing
7-81.40	7416	Tobacco worker, conditioning
7-81.50	7416	Stemmer, tobacco
7-81.50	7416	Stripper, tobacco leaf
7-81.50	7416	Tobacco worker, leaf stemming
7-81.50	7416	Tobacco worker, leaf stripping
7-81.60	8279	Machine-operator, stripping/tobacco-leaf
7-81.70	7416	Cutter, tobacco
7-81.70	8279	Machine-operator, cutting/tobacco leaf
7-81.70	7416	Tobacco worker, cutting
7-81.90	7416	Drier, tobacco
7-81.90	7416	Dryer, tobacco
7-81.90	7416	Flavourer, tobacco
7-81.90	7416	Stover, tobacco
7-81.90	7416	Tobacco worker, drying
7-82.20	7416	Maker, cigar
7-82.20	7416	Moulder, cigar
7-82.20	7416	Roller, cigar
7-82.30	8279	Machine-operator, cigar production
7-82.90	7416	Presser, cigar
7-82.90	7416	Sorter, cigar
7-83.10	7416	Maker, cigarette
7-83.20	8279	Machine-operator, cigarette production
7-89.20	7416	Blender, snuff
7-89.20	7416	Drier, snuff
7-89.20	7416	Grinder, snuff
7-89.20	7416	Maker, snuff
7-89.20	7416	Mixer, snuff
7-89.20	7416	Screener, snuff
7-89.90	7416	Maker, tobacco cake
7-89.90	7416	Maker, tobacco plug
7-91.10	7433	Tailor
7-91.20	7433	Tailor, bespoke
7-91.20	7433	Tailor, garment/made-to-measure
7-91.30	7433	Tailor, garment/ready-to-wear
7-91.40	7433	Dressmaker
7-91.40	7433	Maker, gown
7-91.90	7433	Dressmaker, theatrical
7-91.90	7332	Handicraft worker, garments
7-91.90	7433	Maker, blouse
7-91.90	7433	Maker, corset
7-91.90	7433	Maker, lingerie
7-91.90	7433	Maker, shirt
7-91.90	7433	Tailor, alteration
7-91.90	7433	Tailor, theatrical

7-92.20	7434	Fur tailor
7-92.20	7434	Furrier
7-92.30	7435	Pattern-maker, fur
7-92.40	7434	Grader, fur
7-92.40	7434	Matcher, fur
7-92.40	7434	Sorter, fur
7-92.50	7434	Cutter, fur
7-92.60	7434	Nailer, fur
7-92.90	7434	Trimmer, fur
7-93.10	8269	Machine-operator, hat making
7-93.20	7433	Maker, hat
7-93.20	7433	Milliner
7-93.30	8269	Blocker, hat
7-93.30	8269	Machine-operator, blocking/hats
7-93.90	7433	Maker, cap
7-94.10	8269	Machine-operator, pattern-making/fur
7-94.10	8269	Machine-operator, pattern-making/leather
7-94.10	8269	Machine-operator, pattern-making/textiles
7-94.20	7435	Pattern-maker, garment
7-94.30	7435	Pattern-maker, caps
7-94.30	7435	Pattern-maker, hats
7-94.40	8269	Machine-operator, mattress production
7-94.40	7435	Marker, garment
7-94.50	7435	Cutter, garment
7-94.50	7435	Cutter, tailor's
7-94.50	8269	Machine-operator, cutting/garments
7-94.50	8269	Machine-operator, cutting/textiles
7-94.70	7435	Cutter, glove
7-94.90	7435	Cutter, mattress
7-94.90	7435	Cutter, sail
7-94.90	7435	Cutter, tent
7-94.90	7435	Cutter, umbrella
7-94.90	7435	Cutter, upholstery
7-94.90	7435	Pattern-maker, gloves
7-94.90	7435	Pattern-maker, mattresses
7-94.90	7435	Pattern-maker, sails
7-94.90	7435	Pattern-maker, tents
7-94.90	7435	Pattern-maker, umbrellas
7-94.90	7435	Pattern-maker, upholstery
7-95.10	7436	Seamstress
7-95.10	7436	Sewer
7-95.10	7436	Sewer, garments
7-95.10	7436	Sewer, textile
7-95.40	7436	Sewer, fur
7-95.50	8263	Machine-operator, sewing
7-95.50	8263	Machine-operator, sewing/embroidery
7-95.50	8263	Machine-operator, sewing/fur
7-95.50	8263	Machine-operator, sewing/garments
7-95.50	8263	Machine-operator, sewing/hats
7-95.50	8263	Machine-operator, sewing/textile products
7-95.50	8263	Machine-operator, sewing/upholstery
7-95.60	7436	Embroiderer
7-95.70	8262	Machine-operator, embroidery
7-95.90	7436	Sewer, hat
7-95.90	7436	Sewer, mattress
7-95.90	7436	Sewer, sail
7-95.90	7436	Sewer, tent
7-95.90	7436	Sewer, upholstery
7-96.20	7437	Upholsterer, furniture
7-96.30	7437	Upholsterer, aircraft
7-96.30	7437	Upholsterer, automobile
7-96.30	7437	Upholsterer, railway carriage
7-96.30	7437	Upholsterer, vehicle
7-96.40	7437	Maker, mattress
7-96.90	7437	Maker, bedding
7-96.90	7437	Maker, furniture/soft furnishing
7-96.90	7437	Maker, quilt
7-96.90	7437	Maker, soft furnishing
7-96.90	7437	Upholsterer, soft furnishing
7-99.20	7436	Maker, awning
7-99.20	7436	Maker, sail, tent and awning
7-99.20	7436	Maker, tent
7-99.30	7436	Maker, umbrella
7-99.90	8286	Assembler, textile products
7-99.90	8262	Machine-operator, carpet production
7-99.90	7436	Maker, artificial flower
7-99.90	7436	Maker, carpet
8-01.10	8266	Machine-operator, footwear production
8-01.10	8266	Machine-operator, shoe production
8-01.10	7442	Maker, footwear
8-01.10	7442	Shoe-maker
8-01.10	7442	Shoe-maker, bespoke
8-01.20	8266	Machine-operator, footwear production/orthopaedic
8-01.20	7442	Maker, footwear/orthopaedic
8-01.20	7442	Maker, surgical footwear
8-01.20	7442	Shoe-maker, orthopaedic
8-01.30	7442	Cobbler
8-01.30	7442	Repairer, footwear

ISCO-68

8-01.90	8266	Machine-operator, foot-wear production/raffia
8-01.90	8266	Machine-operator, footwear production/sports
8-01.90	7442	Maker, footwear/sport
8-01.90	7442	Maker, sports equipment/footwear
8-01.90	7442	Shoe-maker, sports
8-02.15	7442	Pattern-maker, footwear
8-02.20	7442	Cutter, footwear/clicker
8-02.25	7442	Cutter, footwear
8-02.30	7442	Burnisher, footwear/uppers
8-02.30	7442	Cementer, footwear/uppers
8-02.30	7442	Fitter, footwear/uppers
8-02.30	7442	Folder, footwear/uppers
8-02.30	7442	Preparer, footwear/uppers
8-02.30	7442	Skiver, footwear
8-02.35	7442	Presser, footwear/soles
8-02.40	7442	Channeller, footwear/soles
8-02.40	7442	Fitter, footwear/soles
8-02.40	7442	Grader, footwear/soles
8-02.40	7442	Preparer, footwear/soles
8-02.40	7442	Rounder, footwear
8-02.40	7442	Sorter, footwear
8-02.40	7442	Splitter, footwear
8-02.45	7442	Laster, footwear
8-02.50	8263	Machine-operator, sewing/footwear
8-02.50	7436	Sewer, footwear
8-02.55	7442	Burnisher, footwear/heels
8-02.55	7442	Finisher, footwear
8-02.55	7442	Stainer, footwear
8-02.55	7442	Taker-off, footwear finishing
8-02.55	7442	Trimmer, footwear finishing
8-02.90	7442	Eyeletter, footwear
8-02.90	7442	Polisher, footwear
8-02.90	7442	Socker, footwear
8-03.10	7332	Handicraft worker, leather
8-03.10	7332	Handicraft worker, leather accessories
8-03.10	7442	Maker, leather goods
8-03.20	7442	Maker, harness
8-03.20	7442	Maker, saddle
8-03.20	7442	Saddler
8-03.30	7442	Cutter, leather
8-03.30	8265	Machine-operator, cutting/leather
8-03.40	7436	Sewer, leather
8-03.50	8263	Machine-operator, sewing/leather
8-03.60	8286	Assembler, leather products
8-03.90	7442	Maker, horse collar
8-03.90	7442	Maker, panel/saddlery
8-03.90	7442	Maker, whip
8-11.10	8285	Assembler, furniture/wood and related materials
8-11.10	8285	Assembler, wood products
8-11.10	8240	Machine-operator, wood products
8-11.20	7422	Cabinet-maker
8-11.20	7422	Maker, cabinet
8-11.90	7422	Maker, chair
8-11.90	7422	Maker, clock case
8-11.90	7422	Maker, instrument case
8-11.90	7422	Maker, piano case
8-12.05	7423	Setter, woodworking machine
8-12.08	8240	Machine-operator, woodworking
8-12.10	7423	Setter-operator, woodworking machine
8-12.20	7423	Sawyer, precision woodworking
8-12.20	7423	Sawyer, wood
8-12.20	7423	Setter-operator, fret-saw/woodworking
8-12.20	7423	Setter-operator, jigsaw/woodworking
8-12.30	8240	Lathe-operator, woodworking
8-12.30	7423	Turner, wood
8-12.30	7423	Wood tuner
8-12.30	7423	Wood turner
8-12.40	7423	Setter-operator, lathe/woodworking
8-12.50	7423	Setter-operator, shaping machine/woodworking
8-12.60	7423	Setter-operator, routing machine/woodworking
8-12.70	7423	Setter-operator, planing machine/woodworking
8-12.80	8240	Machine-operator, carving/wood
8-12.80	7423	Setter-operator, carving machine/woodworking
8-12.90	7423	Borer, wood
8-12.90	8240	Machine-operator, engraving/wood
8-12.90	8240	Machine-operator, etching/wood
8-12.90	8240	Machine-operator, finishing/wood
8-12.90	8240	Machine-operator, polishing/wood
8-12.90	7422	Tenoner
8-12.90	7423	Woodworker, dovetailing
8-12.90	7423	Woodworker, dowelling
8-12.90	7423	Woodworker, morticing
8-12.90	7423	Woodworker, sanding
8-12.90	7423	Woodworker, tenoning
8-19.20	7422	Builder, coach-body/wooden
8-19.20	7422	Builder, vehicle-body/wooden
8-19.20	7422	Builder, vehicle-frame/wooden
8-19.25	7422	Cart-wright

8-19.25	7422	Wheel-wright
8-19.30	7422	Cooper
8-19.30	7422	Maker, barrel
8-19.30	7422	Maker, cask
8-19.30	7422	Maker, tank/wooden
8-19.35	7422	Pattern-maker, wood patterns
8-19.40	7422	Maker, model/wooden
8-19.45	7422	Carver, wood
8-19.50	7422	Veneer applier
8-19.55	7422	Finisher, wooden furniture
8-19.55	8240	Machine-operator, furniture production
8-19.55	7422	Stainer, wooden furniture
8-19.55	7422	Varnisher, wooden furniture
8-19.60	7422	Maker, pipe/smoking
8-19.60	7422	Maker, pipe/smoking (wood)
8-19.65	7422	Inlayer, marquetry
8-19.90	7422	Bender, wood
8-19.90	7331	Handicraft worker, wooden articles
8-19.90	8240	Machine-operator, bending/wood
8-19.90	8240	Machine-operator, marking/wood
8-19.90	8240	Machine-operator, sports equipment/wood
8-19.90	7422	Maker, clog
8-19.90	7422	Maker, coffin
8-19.90	7422	Maker, ladder/wood
8-19.90	7422	Maker, picture frame
8-19.90	7422	Maker, sports equipment/wood
8-19.90	7422	Marker, woodworking
8-20.10	8212	Machine-operator, mineral products
8-20.10	8212	Machine-operator, stone products
8-20.20	7113	Cutter-finisher, stone
8-20.20	7113	Dresser, stone
8-20.20	7113	Finisher, stone
8-20.20	7113	Grinder, slate
8-20.20	7113	Grinder, stone
8-20.20	8112	Machine-operator, cutting/stone
8-20.20	8212	Machine-operator, finishing/stone
8-20.20	8112	Machine-operator, grinding/stone
8-20.20	8112	Machine-operator, planing/stone
8-20.20	8212	Machine-operator, polishing/stone
8-20.20	8112	Machine-operator, sawing/stone
8-20.20	7113	Planer, stone
8-20.20	7113	Polisher, granite
8-20.20	7113	Polisher, marble
8-20.20	7113	Polisher, slate
8-20.20	7113	Polisher, stone
8-20.20	7113	Sawyer, stone
8-20.30	7113	Grader, stone
8-20.40	7113	Stonework layout worker
8-20.40	7113	Stoneworker
8-20.50	8212	Lathe-operator, stoneworking
8-20.50	8212	Machine-operator, cutting/stone products
8-20.50	7113	Setter-operator, lathe/stone
8-20.50	7113	Tuner, stone
8-20.60	7113	Cutter, stone
8-20.60	7113	Cutter, stone/lettering
8-20.70	7113	Carver, stone
8-20.70	7331	Handicraft worker, stone articles
8-20.70	8212	Machine-operator, carving/stone products
8-20.80	7113	Carver-setter, monument
8-20.80	7113	Mason, monument
8-20.90	7113	Driller, stone
8-20.90	8112	Machine-operator, drilling/stone
8-20.90	8212	Machine-operator, engraving/stone
8-20.90	7113	Sandblaster, stonecutting
8-20.90	7113	Shotblaster, stonecutting
8-31.10	7221	Blacksmith
8-31.10	7221	Farrier
8-31.10	7221	Smith, agricultural implement
8-31.10	7221	Smith, anvil
8-31.10	7221	Toolsmith
8-31.20	7221	Drop forger
8-31.20	7221	Hammer-smith
8-31.20	7221	Hammer-smith, forge
8-31.20	8211	Machine-operator, forging/metal
8-31.30	7221	Drop-hammer worker
8-31.40	7221	Forging-press worker
8-31.40	7221	Press-operator, forging/metal
8-31.40	7221	Smith, bulldozer
8-31.90	7221	Driver, forge hammer
8-31.90	9322	Striker, blacksmith's
8-32.20	8211	Machine-operator, tool production
8-32.20	7222	Maker, press tool
8-32.20	7222	Maker, tap-die
8-32.20	7222	Maker, tool
8-32.20	7222	Maker, tool and die
8-32.20	7222	Toolmaker
8-32.30	7222	Maker, gauge
8-32.30	7222	Maker, jig-gauge
8-32.40	7222	Pattern-maker, metal foundry
8-32.50	7222	Marker, metal
8-32.90	7222	Finisher, die
8-32.90	7222	Maker, template
8-32.90	7222	Maker, tool/diamond-pointed
8-32.90	8331	Operator, forestry machinery
8-33.05	7223	Setter, machine tool
8-33.05	7223	Setter, metalworking machine

ISCO-68

8-33.05	7223	Setter, metalworking machine
8-33.10	7223	Setter-operator, machine tool
8-33.10	7223	Setter-operator, metalworking machine
8-33.20	7223	Setter-operator, lathe/ metalworking
8-33.20	7223	Turner
8-33.30	7223	Setter-operator, milling machine/ metalworking
8-33.40	7223	Setter-operator, planing machine/ metalworking
8-33.50	7223	Setter-operator, boring machine/ metalworking
8-33.60	7223	Setter-operator, drilling machine/ metalworking
8-33.60	7223	Setter-operator, reaming machine/ metalworking
8-33.70	7223	Setter-operator, grinding machine/ metalworking
8-33.70	7223	Setter-operator, precision-grinding machine/metalworking
8-33.80	7223	Setter-operator, honing machine/ metalworking
8-33.85	7223	Setter-operator, numerical control machine/metalworking
8-33.90	7223	Setter-operator, cutting machine/ metalworking
8-33.90	7223	Setter-operator, die-sinking machine/metalworking
8-33.90	7223	Setter-operator, lapping machine/ metalworking
8-33.90	7223	Setter-operator, routing machine/ metalworking
8-33.90	7223	Setter-operator, shaping machine/ metalworking
8-34.10	8211	Machine-operator, machine tool
8-34.10	8211	Machine-operator, metal products
8-34.10	8211	Operator, machine-tool
8-34.20	8211	Lathe-operator, capstan/ metalworking
8-34.20	8211	Lathe-operator, centre/ metalworking
8-34.20	8211	Lathe-operator, engine/ metalworking
8-34.20	8211	Lathe-operator, metalworking
8-34.20	8211	Lathe-operator, turret/ metalworking
8-34.30	8211	Machine-operator, milling/metal
8-34.40	8211	Machine-operator, planing/metal
8-34.50	8211	Machine-operator, boring/metal
8-34.60	7223	Borer, metal
8-34.60	7223	Driller, metal
8-34.60	8211	Machine-operator, drilling/metal
8-34.60	8211	Machine-operator, reaming/metal
8-34.65	8211	Machine-operator, grinding/metal
8-34.65	8211	Machine-operator, precision grinding/metal
8-34.70	8211	Machine-operator, honing/metal
8-34.75	8211	Machine-operator, sawing/metal
8-34.80	8211	Machine-operator, automatic transfer/components
8-34.90	8211	Machine-operator, lapping/metal
8-34.90	8211	Machine-operator, shaping/metal
8-35.20	7224	Burnisher, metal
8-35.20	7224	Finisher, metal
8-35.20	8211	Machine-operator, burnishing/ metal
8-35.20	8223	Machine-operator, finishing/metal
8-35.20	8223	Machine-operator, laminating/ metal
8-35.20	8223	Machine-operator, polishing/metal
8-35.20	8211	Machine-operator, sharpening/ metal
8-35.30	7224	Grinder, machine tool
8-35.30	7224	Grinder, metal
8-35.30	8211	Machine-operator, grinding/ machine-tool
8-35.30	7224	Wheel-grinder, metal
8-35.40	7224	Grinder, tool
8-35.40	8211	Machine-operator, grinding/tool
8-35.40	7224	Sharpener, cutting instruments
8-35.40	7224	Sharpener, knife
8-35.40	7224	Sharpener, tool
8-35.50	7224	Repairer, saw
8-35.50	7224	Sharpener, saw
8-35.60	7224	Grinder, textile carding machine
8-35.90	7224	Buffer, metal
8-35.90	8211	Machine-operator, buffing/metal
8-35.90	7224	Polisher, metal
8-35.90	7224	Polisher, metal/emery polishing
8-35.90	7224	Polisher, metal/mirror-finish
8-35.90	7224	Polisher, metal/sand polishing
8-35.90	7224	Sharpener, itinerant
8-39.20	7222	Gunsmith
8-39.30	7222	Locksmith
8-39.40	8211	Machine-operator, spinning/metal
8-39.40	7223	Spinner, metal
8-39.40	7223	Spinner, sheet-metal
8-39.50	7221	Former, metal
8-39.50	8211	Machine-operator, forming/metal
8-39.60	8211	Press-operator, metal/except forging
8-39.60	8211	Press-operator, punching/metal
8-39.60	8211	Press-operator, stamping/metal
8-39.70	8211	Machine-operator, bending/metal
8-39.80	8211	Machine-operator, cutting/metal
8-39.80	8211	Machine-operator, shearing/metal

8-39.80	8211	Operator, power-shear
8-39.90	8211	Machine-operator, cable production
8-39.90	8211	Machine-operator, engraving/metal
8-39.90	8211	Machine-operator, minting/metal
8-39.90	8211	Machine-operator, needle production
8-39.90	8211	Machine-operator, nut production/metal
8-39.90	8211	Machine-operator, pipe production
8-39.90	8211	Machine-operator, rivet production
8-39.90	8211	Machine-operator, sports equipment/metal
8-39.90	8211	Machine-operator, wire goods production
8-39.90	8211	Machine-operator, wiring/electric
8-41.05	7233	Fitter, industrial machinery
8-41.10	8281	Assembler, industrial machinery
8-41.10	8281	Assembler, mechanical machinery
8-41.10	8281	Assembler, vehicle
8-41.10	8281	Machine-operator, assembly line/vehicles
8-41.10	8281	Machine-operator, assembly-line/aircraft
8-41.15	8281	Assembler, engine/internal combustion
8-41.15	8281	Assembler, engine/motor vehicles
8-41.15	7231	Fitter, engine/motor-vehicle
8-41.20	8281	Assembler, aircraft
8-41.20	8281	Assembler, engine/aircraft
8-41.20	7232	Fitter, engine/aircraft
8-41.25	8281	Assembler, engine/marine
8-41.25	7233	Fitter, engine/marine
8-41.30	8281	Assembler, turbine
8-41.30	7233	Fitter, turbine
8-41.35	8281	Assembler, machine-tool
8-41.35	7233	Fitter, machine-tool
8-41.35	7233	Fitter, metalworking machinery
8-41.40	8281	Assembler, mining machinery
8-41.40	7233	Fitter, mining machinery
8-41.45	8281	Assembler, printing machinery
8-41.45	7233	Fitter, printing machinery
8-41.50	8281	Assembler, textile machinery
8-41.50	7233	Fitter, textile machinery
8-41.55	8281	Assembler, woodworking machinery
8-41.55	7233	Fitter, woodworking machinery
8-41.60	8281	Assembler, agricultural machinery
8-41.60	7233	Fitter, agricultural machinery
8-41.65	8281	Assembler, earth-moving equipment
8-41.65	7233	Fitter, earth-moving equipment
8-41.70	8283	Assembler, office machinery
8-41.70	7233	Fitter, office machinery
8-41.75	7233	Erector-installer, agricultural machinery
8-41.75	7233	Erector-installer, industrial machinery
8-41.80	7233	Erector, refrigeration and air-conditioning equipment
8-41.80	7233	Mechanic, air-conditioning equipment
8-41.80	7233	Mechanic, refrigeration and air-conditioning equipment
8-41.80	7233	Mechanic, refrigeration equipment
8-41.85	7232	Erector, metal airframe
8-41.85	7232	Fitter-assembler, airframe
8-41.90	8281	Assembler, engines/steam
8-41.90	7233	Fitter, engine/steam
8-42.20	8283	Assembler, chronometer
8-42.20	8283	Assembler, clock
8-42.20	8283	Assembler, watch
8-42.20	8211	Machine-operator, clock production
8-42.20	8211	Machine-operator, watch production
8-42.20	7311	Maker, clock
8-42.20	7311	Maker, watch
8-42.25	7311	Repairer, clock
8-42.25	7311	Repairer, watch
8-42.25	7311	Watch adjuster
8-42.30	7311	Balancer, scale
8-42.30	7311	Calibrator, precision instrument
8-42.30	7311	Maker, barometer
8-42.30	7311	Maker, instrument/meteorological
8-42.30	7311	Maker, instrument/nautical
8-42.30	7311	Maker, instrument/precision
8-42.30	7311	Repairer, instrument/precision
8-42.35	7311	Maker, instrument/optical
8-42.35	7311	Repairer, camera
8-42.35	7311	Repairer, instrument/optical
8-42.40	8283	Assembler, precision instrument
8-42.40	7311	Maker, photographic equipment
8-42.40	7311	Maker, precision instrument
8-42.45	7311	Maker, artificial limb
8-42.45	7311	Maker, brace/orthopaedic
8-42.45	7311	Maker, orthopaedic appliance
8-42.45	7311	Maker, surgical appliance
8-42.45	7311	Repairer, orthopaedic appliance
8-42.50	7311	Maker, dental prosthesis
8-42.50	7311	Mechanic, dental
8-42.50	7311	Repairer, dental prosthesis
8-42.90	7311	Maker, instrument/dental
8-42.90	7311	Maker, instrument/scientific
8-42.90	7311	Maker, instrument/surgical

ISCO-68

8-42.90	7311	Repairer, instrument/dental
8-42.90	7311	Repairer, instrument/scientific
8-42.90	7311	Repairer, instrument/surgical
8-42.90	7311	Repairer, photographic equipment
8-42.90	7311	Repairer, surgical appliance
8-43.20	7231	Mechanic, automobile
8-43.20	7231	Mechanic, engine/diesel (motor vehicle)
8-43.20	7231	Mechanic, engine/motor vehicle
8-43.20	7231	Mechanic, garage
8-43.20	7231	Mechanic, motor vehicle
8-43.30	7231	Mechanic, motor truck
8-43.30	7231	Mechanic, truck
8-43.40	7231	Mechanic, motor cycle
8-43.90	7231	Mechanic, automobile transmission
8-43.90	7231	Mechanic, bus
8-43.90	7231	Mechanic, motor-vehicle transmission
8-43.90	7231	Mechanic, tractor
8-43.90	7231	Repairer, motor vehicle
8-43.90	7231	Tuner, engine-driving
8-43.90	7231	Tuner, vehicle engine
8-44.10	7232	Aeromechanic
8-44.10	7232	Repairer, engine/aircraft
8-44.20	7232	Mechanic, engine/aircraft
8-49.10	7233	Mechanic, industrial machinery
8-49.15	7233	Mechanic, engine/steam
8-49.20	7233	Mechanic, engine/diesel (except motor vehicle)
8-49.25	7233	Mechanic, turbine
8-49.30	7233	Mechanic, machine tool
8-49.35	7233	Mechanic, mining machinery
8-49.40	7233	Mechanic, printing machinery
8-49.45	7233	Mechanic, textile machinery
8-49.50	7233	Mechanic, woodworking machinery
8-49.55	7233	Mechanic, agricultural machinery
8-49.55	7233	Mechanic, farm machinery
8-49.60	7233	Mechanic, construction machinery
8-49.60	7233	Mechanic, earth-moving equipment
8-49.65	7243	Mechanic, electronics/accounting-machine
8-49.65	7243	Mechanic, electronics/business machine
8-49.65	7243	Mechanic, electronics/calculating machine
8-49.65	7243	Mechanic, electronics/office machine
8-49.65	7233	Mechanic, typewriter
8-49.70	7233	Fitter, plant maintenance
8-49.70	7233	Mechanic, plant maintenance
8-49.70	7233	Millwright
8-49.75	7231	Repairer, bicycle
8-49.75	7231	Repairer, pedal cycle
8-49.80	7233	Oiler and greaser
8-49.85	3152	Inspector, quality/mechanical products
8-49.90	8281	Assembler, metal products
8-49.90	7233	Mechanic, ship
8-49.90	7442	Shoe-maker, raffia
8-51.10	7241	Fitter, electrical
8-51.20	7241	Fitter, dynamo
8-51.20	7241	Fitter, electrical/generator
8-51.20	7241	Fitter, electrical/magneto
8-51.20	7241	Fitter, electrical/motor
8-51.30	7241	Fitter, electrical/transformer
8-51.40	7241	Fitter, electrical/control apparatus
8-51.40	7241	Fitter, electrical/rheostat
8-51.40	7241	Fitter, electrical/switchgear
8-51.50	7241	Fitter, electrical/instruments
8-51.60	7241	Fitter, electrical/elevator and related equipment
8-51.90	7241	Builder, armature
8-51.90	7241	Builder, commutator
8-51.90	7241	Fitter, electrical/refrigeration and air-conditioning
8-51.90	7241	Fitter, electrical/signalling equipment
8-51.90	8211	Machine-operator, armature production
8-51.90	8211	Machine-operator, commutator production
8-52.10	7242	Fitter, electronics
8-52.10	7242	Fitter, electronics/prototype
8-52.10	7243	Mechanic, electronics
8-52.10	7243	Repairer, electronics equipment
8-52.10	7243	Servicer, electronics equipment
8-52.20	7242	Fitter, electronics/audio-visual equipment
8-52.20	7242	Fitter, electronics/radar
8-52.20	7242	Fitter, electronics/radio
8-52.20	7242	Fitter, electronics/telecommunications equipment
8-52.20	7242	Fitter, electronics/television
8-52.30	7242	Fitter, electronics/medical equipment
8-52.40	7242	Fitter, electronics/computer equipment
8-52.40	7242	Fitter, electronics/data-processing equipment
8-52.40	7243	Mechanic, electronics/computer

8-52.50	7242	Fitter, electronics/industrial equipment
8-52.60	7242	Fitter, electronics/signalling equipment
8-52.60	7242	Fitter, electronics/signalling systems
8-52.90	7242	Fitter, electronics/instruments
8-52.90	7242	Fitter, electronics/meteorological equipment
8-53.20	8282	Assembler, electrical equipment
8-53.30	8283	Assembler, audio-visual equipment
8-53.30	8290	Assembler, composite products
8-53.30	8283	Assembler, electronic equipment
8-53.30	8283	Assembler, radio
8-53.30	8283	Assembler, television
8-53.40	8282	Machine-operator, winding/armature
8-53.40	8282	Machine-operator, winding/rotor coil
8-53.40	8282	Machine-operator, winding/stator coil
8-53.40	8282	Machine-operator, winding/transformer coil
8-53.50	9321	Winder, armature/hand
8-53.50	9321	Winder, coil/hand
8-53.50	9321	Winder, filament/hand
8-53.50	9321	Winder, rotor coil/hand
8-53.50	9321	Winder, stator coil/hand
8-53.50	9321	Winder, transformer coil/hand
8-53.90	8282	Assembler, electrical components
8-53.90	8283	Assembler, electronic components
8-53.90	8283	Assembler, hearing aid
8-53.90	8283	Assembler, microelectronics equipment
8-53.90	8171	Machine-operator, automated assembly line
8-53.90	8290	Machine-operator, silicon chip production
8-53.90	8283	Machine-operator, winding/filament
8-53.90	8171	Operator, assembly-line/automated
8-54.20	7243	Mechanic, electronics/audio-visual equipment
8-54.20	7243	Mechanic, electronics/radio
8-54.20	7243	Mechanic, electronics/television
8-54.20	7243	Repairer, electronics equipment/audio-visual
8-54.20	7243	Repairer, electronics equipment/radio
8-54.20	7243	Repairer, electronics equipment/television
8-54.20	7243	Servicer, electronics equipment/audio-visual
8-54.20	7243	Servicer, electronics equipment/radio
8-54.20	7243	Servicer, electronics equipment/television
8-54.90	7243	Erector, radio aerial
8-54.90	7243	Erector, television aerial
8-55.10	7137	Electrician
8-55.20	7137	Electrician, building
8-55.20	7137	Electrician, building/electrical installation
8-55.30	7241	Electrician, aircraft
8-55.35	7241	Electrician, ship
8-55.40	7241	Electrician, locomotive
8-55.40	7241	Electrician, motor vehicle
8-55.40	7241	Electrician, tram
8-55.40	7241	Electrician, vehicle
8-55.50	7137	Electrician, stage and studio
8-55.50	7137	Electrician, theatre
8-55.60	7137	Electrician, building maintenance
8-55.60	7137	Electrician, building/electrical maintenance
8-55.70	7137	Electrician, building repairs
8-55.70	7241	Mechanic, electrical
8-55.70	7241	Repairer, electrical equipment
8-55.70	7241	Servicer, electrical equipment
8-55.90	7137	Electrician, mine
8-55.90	7137	Electrician, neon-lighting
8-56.20	7244	Installer, telegraph
8-56.20	7244	Installer, telephone
8-56.30	7244	Mechanic, telegraph
8-56.30	7244	Mechanic, telephone
8-56.30	7244	Servicer, telegraph
8-56.30	7244	Servicer, telephone
8-57.20	7245	Cable worker, electric power/overhead cables
8-57.20	7245	Line worker, electric power
8-57.20	7245	Wire worker, electric power/overhead wires
8-57.30	7245	Cable worker, electric traction/overhead cables
8-57.30	7245	Line worker, electric traction
8-57.30	7245	Wire worker, electric traction/overhead wires
8-57.40	7245	Cable worker, telegraph
8-57.40	7245	Cable worker, telephone
8-57.40	7245	Line worker, telegraph
8-57.40	7245	Line worker, telephone
8-57.40	7245	Wire worker, telegraph
8-57.40	7245	Wire worker, telephone

8-72.90	7212	Setter-operator, soldering/jewellery
8-72.90	7212	Setter-operator, soldering/metal
8-72.90	7212	Solderer, dip
8-72.90	7212	Solderer, furnace
8-72.90	7212	Solderer, torch
8-73.10	8284	Assembler, metal products
8-73.10	7213	Sheet-metal worker
8-73.20	7213	Marker, sheet metal
8-73.30	7213	Coppersmith
8-73.30	7213	Sheet-metal worker, copper
8-73.40	7213	Sheet-metal worker, tin
8-73.40	7213	Tinsmith
8-73.50	7213	Boilersmith
8-73.50	8211	Machine-operator, boiler production
8-73.50	7213	Maker, boiler
8-73.60	7213	Sheet-metal worker, ornamental
8-73.70	7213	Beater, vehicle panel
8-73.80	7213	Beater, aircraft panel
8-73.80	8281	Machine-operator, assembly-line/except vehicles and aircraft
8-73.80	7213	Sheet-metal worker, aircraft
8-73.80	7213	Sheet-metal worker, vehicles
8-73.90	8284	Assembler, furniture/sheet-metal
8-73.90	7213	Sheet-metal worker, furniture
8-74.10	7214	Erector, structural metal
8-74.10	7214	Preparer, structural metal
8-74.20	7214	Loftsman, structural metal
8-74.20	7214	Loftswoman, structural metal
8-74.20	7214	Marker, structural metal
8-74.30	7214	Structural steel worker, workshop
8-74.40	7214	Erector, constructional steel
8-74.50	7214	Erector, ship beam and frame
8-74.50	7214	Shipwright, metal
8-74.55	7214	Plater, ship
8-74.60	7214	Riveter
8-74.65	8211	Machine-operator, riveting
8-74.70	7214	Riveter, pneumatic
8-74.90	7214	Bender, metal plate
8-74.90	8131	Machine-operator, bending/glass
8-80.10	7313	Jeweller
8-80.10	8212	Machine-operator, industrial-diamonds production
8-80.20	7313	Repairer, jewellery
8-80.30	7313	Cutter-polisher, gems
8-80.30	7313	Cutter-polisher, industrial diamonds
8-80.30	7313	Cutter-polisher, jewels
8-80.30	7313	Lapidary
8-80.30	8212	Machine-operator, cutting/industrial diamonds

8-80.30	8212	Machine-operator, polishing/industrial diamonds
8-80.30	7313	Polisher, industrial diamonds
8-80.30	7313	Sawyer, industrial diamonds
8-80.40	7313	Setter, gem
8-80.40	7313	Setter, jewels
8-80.50	7313	Goldsmith
8-80.50	7313	Pewtersmith
8-80.50	7313	Silversmith
8-80.60	7313	Roller, precious-metal
8-80.70	7313	Gold beater
8-80.70	7313	Maker, precious-metal leaf
8-80.80	7313	Engraver, jewellery
8-80.90	7313	Caster, jewellery moulds
8-80.90	7313	Cutter, precious metal
8-80.90	7313	Driller, precious metals
8-80.90	7313	Enameller, jewellery
8-80.90	7313	Hammer-smith, precious-metal articles
8-80.90	7313	Maker, precious-metal chain
8-80.90	7313	Mounter, jewellery
8-80.90	7313	Polisher, jewellery
8-80.90	7313	Spinner, precious metal
8-91.10	7322	Glass worker
8-91.10	7322	Grinder, glass
8-91.10	8131	Machine-operator, cutting/glass
8-91.10	8131	Machine-operator, grinding/glass
8-91.20	7322	Blower, glass
8-91.24	7322	Blower, scientific glass
8-91.28	8131	Machine-operator, blowing/glass
8-91.28	8131	Machine-operator, bottle production
8-91.32	7322	Moulder, glass lens
8-91.36	8131	Machine-operator, moulding/glass
8-91.36	8131	Machine-operator, pressing/glass
8-91.40	8131	Machine-operator, drawing/glass
8-91.44	8131	Machine-operator, rolling/plate-glass
8-91.48	8131	Machine-operator, polishing/plate-glass
8-91.52	8131	Kiln-operator, float-glass bath
8-91.56	7322	Cutter, glass
8-91.60	7322	Cutter, glass/optical
8-91.60	7322	Slicer, optical glass
8-91.60	7322	Slitter, optical glass
8-91.64	7322	Beveller, glass
8-91.64	7322	Grinder, glass edge
8-91.68	7322	Grinder, glass lens
8-91.72	8131	Machine-operator, polishing/glass lens
8-91.72	7322	Polisher, glass/lenses
8-91.76	8131	Machine-operator, glass rod production

8-95.90	8131	Machine-operator, plating/glass
8-95.90	7324	Toucher-up, ceramics decoration
8-95.90	7324	Tracer, ceramics decoration
8-99.20	8139	Machine-operator, mixing/glass
8-99.30	8139	Machine-operator, grinding/clay
8-99.30	8139	Machine-operator, mixing/clay
8-99.40	8139	Machine-operator, clay slips production
8-99.50	8139	Kiln-operator, frit
8-99.50	8139	Machine-operator, glaze production
8-99.50	8139	Machine-operator, grinding/glaze
8-99.50	8139	Machine-operator, mixing/glaze
8-99.60	8139	Machine-operator, mixing/abrasives
8-99.70	8139	Machine-operator, glass-fibre production
8-99.90	8139	Operator, pug-mill/clay
8-99.90	8139	Press-operator, filtering/clay
9-01.10	8232	Machine-operator, plastic products
9-01.10	8232	Machine-operator, plastics production
9-01.20	8231	Machine-operator, compounding/rubber
9-01.20	8231	Machine-operator, extruding/rubber
9-01.20	8231	Machine-operator, milling/rubber
9-01.20	8231	Machine-operator, rubber processing
9-01.25	8231	Operator, calender/rubber
9-01.30	8231	Machine-operator, moulding/tyres
9-01.35	8231	Machine-operator, moulding/rubber
9-01.40	8284	Assembler, rubber products
9-01.50	8232	Machine-operator, injection moulding/plastics
9-01.55	8232	Machine-operator, compression moulding/plastics
9-01.60	8232	Machine-operator, extruding/plastics
9-01.65	8232	Machine-operator, laminating/plastics
9-01.70	8284	Assembler, plastic products
9-01.80	8232	Machine-operator, fabrication/plastic products
9-01.90	8232	Machine-operator, buffing/plastics
9-01.90	8232	Machine-operator, carving/plastics
9-01.90	8232	Machine-operator, casting/plastic products
9-01.90	8231	Machine-operator, coating/rubber
9-01.90	8232	Machine-operator, cutting/plastics
9-01.90	8232	Machine-operator, drilling/plastics

9-01.90	8231	Machine-operator, embossing/rubber
9-01.90	8232	Machine-operator, etching/plastics
9-01.90	8232	Machine-operator, finishing/plastics
9-01.90	8232	Machine-operator, grinding/plastics
9-01.90	8232	Machine-operator, moulding/plastics
9-01.90	8231	Machine-operator, rubber products
9-01.90	8231	Machine-operator, vulcanising/rubber goods
9-02.30	8231	Machine-operator, vulcanising/tyres
9-02.40	8231	Machine-operator, rebuilding/tyres
9-02.90	8231	Machine-operator, tyre production
9-10.10	8286	Assembler, paperboard products
9-10.10	7331	Handicraft worker, paper articles
9-10.10	8253	Machine-operator, paper products
9-10.10	8253	Machine-operator, paperboard products
9-10.30	8253	Machine-operator, paper box production
9-10.40	8253	Machine-operator, lining/cardboard
9-10.50	8253	Machine-operator, cutting/paper-boxes
9-10.50	8253	Machine-operator, folding/paper boxes
9-10.70	8253	Machine-operator, envelope and paper bag production
9-10.80	8253	Machine-operator, cellophane bag production
9-10.80	8253	Machine-operator, polythene bag production
9-10.90	8253	Machine-operator, cardboard products
9-10.90	8253	Machine-operator, embossing/paper
9-21.10	7341	Printer
9-21.10	7341	Printer, job
9-21.20	7341	Compositor, printing
9-21.20	7341	Typesetter
9-21.30	7341	Intertype operator
9-21.30	7341	Linotyper
9-21.30	7341	Typesetter, linotype
9-21.30	7341	Typographer
9-21.35	7341	Monotyper
9-21.40	8251	Machine-operator, casting/printing type
9-21.40	7341	Setter, printing machine

ISCO-68

9-27.20	7344	Developer, film/colour
9-27.20	7344	Developer, negative/colour
9-27.20	7344	Developer, photograph/colour
9-27.20	7344	Developer, positive/colour
9-27.30	7344	Darkroom worker, film developing/ black and white photography
9-27.30	7344	Developer, film/black-and-white
9-27.30	7344	Developer, negative/black-and-white
9-27.30	7344	Developer, photograph/black-and-white
9-27.30	7344	Developer, positive/black-and-white
9-27.30	8224	Machine-operator, developing/ photography
9-27.30	8224	Machine-operator, film developing
9-27.30	8224	Machine-operator, photographic film developing
9-27.30	8224	Machine-operator, printing/ photography (black and white)
9-27.40	7344	Darkroom worker, photograph printing
9-27.40	8224	Machine-operator, printing/ photography (colour)
9-27.40	7344	Printer, film
9-27.40	7344	Printer, photograph
9-27.50	7344	Darkroom worker, photograph enlarging
9-27.50	7344	Enlarger, photograph
9-27.50	8224	Machine-operator, enlarging/ photography
9-27.50	7344	Printer, projection
9-27.90	7344	Developer, film/x-ray
9-27.90	7344	Developer, photographic plate
9-27.90	7344	Developer, print
9-27.90	8224	Machine-operator, developing/ motion picture film
9-29.20	7346	Cutter, stencil/silk-screen
9-29.30	7346	Printer, silk-screen
9-29.30	7346	Stenciller, silk-screen
9-29.40	7346	Printer, block
9-29.50	7346	Printer, textile
9-29.90	7346	Embosser, paper
9-29.90	7346	Maker, stencil/silk-screen
9-29.90	7346	Stamper, heraldic printing
9-31.20	7141	Brush-painter, construction
9-31.20	7141	Outside painter, construction
9-31.20	7141	Painter, building
9-31.20	7141	Painter, construction
9-31.20	7141	Painter, house
9-31.20	7141	Painter, outside/construction
9-31.20	7141	Painter-decorator, buildings
9-31.20	7141	Spray-painter, construction
9-31.30	7141	Painter, ship's hull
9-31.30	7141	Painter, structural steel
9-31.90	7141	Painter, motion picture set
9-31.90	7141	Painter, stage scenery
9-31.90	7141	Whitewasher
9-39.10	7142	Painter, manufactured articles
9-39.10	7142	Varnisher, manufactured articles
9-39.20	7324	Painter, decorative
9-39.30	7324	Brush-painter, except construction
9-39.30	7324	Spray-painter, except construction
9-39.40	7324	Dipper, metal articles
9-39.50	7324	Letterer, sign-writing
9-39.50	7324	Painter, decorative/sign
9-39.50	7324	Signpainter
9-39.50	7324	Sign-writer
9-39.60	7142	Painter, automobile
9-39.60	7142	Painter, vehicle
9-39.60	7142	Varnisher, vehicle
9-39.90	8223	Machine-operator, painting/metal
9-39.90	8240	Machine-operator, painting/wood
9-39.90	8281	Machine-operator, vehicle assembly
9-39.90	8290	Operator, marking equipment/ roads
9-39.90	7142	Painter, metal
9-39.90	7142	Varnisher, metal
9-41.20	7312	Maker, instrument/musical (string)
9-41.20	7312	Maker, violin
9-41.20	7312	Repairer, instrument/musical (string)
9-41.30	7312	Maker, instrument/musical (woodwind)
9-41.30	7312	Tone regulator, musical instruments
9-41.40	7312	Maker, instrument/musical (brass)
9-41.40	7312	Maker, instrument/musical (metal wind)
9-41.40	7312	Repairer, instrument/musical (wind)
9-41.50	7312	Maker, accordion
9-41.50	7312	Maker, piano accordion
9-41.60	7312	Builder, organ
9-41.60	7312	Maker, organ
9-41.60	7312	Maker, organ/bellow
9-41.60	7312	Maker, organ/pipe
9-41.70	7312	Maker, piano
9-41.70	7312	Maker, piano/key
9-41.70	7312	Maker, piano/sound-board
9-41.70	7312	Stringer, piano
9-41.80	7312	Tuner, accordion
9-41.80	7312	Tuner, musical instrument
9-41.80	7312	Tuner, organ

ISCO-68

9-52.20	7123	Shutterer, concrete moulding
9-52.30	7123	Iron worker, concrete reinforcement
9-52.40	7123	Finisher, cement
9-52.40	7123	Finisher, concrete
9-52.40	8212	Machine-operator, finishing/concrete
9-52.50	7123	Terrazzo worker
9-53.10	7131	Roofer
9-53.20	7131	Roofer, slate
9-53.20	7131	Roofer, tile
9-53.30	7131	Roofer, composite materials
9-53.40	7131	Roofer, asphalt
9-53.50	7131	Roofer, metal
9-53.60	7131	Thatcher
9-53.90	7131	Roofer, wood-shingle
9-54.10	7124	Carpenter
9-54.10	7124	Joiner
9-54.15	7124	Carpenter, construction
9-54.15	7124	Carpenter, first fixing
9-54.20	7124	Carpenter, second fixing
9-54.20	7124	Carpenter-joiner
9-54.20	7124	Joiner, construction
9-54.30	7124	Carpenter, stage
9-54.30	7124	Carpenter, theatre
9-54.40	7124	Shipwright, wood
9-54.45	7124	Joiner, ship
9-54.50	7124	Boatbuilder, wood
9-54.50	7124	Builder, barge/wooden
9-54.55	7124	Carpenter, ship's
9-54.60	7124	Joiner, aircraft
9-54.70	7124	Carpenter, bench
9-54.70	7124	Fitter, shop
9-54.70	7124	Joiner, bench
9-54.70	7124	Shopfitter
9-54.75	7132	Floor layer, parquetry
9-54.75	7132	Parquetry worker
9-54.90	7129	Billboard erector
9-54.90	7124	Carpenter, bridge
9-54.90	7124	Carpenter, maintenance
9-54.90	7124	Carpenter, mine
9-54.90	7124	Carpenter, wharf
9-54.90	7129	Erector, billboard
9-54.90	7132	Floor layer, wood block
9-54.90	7132	Layer, wood block
9-54.90	7124	Maker, mast and spar/wood
9-55.10	7133	Plasterer
9-55.20	7133	Plasterer, ornamental
9-55.30	7133	Mason, stucco
9-55.30	7133	Plasterer, stucco
9-55.40	7133	Plasterer, fibrous sheet
9-56.10	7134	Insulation worker
9-56.20	7134	Insulation worker, building
9-56.30	8290	Machine-operator, insulation
9-56.40	7134	Insulation worker, acoustical
9-56.40	7134	Insulation worker, sound-proofing
9-56.50	7134	Insulation worker, boiler and pipe
9-56.50	7134	Lagger, boiler and pipe
9-56.60	7134	Insulation worker, refrigeration and air-conditioning equipment
9-57.10	7135	Glazier
9-57.20	7135	Glazier, building
9-57.20	7135	Glazier, double glazing
9-57.20	7135	Glazier, structural
9-57.20	7135	Setter, glass/buildings
9-57.30	7135	Glazier, patent roofing
9-57.30	7135	Glazier, roofing
9-57.40	7135	Fitter, plate-glass
9-57.40	7135	Glazier, plate-glass
9-57.50	7135	Glazier, leaded-glass
9-57.50	7135	Glazier, stained-glass
9-57.50	7135	Setter, artistic/glass
9-57.60	7135	Glazier, vehicle
9-59.10	7129	Builder, house/non-traditional materials
9-59.10	7121	Builder, house/traditional materials
9-59.10	7129	Housebuilder, non-traditional materials
9-59.10	7121	Housebuilder, traditional materials
9-59.20	9313	Handyman, building maintenance
9-59.20	9313	Handywoman, building maintenance
9-59.20	7129	Maintenance worker, building
9-59.20	7129	Repairer, building
9-59.20	7129	Repairer, chimney
9-59.25	7141	Painter-decorator, wallcarpeting
9-59.25	7141	Painter-decorator, wallcovering
9-59.25	7141	Painter-decorator, wallpapering
9-59.25	7141	Paperhanger
9-59.25	7141	Wallpaper hanger
9-59.30	7129	Steeplejack
9-59.40	7129	Rigger, scaffolding
9-59.40	7129	Scaffolder
9-59.45	7129	Demolition worker
9-59.45	7129	Wrecker, building
9-59.50	7136	Jointer, pipe-laying
9-59.50	7129	Layer, drain
9-59.50	7136	Layer, pipe
9-59.50	7136	Layer-jointer, mains pipes
9-59.50	8290	Machine-operator, drain installation
9-59.50	8290	Machine-operator, pipe installation
9-59.50	7136	Pipeline worker

ISCO-68

391

ISCO-68

9-79.20	8334	Operator, truck/fork-lift
9-79.20	8334	Operator, truck/industrial
9-79.20	8334	Operator, truck/lifting
9-79.30	8324	Driver, dumper truck
9-79.30	8324	Driver, truck/dumper
9-79.40	8324	Operator, shuttle-car/mine
9-79.40	8324	Operator, shuttle-car/quarry
9-79.50	8331	Driver, lumber carrier
9-79.50	8331	Driver, timber carrier
9-79.90	8333	Operator, cable car
9-79.90	8333	Operator, chair-lift
9-79.90	8333	Operator, conveyer
9-79.90	8333	Operator, elevator/material-handling
9-79.90	8333	Operator, ropeway/aerial
9-81.20	8340	Boatswain
9-81.30	8340	Crewman
9-81.30	8340	Crewwoman
9-81.30	8340	Sailor
9-81.30	8340	Seaman, able
9-81.30	8340	Seawoman, able
9-81.40	8340	Deck hand, ship
9-81.40	8340	Hand, deck
9-81.40	8340	Seaman, ordinary
9-81.40	8340	Seawoman, ordinary
9-81.90	8340	Boatman
9-81.90	8340	Boatman, ferry
9-81.90	8340	Boatman, motor
9-81.90	8340	Boatman, tug
9-81.90	8340	Boatwoman
9-81.90	8340	Boatwoman, ferry
9-81.90	8340	Boatwoman, motor
9-81.90	8340	Boatwoman, tug
9-81.90	8340	Coxswain, lifeboat
9-81.90	8340	Crewman, dredger
9-81.90	8340	Crewman, yacht
9-81.90	8340	Crewwoman, dredger
9-81.90	8340	Crewwoman, yacht
9-81.90	8340	Hand, cable-ship
9-81.90	8340	Lifeboatman
9-81.90	8340	Lifeboatwoman
9-81.90	8340	Lighterman
9-81.90	8340	Lighterwoman
9-81.90	8340	Lightshipman
9-81.90	8340	Lightshipwoman
9-81.90	8340	Operator, barge
9-81.90	8340	Waterman
9-81.90	8340	Waterwoman
9-82.20	8162	Fireperson, ship
9-82.20	8162	Operator, boiler/ship
9-82.20	8162	Stoker, ship
9-82.30	7233	Oiler and greaser, ship
9-83.20	8311	Driver, locomotive
9-83.20	8311	Driver, railway engine
9-83.20	8311	Driver, railway engine/mine
9-83.20	8311	Driver, railway engine/quarry
9-83.20	8311	Driver, train
9-83.30	8162	Fireperson, locomotive boiler
9-83.30	8162	Operator, boiler/locomotive
9-83.40	8311	Driver-assistant, locomotive
9-83.40	8311	Driver-assistant, railway-engine
9-83.40	8311	Driver-assistant, train
9-83.50	8311	Driver, elevated train
9-83.50	8311	Driver, train/elevated
9-83.50	8311	Driver, train/underground
9-83.50	8311	Driver, underground train
9-83.60	8311	Driver, engine/mine
9-83.60	8311	Driver, engine/quarry
9-83.60	8311	Driver, locomotive/mine
9-83.60	8311	Driver, locomotive/quarry
9-83.90	8311	Driver, shunting-engine
9-84.20	8312	Braker, train/freight
9-84.20	8312	Guard, freight train
9-84.20	8312	Guard, goods train
9-84.30	8312	Signaller, railway
9-84.40	8312	Braker, railway
9-84.40	8312	Coupler, railway yard
9-84.40	8312	Shunter, railway
9-84.50	8312	Braker, train/mine
9-84.50	8312	Braker, train/quarry
9-85.20	8323	Driver, streetcar
9-85.20	8323	Driver, tram
9-85.20	8323	Driver, tramcar
9-85.30	8322	Driver, cab
9-85.30	8322	Driver, taxi
9-85.30	8322	Driver, taxi/motor-tricycle
9-85.40	8323	Driver, bus
9-85.40	8323	Driver, motor bus
9-85.40	8323	Driver, trolley-bus
9-85.50	8324	Driver, lorry
9-85.50	8322	Driver, van
9-85.60	8324	Driver, tanker
9-85.60	8324	Driver, trailer-truck
9-85.60	8324	Driver, truck
9-85.60	8324	Driver, truck/heavy
9-85.70	8321	Dispatch rider
9-85.70	8321	Driver, dispatch
9-85.70	8321	Driver, motor cycle
9-85.70	8321	Driver, motor tricycle
9-85.70	8321	Driver, motor tricycle/goods
9-85.70	8321	Motor-cyclist

9-85.70	8321	Rider, dispatch
9-85.70	8321	Rider, motor cycle
9-85.90	8322	Chauffeur, motor-car
9-85.90	8322	Driver, ambulance
9-85.90	8322	Driver, car
9-85.90	8322	Driver, car-delivery
9-85.90	8322	Driver, mail van
9-85.90	8322	Driver, motor car
9-85.90	8322	Driver, postal van
9-85.90	3340	Instructor, driving
9-86.20	9332	Driver, animal-drawn vehicle/road
9-86.30	9332	Driver, animal-drawn vehicle/mine
9-86.30	9332	Driver, animal-drawn vehicle/quarry
9-86.30	9332	Driver, animal/mine
9-86.30	9332	Driver, animal/quarry
9-86.90	9332	Driver, animal train
9-86.90	9332	Driver, animal train/camel
9-86.90	9332	Driver, animal train/mule
9-86.90	9332	Driver, elephant
9-86.90	9332	Mahout
9-89.20	3115	Dockmaster, dry dock
9-89.20	3115	Dockmaster, graving dock
9-89.30	8333	Lock-keeper, canal or port
9-89.30	8333	Operator, lock/canal or port
9-89.40	8340	Keeper, lighthouse
9-89.40	8340	Lighthouse keeper
9-89.50	9331	Bicyclist
9-89.50	9331	Driver, pedal vehicle
9-89.50	9331	Driver, tricycle/non-motorised
9-89.50	9331	Rider, bicycle
9-89.50	9331	Rider, tricycle
9-89.50	9331	Tricyclist
9-89.90	8333	Attendant, dry dock
9-89.90	9331	Berther, dock
9-89.90	9331	Driver, rickshaw
9-89.90	8333	Operator, sluice/dock
9-89.90	8333	Sluiceman, dock
9-89.90	8333	Sluicewoman, dock
9-99.10	9321	Bottle sorter
9-99.10	9132	Cleaner, factory
9-99.10	9142	Cleaner, vehicles
9-99.10	9162	Coalman
9-99.10	9162	Coalwoman
9-99.10	9161	Collector, garbage
9-99.10	9161	Collector, refuse
9-99.10	9331	Driver, handtruck
9-99.10	9161	Dustman
9-99.10	9161	Dustwoman
9-99.10	8290	Handyman

9-99.10	9313	Handywoman
9-99.10	9313	Hod carrier
9-99.10	9321	Labourer, assembling
9-99.10	9312	Labourer, construction
9-99.10	9313	Labourer, construction/buildings
9-99.10	9312	Labourer, construction/dams
9-99.10	9312	Labourer, construction/roads
9-99.10	9313	Labourer, demolition
9-99.10	9312	Labourer, digging/ditch
9-99.10	9312	Labourer, digging/grave
9-99.10	9312	Labourer, digging/trench
9-99.10	9213	Labourer, fishery
9-99.10	9212	Labourer, forestry
9-99.10	9213	Labourer, hunting
9-99.10	9312	Labourer, maintenance
9-99.10	9312	Labourer, maintenance/dams
9-99.10	9312	Labourer, maintenance/roads
9-99.10	9322	Labourer, manufacturing
9-99.10	9162	Labourer, odd-jobbing
9-99.10	9211	Labourer, roustabout
9-99.10	9213	Labourer, trapping
9-99.10	9312	Labourer, tube well
9-99.10	9312	Labourer, water well
9-99.10	9312	Land clearer
9-99.10	9312	Navvy
9-99.10	9162	Odd-job person
9-99.10	9312	Shoveller
9-99.10	9313	Stacker, building construction
9-99.10	9212	Stump-grubber
9-99.10	9162	Sweeper, factory
9-99.10	9162	Sweeper, house
9-99.10	9162	Sweeper, park
9-99.10	9162	Sweeper, street
9-99.10	9162	Sweeper, yard
9-99.10	9312	Trackman, railway
9-99.10	9312	Trackwoman, railway
9-99.10	9132	Washer, hand/dishes
9-99.10	9322	Washer, hand/manufacturing process
9-99.10	9120	Washer, hand/street (car windows)
9-99.10	9142	Washer, hand/vehicle

See Introduction, Supervisor
See Introduction, Teacher, private lessons
See Introduction, Working proprietor

ISCO-68

Alphabetical index of occupational titles

A

1-99.40	2419	Account executive, advertising
1-10.10	2411	Accountant
1-10.20	2411	Accountant, auditing
1-10.10	2411	Accountant, chartered
1-10.10	2411	Accountant, company
1-10.90	2411	Accountant, cost
1-10.10	2411	Accountant, municipal
1-10.10	2411	Accountant, public
7-13.70	3117	Acidiser, oil and gas well
1-75.40	3474	Acrobat
1-73.20	2455	Actor
1-73.20	2455	Actor, character
1-73.20	2455	Actor, comic
1-73.20	2455	Actor, dramatic
1-73.20	2455	Actor, film
0-82.50	2121	Actuary
4-43.30	3417	Adjuster, claims
4-43.30	3417	Adjuster, claims/insurance
3-21.20	3431	Administrative secretary
2-02.10	1120	Administrator, city
2-02.10	1120	Administrator, government
2-02.10	1120	Administrator, intergovernmental organisation
4-31.30	3415	Adviser, after-sales service
0-53.60	3213	Adviser, agricultural
1-94.30	2412	Adviser, careers
1-39.20	2351	Adviser, education
1-39.20	2351	Adviser, education methods
0-53.60	3213	Adviser, farming
0-53.60	3213	Adviser, forestry
1-29.10	2429	Adviser, legal
1-39.20	2351	Adviser, teaching methods
1-21.10	2421	Advocate
1-75.50	3474	Aerialist
0-12.20	2111	Aerodynamicist
8-44.10	7232	Aeromechanic
1-99.90	3422	Agent, clearing
1-99.90	3423	Agent, employment
4-41.30	3413	Agent, estate
1-99.90	3422	Agent, forwarding
4-41.90	3412	Agent, group insurance
4-41.30	3413	Agent, house
5-82.30	3450	Agent, inquiry/police
4-41.20	3412	Agent, insurance
1-99.90	3429	Agent, literary
1-99.90	3429	Agent, musical performance
4-22.30	3416	Agent, procurement
4-41.30	3413	Agent, property
4-22.30	3416	Agent, purchasing
4-32.20	3415	Agent, sales/commercial
4-31.20	3415	Agent, sales/engineering
4-32.30	3415	Agent, sales/manufacturing
4-31.20	3415	Agent, sales/technical
1-99.90	3422	Agent, shipping
1-99.90	3429	Agent, sports
1-99.90	3429	Agent, theatrical
0-53.20	2213	Agricultural scientist
0-53.20	2213	Agronomist
5-99.40	5132	Aid, dental
5-99.40	5132	Aid, nursing/clinic
5-99.40	5133	Aid, nursing/home
5-99.40	5132	Aid, nursing/hospital
5-99.50	5139	Aid, pharmacy
5-99.60	5139	Aid, veterinary
1-93.20	3460	Almoner, associate professional
1-93.20	2446	Almoner, professional
2-02.10	1120	Ambassador
5-99.40	5132	Ambulance man
5-99.40	5132	Ambulance woman
0-61.20	2221	Anaesthetist
0-23.90	2131	Analyst, communications/computers
0-23.90	2149	Analyst, communications/except computers
0-23.90	2131	Analyst, database/computers
1-94.40	2412	Analyst, job
0-90.30	2419	Analyst, market research
1-94.40	2412	Analyst, occupational
0-82.40	2121	Analyst, operations research
0-83.10	2131	Analyst, systems/computers
0-83.10	2149	Analyst, systems/except computers
0-52.20	2212	Anatomist
0-52.80	2213	Animal scientist
7-26.20	8123	Annealer
1-79.20	3472	Announcer, news
1-79.20	3472	Announcer, radio
1-79.20	3472	Announcer, television
7-28.90	8223	Anodiser
1-92.40	2442	Anthropologist
6-12.90	6123	Apiarist
6-29.20	6123	Apiary worker, skilled

1-29.10	2429	Appeals referee, social security claims
4-43.30	3417	Appraiser
0-53.30	2213	Arboriculturist
1-92.40	2442	Archaeologist
1-41.20	2460	Archbishop
0-21.20	2141	Architect, building
0-21.20	2141	Architect, interior
0-21.40	2141	Architect, landscape
0-24.50	2145	Architect, marine
0-24.50	2145	Architect, naval
1-91.30	2431	Archivist
1-72.20	2454	Arranger, ballet
1-71.30	2453	Arranger, music
1-62.20	2452	Artist, commercial
1-61.90	2452	Artist, creative
1-62.40	2452	Artist, fashion creation
1-62.20	2452	Artist, graphic
1-75.90	3474	Artist, high-wire
1-61.30	2452	Artist, landscape
1-61.30	2452	Artist, paintings
1-62.20	2452	Artist, poster
1-79.90	3474	Artist, strip-tease
1-75.90	3474	Artist, tight-rope
1-75.50	3474	Artist, trapeze
1-61.90	2452	Artist-painter
0-26.30	2147	Assayer
8-41.60	8281	Assembler, agricultural machinery
8-41.20	8281	Assembler, aircraft
8-53.30	8283	Assembler, audio-visual equipment
8-42.20	8283	Assembler, chronometer
8-42.20	8283	Assembler, clock
8-53.30	8290	Assembler, composite products
8-41.65	8281	Assembler, earth-moving equipment
8-53.90	8282	Assembler, electrical components
8-53.20	8282	Assembler, electrical equipment
8-53.90	8283	Assembler, electronic components
8-53.30	8283	Assembler, electronic equipment
8-41.20	8281	Assembler, engine/aircraft
8-41.15	8281	Assembler, engine/internal combustion
8-41.25	8281	Assembler, engine/marine
8-41.15	8281	Assembler, engine/motor vehicles
8-41.90	8281	Assembler, engines/steam
8-73.90	8284	Assembler, furniture/sheet-metal
8-11.10	8285	Assembler, furniture/wood and related materials
8-53.90	8283	Assembler, hearing aid
8-41.10	8281	Assembler, industrial machinery
8-03.60	8286	Assembler, leather products
8-41.35	8281	Assembler, machine tool
8-41.10	8281	Assembler, mechanical machinery

8-49.90	8281	Assembler, metal products
8-73.10	8284	Assembler, metal products
8-53.90	8283	Assembler, microelectronics equipment
8-41.40	8281	Assembler, mining machinery
8-41.70	8283	Assembler, office machinery
9-10.10	8286	Assembler, paperboard products
9-01.70	8284	Assembler, plastic products
8-42.40	8283	Assembler, precision instrument
8-41.45	8281	Assembler, printing machinery
8-53.30	8283	Assembler, radio
6-31.40	6141	Assembler, raft
9-01.40	8284	Assembler, rubber products
8-53.30	8283	Assembler, television
8-41.50	8281	Assembler, textile machinery
7-99.90	8286	Assembler, textile products
8-41.30	8281	Assembler, turbine
8-41.10	8281	Assembler, vehicle
8-42.20	8283	Assembler, watch
8-11.10	8285	Assembler, wood products
8-41.55	8281	Assembler, woodworking machinery
4-43.30	3417	Assessor, claims
4-43.30	3417	Assessor, insurance
4-43.30	3417	Assessor, loss
0-84.90	3434	Assistant, accounting
0-84.90	3434	Assistant, actuarial
3-93.90	3432	Assistant, bank
3-93.40	3432	Assistant, barrister's
3-93.50	3432	Assistant, broker's
0-34.90	3121	Assistant, computer/ communications
0-34.90	3121	Assistant, computer/database analysis
0-34.90	3121	Assistant, computer/engineering
0-34.90	3121	Assistant, computer/programming
0-34.90	3121	Assistant, computer/systems analysis
0-34.90	3121	Assistant, computer/systems design
0-34.90	3121	Assistant, computer/users' services
3-93.20	3431	Assistant, correspondence
0-64.20	3225	Assistant, dental
0-64.30	3225	Assistant, dental/school service
3-93.50	3432	Assistant, insurance/adjustment
3-93.50	3432	Assistant, insurance/claims
3-93.50	3432	Assistant, insurance/policy
3-93.40	3432	Assistant, legal
0-84.90	3434	Assistant, mathematical
0-62.10	3221	Assistant, medical
0-62.10	3221	Assistant, medical/family planning
1-63.50	3131	Assistant, motion picture

0-68.10	3228	Assistant, pharmaceutical
4-51.90	5220	Assistant, shop/orders
3-93.40	3432	Assistant, solicitor's
0-84.90	3434	Assistant, statistical
0-66.10	3227	Assistant, veterinary
0-66.10	3227	Assistant, veterinary/artificial insemination
1-99.60	5151	Astrologer
0-12.10	2111	Astronomer
0-13.50	2111	Astronomer, radio
0-13.50	2111	Astrophysicist
1-80.20	3475	Athlete
5-99.70	5111	Attendant, airport
5-99.90	9152	Attendant, amusement park
5-70.70	5141	Attendant, bath
5-70.70	5141	Attendant, bath/hot-room
5-70.70	5141	Attendant, bath/sauna
5-70.70	5141	Attendant, bath/turkish
5-32.90	5123	Attendant, canteen
5-99.90	9152	Attendant, cloakroom
5-99.40	5132	Attendant, dental
9-89.90	8333	Attendant, dry dock
5-99.90	9152	Attendant, fairground
5-99.40	5132	Attendant, first-aid
5-99.70	5111	Attendant, flight

5-99.90	9152	Attendant, fun-fair
5-92.90	5143	Attendant, funeral
5-99.40	5132	Attendant, hospital
5-99.90	9152	Attendant, lavatory
5-99.90	9151	Attendant, lift
5-99.40	5133	Attendant, nursing/home
5-99.40	5132	Attendant, nursing/except home
5-99.90	9152	Attendant, parking lot
4-51.90	5220	Attendant, petrol pump
5-99.90	9152	Attendant, rest-room
5-32.90	5123	Attendant, restaurant seating
5-40.35	5131	Attendant, schoolchildren
4-51.90	5220	Attendant, service station/ automobiles
5-99.70	5111	Attendant, ship's cabin
4-51.30	5220	Attendant, shop
3-91.40	4131	Attendant, tool crib
5-92.90	5143	Attendant, undertaker's
1-21.10	2421	Attorney
1-29.10	2429	Attorney, insurance claims
4-43.20	3417	Auctioneer
1-10.20	2411	Auditor
1-51.20	2451	Author
0-64.20	3225	Auxiliary, dental

B

0-52.50	2211	Bacteriologist
0-52.50	2211	Bacteriologist, agricultural
0-52.50	2211	Bacteriologist, dairy
0-52.50	2211	Bacteriologist, fishery
0-52.50	2211	Bacteriologist, food
0-52.50	2211	Bacteriologist, industrial
0-52.50	2211	Bacteriologist, medical
0-52.50	2211	Bacteriologist, pharmaceutical
0-52.50	2211	Bacteriologist, soil
0-52.50	2211	Bacteriologist, veterinary
9-71.50	9322	Bagger, hand
5-89.90	3432	Bailiff
7-76.10	7412	Baker
7-76.90	7412	Baker, biscuit
7-76.20	7412	Baker, bread
7-76.30	7412	Baker, pastry
8-42.30	7311	Balancer, scale
7-52.90	8261	Baller, thread and yarn
1-72.30	2454	Ballerina
0-12.20	2111	Ballistician
1-71.35	3473	Band leader
1-71.35	3473	Bandmaster
9-73.45	8333	Banksman, mine
9-73.45	8333	Bankswoman, mine
5-70.30	5141	Barber

1-71.45	2453	Baritone
5-10.50	1315	Barkeeper
1-21.10	2421	Barrister
5-32.50	5123	Bartender
1-71.40	2453	Bassoonist
6-49.90	9213	Beachcomber
8-73.80	7213	Beater, aircraft panel
8-73.70	7213	Beater, vehicle panel
5-70.40	5141	Beautician
5-70.60	5141	Beautician, make-up/stage
5-70.20	5141	Beautician, make-up/studio
6-29.20	6123	Beekeeper
6-29.20	6123	Beekeeping worker, skilled
5-99.90	9151	Bellboy
8-91.80	7322	Bender, glass
8-74.90	7214	Bender, metal plate
8-19.90	7422	Bender, wood
9-89.90	9331	Berther, dock
8-91.64	7322	Beveller, glass
9-89.50	9331	Bicyclist
9-54.90	7129	Billboard erector
5-99.90	9120	Billposter
0-52.30	2212	Biochemist
1-51.20	2451	Biographer
0-51.10	2211	Biologist

0-51.90	2211	Biologist, fresh-water
0-51.90	2211	Biologist, marine
0-51.90	2211	Biologist, molecular
0-81.30	2122	Biometrician
0-52.90	2212	Biophysicist
1-41.20	2460	Bishop
8-31.10	7221	Blacksmith
7-11.50	7112	Blaster
7-56.15	7431	Bleacher, fibre/textiles
7-51.25	7431	Blender, fibre/textiles
7-89.20	7416	Blender, snuff
7-81.30	7416	Blender, tobacco
7-93.30	8269	Blocker, hat
8-91.20	7322	Blower, glass
8-91.24	7322	Blower, scientific glass
7-29.20	7224	Bluer, metal
9-54.50	7124	Boatbuilder, wood
9-81.90	8340	Boatman
9-81.90	8340	Boatman, ferry
9-81.90	8340	Boatman, motor
9-81.90	8340	Boatman, tug
9-81.20	8340	Boatswain
9-81.90	8340	Boatwoman
9-81.90	8340	Boatwoman, ferry
9-81.90	8340	Boatwoman, motor
9-81.90	8340	Boatwoman, tug
5-89.90	5169	Bodyguard
8-73.50	7213	Boilersmith
7-11.60	7111	Bolter, roof/mine
7-79.40	7411	Boner, fish
7-73.90	7411	Boner, meat
1-41.20	2460	Bonze
9-26.20	7345	Bookbinder
9-26.20	7345	Bookbinding sewer
3-31.10	3433	Bookkeeper
3-31.10	3433	Bookkeeper, ledger
5-99.20	4213	Bookmaker
5-99.20	4213	Bookmaker, betting pool
5-99.20	4213	Bookmaker, pari-mutuel system
5-99.20	4213	Bookmaker, ticket writing
5-99.20	4213	Bookmaker, totalisator
8-91.90	7322	Borer, glass
8-34.60	7223	Borer, metal
8-12.90	7423	Borer, wood
0-51.20	2211	Botanist
0-51.20	2211	Botanist, ecology
0-51.20	2211	Botanist, economic
0-51.20	2211	Botanist, histology
0-51.20	2211	Botanist, mycology
0-51.20	2211	Botanist, soil
0-51.20	2211	Botanist, taxonomy
9-99.10	9321	Bottle sorter
9-71.50	9322	Bottler, hand
1-80.20	3475	Boxer
9-59.90	7129	Bracer, construction
9-84.40	8312	Braker, railway
9-84.20	8312	Braker, train/freight
9-84.50	8312	Braker, train/mine
9-84.50	8312	Braker, train/quarry
8-72.45	7212	Brazier
8-72.45	7212	Brazier, flame
8-72.90	7212	Brazier, furnace
8-72.45	7212	Brazier, induction
6-12.90	6129	Breeder, bird
6-24.40	6121	Breeder, cat
6-12.40	6121	Breeder, cattle
6-24.40	6121	Breeder, dog
6-12.90	6129	Breeder, game bird
6-12.90	6129	Breeder, laboratory animal
6-12.90	6129	Breeder, laboratory animal/mice
6-12.90	6129	Breeder, lion
6-12.60	6122	Breeder, poultry
6-12.90	6129	Breeder, reindeer
6-12.90	6129	Breeder, reptile
6-12.90	6129	Breeder, reptile/snake
6-12.90	6129	Breeder, snail
6-12.40	6121	Breeder, stud
7-78.10	8278	Brewer
9-51.25	7122	Bricklayer, chimney
9-51.20	7122	Bricklayer, construction
9-51.30	7122	Bricklayer, firebrick
9-51.30	7122	Bricklayer, furnace lining
9-51.90	7122	Bricklayer, ingot mould lining
9-51.30	7122	Bricklayer, kiln
9-51.30	7122	Bricklayer, oven
7-74.50	7411	Briner, foodstuffs
4-10.20	3421	Broker, commodity
4-41.40	3411	Broker, foreign exchange
4-41.20	3412	Broker, insurance
4-41.40	3411	Broker, investment
4-41.40	3411	Broker, securities
4-10.20	3421	Broker, shipping
4-41.40	3411	Broker, stocks and shares
4-10.20	3421	Broker, trade
9-31.20	7141	Brush-painter, construction
9-39.30	7324	Brush-painter, except construction
6-31.20	6141	Bucker, logging
6-23.90	6112	Budder-grafter, fruit tree
6-27.30	6113	Budder-grafter, shrubs
7-61.90	7441	Buffer, leather
8-35.90	7224	Buffer, metal
8-51.90	7241	Builder, armature
9-54.50	7124	Builder, barge/wooden
9-51.25	7122	Builder, chimney
8-19.20	7422	Builder, coach-body/wooden
8-51.90	7241	Builder, commutator

C

3-31.60	4211	Cashier, store
9-52.20	7123	Caster, concrete products
9-23.30	7342	Caster, electrotype
8-80.90	7313	Caster, jewellery moulds
7-24.20	7221	Caster, metal
8-92.35	7321	Caster, pottery and porcelain
9-23.20	7342	Caster, stereotype
5-99.90	9151	Cellarman
5-99.90	9151	Cellarwoman
1-71.40	2453	Cellist
8-02.30	7442	Cementer, footwear/uppers
7-13.50	3117	Cementer, oil and gas wells
3-10.10	3449	Censor, government administration
2-11.10	1210	Chairperson, enterprise
2-11.10	1210	Chairperson, organisation
2-11.10	1141	Chairperson, political party
5-40.50	9132	Chambermaid
2-01.10	1110	Chancellor, government
2-11.10	1210	Chancellor, university
8-02.40	7442	Channeller, footwear/soles
1-41.20	2460	Chaplain
5-40.20	9131	Charworker, domestic
5-52.20	9132	Charworker, factory
5-52.20	9132	Charworker, hotel
5-52.20	9132	Charworker, office
5-52.20	9132	Charworker, restaurant
9-85.90	8322	Chauffeur, motor-car
5-31.20	5122	Chef de cuisine
0-11.10	2113	Chemist
0-11.50	2113	Chemist, analytical
0-11.40	2113	Chemist, corrosion
0-11.40	2113	Chemist, crystallography
0-11.20	2113	Chemist, detergents
0-11.20	2113	Chemist, dye
0-11.20	2113	Chemist, food
0-11.30	2113	Chemist, glass
0-11.30	2113	Chemist, inorganic
0-11.20	2113	Chemist, leather
0-11.30	2113	Chemist, metallurgical
0-11.40	2113	Chemist, nuclear
0-11.20	2113	Chemist, organic
0-11.20	2113	Chemist, paint
0-11.20	2113	Chemist, petroleum
0-11.90	2113	Chemist, pharmaceutical
0-11.40	2113	Chemist, physical
0-11.20	2113	Chemist, plastics
0-11.20	2113	Chemist, polymer
0-11.50	2113	Chemist, quality control
0-11.20	2113	Chemist, rubber
0-11.20	2113	Chemist, textile
2-02.10	1120	Chief constable, police
0-43.15	3141	Chief engineer, ship
2-11.10	1210	Chief executive, enterprise
2-11.10	1210	Chief executive, enterprise/agriculture
2-11.10	1210	Chief executive, enterprise/business services
2-11.10	1210	Chief executive, enterprise/cleaning
2-11.10	1210	Chief executive, enterprise/communications
2-11.10	1210	Chief executive, enterprise/construction
2-11.10	1210	Chief executive, enterprise/cultural activities
2-11.10	1210	Chief executive, enterprise/education
2-11.10	1210	Chief executive, enterprise/fishing
2-11.10	1210	Chief executive, enterprise/forestry
2-11.10	1210	Chief executive, enterprise/health
2-11.10	1210	Chief executive, enterprise/hotel
2-11.10	1210	Chief executive, enterprise/hunting
2-11.10	1210	Chief executive, enterprise/manufacturing
2-11.10	1210	Chief executive, enterprise/personal care
2-11.10	1210	Chief executive, enterprise/recreation
2-11.10	1210	Chief executive, enterprise/restaurant
2-11.10	1210	Chief executive, enterprise/retail trade
2-11.10	1210	Chief executive, enterprise/social work
2-11.10	1210	Chief executive, enterprise/sporting activities
2-11.10	1210	Chief executive, enterprise/storage
2-11.10	1210	Chief executive, enterprise/transportation
2-11.10	1210	Chief executive, enterprise/travel agency
2-11.10	1210	Chief executive, enterprise/wholesale trade
2-11.10	1210	Chief executive, organisation
2-11.10	1210	Chief executive, organisation/cultural activities
2-11.10	1210	Chief executive, organisation/education
2-11.10	1210	Chief executive, organisation/extra-territorial organisations
2-11.10	1210	Chief executive, organisation/fishing
2-11.10	1210	Chief executive, organisation/forestry
2-11.10	1210	Chief executive, organisation/health
2-11.10	1210	Chief executive, organisation/public administration
2-11.10	1210	Chief executive, organisation/recreation

3-94.90	4222	Clerk, information	3-21.50	4112	Clerk, telex
3-94.90	4222	Clerk, inquiries	3-31.60	4221	Clerk, ticket issuing/travel
3-93.50	3432	Clerk, insurance	3-31.60	4211	Clerk, ticket issuing/except travel
3-39.40	4122	Clerk, investment	3-31.60	4211	Clerk, toll collection
3-39.90	4121	Clerk, invoice	3-99.90	4133	Clerk, transport
3-41.20	4114	Clerk, invoicing machine	3-94.40	4221	Clerk, travel
3-93.40	3432	Clerk, judge's	3-94.40	4221	Clerk, travel /airlines
3-21.90	4111	Clerk, justowriting	3-94.40	4221	Clerk, travel /railway
3-93.40	3432	Clerk, law	3-94.40	4221	Clerk, travel agency
3-31.20	4121	Clerk, ledger	3-94.40	4221	Clerk, travel agency/bookings
3-95.20	4141	Clerk, library	3-94.40	4221	Clerk, travel agency/reservations
3-95.20	4141	Clerk, library/acquisitions	3-21.40	4111	Clerk, typing
3-93.90	4190	Clerk, list/addresses	3-39.30	4121	Clerk, wages
3-99.90	4190	Clerk, list/mail	3-91.40	4131	Clerk, warehouse
3-93.90	4143	Clerk, listing	3-91.50	4131	Clerk, weighing
3-70.90	4142	Clerk, mail/dispatch	3-91.50	4131	Clerk, weighing/scale
3-70.20	4142	Clerk, mail/sorting	3-91.50	4131	Clerk, weighing/tally
3-39.40	4122	Clerk, mortgage	3-21.40	4112	Clerk, word processing
3-31.20	4121	Clerk, office cash	0-13.40	2112	Climatologist
3-92.20	4132	Clerk, order/materials	6-31.30	6141	Climber, logging
3-39.30	4121	Clerk, payroll	7-11.90	7111	Clipper, mine
3-99.50	4141	Clerk, photocopying	1-75.20	3474	Clown
3-92.20	4132	Clerk, planning/materials	1-80.30	3475	Coach, athletic
3-31.70	4212	Clerk, post office counter	1-80.30	3475	Coach, games
3-41.20	4114	Clerk, posting machine	1-80.30	3475	Coach, sports
3-93.40	3432	Clerk, probate	9-99.10	9162	Coalman
3-92.30	4132	Clerk, production planning	9-99.10	9162	Coalwoman
3-92.30	4132	Clerk, production planning/ coordination	5-89.90	5169	Coastguard
			8-01.30	7442	Cobbler
3-92.30	4132	Clerk, production planning/ schedule	3-99.30	4143	Coder, clerical
			3-99.30	4143	Coder, clerical/data-processing
3-99.40	4143	Clerk, proof-reading	3-99.30	4143	Coder, clerical/statistics
3-99.40	4143	Clerk, proof-reading/printing	9-26.20	7345	Collator, bookbinding
3-39.40	4122	Clerk, rating	3-39.90	4215	Collector, charity
3-93.30	4190	Clerk, records/personnel	3-31.60	9153	Collector, coin machine
3-99.50	4141	Clerk, reproduction processes/ office	3-31.60	9153	Collector, coin meter
			3-39.90	4215	Collector, debt
3-39.30	4121	Clerk, salaries	9-99.10	9161	Collector, garbage
3-92.20	4132	Clerk, schedule/materials	3-39.90	4215	Collector, payment
3-99.90	4143	Clerk, scripts	9-99.10	9161	Collector, refuse
3-39.40	4122	Clerk, securities	3-39.90	4215	Collector, rent
3-99.20	4122	Clerk, statistical	3-31.60	9152	Collector, ticket
3-91.30	4131	Clerk, stock	3-31.60	9153	Collector, turnstile
3-91.30	4131	Clerk, stock/control	3-31.60	9153	Collector, vending machine
3-91.30	4131	Clerk, stock/control (inventory)	3-31.60	9153	Collector, vending machine/money
3-91.30	4131	Clerk, stock/control (records)	3-31.60	9153	Collector, vending machine/tokens
3-91.30	4131	Clerk, stock/records	1-59.15	2451	Columnist
3-91.40	4131	Clerk, stock/storeroom	7-51.45	7431	Comber, fibre/textiles
3-91.40	4131	Clerk, supply	1-75.20	3474	Comic, circus
3-39.40	4122	Clerk, tax	1-59.90	2451	Commentator, extempore
3-21.50	4112	Clerk, telefax	1-59.35	2451	Commentator, news
3-21.50	4112	Clerk, telegraph	1-59.90	2451	Commentator, sports
3-21.50	4112	Clerk, teleprinter	4-32.20	3415	Commercial traveller

1-51.30	2451	Critic, art
1-51.30	2451	Critic, book
1-51.30	2451	Critic, drama
1-51.30	2451	Critic, film
1-51.30	2451	Critic, literary
1-51.30	2451	Critic, music
1-51.30	2451	Critic, radio
1-51.30	2451	Critic, television
7-59.30	7432	Crocheter
0-53.20	2213	Crop research scientist
6-31.20	6141	Cross-cutter, logging
5-99.30	4213	Croupier
5-99.30	4213	Croupier, gambling-table
6-32.40	6141	Cruiser, timber
0-11.40	2113	Crystallographer
6-49.90	6151	Cultivator, algae
6-29.90	6113	Cultivator, mushroom
6-49.90	6151	Cultivator, pearl
1-41.20	2460	Curate
1-91.40	2431	Curator, art gallery
1-91.40	2431	Curator, museum
7-74.50	7411	Curer, bacon
7-74.50	7411	Curer, fish
7-74.50	7411	Curer, meat
1-39.20	2351	Curricula developer
7-61.50	7441	Currier, leather
8-94.20	7323	Cutter, crystal glass
7-79.40	7411	Cutter, fish
8-02.25	7442	Cutter, footwear
8-02.20	7442	Cutter, footwear/clicker
7-92.50	7434	Cutter, fur
7-94.50	7435	Cutter, garment
8-91.56	7322	Cutter, glass
8-91.60	7322	Cutter, glass/optical

7-94.70	7435	Cutter, glove
8-94.20	7323	Cutter, intaglio glass
8-03.30	7442	Cutter, leather
7-94.90	7435	Cutter, mattress
7-73.30	7411	Cutter, meat
6-31.90	6141	Cutter, pole and pile
8-80.90	7313	Cutter, precious metal
6-31.90	6141	Cutter, railway tie
7-94.90	7435	Cutter, sail
6-31.90	6141	Cutter, sleeper
9-29.20	7346	Cutter, stencil/silk-screen
8-20.60	7113	Cutter, stone
8-20.60	7113	Cutter, stone/lettering
6-22.90	9211	Cutter, sugar cane
7-76.60	7412	Cutter, sugar confectionery
7-94.50	7435	Cutter, tailor's
7-94.90	7435	Cutter, tent
6-31.20	6141	Cutter, timber/forestry
7-81.70	7416	Cutter, tobacco
7-94.90	7435	Cutter, umbrella
7-94.90	7435	Cutter, upholstery
8-20.20	7113	Cutter-finisher, stone
8-80.30	7313	Cutter-polisher, gems
8-80.30	7313	Cutter-polisher, industrial diamonds
8-80.30	7313	Cutter-polisher, jewels
9-51.55	7132	Cutter-setter, mosaic
8-94.90	7323	Cutter-shaper, decorative glass
7-12.90	8112	Cyanide worker, separation equipment
1-80.20	3475	Cycle racer
0-51.90	2211	Cytologist
0-52.90	2211	Cytologist, animal
0-52.90	2211	Cytologist, plant

D

1-72.30	2454	Dancer, ballet
1-72.30	2454	Dancer, ballroom
1-72.30	3473	Dancer, chorus
1-72.30	3473	Dancer, night-club
1-72.30	3473	Dancer, tap
9-27.30	7344	Darkroom worker, film developing/ black and white photography
9-27.20	7344	Darkroom worker, film developing/ colour photography
9-27.50	7344	Darkroom worker, photograph enlarging
9-27.40	7344	Darkroom worker, photograph printing
0-84.20	2131	Database administrator
2-19.90	1229	Dean
9-81.40	8340	Deck hand, ship

8-95.40	7324	Decorator, ceramics
8-95.50	7324	Decorator, ceramics/aerographing
8-95.30	7324	Decorator, ceramics/freehand painting
8-95.50	7324	Decorator, ceramics/spray-painting
1-62.50	3471	Decorator, display
1-62.50	3471	Decorator, display/windows
1-62.30	3471	Decorator, interior
1-62.30	3471	Decorator, motion picture set
8-95.30	7324	Decorator, pottery
7-61.30	7441	Dehairer, hide
3-70.40	9151	Deliverer, hand
4-52.40	9151	Deliverer, hand/newspapers
0-81.30	2122	Demographer
9-59.45	7129	Demolition worker
4-51.50	5220	Demonstrator

1-62.30	3471	Designer, decoration
1-62.50	3471	Designer, display
1-62.50	3471	Designer, display/windows
1-62.40	3471	Designer, dress
1-62.50	3471	Designer, exhibition
1-62.40	3471	Designer, fashion
1-62.40	3471	Designer, furniture
1-62.20	3471	Designer, graphic
1-62.40	3471	Designer, industrial products
1-62.30	3471	Designer, interior decoration
1-62.40	3471	Designer, jewellery
0-24.70	2145	Designer, motor-car
1-62.40	3471	Designer, package
1-62.20	3471	Designer, poster
1-62.90	3471	Designer, scenery
1-62.90	3471	Designer, stage set
0-23.90	2131	Designer, systems/computers
0-23.90	2149	Designer, systems/except computers
1-62.40	3471	Designer, textile
1-62.20	3471	Designer, typographical
5-82.30	3450	Detective
5-89.20	3450	Detective, store
9-27.30	7344	Developer, film/black-and-white
9-27.20	7344	Developer, film/colour
9-27.90	7344	Developer, film/x-ray
9-27.30	7344	Developer, negative/black-and-white
9-27.20	7344	Developer, negative/colour
9-27.30	7344	Developer, photograph/black-and-white
9-27.20	7344	Developer, photograph/colour
9-27.90	7344	Developer, photographic plate
9-27.30	7344	Developer, positive/black-and-white
9-27.20	7344	Developer, positive/colour
9-27.90	7344	Developer, print
0-69.10	3223	Dietician
0-69.10	3223	Dietician, therapeutic
9-59.55	7136	Digger, well
2-02.10	1120	Diplomatic representative, embassy
8-95.60	7321	Dipper, ceramics
9-39.40	7324	Dipper, metal articles
7-76.90	7412	Dipper, sugar confectionery
7-81.40	7416	Dipper, tobacco
7-31.30	7421	Dipper, wood treatment
1-73.40	2455	Director, motion picture
1-71.90	1229	Director, musical
1-73.40	2455	Director, radio
1-39.40	1210	Director, school
1-73.30	2455	Director, stage
1-73.40	2455	Director, television
1-73.30	2455	Director, theatrical
2-11.10	1142	Director-general, employers' organisation
2-11.10	1210	Director-general, enterprise
2-11.10	1210	Director-general, enterprise/agriculture
2-11.10	1210	Director-general, enterprise/business services
2-11.10	1210	Director-general, enterprise/cleaning
2-11.10	1210	Director-general, enterprise/communications
2-11.10	1210	Director-general, enterprise/construction
2-11.10	1210	Director-general, enterprise/cultural activities
2-11.10	1210	Director-general, enterprise/education
2-11.10	1210	Director-general, enterprise/fishing
2-11.10	1210	Director-general, enterprise/forestry
2-11.10	1210	Director-general, enterprise/health
2-11.10	1210	Director-general, enterprise/hotel
2-11.10	1210	Director-general, enterprise/hunting
2-11.10	1210	Director-general, enterprise/manufacturing
2-11.10	1210	Director-general, enterprise/personal care
2-11.10	1210	Director-general, enterprise/recreation
2-11.10	1210	Director-general, enterprise/restaurant
2-11.10	1210	Director-general, enterprise/retail trade
2-11.10	1210	Director-general, enterprise/social work
2-11.10	1210	Director-general, enterprise/sporting activities
2-11.10	1210	Director-general, enterprise/storage
2-11.10	1210	Director-general, enterprise/transportation
2-11.10	1210	Director-general, enterprise/travel agency
2-11.10	1210	Director-general, enterprise/wholesale trade
2-02.10	1120	Director-general, government administration/regional
2-02.10	1120	Director-general, government department
2-02.10	1120	Director-general, intergovernmental organisation
2-11.10	1210	Director-general, organisation
2-11.10	1210	Director-general, organisation/cultural activities
2-11.10	1210	Director-general, organisation/education

2-11.10	1210	Director-general, organisation/ extra-territorial organisations
2-11.10	1210	Director-general, organisation/ fishing
2-11.10	1210	Director-general, organisation/ forestry
2-11.10	1210	Director-general, organisation/ health
2-11.10	1210	Director-general, organisation/ public administration
2-11.10	1210	Director-general, organisation/ recreation
2-11.10	1210	Director-general, organisation/ social work
2-11.10	1210	Director-general, organisation/ sporting activities
1-79.30	3472	Disc jockey
9-85.70	8321	Dispatch rider
3-59.70	4133	Dispatcher, clerical/aircraft
3-59.90	4133	Dispatcher, clerical/boat
3-59.40	4133	Dispatcher, clerical/bus
3-59.90	4133	Dispatcher, clerical/gas pipelines
3-59.90	4133	Dispatcher, clerical/oil pipelines
3-59.25	4133	Dispatcher, clerical/railway
3-59.40	4133	Dispatcher, clerical/road transport (*except bus and truck)
3-59.25	4133	Dispatcher, clerical/train
3-59.40	4133	Dispatcher, clerical/truck
9-61.70	8161	Dispatcher, load/electrical power station
6-49.90	6152	Diver, oyster
6-49.90	6152	Diver, pearl
9-59.60	7216	Diver, salvage
6-49.90	6152	Diver, sponge
9-71.20	9333	Docker
9-89.20	3115	Dockmaster, dry dock
9-89.20	3115	Dockmaster, graving dock
0-61.05	2221	Doctor, medical
0-61.20	2221	Doctor, medical/anaesthetics
0-61.20	2221	Doctor, medical/cardiology
0-61.20	2221	Doctor, medical/dermatology
0-61.20	2221	Doctor, medical/gynaecology
0-61.90	2221	Doctor, medical/medical insurance consultancy
0-52.40	2221	Doctor, medical/neurology
0-61.20	2221	Doctor, medical/obstetrics
0-61.20	2221	Doctor, medical/ophthalmology
0-61.20	2221	Doctor, medical/osteopathy
0-61.20	2221	Doctor, medical/otolaryngology
0-61.20	2221	Doctor, medical/pediatrics
0-61.20	2221	Doctor, medical/psychiatry
0-61.20	2221	Doctor, medical/radiology
1-91.90	2432	Documentalist

7-54.90	9322	Doffer, cloth
5-99.90	9152	Doorkeeper
1-29.10	2429	Drafter, parliamentary
1-51.20	2451	Dramatist
0-32.10	3118	Draughtsperson
0-32.50	3118	Draughtsperson, architectural
0-32.60	3118	Draughtsperson, cartographical
0-32.20	3118	Draughtsperson, die
0-32.10	3118	Draughtsperson, engineering
0-32.40	3118	Draughtsperson, engineering/civil
0-32.30	3118	Draughtsperson, engineering/ electrical
0-32.30	3118	Draughtsperson, engineering/ electronics
0-32.90	3118	Draughtsperson, engineering/ heating and ventilation systems
0-32.20	3118	Draughtsperson, engineering/ marine
0-32.20	3118	Draughtsperson, engineering/ mechanical
0-32.40	3118	Draughtsperson, engineering/ structural
0-32.20	3118	Draughtsperson, engineering/ aeronautical
0-32.90	3118	Draughtsperson, geological
0-32.20	3118	Draughtsperson, jig and tool
0-32.80	3118	Draughtsperson, lithographic
0-32.70	3118	Draughtsperson, technical
0-32.60	3118	Draughtsperson, topographical
7-51.50	7431	Drawer, fibre/textiles
7-11.90	7111	Drawer, prop/mine
7-11.90	7111	Drawer, prop/quarry
7-11.90	7111	Drawer, timber/mine
7-11.90	7111	Drawer, timber/quarry
7-27.20	7221	Drawer, wire
7-54.20	7432	Drawer-in, textile weaving
7-79.40	7411	Dresser, fish
7-73.10	7411	Dresser, meat
7-62.10	7441	Dresser, pelt
7-73.90	7411	Dresser, poultry
8-20.20	7113	Dresser, stone
7-73.90	7411	Dresser, tripe
5-70.90	5141	Dresser, wig/stage
7-91.40	7433	Dressmaker
7-91.90	7433	Dressmaker, theatrical
7-89.20	7416	Drier, snuff
7-81.90	7416	Drier, tobacco
8-91.90	7322	Driller, glass
8-34.60	7223	Driller, metal
8-92.90	7321	Driller, pottery
8-80.90	7313	Driller, precious metals
8-20.90	7113	Driller, stone
9-85.90	8322	Driver, ambulance
9-86.30	9332	Driver, animal-drawn vehicle/mine

9-86.30	9332	Driver, animal-drawn vehicle/ quarry
9-86.20	9332	Driver, animal-drawn vehicle/road
9-86.90	9332	Driver, animal train
9-86.90	9332	Driver, animal train/camel
9-86.90	9332	Driver, animal train/mule
9-86.30	9332	Driver, animal/mine
9-86.30	9332	Driver, animal/quarry
9-74.30	8332	Driver, bulldozer
9-85.40	8323	Driver, bus
9-85.30	8322	Driver, cab
9-73.40	8333	Driver, cage/mine
9-85.90	8322	Driver, car
9-85.90	8322	Driver, car-delivery
9-74.25	8332	Driver, digger/trench digging
9-85.70	8321	Driver, dispatch
9-79.30	8324	Driver, dumper truck
9-86.90	9332	Driver, elephant
9-83.50	8311	Driver, elevated train
9-83.60	8311	Driver, engine/mine
9-83.60	8311	Driver, engine/quarry
9-74.20	8332	Driver, excavating machine
6-28.90	9332	Driver, farm equipment/non-motorised
8-31.90	7221	Driver, forge hammer
9-99.10	9331	Driver, handtruck
9-83.20	8311	Driver, locomotive
9-83.60	8311	Driver, locomotive/mine
9-83.60	8311	Driver, locomotive/quarry
9-85.50	8324	Driver, lorry
9-79.50	8331	Driver, lumber carrier
9-85.90	8322	Driver, mail van
9-85.40	8323	Driver, motor bus
9-85.90	8322	Driver, motor car
9-85.70	8321	Driver, motor cycle
1-80.20	3475	Driver, motor racing
9-85.70	8321	Driver, motor tricycle
9-85.70	8321	Driver, motor tricycle/goods
9-89.50	9331	Driver, pedal vehicle
9-85.90	8322	Driver, postal van
6-31.40	6141	Driver, raft/logging
9-83.20	8311	Driver, railway engine
9-83.20	8311	Driver, railway engine/mine
9-83.20	8311	Driver, railway engine/quarry
9-89.90	9331	Driver, rickshaw
9-74.45	8332	Driver, road grader and scraper
9-74.50	8332	Driver, road roller
9-83.90	8311	Driver, shunting-engine
9-74.50	8332	Driver, steamroller
9-85.20	8323	Driver, streetcar
9-85.60	8324	Driver, tanker
9-74.60	8332	Driver, tar-spreading machine
9-85.30	8322	Driver, taxi
9-85.30	8322	Driver, taxi/motor-tricycle
9-79.50	8331	Driver, timber carrier
6-28.20	8331	Driver, tractor
9-85.60	8324	Driver, trailer-truck
9-83.20	8311	Driver, train
9-83.50	8311	Driver, train/elevated
9-83.50	8311	Driver, train/underground
9-85.20	8323	Driver, tram
9-85.20	8323	Driver, tramcar
9-74.25	8332	Driver, trench-digging machine
9-89.50	9331	Driver, tricycle/non-motorised
9-85.40	8323	Driver, trolley-bus
9-85.60	8324	Driver, truck
9-79.30	8324	Driver, truck/dumper
9-85.60	8324	Driver, truck/heavy
9-83.50	8311	Driver, underground train
9-85.50	8322	Driver, van
9-83.40	8311	Driver-assistant, locomotive
9-83.40	8311	Driver-assistant, railway-engine
9-83.40	8311	Driver-assistant, train
8-31.20	7221	Drop forger
8-31.30	7221	Drop-hammer worker
6-24.90	9211	Drover, cattle
0-67.10	2224	Druggist
1-71.40	2453	Drummer
5-60.40	9133	Dry-cleaner, hand
7-81.90	7416	Dryer, tobacco
9-99.10	9161	Dustman
9-99.10	9161	Dustwoman
7-61.90	7441	Dyer, leather
7-62.50	7441	Dyer, pelt
7-61.55	7441	Dyer, vat/leather
7-62.90	7441	Dyer, vat/pelt
7-61.90	7441	Dyer-stainer
7-61.55	7441	Dyer-stainer, leather
7-61.90	7441	Dyer-stainer, spray

E

0-51.90	2211	Ecologist
0-51.30	2211	Ecologist, animal
0-51.20	2211	Ecologist, plant
0-90.10	2441	Econometrician
0-90.10	2441	Economist
0-90.20	2441	Economist, agricultural
0-90.10	2441	Economist, econometrics
0-90.20	2441	Economist, finance
0-90.20	2441	Economist, international trade
0-90.20	2441	Economist, labour

Alphabetical index

0-23.05	2143	Engineer, electrical/high voltage
0-23.10	2144	Engineer, electronics
0-23.90	2144	Engineer, electronics/computer hardware design
0-23.90	2144	Engineer, electronics/information engineering
0-23.90	2144	Engineer, electronics/instrumentation
0-23.90	2144	Engineer, electronics/semiconductors
0-41.50	3143	Engineer, flight
0-24.30	2145	Engineer, gas turbine
0-52.90	2211	Engineer, genetics
0-22.55	2142	Engineer, hydraulics
0-22.55	2142	Engineer, hydrology
0-28.90	2149	Engineer, industrial
0-28.10	2149	Engineer, industrial efficiency
0-28.90	2149	Engineer, industrial layout
0-24.30	2145	Engineer, internal combustion engine
0-22.55	2142	Engineer, irrigation
0-24.30	2145	Engineer, jet engine
0-24.30	2145	Engineer, locomotive engine
0-24.90	2145	Engineer, lubrication
0-24.40	2145	Engineer, marine
0-24.10	2145	Engineer, mechanical
0-24.60	2145	Engineer, mechanical/aeronautics
0-29.30	2145	Engineer, mechanical/agriculture
0-24.80	2145	Engineer, mechanical/air-conditioning
0-24.70	2145	Engineer, mechanical/automotive
0-24.30	2145	Engineer, mechanical/diesel
0-24.30	2145	Engineer, mechanical/gas turbine
0-24.80	2145	Engineer, mechanical/heating, ventilation and refrigeration
0-24.20	2145	Engineer, mechanical/industrial machinery and tools
0-24.90	2145	Engineer, mechanical/instruments
0-24.40	2145	Engineer, mechanical/motors and engines (marine)
0-24.30	2145	Engineer, mechanical/motors and engines (except marine)
0-24.50	2145	Engineer, mechanical/naval
0-24.85	2145	Engineer, mechanical/nuclear power
0-24.80	2145	Engineer, mechanical/refrigeration
0-24.50	2145	Engineer, mechanical/ship construction
0-28.20	2419	Engineer, methods
0-27.10	2147	Engineer, mining
0-27.20	2147	Engineer, mining/coal
0-27.90	2147	Engineer, mining/diamonds
0-27.30	2147	Engineer, mining/metal
0-27.40	2147	Engineer, mining/petroleum and natural gas
0-24.30	2145	Engineer, motor
0-25.90	2146	Engineer, natural gas production and distribution
0-24.50	2145	Engineer, naval
0-24.85	2145	Engineer, nuclear power
0-25.20	2146	Engineer, petroleum
0-28.20	2149	Engineer, planning
0-28.10	2149	Engineer, production
0-29.90	2149	Engineer, robotics
0-28.90	2149	Engineer, safety
0-22.50	2142	Engineer, sanitary
0-43.20	3141	Engineer, ship
0-43.20	3141	Engineer, ship
0-24.50	2145	Engineer, ship construction
0-43.20	3141	Engineer, ship/first
0-43.20	3141	Engineer, ship/second
0-43.20	3141	Engineer, ship/third
0-43.20	3141	Engineer, ship/fourth
0-23.90	2131	Engineer, software
0-23.90	2131	Engineer, systems/computers
0-23.90	2149	Engineer, systems/except computers
0-23.40	2144	Engineer, telecommunications
0-23.90	2144	Engineer, telecommunications/aerospace
0-23.90	2144	Engineer, telecommunications/radar
0-23.90	2144	Engineer, telecommunications/radio
0-23.90	2144	Engineer, telecommunications/signal systems
0-23.40	2144	Engineer, telecommunications/telegraph
0-23.40	2144	Engineer, telecommunications/telephone
0-23.90	2144	Engineer, telecommunications/television
0-28.30	2149	Engineer, time and motion study
0-29.50	2141	Engineer, traffic
0-23.30	2143	Engineer, transmission/electric power
0-28.30	2149	Engineer, work study
8-94.20	7323	Engraver, glass
8-80.80	7313	Engraver, jewellery
9-24.30	7343	Engraver, printing/linoleum block
9-24.15	7343	Engraver, printing/lithographic stone
9-24.20	7343	Engraver, printing/metal die
9-24.20	7343	Engraver, printing/metal plate
9-24.40	7343	Engraver, printing/metal roller
9-24.90	7343	Engraver, printing/music printing
9-24.45	7343	Engraver, printing/pantograph
9-25.10	7343	Engraver, printing/photogravure
9-24.30	7343	Engraver, printing/rubber block

9-24.30	7343	Engraver, printing/wood block
1-61.50	2452	Engraver-etcher, artistic
9-27.50	7344	Enlarger, photograph
0-51.30	2211	Entomologist
0-52.40	2212	Epidemiologist
0-65.90	2223	Epidemiologist, veterinary
9-54.90	7129	Erector, billboard
8-74.40	7214	Erector, constructional steel
8-41.85	7232	Erector, metal airframe
9-59.90	7129	Erector, prefabricated buildings
8-54.90	7243	Erector, radio aerial
8-41.80	7233	Erector, refrigeration and air-conditioning equipment
8-74.50	7214	Erector, ship beam and frame
8-74.10	7214	Erector, structural metal
8-54.90	7243	Erector, television aerial
8-41.75	7233	Erector-installer, agricultural machinery
8-41.75	7233	Erector-installer, industrial machinery
3-70.40	9120	Errand boy
3-70.40	9120	Errand girl
5-99.90	5149	Escort, social
1-51.20	2451	Essayist
0-36.90	3116	Estimator, engineering/chemical
0-33.20	3112	Estimator, engineering/civil
0-34.90	3113	Estimator, engineering/electrical
0-34.90	3114	Estimator, engineering/electronics
0-35.90	3115	Estimator, engineering/mechanical
8-94.30	7323	Etcher, glass
9-24.60	7343	Etcher, printing/metal engraving
9-24.60	7343	Etcher, printing/metal plate
9-24.60	7343	Etcher, printing/metal roller
9-25.50	7343	Etcher, printing/photogravure
1-92.40	2442	Ethnologist
1-95.20	2444	Etymologist
1-41.40	3480	Evangelist
7-73.90	7411	Eviscerator, animal
7-54.70	3152	Examiner, cloth
7-54.70	3152	Examiner, fabrics
3-10.10	3439	Executive secretary, committee
3-10.10	3439	Executive secretary, consular office
3-10.10	3439	Executive secretary, government administration
3-10.10	3439	Executive secretary, non-government administration
7-79.90	7414	Expeller, oil
5-99.90	7143	Exterminator
8-02.90	7442	Eyeletter, footwear

F

1-49.20	3242	Faith healer
0-53.60	3213	Farm demonstrator
6-24.20	6121	Farm worker, skilled/cattle
6-23.90	6112	Farm worker, skilled/cocoa
6-23.90	6112	Farm worker, skilled/coffee
6-22.40	6111	Farm worker, skilled/cotton
6-25.10	6121	Farm worker, skilled/dairy
6-24.50	6121	Farm worker, skilled/domestic fur-bearing animals
6-12.20	6111	Farm worker, skilled/field crops
6-49.20	6151	Farm worker, skilled/fish
6-22.90	6111	Farm worker, skilled/flax
6-23.20	6112	Farm worker, skilled/fruit
6-22.90	6111	Farm worker, skilled/groundnut
6-23.20	6112	Farm worker, skilled/grove
6-23.90	6112	Farm worker, skilled/hops
6-29.50	6111	Farm worker, skilled/irrigation
6-22.90	6111	Farm worker, skilled/jute
6-24.10	6121	Farm worker, skilled/livestock
6-24.10	6124	Farm worker, skilled/mixed animal husbandry
6-11.10	6114	Farm worker, skilled/mixed crop
6-21.05	6130	Farm worker, skilled/mixed farming
6-29.90	6113	Farm worker, skilled/mushroom
6-24.50	6129	Farm worker, skilled/non-domesticated fur-bearing animals
6-27.30	6113	Farm worker, skilled/nursery
6-23.20	6112	Farm worker, skilled/orchard
6-24.90	6129	Farm worker, skilled/ostrich
6-49.30	6151	Farm worker, skilled/oyster
6-24.40	6121	Farm worker, skilled/pig
6-22.20	6111	Farm worker, skilled/potato
6-26.10	6122	Farm worker, skilled/poultry
6-22.50	6111	Farm worker, skilled/rice
6-23.50	6112	Farm worker, skilled/rubber
6-49.90	6151	Farm worker, skilled/seafood
6-24.30	6121	Farm worker, skilled/sheep
6-23.20	6112	Farm worker, skilled/shrub crop
6-11.10	6210	Farm worker, skilled/subsistence farming
6-22.20	6111	Farm worker, skilled/sugar-beet
6-22.60	6111	Farm worker, skilled/sugar-cane
6-23.40	6112	Farm worker, skilled/tea
6-22.90	6111	Farm worker, skilled/tobacco
6-23.20	6112	Farm worker, skilled/tree crop
6-22.20	6111	Farm worker, skilled/vegetables
6-23.30	6112	Farm worker, skilled/vineyard
6-22.30	6111	Farm worker, skilled/wheat
6-12.20	6111	Farmer, alfalfa
6-12.90	6123	Farmer, apiary
6-12.60	6122	Farmer, battery
6-12.90	6123	Farmer, beekeeping

6-12.40	6121	Farmer, cattle
6-12.20	6111	Farmer, cereal
6-12.60	6122	Farmer, chicken
6-12.30	6112	Farmer, cocoa
6-12.30	6112	Farmer, coconut
6-12.30	6112	Farmer, coffee
6-12.30	6112	Farmer, copra
6-12.20	6111	Farmer, corn
6-12.20	6111	Farmer, cotton
6-12.50	6121	Farmer, dairy
6-12.60	6122	Farmer, duck
6-12.60	6122	Farmer, egg production
6-12.20	6111	Farmer, field crop
6-12.20	6111	Farmer, field vegetable
6-49.20	6151	Farmer, fish
6-12.20	6111	Farmer, flax
6-12.30	6112	Farmer, fruit
6-12.40	6121	Farmer, fur/domestic animals
6-24.50	6129	Farmer, fur/non-domesticated animals
6-12.60	6122	Farmer, goose
6-12.20	6111	Farmer, grain
6-12.20	6111	Farmer, groundnut
6-12.30	6112	Farmer, hop
6-12.40	6121	Farmer, horse breeding
6-12.40	6121	Farmer, horse raising
6-12.20	6111	Farmer, jute
6-12.40	6121	Farmer, livestock
6-12.20	6111	Farmer, maize
6-12.50	6121	Farmer, milk
6-12.90	6124	Farmer, mixed-animal husbandry
6-11.10	6114	Farmer, mixed crop
6-11.10	6130	Farmer, mixed farming
6-12.30	6112	Farmer, nut
6-12.30	6112	Farmer, orchard
6-49.30	6151	Farmer, oyster
6-24.90	6121	Farmer, pelt
6-12.40	6121	Farmer, pig
6-12.60	6122	Farmer, poultry/hatching and breeding
6-12.40	6121	Farmer, ranch
6-12.20	6111	Farmer, rice
6-23.30	6112	Farmer, rubber
6-12.30	6112	Farmer, rubber plantation
6-49.20	6151	Farmer, seafood
6-12.90	6123	Farmer, sericulture
6-24.40	6121	Farmer, sheep
6-12.40	6121	Farmer, sheep raising
6-24.40	6121	Farmer, sheep/astrakhan
6-12.30	6112	Farmer, shrub crop
6-12.90	6123	Farmer, silkworm raising
6-12.20	6111	Farmer, sisal
6-12.20	6111	Farmer, soya-bean
6-12.40	6121	Farmer, stud breeding
6-11.10	6210	Farmer, subsistence farming
6-12.20	6111	Farmer, sugar-beet
6-12.20	6111	Farmer, sugar-cane
6-23.30	6112	Farmer, tea
6-12.30	6112	Farmer, tea plantation
6-12.20	6111	Farmer, tobacco
6-12.30	6112	Farmer, tree crop
6-12.60	6122	Farmer, turkey
6-12.20	6111	Farmer, vegetable
6-23.30	6112	Farmer, vineyard
6-12.30	6112	Farmer, viniculture
6-12.20	6111	Farmer, wheat
8-31.10	7221	Farrier
6-31.20	6141	Feller, logging
6-31.20	6141	Feller-bucker, tree
7-61.25	7441	Fellmonger
7-29.30	8223	Fettler
7-51.40	7431	Fibre lapper, textiles
7-79.40	7411	Filleter, fish
7-43.20	8153	Filter-press operator, chemical and related materials
9-26.40	7345	Finisher, book
7-29.30	7224	Finisher, cast metal articles
9-52.40	7123	Finisher, cement
9-52.40	7123	Finisher, concrete
8-32.90	7222	Finisher, die
8-02.55	7442	Finisher, footwear
8-91.90	7322	Finisher, glass
8-35.20	7224	Finisher, metal
7-62.60	7441	Finisher, pelt
9-25.60	7343	Finisher, photo-engraving/printing plates
8-20.20	7113	Finisher, stone
8-19.55	7422	Finisher, wooden furniture
5-81.90	3151	Fire investigator
5-81.10	5161	Fire-fighter
5-81.40	5161	Fire-fighter, aircraft accidents
6-32.50	5161	Fire-fighter, forest
9-51.30	7122	Firebrick layer
9-69.30	8162	Fireperson, boiler plant
9-83.30	8162	Fireperson, locomotive boiler
9-82.20	8162	Fireperson, ship
6-41.30	6152	Fisherman, coastal waters
6-41.20	6153	Fisherman, deep-sea
6-41.30	6152	Fisherman, inland waters
6-49.50	6154	Fisherman, seal
6-41.30	6152	Fisherwoman, coastal waters
6-41.20	6153	Fisherwoman, deep-sea
6-41.30	6152	Fisherwoman, inland waters
6-49.40	6154	Fisherwoman, seal
6-41.30	6152	Fishery worker, skilled/coastal waters

9-71.20	9333	Freight handler
5-89.90	7216	Frogman, salvage
5-89.90	7216	Frogwoman, salvage
8-94.40	7323	Froster, glass sandblasting
5-92.10	5143	Funeral director
7-92.20	7434	Fur tailor
8-93.30	8131	Furnace-operator, annealing/glass
7-26.20	8123	Furnace-operator, annealing/metal
7-26.40	8123	Furnace-operator, case-hardening/metal
7-42.40	8152	Furnace-operator, chemical and related processes
7-21.70	8121	Furnace-operator, converting/non-ferrous metal
7-21.10	8121	Furnace-operator, converting/steel
7-21.50	8121	Furnace-operator, converting/steel (bessemer furnace)
7-21.40	8121	Furnace-operator, converting/steel (oxygen furnace)
7-21.50	8121	Furnace-operator, converting/steel (thomas furnace)
8-93.20	8131	Furnace-operator, glass production
7-26.30	8123	Furnace-operator, hardening/metal
7-26.30	8123	Furnace-operator, heat-treating/metal
8-93.30	8131	Furnace-operator, lehr
7-23.20	8122	Furnace-operator, melting/metal
7-23.20	8122	Furnace-operator, melting/metal (crucible furnace)
7-23.30	8122	Furnace-operator, melting/metal (cupola furnace)
7-23.20	8122	Furnace-operator, melting/metal (electric-arc furnace)
7-23.20	8122	Furnace-operator, melting/metal (open-hearth furnace)
7-23.20	8122	Furnace-operator, melting/metal (reverberatory furnace)
7-21.90	8121	Furnace-operator, puddling
7-21.70	8121	Furnace-operator, refining/non-ferrous metal
7-21.10	8121	Furnace-operator, refining/steel
7-21.60	8121	Furnace-operator, refining/steel (electric-arc furnace)
7-21.30	8121	Furnace-operator, refining/steel (open-hearth furnace)
9-69.60	8163	Furnace-operator, refuse disposal
7-23.40	8122	Furnace-operator, reheating/metal
8-93.20	8131	Furnace-operator, smelting/glass
7-21.10	8121	Furnace-operator, smelting/metal
7-21.20	8121	Furnace-operator, smelting/metal (blast furnace)
8-93.40	8131	Furnace-operator, tempering/glass
9-71.90	9333	Furniture mover
7-92.20	7434	Furrier

G

6-49.90	6154	Game beater
6-49.90	5169	Game-warden
6-49.90	6129	Gamekeeper
5-89.30	5163	Gaoler
6-27.40	6113	Gardener
6-12.70	6113	Gardener, greenhouse
6-27.40	6113	Gardener, jobbing
6-29.60	6113	Gardener, park
6-27.30	6113	Gardener, seed propagation
8-91.90	7322	Gatherer, glass
6-49.90	9213	Gatherer, seaweed
6-49.90	9213	Gatherer, shellfish
1-92.90	2443	Genealogist
6-00.20	1311	General manager, agriculture
5-00.90	1315	General manager, boarding-house
2-11.10	1317	General manager, business services
5-00.90	1315	General manager, cafe
5-00.90	1315	General manager, camping site
5-00.90	1315	General manager, canteen
5-10.90	1315	General manager, caravan park
2-11.10	1318	General manager, cleaning
2-11.10	1316	General manager, communications
2-11.10	1313	General manager, construction
2-11.10	1319	General manager, cultural activities
2-11.10	1319	General manager, education
6-00.20	1311	General manager, fishing
6-00.20	1311	General manager, forestry
5-10.40	1315	General manager, guest-house
2-11.10	1319	General manager, health
5-00.90	1315	General manager, hostel
5-10.20	1315	General manager, hotel
6-00.20	1311	General manager, hunting
5-10.20	1315	General manager, inn
5-10.90	1315	General manager, lodging-house
2-11.10	1312	General manager, manufacturing
5-00.20	1315	General manager, motel
2-11.10	1318	General manager, personal care
2-11.10	1319	General manager, recreation
5-00.90	1315	General manager, refreshment-room
5-00.30	1315	General manager, restaurant
4-00.30	1314	General manager, retail trade

6-12.30	6112	Grower, coconut	9-84.20	8312	Guard, goods train
6-12.30	6112	Grower, coffee	5-89.40	9152	Guard, museum
6-12.20	6111	Grower, field crop	5-82.40	5162	Guard, police force
6-12.20	6111	Grower, field vegetable	5-89.30	5163	Guard, prison
6-12.70	6113	Grower, flower	3-60.20	5112	Guard, railway
6-12.70	6113	Grower, horticultural nursery	5-82.40	5169	Guard, security
6-12.70	6113	Grower, market gardening	5-91.30	5113	Guide, art gallery
6-12.90	6113	Grower, mushroom	5-91.30	5113	Guide, museum
6-12.70	6113	Grower, nursery	5-91.20	5113	Guide, travel
6-12.70	6113	Grower, nursery/bulbs	5-91.90	5113	Guide, travel/alpine
6-12.70	6113	Grower, nursery/seeds	5-91.30	5113	Guide, travel/art gallery
6-12.90	6113	Grower, nursery/spices	5-40.90	5113	Guide, travel/bus
6-12.70	6113	Grower, nursery/vegetables	5-91.90	5113	Guide, travel/fishing
6-12.90	6113	Grower, osier	5-91.90	5113	Guide, travel/game park
6-12.90	6113	Grower, reed	5-91.90	5113	Guide, travel/hunting
6-12.70	6113	Grower, rose	5-91.90	5113	Guide, travel/industrial establishment
6-12.30	6112	Grower, rubber			
6-12.30	6112	Grower, shrub crop	5-91.30	5113	Guide, travel/museum
6-12.20	6111	Grower, soya-bean	5-91.90	5113	Guide, travel/safari
6-12.20	6111	Grower, sugar-beet	5-91.30	5113	Guide, travel/sightseeing
6-12.20	6112	Grower, tree crop	1-71.40	2453	Guitarist
6-12.70	6113	Grower, tulip	8-39.20	7222	Gunsmith
5-89.40	9152	Guard, art gallery	0-79.90	3226	Gymnast, remedial
5-89.90	5169	Guard, beach	0-61.20	2221	Gynaecologist
9-84.20	8312	Guard, freight train			

H

5-70.30	5141	Hairdresser	6-23.90	9211	Hand, harvest/orchard
5-70.30	5141	Hairdresser, men	5-52.90	9132	Hand, kitchen
5-70.20	5141	Hairdresser, women	6-24.20	9211	Hand, ranch/cattle
8-31.20	7221	Hammer-smith	6-24.30	9211	Hand, ranch/sheep
8-31.20	7221	Hammer-smith, forge	7-54.90	9322	Hand, shuttle
8-80.90	7313	Hammer-smith, precious-metal articles	9-42.20	7331	Handicraft worker, basketry
			9-49.60	7331	Handicraft worker, candlemaking
9-81.90	8340	Hand, cable-ship	7-54.35	7332	Handicraft worker, carpets
7-74.90	9322	Hand, cannery	7-55.50	7332	Handicraft worker, garment knitting
9-81.40	8340	Hand, deck			
6-21.05	9211	Hand, farm	7-91.90	7332	Handicraft worker, garments
6-23.20	9211	Hand, farm/citrus fruit	8-03.10	7332	Handicraft worker, leather
6-22.40	9211	Hand, farm/cotton picking	8-03.10	7332	Handicraft worker, leather accessories
6-25.10	9211	Hand, farm/dairy			
6-22.10	9211	Hand, farm/field crops	9-10.10	7331	Handicraft worker, paper articles
6-23.20	9211	Hand, farm/fruit picking	9-42.20	7331	Handicraft worker, reed weaving
6-24.50	9211	Hand, farm/fur-bearing animals	9-42.90	7331	Handicraft worker, straw articles
6-24.10	9211	Hand, farm/livestock	8-20.70	7331	Handicraft worker, stone articles
6-25.90	9211	Hand, farm/milch	7-54.30	7332	Handicraft worker, textile weaving
6-25.90	9211	Hand, farm/milking	7-54.90	7332	Handicraft worker, textiles
6-23.20	9211	Hand, farm/orchard	8-19.90	7331	Handicraft worker, wooden articles
6-29.30	9211	Hand, farm/silk worms	9-71.20	9333	Handler, freight
6-23.90	9211	Hand, farm/tea plucking	8-92.90	7321	Handler, pottery
6-21.10	9211	Hand, harvest	9-99.10	9313	Handyman
6-22.90	9211	Hand, harvest/field crops	9-59.20	9313	Handyman, building maintenance

9-99.10	9313	Handywoman
9-59.20	9313	Handywoman, building maintenance
1-71.40	2453	Harpist
6-49.40	6154	Harpooner, whale
6-49.20	6151	Hatcher, fish
6-12.60	6122	Hatcher-breeder, poultry
6-49.20	6151	Hatchery worker, skilled/fish
6-26.20	6122	Hatchery worker, skilled/poultry
4-52.20	9112	Hawker
1-39.40	1229	Head teacher
2-02.10	1120	Head, chancery
2-19.90	1229	Head, college faculty
2-02.10	1120	Head, government department
2-19.90	1229	Head, university faculty
2-01.10	1130	Head, village
1-93.40	1229	Headmaster
1-93.40	1229	Headmistress
0-79.90	3241	Healer, drugless treatment
1-49.20	3242	Healer, faith
0-79.90	3241	Healer, herbal
0-79.90	3241	Healer, village
0-71.30	2230	Health visitor
5-40.20	9131	Helper, domestic
5-40.90	9131	Helper, domestic/parlour
6-21.10	9211	Helper, farm
5-40.90	9131	Helper, kitchen/domestic
5-32.90	9132	Helper, kitchen/non-domestic
6-31.30	6141	High climber, logging
2-02.10	1120	High commissioner, government
0-51.90	2211	Histologist
0-51.30	2211	Histologist, animal
0-51.20	2211	Histologist, plant
0-52.60	2212	Histopathologist
1-92.60	2443	Historian
1-92.60	2443	Historian, economic
1-92.60	2443	Historian, political
1-92.60	2443	Historian, social
9-99.10	9313	Hod carrier
1-99.30	2419	Home economist
0-79.90	3229	Homeopath
6-24.90	6129	Horse-breaker
6-12.70	6113	Horticultural grower
6-27.30	6113	Horticultural worker, skilled
0-53.30	2213	Horticulturist
5-99.90	5149	Host, club
5-99.90	5149	Hostess, club
7-49.40	8159	Hot-cell technician
5-40.20	9131	Houseboy
9-59.10	7129	Housebuilder, non-traditional materials
9-59.10	7121	Housebuilder, traditional materials
1-93.20	3460	Housefather, associate professional
1-93.20	2446	Housefather, professional
5-20.20	5121	Housekeeper
5-20.20	5121	Housekeeper, executive
5-40.20	9131	Housemaid
1-93.40	3460	Housemaster, associate professional/approved school
1-93.40	2446	Housemaster, professional/ approved school
1-93.20	3460	Housemother, associate professional
1-93.20	2446	Housemother, professional
6-49.60	6154	Hunter
6-49.50	6154	Hunter, seal
6-49.50	6154	Hunter, whale
0-51.90	2211	Hydrobiologist
0-12.20	2111	Hydrodynamicist
0-13.20	2114	Hydrologist
0-64.40	3225	Hygienist, dental
0-64.40	3225	Hygienist, oral
1-79.90	3474	Hypnotist

I

0-51.30	2211	Ichthyologist
1-75.30	3474	Illusionist
1-62.20	3471	Illustrator, advertising
1-62.20	3471	Illustrator, book
0-32.70	3118	Illustrator, engineering
0-32.70	3118	Illustrator, technical
1-41.20	2460	Imam
1-79.90	3474	Imitator
1-79.90	3474	Imitator, animal noise
0-51.90	2211	Immunologist
1-73.90	2455	Impersonator
9-21.50	7341	Imposer, printing
7-31.30	7421	Impregnator, wood
1-74.20	1229	Impresario
1-91.90	2432	Information scientist, business services
1-91.90	2432	Information scientist, technical information
8-19.65	7422	Inlayer, marquetry
5-10.20	1315	Innkeeper
3-10.10	3441	Inspector, border
5-89.90	3151	Inspector, building
3-10.10	3449	Inspector, civil service
4-43.30	3417	Inspector, claims
3-59.30	4133	Inspector, clerical/railway transport service

3-59.45	4133	Inspector, clerical/road transport service
3-10.10	3441	Inspector, customs
5-81.20	3151	Inspector, fire
3-10.10	3449	Inspector, government administration
4-43.30	3417	Inspector, insurance claims
3-10.10	3444	Inspector, licensing
3-10.10	3152	Inspector, occupational safety
3-10.10	3443	Inspector, pensions
5-82.30	3450	Inspector, police
3-10.10	3449	Inspector, price
9-49.80	3152	Inspector, product safety
9-49.80	3152	Inspector, quality
8-59.20	3152	Inspector, quality/electrical products
8-59.20	3152	Inspector, quality/electronic products
7-54.70	3152	Inspector, quality/fabrics
9-49.80	3152	Inspector, quality/industrial processes
8-49.85	3152	Inspector, quality/mechanical products
9-49.80	3152	Inspector, quality/products
9-49.80	3152	Inspector, quality/services
3-10.10	3152	Inspector, safety and health
1-93.90	3152	Inspector, safety and health/child care
3-10.10	3152	Inspector, safety and health/consumer protection
3-10.10	3152	Inspector, safety and health/electricity
3-10.10	3152	Inspector, safety and health/establishments
3-10.10	3152	Inspector, safety and health/factories
3-10.10	3152	Inspector, safety and health/industrial waste-processing
3-10.10	3152	Inspector, safety and health/labour
3-10.10	3152	Inspector, safety and health/pollution

3-10.10	3152	Inspector, safety and health/shops
3-10.10	3152	Inspector, safety and health/vehicles
3-10.10	3152	Inspector, safety and health/working conditions
0-79.40	3222	Inspector, sanitary
1-39.50	2352	Inspector, school
3-10.10	3442	Inspector, tax
9-49.80	3152	Inspector, vehicles/technical standards inspection
3-10.10	3449	Inspector, wage
3-10.10	3449	Inspector, weights and measures
2-02.10	1120	Inspector-general, police
8-56.20	7244	Installer, telegraph
8-56.20	7244	Installer, telephone
1-80.90	3475	Instructor, billiards
1-80.90	3475	Instructor, bridge
1-80.90	3475	Instructor, chess
9-85.90	3340	Instructor, driving
0-41.60	3340	Instructor, flying
1-80.30	3340	Instructor, sailing
1-80.30	3475	Instructor, sports
1-71.40	2453	Instrumentalist
9-56.10	7134	Insulation worker
9-56.40	7134	Insulation worker, acoustical
9-56.50	7134	Insulation worker, boiler and pipe
9-56.20	7134	Insulation worker, building
9-56.60	7134	Insulation worker, refrigeration and air-conditioning equipment
9-56.40	7134	Insulation worker, sound-proofing
4-41.20	3412	Insurance broker
1-95.40	2444	Interpreter
9-21.30	7341	Intertype operator
1-94.20	2412	Interviewer, employment
1-79.20	3472	Interviewer, media
9-52.30	7123	Iron worker, concrete reinforcement
5-60.70	9133	Ironer, hand
6-29.50	6111	Irrigation worker, skilled

J

7-53.50	8262	Jacquard card cutter
7-53.90	8262	Jacquard card lacer
7-53.40	7435	Jacquard design copyist
5-51.30	9141	Janitor
8-80.10	7313	Jeweller
8-92.30	7321	Jiggerer, pottery and porcelain
4-41.90	3411	Jobber, stock
1-80.20	3475	Jockey
9-54.10	7124	Joiner
9-54.60	7124	Joiner, aircraft

9-54.70	7124	Joiner, bench
9-54.20	7124	Joiner, construction
9-54.45	7124	Joiner, ship
8-57.50	7245	Jointer, cable
8-57.50	7245	Jointer, cable/electric
8-57.50	7245	Jointer, cable/telegraph
8-57.50	7245	Jointer, cable/telephone
9-59.50	7136	Jointer, pipe-laying
8-92.30	7321	Jollier, pottery and porcelain
1-59.15	2451	Journalist

K

L

8-80.30	7313	Lapidary
8-02.45	7442	Laster, footwear
8-34.20	8211	Lathe-operator, capstan/ metalworking
8-34.20	8211	Lathe-operator, centre/ metalworking
7-32.40	8141	Lathe-operator, cutting/veneer
7-32.10	8141	Lathe-operator, cutting/wood
8-34.20	8211	Lathe-operator, engine/ metalworking
8-34.20	8211	Lathe-operator, metalworking
8-20.50	8212	Lathe-operator, stoneworking
8-34.20	8211	Lathe-operator, turret/ metalworking
8-12.30	8240	Lathe-operator, woodworking
5-60.10	9133	Launderer, hand
1-21.10	2421	Lawyer
1-21.10	2421	Lawyer, civil
1-21.10	2421	Lawyer, conveyancing
1-21.10	2421	Lawyer, criminal
1-21.10	2421	Lawyer, litigation
1-41.40	3480	Lay preacher
1-49.90	3480	Lay worker
9-59.70	7132	Layer, composition tile
9-59.50	7129	Layer, drain
9-54.75	7132	Layer, parquetry
9-59.50	7136	Layer, pipe
9-59.70	7132	Layer, tile
9-59.90	7245	Layer, underground cable
9-54.90	7132	Layer, wood block
9-59.50	7136	Layer-jointer, mains pipes
9-22.90	7341	Layer-on, printing press
2-11.10	1141	Leader, political party
2-11.10	1142	Leader, trade union
1-31.10	2310	Lecturer, college
1-31.10	2310	Lecturer, university
9-39.50	7324	Letterer, sign-writing
1-95.20	2444	Lexicographer
1-91.20	2432	Librarian
5-89.90	5169	Life-guard
9-81.90	8340	Lifeboatman
9-81.90	8340	Lifeboatwoman
9-81.90	8340	Lighterman
9-81.90	8340	Lighterwoman
9-89.40	8340	Lighthouse keeper
9-81.90	8340	Lightshipman
9-81.90	8340	Lightshipwoman
8-57.20	7245	Line worker, electric power
8-57.30	7245	Line worker, electric traction
8-57.40	7245	Line worker, telegraph
8-57.40	7245	Line worker, telephone
1-95.20	2444	Linguist
9-21.30	7341	Linotyper
9-71.35	9333	Loader, aircraft
9-71.40	9333	Loader, boat
9-71.40	9333	Loader, boat/gases
9-71.20	9333	Loader, boat/liquids
9-71.90	9333	Loader, furniture
9-71.30	9333	Loader, railway vehicles
9-71.30	9333	Loader, road vehicles
9-71.30	9333	Loader, road vehicles/lorry
9-71.30	9333	Loader, road vehicles/truck
9-71.20	9333	Loader, ship
9-71.40	9333	Loader, ship/gases
9-71.20	9333	Loader, ship/liquids
9-89.30	8333	Lock-keeper, canal or port
8-39.30	7222	Locksmith
8-74.20	7214	Loftsman, structural metal
8-74.20	7214	Loftswoman, structural metal
6-31.10	6141	Logger
9-71.20	9333	Longshoreman
9-71.20	9333	Longshorewoman
6-31.10	6141	Lumberjack

M

9-43.90	8212	Machine-operator, abrasive-coatings production
9-49.90	8222	Machine-operator, ammunition products
8-51.90	8211	Machine-operator, armature production
9-43.40	8212	Machine-operator, artificial stone products
9-43.30	8212	Machine-operator, asbestos-cement products
8-41.10	8281	Machine-operator, assembly line/ vehicles
8-41.10	8281	Machine-operator, assembly-line/ aircraft
8-73.80	8281	Machine-operator, assembly-line/ except vehicles and aircraft
8-53.90	8171	Machine-operator, automated assembly line
8-34.80	8211	Machine-operator, automatic transfer/components
7-76.90	8274	Machine-operator, bakery products
8-74.90	8131	Machine-operator, bending/glass
8-39.70	8211	Machine-operator, bending/metal
8-19.90	8240	Machine-operator, bending/ wood
7-79.90	8275	Machine-operator, blanching/ edible nuts

7-49.90	8229	Machine-operator, halogen gas production
7-93.10	8269	Machine-operator, hat making
7-61.35	8265	Machine-operator, hide processing
8-34.70	8211	Machine-operator, honing/metal
7-71.90	8273	Machine-operator, hulling/grain
7-71.90	8273	Machine-operator, husking/grain
7-49.90	8229	Machine-operator, hydrogen gas production
9-69.70	8163	Machine-operator, ice production
8-80.10	8212	Machine-operator, industrial-diamonds production
9-01.50	8232	Machine-operator, injection moulding/plastics
9-56.30	8290	Machine-operator, insulation
7-24.90	8211	Machine-operator, jewellery production
7-55.10	8262	Machine-operator, knitting
7-55.20	8262	Machine-operator, knitting/garment
7-55.30	8262	Machine-operator, knitting/hosiery
9-71.60	8290	Machine-operator, labelling
7-54.50	8262	Machine-operator, lace production
8-35.20	8223	Machine-operator, laminating/metal
9-01.65	8232	Machine-operator, laminating/plastics
8-34.90	8211	Machine-operator, lapping/metal
7-51.40	8261	Machine-operator, lapping/ribbon
7-51.40	8261	Machine-operator, lapping/sliver
7-51.40	8261	Machine-operator, lapping/textile fibres
5-60.20	8264	Machine-operator, laundering
5-60.60	8264	Machine-operator, laundry
7-49.90	8229	Machine-operator, lead production
7-61.50	8265	Machine-operator, leather preparing
9-10.40	8253	Machine-operator, lining/cardboard
9-49.30	8229	Machine-operator, linoleum production
7-78.90	8278	Machine-operator, liqueur production
8-34.10	8211	Machine-operator, machine tool
7-12.90	8112	Machine-operator, magnetic ore processing
7-78.20	8278	Machine-operator, malting/spirits
7-79.90	8275	Machine-operator, margarine processing
9-71.60	8290	Machine-operator, marking/goods
8-19.90	8240	Machine-operator, marking/wood
9-49.90	8222	Machine-operator, match production
7-94.40	8269	Machine-operator, mattress production
7-73.30	8271	Machine-operator, meat processing
7-73.90	8271	Machine-operator, meat products
8-34.10	8211	Machine-operator, metal products
7-75.90	8272	Machine-operator, milk powder production
7-75.90	8272	Machine-operator, milk processing
7-41.30	8151	Machine-operator, milling/chemical and related processes
7-71.20	8273	Machine-operator, milling/grain
8-34.30	8211	Machine-operator, milling/metal
7-12.40	8112	Machine-operator, milling/minerals
7-71.90	8273	Machine-operator, milling/mustard seeds
7-79.20	8275	Machine-operator, milling/oil-seed
7-71.30	8273	Machine-operator, milling/rice
9-01.20	8231	Machine-operator, milling/rubber
7-71.40	8273	Machine-operator, milling/spices
7-12.40	8112	Machine-operator, milling/stone
7-32.10	8141	Machine-operator, milling/wood
7-12.10	8112	Machine-operator, mineral processing
8-20.10	8212	Machine-operator, mineral products
7-11.40	8111	Machine-operator, mining/continuous
8-39.90	8211	Machine-operator, minting/metal
8-99.60	8139	Machine-operator, mixing/abrasives
7-41.40	8151	Machine-operator, mixing/chemical and related processes
8-99.30	8139	Machine-operator, mixing/clay
7-59.45	8265	Machine-operator, mixing/fur fibre
8-99.20	8139	Machine-operator, mixing/glass
8-99.50	8139	Machine-operator, mixing/glaze
7-26.90	8123	Machine-operator, mixing/metal
8-91.36	8131	Machine-operator, moulding/glass
7-25.40	8211	Machine-operator, moulding/metal
9-01.90	8232	Machine-operator, moulding/plastics
9-01.35	8231	Machine-operator, moulding/rubber
9-01.30	8231	Machine-operator, moulding/tyres
8-39.90	8211	Machine-operator, needle production
7-54.65	8262	Machine-operator, net production
7-76.40	8274	Machine-operator, noodle production
8-39.90	8211	Machine-operator, nut production/metal
9-71.55	8290	Machine-operator, packing
8-95.50	8131	Machine-operator, painting/ceramics
8-95.20	8131	Machine-operator, painting/glass
9-39.90	8223	Machine-operator, painting/metal

9-01.90	8231	Machine-operator, rubber processing
9-49.50	8231	Machine-operator, rubber stamp production
8-34.75	8211	Machine-operator, sawing/metal
8-20.20	8112	Machine-operator, sawing/stone
7-32.20	8141	Machine-operator, sawing/wood
9-71.55	8290	Machine-operator, sealing
7-31.20	8141	Machine-operator, seasoning/wood
7-95.50	8263	Machine-operator, sewing
7-95.50	8263	Machine-operator, sewing/embroidery
8-02.50	8263	Machine-operator, sewing/footwear
7-95.50	8263	Machine-operator, sewing/fur
7-95.50	8263	Machine-operator, sewing/garments
7-95.50	8263	Machine-operator, sewing/hats
8-03.50	8263	Machine-operator, sewing/leather
7-95.50	8263	Machine-operator, sewing/textile products
7-95.50	8263	Machine-operator, sewing/upholstery
8-34.90	8211	Machine-operator, shaping/metal
7-32.90	8141	Machine-operator, shaping/wood
8-35.20	8211	Machine-operator, sharpening/metal
7-32.90	8141	Machine-operator, shaving/wood
8-39.80	8211	Machine-operator, shearing/metal
8-01.10	8266	Machine-operator, shoe production
7-29.30	8223	Machine-operator, shotblasting/metal
7-56.50	8264	Machine-operator, shrinking/textiles
8-53.90	8290	Machine-operator, silicon chip production
7-56.65	8264	Machine-operator, silk weighting
7-52.50	8261	Machine-operator, skeining/thread and yarn
7-78.10	8278	Machine-operator, soft-drinks production
8-39.40	8211	Machine-operator, spinning/metal
7-49.35	8261	Machine-operator, spinning/synthetic-fibre
7-52.20	8261	Machine-operator, spinning/thread and yarn
9-72.10	8290	Machine-operator, splicing/cable and rope
7-12.20	8112	Machine-operator, splitting/stone
7-52.50	8261	Machine-operator, spooling/thread and yarn
8-39.90	8211	Machine-operator, sports equipment/metal
8-19.90	8240	Machine-operator, sports equipment/wood
7-28.50	8223	Machine-operator, spraying/metal
7-61.55	8265	Machine-operator, staining/leather
7-74.20	8271	Machine-operator, sterilising/fish
7-74.20	8275	Machine-operator, sterilising/fruit
7-74.20	8271	Machine-operator, sterilising/meat
7-74.20	8275	Machine-operator, sterilising/vegetables
7-12.10	8112	Machine-operator, stone processing
8-20.10	8212	Machine-operator, stone products
7-81.60	8279	Machine-operator, stripping/tobacco-leaf
7-72.10	8276	Machine-operator, sugar production
7-49.35	8159	Machine-operator, synthetic-fibre production
7-61.45	8265	Machine-operator, tanning
7-77.10	8277	Machine-operator, tea-leaf processing
8-93.40	8131	Machine-operator, tempering/glass
7-26.50	8123	Machine-operator, tempering/metal
7-32.90	8141	Machine-operator, tempering/wood
7-51.10	8261	Machine-operator, textile fibre preparing
7-54.25	8262	Machine-operator, threading/loom
7-81.10	8279	Machine-operator, tobacco processing
7-81.10	8279	Machine-operator, tobacco products
7-44.90	8221	Machine-operator, toiletries production
8-32.20	8211	Machine-operator, tool production
9-49.90	8211	Machine-operator, toy production/metal
9-49.90	8240	Machine-operator, toy production/wood
7-31.30	8141	Machine-operator, treating/wood
7-52.40	8261	Machine-operator, twining/thread and yarn
7-52.40	8261	Machine-operator, twisting/thread and yarn
9-02.90	8231	Machine-operator, tyre production
7-79.90	8275	Machine-operator, vegetable juice production
7-74.90	8275	Machine-operator, vegetable processing
9-39.90	8281	Machine-operator, vehicle assembly
7-78.70	8278	Machine-operator, vinegar making
9-01.90	8231	Machine-operator, vulcanising/rubber goods

9-02.30	8231	Machine-operator, vulcanising/tyres
7-54.15	8262	Machine-operator, warping/beam (textile weaving)
9-71.55	8278	Machine-operator, washing/bottles
7-73.90	8271	Machine-operator, washing/carcasses
7-49.90	8229	Machine-operator, washing/chemical and related materials
7-56.35	8264	Machine-operator, washing/cloth
7-74.90	8275	Machine-operator, washing/fruit
7-61.90	8265	Machine-operator, washing/hide
5-60.20	8264	Machine-operator, washing/laundry
7-12.90	8112	Machine-operator, washing/minerals
7-51.90	8261	Machine-operator, washing/textile fibres
7-74.90	8275	Machine-operator, washing/vegetables
7-56.35	8264	Machine-operator, washing/yarn
8-42.20	8211	Machine-operator, watch production
7-56.60	8264	Machine-operator, waterproofing/cloth
7-56.60	8264	Machine-operator, waterproofing/fabric
7-56.60	8264	Machine-operator, waterproofing/textiles
7-54.40	8262	Machine-operator, weaving
7-54.60	8262	Machine-operator, weaving/carpets
7-54.40	8262	Machine-operator, weaving/fabrics
7-54.45	8262	Machine-operator, weaving/jacquard
7-54.50	8262	Machine-operator, weaving/laces
8-72.25	8211	Machine-operator, welding/metal
8-53.40	8282	Machine-operator, winding/armature
8-53.90	8283	Machine-operator, winding/filament
8-53.40	8282	Machine-operator, winding/rotor coil
8-53.40	8282	Machine-operator, winding/stator coil
7-52.50	8261	Machine-operator, winding/thread and yarn
8-53.40	8282	Machine-operator, winding/transformer coil
8-39.90	8211	Machine-operator, wire goods production
8-39.90	8211	Machine-operator, wiring/electric
7-32.10	8141	Machine-operator, wood processing
8-11.10	8240	Machine-operator, wood products
8-12.08	8240	Machine-operator, woodworking
9-71.55	8290	Machine-operator, wrapping
1-75.30	3474	Magician
1-22.10	2422	Magistrate
9-86.90	9332	Mahout
5-40.50	9132	Maid, chamber
5-40.30	5142	Maid, lady's
5-40.90	9133	Maid, linen
5-40.30	5142	Maid, personal
3-70.30	4142	Mailman
3-70.30	4142	Mailwoman
9-59.20	7129	Maintenance worker, building
5-32.20	5123	Maitre d'hotel
5-70.60	5141	Make-up artist, stage
5-70.60	5141	Make-up artist, studio
9-41.50	7312	Maker, accordion
7-99.90	7436	Maker, artificial flower
8-42.45	7311	Maker, artificial limb
7-99.20	7436	Maker, awning
8-42.30	7311	Maker, barometer
8-19.30	7422	Maker, barrel
9-42.20	7424	Maker, basket
7-96.90	7437	Maker, bedding
7-76.90	7412	Maker, biscuit
7-91.90	7433	Maker, blouse
8-73.50	7213	Maker, boiler
8-42.45	7311	Maker, brace/orthopaedic
7-59.20	7432	Maker, braid
9-21.90	7341	Maker, braille plate
9-42.40	7424	Maker, broom
9-42.30	7424	Maker, brush
7-75.30	7413	Maker, butter
8-11.20	7422	Maker, cabinet
7-93.90	7433	Maker, cap
7-99.90	7436	Maker, carpet
8-19.30	7422	Maker, cask
8-11.90	7422	Maker, chair
7-75.30	7413	Maker, cheese
7-76.90	7412	Maker, chewing-gum
7-76.50	7412	Maker, chocolate
7-82.20	7416	Maker, cigar
7-83.10	7416	Maker, cigarette
8-42.20	7311	Maker, clock
8-11.90	7422	Maker, clock case
8-19.90	7422	Maker, clog
8-19.90	7422	Maker, coffin
7-76.60	7412	Maker, confectionery
7-91.90	7433	Maker, corset
7-75.10	7413	Maker, dairy products
8-42.50	7311	Maker, dental prosthesis
9-41.90	7312	Maker, drum
7-59.40	7432	Maker, fishing net
8-01.10	7442	Maker, footwear
8-01.20	7442	Maker, footwear/orthopaedic

9-49.90	7424	Maker, footwear/raffia
8-01.90	7442	Maker, footwear/sport
7-79.90	7414	Maker, fruit juice
9-42.50	7424	Maker, furniture/basket
9-42.50	7422	Maker, furniture/cane
7-96.90	7437	Maker, furniture/soft furnishing
9-42.50	7424	Maker, furniture/wicker
8-32.30	7222	Maker, gauge
7-91.40	7433	Maker, gown
8-03.20	7442	Maker, harness
7-93.20	7433	Maker, hat
8-03.90	7442	Maker, horse collar
7-75.50	7413	Maker, ice-cream
8-11.90	7422	Maker, instrument case
8-42.90	7311	Maker, instrument/dental
8-42.30	7311	Maker, instrument/meteorological
9-41.40	7312	Maker, instrument/musical (brass)
9-41.40	7312	Maker, instrument/musical (metal wind)
9-41.20	7312	Maker, instrument/musical (string)
9-41.30	7312	Maker, instrument/musical (woodwind)
8-42.30	7311	Maker, instrument/nautical
8-42.35	7311	Maker, instrument/optical
8-42.30	7311	Maker, instrument/precision
8-42.90	7311	Maker, instrument/scientific
8-42.90	7311	Maker, instrument/surgical
7-24.90	7313	Maker, jewellery
8-32.30	7222	Maker, jig-gauge
8-19.90	7422	Maker, ladder/wood
8-03.10	7442	Maker, leather goods
7-91.90	7433	Maker, lingerie
6-31.40	6141	Maker, log-raft
9-54.90	7124	Maker, mast and spar/wood
7-96.40	7437	Maker, mattress
8-19.40	7422	Maker, model/wooden
7-59.40	7432	Maker, net
7-76.40	7412	Maker, noodle
9-41.60	7312	Maker, organ
9-41.60	7312	Maker, organ/bellow
9-41.60	7312	Maker, organ/pipe
8-42.45	7311	Maker, orthopaedic appliance
8-03.90	7442	Maker, panel/saddlery
7-34.60	7422	Maker, paper
7-76.30	7412	Maker, pastry
8-42.40	7311	Maker, photographic equipment
9-25.40	7343	Maker, photogravure/printing plate
9-41.70	7312	Maker, piano
9-41.50	7312	Maker, piano accordion
8-11.90	7422	Maker, piano case
9-41.70	7312	Maker, piano/key
9-41.70	7312	Maker, piano/sound-board
8-19.90	7422	Maker, picture frame
7-76.30	7412	Maker, pie
8-19.60	7422	Maker, pipe/smoking
8-19.60	7422	Maker, pipe/smoking (wood)
8-92.20	7321	Maker, pottery and porcelain mould
8-92.90	7321	Maker, pottery spout
8-80.90	7313	Maker, precious-metal chain
8-80.70	7313	Maker, precious-metal leaf
8-42.40	7311	Maker, precision instrument
8-32.20	7222	Maker, press tool
7-96.90	7437	Maker, quilt
8-03.20	7442	Maker, saddle
7-59.40	7432	Maker, safety net
7-99.20	7436	Maker, sail, tent and awning
7-73.40	7411	Maker, sausage
7-91.90	7433	Maker, shirt
7-89.20	7416	Maker, snuff
7-96.90	7437	Maker, soft furnishing
7-76.30	7412	Maker, sponge cake
8-01.90	7442	Maker, sports equipment/footwear
8-19.90	7422	Maker, sports equipment/wood
9-24.90	7343	Maker, stencil/printing plate
9-29.90	7346	Maker, stencil/silk-screen
9-49.90	7411	Maker, string/gut
7-72.10	7414	Maker, sugar/traditional methods
8-42.45	7311	Maker, surgical appliance
8-01.20	7442	Maker, surgical footwear
8-19.30	7422	Maker, tank/wooden
8-32.20	7222	Maker, tap-die
7-54.35	7432	Maker, tapestry
8-32.90	7222	Maker, template
7-99.20	7436	Maker, tent
7-89.90	7416	Maker, tobacco cake
7-89.90	7416	Maker, tobacco plug
8-32.20	7222	Maker, tool
8-32.20	7222	Maker, tool and die
8-32.90	7222	Maker, tool/diamond-pointed
9-49.40	7436	Maker, toy/dolls and stuffed toys
9-49.90	7223	Maker, toy/metal
9-49.90	7436	Maker, toy/soft toys
9-49.40	7436	Maker, toy/stuffed toys
9-49.90	7424	Maker, toy/wooden
7-99.30	7436	Maker, umbrella
7-79.90	7414	Maker, vegetable juice
9-41.20	7312	Maker, violin
8-42.20	7311	Maker, watch
8-03.90	7442	Maker, whip
9-49.90	7433	Maker, wig
9-41.90	7312	Maker, xylophone
7-78.40	7412	Maker, yeast
9-21.90	7341	Maker-up, photo-typesetting
9-21.45	7341	Maker-up, printing
7-78.20	8278	Maltster

0-51.30	2211	Mammalogist
2-11.10	1210	Managing director, enterprise
2-11.10	1210	Managing director, enterprise/ agriculture
2-11.10	1210	Managing director, enterprise/ business services
2-11.10	1210	Managing director, enterprise/ cleaning
2-11.10	1210	Managing director, enterprise/ communications
2-11.10	1210	Managing director, enterprise/ construction
2-11.10	1210	Managing director, enterprise/ cultural activities
2-11.10	1210	Managing director, enterprise/ education
2-11.10	1210	Managing director, enterprise/ fishing
2-11.10	1210	Managing director, enterprise/ forestry
2-11.10	1210	Managing director, enterprise/ health
2-11.10	1210	Managing director, enterprise/ hotel
2-11.10	1210	Managing director, enterprise/ hunting
2-11.10	1210	Managing director, enterprise/ manufacturing
2-11.10	1210	Managing director, enterprise/ personal care
2-11.10	1210	Managing director, enterprise/ recreation
2-11.10	1210	Managing director, enterprise/ restaurant
2-11.10	1210	Managing director, enterprise/retail trade
2-11.10	1210	Managing director, enterprise/ social work
2-11.10	1210	Managing director, enterprise/ sporting activities
2-11.10	1210	Managing director, enterprise/ storage
2-11.10	1210	Managing director, enterprise/ transport
2-11.10	1210	Managing director, enterprise/ travel agency
2-11.10	1210	Managing director, enterprise/ wholesale trade
2-11.10	1210	Managing director, organisation
2-11.10	1210	Managing director, organisation/ cultural activities
2-11.10	1210	Managing director, organisation/ education
2-11.10	1210	Managing director, organisation/ extra-territorial organisations
2-11.10	1210	Managing director, organisation/ fishing
2-11.10	1210	Managing director, organisation/ forestry
2-11.10	1210	Managing director, organisation/ health
2-11.10	1210	Managing director, organisation/ public administration
2-11.10	1210	Managing director, organisation/ recreation
2-11.10	1210	Managing director, organisation/ social work
2-11.10	1210	Managing director, organisation/ sporting activities
5-70.50	5141	Manicurist
7-22.70	8122	Manipulator, rolling-mill
4-51.40	5210	Mannequin
5-40.30	5142	Manservant
0-32.60	2148	Map maker
7-94.40	7435	Marker, garment
8-94.90	7323	Marker, glass engraving
8-32.50	7222	Marker, metal
8-73.20	7213	Marker, sheet metal
8-74.20	7214	Marker, structural metal
6-32.90	6141	Marker, timber
6-32.90	6141	Marker, tree
8-19.90	7422	Marker, woodworking
6-27.20	6113	Market gardener
6-27.20	6113	Market gardening worker, skilled
8-20.80	7113	Mason, monument
9-55.30	7133	Mason, stucco
0-76.40	3226	Masseur
0-76.40	3226	Masseuse
3-51.10	1226	Master, railway station
0-42.20	3142	Master, ship/inland waterways
0-42.15	3142	Master, ship/sea
7-92.40	7434	Matcher, fur
0-82.50	2121	Mathematician, actuarial science
0-82.30	2121	Mathematician, applied mathematics
0-82.20	2121	Mathematician, pure mathematics
0-71.10	2230	Matron
5-20.60	5121	Matron, housekeeping
2-01.10	1110	Mayor
8-49.55	7233	Mechanic, agricultural machinery
8-41.80	7233	Mechanic, air-conditioning equipment
8-43.20	7231	Mechanic, automobile
8-43.90	7231	Mechanic, automobile transmission
8-43.90	7231	Mechanic, bus
8-49.60	7233	Mechanic, construction machinery
8-42.50	7311	Mechanic, dental
8-49.60	7233	Mechanic, earth-moving equipment
8-55.70	7241	Mechanic, electrical

8-52.10	7243	Mechanic, electronics
8-49.65	7243	Mechanic, electronics/accounting-machine
8-54.20	7243	Mechanic, electronics/audio-visual equipment
8-49.65	7243	Mechanic, electronics/business machine
8-49.65	7243	Mechanic, electronics/calculating machine
8-52.40	7243	Mechanic, electronics/computer
8-49.65	7243	Mechanic, electronics/office machine
8-54.20	7243	Mechanic, electronics/radio
8-54.20	7243	Mechanic, electronics/television
8-44.20	7232	Mechanic, engine/aircraft
8-43.20	7231	Mechanic, engine/diesel (motor vehicle)
8-49.20	7233	Mechanic, engine/diesel (except motor vehicle)
8-43.20	7231	Mechanic, engine/motor vehicle
8-49.15	7233	Mechanic, engine/steam
8-49.55	7233	Mechanic, farm machinery
8-43.20	7231	Mechanic, garage
8-49.10	7233	Mechanic, industrial machinery
8-49.30	7233	Mechanic, machine tool
8-49.35	7233	Mechanic, mining machinery
8-43.40	7231	Mechanic, motor cycle
8-43.30	7231	Mechanic, motor truck
8-43.20	7231	Mechanic, motor vehicle
8-43.90	7231	Mechanic, motor-vehicle transmission
8-49.70	7233	Mechanic, plant maintenance
8-49.40	7233	Mechanic, printing machinery
8-41.80	7233	Mechanic, refrigeration and air-conditioning equipment
8-41.80	7233	Mechanic, refrigeration equipment
8-49.90	7233	Mechanic, ship
8-56.30	7244	Mechanic, telegraph
8-56.30	7244	Mechanic, telephone
8-49.45	7233	Mechanic, textile machinery
8-43.90	7231	Mechanic, tractor
8-43.30	7231	Mechanic, truck
8-49.25	7233	Mechanic, turbine
8-49.65	7233	Mechanic, typewriter
8-49.50	7233	Mechanic, woodworking machinery
0-61.05	2221	Medical practitioner
2-01.10	1110	Member, parliament
4-10.30	1314	Merchant, retail trade
4-10.20	1314	Merchant, wholesale trade
3-70.40	9151	Messenger
3-70.40	9151	Messenger boy
3-70.40	9151	Messenger girl
3-70.40	9151	Messenger, office
3-70.40	9151	Messenger, telegraph
0-26.20	2147	Metallurgist, extractive
0-26.30	2147	Metallurgist, foundry
0-26.30	2147	Metallurgist, physical
0-26.90	2147	Metallurgist, radioactive minerals
0-26.30	2147	Metallurgist-assayer
0-13.40	2112	Meteorologist
0-13.40	2112	Meteorologist, climatology
0-13.40	2112	Meteorologist, weather forecasting
3-31.90	9153	Meter reader
1-71.45	2453	Mezzo-soprano
0-52.50	2211	Microbiologist
0-13.30	2114	Micropalaeontologist
1-63.90	3131	Microphotographer
0-74.10	3232	Midwife, associate professional
0-73.10	3232	Midwife, associate professional/district
0-73.10	2230	Midwife, professional
0-73.10	2230	Midwife, professional/district
7-93.20	7433	Milliner
8-49.70	7233	Millwright
3-99.50	4141	Mimeographer
7-11.05	7111	Miner
7-11.90	7111	Miner, hydraulic/placer mining
7-11.05	7111	Miner, surface
7-11.05	7111	Miner, underground
0-13.90	2114	Mineralogist
2-01.10	1110	Minister, government
2-01.10	1110	Minister, government/junior
1-41.20	2460	Minister, religion
1-41.30	2460	Missionary
7-76.20	7412	Mixer, bread dough
7-76.50	7412	Mixer, chocolate
9-74.70	7123	Mixer, concrete
7-76.30	7412	Mixer, flour confectionery
7-76.30	7412	Mixer, pie paste
7-89.20	7416	Mixer, snuff
7-76.60	7412	Mixer, sugar confectionery
7-81.30	7416	Mixer, tobacco
4-51.90	5210	Model, advertising
5-99.90	5210	Model, artist's
4-51.40	5210	Model, clothing display
4-51.40	5210	Model, fashion
8-92.15	7321	Modeller, pottery and porcelain
1-61.20	2452	Modeller, sculpture
3-31.50	4212	Money changer
4-90.20	4214	Money-lender
1-41.40	3480	Monk, associate professional
1-41.20	2460	Monk, professional
9-21.35	7341	Monotyper
1-95.20	2444	Morphologist
5-92.20	5143	Mortician
9-85.70	8321	Motor-cyclist

8-92.60	7321	Moulder, abrasive wheel
8-92.40	7321	Moulder, brick and tile
7-76.90	7412	Moulder, chocolate
7-82.20	7416	Moulder, cigar
9-23.30	7342	Moulder, electrotype
8-91.90	7322	Moulder, glass
8-91.32	7322	Moulder, glass lens
7-25.10	7211	Moulder, metal castings
7-25.20	7211	Moulder, metal castings/bench
7-25.30	7211	Moulder, metal castings/floor and pit
7-25.30	7211	Moulder, metal castings/pit

7-25.20	7211	Moulder, metal castings/stump
7-25.20	7211	Moulder, metal castings/tub
9-23.20	7342	Moulder, stereotype
8-80.90	7313	Mounter, jewellery
9-25.90	7343	Mounter, photo-engraving/printing plates
9-25.90	7343	Mounter, photogravure/printing
1-71.40	2453	Musician, instrumental
1-71.40	3473	Musician, night-club
1-71.40	3473	Musician, street
1-71.20	2453	Musicologist
0-51.20	2211	Mycologist

N

7-92.60	7434	Nailer, fur
5-40.35	5131	Nanny
0-79.90	3241	Naturopath
0-41.40	3143	Navigator, flight
9-99.10	9312	Navvy
0-52.40	2221	Neurologist
0-52.60	2212	Neuropathologist
0-61.30	2221	Neurosurgeon
1-79.20	3472	Newscaster
4-52.40	9112	Newsvendor
7-26.40	8123	Nitrider
1-29.10	2429	Notary
1-51.20	2451	Novelist
1-99.60	5152	Numerologist
1-41.40	3480	Nun, associate professional
1-41.20	2460	Nun, professional
0-72.10	3231	Nurse, associate professional
0-71.20	3231	Nurse, associate professional/anaesthetics
0-71.10	3231	Nurse, associate professional/charge
0-71.10	3231	Nurse, associate professional/clinic
0-71.90	3231	Nurse, associate professional/consultant
0-71.10	3231	Nurse, associate professional/district
0-71.40	3231	Nurse, associate professional/industrial
0-71.20	3231	Nurse, associate professional/maternity

0-71.20	3231	Nurse, associate professional/obstetrics
0-71.40	3231	Nurse, associate professional/occupational health
0-71.20	3231	Nurse, associate professional/orthopaedic
0-71.20	3231	Nurse, associate professional/pediatric
0-71.20	3231	Nurse, associate professional/psychiatric
0-71.90	3231	Nurse, associate professional/school
0-71.10	2230	Nurse, professional
0-71.20	2230	Nurse, professional/anaesthetics
0-71.10	2230	Nurse, professional/charge
0-71.10	2230	Nurse, professional/clinic
0-71.90	2230	Nurse, professional/consultant
0-71.10	2230	Nurse, professional/district
0-71.40	2230	Nurse, professional/industrial
0-71.20	2230	Nurse, professional/maternity
0-71.20	2230	Nurse, professional/obstetrics
0-71.40	2230	Nurse, professional/occupational health
0-71.20	2230	Nurse, professional/orthopaedic
0-71.20	2230	Nurse, professional/pediatric
0-71.20	2230	Nurse, professional/psychiatric
0-71.90	2230	Nurse, professional/school
5-40.35	5131	Nursemaid
6-12.70	6113	Nurseryman
6-12.70	6113	Nurserywoman
0-69.20	3223	Nutritionist

O

1-71.40	2453	Oboist
0-61.20	2221	Obstetrician
0-13.30	2114	Oceanographer, geological
0-13.20	2114	Oceanographer, geophysical

9-99.10	9162	Odd-job person
7-73.90	7411	Offal worker
3-10.10	3449	Officer, civil defence
3-10.10	3449	Officer, civil service commission

3-10.10	3442	Officer, excise
3-10.10	3444	Officer, immigration
1-94.20	2412	Officer, industrial relations
1-99.90	3423	Officer, job placement
3-10.10	3444	Officer, licensing
1-94.30	2412	Officer, occupational guidance
3-10.10	3441	Officer, passport checking
3-10.10	3444	Officer, passport issuing
3-10.10	3443	Officer, pensions
1-94.20	2412	Officer, personnel
1-94.90	2412	Officer, personnel safety
1-59.55	2419	Officer, press liaison
0-71.10	3231	Officer, principal nursing/associate professional
0-71.10	2230	Officer, principal nursing/ professional
1-59.55	2419	Officer, public information
1-59.55	2419	Officer, public relations
0-42.30	3142	Officer, ship/deck
0-42.30	3142	Officer, ship/navigation
3-80.50	3132	Officer, ship/radio
3-10.10	3443	Officer, social benefits
3-10.10	3443	Officer, social security claims
1-94.20	2412	Officer, staff training
3-10.10	3442	Officer, tax
1-99.90	3423	Officer, youth employment
3-10.10	3439	Official, consular
3-10.10	3449	Official, electoral
2-01.10	1110	Official, legislative
1-80.40	3475	Official, sports
8-49.80	7233	Oiler and greaser
9-82.30	7233	Oiler and greaser, ship
0-53.30	2213	Olericulturist
9-73.45	8333	Onsetter, mine
7-51.90	7431	Opener, fibre/textiles
6-28.20	8331	Operator, agricultural machinery
3-59.60	3144	Operator, air-traffic control equipment
8-53.90	8171	Operator, assembly-line/ automated
8-61.30	3131	Operator, audio equipment/radio
8-61.30	3131	Operator, audio equipment/ television
0-79.90	3133	Operator, audiometric equipment
7-42.90	8152	Operator, autoclave/chemical and related processes
7-74.20	8275	Operator, autoclave/fruit and vegetables
7-74.20	8271	Operator, autoclave/meat and fish
7-79.30	8275	Operator, autoclave/oils and fats
6-28.20	8331	Operator, baler/farm
7-32.30	8141	Operator, band saw
9-81.90	8340	Operator, barge
7-33.60	8142	Operator, beater/paper pulp

7-49.15	8159	Operator, bleacher/chemicals
7-33.50	8142	Operator, bleacher/paper
7-45.60	8155	Operator, blender/petroleum and natural gas refining (ethyl)
9-73.90	8333	Operator, boat/derrick
9-69.30	8162	Operator, boiler plant/steam
7-42.20	8152	Operator, boiler/chemical and related processes
9-83.30	8162	Operator, boiler/locomotive
7-33.40	8142	Operator, boiler/paper pulp
9-82.20	8162	Operator, boiler/ship
7-13.80	8113	Operator, boring equipment/wells
7-12.80	8112	Operator, breaker/gyratory
9-73.55	8333	Operator, bridge
9-73.55	8333	Operator, bridge/bascule
9-73.55	8333	Operator, bridge/opening
9-73.55	8333	Operator, bridge/swing
8-61.90	3132	Operator, broadcasting equipment/ field
8-61.30	3132	Operator, broadcasting equipment/ radio
8-61.30	3132	Operator, broadcasting equipment/ telecine
8-61.90	3132	Operator, broadcasting equipment/ television
8-61.30	3132	Operator, broadcasting equipment/ video
9-74.30	8332	Operator, bulldozer
7-49.30	8159	Operator, burner/charcoal production
7-42.40	8152	Operator, burner/chemical and related processes
7-49.20	8159	Operator, burner/coke production
9-79.90	8333	Operator, cable car
9-73.45	8333	Operator, cage/mine
7-42.40	8152	Operator, calciner/chemical and related processes
9-01.25	8231	Operator, calender/rubber
7-56.70	8264	Operator, calender/textiles
1-63.60	3131	Operator, camera/cinematography
1-63.60	3131	Operator, camera/motion picture
1-63.70	3131	Operator, camera/television
7-26.40	8123	Operator, carbonation equipment/ metal
7-72.40	8276	Operator, carbonation equipment/ sugar refining
7-42.90	8152	Operator, cement production plant
7-43.40	8153	Operator, centrifugal separator/ chemical and related processes
9-79.90	8333	Operator, chair-lift
7-42.40	8152	Operator, chemical and related processing plant
7-49.90	8159	Operator, chemical processing plant/electric cells

7-49.40	8159	Operator, chemical processing plant/radioactive materials
7-33.30	8142	Operator, chipper/paper pulp
5-60.90	8264	Operator, cleaning equipment/carpets
7-56.35	8264	Operator, cleaning equipment/cloth
5-60.20	8264	Operator, cleaning equipment/laundry
7-29.40	8223	Operator, cleaning equipment/metal
7-56.35	8264	Operator, cleaning equipment/textiles
7-49.20	8159	Operator, coke production plant
6-28.20	8331	Operator, combiner/agricultural
7-34.90	8143	Operator, combiner/paper production
7-45.60	8155	Operator, compounder/petroleum and natural gas refining
9-69.20	8163	Operator, compressor/air
9-69.25	8163	Operator, compressor/gas
3-42.20	3122	Operator, computer peripheral equipment
3-42.20	3122	Operator, computer peripheral equipment/console
3-42.90	3122	Operator, computer peripheral equipment/high-speed printer
9-74.75	8212	Operator, concrete-mixing plant
7-12.80	8112	Operator, cone/mine
7-45.50	8155	Operator, control-panel/petroleum and natural gas refinery
8-61.30	3132	Operator, control-room equipment/radio
8-61.30	3132	Operator, control-room equipment/television
7-44.40	8154	Operator, converter/chemical processes (except petroleum and natural gas)
9-79.90	8333	Operator, conveyer
7-42.20	8152	Operator, cooking equipment/chemical and related processes
7-78.30	8278	Operator, cooking equipment/malt
9-69.70	8163	Operator, cooling plant
9-73.10	8333	Operator, crane
9-73.20	8333	Operator, crane/bridge
9-73.30	8333	Operator, crane/crawler
9-73.90	8333	Operator, crane/floating
9-73.20	8333	Operator, crane/gantry
9-73.90	8333	Operator, crane/locomotive
9-73.30	8333	Operator, crane/mobile
9-73.90	8333	Operator, crane/railway
9-73.25	8333	Operator, crane/stationary jib
9-73.27	8333	Operator, crane/tower
9-73.30	8333	Operator, crane/tractor
7-72.50	8276	Operator, crystallising equipment/sugar refining
7-32.90	8141	Operator, cut-off saw/barrel staves
7-32.90	8141	Operator, cut-off saw/log staves
7-43.50	8153	Operator, dehydrator/oilfield
7-13.20	8113	Operator, derrick/oil and gas wells
9-69.90	8163	Operator, desilting basin
9-21.55	7341	Operator, desktop publishing equipment
8-92.50	8139	Operator, die-press/pottery and porcelain
7-72.30	8276	Operator, diffuser/beet sugar
7-33.40	8142	Operator, digester/paper pulp
9-74.25	8332	Operator, digger/trench digging
7-44.20	8154	Operator, distiller/batch (chemical processes except petroleum and natural gas)
7-44.30	8154	Operator, distiller/continuous (chemical processes except petroleum and natural gas)
7-45.40	8155	Operator, distiller/petroleum and natural gas refining
7-44.90	8154	Operator, distiller/turpentine
7-44.90	8221	Operator, distilling equipment/perfume
9-73.50	8333	Operator, donkey engine
9-73.55	8333	Operator, drawbridge
9-74.35	8332	Operator, dredge
7-42.40	8152	Operator, drier/chemical and related processes
7-13.40	8113	Operator, drilling equipment/cable (oil and gas wells)
7-13.30	8113	Operator, drilling equipment/rotary (oil and gas wells)
7-13.80	8113	Operator, drilling equipment/wells
9-74.90	8332	Operator, drilling plant
8-62.90	3131	Operator, dubbing equipment
9-74.90	8332	Operator, earth-boring machinery/construction
9-74.10	8332	Operator, earth-moving equipment
9-61.90	8161	Operator, electric power plant
0-79.90	3133	Operator, electrocardiograph equipment
0-79.90	3133	Operator, electroencephalograph equipment
9-79.90	8333	Operator, elevator/material-handling
7-74.90	8275	Operator, evaporation equipment/food essences
7-44.50	8154	Operator, evaporator/chemical processes (except petroleum and natural gas)
9-74.20	8332	Operator, excavator
7-43.20	8153	Operator, expeller/chemical and related materials
7-43.90	8153	Operator, extractor/chemical and related materials

7-44.40	8154	Operator, reactor/chemical processes (except petroleum and natural gas)
9-61.40	8161	Operator, reactor/nuclear-power
8-62.20	3131	Operator, recording equipment/ discs
8-62.20	3131	Operator, recording equipment/ sound
8-62.90	3131	Operator, recording equipment/ sound mixing
8-62.20	3131	Operator, recording equipment/ tape
8-61.30	3131	Operator, recording equipment/ video
8-62.20	3131	Operator, recording equipment/ wire
9-61.90	8161	Operator, rectifier/electric current
7-33.90	8142	Operator, refinery/paper pulp
7-45.30	8155	Operator, refinery/petroleum and natural gas
9-69.70	8163	Operator, refrigeration system
9-69.90	8163	Operator, reservoir/water
7-42.40	8152	Operator, retort/chemical and related processes
7-49.25	8159	Operator, retort/coal gas
9-74.60	8332	Operator, road surface laying machinery
9-74.50	8332	Operator, road-roller
7-42.30	8152	Operator, roasting equipment/ chemical and related processes
7-77.60	8277	Operator, roasting equipment/ cocoa-bean
7-77.50	8277	Operator, roasting equipment/ coffee
0-39.90	8172	Operator, robot
7-71.20	8273	Operator, rolling-mill/grain
7-22.50	8122	Operator, rolling-mill/non-ferrous metal
7-22.60	8122	Operator, rolling-mill/seamless pipe and tube
7-71.40	8273	Operator, rolling-mill/spices
7-22.40	8122	Operator, rolling-mill/steel (cold-rolling)
7-22.30	8122	Operator, rolling-mill/steel (continuous)
7-22.20	8122	Operator, rolling-mill/steel (hot-rolling)
9-79.90	8333	Operator, ropeway/aerial
7-49.90	8159	Operator, rubber processing plant
8-94.40	8131	Operator, sandblasting equipment/ glass
7-29.30	8223	Operator, sandblasting equipment/ metal
7-32.10	8141	Operator, sawmill
7-32.30	8141	Operator, sawmill/band-saw
0-77.90	3133	Operator, scanning equipment
3-42.90	3133	Operator, scanning equipment/ optical
7-43.90	8153	Operator, screener/chemical and related materials
7-33.90	8142	Operator, screener/paper pulp
7-43.40	8153	Operator, separator/chemical and related processes
9-69.90	8163	Operator, sewage plant
9-74.20	8332	Operator, shovel/mechanical
9-79.40	8324	Operator, shuttle-car/mine
9-79.40	8324	Operator, shuttle-car/quarry
7-43.90	8153	Operator, sifting equipment/ chemical and related materials
9-89.90	8333	Operator, sluice/dock
9-61.90	8161	Operator, solar power plant
7-42.90	8152	Operator, spray-drier/chemical and related processes
9-74.60	8332	Operator, spreader/asphalt
9-74.55	8332	Operator, spreader/concrete paving (construction)
9-74.90	8332	Operator, spreader/stone (construction)
9-74.60	8332	Operator, spreader/tar
9-69.30	8162	Operator, steam engine
9-61.20	8161	Operator, steam power plant
7-45.30	8155	Operator, still-pump/petroleum and natural gas refining
7-44.20	8154	Operator, still/batch (chemical processes except petroleum and natural gas)
7-44.30	8154	Operator, still/continuous (chemical processes except petroleum and natural gas)
7-44.90	8221	Operator, still/perfume
7-45.40	8155	Operator, still/petroleum and natural gas refining
7-44.90	8278	Operator, still/spirits
7-44.90	8154	Operator, still/turpentine
7-12.10	8112	Operator, stone-processing plant
8-61.30	3131	Operator, studio equipment/radio
8-61.30	3131	Operator, studio equipment/ television
7-34.40	8143	Operator, supercalender
9-61.60	8161	Operator, switchboard/electrical power station
9-61.60	8161	Operator, switchboard/power station generator
7-49.35	8159	Operator, synthetic-fibre production plant
9-74.90	8332	Operator, tamping machinery/ construction
3-59.75	3132	Operator, telecommunications equipment
3-80.40	3132	Operator, telegraphic equipment
6-28.20	8331	Operator, thresher
9-61.90	8161	Operator, tidal power plant

8-61.20	3132	Operator, transmitting equipment/ radio
8-61.20	3132	Operator, transmitting equipment/ television
7-45.20	8155	Operator, treater/desulphurisation (petroleum and natural gas refining)
7-45.20	8155	Operator, treater/petroleum and natural gas refining
7-49.40	8159	Operator, treater/radioactive waste
9-69.50	8163	Operator, treater/water
7-43.50	8153	Operator, treating equipment/ crude oil
9-79.20	8334	Operator, truck/fork-lift
9-79.20	8334	Operator, truck/industrial
9-79.20	8334	Operator, truck/lifting
9-74.90	8332	Operator, tunnelling machinery/ construction
9-61.50	8161	Operator, turbine/electricity generation
9-61.50	8161	Operator, turbine/power station
7-74.40	8275	Operator, vacuum oven/foodstuffs
7-44.50	8154	Operator, vacuum pan/chemical and related processes (except petroleum and natural gas)
7-75.90	8272	Operator, vacuum pan/condensed milk
7-74.90	8275	Operator, vacuum pan/food essences
7-81.40	8279	Operator, vacuum-conditioner/ tobacco processing

9-69.80	8163	Operator, ventilation equipment
9-69.50	8163	Operator, water purification plant
9-69.50	8163	Operator, water treatment plant
9-73.50	8333	Operator, winch
9-61.90	8161	Operator, wind-energy plant/ electric power generating
7-78.50	8278	Operator, winemaking plant
7-32.10	8141	Operator, wood-processing plant
0-61.20	2221	Ophthalmologist
0-75.30	3224	Optician, dispensing
0-75.20	3224	Optician, ophthalmic
0-75.20	3224	Optometrist
1-71.30	2453	Orchestrator
5-99.40	5132	Orderly
1-99.90	3414	Organiser, travel
1-71.40	2453	Organist
0-51.30	2211	Ornithologist
0-63.20	2222	Orthodontist
0-79.90	3229	Orthoepist
0-79.90	3229	Orthophonist
0-75.20	3229	Orthoptist
0-79.20	2221	Osteopath
0-79.20	3226	Osteopath, lay
0-61.20	2221	Otolaryngologist
9-31.20	7141	Outside painter, construction
7-76.90	7412	Oven worker, biscuits
7-76.20	7412	Oven worker, bread
7-76.30	7412	Oven worker, flour confectionery

P

9-71.50	9322	Packer, hand
9-39.60	7142	Painter, automobile
9-31.20	7141	Painter, building
9-31.20	7141	Painter, construction
9-39.20	7324	Painter, decorative
8-95.30	7324	Painter, decorative/ceramics
8-95.20	7324	Painter, decorative/glass
9-39.50	7324	Painter, decorative/sign
9-31.20	7141	Painter, house
9-39.10	7142	Painter, manufactured articles
9-39.90	7142	Painter, metal
1-61.90	2452	Painter, miniatures
9-31.90	7141	Painter, motion picture set
9-31.20	7141	Painter, outside/construction
1-61.30	2452	Painter, portrait
9-31.30	7141	Painter, ship's hull
9-31.90	7141	Painter, stage scenery
9-31.30	7141	Painter, structural steel
9-39.60	7142	Painter, vehicle
9-31.20	7141	Painter-decorator, buildings

9-59.25	7141	Painter-decorator, wallcarpeting
9-59.25	7141	Painter-decorator, wallcovering
9-59.25	7141	Painter-decorator, wallpapering
0-13.30	2114	Palaeontologist
1-99.60	5152	Palmist
9-59.25	7141	Paperhanger
0-51.30	2211	Parasitologist
1-49.90	3480	Parish worker
2-01.10	1110	Parliamentarian
1-93.40	3460	Parole officer, associate professional
1-93.40	2446	Parole officer, professional
9-54.75	7132	Parquetry worker
5-99.90	5149	Partner, dancing
1-41.20	2460	Pastor
6-12.40	9211	Pastoralist
5-31.40	7421	Pastry-cook
1-99.20	2419	Patent agent
0-52.60	2212	Pathologist
0-52.65	2212	Pathologist, animal

0-52.60	2212	Pathologist, clinical
0-52.60	2212	Pathologist, forensic
0-52.60	2212	Pathologist, histopathology
0-52.60	2212	Pathologist, medical
0-52.60	2212	Pathologist, neuropathology
0-52.90	2212	Pathologist, plant
0-52.60	2212	Pathologist, surgical
0-52.65	2212	Pathologist, veterinary
5-89.90	5169	Patrolman, beach
6-32.50	5161	Patrolman, forest fire
5-82.20	5162	Patrolman, police
5-89.40	5169	Patrolman, security
5-89.90	5169	Patrolwoman, beach
5-81.10	5161	Patrolwoman, forest fire
5-82.20	5162	Patrolwoman, police
5-89.40	5169	Patrolwoman, security
7-94.30	7435	Pattern-maker, caps
8-02.15	7442	Pattern-maker, footwear
7-92.30	7435	Pattern-maker, fur
7-94.20	7435	Pattern-maker, garment
7-94.90	7435	Pattern-maker, gloves
7-94.30	7435	Pattern-maker, hats
7-94.90	7435	Pattern-maker, mattresses
8-32.40	7222	Pattern-maker, metal foundry
7-94.90	7435	Pattern-maker, sails
7-94.90	7435	Pattern-maker, tents
7-94.90	7435	Pattern-maker, umbrellas
7-94.90	7435	Pattern-maker, upholstery
8-19.35	7422	Pattern-maker, wood patterns
9-51.60	7122	Paviour
4-90.20	4214	Pawnbroker
2-02.10	1120	Paymaster-general, government
0-61.20	2221	Pediatrician
4-52.20	9112	Pedlar
0-63.20	2222	Pedodontist
1-92.20	2442	Penologist
1-71.40	2453	Percussionist
0-63.20	2222	Periodontist
0-13.30	2114	Petrologist
8-80.50	7313	Pewtersmith
0-67.10	2224	Pharmacist
0-67.10	2224	Pharmacist, hospital
0-11.90	2113	Pharmacist, industrial
0-67.10	2224	Pharmacist, retail
0-52.70	2212	Pharmacologist
0-52.70	2212	Pharmacologist, toxicology
1-95.20	2444	Philologist
1-95.20	2444	Philologist, etymology
1-95.20	2444	Philologist, graphology
1-95.20	2444	Philologist, lexicography
1-95.20	2444	Philologist, linguistics
1-95.20	2444	Philologist, morphology
1-95.20	2444	Philologist, phonology
1-95.20	2444	Philologist, semantics
1-92.70	2443	Philosopher
1-92.70	2443	Philosopher, political
1-95.20	2444	Phonologist
9-21.55	7341	Photo type-setter, printing
9-21.55	7341	Photo-composer, printing
9-25.10	7343	Photo-engraver
0-31.50	2148	Photogrammetrist
1-63.10	3131	Photographer
1-63.30	3131	Photographer, advertising
1-63.90	3131	Photographer, aerial
1-63.90	3131	Photographer, architecture
1-63.30	3131	Photographer, commercial
1-63.90	3131	Photographer, commercial illustration
1-63.30	3131	Photographer, fashion
1-63.30	3131	Photographer, industrial
1-63.90	3131	Photographer, medical
1-63.90	3131	Photographer, microphotography
1-63.40	3131	Photographer, news
9-25.20	7343	Photographer, photogravure
1-63.90	3131	Photographer, police
1-63.20	3131	Photographer, portrait
1-63.40	3131	Photographer, press
1-63.90	3131	Photographer, scientific
9-25.20	7343	Photolithographer
0-61.05	2221	Physician
0-12.10	2111	Physicist
0-12.50	2111	Physicist, acoustics
0-13.50	2111	Physicist, astronomy
0-12.80	2111	Physicist, atomic
0-12.20	2111	Physicist, ballistics
0-12.60	2111	Physicist, electricity and magnetism
0-12.70	2111	Physicist, electronics
0-12.30	2111	Physicist, heat
0-12.20	2111	Physicist, hydrodynamics
0-12.40	2111	Physicist, light
0-12.20	2111	Physicist, mechanics
0-12.80	2111	Physicist, molecular
0-12.80	2111	Physicist, nuclear
0-12.50	2111	Physicist, optics
0-12.20	2111	Physicist, rheology
0-12.90	2111	Physicist, solid-state
0-12.50	2111	Physicist, sound
0-12.90	2111	Physicist, theoretical
0-12.30	2111	Physicist, thermodynamics
0-52.40	2212	Physiologist
0-52.40	2212	Physiologist, animal
0-52.40	2212	Physiologist, endocrinology
0-52.40	2212	Physiologist, epidemiology
0-52.40	2212	Physiologist, neurology
0-52.40	2212	Physiologist, plant

0-76.20	3226	Physiotherapist
1-71.40	2453	Pianist
6-22.90	9211	Picker, cotton
7-51.30	7431	Picker, fibre/textiles
6-23.90	9211	Picker, fruit
7-74.50	7411	Pickler, fish
7-74.50	7414	Pickler, fruit
7-74.50	7411	Pickler, meat
7-62.90	7441	Pickler, pelt
7-74.50	7414	Pickler, vegetables
7-11.60	7111	Piler, mine
0-41.30	3143	Pilot, aircraft
0-41.60	3340	Pilot, check
0-41.20	3143	Pilot, helicopter
0-42.90	3142	Pilot, hovercraft
0-41.20	3143	Pilot, seaplane
0-42.40	3142	Pilot, ship
0-41.30	3143	Pilot, test
9-59.50	7136	Pipeline worker
0-51.30	2211	Pisciculturist
9-52.10	7123	Placer, concrete
8-20.20	7113	Planer, stone
0-21.30	2141	Planner, town
0-29.50	2141	Planner, traffic
0-21.30	2141	Planner, urban
6-23.50	6112	Plantation worker, skilled/rubber
6-23.10	6112	Plantation worker, skilled/shrub crop
6-23.40	6112	Plantation worker, skilled/tea
6-23.10	6112	Plantation worker, skilled/tree crop
6-12.30	6112	Planter, copra
6-12.20	6111	Planter, cotton
6-32.90	6141	Planter, forestry
6-12.20	6111	Planter, sugar-cane
6-12.30	6112	Planter, tea
6-12.20	6111	Planter, tobacco
9-55.10	7133	Plasterer
9-55.40	7133	Plasterer, fibrous sheet
9-55.20	7133	Plasterer, ornamental
9-55.30	7133	Plasterer, stucco
8-74.55	7214	Plater, ship
1-80.20	3475	Player, sports
1-51.20	2451	Playwright
6-23.90	9211	Plucker, tea
7-62.40	7441	Plucker-trimmer, pelt
8-71.05	7136	Plumber
8-71.90	7136	Plumber, chemical
8-71.30	7136	Plumber, ship
8-57.50	7245	Plumber-jointer, electric cable
0-79.90	3226	Podiatrist
1-51.20	2451	Poet
5-82.20	5162	Police officer
5-82.20	5162	Police officer, harbour
5-82.20	5162	Police officer, river
5-82.20	5162	Police officer, traffic
8-02.90	7442	Polisher, footwear
8-91.90	7322	Polisher, glass
8-91.72	7322	Polisher, glass/lenses
8-20.20	7113	Polisher, granite
8-80.30	7313	Polisher, industrial diamonds
8-80.90	7313	Polisher, jewellery
7-61.90	7441	Polisher, leather
8-20.20	7113	Polisher, marble
8-35.90	7224	Polisher, metal
8-35.90	7224	Polisher, metal/emery polishing
8-35.90	7224	Polisher, metal/mirror-finish
8-35.90	7224	Polisher, metal/sand polishing
5-99.90	9120	Polisher, shoes
8-20.20	7113	Polisher, slate
8-20.20	7113	Polisher, stone
1-92.70	2443	Political scientist
0-53.30	2213	Pomologist
1-41.20	2460	Poojari
9-71.45	9333	Porter, cold-storage
9-71.45	9333	Porter, fish
9-71.45	9333	Porter, food market
9-71.45	9333	Porter, fruit
9-71.30	9333	Porter, goods-loading
5-40.55	9152	Porter, hotel
9-71.90	9151	Porter, luggage
9-71.45	9333	Porter, meat
9-71.45	9333	Porter, shop
9-71.45	9333	Porter, warehouse
3-70.30	4142	Post carrier
3-70.40	9151	Post-runner
3-70.30	4142	Postman
3-52.10	1226	Postmaster
2-02.10	1120	Postmaster-general, government
3-70.30	4142	Postwoman
8-92.10	7321	Potter
0-79.90	3229	Practitioner, homeopathic
1-41.40	3480	Preacher, lay
7-12.70	8112	Precipitator, gold
7-12.70	8112	Precipitator, silver
7-51.10	7431	Preparer, fibre/textiles
8-02.40	7442	Preparer, footwear/soles
8-02.30	7442	Preparer, footwear/uppers
8-74.10	7214	Preparer, structural metal
7-74.90	7414	Preserver, fruit
7-79.90	7414	Preserver, fruit juice
7-74.90	7411	Preserver, sauces and condiments
7-74.90	7414	Preserver, vegetable
7-79.90	7414	Preserver, vegetable juice
2-11.10	1142	President, employers' organisation
2-11.10	1210	President, enterprise
2-01.10	1110	President, government

Alphabetical index of occupational titles

————————————————— Q —————————————————

9-49.80	3152	Quality inspector
8-59.20	3152	Quality inspector, electrical products
8-59.20	3152	Quality inspector, electronic products
8-59.85	3152	Quality inspector, mechanical products
9-49.80	3152	Quality inspector, processes
9-49.80	3152	Quality inspector, products
9-49.80	3152	Quality inspector, services
7-11.10	7111	Quarrier

————————————————— R —————————————————

1-41.20	2460	Rabbi
1-80.20	3475	Racer, cycle
0-61.20	2221	Radiologist
6-12.40	6121	Raiser, cattle
6-12.90	6129	Raiser, laboratory animal
6-12.90	6129	Raiser, ostrich
6-12.40	6121	Raiser, pig
6-12.40	6121	Raiser, sheep
6-12.90	6123	Raiser, silkworm
6-12.40	6121	Rancher, cattle
6-32.90	6141	Ranger, forest
1-31.10	2310	Reader, university
4-41.30	3413	Realtor
3-94.10	4222	Receptionist
3-94.30	4222	Receptionist, dental
3-94.20	4222	Receptionist, hotel
3-94.30	4222	Receptionist, medical
1-41.20	2460	Rector, religion
1-80.40	3475	Referee, sports
7-76.50	7412	Refiner, chocolate
2-02.10	1120	Registrar-general, government
1-41.40	3480	Religious worker
9-71.90	9333	Remover, furniture
9-71.90	9333	Remover, household goods
8-49.75	7231	Repairer, bicycle
9-59.20	7129	Repairer, building
8-42.35	7311	Repairer, camera
9-59.20	7129	Repairer, chimney
8-42.25	7311	Repairer, clock
8-42.50	7311	Repairer, dental prosthesis
8-55.70	7241	Repairer, electrical equipment
8-52.10	7243	Repairer, electronics equipment
8-54.20	7243	Repairer, electronics equipment/audio-visual
8-54.20	7243	Repairer, electronics equipment/radio
8-54.20	7243	Repairer, electronics equipment/television
8-44.10	7232	Repairer, engine/aircraft
7-54.75	7432	Repairer, fabrics
8-01.30	7442	Repairer, footwear
8-42.90	7311	Repairer, instrument/dental
9-41.90	7312	Repairer, instrument/musical (percussion)
9-41.20	7312	Repairer, instrument/musical (string)
9-41.40	7312	Repairer, instrument/musical (wind)
8-42.35	7311	Repairer, instrument/optical
8-42.30	7311	Repairer, instrument/precision
8-42.90	7311	Repairer, instrument/scientific
8-42.90	7311	Repairer, instrument/surgical
8-80.20	7313	Repairer, jewellery
8-43.90	7231	Repairer, motor vehicle
8-42.45	7311	Repairer, orthopaedic appliance
8-49.75	7231	Repairer, pedal cycle
8-42.90	7311	Repairer, photographic equipment
8-35.50	7224	Repairer, saw
8-42.90	7311	Repairer, surgical appliance
8-42.25	7311	Repairer, watch
3-21.30	3431	Reporter, administrative/court
3-21.30	3431	Reporter, administrative/verbatim
1-59.30	2451	Reporter, journalism/media
1-59.30	2451	Reporter, journalism/media (crime)
1-59.30	2451	Reporter, journalism/media (fashion)
1-59.30	2451	Reporter, journalism/media (newspapers)
1-59.30	2451	Reporter, journalism/media (sports)
4-42.20	3429	Representative, business services
4-42.30	3429	Representative, business services/advertising
4-42.20	3429	Representative, business services/advertising space
2-02.10	1120	Representative, diplomatic
4-32.20	3415	Representative, sales/commercial
4-31.20	3415	Representative, sales/engineering
4-32.30	3415	Representative, sales/manufacturing
4-31.20	3415	Representative, sales/technical
5-10.30	1315	Restaurateur
1-61.60	2452	Restorer, picture

4-10.30	1314	Retailer
9-25.30	7343	Retoucher, photogravure
9-25.60	7343	Retoucher, printing plates
0-12.20	2111	Rheologist
7-55.40	7432	Ribbon lapper
9-89.50	9331	Rider, bicycle
9-85.70	8321	Rider, dispatch
9-85.70	8321	Rider, motor cycle
6-31.40	6141	Rider, timber
9-89.50	9331	Rider, tricycle
9-72.05	7215	Rigger
9-72.40	7215	Rigger, aircraft
9-72.05	7215	Rigger, hoisting equipment
9-72.20	7215	Rigger, hoisting equipment/ construction
9-72.50	7215	Rigger, oil and gas well
9-72.90	7215	Rigger, railway cable
9-59.40	7129	Rigger, scaffolding
9-72.30	7215	Rigger, ship
9-72.90	7215	Rigger, ski-lift

8-74.60	7214	Riveter
8-74.70	7214	Riveter, pneumatic
7-11.90	7111	Robber, timber/mine
7-82.20	7416	Roller, cigar
8-80.60	7313	Roller, precious metal
7-76.60	7412	Roller, sugar confectionery
9-53.10	7131	Roofer
9-53.40	7131	Roofer, asphalt
9-53.30	7131	Roofer, composite materials
9-53.50	7131	Roofer, metal
9-53.20	7131	Roofer, slate
9-53.20	7131	Roofer, tile
9-53.90	7131	Roofer, wood-shingle
8-02.40	7442	Rounder, footwear
4-52.20	9113	Roundsman, distribution/retail
4-52.20	9113	Roundswoman, distribution/retail
7-51.55	7431	Rover, fibre/textiles
8-95.40	7324	Rubber stamper, ceramics
3-70.40	9151	Runner post
3-70.40	9151	Runner, messages

S

8-03.20	7442	Saddler
9-81.30	8340	Sailor
4-41.40	3411	Salesperson, bond
4-42.20	3429	Salesperson, business services
4-42.30	3429	Salesperson, business services/ advertising
4-42.30	3429	Salesperson, business services/ advertising space
4-32.20	3415	Salesperson, commercial
4-52.30	9113	Salesperson, door-to-door
4-31.20	3415	Salesperson, engineering
4-51.30	5230	Salesperson, kiosk
4-32.30	3415	Salesperson, manufacturing
4-51.30	5230	Salesperson, market
4-41.30	3413	Salesperson, property
4-41.30	3413	Salesperson, real-estate
4-51.30	5220	Salesperson, retail establishment
4-41.40	3411	Salesperson, securities
4-51.30	5220	Salesperson, shop
4-51.30	5230	Salesperson, street stall
4-31.20	3415	Salesperson, technical
4-52.30	9113	Salesperson, telephone
4-32.20	3415	Salesperson, travelling
4-51.20	5220	Salesperson, wholesale establishment
7-75.90	8272	Salter, cheese
7-74.50	7411	Salter, fish
7-74.50	7411	Salter, meat
5-81.30	5161	Salvageman, fire

5-81.30	5161	Salvagewoman, fire
1-41.40	3480	Salvationist
7-11.90	7111	Sampler, core
7-11.70	7111	Sampler, mine
7-11.90	7111	Sampler, quarry
9-59.75	7143	Sandblaster, building exteriors
8-94.40	7323	Sandblaster, glass decorating
8-20.90	7113	Sandblaster, stonecutting
0-79.40	3222	Sanitarian
7-32.20	8141	Sawyer, edge
8-80.30	7313	Sawyer, industrial diamonds
8-12.20	7423	Sawyer, precision woodworking
7-32.10	8141	Sawyer, sawmill
8-20.20	7113	Sawyer, stone
8-12.20	7423	Sawyer, wood
1-71.40	2453	Saxophonist
9-59.40	7129	Scaffolder
6-31.90	6141	Scaler, log
7-51.20	7431	Scourer, wool
7-89.20	7416	Screener, snuff
3-93.90	4144	Scribe
1-61.20	2452	Sculptor
9-81.30	8340	Seaman, able
9-81.40	8340	Seaman, ordinary
7-95.10	7436	Seamstress
9-81.30	8340	Seawoman, able
9-81.40	8340	Seawoman, ordinary
3-21.20	4115	Secretary
3-21.20	3431	Secretary, administrative

2-02.10	1120	Secretary, embassy
3-10.10	3439	Secretary, executive/committee
3-10.10	3439	Secretary, executive/consular office
3-10.10	3439	Secretary, executive/government administration
3-10.10	3439	Secretary, executive/non-government administration
2-01.10	1110	Secretary, government/legislative
2-02.10	1120	Secretary, government/non-legislative
2-01.10	1110	Secretary, state
3-21.20	4115	Secretary, stenography
3-21.20	4115	Secretary, stenography/typing
3-21.20	4115	Secretary, typing
3-21.20	4115	Secretary, word processing
2-11.10	1142	Secretary-general, employers' organisation
2-11.10	1143	Secretary-general, environment protection organisation
2-02.10	1120	Secretary-general, government administration
2-02.10	1120	Secretary-general, government administration/deputy
2-11.10	1143	Secretary-general, human rights organisation
2-11.10	1143	Secretary-general, humanitarian organisation
2-11.10	1141	Secretary-general, political party
2-11.10	1143	Secretary-general, Red Crescent organisation
2-11.10	1143	Secretary-general, Red Cross organisation
2-11.10	1143	Secretary-general, special-interest organisation
2-11.10	1142	Secretary-general, trade union
2-11.10	1143	Secretary-general, wild life protection organisation
0-13.20	2114	Seismologist
1-95.20	2444	Semasiologist
2-01.10	1110	Senator
2-11.10	1142	Senior official, employers' organisation
2-02.10	1120	Senior official, government
2-11.10	1143	Senior official, humanitarian organisation
2-11.10	1141	Senior official, political party
2-11.10	1143	Senior official, special-interest organisation
2-11.10	1142	Senior official, trade union
6-29.30	6123	Sericultural worker, skilled
6-12.90	6123	Sericulturist
8-55.70	7241	Servicer, electrical equipment
8-52.10	7243	Servicer, electronics equipment
8-54.20	7243	Servicer, electronics equipment/audio-visual
8-54.20	7243	Servicer, electronics equipment/radio
8-54.20	7243	Servicer, electronics equipment/television
8-56.30	7244	Servicer, telegraph
8-56.30	7244	Servicer, telephone
9-57.50	7135	Setter, artistic/glass
8-80.40	7313	Setter, gem
9-57.20	7135	Setter, glass/buildings
8-80.40	7313	Setter, jewels
7-53.30	7432	Setter, knitting-machine
7-53.20	7432	Setter, loom
8-33.05	7223	Setter, machine tool
9-51.45	7132	Setter, marble
8-33.05	7223	Setter, metalworking machine
9-21.40	7341	Setter, printing machine
9-51.50	7132	Setter, tile
8-12.05	7423	Setter, woodworking machine
8-33.50	7223	Setter-operator, boring machine/metalworking
8-12.80	7423	Setter-operator, carving machine/woodworking
9-21.40	7341	Setter-operator, casting machine/printing type
8-33.90	7223	Setter-operator, cutting machine/metalworking
8-33.90	7223	Setter-operator, die-sinking machine/metalworking
8-33.60	7223	Setter-operator, drilling machine/metalworking
7-27.50	7223	Setter-operator, extruding machine/metalworking
8-12.20	7423	Setter-operator, fret-saw/woodworking
8-33.70	7223	Setter-operator, grinding machine/metalworking
8-33.80	7223	Setter-operator, honing machine/metalworking
8-12.20	7423	Setter-operator, jigsaw/woodworking
8-33.90	7223	Setter-operator, lapping machine/metalworking
8-91.90	7322	Setter-operator, lathe/glass
8-33.20	7223	Setter-operator, lathe/metalworking
8-20.50	7113	Setter-operator, lathe/stone
8-12.40	7423	Setter-operator, lathe/woodworking
8-33.10	7223	Setter-operator, machine tool
8-33.10	7223	Setter-operator, metalworking machine
8-33.30	7223	Setter-operator, milling machine/metalworking
8-33.85	7223	Setter-operator, numerical control machine/metalworking

8-33.40	7223	Setter-operator, planing machine/ metalworking
8-12.70	7423	Setter-operator, planing machine/ woodworking
8-33.70	7223	Setter-operator, precision-grinding machine/metalworking
8-33.60	7223	Setter-operator, reaming machine/ metalworking
8-33.90	7223	Setter-operator, routing machine/ metalworking
8-12.60	7423	Setter-operator, routing machine/ woodworking
8-33.90	7223	Setter-operator, shaping machine/ metalworking
8-12.50	7423	Setter-operator, shaping machine/ woodworking
8-72.90	7212	Setter-operator, soldering
8-72.90	7212	Setter-operator, soldering/jewellery
8-72.90	7212	Setter-operator, soldering/metal
8-12.10	7423	Setter-operator, woodworking machine
7-95.10	7436	Sewer
8-02.50	7436	Sewer, footwear
7-95.40	7436	Sewer, fur
7-95.10	7436	Sewer, garments
7-95.90	7436	Sewer, hat
8-03.40	7436	Sewer, leather
7-95.90	7436	Sewer, mattress
7-95.90	7436	Sewer, sail
7-95.90	7436	Sewer, tent
7-95.10	7436	Sewer, textile
7-95.90	7436	Sewer, upholstery
5-51.40	9141	Sexton
7-73.20	7411	Shactor
4-41.40	3411	Sharebroker
8-35.40	7224	Sharpener, cutting instruments
8-35.90	7224	Sharpener, itinerant
8-35.40	7224	Sharpener, knife
8-35.50	7224	Sharpener, saw
8-35.40	7224	Sharpener, tool
7-62.90	7441	Shaver, fur
6-24.90	6121	Shearer, sheep
8-73.10	7213	Sheet-metal worker
8-73.80	7213	Sheet-metal worker, aircraft
8-73.30	7213	Sheet-metal worker, copper
8-73.90	7213	Sheet-metal worker, furniture
8-73.60	7213	Sheet-metal worker, ornamental
8-73.40	7213	Sheet-metal worker, tin
8-73.80	7213	Sheet-metal worker, vehicles
6-24.30	6121	Shepherd
7-28.90	8223	Sherardiser
5-99.90	9120	Shiner, shoes
0-42.30	3142	Shipmate
8-74.50	7214	Shipwright, metal
9-54.40	7124	Shipwright, wood
5-99.90	9120	Shoe-black
5-99.90	9120	Shoe-polisher
5-99.90	9120	Shoe-shiner
8-01.10	7442	Shoe-maker
8-01.10	7442	Shoe-maker, bespoke
8-01.20	7442	Shoe-maker, orthopaedic
8-49.90	7442	Shoe-maker, raffia
8-01.90	7442	Shoe-maker, sports
7-13.90	3117	Shooter, oil and gas wells
9-54.70	7124	Shopfitter
4-10.30	1314	Shopkeeper
9-59.90	7129	Shorer, construction
8-20.90	7113	Shotblaster, stonecutting
7-11.50	7112	Shotfirer
9-99.10	9312	Shoveller
9-84.40	8312	Shunter, railway
9-52.20	7123	Shutterer, concrete moulding
9-84.30	8312	Signaller, railway
9-39.50	7324	Signpainter
9-39.50	7324	Sign-writer
8-95.70	7324	Silverer, glass
8-95.70	7324	Silverer, mirror
8-80.50	7313	Silversmith
0-53.40	2213	Silviculturist
1-71.45	2453	Singer, bass
1-71.45	2453	Singer, choir
1-71.45	2453	Singer, concert
1-71.45	2453	Singer, jazz
1-71.40	3473	Singer, night-club
1-71.45	2453	Singer, opera
1-71.45	2453	Singer, popular music
1-71.45	3473	Singer, street
9-59.55	7136	Sinker, well
0-71.10	3231	Sister, nursing/associate professional
0-71.10	2230	Sister, nursing/professional
1-71.40	2453	Sitar player
7-73.90	7411	Skinner, animal
0-42.90	3142	Skipper, yacht
8-02.30	7442	Skiver, footwear
7-73.20	7411	Slaughterer
8-91.60	7322	Slicer, optical glass
8-91.60	7322	Slitter, optical glass
7-51.40	7431	Sliver lapper
9-89.90	8333	Sluiceman, dock
9-89.90	8333	Sluicewoman, dock
8-31.10	7221	Smith, agricultural implement
8-31.10	7221	Smith, anvil
8-31.40	7221	Smith, bulldozer
7-74.60	7411	Smokehouse worker, fish
7-74.60	7411	Smokehouse worker, meat
1-92.20	2442	Social pathologist

1-93.10	3460	Social worker, associate professional
1-93.30	3460	Social worker, associate professional/community centre
1-93.30	3460	Social worker, associate professional/cultural centre
1-93.40	3460	Social worker, associate professional/delinquency
1-93.10	3460	Social worker, associate professional/enterprise
1-93.90	3460	Social worker, associate professional/family planning
1-93.90	3460	Social worker, associate professional/home-help service
1-93.20	3460	Social worker, associate professional/medical
1-93.40	3460	Social worker, associate professional/probation
1-93.50	3460	Social worker, associate professional/psychiatric
1-93.10	2446	Social worker, professional
1-93.30	2446	Social worker, professional/community centre
1-93.30	2446	Social worker, professional/cultural centre
1-93.40	2446	Social worker, professional/delinquency
1-93.10	2446	Social worker, professional/enterprise
1-93.90	2446	Social worker, professional/family planning
1-93.90	2446	Social worker, professional/home-help service
1-93.20	2446	Social worker, professional/medical
1-93.40	2446	Social worker, professional/probation
1-93.50	2446	Social worker, professional/psychiatric
1-92.20	2442	Sociologist
1-92.20	2442	Sociologist, criminology
1-92.20	2442	Sociologist, industrial
1-92.20	2442	Sociologist, penology
1-92.20	2442	Sociologist, social pathology
8-02.90	7442	Socker, footwear
0-23.90	2131	Software engineer
0-53.50	2213	Soil scientist
8-72.60	7212	Solderer
8-72.90	7212	Solderer, dip
8-72.90	7212	Solderer, furnace
8-72.90	7212	Solderer, torch
1-21.10	2421	Solicitor
1-71.45	2453	Soprano
7-82.90	7416	Sorter, cigar
8-02.40	7442	Sorter, footwear
7-92.40	7434	Sorter, fur
8-62.90	3131	Sound mixer
2-01.10	1110	Speaker
1-39.30	2351	Specialist, audio-visual and other teaching aids
1-39.30	2351	Specialist, audio-visual teaching aids
0-28.10	2419	Specialist, business efficiency
5-81.20	3151	Specialist, fire prevention
1-94.20	2412	Specialist, personnel
0-28.20	2419	Specialist, sales promotion methods
1-39.30	2351	Specialist, teaching aids
1-39.30	2351	Specialist, visual teaching aids
8-39.40	7223	Spinner, metal
8-80.90	7313	Spinner, precious metal
8-39.40	7223	Spinner, sheet-metal
7-52.20	7432	Spinner, thread and yarn
9-72.60	7215	Spinner-squeezer, cable
9-72.60	7215	Spinner-squeezer, wire
9-72.10	7215	Splicer, cable and rope
7-73.90	7411	Splitter, carcass
8-02.40	7442	Splitter, footwear
7-61.40	7441	Splitter, hide
7-12.20	7113	Splitter, stone
6-49.90	6152	Sponge hooker
1-80.20	3475	Sportsman, professional
1-80.20	3475	Sportwoman, professional
5-60.50	9133	Spotter, dry-cleaning
9-31.20	7141	Spray-painter, construction
9-39.30	7324	Spray-painter, except construction
7-28.50	7142	Sprayer, metal
6-24.90	9211	Stable lad
9-99.10	9313	Stacker, building construction
1-74.90	1229	Stage manager
8-02.55	7442	Stainer, footwear
7-61.55	7441	Stainer, leather
8-19.55	7422	Stainer, wooden furniture
9-29.90	7346	Stamper, heraldic printing
3-51.10	1226	Station master, railway
0-81.10	2122	Statistician
0-81.30	2122	Statistician, agricultural
0-81.30	2122	Statistician, applied statistics
0-81.30	2122	Statistician, biometrics
0-81.30	2122	Statistician, biostatistics
0-81.30	2122	Statistician, demography
0-81.30	2122	Statistician, economics
0-81.30	2122	Statistician, education
0-81.30	2122	Statistician, engineering
0-81.30	2122	Statistician, finance
0-81.30	2122	Statistician, health
0-81.20	2122	Statistician, mathematical
0-81.30	2122	Statistician, opinion-polling

T

7-76.20	7412	Table hand, bread
7-76.30	7412	Table hand, flour confectionery
7-91.10	7433	Tailor
7-91.90	7433	Tailor, alteration
7-91.20	7433	Tailor, bespoke
7-91.20	7433	Tailor, garment/made-to-measure
7-91.30	7433	Tailor, garment/ready-to-wear
7-91.90	7433	Tailor, theatrical
8-02.55	7442	Taker-off, footwear finishing
9-22.90	7341	Taker-off, printing press
1-41.20	2460	Talapoin
1-79.90	3474	Tamer, wild animal
7-61.45	7441	Tanner
7-61.45	7441	Tanner, hide
7-61.45	7441	Tanner, leather
6-29.40	6112	Tapper, maple syrup
6-29.40	6112	Tapper, pine resin
6-23.90	6112	Tapper, rubber tree
6-29.40	6112	Tapper, toddy
7-77.20	7415	Taster, coffee
7-74.90	7415	Taster, food
7-74.90	7415	Taster, juice
7-78.60	7415	Taster, liquor
7-77.20	7415	Taster, tea
7-78.60	7415	Taster, wine
1-62.90	3471	Tattooist
9-49.20	3211	Taxidermist
0-51.90	2211	Taxonomist
0-51.30	2211	Taxonomist, animal
0-51.20	2211	Taxonomist, plant
1-34.90	3320	Teacher, kindergarten/associate professional
1-34.90	2332	Teacher, kindergarten/professional
1-34.20	3320	Teacher, nursery/associate professional
1-34.20	2332	Teacher, nursery/professional
1-31.10	2310	Teacher, post-secondary education
1-31.45	2310	Teacher, post-secondary education/accountancy
1-31.90	2310	Teacher, post-secondary education/advertising
1-31.60	2310	Teacher, post-secondary education/agricultural science
1-31.60	2310	Teacher, post-secondary education/agronomy
1-31.30	2310	Teacher, post-secondary education/anatomy
1-31.60	2310	Teacher, post-secondary education/animal husbandry
1-31.65	2310	Teacher, post-secondary education/anthropology
1-31.65	2310	Teacher, post-secondary education/archaeology
1-31.25	2310	Teacher, post-secondary education/architecture
1-31.90	2310	Teacher, post-secondary education/art
1-31.70	2310	Teacher, post-secondary education/art criticism
1-31.70	2310	Teacher, post-secondary education/art history
1-31.20	2310	Teacher, post-secondary education/astronomy
1-31.30	2310	Teacher, post-secondary education/bacteriology
1-31.20	2310	Teacher, post-secondary education/biochemistry
1-31.30	2310	Teacher, post-secondary education/biology
1-31.30	2310	Teacher, post-secondary education/botany
1-31.45	2310	Teacher, post-secondary education/business management
1-31.20	2310	Teacher, post-secondary education/chemistry
1-31.75	2310	Teacher, post-secondary education/chiropractic
1-31.45	2310	Teacher, post-secondary education/commerce
1-31.40	2310	Teacher, post-secondary education/community development
1-31.90	2310	Teacher, post-secondary education/computer science
1-31.80	2310	Teacher, post-secondary education/construction technology
1-31.90	2310	Teacher, post-secondary education/dancing
1-31.65	2310	Teacher, post-secondary education/demography
1-31.30	2310	Teacher, post-secondary education/dentistry
1-31.75	2310	Teacher, post-secondary education/dietetics
1-31.90	2310	Teacher, post-secondary education/drama
1-31.45	2310	Teacher, post-secondary education/economics
1-31.55	2310	Teacher, post-secondary education/education
1-31.25	2310	Teacher, post-secondary education/engineering
1-31.25	2310	Teacher, post-secondary education/engineering (chemical)
1-31.25	2310	Teacher, post-secondary education/engineering (civil)
1-31.25	2310	Teacher, post-secondary education/engineering (electrical)

1-31.65	2310	Teacher, post-secondary education/philosophy
1-31.20	2310	Teacher, post-secondary education/physical sciences
1-31.20	2310	Teacher, post-secondary education/physics
1-31.75	2310	Teacher, post-secondary education/physiotherapy
1-31.65	2310	Teacher, post-secondary education/political science
1-31.65	2310	Teacher, post-secondary education/prehistory
1-31.65	2310	Teacher, post-secondary education/psychology
1-31.90	2310	Teacher, post-secondary education/public administration
1-31.30	2310	Teacher, post-secondary education/public health
1-31.75	2310	Teacher, post-secondary education/radiology
1-31.65	2310	Teacher, post-secondary education/religion
1-31.90	2310	Teacher, post-secondary education/sales methods
1-31.90	2310	Teacher, post-secondary education/sculpture
1-31.60	2310	Teacher, post-secondary education/silviculture
1-31.65	2310	Teacher, post-secondary education/social science
1-31.65	2310	Teacher, post-secondary education/sociology
1-31.40	2310	Teacher, post-secondary education/statistics
1-31.90	2310	Teacher, post-secondary education/telecommunications services
1-31.80	2310	Teacher, post-secondary education/textile technology
1-31.65	2310	Teacher, post-secondary education/theology
1-31.90	2310	Teacher, post-secondary education/trade unionism
1-31.90	2310	Teacher, post-secondary education/transport services
1-31.30	2310	Teacher, post-secondary education/veterinary science
1-31.30	2310	Teacher, post-secondary education/zoology
1-34.20	3320	Teacher, pre-primary education/associate professional
1-34.20	2332	Teacher, pre-primary education/professional
1-33.20	3310	Teacher, primary education/associate professional
1-33.90	2331	Teacher, primary education/professional
1-33.90	3310	Teacher, primary education/reading (associate professional)
1-33.90	2331	Teacher, primary education/reading (professional)
1-33.90	3310	Teacher, primary education/writing (associate professional)
1-33.90	2331	Teacher, primary education/writing (professional)
		Teacher, private lessons (see Introduction)
1-35.90	3330	Teacher, remedial/associate professional
1-35.90	2340	Teacher, remedial/professional
1-32.10	2320	Teacher, secondary education
1-32.90	2320	Teacher, secondary education/adult literacy
1-32.70	2320	Teacher, secondary education/agricultural science
1-32.40	2320	Teacher, secondary education/archaeology
1-32.50	2320	Teacher, secondary education/art
1-32.50	2320	Teacher, secondary education/art history
1-32.30	2320	Teacher, secondary education/biology
1-32.30	2320	Teacher, secondary education/botany
1-32.80	2320	Teacher, secondary education/bricklaying
1-32.30	2320	Teacher, secondary education/chemistry
1-32.60	2320	Teacher, secondary education/commercial and secretarial
1-32.60	2320	Teacher, secondary education/commercial subjects
1-32.80	2320	Teacher, secondary education/computer science
1-32.50	2320	Teacher, secondary education/dancing
1-32.75	2320	Teacher, secondary education/domestic science
1-32.50	2320	Teacher, secondary education/drama
1-32.40	2320	Teacher, secondary education/economics
1-32.80	2320	Teacher, secondary education/engineering
1-32.50	2320	Teacher, secondary education/fine arts
1-32.40	2320	Teacher, secondary education/geography
1-32.30	2320	Teacher, secondary education/geology
1-32.40	2320	Teacher, secondary education/government
1-32.80	2320	Teacher, secondary education/handicrafts and crafts

1-32.40	2320	Teacher, secondary education/ history
1-32.15	2320	Teacher, secondary education/ language
1-32.15	2320	Teacher, secondary education/ languages and literature
1-32.30	2320	Teacher, secondary education/life sciences
1-32.15	2320	Teacher, secondary education/ linguistics
1-32.15	2320	Teacher, secondary education/ literature
1-32.20	2320	Teacher, secondary education/ mathematics
1-32.80	2320	Teacher, secondary education/ metalwork
1-32.50	2320	Teacher, secondary education/ music
1-32.30	2320	Teacher, secondary education/ natural science
1-32.75	2320	Teacher, secondary education/ nursing
1-32.90	2320	Teacher, secondary education/ pedagogy
1-32.90	2320	Teacher, secondary education/ philosophy
1-32.80	2320	Teacher, secondary education/ photography
1-32.90	2320	Teacher, secondary education/ physical education
1-32.30	2320	Teacher, secondary education/ physics
1-32.80	2320	Teacher, secondary education/ printing
1-32.40	2320	Teacher, secondary education/ religion
1-32.50	2320	Teacher, secondary education/ sculpture
1-32.60	2320	Teacher, secondary education/ secretarial subjects
1-32.40	2320	Teacher, secondary education/ social studies
1-32.40	2320	Teacher, secondary education/ sociology
1-32.80	2320	Teacher, secondary education/ stonemasonry
1-32.80	2320	Teacher, secondary education/ technical drawing
1-32.80	2320	Teacher, secondary education/ technical education
1-32.60	2320	Teacher, secondary education/ typing
1-32.80	2320	Teacher, secondary education/ vocational training
1-32.80	2320	Teacher, secondary education/ woodwork
1-32.30	2320	Teacher, secondary education/ zoology
1-35.20	3330	Teacher, special education/for the blind (associate professional)
1-35.20	2340	Teacher, special education/for the blind (professional)
1-35.30	3330	Teacher, special education/for the deaf (associate professional)
1-35.30	2340	Teacher, special education/for the deaf (professional)
1-35.90	3330	Teacher, special education/for the dumb (associate professional)
1-35.90	2340	Teacher, special education/for the dumb (professional)
1-35.40	3330	Teacher, special education/for the mentally handicapped (associate professional)
1-35.40	2340	Teacher, special education/for the mentally handicapped (professional)
1-35.90	3330	Teacher, special education/for the physically handicapped (associate professional)
1-35.90	2340	Teacher, special education/for the physically handicapped (professional)
1-35.90	3330	Teacher, special education/ remedial (associate professional)
1-35.90	2340	Teacher, special education/ remedial (professional)
7-51.90	7431	Teaser, textiles
0-54.90	3212	Technician, agronomy
3-59.50	3145	Technician, air traffic safety
0-54.20	3211	Technician, anatomy
0-54.90	3212	Technician, arboriculture
0-14.90	3111	Technician, astronomy
0-54.20	3211	Technician, bacteriology
0-54.20	3211	Technician, biochemistry
0-54.20	3211	Technician, biology
0-54.20	3211	Technician, biophysics
0-54.30	3211	Technician, blood-bank
0-54.20	3211	Technician, botany
0-14.20	3111	Technician, chemistry
0-34.90	3121	Technician, computer
0-54.90	3212	Technician, crop research
0-54.30	3211	Technician, cytology
0-54.20	3211	Technician, ecology
0-35.30	3115	Technician, engineering/ aeronautics
0-34.90	3114	Technician, engineering/aerospace
0-36.90	3116	Technician, engineering/chemical
0-36.90	3116	Technician, engineering/chemical process
0-33.10	3112	Technician, engineering/civil
0-33.90	3112	Technician, engineering/civil (construction)

0-33.90	3112	Technician, engineering/civil (dredging)
0-33.90	3112	Technician, engineering/civil (hydraulics)
0-33.90	3112	Technician, engineering/civil (hydrology)
0-33.90	3112	Technician, engineering/civil (irrigation)
0-33.90	3112	Technician, engineering/civil (public health)
0-33.90	3112	Technician, engineering/civil (sanitary)
0-33.90	3112	Technician, engineering/civil (soil mechanics)
0-33.90	3112	Technician, engineering/civil (structural)
0-34.05	3113	Technician, engineering/electrical
0-34.90	3113	Technician, engineering/electrical (electric illumination)
0-34.90	3113	Technician, engineering/electrical (electric power distribution)
0-34.90	3113	Technician, engineering/electrical (electric power transmission)
0-34.90	3113	Technician, engineering/electrical (electric traction)
0-34.20	3113	Technician, engineering/electrical (high voltage)
0-34.90	3113	Technician, engineering/electrical systems
0-34.10	3114	Technician, engineering/electronics
0-34.90	3114	Technician, engineering/electronics (computer hardware design)
0-34.90	3114	Technician, engineering/electronics (information engineering)
0-34.90	3114	Technician, engineering/electronics (instrumentation)
0-34.90	3114	Technician, engineering/electronics (semiconductors)
0-39.30	3119	Technician, engineering/industrial efficiency
0-39.20	3119	Technician, engineering/industrial layout
0-35.20	3115	Technician, engineering/marine
0-35.10	3115	Technician, engineering/mechanical
0-35.30	3115	Technician, engineering/mechanical (aeronautics)
0-35.90	3115	Technician, engineering/mechanical (agriculture)
0-35.50	3115	Technician, engineering/mechanical (air-conditioning)
0-35.90	3115	Technician, engineering/mechanical (automotive)
0-35.20	3115	Technician, engineering/mechanical (diesel)
0-35.20	3115	Technician, engineering/mechanical (gas turbine)
0-35.50	3115	Technician, engineering/mechanical (heating, ventilation and refrigeration)
0-35.90	3115	Technician, engineering/mechanical (industrial machinery and tools)
0-35.90	3115	Technician, engineering/mechanical (instruments)
0-35.20	3115	Technician, engineering/mechanical (internal combustion)
0-35.20	3115	Technician, engineering/mechanical (jet engine)
0-35.20	3115	Technician, engineering/mechanical (locomotive engine)
0-35.90	3115	Technician, engineering/mechanical (lubrication)
0-35.90	3115	Technician, engineering/mechanical (marine)
0-35.20	3115	Technician, engineering/mechanical (motor)
0-35.90	3115	Technician, engineering/mechanical (naval)
0-35.90	3115	Technician, engineering/mechanical (nuclear power)
0-35.50	3115	Technician, engineering/mechanical (refrigeration)
0-35.90	3115	Technician, engineering/mechanical (ship construction)
0-39.20	3119	Technician, engineering/methods
0-38.10	3117	Technician, engineering/mining
0-38.90	3117	Technician, engineering/mining (coal)
0-38.90	3117	Technician, engineering/mining (diamonds)
0-38.90	3117	Technician, engineering/mining (metal)
0-38.20	3117	Technician, engineering/mining (petroleum and natural gas)
0-35.20	3115	Technician, engineering/motor and engine
0-36.90	3116	Technician, engineering/natural gas production and distribution
0-35.90	3115	Technician, engineering/naval
0-35.90	3115	Technician, engineering/nuclear power
0-36.20	3116	Technician, engineering/petroleum
0-39.20	3119	Technician, engineering/planning
0-39.20	3119	Technician, engineering/production
0-39.90	3119	Technician, engineering/safety
0-34.90	3121	Technician, engineering/systems (computers)

0-39.90	3119	Technician, engineering/systems (except computers)
0-34.30	3114	Technician, engineering/ telecommunications
0-34.90	3114	Technician, engineering/ telecommunications (aerospace)
0-34.90	3114	Technician, engineering/ telecommunications (radar)
0-34.90	3114	Technician, engineering/ telecommunications (radio)
0-34.90	3114	Technician, engineering/ telecommunications (signal systems)
0-34.90	3114	Technician, engineering/ telecommunications (telegraph)
0-34.90	3114	Technician, engineering/ telecommunications (telephone)
0-34.90	3114	Technician, engineering/ telecommunications (television)
0-39.30	3119	Technician, engineering/time and motion study
0-39.90	3119	Technician, engineering/value
0-39.30	3119	Technician, engineering/work study
0-54.90	3212	Technician, floriculture
0-54.90	3212	Technician, forestry
0-54.20	3211	Technician, genetics
0-14.90	3111	Technician, geology
0-14.90	3111	Technician, geophysics
0-54.30	3211	Technician, haematology
0-54.30	3211	Technician, histology
0-54.90	3212	Technician, horticulture
0-54.30	3211	Technician, medical science
0-37.90	3117	Technician, metallurgy/assaying
0-37.20	3117	Technician, metallurgy/extractive
0-37.30	3117	Technician, metallurgy/foundry
0-37.30	3117	Technician, metallurgy/physical
0-37.90	3117	Technician, metallurgy/radioactive minerals
0-14.90	3111	Technician, meteorology
0-14.90	3111	Technician, oceanography
0-54.90	3212	Technician, olericulture
0-79.50	3226	Technician, orthopaedic
0-54.20	3211	Technician, pathology
0-54.20	3211	Technician, pharmacology
0-14.30	3111	Technician, physics
0-54.20	3211	Technician, physiology
0-54.90	3212	Technician, pomology
0-79.50	3226	Technician, prosthetic
0-39.90	3119	Technician, quantity surveying
0-35.90	3123	Technician, robot
0-54.30	3211	Technician, serology
0-54.90	3212	Technician, silviculture
0-54.90	3212	Technician, soil science
8-62.90	3131	Technician, sound-effects
8-62.90	3131	Technician, sound-testing
8-62.20	3131	Technician, sound/studio (radio)
8-62.20	3131	Technician, sound/studio (television)
0-33.30	3112	Technician, surveying
0-54.30	3211	Technician, tissue
0-54.20	3211	Technician, zoology
0-29.40	2146	Technologist, brewing
0-22.90	2142	Technologist, building materials
0-29.90	2149	Technologist, cement
0-29.20	2149	Technologist, ceramics
0-25.90	2146	Technologist, chemical process
0-25.10	2146	Technologist, engineering/ chemical
0-22.10	2142	Technologist, engineering/civil
0-23.90	2143	Technologist, engineering/ electrical
0-23.90	2144	Technologist, engineering/ electronics
0-24.90	2145	Technologist, engineering/ mechanical
0-23.90	2144	Technologist, engineering/ telecommunications
0-27.90	2147	Technologist, extractive
0-29.40	2146	Technologist, fibre
0-29.40	2146	Technologist, food and drink
0-25.90	2146	Technologist, fuel
0-29.20	2149	Technologist, glass
0-29.90	2149	Technologist, leather
0-29.90	2149	Technologist, packaging
0-25.90	2146	Technologist, paint
0-29.40	2146	Technologist, paper
0-25.90	2146	Technologist, plastics
0-25.90	2146	Technologist, polymer
0-29.90	2149	Technologist, printing
0-25.90	2146	Technologist, rubber
0-29.90	2149	Technologist, textiles
0-25.90	2146	Technologist, tyre
0-24.90	2145	Technologist, welding
0-29.90	2149	Technologist, wood
3-80.40	3132	Telegrapher
3-80.20	4223	Telephonist
3-21.50	4112	Teletypist
3-31.40	4212	Teller, bank
7-76.90	7412	Temperer, chocolate
7-12.50	8112	Tender, jig
9-73.45	8333	Tender, skip
9-69.90	8163	Tender, water dam
8-12.90	7422	Tenoner
1-71.45	2453	Tenor
9-52.50	7123	Terrazzo worker
0-41.30	3143	Test pilot, aircraft
9-53.60	7131	Thatcher
1-49.90	2460	Theologian

U

7-96.30	7437	Upholsterer, aircraft
7-96.30	7437	Upholsterer, automobile
7-96.20	7437	Upholsterer, furniture
7-96.30	7437	Upholsterer, railway carriage

7-96.90	7437	Upholsterer, soft furnishing
7-96.30	7437	Upholsterer, vehicle
5-99.90	9152	Usher

V

0-66.10	3227	Vaccinator, veterinary
5-40.30	5142	Valet
5-40.90	5142	Valet, hotel
5-40.30	5142	Valet, personal
4-43.30	3417	Valuer
3-21.90	4111	Varitypist
9-39.10	7142	Varnisher, manufactured articles
9-39.90	7142	Varnisher, metal
9-39.60	7142	Varnisher, vehicle
8-19.55	7422	Varnisher, wooden furniture
4-52.20	9111	Vendor, fresh-water
4-52.40	9112	Vendor, newspapers
4-90.90	9111	Vendor, refreshments
4-90.90	9111	Vendor, refreshments/cinema
4-90.90	9111	Vendor, refreshments/theatre

4-52.20	9111	Vendor, street/food
4-52.20	9112	Vendor, street/non-food products
4-90.90	9112	Vendor, theatre programme
8-19.50	7422	Veneer applier
1-79.90	3474	Ventriloquist
3-21.30	3431	Verbatim reporter
5-51.40	9141	Verger
0-65.10	2223	Veterinarian
0-65.10	2223	Veterinarian, epidemiology
0-65.10	2223	Veterinarian, surgery
1-41.20	2460	Vicar
6-12.30	6112	Viniculturist
1-71.40	2453	Violinist
9-41.80	7312	Voicer, organ
0-13.20	2114	Volcanologist

W

5-32.10	5123	Waiter
5-32.30	5123	Waiter, banquet
5-32.30	5123	Waiter, formal
5-32.20	5123	Waiter, head
5-32.10	5123	Waiter, railway dining car
5-32.40	5123	Waiter, wine
5-32.10	5123	Waitress
5-32.30	5123	Waitress, banquet
5-32.30	5123	Waitress, formal
5-32.20	5123	Waitress, head
5-32.10	5123	Waitress, railway dining car
5-32.40	5123	Waitress, wine
9-59.25	7141	Wallpaper hanger
6-49.90	5169	Warden, bird sanctuary
5-20.90	5121	Warden, camp
1-93.30	3460	Warden, community centre/associate professional
1-93.30	2446	Warden, community centre/professional
5-20.90	5121	Warden, dormitory
5-89.30	5163	Warden, prison
1-93.40	3460	Warden, probation home/associate professional
1-93.40	2446	Warden, probation home/professional
5-89.90	5169	Warden, traffic
6-49.90	5169	Warden, wild life
5-89.30	5163	Warder, prison

5-40.70	7433	Wardrobe mistress, stage and studio
7-73.90	9322	Washer, hand/carcass
5-60.90	9322	Washer, hand/cloth
9-99.10	9132	Washer, hand/dishes
7-56.35	9322	Washer, hand/fibre
7-61.90	9322	Washer, hand/hide
5-60.10	9133	Washer, hand/laundry
9-99.10	9322	Washer, hand/manufacturing process
9-99.10	9120	Washer, hand/street (car windows)
9-99.10	9142	Washer, hand/vehicle
5-60.90	9322	Washer, hand/yarn
8-42.25	7311	Watch adjuster
5-89.40	9152	Watchman
5-89.40	9152	Watchman, night
5-89.40	9152	Watchwoman
5-89.40	9152	Watchwoman, night
9-81.90	8340	Waterman
9-81.90	8340	Waterwoman
8-94.90	7323	Waxer, glass sandblasting
9-42.20	7424	Weaver, basket
7-54.55	7432	Weaver, carpet
7-54.30	7432	Weaver, cloth
7-54.45	7432	Weaver, jacquard
9-42.90	7424	Weaver, straw

7-54.35	7432	Weaver, tapestry
8-72.10	7212	Welder
8-72.15	7212	Welder, acetylene
8-72.35	7212	Welder, butt
8-72.35	7212	Welder, contact
8-72.20	7212	Welder, electric arc
8-72.35	7212	Welder, flash
8-72.15	7212	Welder, gas
8-72.10	7212	Welder, gas and electric
8-72.15	7212	Welder, oxy-acetylene
8-72.35	7212	Welder, resistance
8-72.35	7212	Welder, seam
8-72.35	7212	Welder, spot
8-72.30	7212	Welder, thermite
1-93.20	3460	Welfare worker, associate professional
1-93.50	3460	Welfare worker, associate professional/mental health
1-93.20	3460	Welfare worker, associate professional/moral welfare
1-93.20	3460	Welfare worker, associate professional/prison
1-93.90	3460	Welfare worker, associate professional/the deaf
1-93.90	3460	Welfare worker, associate professional/the physically handicapped
1-93.20	2446	Welfare worker, professional
1-93.50	2446	Welfare worker, professional/mental health
1-93.20	2446	Welfare worker, professional/moral welfare
1-93.20	2446	Welfare worker, professional/prison
1-93.90	2446	Welfare worker, professional/the deaf
1-93.90	2446	Welfare worker, professional/the physically handicapped
3-59.90	4133	Wharfinger
8-35.30	7224	Wheel-grinder, metal
8-19.25	7422	Wheel-wright
9-31.90	7141	Whitewasher
4-10.20	1314	Wholesaler
7-51.90	7431	Willeyer
8-53.50	9321	Winder, armature/hand
8-53.50	9321	Winder, coil/hand
8-53.50	9321	Winder, filament/hand
8-53.50	9321	Winder, rotor coil/hand
8-53.50	9321	Winder, stator coil/hand
8-53.50	9321	Winder, transformer coil/hand
6-12.30	6112	Winegrower
7-77.90	8277	Winnower, cocoa-bean
8-57.20	7245	Wire worker, electric power/overhead wires
8-57.90	7245	Wire worker, electric power/underground wires
8-57.30	7245	Wire worker, electric traction/overhead wires
8-57.40	7245	Wire worker, telegraph
8-57.40	7245	Wire worker, telephone
7-32.70	7421	Wood grader
7-31.90	7421	Wood incising worker
7-31.20	7421	Wood seasoner
7-31.30	7421	Wood treater
8-12.30	7423	Wood tuner
8-12.30	7423	Wood turner
6-31.90	6141	Woodcutter, forest
6-32.30	6141	Woodman
6-32.30	6141	Woodwoman
8-12.90	7423	Woodworker, dovetailing
8-12.90	7423	Woodworker, dowelling
8-12.90	7423	Woodworker, morticing
8-12.90	7423	Woodworker, sanding
8-12.90	7423	Woodworker, tenoning
7-31.90	7421	Woodworker, treating
		Working proprietor (see Introduction)
9-71.50	9322	Wrapper, hand
9-59.45	7129	Wrecker, building
1-80.20	3475	Wrestler
1-51.20	2451	Writer
1-59.90	2451	Writer, continuity
1-59.90	2451	Writer, drama
1-59.15	2451	Writer, feature
1-59.65	2451	Writer, handbook
1-59.90	2451	Writer, lyric
1-59.60	2451	Writer, public information
1-59.60	2451	Writer, publicity
1-59.90	2451	Writer, scenario
1-59.90	2451	Writer, script
1-51.20	2451	Writer, short story
1-59.90	2451	Writer, song
1-59.65	2451	Writer, technical

Y

3-59.35	4133	Yardmaster, railway		1-99.90	3423	Youth employment officer

Z

ILO statistical publications

Data dissemination

Year Book of Labour Statistics (annual). Trilingual
ISBN 92-2-006426-X, 49th issue 1989-90.
ISSN 0084-3857   150 Swiss francs
(Chapters I-III are also available on diskette).

Year Book of Labour Statistics: Retrospective edition on population censuses, 1945-89 Trilingual
ISBN 92-2-006428-6   170 Swiss francs
(Also available on diskette.)

Bulletin of Labour Statistics (quarterly with supplements in the intervening months). Trilingual
ISSN 0007-4950.
Annual subscription (1991)   95 Swiss francs
Price per issue   25 Swiss francs

Results of October Inquiry on occupational wages and hours of work and retail price of selected food items (special annual issue of the Bulletin). Trilingual
ISSN 0007-4950   25 Swiss francs

The Cost of Social Security: Twelfth international inquiry, 1981-83 Trilingual
ISBN 92-2-006423-5   ISSN 0538-8295
                                      50 Swiss francs

Forthcoming:
The Cost of Social Security: Thirteenth international inquiry, 1984-86 Trilingual
ISBN 92-2-006430-8   ISSN 0538-8295

Economically active population, 1950-2025:

Vol. I: Asia Trilingual
            ISBN 92-2-005345-4   37.50 Swiss francs
            ISSN 0258-0489

Vol. II: Africa Trilingual
            ISBN 92-2-005346-2   40 Swiss francs
            ISSN 0258-0489

Vol. III: Latin America Trilingual
            ISBN 92-2-005347-0   32.50 Swiss francs
            ISSN 0258-0489

Vol. IV: Northern America, Europe, Oceania and USSR Trilingual
            ISBN 92-2-005348-9   37.50 Swiss francs
            ISSN 0258-0489

Vol. V: World Summary Trilingual
            ISBN 92-2-005349-7   32.50 Swiss francs
            ISSN 0258-0489

Vol. VI: Methodological supplement
            ISBN 92-2-105424-1
            ISSN 1012-0440   35 Swiss francs
(Also available on magnetic tape or diskettes.)

Statistical Sources and Methods

Vol. 1: Consumer price indices
         ISBN 92-2-106093-4   32.50 Swiss francs
         ISSN 0255-3465

Vol. 2: Employment, wages and hours of work (establishment surveys)
         ISBN 92-2-105492-6   32.50 Swiss francs
         ISSN 0255-3465

Vol. 3: Economically active population, employment, unemployment, and hours of work (household surveys)
         ISBN 92-2-106448-4   42.50 Swiss francs
         ISSN 0255-3465

Vol. 4: Employment, unemployment, wages and hours of work (administrative records and related sources)
         ISBN 92-2-106406-9   32.50 Swiss francs
         ISSN 0255-3465

Vol. 5: Total and economically active population, employment and unemployment (population censuses)
         ISBN 92-2-106447-6   32.50 Swiss francs
         ISSN 0255-3465

Manuals

An integrated system of wages statistics: A manual on methods
ISBN 92-2-102007-X   35 Swiss francs
(limp cover)
ISBN 92-2-102019-3   45 Swiss francs
(hard cover)

Consumer price indices: An ILO manual
ISBN 92-2-106436-0   27.50 Swiss francs

Surveys of economically active population, employment, unemployment and underemployment: An ILO manual on concepts and methods
ISBN 92-2-106516-2   40 Swiss francs

Occupations: An ILO manual on the development and use of national standard classifications of occupations (forthcoming).

Statistical standards

Current international recommendations on labour statistics
ISBN 92-2-106433-6   17.50 Swiss francs

Prices subject to change without notice.